Leaders of the American Civil War

D0146917

LEADERS OF THE AMERICAN CIVIL WAR

A Biographical and Historiographical Dictionary

Edited by **Charles F. Ritter**
and
Jon L. Wakelyn

GREENWOOD PRESS
Westport, Connecticut

Library of Congress Cataloging-in-Publication Data

Leaders of the American Civil War : a biographical and historiographical
   dictionary / edited by Charles F. Ritter and Jon L. Wakelyn.
    p. cm.
  Includes bibliographical references and index.
  ISBN 0–313–29560–3 (alk. paper)
  1. United States—History—Civil War, 1861–1865—Biography—
Dictionaries. 2. United States—History—Civil War, 1861–1865—
Historiography—Dictionaries. I. Ritter, Charles F., 1937– .
II. Wakelyn, Jon L., 1938– .
E467.L43   1998
973.7'092'2
[B]—dc21   98–12156

British Library Cataloguing in Publication Data is available.

Library of Congress Catalog Card Number: 98–12156
ISBN: 0–313–29560–3

First published in 1998

Greenwood Press, 88 Post Road West, Westport, CT 06881
An imprint of Greenwood Publishing Group, Inc.

Printed in the United States of America

The paper used in this book complies with the
Permanent Paper Standard issued by the National
Information Standards Organization (Z39.48–1984).

10 9 8 7 6 5 4 3 2 1

To the memory of Thomas Lawrence Connelly,
scholar, teacher, Tennessean

CONTENTS

PREFACE

For the leaders included in this volume, the Civil War constituted the major event of their lives. For most of them, their participation in that war was also the major activity and accomplishment of their busy and important careers. They have been selected for inclusion in this dictionary, then, because of their various major contributions to that war. A number of the leaders included in this book have been regarded as some of the most important and greatest leaders in this country's history. Some, however, have neither received full due for their contributions to the war nor been regarded as great leaders. But each of them, in the many different kinds of service needed in modern warfare, made a major impact on his or her respective side's war effort. All forty-seven, it will be shown, deserve to be called important leaders of the Civil War.

Because the study of warfare continues to evolve, we have become increasingly aware of its complicated nature and the types of activity required for its function. Although the great military officers remain the central focus of leadership in warfare, and make up the major category of those included in this volume, other leaders, too, deserve study. Civilian political leaders Abraham Lincoln and Jefferson Davis, as presidents and commanders in chief of their respective war machines, used their most important government subordinates to make and carry out war policies. Those so-called lesser governmental and political leaders were integral to the war's functioning. Government leaders supported the activities of the military leaders, as they provided food, clothing, and armaments and delivered personnel to the front lines. In the Civil War, the interaction of central and state authorities was crucial to the recruitment of troops and to financing the war. War governors' activities thus became important to the success or failure of the war effort. In addition, members of the congressional leadership bridged the gap between state and central policies, and the most important of them dealt with the legislative policies of the central governments. Behind the lines, a number of leaders, often neglected by students of warfare, had major parts in the war effort. Businessmen, bankers, and manufacturers provided the resources of war. Jay Cooke, the Union's major fund-raiser, and Joseph Anderson, the Confederacy's most important arms maker, fitted into this category. Perhaps equally important were those civilian leaders who contributed to the morale of each side. Thus, preachers and journalists have come in for critical reappraisal. Finally, women in key positions to counsel and to provide support for other leaders are regarded as important leaders. The most important leaders from each of these categories make up those included in this biographical dictionary.

Those who have been included in this dictionary have had their life stories studied in similar fashion. Their upbringing, family life, education, relation to their age cohort, and prewar experience are discussed as preparation for their participation in the war. Why those leaders would give so much of themselves to the war effort has been a question asked of their upbringing and training. Wartime activities, of course, take up the central place in these entries. The positions they held and the places of their action have been discussed in full. More important, the interaction of those leaders with other leaders has been described and analyzed. A few built upon their war activities to fashion important contributions to the postwar period. Ulysses S. Grant and Andrew Johnson are examples of this group. However, no matter how much these leaders influenced events during the entire war era, their wartime experiences and accomplishments are the central focus of this dictionary. How they fared during the postwar period, what they did to enhance their wartime reputations, and how their war experience continued to influence their lives are discussed in depth. Each entry is cross-referenced, indicating other biographical subjects who also appear as entries.

A secondary, but most important, part of this dictionary discusses how the leaders wanted to be remembered in history and how history has evaluated their accomplishments. The last part of each entry includes an evaluation of how historians have regarded these leaders. Thus, those leaders' reputations have been analyzed historiographically. The leaders' views of themselves, the support or criticism of postwar memoirists and biographers, and the verdict of early historians are included in the bibliographical section. In addition, the best modern historical studies of their lives have been used to assess their contributions to the war. A chronological bibliography, from the earliest works to the present, concludes each entry. To set this study into historical context, the introduction critiques how students of their lives, from witnesses to their accomplishments to modern historians, have regarded their reputations.

The purpose of this dictionary, then, has been to study the lives of many of the Civil War's most important leaders by providing the reader with an up-to-date analysis of their activities, the ways they achieved fame, and the reasons why their reputations are what they are today. The late Thomas Lawrence Connelly, a modern historian of the many types of Civil War leaders, profoundly influenced the organization and purpose of this volume. Connelly both evaluated leadership reputation building and analyzed leadership accomplishment. For his contribution to our understanding of the relationship between accomplishments and reputation making, we dedicate this book to Tom's memory.

We also have a number of other people to thank for the final shape of this dictionary. Charles Ritter would like to thank the library and staff of Notre Dame College in Maryland, while Jon L. Wakelyn thanks the library staffs at the Catholic University of America and Kent State University for help in finding rare sources. David Kelly of the reference division of the Library of Congress was a major source of goodwill and bibliographical references for both of us. Besides contributing to the volume, Fred Blue, Herman Hattaway, John Hubbell, Leonne Hudson, John Marszalek, Jim Rawley, and Steven Woodworth have given us excellent advice on analyzing the wartime accomplishments of the leaders included in this volume. Those who advised us may not agree with all of our assessments, and certainly they are not to be held accountable for any of our mistakes. Wakelyn wishes, in addition, to thank John Allen, Michael Connolly, Clayton Jewett, and Kenneth Nivison, his graduate students at Catholic University, for the privilege of being their adviser. Frank Vandiver, mentor, friend, and colleague of Tom Connelly and Jon L. Wakelyn, shared with us his expertise on the Civil War. One would think that he would have lost patience or at least interest. Last, but not least, we thank our wives—Pam and Joyce—who suffered much from hearing about this joint effort.

INTRODUCTION: THE MAKING AND MEANING OF GREATNESS

Biography is the most popular form of history and the most problematic endeavor for the professional historian. Few present-day academic historians try their hand at biography, yet their students demand that biography have a place in the classroom. Professors often resist their students' requests because they find teaching biography difficult. One major reason for this difficulty is the persistent problem of contextualizing the subject's life and evaluating the importance of that person to the historical period in which he or she lived. Too often, the historians and their students also find that the many books and articles they read about a leader's life reveal contradictions and disagreements among scholars that both confuse and distort the process of evaluation.

One group of leaders who have proved particularly difficult to evaluate for scholarly research and teaching are the great heroes of the U.S. Civil War. That is because many modern scholars have relied on the memoirs of the participants in the Civil War, as well as their contemporary biographers and historians, to assess their activities. But often those original sources prove disadvantageous to adequate analysis of the leaders' accomplishments. Those early authors concentrated mainly on personality to the detriment of rigorous evaluation of the leaders' wartime activities. Only recently have a number of "new" military historians gone beyond those older sources to develop sophisticated means to study types of war leaders and evaluate their contribution to the total wartime experience. If they use those early works, these new military historians are careful to ignore the battles over personality and to focus on the actual descriptions of events the leaders participated in.[1]

The historians who have written the entries in this dictionary place these great leaders' lives in historical context by showing how others have judged their accomplishments since that first generation of primary witnesses. To achieve their purpose, the contributors describe those leaders' family history, childhood, education, and prewar career patterns to show how those leaders prepared for the central years of their lives. They evaluate their subjects' wartime accomplishments and assess those leaders' reputations at the war's end. Some of those Civil War leaders received enough publicity and fame during the war to make them immediate heroic figures; others' importance grew or dimmed in the years after the war. In each case, our contributors assess their sustaining, growing, or diminishing reputations through a historiographical survey of the leaders' lives and accomplishments.

Those who achieved leadership roles in that war regarded it as the major event of their lives. The war provided opportunity for both young and old, for those whose careers had reached a dead end in the 1850s, and for those just beginning or ending their life's endeavors. For all, it was the most important event in their lives, and they wished to emerge from the conflict with positive reputations. In the so-called postwar battle of the books, the former leaders and their partisans squabbled and fought to protect or to regain a place in the nation's history.[2] In a number of their memoirs, ex-generals like James Longstreet and Joseph E. Johnston actually damaged their own cause. But others, such as Ulysses S. Grant and William T. Sherman, by the sheer importance of their own reputations and the high regard contemporaries held for their memoirs, often sealed the fate of some or resurrected lesser leaders' reputations. Thus, the connection between the actual accomplishments of these leaders and their efforts to use their memoirs to influence the way history would regard them is an important subject for this volume.

The most gifted recent Civil War historian to suggest the link between contemporary reputation making and the way history has treated leaders' careers is the late Thomas L. Connelly. While studying the Confederate Army of Tennessee, Connelly sought an explanation as to why there was a lack of cooperation between the Confederate east and west. Determined to get at the heart of what he believed was the Confederacy's fatal flaw, Connelly studied in depth military and civilian organization, politics, strategy, and other activities. His analysis led him to the career of Robert E. Lee, who became for Connelly a flawed commander.

Connelly's view that Lee often failed in battle and that he betrayed the Confederate war effort in the West ran counter to the Virginian's high-toned reputation. That insight led Connelly to study historical reputation making. He discovered that the earliest historical verdict on Lee was mixed, with some writers praising his actions and others questioning just how able a general he was. Yet shortly after the war, Lee's reputation began to rise to the point where it remains today—virtually unassailable. Connelly argued that a Virginia-led plot built up Lee's importance, perhaps to use Lee to retain Virginia's preeminent place in history. Whether through plot or some deeper reason, it is clear that former Confederate general Jubal Early created a Lee propaganda machine that turned an excellent wartime commander into the South's greatest hero. History has not looked back, and through the efforts of Douglas S. Freeman, Lee's actions shine, diminishing even his most faithful lieutenants by comparison.

Connelly demurred forcefully. His efforts have persuaded other historians to study how memoirists, contemporary historians, and biographers have attempted to influence the historical record.[3]

Connelly's work suggests that a number of civilians also emerged as important leaders, their lives instrumental to the complex requirements of conducting that first modern war. In *The Politics of Command*, Connelly and Archer Jones demonstrate the importance to the war of a civilian cohort of publicist-propagandists, politicians, major bureaucrats, and other government officials. Connelly and Jones show how the military leaders formed ''concentration blocs'' or advocates in the Confederate Congress and the cabinet, who not only supported their careers but aided or hindered their ability to fight.[4] Therefore, the major congressional and governmental leaders from both sides so influenced the war effort that without them the results might have been quite different. This is so especially in the chain of command that extended from the Secretary of War to his staff to the producers and deliverers of the materiel of warfare. Connelly's mentor Frank E. Vandiver and Vandiver's great teacher Charles W. Ramsdell studied these leaders brilliantly.[5] We follow in their path, identifying other important civilians who contributed to the command and support structure and showing how their wartime activities affected their postwar reputations.

Other civilians who at first glance may not seem to belong in the category of great leaders also made crucial contributions to the war. The political culture of warfare, if even now poorly understood, produced a number of crucial leaders. Newspaper writers and editors helped to shape public opinion and to spread government and military propaganda to the citizenry. Preachers espoused total commitment and also helped in the pageantry so crucial to war as they presided over the funerals of fallen heroes. Equally important were the women, both as partners of the leaders and as participants in various aspects of the war effort. Their contributions should help us grasp the totality of the war.

One civilian leader, Walt Whitman, looms large in the history of those times because his actions and his values reflected the message and the meaning of the Civil War. A poet and hospital volunteer, Whitman encapsulated the tragedy and the grandeur of the war by bridging the gap between ordinary soldiers and the highest leadership of the Union, President Abraham Lincoln. This humble poet's activities—he spent most of the war as a male nurse—did not make him a great leader, but his devotion to humanity and his articulation of Union values did.[6]

Thanks to the writings of Whitman and the publicists, Civil War leaders' modern reputations began to take shape during the war itself and shortly after it had ended. Contemporary publicists etched a portrait of these leaders on the public consciousness, which in some cases remains fixed to this day. Take, for example, the reputation created during the war of Union commander George B. McClellan. Because he left military service but remained in the public eye, McClellan was forced to watch as his accomplishments were diminished while the war was being fought around him. McClellan's run for the presidency in

1864 did not help his reputation. His boosters declared him a war Democrat and heroic figure victimized by radical Republicans. The Republican party, renamed the Union party, put its propaganda machine to work on the former general and destroyed his reputation in order to win the election. McClellan's shortcomings—being overcautious and slow—thus became magnified as the Republican party press caricatured his wartime actions. That image stuck, and historians have used it against him ever since.[7]

Then there were the fallen warriors, those heroes killed during the war. At their funerals, preachers and politicians magnified their accomplishments. For example, the flawed soldier Leonidas Polk had a funeral full of pomp and splendor that lamented the loss of his genius. But even his tragic death did not make history turn him into a great warrior. The same fate did not await "Stonewall" Jackson, lauded by Yankee and Confederate alike. In a biography written after his death, a Northern writer sought to use the fallen hero's life to reconcile both sides in that bloody war to heal sectional hatreds. Yet in the South, a Virginia officer writing in 1863 used Jackson's untimely death to buck up a dispirited Confederacy so as to stir up further resistance. If that author did not succeed in reviving Southern morale, he did manage to assist the propaganda mill as it churned out copy on the irreplaceable and indispensable captain.[8] Jackson's reputation profited from his early death, as his failures were forgotten and his accomplishments remembered. That has been the judgment of most historians.

As the war came to an end, a second wave of commentators, usually journalists who themselves belong in the category of wartime leaders, began to write about those leaders who had survived. Actually, the efforts at reputation making by Charles Dana and Edward A. Pollard began during the war itself. Dana, the New York journalist, publicist, and Undersecretary of War, held a unique position from which to help form positive reputations of Union leaders. When Secretary of War Edwin Stanton sent him to Shiloh to find out whether Grant had been drunk there, Dana seized the opportunity to describe the general as a heroic man of action. His rendering of Grant's deeds helped to raise the general in the public eye and in the estimation of President Lincoln. Dana turned Grant's tenacity and plodding doggedness into a symbol of the Union's own preoccupation with restoration at any cost. Dana's dislike for George Meade and praise for Philip Sheridan also influenced later historical verdicts on their respective wartime accomplishments.[9] Grant's famous *Memoirs* confirmed the newspaperman's sentiments and helped determine how history has seen those lesser lieutenants. Thanks in part to Dana, with only an occasional demure, later historians have regarded Grant as the Union's most famous military leader.

Edward A. Pollard, Richmond journalist and self-styled critic of soldier and civilian alike, began his doom-filled history of Confederate failure early in the war. A vagabond and bitter intellectual masquerading as a newspaperman, Pollard hated President Jefferson Davis and all who were allied with him. Independent politicos and stubborn generals who disliked Davis rose in Pollard's estimation. Thus, Pierre G. T. Beauregard was heroic because he hated Davis.

Pollard dismissed cabinet members and Davis allies Judah P. Benjamin and Christopher G. Memminger as being unequal to their tasks. He also contributed to the Jackson and Lee mystiques. In Pollard's view, their principal accomplishment was their independence of command, which helped them circumvent the faulty orders of their commander in chief. Unwittingly, Pollard created a picture of a chaotic Confederacy made up of ruggedly independent heroes who rejected nearly all forms of cooperative military and political activities.[10] Some war participants, who later set down their own impressions, attempted to distance themselves from that vituperative and rebellious journalist. But Pollard, like his Northern counterpart Dana, had the last laugh. His biased accounts had enormous influence on how a number of future historians evaluated Confederate leadership abilities.

In addition to the early efforts of those journalists, secondary leaders close to the scenes of action, both military and civilian, eventually published their own impressions of the quality of wartime leadership. Few of them have had more lasting influence on how history has treated Southern leaders than famous Confederate War Department clerk John B. Jones. A former journalist and novelist, Jones kept a biting and sarcastic diary in which he set down critical sketches of those who led the Confederacy. Published in 1866, the *Rebel War Clerk's Diary* contained pithy comments on the qualities of civilian and military commanders. In it he described President Jefferson Davis as a committed but sickly leader who seemed more concerned with being consistent than with victory. Like Pollard, Jones found his heroes among those who disliked the president and his villains among Davis's friends. Thus, Joseph E. Johnston came in for praise when he maligned the abilities of Secretary of War Judah P. Benjamin. Likewise, Lee's actions on the peninsula in 1862 were brilliant, but his failure to follow up his advantage was Davis's fault. Describing his approach in the *Diary*, Jones said, "My chronicles are designed to assist history, and to supply the smaller incidents and details which the grand historians would be likely to omit."[11] Assist he did, to the disadvantage of those "grand historians."

While Davis, leader of the losing side, suffered in reputation, the Union's president was elevated to iconographic status by his faithful secretaries John Hay and John G. Nicolay. In a multivolume biography of the fallen president, Nicolay and Hay portrayed Lincoln as steadfast, politically brilliant, and the war's moral center. Those who opposed Lincoln or stood in his way, like William H. Seward and Salmon P. Chase, were chastised. Similarly, McClellan, Joseph Hooker, Irwin McDowell, and Ambrose Burnside, who never understood the war's purpose and never followed orders properly, were dismissed as failures. Nicolay and Hay see Henry Halleck, Edwin Stanton, and especially Grant as truly great because they cooperated with the chief. These volumes reek with insider information, filled with the stuff historians like to use. Thus, those leaders seen as second-rate by the diarist and the secretaries have never recovered their reputations, as historians continue to use those eyewitness sources to form their own views of leadership during the Civil War.[12]

Shortly after the war, the great captains themselves began their own efforts
to set the record straight about their places in history. Some wrote because they
needed the money or because their lives were so important that the public clamored for their memories. Later, old and infirm former leaders, inspired by attacks
on their reputations in others' memoirs and fretful over the depictions of their
accomplishments, took to their desks to recoup their places in history. A few
died too early to produce memoirs; so history is spared their confessions, child-
ish recriminations, and hate-filled commentary. The Union general George Thomas, for instance, probably had his reputation damaged by dying before he could
produce a memoir. Others, like Lee, no doubt rose in history's eyes because he
did little recriminating or attacking in print. But all of those who wrote their
memoirs were obsessed with their places in the war. Even years after the event,
the war defined their very manhood, and they felt they had to defend the importance of their roles in it. Obviously, in their efforts at self-aggrandizement,
their records influenced the way the future wrote about their greatness.

If many of those leaders wrote in positive terms of their accomplishments,
some memoirists questioned the purpose of their cause. Many, like Alexander
Stephens, became obsessive revisionists as they shifted the meaning of the war
to suit their postwar needs. Yet these memoirs have no regrets for the many
who died because of their actions. Preoccupied with their places in history, they
cannot comment about the costs of war to those they commanded or governed.
Duty seems to have been everything. There is no mourning, no remorse, and
for their souls, perhaps no peace.

The nature of command perhaps taught the leaders never to apologize. That
is why even questionable behavior is cast in a positive light. Take, for example,
the swashbuckling saga of *Memoirs of Service Afloat* by the Confederate "privateer," admiral, Raphael Semmes. In his hurriedly published 1869 memoirs,
Semmes explained his burning and sinking of defenseless Union merchant ships
as an expression of modern total war. It denied his enemy access to goods from
abroad. To show the success of Semmes's memoirs on later interpretation of his
deeds, there is no hint of this war on civilians at the Semmes Museum in Mobile.
The visitor only sees the exploits of a great navy hero in armed conflict with
Union ships of war.[13]

Those memoirs published early after the war were paltry efforts at rectification
and obfuscation compared to the works of the great leaders written years after
the war. Some, like the memoirs of Grant and Sherman, are great works of art
that give much insight into military genius. Grant, who understood his audience
and perhaps the future, placed himself in the background, never appeared flashy,
yet showed himself in command of all situations. He had the genius to pretend
he was ordinary and still reveal just how extraordinary he was. Of course,
as he elevated himself, Grant just had to tell the truth about others. In his wake,
he left a bloodstained record of his subordinates' failures. Sherman, too, sought
to convey a public image. He appears as he fought: brutal, sure of himself,
conceding only one peer, Grant.[14] So much has been written about these two

great generals based on their own memoirs that perhaps it is time to set aside their writings and find other ways to assess their genius.

Less significant, or as well written as those of Grant and Sherman, are a host of other personal memoirs designed to build or restore reputations. Few can compare to the apparent self-effacement of Philip Sheridan, the little man who was in the right place enough times to make his exploits legendary. His purpose in writing, he claimed, was certainly not to give his own actions "an unmerited prominence." Instead, "the importance of the subject-matter of my narrative is my own claim on the reader's attention." Then, in two volumes of over 1,000 pages, we get the story of the immigrant boy who rose to fame through hard work and military genius. Of course, to raise himself, others had to fall. For example, he claims he saved General William Rosecrans at Murfreesboro. Accordingly, Sheridan insists that he, and not General George Thomas, was really the hero of Missionary Ridge. Sheridan also diminishes Meade's role at the siege of Petersburg and the final victory at Appomattox Courthouse.[15] Grant defended Sheridan in his *Memoirs*, as little Phil gleefully pointed out. No one today doubts Sheridan's accomplishments. But his *Memoirs* have too much influenced historians' evaluation of his services to the Union cause.

If the Union leaders at times diminished one another, the Confederate leaders' "battle of the books," which involved both enormous personal pride and justification for defeat, revealed smarmy personal feuds. For instance, Joseph E. Johnston's 1874 work, written in response to ex-President Jefferson Davis's memoir and the Virginia historical machine's attempt to label him "Retreatin' Joe," emasculates the reputations of Braxton Bragg, Davis, and Pierre G. T. Beauregard.[16] Indeed, Beauregard himself went so far to help his cause as to publish his memoir in the guise of a biography written by one of his faithful subordinates. He wrote the 1884 *Military Operations of General Beauregard* to even the score with ex-President Davis, who in 1881 had attacked his competence and even claimed the great Creole had feigned illness to avoid combat.[17] Similarly, James Longstreet struggled against the Virginia historical machine's protection of Lee's reputation. In *From Manassas to Appomattox*, he lashed out at the incompetency of others, especially Lee. Taking on the great icon was bad enough, but when Longstreet became a postwar Republican party supporter, he sealed his historical fate, and historians until recently have judged him accordingly.[18]

The saddest of all the ex-Confederate memoirs are those of John Bell Hood, too aptly entitled *Advance and Retreat*. Published by a man broken in health and spirit, they reveal wrenching attempts to explain wartime actions to the public and to himself. Hood argued that he always obeyed orders and that he followed the tactics of the offensive as taught by his two heroes, Jackson and Lee. It was almost as if the gallant Hood believed that by association with greatness he could absolve himself of guilt. He used the early sections of the memoir to prepare the reader for 1864, when he would have to explain his actions from Atlanta to Nashville. He blames Joseph E. Johnston for his failure in that campaign, but his own description of events exposes his incompetence. Among all the great Confederate apologists, Hood's work remains the most obtuse, as it reveals a leader who never understood why he had led all those young men to needless slaughter.[19]

The Civil War's military leaders' self-explanations and attacks on others, thus, only marginally assist us to assess their authors' actions and value to the war. But too often those leaders' evaluations of their peers have been used by their apologists or opponents to create a false record of others' leadership accomplishments. All of the losers in the war reveal their lasting hurt because of personal failure. The victors did not have that problem, yet they, too, distorted the facts in order to elevate themselves. As the authors of these entries demonstrate, too many historians have believed these memorists' views of their own careers and of others' personalities and have supported that false record of the great leaders' accomplishments. They also comment on what those leaders themselves revealed about the ways they fought the first modern war.

If the military leaders attempted to distort their roles in history, the great civilian leaders also used memoirs to assert their version of the war's purpose, to affirm their accomplishments, to harm the careers of their foes, and even to revise why they served in the first place. Union Secretary of the Treasury Salmon P. Chase's *Diary* is notorious for its slander of others. In it Chase attacked Edwin Stanton and other cabinet members who had been his allies. He claimed that they had failed in their offices and that only he had been a successful cabinet member, loyal to the president.[20] Chase's false rendering of Union government careers unfortunately has become a major source for a number of historians. Another diarist, former Union Secretary of the Navy Gideon Welles, was even more of a revisionist than Chase. The puritan New Englander hated everyone and thought he was surrounded by incompetence. For example, Welles depicted Stanton as a half-mad, frantic, and incompetent judge of military needs.[21] Welles's *Diary* has been an important source for historians because it reads like the objective views of a talented leader who did understand the cost of war. In reality, the *Diary* is an effort by one who sought to secure his place in history by diminishing others.

In a class by themselves are the so-called histories of the Civil War by the vice president and the president of the Confederacy. In them they explained away their own shortcomings and mistakes, and they attempted to revise the very reasons why the nation went to war. In *A Constitutional View of the Late War between the States*, former Confederate Vice President Alexander H. Stephens claimed that his first loyalty was to Georgia and state's rights. Gone is any reference to his famous "cornerstone" speech in which he asserted that the South's need to protect slavery had caused the war. In his postwar analysis of the war, Stephens argued for the rights of local self-government, which some historians see as his own reason to resist the very Confederacy that had been formed to protect slave society. The wizened, diminutive, enigmatic leader wrote a veiled defense of why he spent most of the war sulking at home in Georgia.

His dislike of the overbearing Jefferson Davis, a government centralizer willing to do anything to preserve secession, is apparent in his so-called historical narrative. At the end of the book, Stephens becomes the reconstructionist politician, eager to demonstrate that "two-thirds of those who had voted for secession, did so, . . . with a view to a more certain re-formation of the Union."[22]

If Stephens was the contrite revisionist, former President Jefferson Davis, in his 1881 *The Rise and Fall of the Confederate Government*, became the bitterender fighting for a just cause. He too obviated the slavery issue and claimed the war had been fought over Southern political rights. But Davis also set out to revise his own role in the war, to claim that he was surrounded by enemies who resisted his entreaties to fight on at all cost. His greatest animosity was toward state's righters such as Georgia Governor Joseph E. Brown, whom he insisted sabotaged the Confederacy. Johnston, Beauregard, and other generals also had undermined the Confederacy by their poor military performances. Even the Southern people came in for criticism because they refused to fight on to victory. Nowhere did Davis blame himself.[23] Historians have mined this trove of half-truths and have exposed Davis's flaws, but they also have acceded uncritically to his list of failed leaders and accepted his reasons for their incompetence.

The memoirs of a second level of leaders who were in the front line of the Washington and Richmond political whirl compounded the problem for present-day historians who seek to understand competence and achievement. These observers from the corridors of power reinforce the messy history of recrimination and distortion written by their heroes or enemies. The memoirs of these witnesses require comment, if only to reinforce the warning to consider the source, even when it is primary.

The most vicious of these political observers cast his effort as a reminiscence. As former Confederate Congressman Henry S. Foote stated in *Casket of Reminiscences*, he had "no apology to make for certain unkind strictures" about some of the leaders in Richmond. For Foote, Davis and his government were to blame for causing the war and for defeat. He accused Secretary of War James A. Seddon of possessing no other talent for conducting the war than that he was an ally of the Confederate president. Foote's hatred for Judah P. Benjamin, whom he insisted had been a war profiteer, spilled over, as he even resurrected a scandal from Benjamin's college days. Furthermore, Foote found Davis's loyalty to the vain, selfish, intriguing Braxton Bragg unconscionable. A former secessionist congressman turned unionist, Foote claimed Davis sabotaged the Hampton Roads Conference deliberately to ensure the war would continue. Lee became a hero for Foote because he did his duty even though his heart was never in the war. Johnston and Beauregard received praise because they hated Davis and because they questioned carrying the war beyond the Confederacy's ability to prevail.[24] In short, Foote's bitterness toward the Confederate leadership certainly makes his judgment of their actions suspect.

Others of the gray persuasion contributed to the crescendo of criticism and praise that influences the way modern historians judge wartime leadership accomplishment. General Richard Taylor, in his highly regarded *Destruction and Reconstruction* of 1879, supported President Davis by diminishing the significance of the activities of Johnston and Beauregard. Because he himself had been an important Confederate general, this son of a former U.S. president produced a memoir that has been used by historians without critical evaluation of the author's motives. Thus, his portrayal of Albert S. Johnston as the Confederacy's great hope who was killed too soon has found a favorable place in history. That Johnston was Davis's favorite no doubt influenced Taylor's lack of objectivity on that great hero's importance.[25] Likewise, John B. Gordon, the former general turned Georgia politician, was such a fine soldier himself that historians have tended to regard him as objective. But Gordon wrote his memoirs in later life, during his service in the U.S. Senate, when he hoped to heal sectional wounds. However, he still maligned General John Pemberton for losing Vicksburg. Gordon had served under Lee, and he contributed much to the legend growing around him. Lee's greatness, according to that lieutenant, was his undying love for the Union and his quick adjustment to Confederate defeat.[26]

Others of these secondary historian-memoirists, writing near the century's end, contributed to the existing belief that the politicians had failed and the generals had succeeded. For example, the veteran John Wise, son of a Virginia governor, in his *The End of an Era* of 1899, damned the politicians and praised the warriors. "It seemed to me," he wrote, "that the men interested with the civic administration of the Confederate government were not of as fine clay as her immortal soldier."[27] Supporting Wise, former Confederate congressman John Goode, in his much admired *Recollections of a Lifetime*, published in 1906, affirmed the verdict of political incompetence.[28] To the detriment of careful analysis of the politics of war, modern historians have relied too much on so-called objective contemporaries from that second rank of leaders like Wise and Goode. By the end of the century, the participants in the Civil War had left a record that would greatly influence the first generation of professional historians who set about to assess the qualities of leadership among the Confederates.

Eyewitness accounts from the second rank of Union leaders, writing less to blame than to praise, have also influenced the way later historians evaluated the Union's greatest leaders. For example, ex-General Lew Wallace, in his *Autobiography* of 1906, bragged about his own exploits during the war. Yet he also contributed to the Grant legend as he heaped praise upon that leader for having saved him from unfair dismissal. More a biographer of Grant and Sherman than of his own life, Wallace attempted to destroy what he considered lesser lights like Halleck who had not fought in the field.[29] In a similar vein, former General Grenville M. Dodge, in his 1914 *Personal Recollections*, praised "the patience, the firmness, the resolution with which" Sherman "pursued his difficult campaign against Johnston from Chattanooga to Atlanta," as "one of the finest achievements in history." Not content to rest on that hyperbolic statement, Dodge added to the Sherman legend when he claimed the March to the Sea made his reputation "for all time."[30] The infamous Benjamin Butler wrote his *Autobiography and Personal Reminiscences* in 1892 to gain absolution for his behavior at New Orleans and his failure at Petersburg. One of the most conspicuous "political" generals, Butler lashed out at West Point–trained soldiers and praised civilian loyalty to the cause. He argued that Henry Halleck, his most bitter enemy, had no political sense and misjudged Butler's abilities. Only Grant, whom Halleck had deceived about Butler, received praise for understanding the "Beast's" place in the war.[31] These self-serving secondary Union leaders heaped praise and blame upon certain of their superiors, which were bound to influence the first generation of professional historians.

Perhaps the most dangerously biased sources for future scholars were those lesser wartime leaders who wrote the early biographies of the great Civil War leaders based supposedly on primary sources and eyewitness accounts. Some of them had been aides who saved the private correspondence of their superiors, which they used to tell their versions of the truth. Another group of them had become the former war leaders' assistants after the war. When their heroes at last died, these men were there to clear up the record and to remind the nation of the sacrifices those great leaders had made for the cause. In their attempts to capture the essence of their leaders' qualities, or to recapture their lost glory, they became the first of a long line of biographer keepers of the flame.

William Preston Johnston had never served with his father, but nevertheless he wrote an important biography of him in 1878. Using interviews with his father's former aides, William contributed to the legend of the fallen warrior who would surely have won the war in the West had he lived. To make his father a hero, William had to attack Beauregard's actions at Shiloh. It was, he claimed, "Borry's" "fatal order to retire" on the second day that lost the battle his father had won the day before.[32] Historians have used that argument to fault Beauregard. The intrepid war clerk John B. Jones also wrote an early biography of Lee in which he used Lee's dispatches and personal correspondence to create an air of reality about his romantic tale. In order to allow the true hero to emerge unscathed from criticism, Jones had to overcome two questionable aspects of the great man's life, one a sentiment and the other an action. Some of Lee's contemporaries had claimed that Lee entered the war reluctantly and "that he was ready to abandon it long before he did." In reality, said Jones, Lee "stood firm to the last." Jones also rejected the notion that Lee could have fought on after Appomattox. In reality, says Jones, Grant accepted Lee's terms of surrender.[33] So it goes with the Lee legend of great sacrifice and love of country. Only recently does Emory Thomas raise again the question of Lee's devotion to the Confederate cause.[34] One supposes, however, that no mere mortal will be able to revise the legend of Bobby Lee. Others of the great warriors have not been so fortunate. For instance, in an edited memoir, thinly disguised as biography, Bradley T. Johnson unsuccessfully attempted to revise upward the reputation of Joseph E. Johnston.[35]

There are also a number of biographies of controversial civilian leaders, often written by aides who wanted to help their heroes' later careers by reminding voters of what they had done in the war. Herbert Fielder wrote a campaign biography for Joseph E. Brown in which he attempted to explain that the ex-Georgia governor had never turned against the Confederacy.[36] If that form of hagiography helped to get Brown back into Georgia politics, later historians have used it to bury him in a sea of disloyalty. Likewise, a number of biographers have sought to dispute the charges that Indiana war governor Oliver P. Morton had run roughshod over the civil rights of Democrats. William M. French and William Dudley Foulke, apologists who knew him, claimed Morton only acted to support those who wanted to restore the Union. Charles M. Walker, the newspaperman, used the familiar tactic of writing a retrospective in a funeral announcement to affirm Morton's place in midwestern and American history. To the charge that Morton had profited in office, Walker replied he had died poor. To the accusation that the former governor had been an atheist, Walker responded that he believed in the "truths of Christianity." Walker was confident that the future would honor Morton.[37] He was wrong, and history is poorer for its ignorance of Morton and the other great governors who supported the Union war effort.

Perhaps the most valuable of those early biographies, some of which have given historians much useful evidence on the personal lives and personalities of the most important political leaders, is flame keeper Varina Howell Davis's *Jefferson Davis, a Memoir*. Published in 1890 and written from Davis's own notes, Varina Davis hoped to restore the late Confederate president's reputation. Of course, in order to elevate her husband, Mrs. Davis had to diminish others. She revived the old wars with Beauregard and Johnston. She vilified the traitors Joe Brown and Alexander Stephens. To elicit sympathy for Davis, she retold the story of his imprisonment after the war in excruciating detail. She recounted how his loyal soldiers invited him to speak at their reunions and called him the greatest of their political leaders. But Mrs. Davis also unwittingly described an insensitive leader who never seemed able to rally his troops during the war. In short, she revealed an imperious president who conducted the war himself, served as his own cabinet leader, and stubbornly fought with Congress, forcing most of its members to resist his entreaties.[38] By using her husband's own words to discuss the failings of others, she created a record that later historians have used against him.

Those efforts at memoir writing, early history, and biography—over thirty-five years of apologetics, rationalizations, and recriminations, North and South—have contributed to modern analyists' depiction of the performances of Civil War leaders. Because the authors of those first works of historical reconstruction were close to the action, their accounts seem credible. Yet when modern historians rely on those early historical writings and other primary sources to assess the true character of those leaders, they depended on flawed sources that focused on the war leaders' personalities rather than on their substance and accomplishments. Used with care, however, these works can be revealing.

A few modern scholars who have written about the first generation of professional Civil War historians have understood the problem of early historical revisionism and have placed the works of those authors into historical context. Unfortunately, most of those recent efforts at historiography, at least those published about historians who wrote down to World War II, have been more concerned with the coming of the Civil War than with the war itself, the performance of wartime leaders, or the social and cultural impact of the war. Nevertheless, one major study, Thomas Pressly's *Americans Interpret Their Civil War*, helps us to begin to ask how to study the qualities of leadership and to evaluate impact and accomplishment.[39]

According to Pressly, the first generation of professional Civil War historians began to appear during the 1880s. They scoured the *Official Record* and dipped into the older primary sources to offer new interpretations of those events. Pressly calls them the ''national'' historians because they favored the Northern victory, advocated sectional reconciliation, and regarded the war as the defining moment when the United States emerged as a major industrial world power. The most important of these early professionals were James Ford Rhodes, John Bach McMaster, Edward Channing, and Albert Bushnell Hart. All wrote for an educated audience, and all painted on a broad nationalist canvas. Most were racist to the extent that they believed the war had been fought over the nation's future, not over slavery, and they accepted a postwar segregated society. However, their works hardly deviated from the earlier versions of heroes and failures. Lincoln, depicted as a conservative Unionist, was the crucial leader, while they saw Jefferson Davis as devious and a failure. Grant and Sherman succeeded as Union generals, and McClellan failed. Most of those ''nationalist'' historians belonged to the Republican party, and their political heroes were of that same persuasion. Many of them praised Lee, not for his military exploits but because he came to symbolize national reconciliation. But those historians were mainly interested in the great forces of modern warfare, in machinery and governance, which became the war's true heroes. Thus, they generally failed to make critical evaluations of individual accomplishments.[40]

Occasionally, a historian wrote a biography to reappraise an important life. One such scholar was University of Chicago professor and later diplomat William E. Dodd, the first professional analyst of Jefferson Davis's performance. Although he believed Davis failed to spark a ''vital nation,'' Dodd hoped that an educated public was prepared to make ''a just estimate'' of the ex-Confederate president's accomplishments. More important, Dodd wanted to forgive Davis and to include him in the pantheon of great Americans. Knowing it was impossible ''to speak dispassionately,'' Dodd sought the middle ground between the devil theory of history and the need for national reunification. In doing so, Dodd misread Davis's own writings in order to forgive the ex-president's wartime errors because of his so-called conversion to nationalism during the 1880s. A Democrat, Dodd also found Davis's argument for the federal principle important in a time when government was corrupt, overstuffed, and in need of reform. He had pled the former president's case, but at the end, he insisted he had made no verdict on Davis's wartime performance.[41]

Another group of historians and writers, many of whom used the works of the wartime participants indiscriminately, began to publish during and after World War I. Known as the neo-Confederates, they adopted the view that the Civil War destroyed a great nation. Most of them were from the South, and they refought the war and reevaluated its leaders with hopes of at long last winning a Southern peace. To be sure, Ulrich B. Phillips and William P. Trent, the best of these Southern historians, supported reconciliation and growth and described the great leaders as those who ultimately supported the entire nation. But the neo-Confederates became important writers and have had a lasting impact upon a number of later historians. The manifesto of this group of young men who lived near Vanderbilt University in Nashville, Tennessee, was the 1930 anti-industrial book *I'll Take My Stand*. Later using biography to give his readers a dose of Southern values, one of them, Allen Tate, wrote in praise of "Stonewall" Jackson and Jefferson Davis as yeomen farmers who ably led the Southern cause. Another neo-Confederate, Stark Young, in his 1934 novel *So Red the Rose*, attacked Sherman as a maniacal modernist who destroyed all that was good in the past.[42] As critic Daniel Aaron stated, the historical and biographical works of those neo-Confederates produced a "series of psychologically simplistic portraits of rather complex personalities."[43] Indeed, the neo-Confederates perpetuated the post–Civil War generation's judgment on great lives based on personality and had offered no serious evaluation of leadership merit.

Ironically, the neo-Confederates connected with a group of revisionist historians, who also believed the Civil War had caused more problems than it solved. Personally buffeted by World War I, this group of professional historians also worried over the economic depression and feared impending world war. They, too, insisted that the Civil War could have been avoided. For Charles W. Ramsdell, Frank L. Owsley, E. Merton Coulter, and James G. Randall—all giants of historical scholarship who wrote between the world wars—a blundering generation of politicos had precipitated a needless war. Their heroes were nationalists. Randall, for example, made Lincoln into a moderate who sought a conservative solution to the Civil War. Coulter believed that most Confederate leaders failed, and he attacked the Southern civilian leaders in particular for continuing an unwinnable war.[44]

If the interwar period spawned a reaction against war in a number of historians, others belonged to what Pressly called the "new nationalist" interpreters of the Civil War. Appearing during the 1930s among those who resisted the rise of Nazi Germany, one of the most important of this group was Douglas S. Freeman, the biographer of George Washington and Robert E. Lee. In his 1942 *Lee's Lieutenants*, this Richmond newspaperman claimed that Lee was a successful hero because when the cause was lost, he quickly advocated restoration of the Union. His harsh judgment of most Confederate generals because they had not supported Lee adequately was a veiled criticism of those who failed to prepare to defend the nation in his own time.[45]

Allan Nevins's efforts to describe how the Civil War had prepared a modern industrial power to resist Hitler were perhaps less disrespectful of historical truth than Freeman's desire to change a Confederate into a national hero. Another newspaperman turned historian, Nevins had the gift of brilliant narrative style and the ability to recapture the essence of a leader in a brief word picture. If he found fault with the personalities of many of the lesser leaders, those who saved the nation became his heroes. According to Nevins, the Civil War hastened modern industrial development and produced the strong central state that now faced a hostile Europe. For him and other "new nationalist" historians, bureaucrats, businessmen, and others who built the machinery of warfare became the Civil War's heroes, and their lives required as much analysis as those of the traditional warriors and politicos.[46]

Understanding modern war's need for new kinds of leaders, Nevins linked "new nationalist" ideals to the qualities of Civil War leadership. He praised leaders who had an "instinct for the spirit and needs of a critical time." Thus he claimed that Jefferson Davis's flaws were a preoccupation with immediate issues of military combat while he ignored "political problems and civil issues." According to Nevins, Davis, Robert M. T. Hunter, and Louis T. Wigfall, all failed as Confederate civilian leaders because they could not establish the economic structure necessary to mold a national defense. Nevins also made judgments on who was most important to the North's war effort. Lincoln, uncompromising leader, was the ablest of them all. Grant and Sherman, who were willing to adopt any means to save the Union, joined the pantheon of great leaders.[47] Thus, Nevins and others had begun to develop criteria for assessing leadership quality and accomplishment.

Since World War II, most works on the Civil War have not attempted a systematic analysis of the qualities of leadership and have generally relied on the much older verdicts of those who participated in the war itself. One finds little commentary on the qualities of leaders in the most recent grand synthesis of the Civil War, James McPherson's 1988 Pulitzer Prize–winning *Battle Cry of Freedom*. McPherson's brilliant old-fashioned narrative account simply shows no understanding of how the war was fought.[48] An ambivalence toward the study of warfare in McPherson's work and in many other of today's academic historians may explain this absence. Does that mean that there is no interest among historians in assessing accomplishment? Are we back to the original problem that provoked this present study of biography—the means of analyzing great lives?

Fortunately, as the entries in this volume show, a number of other recent historians have made enormous strides in the study of modern warfare, especially regarding individual and collective leadership performance. They use quite carefully the work of the earliest generation of eyewitnesses who so distorted the historical record. Only where those early authors wrote about how the war was fought do these new historians make use of them. Two of the best modern syntheses of the Civil War—Herman Hattaway and Archer Jones's 1983 *How the North Won the Civil War* and Jones, Hattaway, and others' 1986 *Why the South Lost the Civil War*—offer new ways to evaluate how the war was fought and the role of its participants in victory and defeat. Together these books reveal a profound knowledge of the art of war and therefore of the war's artists.[49]

The authors of *Why the South Lost the Civil War* have dispensed with some of the cherished older arguments for Confederate defeat. While the new historians may concentrate too much on morale and loyalty as actors in the Confederacy's demise, they nevertheless show how valuable certain leaders' contributions were to the cause. More important, they question the criteria that some authors use to claim that the Union had better generals, and they ask for more sophisticated means to assess military abilities. The authors also cite the splendid work of Paul Escott, who shows how Jefferson Davis failed to keep up Southern morale and how Governor Joe Brown of Georgia deserved much credit for feeding the soldiers' families and thus keeping up their will to fight.[50] They also understand the importance of religion and religious leaders to the war. Above all, these historians' analysis of "a tight relationship of military and civilian decision making" has influenced other studies of just who were the most important and the most able wartime leaders.

In *How the North Won the Civil War*, the authors unite the context for action and the evaluation of leadership ability. They cite the excellent writings of John G. Moore, June I. Gow, Michael Howard, and Brien Holden Reid, which show how those in military operations developed knowledge of logistics, transportation, and the terrain.[51] These recent military historians have built on the pioneer work of Frank E. Vandiver and others to understand just how important activity behind the lines was to the war itself.[52] Hattaway and Jones's verdict that "an army which lived off the country could not both forage and fight" reopens the significance of geography to the war. These authors also state that those who wrote from a perspective too close to the war claimed that certain military actions were more important than they in fact were. They therefore mostly avoid using those old accounts, especially because those original authors often failed to assess the context for success adequately.

Hattaway and Jones also concentrate on new views of leadership activities. They have used books by students of psychology and opinion, such as Michael Adams's 1978 *Our Masters the Rebels*. Adams exposes flaws in the leaders' belief systems that possibly influenced the way they fought.[53] That Davis wore himself out because of his compulsion to command all aspects of the war shows something of his inner psychological needs. Hattaway and Jones's analysis of self-enhancement through use of prewar personal connections, reminiscent of Connelly and Jones in their 1973 *The Politics of Command*, reveals why some leaders had the opportunity to command, while others were never given the chance.[54] Their use of the power of public opinion, the actuality of democracy, and decision making show us another context for evaluating leadership. In doing so, Hattaway and Jones reveal that all of those Civil War leaders were handicapped by an ignorant public that demanded victory in battle when many of the leaders understood that modern war gave few clear-cut victories.[55] That the public encouraged Grant to pursue "total" war no doubt gave him the will to persevere in his activities against Southern noncombatants. Davis's political blunders also must be seen as pressured responses to the negative public opinion made by the partisan press. Jones and Hattaway's combining psychological analysis and study of public opinion has assisted the historians who have contributed to this volume to evaluate the context needed for the assessment of leadership ability.

Jones and Hattaway's and Connelly and Jones's work also uncovers the relationship of politics to warfare and thus suggests renewed concentration on the institutional setting for warfare. Although the best of recent studies on this subject, Richard Bensel's 1992 *Yankee Leviathan*, makes little judgment on leadership, it does explain the relationship between methods of governance and wartime activities. For example, success in mobilization for war was related to tensions between federal and state governments. Bensel also focuses on the federal Congress to understand the executive and legislative battles that so influenced the decisions of where and how to fight. Bensel suggests that strong, knowledgeable, and committed leaders at times transcended "bureaucratic autonomy" but rarely partisanship. There is a hint here that partisan political memoirs have distorted the way we evaluate leadership accomplishments.[56]

All of these new and more sophisticated means to study warfare acknowledge Thomas L. Connelly's pioneering study of propaganda and image making, and of molding the careers of friends, which helps historians sort out the true accomplishments of those great Civil War leaders. Those who have learned from Connelly are asking other questions about wartime activities and postwar image making. One such effort by Craig L. Symonds undertakes the thankless task of revising the interpretation of the nearly unfathomable military career of Joseph E. Johnston. Symonds carefully analyzes what others said to diminish Johnston. He then shows how Johnston attempted to defend himself in print—and hurt his reputation by doing so. "For the rest of his life," says Symonds, "he would fight a furious rearguard action in defense of his reputation." Johnston indeed had written to justify his own personal honor and, in doing so, as Symonds shows, gravely distorted his own and many others' accomplishments. But Symonds also carefully followed Johnston's wartime actions as described in his memoirs and came to appreciate what that beleaguered general was up against in fighting a modern war.[57]

All of these recent works have revealed the dangers for those who have used those first efforts at historical writings to understand how to evaluate the careers of the Civil War leaders included in this volume. A most thoughtful student of the Civil War era, Merrill Peterson, in his 1994 *Lincoln in American Memory*, has brilliantly addressed the issue of the development over time of great leaders' reputations. By using the developmental approach, he has confirmed one purpose of this volume. In analyzing the evolution of Lincoln's reputation, Peterson has also confirmed Connelly's method of getting at the real accomplishments of other great Civil War leaders.[58] Perhaps the authors' use in this volume of Connelly's and others' work on ways to evaluate leadership will make biography again worthy of scholarly historical research and give those who teach biography the means to judge the accomplishments of the great leaders of the American Civil War.

NOTES

1. Thomas L. Connelly and Archer Jones, *The Politics of Command* (Baton Rouge: Louisiana State University Press, 1973); Herman Hattaway and Archer Jones, *How the North Won the Civil War* (Urbana: University of Illinois Press, 1983); Edward Hagerman, *The American Civil War and the Origins of Modern Warfare* (Indianapolis: Indiana University Press, 1988); Joseph T. Glatthaar, *Partners in Command* (New York: Free Press, 1994).

2. Anne Rose, *Victorianism and the American Civil War* (New York: Cambridge University Press, 1995), chap. 7.

3. Thomas L. Connelly, *The Marble Man* (Baton Rouge: Louisiana State University Press, 1973), esp. chaps. 2 and 3; Walter Piston, *Lee's Tarnished Lieutenant* (Athens: University of Georgia Press, 1987).

4. Connelly and Jones, *The Politics of Command*, 48–49.

5. Frank E. Vandiver, *Ploughshares into Swords* (Austin: University of Texas Press, 1952); Charles W. Ramsdell, *Behind the Lines in the Southern Confederacy* (Baton Rouge: Louisiana State University Press, 1944).

6. David S. Reynolds, *Walt Whitman's America* (New York: Alfred A. Knopf, 1996).

7. See Thomas Rowland, *In the Shadow of Grant and Sherman* (Kent, Ohio: Kent State University Press, 1998).

8. Markinfield Addey, *Life and Military Career of Thomas Jonathan Jackson* (New York: Charles T. Evans, 1863); Thomas Jackson Arnold, *Early Life and Letters of Thomas J. Jackson* (Richmond, Va.: Fleming H. Kavell Co., 1916).

9. Charles A. Dana, *Recollections* (New York: D. Appleton and Co., 1902).

10. Edward A. Pollard, *The Lost Cause* (New York: Fairfax Press, 1988); Edward A. Pollard, *Life of Jefferson Davis* (New York: Books for Libraries Press, 1969).

11. John B. Jones, *Rebel War Clerk's Diary at the Confederate States Capital*, 2 vols. (Philadelphia: J. P. Lippincott, 1866), 1:116, 178.

12. John George Nicolay and John Hay, *Abraham Lincoln: A History*, 10 vols. (New York: Charles Scribner, 1890).

13. Raphael Semmes, *Memoirs of Service Afloat, During the War between the States* (Baltimore: Kelly, Piet and Co., 1869).

14. U. S. Grant, *Memoirs and Selected Letters*, 2 vols. (New York: Library of America, 1990); William T. Sherman, *Memoirs*, 2 vols. (Indianapolis: Indiana University Press, 1957).

15. Philip Sheridan, *Personal Memoirs*, 2 vols. (New York: Charles L. Webster, 1888).

16. Joseph E. Johnston, *Narrative of Military Operations* (Indianapolis: Indiana University Press, 1959), 162, 189, 226.

17. Alfred Roman, *The Military Operations of General Beauregard*, 2 vols. (New York: Harper and Row, 1884).

18. James A. Longstreet, *From Manassas to Appomattox* (Indianapolis: Indiana University Press, 1960).

19. John Bell Hood, *Advance and Retreat* (New Orleans: Hood Orphan's Memorial Fund, 1880).

20. Jacob W. Schukers, *Life and Public Service of Samuel Portland Chase* (New York: Scribner, 1894); for the other side, see George C. Gorhan, *Life and Public Service of Edwin M. Stanton*, 2 vols. (New York: Houghton Mifflin, 1899).

21. Gideon Welles, *Diary* (Boston: Houghton Mifflin, 1911).

22. Alexander H. Stephens, *A Constitutional View of the Late War Between the States*, 2 vols. (Philadelphia: National Publishing Co., 1868, 1870), 1:330.

23. Jefferson Davis, *The Rise and Fall of the Confederate Government*, 2 vols. (New York: D. Appleton, 1881); also see George Cary Eggleston, *History of the Confederate War*, 2 vols. (New York: Sturgis and Walter, 1910), 2:322–324.

24. Henry S. Foote, *Casket of Reminiscences* (Washington, D.C.: Chronicle Publishing Co., 1874), preface.

25. Richard Taylor, *Destruction and Reconstruction* (New York: D. Appleton, 1879), 34–36.

26. John B. Gordon, *Reminiscences of the Civil War* (Baton Rouge: Louisiana State University Press, 1993), 118, 166.

27. John S. Wise, *The End of an Era* (Boston: Houghton Mifflin, 1899), 404.

28. John Goode, *Recollections of a Lifetime* (New York: Neale Publishing Co., 1906), 88, 93.

29. Lew Wallace, *An Autobiography*, 2 vols. (New York: Harper, 1906).

30. Grenville M. Dodge, *Personal Recollections* (Council Bluffs, Iowa: Monarch Publishing Co., 1914), 183.

31. Benjamin F. Butler, *Autobiography and Personal Reminiscences* (Boston: A. M. Thayer, 1892).

32. William Preston Johnston, *The Life of Albert Sidney Johnston* (New York: D. Appleton and Co., 1878), vii, viii.

33. John B. Jones, *Personal Reminiscences of General Robert E. Lee* (Baton Rouge: Louisiana State University Press, 1994), 293.

34. Emory Thomas, *Robert E. Lee* (New York: W. W. Norton, 1995).

35. Bradley T. Johnson, *Life of Joseph E. Johnston* (Baltimore: R. H. Woodward & Co., 1891).

36. Herbert Fielder, *Sketch of Life and Times and Speeches of Joseph E. Brown* (Springfield, Mass.: Press of Springfield Print Co., 1883).

37. William Dudley Foulke, *Life of Oliver P. Morton*, 2 vols. (Indianapolis: Bobbs-Merrill, 1899); William M. French, *Life, Speeches, and Public Service of Governor Oliver P. Morton* (Indianapolis: S. L. Marrow, 1900).

38. Varina Howell Davis, *Jefferson Davis, a Memoir*, 2 vols. (1890; Baltimore: Nautical and Aviation Publishing Co. of America, 1990), 2:939, 932.

39. Thomas Pressly, *Americans Interpret Their Civil War* (Princeton: Princeton University Press, 1954).

40. Ibid., chap. 4.

41. William E. Dodd, *Jefferson Davis* (New York: Russell and Russell, 1966).

42. Allen Tate et al., *I'll Take My Stand* (1930; New York: Harper and Row, 1962);

Allen Tate, *Jefferson Davis* (New York: Minton, Balch and Co., 1929); Stark Young, *So Red the Rose* (New York: Charles Scribner's Sons, 1934).

43. Daniel Aaron, *The Unwritten War* (New York: Oxford University Press, 1973).

44. See James G. Randall, *Lincoln*, 4 vols. (New York: Dodd, Mead, 1939–1947); E. Merton Coulter, *History of the Southern Confederacy* (Baton Rouge: Louisiana State University Press, 1949).

45. Douglas Southall Freeman, *Lee's Lieutenants*, 3 vols. (New York: Charles Scribner, 1942–1944), 1:introduction.

46. Allan Nevins, *Ordeal of the Union*, 8 vols. (New York: Charles Scribner, 1949–1971).

47. Allan Nevins, *Statesmanship of the Civil War* (New York: Colliers, 1962), 75, 78, 83, 91.

48. James McPherson, *Battle Cry of Freedom* (New York: Oxford University Press, 1988).

49. Hattaway and Jones, *How the North Won the Civil War*, passim.

50. Paul Escott, *After Secession: Jefferson Davis and the Failure of Confederate Nationalism* (Baton Rouge: Louisiana State University Press, 1978), 74–76.

51. Michael E. Howard, *The Causes of War and Other Essays* (Cambridge: Harvard University Press, 1984); John G. Moore, "Mobility and Strategy in the Civil War," *Military Affairs* 25 (Fall 1961): 68–77; June I. Gow, "Theory and Practice in Confederate Military Administration," *Military Affairs* 39 (October 1975): 119–123; Brien Holden Reid, "Another Look at Grant's Crossing of the James, 1864," *Civil War History* 39 (December 1993): 292–316.

52. Vandiver, *Ploughshares into Swords*, esp. chap. 5.

53. Michael Adams, *Our Masters the Rebels* (Cambridge: Harvard University Press, 1978).

54. Connelly and Jones, *The Politics of Command*, xiii, 48–49.

55. Hattaway and Jones, *How the North Won the Civil War*, 302.

56. Richard Bensel, *Yankee Leviathan* (New York: Cambridge University Press, 1992), esp. chap. 2.

57. Craig L. Symonds, *Joseph E. Johnston: A Civil War Biography* (New York: W. W. Norton, 1992), 125.

58. Merrill Peterson, *The Lincoln Image in American Memory* (New York: Oxford University Press, 1994); John Bodnar, *Remaking America* (Princeton: Princeton University Press, 1992), 206; for dissent on the place of the Civil War in this country's history, see Wilbur Zelinsky, *Nation into State: The Shifting Symbolic Foundation of American Nationalism* (Chapel Hill: University of North Carolina Press, 1988), 241–242.

JOSEPH REID ANDERSON
(February 6, 1813–September 7, 1892)

Jon L. Wakelyn

As president of Richmond's Tredegar Iron Works and brigadier general in the Confederate Army, Joseph Reid Anderson was the South's major manufacturer of military weapons. He was born at "Walnut Hill," the family residence in Batecourt County, Virginia, on February 6, 1813. His father William, descended from Scotch-Irish immigrants, began his career as a surveyor, fought in the War of 1812, and was a staunch Presbyterian and stern master of his household. His mother Anne Thomas came from a successful Maryland plantation family and belonged to the Episcopal Church. The youngest of nine children, the precocious Joseph was sent to Logan's Classical School near Fincastle, Virginia, where many planter's children prepared for their future lives. But young Anderson was not destined to be a planter because there was too little land and he was last on the list of sons. Others of his brothers also gave up on having a future in Virginia agriculture. Two became lawyers, and one a doctor. Their success would some-day come in handy for young Joseph.

So how did that young man make his way in that proud but floundering economic world of his native state? The legend that Joseph left home to strike out for himself is incorrect. Instead, family contacts and his own keen intelligence landed him a place at the United States Military Academy in 1832. Young Joseph, like many bright scientifically and mathematically inclined young men, wanted to become a civil engineer. West Point was almost the only way he could gain such training. He came to the banks of the Hudson River determined to find the means to seek his fortune. An imposing and earnest young man, his peers soon noticed that his work ethic left little time for play. To them he appeared direct, daring, and disciplined. He was seen as a leader because of his good judgment, but a few of his fellow Southern classmates remarked that Anderson lacked interest in any studies but the sciences. Also, his near anti-Southern correctness in behavior earned him few merits among his fellows and few demerits at the academy. But that diligent and ambitious student—he finished number four out of forty-nine cadets—had earned enough respect from his classmates to be named captain of the Corps. He also had realized his earlier ambition by gaining appointment to the elite artillery corps.

Within a year, however, understanding there was no way to rise to prominence in a peacetime army, he resigned his commission to take a position as chief engineer of the Valley Turnpike Company near Winchester, Virginia. Anderson had taken the ideal job to launch himself on the path to success. He would use his skills, family links to the valley, and an insatiable ambition to rise in Virginia public and business life. As chief engineer with a speciality in building paved roads, he was in a position to help link a growing West with the business world of Richmond by building those roads. Soon he had made a name for himself in Winchester, as his attendance at the Norfolk Commercial Convention demonstrated. In late 1836, he married Sallie Archer, the daughter of a Norfolk dock owner and a descendant of the first families of colonial Virginia. Anderson had also begun to represent the interests of an iron company, the Augusta Company.

He held the turnpike job until 1841, when he moved to Richmond to become an agent for the Tredegar Iron Works. Tredegar had been founded in 1837 to make the iron structures to build a growing commercial Richmond. But Anderson soon realized that the company needed a larger market and required a man who was ambitious and willing to work to expand that market. Expand he did, as he soon created a large market for the company's produce. His rise had paralleled the growth of an urban and industrialized upper South.

His descendant Kathleen Bruce's work on Virginia in manufacturing chronicled just how he succeeded. Her book also discussed the many young and ambitious Virginia farm and planter boys who had been forced off their ancestral lands. So many of them had left Virginia to settle in the new Southwest. The antebellum success of the Anderson brothers in Virginia, she hoped, would be a model to future ambitious young Virginians. Indeed it was. Alas, post–Civil War Virginia experienced an even more rapid exodus of its best and brightest youth.

Anderson's rise in that competitive antebellum business, which Bruce so ably chronicled, was based on a combination of intelligence, will, an understanding of the meaning of local public service for business, and super salesmanship. He met the growing Southern demand for Southern-produced iron goods. Anderson also tapped into a growing national market, using his contacts in Washington from his army and valley days, especially his friend John Tanner of the Navy Yard, and the promise of some financial backing from his wife's Archer relatives. In September 1842, he won a contract to produce cannons for the U.S. Department of the Navy.

That successful sales agent at first wanted no part of the production end of the business. But the directors talked him into assisting in reorganizing its productivity capacity. With the profits from the navy contract as well as his in-laws' investments, during the next five years Anderson remodeled the old production plant, streamlined the sales division, and continued to gain contracts in the North, including iron sales to New York businesses and construction developers. According to Kathleen Bruce, he also sold the U.S. government chain cable, tested his own new cannon, and built a new foundry for military goods production. He became an expert in the use of hydrostatic pressure and, after 1845, a specialist in cannon making. By 1860 the U.S. government had bought 1,200 cannons from his company. With aid from the Archers, he set up a shipyard to make iron steamers. Anderson also produced heavy railroad equipment, including engines, for the burgeoning Virginia transportation system.

Anderson's successes for the company and Virginia business also brought him much wealth. In April 1848, he invested $125,000 to become the major proprietor of Tredegar. His efforts had made a national market for the company and had brought much wealth and prestige to Richmond and to the Valley of Virginia. By 1854 the company had become synonymous with his name, and Anderson had become a pillar of the Richmond community and the South's most important producer of iron goods. Anderson's home became a meeting place for ambitious business leaders and politicians alike.

His many services to Richmond and Virginia went far beyond his business activities, however. Anderson set up charity organizations to help the poor and homeless, and he served on the boards of a number of church and civic foundations. As warden of prestigious St. Paul's Episcopal Church, he worked to remodel that old structure. He even took a fling at public political activity. A staunch expansionist Whig, he spoke often of diversified business opportunities for the South, and he lobbied for state investment in internal improvements. Anderson also supported the tariff protectionists in the Federal Congress because he wanted to aid infant industry in his state and the country. In 1847 he was elected to the Richmond city council. In 1852 he became a member of the state legislature. As a member of the legislature, he continued to contribute to local charitable institutions.

But his politics gradually began to change from those of the nationalist Whigs, and in 1856, after his party had collapsed in the South, he joined the Democratic party. Events that he regarded as harmful to his state began to temper his usual conservative positions. He soon took up with the more radical sectionalist wing of the Democratic party. The John Brown raid and its aftermath made him fear for the Union's future. Although he was reluctant to support straight out secession, by 1860 he believed the Southern states should unite to protect their major interests. How had a leader with national political ties and business interests become so radical?

There are a number of theories to explain his behavior. For one thing, Anderson had used slave labor in his factories, and he was committed to protection of that institution. The paucity of skilled foreign labor and the unwillingness of Southern farmers to take menial factory work had led him to develop a factory slave labor force. He often rented slaves from local planters during the fallow season. He trained a number of the slaves to do skilled ''puddling'' work at

Tredegar. For another, Anderson had gradually lost his national market as Northern businesses undercut his prices for iron. The federal government, too, cut back on contracts from his company. Tredegar then began during the 1850s to vigorously pursue a Southern market. Anderson sold iron goods to help build Southern cities and became almost the exclusive producer of railroad engines and track for the growing Southern transportation market. Although Tredegar charged more for iron than its Northern competitors, the fact that it was a Southern business and that it gave favorable purchase terms to Southern concerns soon made the company's market almost exclusively Southern. Those purchase terms, which amounted to loans to Southern businesses, Charles Dew suggests, meant that Anderson was too heavily invested in the South not to support the Southern Confederacy. His heart, or national feeling, therefore, was where his investments were.

Still, it was not until January 1861 that Anderson believed civil war inevitable. He welcomed the war. At first there were cancellations of some Southern contracts, and some Southern customers, especially state governments, had to suspend payment on their purchases of weapons. Adroitly, Anderson positioned Tredegar as the major munitions producer for three states, North Carolina, South Carolina, and Georgia, all of whom had coasts to protect and all of whom had few means of defending themselves. He offered to produce ordnance for those states, and he soon became their most important arms supplier. Those southeastern state contacts would be of much service to his company as the war deepened. Anderson would also become the largest and most important supplier of all weapons to the Confederate States' military, army and navy.

This West Point graduate wanted to be more than an iron maker, however. He wanted to test his skills as a military commander. His first miltary test was to provide for the defense of Richmond and his own iron works. Anderson organized a number of his employees into the Tredegar Battalion, which he commanded. In September 1861, he asked for line command duties, and President Jefferson Davis (q.v.) reluctantly named this iron maker a brigadier general. The president placed Anderson in charge of the defenses around the Cape Fear River in North Carolina. But that was not enough action, so he asked for duty in the upcoming Peninsula Campaign against the Northern invaders. In April 1862, he opposed Union general Irwin McDowell at Fredericksburg and helped forestall that Union advance. He served ably in the June 1862 defense at Mechanicsville and Gaines Mill. The businessman general won praise from General Joseph E. Johnston (q.v.). At Frayser's Farm, however, in heavy combat, he received a wound that disabled him for the duration of the Peninsula Campaign.

Finally, realizing he was needed to conduct affairs at Tredegar, Anderson resigned his command on July 19, 1862. To the relief of President Davis and ordnance officer Josiah Gorgas (q.v.), their arms manufacturer would return to what the Confederacy wanted him to do. During the rest of the war, despite severe production handicaps owing to the paucity of labor and the inability to get to Southern mines, he would serve the Confederacy as its most important arms producer.

In 1861 Anderson had offered to sell his company to the Confederate government and to stay on as its manager for a nominal fee. But the government resisted privatization and preferred the market mechanism and patriotic loyalty to persuade the private sector to sell at a fair price. At first Anderson was the only producer of cannons for the army, and despite a shortage of skilled artisans, he managed to supply weapons for the army and coastal defense. Anderson used local businesses to produce new materials for his factory, and he reorganized them to give him a nearly integrated production system from mine to factory.

Although some of his early weapons were of shoddy make, Anderson soon managed to improve his smelter system to make a sturdy cannon. The government's needs also exceeded his factory's capacity, so he built new works in Richmond, as he worked closely with Josiah Gorgas, chief of ordnance, to make timely shipments to the areas where weapons were needed most. Anderson's designs for heavy guns, especially the rifled Columbia, were used at the defense of the new Confederate forts in Tennessee, Forts Henry and Donelson. In 1861 Anderson made iron plate and marine engines for Secretary Stephen Mallory's (q.v.) navy and, with the assistance of maritime engineer John Mercer Brooks, outfitted the fabled *Merrimack*. Anderson also built machinery, engines, and lockers, as well as made the torpedoes for the coastal ironclad C.S.S. *Mississippi*. Although never able to meet the demand for railroad materials, and by 1862 weapon production forced Tredegar out of engine building, the company did provide axles, spikes, and rails for the private companies who sold to the government.

By late 1862, the raw materials necessary to make weapons could not be produced fast enough for Tredegar's production schedule, and often the plant lay idle. Anderson tried to revive the pig iron industry, but he was never satisfied with the quantity of raw goods he produced. The price of finished goods rose to meet inflation, and Anderson soon found himself at odds with his friend President Davis. War Secretary George W. Randolph defended Anderson's pricing system, but when James Seddon (q.v.) took over at the department, there ensued nasty scenes and mutual accusations between those two loyal Virginians. But Anderson continued. He bought coal mines and tried to find ways to equip their furnaces. By 1863 it was clear that Tredegar war supplies could no longer reach lower and southwest defenses, so Anderson joined George W. Rains in advocating building additional plants in Georgia and Alabama. Then the finances of the Confederate government began to break down. Historian Charles W. Ramsdell maintained that the government's failure to finance the war forced producers like Anderson to falter on their contracts.

If Tredegar could not get paid, Anderson still managed to find resourceful ways to raise needed funds for his employees. He purchased cotton to send through the blockade, not only to buy European raw goods for production but to allow him to protect his interests by investing abroad. Anderson also knew that healthy and well-fed workers were most essential to produce needed weapons. As such, he set up a farm to feed, and a factory to produce clothing for, his employees and their families. He was forced to expand the use of slave labor because foreigners would no longer come south and because the government threatened to draft his white skilled laborers. Try as he might to persuade authorities of the need for that labor, he constantly had to battle against the draft.

If Anderson fought hard to keep the factory labor system afloat, he tried even harder during the last year of the war to manufacture iron goods. But the Ordnance Bureau was no longer able to procure raw goods for him. The lower South, where the factories were, had fallen to the Yankees. Then Anderson could no longer produce long-range batteries, and he had to settle for short-range weapons. As the government could not pay its bills, and there were employees to feed, the business leader was forced to sell military goods to private companies. Even as troop numbers dwindled during the siege of Petersburg, Anderson worked to deliver the necessary weapons to the Army of Northern Virginia. In April 1865, as the government collapsed around him, Anderson used his own employees as guards to protect the iron works from looters. At the last, he seemed even at war with his own countrymen. The Confederate government owed Tredegar's owner $900,000.

After the war ended, that business leader was left to look after himself and the Archer and Anderson families. In debt, with a damaged business, he took advantage of the disruption around him to petition for pardon. Some Virginians allowed that he was too quick to desert the Confederacy, but he knew an idle factory would soon go bankrupt. Too, Anderson feared federal confiscation of his business. So he went to work to help restore authority in Richmond, and late in April 1865, he took the oath of loyalty to the old nation. He supported Virginia Unionist governor Francis H. Pierpont. His reward was a presidential pardon on September 21, 1865. As Dew said: "His pro-Johnson sympathies would soon aid materially in his quest for northern capital" (316). Anderson dealt off some property to a New York business, sold what cotton he had left, and retrieved his finances tucked away in an English bank.

In February 1867, Anderson organized the Tredegar Company by borrowing needed capital in the North. He used ex-slaves in the factory, and he paid them a decent salary. As the South slowly stirred to life, Tredegar became its major producer of iron for railroads. The old angle of selling mainly in the South was restored. This time he did not try to manufacture iron but instead bought iron materials from the North. By 1873 the company was again a success, but impending depression soon sent it into receivership in 1876. Anderson lacked the funds to turn from iron to steel goods, and the rich veins of ore in northern Alabama soon meant that Birmingham would replace Richmond as the South's industrial center. So Anderson was reduced to producing overpriced goods for a local Virginia market. Tredegar continued even after his death. The company finally went out of business in the 1930s. As for Anderson, he often spent time on his farm and grew progressively weaker but continued to hope that a restored

Norfolk and the help of his Archer kin would give him one more chance as a great business leader. But he had to settle for the public service of church and civic work. On holiday to escape the Richmond heat, Joseph Anderson died at Isles of Shoals, New Hampshire, on September 7, 1892.

What of his reputation as the Confederacy's great iron maker? At the end of the Civil War, despite his rush to rejoin the Union, he was regarded as a man who had persevered in the face of shortages of labor and raw goods and financial deficits to give enormous help to the Confederacy. He was considered an administrative and production genius, and he received the praise of Josiah Gorgas and Jefferson Davis. His friend and ally George Washington Rains, in his *History of the C.S. Powder Works* (1882), claimed for him great service to the war effort. Since that time, the Rains's opinion as clarified and expanded by Charles W. Ramsdell in *Behind the Lines in the Southern Confederacy* (1944) has given Anderson a place in the firmament of great Confederate leaders. His kinswoman Kathleen Bruce in 1930 made the major connection of Anderson's war contribution with his Southern business genius. If the war had not happened, said Bruce, Anderson would have been considered one of the South's finest and most important industrialists. In a study of the country's most important industrialists, *History of American Business Leaders* (1940), even Yankee Fritz Redlich gratuitously acknowledged Anderson as one of the great organizers and entrepreneurs of his generation despite coming from the backward South.

Of course, it is Anderson's contribution to the Southern Confederacy that is of most importance in assessing him. In that evaluation, there is no doubt. Charles Black, in *Railroads of the Confederate States* (1960), claims that Anderson was a success even if the Confederate government failed. Bruce gives little attention in her book to the Civil War but still lauds her kinsman for his loyalty and his contributions. But Bruce is virtually alone in her argument for a truly capitalist prewar South that trained Anderson to assist the Confederacy. More often, Anderson is seen as an anomaly among an Old South business elite usually more concerned with slavery than with business success. Robert Starobin, in his classic *Industrial Slavery in the Old South* (1970), suggests that the use of slave factory labor by most so-called industrialists was more an explanation of Southern backwardness in labor than recognition of slaves as vital to business expansion. Until Anderson's business activities are studied alongside a reevaluation of Old South business capitalism, it is Dew's comprehensive analysis of 1966 that will have to serve as the best guide to where history places Anderson as a Confederate leader. But Dew leaves one a bit confused. In his reading, Anderson had to function in a backward South. Dew concludes that Anderson's business practices and lack of loyalty to the Confederate cause revealed a national leader trapped in a second-class business environment. Anderson, in fact, was a loyal and brilliant business leader.

BIBLIOGRAPHY

George Washington Rains, *History of the Confederate States Powder Works* (1882; New-
    burgh, N.Y.: Newburgh Daily News, 1979).

S. F. H. Tarrant, ed., *Hon. Daniel Pratt: A Biography* (Richmond, Va.: Whittet and Shep-
    person, 1904).

Kathleen Bruce, *Virginia Iron Manufacture in the Slave Era* (New York: Century Co.,
    1930).

Fritz Redlich, *History of American Business Leaders*, 2 vols. (Ann Arbor, Mich.: Ed-
    wards Bros., 1940–1951).

Charles W. Ramsdell, *Behind the Lines in the Southern Confederacy* (1928; Baton
    Rouge: Louisiana State University Press, 1944).

Frank E. Vandiver, *Ploughshares into Swords: Josiah Gorgas* (Austin: University of
    Texas Press, 1952).

Charles B. Dew, *Ironmaker to the Confederacy: Joseph R. Anderson and the Tredegar
    Iron Works* (New Haven, Conn.: Yale University Press, 1966).

Robert S. Starobin, *Industrial Slavery in the Old South* (New York: Oxford University
    Press, 1970).

CLARA BARTON
(December 25, 1821–April 13, 1912)

Charles F. Ritter

Clara Barton was working as a copyist in the U.S. Patent Office when the Civil War began. Like many women in 1861, she responded quickly to the need for care of the wounded troops who flooded into Washington City, but Barton soon emerged not only as a caregiver but as a one-woman distribution center of medical and other supplies to the tragically underequipped hospitals. Defying all convention and considerable official disapproval, Barton was soon close to the field of battle, bringing her nurturing and her supply wagons to the wounded. Because of her riveted focus on succoring the wounded and dying in total disregard for her own welfare, Barton built a reputation as "the Angel of the Battlefield." Capitalizing on that reputation and the skills she derived from her experiences, Barton went on to a forty-year career spearheading the American Red Cross and leading various relief operations. Her reputation for bravery and humanitarianism was such that U.S. Senator George F. Hoar was moved to proclaim, "Clara Barton, where will you find the *man* to equal her?" (Bacon-Foster, 1).

Born in North Oxford, Massachusetts, on Christmas Day in 1821, Clarissa Hartowe Barton was named after an aunt who herself had been named for Samuel Richardson's unfortunate romantic heroine. Barton was the fifth and youngest child by ten years of Stephen Barton, Jr., and Sara (Stone) Barton, who was thirteen years her husband's junior. Stephen Barton farmed in Oxford, led the town militia, and served in various town offices. He was a veteran of the Indian wars and served for three years with Anthony Wayne, an experience that became a touchstone of his life and, through him, his daughter Clara's, whose head he filled with stories of the glories of combat. Sara Stone Barton, a hard-working, erratic woman given to fits of temper and profanity, left Clara's upbringing to her siblings, leading Clara to say later in life that she had six parents.

Barton was educated in North Oxford schools, and at age eleven, she began a two-year period nursing her brother David who was injured in a fall. Commencing a career as a teacher in North Oxford in 1839, Barton quickly earned a reputation for high academic standards and effective discipline. She demonstrated her commitment to principles of equality and fairness—a characteristic inherited from her Universalist parents—when she demanded from the school board equal pay for equal work.

In 1850, after a decade of successful teaching, Barton, at age twenty-nine, enrolled in the Clinton Liberal Institute, in Clinton, New York, in order to continue her education. Two years later, out of money, she was teaching again, first in Cedarville, New Jersey, and then in Bordentown. It was in Bordentown that Barton experienced her first success at persuading public authorities to take a progressive road. Schooling in New Jersey operated on a for-fee basis, which offended Barton's equalitarian sensibilities. She persuaded the town leaders to experiment with a free school, such as she had known in Massachusetts. In one year, enrollment jumped from 6 to 600 pupils, and the town added a second school. Yet when Bordentown officials chose the director of the new free school, they hired a man at $500 a year and appointed Barton his "female assistant" at $250, on the grounds that the task of running the school was too complex for a woman. Barton quit in 1854, ending her teaching career, and moved to Washington, D.C.

In the nation's capital, Barton found the first of a long series of mentors and patrons who appreciated her talents—Charles Mason, the head of the Patent Office. Introduced to her by Massachusetts congressman Charles DeWitt, whom Barton had sought out, Mason hired her as a Patent Office clerk at $1,400 a year, one of the first women to work for the federal government and at a salary comparable to that of male clerks. Although progressive in his thinking, Mason had to be discreet in his actions—he hid Barton in his annual report to the more conventional Secretary of the Interior. When Mason left the Patent Office temporarily in 1856, Interior Secretary Robert McCelland reduced Barton to doing piecework at $.10 per 100 words and doing her copying at home rather than mix " 'the two sexes within the walls of a public office' " (Pryor, 59). Mason soon returned and elevated Barton to her former, albeit sub-rosa, clerk's position and salary.

Barton's tenure at the Patent Office was short-lived. Her patron Congressman DeWitt was defeated in the 1856 election, and Charles Mason retired for good when a new Secretary of the Interior took over. Reluctantly, Barton returned to North Oxford and tended to family matters, but she was restless and without purpose. " 'I must not rust much longer,' " she wrote to her nephew Bernard Vassall, but " 'push out and do *something somewhere*, or *anything anywhere*' " (Pryor, 70).

Through a set of circumstances that still remains unclear—perhaps through the influence of friends like Charles Mason, now a patent attorney in Washington—Barton was called back to the Patent Office and rehired as a copyist making $.08 per 100 words. Ensconced in her former room in Almira Fales's boardinghouse, Barton deliberately sought out Massachusetts Senator Henry

Wilson, chairman of the Military Affairs Committee; he became a lifelong patron and friend.

At age thirty-nine when the Civil War began, Barton was not especially politicized by events. She was not a strong abolitionist and had some sympathy for the South's fear of Northern domination. But she was galvanized into action by the attack on the 6th Massachusetts Regiment in Baltimore on April 19, 1861. This regiment from the Worcester area contained boys Barton had taught—"her boys," she called them (Schurr, 53). She rushed to their camp, tended to their wounds, and rounded up their luggage.

Struck by the lack of preparation for the influx of troops, and taking a lead from her landlady and friend Almira Fales, who began hording supplies with the firing on Ft. Sumter, Barton began to solicit and collect supplies, storing them at first in her room and then in rented storage facilities. In six months, she had three warehouses full of canned goods, bedding, clothes, and other articles. Like other ladies in the capital city, Barton made the rounds of the hospitals, dispensing supplies. She chose this independent path rather than joining Dorothea Dix's (q.v.) Department of Female Nurses or the nursing corps of the U.S. Sanitary Commission because this five-foot-tall dynamo could not work under someone else's direction.

By 1862, Barton had come to the realization that soldiers' deaths from wounds could be reduced if she were to minister to them in the field rather than having them make the arduous trip back to Washington. She was encouraged in this bold decision partly by her father's deathbed admonition to " 'serve my country with all I had, even my life . . . [and to] comfort the afflicted everywhere' " (Pryor, 84).

Massachusetts Governor John Andrew and Senator Henry Wilson thought it a splendid idea, but U.S. military authorities had their doubts. They saw women as an impediment and a distraction at or near the field of battle. Furthermore, in Victorian sensibilities, the battlefield was no place for delicate ladies. Barton would have none of that. More than Dix, more than the fabled Florence Nightingale, Barton defied convention and entered the male world of the battlefield. She did so with the help of the head of the Quartermaster Depot in Washington, Colonel Daniel H. Rucker, whose initial hesitation Barton broke down with a cascade of tears and a declaration that "I want to go to the front" (Oates, 51).

And go she did. With a wagon and driver provided by Colonel Rucker and authorization from Surgeon-General William Hammond, and with her supplies in tow, Barton arrived at Culpeper Court House, a staging and relief area for the battle of Cedar Mountain, on August 13, 1862. There she gave the wounded soldiers food and water and provided clean dressings for their wounds. Two weeks later, on August 31, Barton was at Fairfax Court House tending the wounded from the battle of Second Manassas. Here, for the first time, she dressed wounds on her own authority.

At each battle, Barton moved closer to the fighting and hence put herself in increasingly greater danger. At Antietam on September 17, she arrived on the field as the battle commenced and tended the wounded in a field hospital set up in a barn close to the cornfield. By day's end, she was assisting the chief surgeon. At Fredericksburg in December she was stationed at the Lacy House, across the river from the town, where she witnessed the disastrous laying of the pontoon bridges and the subsequent assault. When the battle moved into the town and on to Marye's Heights, Barton crossed the bridge, under fire, to tend the wounded. There were plenty of female nurses at both Antietam and Fredericksburg, but no woman was as far in front or in so much personal danger as Clara Barton. She became a legend to the troops, who called her "the soldier's friend."

Barton capitalized on her reputation with the troops and the notoriety she received in the press to encourage contributions of money and goods. Her exaggerated, oversentimentalized, overdramatized solicitation letters were widely published. Her celebrity and effectiveness in the field won her unqualified support from many military authorities. Colonel Rucker now wanted her to go into the field and offered her quartermaster supplies. But medical services in the Virginia theater of the war were well staffed and organized by the beginning of 1863, and Barton had far more competition from Dix's nurses and the Sanitary Commission staff. When her brother Daniel was assigned assistant quartermaster in Port Royal, South Carolina, Barton did not hesitate to request that she serve in the Department of the South. Colonel Rucker paved the way for her with a letter of introduction that stated that " 'she acts under the direction of the Surgeon-General, and with the authority of the Secretary of War' " (Oates, 133).

Barton spent most of 1863 in the South. There she passed the spring at Hilton Head—eating, sleeping, horseback riding, and having a languorous affair with Lieutenant Colonel John Elwell, chief quartermaster of the department. In July, however, she moved to the front, witnessed the tragic assault on Battery Wagner, and spent the next two months working in a field hospital on Morris Island. Conflict with one of the surgeons, which sent her into a depression and a siege of diarrhea, resulted in her return to Hilton Head and then to Washington in December.

The well-staffed nursing corps and the well-organized army medical department that Barton encountered on her return suggested that the age of the independent operative was over. Yet as the 1864 Overland Campaign unfolded, Barton found a niche for herself. The high casualties at the Wilderness and Spotsylvania Court House overwhelmed the U.S. Sanitary Commission's medical facilities. In a typical example of Barton's way of getting results in a crisis, she complained to Senator Wilson that the Quartermaster's Department had not sufficiently responded to the wounded, and with Wilson's prodding, Quartermaster General Montgomery Meigs personally went to Fredericksburg with necessary supplies.

When the siege of Petersburg began in June 1864, Barton eschewed the base camp hospitals at City Point, where there were ample Sanitary Commission nurses, and headed instead for the front with a glowing letter of introduction in hand from Senator Wilson to General Benjamin Butler. The two "strong willed mavericks" (Oates, 249) hit it off, and she became the "unofficial matron" (Oates, 265) of the 10th Corps hospital. Six and one-half months later, with her patron Butler removed by General U.S. Grant (q.v.) and another supporter, Dr. Martin Kittinger, resigned, Barton returned to Washington in January 1865 to care for her brother Steven.

Because of her celebrity as the soldiers' friend, Barton received many requests from spouses and parents for information about missing loved ones. From the time she began her relief operations, she had gathered information about the men she treated. Now, with the war winding down and prisoner exchanges resumed, she was inundated with requests. This provided Barton a logical transition from wartime to peacetime relief. For two months, she made the rounds of Washington bureaucrats, trying to find a powerful sponsor for her soldier identification scheme; with the aid of General Ethan Allen Hitchcock, commissioner in charge of prisoner exchanges, she obtained the endorsement of the president himself.

In June 1865, Dorance Atwater contacted Barton. While a prisoner at Andersonville, Atwater had managed to record the names and burial locations of most of the federal prisoners who died there. Barton convinced Secretary of War Edwin Stanton (q.v.) to endorse a reburial project at the infamous prison, and on August 17, 1865, she raised the U.S. flag over the National Cemetery at Andersonville. Although she waged a continuing battle with the War Department over possession and publication of Atwater's list (it was finally published by Horace Greeley in February 1866), this work was a fitting end to her Civil War career.

Now forty-four years old, Barton had no war to engage her energies and was in constant need of money. In 1866, she took to the lecture circuit, describing to rapt audiences the horrors of the battlefield and her own heroic efforts. She crisscrossed the United States for two years, enhancing her reputation at every turn. Although she praised the brave sisterhood—perhaps 18,000 to 20,000 strong—who served the fighting men, Barton was always in the lead.

Her grueling speaking schedule left her exhausted, and in late summer 1869, Barton embarked on a fateful trip to Europe to get some rest. She traveled from London to Paris to Geneva to Sardinia and back to Geneva, where she was the guest of the parents of Jules Golay, a soldier she had nursed back to health at Petersburg. Through the Golays she met Dr. Louis Appia, who was familiar with her work. Appia was a founder of the International Red Cross, and he inquired of Barton as to why the United States had not signed the 1866 Geneva Convention providing for the humane care of wartime wounded and establishing the international relief body. Barton had no answer, but she did have a new *cause célèbre*.

Commitment to that cause was reinforced by her experience during the Franco-Prussian War that erupted in July 1870. Naturally, Barton volunteered to work with the Red Cross in relief operations. Impressed with the organization's bulging supply warehouses, she finally prevailed on Red Cross leaders to allow her and Antoinette Margot to take supplies to the devastated city of Strasbourg, where she worked from October 1870 to June 1871.

Barton's work in Strasbourg gave her an insight that helped set the course of the rest of her life working in relief operations. Although Strasbourg had been heavily shelled by the Germans, Barton was not there to nurse the wounded. Her focus was on what she could do to aid the civilian population. She sensed that monetary handouts would not be effective; what people needed, she thought, was income-producing work. Raising money through her well-established network in the United States, Barton organized Strasbourg women into sewing groups and provided cloth. Soon the women were selling garments in Strasbourg and elsewhere. She and Margot and Dorance Atwater moved on to Paris, which was devastated by its surrender to the Germans and in a chaotic state after the fall of the Commune. But " 'there was nothing at all that we could do in Paris,' " Margot wrote (Pryor, 169). They left in August 1871.

Barton was again exhausted. Returning to London, where she avoided meeting Florence Nightingale (she noted that while she was known as the "Florence Nightingale of America," no one called the Englishwoman the "Clara Barton of Britain" [Pryor, 173]), Barton sailed for the United States on September 30, 1873, to nurse her sister Sally. On board, the apprehensive Barton penned the poem "Have Ye Room?" which concludes:

> Have ye place, each beloved one, a place in your prayer,
> Have ye *work*, my brave countrymen, work for me there?
> . . . .
> *Have* ye place, each beloved one, a place in your prayer,
> Have ye *room*, my dear countrymen, room for me there? (William Barton, 2:85–
> 87)

Taking to her bed for two years, Barton suffered further from the loss in 1876 of her longtime friend Henry Wilson. Entering the Dansville, New York, sanitorium of Dr. James Jackson in the summer of 1876, Barton regained her health under his regimen of rest, recreation, and nutritious food. An important part of her recovery was her growing commitment to founding an American chapter of the Red Cross. She labored for six years to bring this idea to fruition. A strong letter of support and an introduction to President Rutherford B. Hayes from the head of the International Red Cross failed to move top Congressional leaders. Appealing to the isolationist tradition of U.S. foreign policy, they rejected the idea of an American organization affiliating with a foreign group. Barton, who had previously published two laudatory tracts about the international organization, now enlisted the aid of two well-known journalists, Walter Phillips, chief of the Associated Press Washington office, and George Kennan, Phillips's assistant.

Barton's path was complicated, however, by the existence of the Blue Anchors—the Women's National Relief Association—which also had ideas of affiliating with the International Red Cross. She moved swiftly to outflank her competition; she received a ringing endorsement from the head of the Grand Army of the Republic, John A. Logan, and elicited pledges from International Red Cross officials Gustave Moynier and Louis Appia that her organization was the only one in the United States with which they would agree to affiliate. Backed with such endorsements and with favorable wire service copy, Barton obtained a meeting with President James A. Garfield in March 1881. He endorsed her idea, as did Secretary of State James G. Blaine. She even managed to get Secretary of War Robert Todd Lincoln on board.

Continuing her steamrolling, the sixty-year-old Barton incorporated the American Society of the Red Cross in 1881 and was named its first president. Shortly, she opened the first local chapter of the Red Cross in Dansville, New York; soon there were chapters in Rochester and Syracuse. The Michigan forest fire of 1881 was well timed for Barton's purpose; her relief operation there garnered favorable press coverage, and in December, President Chester A. Arthur asked the Senate to accept the Geneva Convention. Congress ratified the convention in March 1882.

For the next twenty-two years, Barton and the American Red Cross were synonymous. She ran the operation out of her home on T Street N.W. in Washington and, after 1890, from Glen Echo, Maryland, a Washington suburb. And there was no end to the natural disasters to which the American Red Cross responded: the Texas famine of 1885; the 1886 Charleston earthquake; a tornado in Mt. Vernon, Illinois, and a yellow fever epidemic in Florida in 1888; the great Johnstown flood, which kept Barton in the field for five months in 1889; and many more. She even took her relief operation abroad, to Russia in relief of famine in 1892, to Armenia in 1896 to deal with the victims of ethnic and religious persecution, and perhaps most famously, to Cuba during the Spanish-American War in 1898. Through it all, Barton was in the field—at age seventy-seven, she was in Cuba supervising operations.

If Barton was in Cuba in 1898, who was at Glen Echo tending to Red Cross business? Rumors about Barton's lax administrative practices and overbearing leadership had been rife for years. Her critics charged that she had no accounts of receipts or expenditures, that she intermingled Red Cross finances with her own, that she mostly ignored local chapters except when she needed them, and that a national organization should have a board of national leaders, not a seventy-year-old woman whose time had obviously passed.

Never one to take criticism lightly, Barton retaliated with an ongoing campaign to keep the Red Cross name before the public while she fought internecine political battles. Her final nemesis was Mabel T. Boardman. Well bred and well connected, Boardman made it her goal to dislodge Barton and professionalize the organization. In an odd series of circumstances, which involved President Theodore Roosevelt and his sister Anna Roosevelt Cowles, Barton found herself abandoned by the nation's top leaders.

Mabel Boardman enlisted Anna Cowles to join her in writing a letter to the president, complaining about Barton's leadership and asking him to withdraw support from the Red Cross. The president complied in a January 1903 letter criticizing Barton's administrative practices and asking that he and his cabinet be removed from the Red Cross board of advisers. Secretary of War William Howard Taft wrote in the *Army-Navy Register* that " 'the present state of the Red Cross [is] deplorable' " (Buckingham, 307).

Although the December 1903 annual Red Cross meeting named Barton president for life, her tenure would not last half a year. That same convention called for a full accounting of Red Cross activities going back to the Johnstown disaster relief operation. Senator Redfield Proctor presided over congressional hearings since the Red Cross had been incorporated by Congress in 1901. Boardman presented her criticisms and Barton's former aide John Morlan made devastating charges of financial irregularities. Barton was vindicated, however, when Morlan, fearful of being exposed as a liar, failed to reappear and Proctor brought the hearings to a quick close. After briefly considering staying on as Red Cross president, Barton realized her time was over, and she resigned on May 14, 1904.

Characteristically, Barton did not remain idle. In 1907 she published *The Story of My Childhood*, the first of a projected three-volume autobiography that she never completed. She also revived an old idea that she had tried unsuccessfully with the Red Cross in 1902, a national first aid association. Incorporated in April 1905, the association sponsored classes in first aid education for a broad range of citizens. The program was such a success that in 1909, based on their claim that Barton had started it as part of the Red Cross, the national organization took it away from her. The eighty-eight-year-old Barton did not put up a fight.

Friends dissuaded her from going to Mexico to run the Mexican Red Cross. Otherwise, she passed her time quietly writing to friends. She attended seances and claimed she contacted President Grant, who responded to her question about the condition of the Red Cross by saying "what a mess they make of it" (Williams, 429).

When Clara Barton died on Good Friday, April 13, 1912, her reputation was secure. Despite Mabel Boardman's decade-long campaign against her, nothing could erase the image of "the Angel of the Battlefield" from the public consciousness. Her life was the stuff of legend even before she died and became more so after.

The first Barton biography, Percy Epler's laudatory *The Life of Clara Barton*, appeared in 1915. Although authorized by the family, Epler's biography did not have the benefit of Barton's papers, which were under the watchful care of Barton family members who retained tight control until 1940. There was also an enormous collection of letters, scrapbooks, and diaries hidden behind a false wall in Barton's Glen Echo home.

William E. Barton, Clara's cousin and chairman of the literary executors' committee, published the most authoritative early work on Barton in 1922. His *Life of Clara Barton* is valuable primarily because he quotes many letters theretofore unavailable. Charles Sumner Young, working on a Barton book at the same time as William Barton, was "precluded the use of data left" by Barton (7), and therefore his *Clara Barton* is a collection of reminiscences.

Blanche Williams was the first Barton biographer to use the entire collection of papers before they were donated to the Library of Congress. Unfortunately, her 1941 *Clara Barton* is a partly fictionalized account without any attribution to documents. Ishbel Ross's *Angel of the Battlefield* (1956) and Clyde Buckingham's *Clara Barton* (1977) are both celebratory affairs that do not contain source citations.

Barton's life has also been the subject of a dozen or so books for children. The best of these largely adulatory volumes is perhaps Leni Hamilton's 1988 *Clara Barton*.

A major contribution to Barton scholarship came with Ellen Langenheim Henle's 1977 Ph.D. dissertation "Against the Fearful Odds: Clara Barton and American Philanthropy." Henle portrays Barton as a flesh-and-blood woman of ambition and passion struggling to carve out a role for herself in a constricted society. As she says in her preface, Barton was "more a politician than a nurse, more middle-class than wealthy, more ambitious than selfless, and a feminist, albeit a 'reluctant' one" (viii).

Two scholarly biographies of Barton have followed Henle's lead. In 1987 Elizabeth Pryor published *Clara Barton: Professional Angel*. Based on meticulous research and written with a critical eye, Pryor offers a Barton who is noble and unselfish, vain and egotistical, generous, controlling, and jealous; all the Clara Bartons are there.

Stephen Oates's account of Barton's Civil War service, entitled *A Woman of Valor*, was published in 1994. His story is as much about the state of medicine and the condition of the army's medical services as it is about Barton. Still, she is the central figure in the story, and Oates captures every aspect of her compelling nature. In 1995, David Burton published a short biography entitled *Clara Barton: In the Service of Humanity*. Based mainly on secondary sources, Burton provides a compact if overly sympathetic account of the great caregiver.

Most of the periodical literature on Barton focuses on her Red Cross experience, such as Cathleen Schurr's "Clara Barton" in *American History Illustrated* (1989). However, Stephen Oates's "Clara Barton's Finest Hour" in a 1993 *Timeline*, and Ellen Langenheim Henle's "Clara Barton, Soldier or Pacifist?" (1978) in *Civil War History* both reflect the new Barton scholarship which locates the source of her Red Cross career in her Civil War work.

BIBLIOGRAPHY

Clara Barton, *The Story of My Childhood* (New York: The Baker and Taylor Company, 1907).

Percy H. Epler, *The Life of Clara Barton* (New York: Macmillan Co., 1915).

Corra Bacon-Foster, *Clara Barton: Humanitarian* (Washington, D.C.: Columbia Historical Society, 1918).

William E. Barton, *The Life of Clara Barton: Founder of the American Red Cross* (Boston: Houghton Mifflin Company, 1922).

Charles Summer Young, *Clara Barton; A Centenary Tribute* (Boston: Richard G. Badger, 1922).

Blanche C. Williams, *Clara Barton; Daughter of Destiny* (Philadelphia: J. B. Lippincott Company, 1941).

Ishbel Ross, *Angel of the Battlefield: The Life of Clara Barton* (New York: Harper and Bros., Publishers, 1956).

Clyde E. Buckingham, *Clara Barton: A Broad Humanity, Philanthropic Efforts on Behalf of the Armed Forces and Disaster Victims, 1860–1900* (Alexandria, Va.: Mount Vernon Publishing Company, 1977).

Ellen Langenheim Henle, ''Against the Fearful Odds: Clara Barton and American Philanthropy,'' (Ph.D. dissertation, Case Western Reserve University, 1977).

Ellen Langenheim Henle, ''Clara Barton, Soldier or Pacifist?'' *Civil War History* 24, no. 2 (1978): 152–160.

Elizabeth Brown Pryor, *Clara Barton: Professional Angel* (Philadelphia: University of Pennsylvania Press, 1987).

Leni Hamilton, *Clara Barton* (New York: Chelsea House Publishers, 1988).

Cathleen Schurr, ''Clara Barton: Founder of the American Red Cross,'' *American History Illustrated* 24, no. 6 (1989): 50–58.

Stephen Oates, ''Clara Barton's Finest Hour,'' *Timeline* 10, no. 1 (1993): 2–17.

Stephen B. Oates, *A Woman of Valor: Clara Barton and the Civil War* (New York: Free Press, 1994).

David H. Burton, *Clara Barton: In the Service of Humanity* (Westport, Conn.: Greenwood Press, 1995).

PIERRE GUSTAVE TOUTANT BEAUREGARD
(May 28, 1818–February 20, 1893)

Herman M. Hattaway and Michael J. C. Taylor

Popular historian Clifford Dowdey, in his 1955 book *The Land They Fought For*, characterized P. G. T. Beauregard as "the Confederacy's first hero." T. Harry Williams began his 1955 biography by declaring that his subject was "the most colorful of all the Confederate generals" (1). Indeed, Beauregard was involved in every phase of the conduct of the war and proved himself a competent commander at a crucial time when the South's command base was diminishing. Although he had defended an agrarian Old South, when defeat came, Beauregard adapted to realities and, in the process, helped to industrialize a New South.

Pierre Gustave Toutant Beauregard was born on May 28, 1818, to a Creole family whose French ancestral ties lead back to the thirteenth century. The fine Beauregard House near Chalmette, Louisiana—an exurb of New Orleans—sits adjacent to the War of 1812 battlefield and is open to the public. Though "Pierre" was added to his name during his Roman Catholic baptism, he preferred Gustave or Gus. Young Gus did not speak a word of English until he was twelve years old, when he was sent to boarding school. Of his childhood and adolescence, Williams concedes that "almost nothing is known" because so few records have survived.

At the lad's urging, Beauregard's father—although he was surprised and perhaps a bit disappointed that his son wanted a military career—arranged for him to study at the U.S. Military Academy at West Point. During his tenure as a cadet, Williams described him as a "grave, reserved, and withdrawn . . . [young man who] excelled in sports, rode a horse beautifully, and made high marks" (7). The young cadet was an outstanding student who in 1838 graduated second in his class. Among his peers were Irwin McDowell, Jubal A. Early, Richard Ewell, Joseph Hooker, and William Tecumseh Sherman (q.v.). After finishing his studies, Beauregard received a commission as a second lieutenant in the prestigious corps of engineers.

For the first five years of his military career, Beauregard was a civil engineer—his most significant duty being the supervision of the topographical and hydrographical surveys of Barataria Bay on the Louisiana Gulf. During this tour of duty, in September 1841, he married Marie Laure Villere, the daughter of a wealthy local planter. By all accounts, the young officer was devoted to Marie, and she bore him two sons, Rene and Henri, to whom he was a dedicated father. In March 1850, Marie died giving birth to a daughter, who was named for her mother. Although he grieved for his wife, Beauregard was devoted to his daughter, whom he described as perfect a human being as he had ever known.

During the Mexican War, Beauregard served with the corps of engineers under Commanding General Winfield Scott. Beauregard's fellow officers included Robert E. Lee (q.v.), George G. Meade (q.v.), and Joseph E. Johnston (q.v.). Beauregard's primary function was to devise topographical surveys for Scott and his subordinate commanders, often with other young officers such as Ulysses S. Grant (q.v.), Thomas J. Jackson (q.v.), and Jubal A. Early.

It was the young lieutenant who influenced General Scott's decision to attack at Chapultepec. Scott informed his immediate staff in late August 1847 that he planned to attack the Mexican capital before Santa Anna could raze his exterior line. When the old general asked for suggestions, Captain Lee voiced his support for one plan, to which Beauregard disagreed. The Creole asserted that a victory at Chapultepec would open two of Santa Anna's most traveled causeways into Mexico City. His arguments convinced Brigadier General Franklin Pierce, who, in turn, convinced Scott.

In the battle itself, Beauregard demonstrated valor as he rode with Johnston, inspiring the foot soldiers with audacious theatrics even while under fire. He was conspicuous and proud, being one of the first to enter Mexico City—and under a heavy barrage of fire as well. Steven Woodworth, in *Jefferson Davis and His Generals*, points out early evidence of Beauregard's touchiness: "Though serving with distinction and receiving plenty of recognition in Scott's reports, Beauregard fumed that he was not singled out for special praise above the other engineers, particularly Robert E. Lee" (73).

Following the war, Beauregard took a leave of absence for health reasons, his health aggravated by the Mexican climate. Later, he returned to New Orleans and labored on behalf of the Franklin Pierce campaign throughout 1852. For his efforts, Beauregard was rewarded by the new president with an appointment as the superintending engineer at New Orleans. The duties of the position did little to satisfy him, however, and according to Williams, Beauregard "displayed a testy impatience with people, especially politicians, who criticized his work or tried to interfere with him" (36).

Beauregard married for a second time, to Caroline Deslonde, the influential sister-in-law of Louisiana's Senator John Slidell. According to Williams, though Beauregard was affectionate toward his new bride, he "did not love her with the ardor he had devoted to Marie Laure" (36). After three years, Beauregard had tired of his military career, believing he had been maliciously slighted by the War Department for promotions he thought himself deserving. Indeed, Steven Woodworth says, "By 1856, Beauregard was so dissatisfied with the army that he considered joining the filibusterer William Walker in his mad adventure at turning Nicaragua into a slave empire" (74). Beauregard ventured into elective politics, running for mayor of New Orleans in 1858. He lost a close race and remained in the military. His family alliance paid handsome dividends when in December 1860 Slidell wrangled him an appointment as superintendent of West Point.

Beauregard enjoyed his post only five days. In December 1860, Louisiana seceded from the Union, and loyal to his state, Beauregard resigned his commission. Although he offered his services to the state without any preconditions, he expected to be named the commanding general of the militia, a position that already had been offered to and accepted by Braxton Bragg (q.v.). After Beauregard enlisted as a private in a Creole company, Slidell called him to a conference with newly inaugurated Confederate President Jefferson Davis (q.v.), which took place on February 26, 1861. Initially impressed with Beauregard, the president offered him the command of the Confederate forces at Charleston, which he accepted. Beauregard became the Confederacy's first general officer; he received a brigadier generalship in the Provisional Army, C.S.A., to rank from March 1, 1861.

The Confederate bombardment of Fort Sumter initiated the most brutal and bloody conflagration in America's history to that time. Beauregard was the first commander of Southern troops to engage in military confrontation with those of the Union. Prior to the shelling of Fort Sumter, there was a genteel semblance maintained between the Confederates and Sumter's defenders, in which the Union commander was allowed to receive comestibles and supplies from Charleston. Upon his arrival, the new Confederate commander found his forces in disarray, ill prepared to carry out Davis's order to take the fortress in the harbor: "I find a great deal in the way of zeal and energy around me, but little professional knowledge and experience" (22). The general chose his personal staff carefully, among them a captain seven years out of West Point, Stephen D. Lee, the future defender of Vicksburg. Lee's duties were to act as acting assistant commissary general, acting assistant quartermaster general, and later acting adjutant general.

Tensions rose between the two forces in early April 1861. President Davis issued a mandate directly ordering Beauregard to force a surrender. In accordance with his instructions, Sumter was also detached from its source of supply. President Abraham Lincoln (q.v.) countered with an order to resupply Sumter and directed Major Robert Anderson to hold Sumter, by force if necessary. These actions produced a situation that did not set well with either commander: Anderson, who had been Beauregard's mentor at West Point, now found his former pupil his enemy. Beauregard wrote a personal note urging his former mentor to surrender the garrison and asked his aides Colonel James Chesnut and Captain Stephen Lee to deliver it. Anderson refused the request but added that "if not hacked to pieces by our batteries he would be starved out in a few days" (Lee Diary). Chesnut and Lee took this statement to mean that the garrison could be taken without a fight.

When negotiations stalled, primarily because Anderson demanded too many concessions, Chesnut and Lee informed Anderson the shelling would begin in one hour. The assault began in the early morning hours and continued throughout the day, with Anderson beginning return fire at dawn. In the end, Beauregard forced Anderson to surrender. Although bombs, shells, and mortar rounds did little real damage, coupled with the fact that the Union officer soon could have been easily resupplied by sea, Beauregard seized the initiative and gained control. After Fort Sumter, in Williams's words, the general became "the South's first paladin" (61). President Davis described the Creole as being "full of talent and of much military experience" and promoted him to the rank of full general in the regular army, to date from July 21, 1861 (Woodworth, 76). This made Beauregard fifth in order of seniority, a fact that much rankled the Creole. He would never forgive Davis for this slight, and as future events unfolded—Grady McWhiney correctly pointed out in several publications and speeches and especially in *Southerners and Other Americans*—he and Davis even came to hate each other (13).

First Manassas, according to Williams, was "a record of bungled orders, sudden shifts in strategy, and final fortunate Victory" (81). Confederate forces made up in the sheer force of their efforts what deficiencies they had in command infrastructure. Of primary importance to the government in Richmond was the protection of Virginia, and two officers were assigned to carry out this directive: Brigadier General P. G. T. Beauregard, near the Union capital of Washington, and General Joseph E. Johnston, to the west in the Shenandoah Valley. President Lincoln, believing Beauregard to have upwards of 35,000 men between Washington and Richmond, ordered General Irvin McDowell to divert Johnston and strike Beauregard before Johnston could reinforce.

Beauregard was outnumbered by his West Point classmate McDowell by 10,000 men but held control of both Centerville and Manassas and the vital railway artery between them. McDowell planned an envelopment. Beauregard had an advantage over his Union rival. In *Elements of Confederate Defeat*, Richard E. Beringer, Herman Hattaway, Archer Jones, and William N. Still, Jr., contend that Beauregard's victory was due to one important factor: "The Confederates, with direct connections to Richmond, had employed the telegraph and the railroad to exploit their interior lines and thereby effect a rapid concentration" (46).

It was critical for Johnston to provide reinforcements to Beauregard in a strike against McDowell, but to do so Johnston had to outmaneuver an opponent in the lower Shenandoah Valley. To divert attention, Johnston dispatched cavalry under J. E. B. Stuart to distract the Union Army long enough for a larger force to board railway transports to the Manassas line. Once McDowell's flanking column made their move toward Bull Run Creek, the Federals made their attack on Beauregard's army, which quickly retreated. As reinforcements arrived, Beauregard ordered a counterattack, and the Union lines faltered and broke. Beauregard and Johnston proclaimed the first Battle of Manassas "an epoch in the history of liberty." Davis was elated: "Too high praise cannot be bestowed, whether for the skill of the principle officers, or for the gallantry of all the troops" (Beringer et al., 41, 43).

Experiences in the battle underscored the problem produced by the Confederacy's national flag being so similar to that of the United States: Unless blown by a strong wind, when hanging limp, it was hard to tell them apart. The flamboyant and ever-active Beauregard designed the now-familiar Confederate battle flag; he had three Cary girls (two sisters and a cousin), who were among the many visitors to be lavishly entertained at his field headquarters, make the first three of them, using material from their undergarments. (At least one of these flags still exists and is on display at the Museum of the Confederacy in New Orleans. The red portions are quite pink. Maybe they always were? Or maybe they just faded over time?)

Beauregard, however, soon began to draw the ire of the president and most of the War Department through his incessant telegrams complaining about Commissary General Lucius B. Northrop and advocating a large-scale offensive to take Washington and Baltimore. At first the president was benign, mollifying over matters that he viewed as petty. But when newspapers printed stories, Davis suspected the general had planted them. The last straw came when Beauregard issued public statements questioning the authority of the Secretary of War to issue instructions to a full commanding general. Although the president respected Beauregard as a commander, Davis wanted him away from the center of power in Richmond.

Beauregard was assigned to be Albert Sidney Johnston's second in command in the Western theater. Though irritated by the president's unwillingness to give him a full command, Beauregard later relished the position under Johnston because of the leeway in planning and execution. Larry J. Daniels, in his book *Shiloh*, provides a good argument that Johnston and Beauregard harmonized rather well—but says that it was "a partnership built upon mutual weaknesses" (125). Beauregard's intelligence network discovered that Grant's forces were in disarray and vulnerable while stationed at Pittsburgh Landing, Tennessee. Beauregard proffered his plan to crush Grant before Don Carlos Buell's approaching reinforcements could arrive. After Johnston agreed, Beauregard ordered the commanders of the Western forces, Leonidas Polk from Columbus and Earl Van Dorn from Arkansas, to Corinth, Mississippi. Davis ordered Bragg to join Johnston and Beauregard. By late March, the forces of the Western theater were united, with numbers over 40,000 strong.

However, as the march began toward Grant's forces, snarls in implementation of Beauregard's plan became evident and necessitated the attack being postponed three days. "Such a scheme should never have been tried," Steven Woodworth writes critically in his 1990 book *Jefferson Davis and His Generals,* "with a hodgepodge army that had been together less than a week and contained many units that had never made a day's march before, but Beauregard could not resist fancy" (96). Woodworth further observed that "the units were to march on different roads, converging and passing between each other at various intersections according to a rigid schedule, in a scheme that was something like the convolution of a modern-day marching band on a monstrous scale" (102). As it unfolded, the lack of troop discipline and breaches of procedure needed for a sneak attack—such as firing a weapon to see if it would work in a damp environment—were enough to dishearten both Beauregard and Bragg, who urged termination. "There is no chance for surprise," Beauregard wailed. "[N]ow they will be entrenched to the eyes" (Williams, 153). Johnston, however, remained resolute: "I would fight them if they were a million," he said to his aide (96).

At the break of dawn on April 6, 1862, the amassed Confederate forces launched a successful surprise attack on Grant's prostrated army. To their credit, though the Union troops fell back gradually, they were potent enough to stagnate a forceful Confederate advance. At an enclave, latter called "the Hornet's Nest," troops under Brigadier General Benjamin Prentis, says Larry Daniel, withstood eight Confederate offensives (215). By the time that their line finally broke at 5:30 in the afternoon, Confederate General Albert Sidney Johnston had been mortally wounded and died. In the end, the battle of Shiloh could be best termed a bloody stalemate, for though both had taken the day—the Confederates on the first day, and the Union on the second day—they had done so with heavy casualties. In his message to President Davis, the new Western commander claimed full victory but, in almost the same breath, he demanded that more troops be dispatched. Davis, having scrounged all he could from other areas, was infuriated by Beauregard's request.

Woodworth is hypercritical of Beauregard's battle plan and, in one of his fiercest strictures, says, "One result of Beauregard's wretched planning was that none of the corps commanders could control his units. . . . Men in battle for the first time found themselves being led by officers they did not know" (99). He also claims that Beauregard compounded his errors when, upon assuming command on the death of Johnston, he did not move his troops back to protect the vital railway interchange at Corinth. As such, according to Woodworth, after the second day "the army could take no more and was about to go to pieces" (102).

Following Shiloh, General Henry Halleck (q.v.) assumed command of Grant and Buell's forces and pressed the Confederates back toward Corinth. Beauregard soon found himself outmanned and outgunned. He deduced that if the Confederates lost the vital railway interchange, "we lose the whole Mississippi Valley and probably our cause." Yet retreat was his only realistic option. What the general had to accomplish, according to T. Harry Williams, was "to deceive the enemy and prevent demarcation among their own troops" (153). In this he was successful, implementing a plan that left the Union commanders awaiting an impending attack that never came.

Upon examination, it was a lack of tenacity that caused Beauregard to abandon Corinth. Woodworth asserts, "Robert E. Lee would successfully defend Virginia against overwhelming forces for two years . . . but Beauregard was not Lee and did not feel up to taking the risks involved" (104). Davis, who was out of patience with the general, was livid at the abandonment of such a vital railway artery without even so much as a fight. As if to make matters worse, the general, following his retreat from Corinth, took an unauthorized medical leave, which destroyed any prestige he had within both the Confederate government and the Southern press.

Davis summarily dismissed Beauregard and replaced him with Braxton Bragg. Bragg, out of courtesy, sought his predecessor's advice as to how to launch a counteroffensive against the Union in Tennessee. Beauregard suggested a strategy similar to that of First Manassas, making optimal use of existing railroad. Also, Beauregard's reputation was still a strong one among Union commanders. During his advance on the Williamsburg Road during the Seven Days Campaign in late June 1862, General George McClellan (q.v.) was disturbed by rumors that Beauregard was to lead the defense of Richmond with 200,000 troops, ignorant of the truth that Beauregard had already been relieved of command and sat idle over a thousand miles away.

Following his dismissal, General Beauregard was not to play a further significant role in the conduct of the war. He spent much of it in command of the defenses of Charleston, South Carolina, where he notably nurtured experimentation and was instrumental in promoting the submarine project that had been moved to that place. He, of course, kept in touch with events and corresponded with his numerous friends and confidants. Thomas Lawrence Connelly and Archer Jones, in their *The Politics of Command* (1973), assert that the so-called Western Concentration Bloc supported Beauregard's grand strategic idea, which in fact was valid and desirable: to stop giving main attention to the war in the East and instead to concentrate and achieve a decisive victory in the West. The strategy, however, was adopted too late and then too halfheartedly implemented (93).

Beauregard had one more brush with fame. By May 1864 he was back in Virginia and probably saved Richmond by discerning and responding to Grant's threat at Petersburg. Grant's plan to force a showdown, says Williams, was "foiled by Beauregard's stubborn defense" (236). With only 2,200 men at his disposal, Beauregard was able to fend off a formidable Union aggression three days in a row, until Lee was able to get reinforcements into place. In this campaign, Beauregard demonstrated both strength and tenacity by digging in and remaining, despite severe supply deficiencies.

During the war's final stages, General Beauregard was put in command of a newly created Military Division of the West, which comprised two Military Departments and John Bell Hood's (q.v.) Army of Tennessee. Beauregard did what he could to save the Western theater, but he misunderstood his authority and ultimately did not do very much, save to facilitate some of the supply arrangements for Hood's ill-fated thrust into Tennessee. Beauregard was met with criticism from Davis. In a letter dated January 8, 1865, to his nephew, Davis stated, "After Sherman started to the South East Genl. Beauregard thought it impossible to overtake him but that his plans might be frustrated by a rapid advance to Tenn." Although the president concurred with the initial point of Beauregard's assessment, he dismissed the latter as "erroneous." After Hood's disastrous failures at Franklin and Nashville, Davis replaced him with Joseph Johnston, rejecting the only other possibility: restoring Beauregard to army command. In a letter dated March 15, 1865, Senator James Chestnut praised Davis for restoring Johnston: "He seems to possess the confidence of the army, and is certainly better than Genl. Beauregard, whose Star is set" (Williams, 139, 142).

Immediately following the conclusion of the war, Beauregard did not take the oath of loyalty, determining it was improper by rules of military protocol to do so until other officers of his rank, primarily Lee and Johnston, had done the same. Neither did he ask for an official reprieve from President Andrew Johnson (q.v.), for in his own estimation, "it is hard to ask a pardon from an adversary you despise" (Williams, 257). Yet by September 1865, Beauregard had reversed his position and wrote to the president, declaring his allegiance to the United States and asking for a pardon. Three years would pass before clemency was given and a further eight years until his full rights of citizenship were restored.

The immediacy of his request was due, in large part, to the general's interest in politics. During the 1868 presidential campaign, at the encouragement of Lee and ex-Confederate Vice President Alexander Stephens (q.v.), he signed a support letter for Democrat Horatio Seymour over General Grant, the Republican candidate. In a letter to the 1872 Democratic candidate Horace Greeley, the general called for reconciliation and for Southerners to abandon their animosities toward the North.

During this time, Beauregard was active in the Reform party, a political movement consisting of conservative New Orleans businessmen whose platform recognized civil and political rights of freed blacks. Their primary aim was to incorporate enough black leaders into an alliance with Democrats to oust Radical Republicans in the Louisiana state legislature. He was also a prime motivator of the Louisiana Unification movement, a political cause—which included both white and black leaders—that sought to oust carpetbag governments and railed against high reconstruction taxes. Although initially the white and black groups cooperated on a bill introduced by Senator John B. Gordon of Georgia, a former general, rancor between the two groups soon emerged, and what seemed to be a potent political force tore itself apart. The experience so soured Beauregard that he never again sought political office. His only other foray into politics was to support an old friend, Winfield Scott Hancock, for the presidency in 1880, against James Garfield. (Beauregard also had an underlying motive: If Hancock were elected, Beauregard hoped he would appoint him to the post of ambassador to France.)

As for earning a living, Beauregard returned to the field he knew best—civil engineering, primarily with the railroads. At first, he was hired as the chief engineer and general superintendent in charge of rebuilding the New Orleans–Jackson–Great Northern Railroad. After conducting a complete survey of the line, Beauregard threw himself into his task, and within nine months, the line had been reestablished between New Orleans and Canton, Mississippi. As revenues soared, Beauregard was named president of the company. After a hostile takeover ousted him, he was asked to do the same type of work for a New Orleans–based city transit company. Through his efforts, the company grew into a profitable enterprise. Yet in less than two years, the general was ousted from his position when the company was bought out by a prosperous tobacco trader; again, Beauregard was out of work and faced with many obligations that had to be met.

Members of the New York Lottery syndicate sought to establish a new enterprise in an area removed from the storm of controversy such gambling enterprises had created in other states. Louisiana seemed the perfect place, for, according to Williams, "churches and schools in New Orleans had conducted lotteries since territorial days" (292). Once Louisiana had been chosen, the syndicate's agent, Charles T. Howard, spent $300,000 to pass a charter through the state legislature, and though the lottery itself was to be tax-exempt, Howard agreed to subsidize the local charity hospital for $40,000 annually from the proceeds. To maintain public interest, and as a measure to guarantee its trustworthiness, Howard sought an established Southern icon with an untarnished reputation to be his spokesman.

This practice was not new. Charles Reagan Wilson points out in his 1980 book, *Baptized in Blood*, that liquor companies, railroad interests, and lotteries "frequently hired Confederate generals to give their efforts respectability" (292). Beauregard was approached by Howard during midspring 1876, following a rash of corruption charges levied against the lottery. The general was leery at first, citing the effect it could have on his reputation, but he eventually accepted the offer. In fiscal terms, it was a positive step for Beauregard in that it became the basis of his recouping a respectable measure of wealth.

The general's duties, says Williams, were to "sit on the platform and supervise the wheels" (297). He also was given the opportunity to select an associate. Beauregard initially offered the position to Wade Hampton, who turned it down following his election to the governorship of South Carolina. Beauregard's second choice was Jubal Early, the commander of the Washington raids, who immediately agreed. The two Confederates were paid with a handsome annual base salary of $10,000, plus expenses and personal appearance fees. In return, Beauregard and Early agreed to "supervise" the drawing process at the four largest contests, to publicly defend the lottery against newspaper attacks, and to utilize their influence to achieve the passage of protective legislation. For the next fifteen years, the enterprise proved lucrative; but in the face of a growing public sentiment against state-sponsored gambling enterprises, and a bill passed in Congress that denied all lottery businesses access to the postal system, the lottery left Louisiana for Honduras in 1894.

Within a few years, war memoirs written by the war's leading participants began making their way to the marketplace and proved popular with the reading public. Soon many others published accounts of their experiences. Primarily, to cash in on this trade, in 1868, the general started to collect documents and to scribble notes for his own personal account of the war. Following five years of work, the project had little to show for the effort. As more war memoirs were made available, Beauregard found a new reason to write—to defend himself against the attacks from his peers as to his effectiveness as a commanding officer. Particularly, Joseph Johnston's account and a biography of Albert Sidney Johnston written by his son, which were highly critical of Beauregard's role in the First Manassas and Shiloh Campaigns, angered the general. He believed his reputation had been sullied. Beauregard employed a close friend, Alfred Roman, to collaborate with him, and by early 1881, the pair had nearly completed their manuscript.

That same year, Jefferson Davis published his exhaustive history, *The Rise and Fall of the Confederate Government.* The president's account contained scathing criticisms of Beauregard, Joseph Johnston, and others whom the ex-president had deemed less than dedicated to the cause. The work reawakened wartime hostilities held by these proud men. Beauregard himself described Davis's two volumes as "an outrage on truth and history" (Williams, 311). But the general's criticisms were not without merit. Incarcerated at Fort Monroe, Davis wrote his wife Varina: "J. E. Johnston and Beauregard were hopeless as to recruiting their forces from the dispersed men of Lee's army, and equally so as to their ability to check Sherman with the forces they had" (Strode, 156). Yet when Davis published his memoirs, the defeat of the Confederacy was due to the poor leadership and strategy of generals such as Johnston and Beauregard and other such field commanders.

What was even more hurtful to the general was that in the five years prior to publication Davis had consulted Beauregard on specific events of the war in which the latter had participated. Beauregard and his collaborator began a rewrite of their manuscript that was to attack the Confederate president at every turn but that would disguise their criticisms under the guise of "the infirmities of age and the severe trials of his prison life" (Strode, 313). It took the pair nearly three years to sell the manuscript, and when it was issued, sales were anemic at best.

Although Beauregard himself was a champion of the "New South," being among those who wanted the region to assert itself with "the influence it formerly asserted in the Councils of the Nation," he also was active in veterans' affairs (Foster, 98). In 1879, when General John Bell Hood and his wife died, leaving a large family of small children to care for with but little means, Beauregard utilized his contacts to publish Hood's memoirs, with all of the proceeds to be used for the Hood family. When the cornerstone for a statue of Robert E. Lee was laid in Richmond in 1887, the governor appointed Beauregard as the grand Marshall of the festivities. Such affinity for the cause ceased when ex-President Jefferson Davis died in 1889. As one of the few surviving full generals of the Confederacy, Beauregard was given the honor of heading the funeral procession. To this request, the old general flatly refused. He said to his family: "I told them I would not do it. We have always been enemies. I cannot pretend I am sorry he is gone. I am no hypocrite" (Basso, 309–310).

During his final years, Beauregard retained the airs of a distinguished gentleman. But as personal tragedies befell him, he lessened his public appearances. The death of his beloved daughter Laure following childbirth was a devastating emotional blow to him, from which he never fully recovered. (Perhaps the two-fold irony that Laure's mother had died while giving her birth added to his sense of tragedy.) Afterward, the general became quite close to her gentle elder daughter Lilian, with whom he spent much of his time. The construction of Laure's marble tomb took several months; but on the day he placed her within it, Lilian died suddenly; Beauregard had her buried that same evening with her mother.

In early February 1893, the old general fell ill with what were later described as stomach cramps. Within days, Beauregard seemed near death, calling out orders to the troops he commanded over thirty years before. Within two weeks, however, he rallied and was taking meals with his family. Late during the night of February 20, 1893, General Beauregard died in his sleep. Edmund Kirby Smith, the last surviving full Confederate general of the war, acted as chief mourner as the remains of the hero of Fort Sumter were buried, with full military honors, within the tomb of the Army of Tennessee in Metairie Cemetery. Throughout the service, a statue of Albert Sidney Johnston, his superior officer in the Western theater, looked down upon the proceedings.

The preeminent extant work on the general is T. Harry Williams's *P. G. T. Beauregard: Napoleon in Gray* (1955). Williams's prose is clear, concise, and lacks the lyrical varnish that gets in the way of a good tale. This book is not just a narrative of "the enigma of his life" but the story of an intriguing man who adapted to a changing South while his contemporaries wallowed in the mire of defeat. We would recommend this book without hesitation to anyone who wants to learn more about the American Civil War or who simply wants a good read. T. Michael Parish of Austin, Texas, is known to be at work on a projected new biography—and given his already demonstrated talent, it doubtless will transcend Williams's study because Williams did not exhaust all of the rich trove of sources known to be extant. In the meantime, some intriguing delineations of Beauregard's abilities and limitations are to be found in Larry J. Daniel's new book, *Shiloh* (1997).

General Beauregard possessed both the knowledge and the talent to have been an asset to the Confederacy's command corps. Emory M. Thomas, in his 1979 book, *The Confederate Nation, 1861–1865*, described him as "a charismatic personality with a flair for the dramatic''; but in the same paragraph he noted that Beauregard was ''a thoughtful soldier, well versed in the military thinking of his time'' (110). His reputation rests primarily on demonstrations of his abilities in three crucial confrontations. As the primary commander at Fort Sumter and First Manassas, he was able to achieve victory when his opponent possessed the advantage. To that Steven Woodworth contends, ''Both affairs could easily have turned out differently, but things had gone Beauregard's way, and he became a national hero'' (75). At Shiloh, crucial time following Johnston's death, Beauregard demonstrated a paralyzing reticence that proved his undoing. In the end, the legacy of General P. G. T. Beauregard was that his enormous ego eclipsed his considerable talent.

BIBLIOGRAPHY

Diary of Stephen D. Lee, University of North Carolina, Chapel Hill.

Hamilton Basso, *Beauregard, the Great Creole* (New York: Charles Scribner's Sons, 1933).

Clifford Dowdy, *The Land They Fought For* (Garden City, N.Y.: Doubleday, 1955).

T. Harry Williams, *P. G. T. Beauregard: Napoleon in Gray* (Baton Rouge: Louisiana State University Press, 1955).

Thomas Lawrence Connelly and Archer Jones, *The Politics of Command* (Baton Rouge: Louisiana State University Press, 1973).

Grady McWhiney, *Southerners and Other Americans* (New York: Basic Books, 1973).

Emory M. Thomas, *The Confederate Nation, 1861–1865* (New York: Harper and Row, 1979).

Charles Reagan Wilson, *Baptised in Blood: The Religion of the Lost Cause, 1865–1920* (Athens: University of Georgia Press, 1980).

Thomas L. Connelly and Barbara Bellows, *God and General Longstreet: The Lost Cause and the Southern Mind* (Baton Rouge: Louisiana State University Press, 1982).

Richard E. Beringer, Herman Hattaway, Archer Jones, and William N. Still, Jr., *Elements of Confederate Defeat: Nationalism, War Aims, and Religion* (Athens: University of Georgia Press, 1988).

Steven E. Woodworth, *Jefferson Davis and His Generals: The Failure of Confederate Command in the West* (Lawrence: University Press of Kansas, 1990).

Richard B. Harwell, *The Confederate Reader: How the South Saw the War* (New York: Barnes and Noble, 1992).

Herman Hattaway and Archer Jones, *How the North Won: A Military History of the Civil War* (Urbana: University of Illinois Press, 1993).

Hudson Strode, ed., *Jefferson Davis: Private Letters 1823–1889* (New York: DeCapo Press, 1995).

Larry J. Daniels, *Shiloh: The Battle that Changed the Civil War* (New York: Simon & Schuster, 1997).

HENRY WARD BEECHER
(June 24, 1813–March 9, 1887)

Jon L. Wakelyn

As the Union's most famous preacher, Henry Ward Beecher's support for the Northern war effort was of incalculable importance. Through work with friends and allies, he influenced President Abraham Lincoln's (q.v.) policies toward slavery. Through his preaching for the cause, Beecher stirred his parishoners on to make great sacrifices for the Union. As the editor of an influential wartime periodical, he wrote important articles and published a number of his sermons, which allowed him to reach an even larger Northern audience with his message. As spokesman for a large number of Northern citizens, that superb preacher-propagandist met with President Lincoln to discuss war policies. If Lincoln did not heed his advice, he did cultivate Beecher's public support. Because he had become a symbol of national sacrifice, the president chose Beecher to give the speech at Fort Sumter in April 1865 to commemorate the Union victory. Historian William G. McLoughlin claims that "no fact better testifies his spiritual leadership . . . than President Lincoln's choice of him as the principal speaker at . . . that ceremony at Fort Sumter'' (x). But membership in a famous family— he was the brother of Harriet Beecher Stowe—and a postwar personal scandal perhaps have overshadowed Beecher's importance to this country in its greatest moment. To give his contribution its rightful importance in history, it is time once again to evaluate his life and what he meant to the Civil War years.

Born in Litchfield, Connecticut, on June 24, 1813, Beecher was the son of the celebrated Congregational minister Lyman Beecher and his wife Roxana Foote. The ninth of eleven children, Henry early was neglected by his busy father and virtually raised by his famous sister Catherine. His closest friend was his sister Harriet, the later celebrated author of *Uncle Tom's Cabin*. When he was three the shy and withdrawn child lost his mother. An aunt, Esther Beecher, took charge of the rebellious youth, as Henry never seemed to get along with his stepmother, Harriet Porter, a rather cold and aloof person. Lyman, a stern but loving father, expected much from his children. He raised them in his own faith and wanted all of them to make contributions to society and to God.

In his youth, Henry seemed withdrawn into a fantasy world, unlike his vibrant and brilliant siblings, and more devoted to fiction than to the Scriptures. At ten he was sent to Miss Sarah Pierce's Female Academy, where he showed himself to be a poor student. When his father pressed him for his confession of religious conversion, Henry felt unable to comply. Because of so many successes in his Litchfield religious revivals, the self-assured Lyman thought he could develop in Henry the self-discipline necessary to academic life and to godly service. Instead, Henry failed miserably. Lyman then sent him on to his sister Catherine's academy in Hartford, but she soon gave up on him as a student. In 1827, Henry attended Mount Pleasant Classical Institute in Amherst, Massachusetts, to prepare for Yale College. Lyman and Henry's older brothers had all gone to Yale, and that New Haven college was nearly seen as a family preserve. Henry continued his scholarly ways, failing math and performing poorly in Latin and Greek, subjects necessary for admission to Yale. Out of desperation, in 1830 Lyman sent his son to the less pressure-filled Amherst, then a college for preparation for the ministry where students were kept under close supervision.

The future great orator hardly thrived at Amherst, even under its benevolent control. He was a poor student, but he did further develop his interests in popular literature there. It was almost as if Henry wanted to get to the heart of popular values and beliefs through the study of fiction. In addition, Henry showed an interest in phrenology, a fashionable and popular pseudoscientific study of the brain's capacity. That interest in popular science remained with Henry throughout his life, as he often used images of nature in his sermons. Early at Amherst Henry joined the antislavery student movement, although he was too cautious to become an outwardly committed abolitionist. He did excell in debate, however, and he joined the Athenian Society to sharpen his talent in public speaking. The college environment also turned Henry from a shy youth into an outwardly gregarious young man who seemed to make friends easily. On a visit to a classmate's home in eastern Massachusetts, Henry met and fell in love with Eunice Bullard. Seven years later they would marry. Because the Beecher family had little money, when college was not in session, Henry rounded out his education by teaching in rural schools.

Sometime during his college days, while separated from Lyman's pressures, Henry became interested in the ministry. Although he never had the conversion experience so popular with his peers who went into the ministry, he came to believe fervently in the gospels and resolved to become a great preacher like his father. Accordingly, upon his graduation from Amherst in 1834, he decided to go west to enter the Presbyterian Lane Seminary in Cincinnati, Ohio. His father, Harriet and her husband Calvin Stowe, and other members of his family had earlier moved to Lane to preach the gospel to the unconverted. While at Lane, Henry, according to his biographer Clifford E. Clark, "learned to judge the limits of public toleration for criticism and social reform" (30). As he became familiar with that thriving border and river city's powerful citizens, he became a follower of the antislavery advocate James Gillespie Birney. But when the seminary erupted over the slavery issue, Henry the student, and his father the preacher, decided to remain with the more conservative element. The radicals went off to found Oberlin in the Western Reserve. That decision typed the Beechers as social and religious reformers but not people who would disrupt local social values. Instead, they would seek reform from within the more established classes.

In 1837, the ambitious Henry left Lane to take up the pulpit at the First Presbyterian Church in Lawrenceburg, Indiana. He then married Eunice, and they soon began to build a family. While at First Presbyterian, Henry helped construct a new school and held revivals, and soon his church and fame began to grow. He used his own life story, images of nature, and vivid language in his sermons. In 1839, the Second Presbyterian Church in Indianapolis called. A thriving city, filled with transplanted New Englanders, it welcomed the moderate reformer and gifted preacher. He held revival after revival in the small towns and villages near Indianapolis. To reach even a larger audience than his church members, Beecher founded and edited the *Indiana Farmer and Gardner*. In 1843, he published a group of sermons, *Lectures to Young Men*, in which he called for self-help to achieve economic success. As a committed public servant, Beecher also became a trustee of nearby Wabash College. During the mid-1840s, he began to preach against slavery, and he made analogies of slave society with a broken family. The theme of the centrality of family to social and political stability became a major message in his sermons.

As Beecher's fame from his sermons, revivals, and publications spread, he came to the attention of important Brooklyn, New York, businessmen who offered him the pulpit of the growing Plymouth Congregational Church in prestigious Brooklyn Heights. The lure of an eastern, urban church, the chance to expand even further his gospel message, and his wife's desire to return to the East prompted Beecher to accept the offer. According to Clark, Beecher's message to his new middle-class flock "combined strong emphasis on individual action with effective peer-group pressure" (72). In his revivals, Beecher spoke of a God of love and caring, not one of Calvinist fear. Whatever the source of his appeal to those people, his church began to grow, he became friendly with the city's cultural and political leaders, and he was on his way to becoming one of the country's most famous preachers.

Fame in the pulpit catapulted Beecher into the public eye and gave that national figure the opportunity to write for important religious magazines. He joined the editorial board of *The Independent* and published in its pages his most famous sermons. Beecher also took positions on many current political issues. He opposed the Mexican War, rejected both national parties, and supported the Free Soil party. In 1848 he took a public stance against slavery, although he did not join the abolitionist movement. In voicing his opposition to the Compromise of 1850, Beecher, as Clifford related, maintained that "slavery

destroyed industry, discipline, and thrift'' (90). Moral suasion became his tactic
as he called for ''passive disobedience'' to the Fugitive Slave Law. At the same
time, Beecher, who seemed to have little time for the poor black people of
Brooklyn, supported the African colonization movement. Increasingly, however,
radical opposition to slavery expansion impressed him. In 1854, he insisted the
Kansas-Nebraska compromise act was a Southern conspiracy. For a time he
became a hothead and actually raised funds to send weapons to support antislave
forces in the Kansas civil war. The guns were called ''Beecher's Bibles.''

As Clifford says, Beecher ''began to play a role in public affairs that few
clergymen have been able to match'' (127). Preaching before large audiences
around the Northeast, he railed against alcohol and called for temperance reform.
The women's rights movement seemed to frighten him, and he spoke out against
expending reform energy on that cause. Possibly under the influence of his
sisters, Catherine and Harriet, he wished to free women from certain domestic
drudgery. But to give them the vote and liberal divorce laws he said would be
a threat to family stability. However, on matters such as public expenditures for
education, Beecher spoke forcefully for an informed people to take their places
in the growing urban manufacturing society that had so nurtured him.

But Beecher's major reform activity was his support of the antislavery cause.
In 1856 he supported the new Republican party and campaigned for antislavery
advocate John Charles Fremont. At first cautious over John Brown's violent
solution to slavery, he later stated that he wanted both freedom and law and
order. In 1860, Beecher and his Plymouth Church flock supported Lincoln and
condemned abolitionist extremists at the same time. But in 1861 he refused any
compromise on secession. Reform was one thing; breaking up the American
family another. Beecher would pour all his efforts into restoring the Union.

In 1861 Beecher was at his full powers as an orator and a feature writer for
the press. With his long, flowing mane, just beginning to gray, he cut a dashing
figure. His full red checks and double chin made him look like a prosperous
minister of a prosperous congregation. Always attired in the best of clothing,
he nevertheless affected a rumpled, slightly disheveled appearance, befitting a
man of God preoccupied with the cause at hand. Even his most hostile biographer, Paxton Hibben, admits that at that time Beecher was the most famous
preacher-orator in the country (179). With talent and energy he would persuade
his unready flock and the entire Northern people to sacrifice on behalf of the
just cause of saving the nation and its democratic government.

As Milton Rugoff says, early ''he addressed recruiting meetings, blessed flags,
preached patriotic sermons'' (389). In short, he urged young men to join up.
Beecher became the recruiter of a citizen's army of Protestant evangelicals,
contrasting the purity of his young warriors with the mongrel New York Irish,
who he claimed sat out the war. In a sermon on camp life that he preached early
in the war, he sought to purify the war effort itself. The war camp was to be a
place of piety, not promiscuity, and should train young men to do battle for the
Lord's war. During the early stages of the war, in addition to personally re-

cruiting troops, Beecher raised money from the Plymouth congregation to arm and feed them. He also persuaded his church leaders to provide for the soldiers' families. He raised the Brooklyn Phalanx brigade and even sent his son to war with his blessing. The actions of those young men, he insisted, proved the success of democracy. Not only were the boys purging their own sinfulness, but as Clark points out, Beecher believed they were reaffirming American "values and ideals" (149).

In addition to delivering sermons and public lectures to soldiers and his parishoners, in the fall of 1861 Beecher became editor in chief of *The Independent*, a New York religious newspaper with a national circulation. He now had an editorial column that many influential people throughout the North read. Beecher used that column to urge on support for the war. But he also wanted to hurry on the victory. Lincoln, for him, was too conciliatory, too tolerant of failure, too cautious on the course of the war. Beecher took General John Charles Frémont's side against the president when that general preemptorily freed slaves in Missouri. Over General George B. McClellan's (q.v.) tepid efforts, the preacher fumed and blamed a weak government. According to Rugoff, Beecher made a "series of almost weekly assaults on the administration" (390). Those columns in his paper made Beecher's criticism of federal war policy a potent force for rousing public opinion to persuade Lincoln on to even bolder action.

In sermons and in editorials, and later in his only novel *Norwood* (1868), Beecher also reflected on activities at the homefront. As stated, he raised funds and urged reform duties on those who stayed behind. He praised the contributions to the war of upper-class women reformers. According to William G. McLoughlin, Beecher believed that the efforts of Northern women on behalf of the United States Sanitary Commission revealed their commitment to the Union cause (207). He spoke eloquently about the sacrifices of Northern women who volunteered in the army hospitals as nurses and attendants. Beecher gave a memorable sermon on the actions of a woman volunteer in the army who had to operate on a soldier after the doctor she worked for had been killed by enemy fire. His persistent theme of contrasting the hedonistic South with the sacrifices of Northern women, McLoughlin points out, showed that "southerners appeared superficial and flighty compared to the deep-natured, persevering northerners" (206).

Perhaps it was Beecher's contrast between the North and the South, or perhaps the victory at Antietam, that convinced him at last to find worth in President Lincoln. Whatever it was, by late 1862 the former critic had become a follower of the administration. In the pulpit and in his editorials, he urged public support for the Republicans in the fall elections. Most important, the once mildly anti-slave advocate now realized that abolition also was the cause of the Union. He supported the preliminary Emancipation Proclamation and argued in favor of the final act of January 1, 1863. In one of his most famous sermons, on January 21, 1863, he harangued his flock on "the Southern Babylon." His topic was the kingdom of despotism and oppression versus the kingdom of God's freedom.

In that sermon, he praised the Emancipation Proclamation for providing the opportunity for black men to fight in the Union Army. Reprinted in Beecher's book of 1863, *Freedom and War*, which became an instant bestseller, the sermon was read by many Northerners. They read that the freedman "is a citizen entitled to self-defense and to the privilege of fighting for his country" (438). That privilege for all Northerners had become a war of no holds barred, to be fought to the bitter end.

Exhausted from his efforts on behalf of the Union, at the urging of his flock, Beecher went to Europe for a rest. Hibben insists without proof that he may have gone to escape scandal. Whatever the reason, Beecher took the opportunity in England to influence its people to support the righteous Northern cause. While he was in England, Beecher's *Freedom and War* was published back home to deliver the message of no compromise, support for Lincoln, the importance of abolition, and the meaning of liberty for a great united American future (iv). Although some historians say he had little influence on British public opinion, U.S. ambassador Charles Francis Adams encouraged the great preacher to speak out. In his October 1863 addresses, Milton Rugoff says "he demonstrated . . . an ability to sustain a line of argument and to orchestrate a variety of appeals" (392). Beecher did much more than that. He gave proof to the English that the Northern people were behind the war effort and that they would fight on to total victory. He stirred his audiences, and they believed his message.

Back home in 1864, Beecher continued to put iron into the spine of the Lincoln administration. When he heard that the president planned to meet with Southern peace commissioners, Beecher rushed to Washington to have an audience with Lincoln to persuade him against any concessions. That Lincoln planned none is secondary to the fact that he was pleased to be seen with the great preacher and to count him an ally. Beecher in turn went on the campaign hustings for Lincoln and again appeared with him in public. The preacher resisted the radical abolitionists who wanted to dump the president. He also spoke out against what he claimed was the pacifist campaign of the Democratic candidate McClellan. Although supposedly bipartisan, Beecher had shifted to the Republican side. In calling for a Republican victory in Congress, he assured his listeners that that party would support the Union cause to victory.

Victory he got. His reward was to be sent to Fort Sumter in April 1865 to give a major address on the restoration of the Union. Rugoff says that Beecher's "official recognition" may have been the high point of "his career" (394). Certainly it was Lincoln's acknowledgment of his contributions to the war. In that "Address at the Fort Sumter Flag Raising," reprinted in Beecher's *Patriotic Addresses* (1887), the preacher harkened back to the war's beginning in unfriendly Confederate fire on the fort in April 1861. Boldly, he stated, "God has stopped the arrogant Rebellion" (678). Slavery was ended, the nation saved, and it was time to reconstruct a free Union. For him, "the sentiment of loyalty and patriotism . . . has been rooted and grounded" (690). Beecher concluded with the hope that the North would welcome back a contrite South, and the South would educate the ex-slaves and make them citizens.

The preacher's hopes were not to be fulfilled. His own activities during Reconstruction would take many twists and turns on the subject of black freedom. Beecher did lobby new president Andrew Johnson (q.v.) to create a Freedman's Bureau and to put Oliver O. Howard, the war hero, in charge of it. Although he cautioned about excessive federal control of the restored South, the preacher nevertheless wanted to give the freedman an opportunity to form a family, to work, and to thrive there. Accordingly, early during Reconstruction he spoke in favor of the vote for the newly freed slaves. He also released a public letter urging quick readmission to the Union of the Southern states. Beecher went on a lecture tour in which he spoke favorably of the president's moderation and cautioned radicals to work for reform through the Republican party. But Beecher became disillusioned with Johnson's pro-Southern views and turned against him. Although the famous cleric seems to have lost the national following he had developed during the war, his insistence that the president was not committed to restoring the American family registered with voters and politicians alike, as they turned against Johnson's disruptive policies.

Beecher also began to lose interest in the plight of the ex-slave as he turned to Northern urban problems. His primary concerns became temperance and what he believed was the chaotic behavior of immigrants. He insisted on the social role of the clergy to speak out on public issues, as he directed his reform activities toward the growing urban middle class. As Clark points out, Beecher championed "a group of people who were both responsible for the increasing industrialization of the period and afraid of it" (187). The preacher championed the gains that could come from individual capitalist endeavor, but he also sensed how personal lives had been roiled by rapid change. For the remainder of his active social ministry, he would preach the theme of growth and adjustment.

This search for a way to ameliorate rapid social change was reflected in Beecher's many publications during that period. What has been called the "new evangelical liberalism" was announced in his essays and sermons printed in the New York *Ledger* and the *Christian Union*, which by 1872 had over 132,000 subscribers. Beecher also published a bestselling *Life of Christ* in 1871. Perhaps his most important written contribution to urban reform was his 1868 pastoral novel *Norwood; or Village Life in New England*. He introduced the novel by saying that "our simple story of domestic life will take us to a point intermediate between the rugged simplicity of a mountain town and the easier life of the cities" (2). On the surface, *Norwood* appears to defend the rural paradise of his imagined western Massachusetts childhood. It even has a stock Southern gentleman who symbolized a simpler, premarket set of values. But *Norwood* also is about the dynamics of competition, of free expression, of the skills to rise in modern society. As Clark says, the novel was a "calculated attempt to humanize and soften the expansion of industrial capitalism" (192). In it also is support for a growing role for women in the industrial, urban world, a role of active participation to sustain the family unit as the best way to endure change.

During those years committed to social reform, Beecher's congregation grew to over 3,000 members. His 1872 lectures at the Yale Divinity School could be considered the high point of his involvement in social issues. But at that time Beecher's life of work and sacrifice began to unravel. He became embroiled in a personal scandal in which a parishoner, Theodore Tilton, accused him of having had an affair with his wife Elizabeth. Denials and counthercharges led to a celebrated court case that forever tarred Beecher's reputation. Hostile biographers, such as Paxton Hibben, believe him to have been guilty. But the best study of the events, Altima Waller's *Reverend Beecher and Mrs. Tilton*, casts doubt on his guilt. More important, Waller insists that the scandal was part of the larger issue of a growing urban New York. As spokesman for a ''liberal Christianity,'' she maintains, Beecher was vulnerable to those who represented a more rigid set of religious values (16). When Beecher's own church leaders rejected claims of his guilt, they did so to protect their own community values. But, Waller points out, the result for Beecher was a retreat into a more private world. ''He was,'' she says, ''never again taken quite so seriously in political or economic matters'' (148).

Waller is only partially correct. In evangelical circles, Beecher was tainted. In politics, he spoke out against political corruption and was heard. In 1884, he supported the Democrat Grover Cleveland against what he believed was a corrupt Republican party. Beecher also opposed labor violence and unfeeling corporate executives. True to his middle road, he abhorred the social controls he saw in the union movement and the excessive selfishness of individualist entrepreneurs. The ordinary middle-class families, his new independent urban settlers, would lead the country, he said. For their sake, Beecher even entered the fray over evolution. His belief in the middle way led Beecher to support both Darwin's natural world and divine immanence. An intelligent people understood, he believed, that Darwinism only strengthened their faith. Beecher's cautious *Evolution and Religion* (1885) called for tolerance of science, for public commitment of the individual to social issues, and for use of science in behalf of the good society. He also became convinced that his own life experiences could be of value, so he began to write his autobiography. But he would never finish. Tired, overworked, in ill health, on March 9, 1887, he died in Brooklyn of a stroke.

There was an immediate public outpouring of grief over the loss of this famous public preacher. The funeral was a public extravaganza. His friend Lyman Abbott called his life ''the story of a successful general'' and ''the story of his successful campaigns'' (vi). Great public figures, Oliver Wendell Holmes, John G. Whittier, and Frederick Douglass (q.v.), spoke at his funeral about the preacher who had helped to save the Union. His political and reform allies from Brooklyn immediately published studies of his life that focused on Beecher's public career. Thomas W. Knox wrote that Beecher ''fearlessly preached freedom for the slave'' and ''converted the English public to a right view of the civil struggle in America'' (iii). For Knox, he was the great war preacher who belonged in the ranks of Lincoln, Charles Sumner (q.v.), and Ulysses S. Grant (q.v.). Another friend, Joseph Howard, Jr., in his 1887 biography, insists Beecher carried New York for Lincoln in 1860. At the end of the war, says Howard, ''he was the first to stretch the hand of reconciliation across the bloody chasm'' (352). The publication of Beecher's *Patriotic Addresses* in 1887 also fixed his wartime activities as the core of his career. In 1891, John B. Howard insisted that ''Lincoln, Grant, and Beecher are generally acknowledged to have been the three greatest men developed by the colossal contests of their era'' (160).

If those contemporaries who had such high regard for Beecher's life made the connection between his fame and the Civil War, it was not long before Beecher's scandal had diminished his importance in religious and historical circles. For years he would be forgotten. If remembered, usually works like that of Paxton Hibben focused on the pompous, overrated war leader and the man who betrayed his trust. It took until 1970 for a critical reappraisal of what Beecher had meant to his times. William G. McLoughlin, in *The Meaning of Henry Ward Beecher*, regards him as the foremost preacher-reformer of the urban Victorian period. Clifford E. Clark, in *Henry Ward Beecher: Spokesman for a Middle Class America*, in 1978 carried McLoughlin's view further. But Clark, who perhaps has studied Beecher's career the most thoroughly of any scholar, did not comment much on his wartime career. Those interested in the sources of Beecher's reform religion, Marie Caskey and Milton Rugoff, nearly bury him in their books on the famous Beecher family. Others of that family get the largest share of analysis. Too, as brilliant a study of the context of the scandal as Altima Waller's *Reverend Beecher and Mrs. Tilton* (1982) is, Beecher's own accomplishments are subsumed under the sexuality issues of the postwar period. Until another biographer studies Beecher as wartime preacher-reformer and understands the centrality of the family and the American middle class to all of his thought and actions, a true assessment of his importance to the Northern cause in the Civil War will be lacking. Yet modern historians of the leaders in that war all acknowledge just how important a role the clergy played in stirring popular support. No one Northern clergyman did more of that than Henry Ward Beecher.

BIBLIOGRAPHY

Henry Ward Beecher, *Freedom and War: Discourses on Topics Suggested by the Times* (Boston: Ticknor and Fields, 1863).

Henry Ward Beecher, *Norwood; or, Village Life in New England* (New York: Charles Scribner and Co., 1868).

Henry Ward Beecher, *Life of Christ* (New York: J. B. Ford, 1871).

Henry Ward Beecher, *Evolution and Religion* (New York: Fords, Howard & Hulbert, 1885).

Lyman Abbott, *Henry Ward Beecher: A Sketch of His Career* (Hartford, Conn.: American Publishing Co., 1887).

Henry Ward Beecher, *Patriotic Addresses* (New York: Fords, Howard & Hulbert, 1887).

Joseph Howard, Jr., *Life of Henry Ward Beecher* (Philadelphia: Hubbard Bros., 1887).

John B. Howard, *Henry Ward Beecher: A Study of His Personality, Career, and Influences in Public Affairs* (New York: Fords, Howard, Hulbert, 1891).

Paxton Hibben, *Henry Ward Beecher: An American Portrait* (New York: George H. Doran Co., 1927).

William G. McLoughlin, *The Meaning of Henry Ward Beecher: An Essay on the Shifting Values of Mid-Victorian America, 1840–1870* (New York: Alfred A. Knopf, 1970).

Marie Caskey, *Chariot of Fire: Religion and the Beecher Family* (New Haven, Conn.: Yale University Press, 1978).

Clifford E. Clark, *Henry Ward Beecher: Spokesman for a Middle Class America* (Champagne: University of Illinois Press, 1978).

Milton Rugoff, *The Beechers: An American Family in the Nineteenth Century* (New York: Harper and Row, 1981).

Altima Waller, *Reverend Beecher and Mrs. Tilton: Sex and Class in Victorian America* (Amherst: University of Massachusetts Press, 1982).

Richard Carwardine, *Evangelicals and Politics in Antebellum America* (New Haven, Conn.: Yale University Press, 1993).

JUDAH PHILIP BENJAMIN
(August 6, 1811–May 6, 1884)

Jon L. Wakelyn

As attorney general, Secretary of War, and Secretary of State at various times in the Confederate government, Judah P. Benjamin may have been the most versatile administrator in Civil War governance. Yet those who have studied his wartime career have been at odds over how to analyze his contribution to the Confederate government. Few have questioned his talents, but many have doubted his loyalties. That he ran off to England and deserted the South after the war's end has not helped his reputation. To make judgment more difficult, Benjamin destroyed his papers, and for all his famous love of publicity, his refusal to enter the "battle" of the memoirists has meant that much of his life story has been cobbled together from disparate sources. But his many duties and role in the Confederate government cannot be ignored. His life, with all its accomplishments and flaws, requires reconstruction and analysis.

The story of this self-made, ambitious leader begins with his birth on August 6, 1811, in what was then the British West Indies. That a European Jewish family somehow came to that place and then journeyed to the southern United States remains somewhat of a mystery, as does much of young Benjamin's early life. It is known that his father, the England-born Philip Benjamin, came from an intellectually inclined Sephardic Jewish family and spent his peripatetic life dependent on relatives and practicing the trade of a small-time shopkeeper. Judah's mother, Rebecca de Mendes, appears to have been the ambitious one in the family, and at least she steeled her son to struggle against adversity. When Judah was quite young, Philip moved his family to the port town of Wilmington, North Carolina, and later to Fayetteville, where a cousin paid for Judah's studies at the Fayetteville Academy.

In 1822, the family once again moved, this time to Charleston, South Carolina, which had a sizable Sephardic community. It was in that cosmopolitan city that young Benjamin thrived, perhaps in the company of such leading Jewish figures as Jacob Cardozo, newspaperman and distinguished economist. Probably the Benjamin family did not travel in such elite circles, but young Judah did have ample opportunity to test his growing intelligence. Again his uncle paid for his schooling and sent the brilliant young man to Yale College in 1825, when he was only fourteen. At that time Yale was known for accepting members of the Southern elite who spent their time gaming and carousing rather than studying, despite the fact that Yale had been the place that had trained the dour John C. Calhoun. Although Benjamin thrived in his studies and as a debater, in 1827 he left New Haven under a permanent cloud of rumor and accusations. Later enemies declared he had been expelled for thievery; others said he was sent down for "ungentlemanly conduct"; but what actually happened remains unclear to this day. What is certain is that Benjamin returned to Charleston, wrote a letter to Yale's president requesting reinstatement, and soon set out for greener pastures. In 1828, barely seventeen, he removed to the exotic, lush Gulf Coast business paradise of New Orleans. He was in search of anonymity and his fortune.

Fortune indeed he made and lost several times; to remain out of the limelight proved impossible. Upon arrival, he gained employment at a bank and began the systematic study of the law. With his keen debate skills, logic of purpose, and vice-like mind, he learned the law and the subtle ways of obtaining clients in that competitive atmosphere. He also discovered that there was a paucity of legal memory in that port city, so in 1834 he wrote the *Digest of the Reported Decisions of the Superior Court of New Orleans and the Supreme Court of Louisiana*. That volume made him well known and brought in many clients, and he grew wealthy. Benjamin also had studied international law, and he became legendary as one of the lawyers on the Creole case, which dealt with slavery in international waters. Like his fellow former Charlestonian, the editor J. D. B. DeBow, he recognized the value of transportation and commerce to the bustling Gulf Coast. He speculated in railroad building and was the prime mover behind the development of a southern Gulf coastal rail line. Benjamin next indulged in sugar planting, both for profit and because he knew of the status planters had in the South. In 1833 he had married the treacherous beauty Natalie St. Martin, who never loved him. Her marriage to him was a matter of convenience. Perhaps only the birth of his beloved daughter kept Benjamin in the marriage. Soon, risky investments forced him to overextend his credit, and he had to sell his plantation. But he returned to the comfort of the law, a profession that would sustain him throughout his life.

The business of the law and its public exposure led him into political life. His ambitions for commercial growth naturally meant that he identified with the Whig party, in New Orleans the party of the best men. In 1842 he entered the state legislature, where he rose to prominence as an expert on parliamentary procedure, and he also became a student in the human frailties attached to political ambition. In 1852 he assisted in writing the revision of the Louisiana constitution, and his fellow solons rewarded him with election to the U.S. Senate. In Washington, his wealth, style, and vast intelligence placed him among the favored few leaders. His business acumen also grew as he realized what profit could be made from good contacts. But sectional squabbles soon roiled that cozy world, and Benjamin found himself forced to take a particularist view of slavery and local rights. The Kansas embroglio wrecked his Whig party, and he drifted into an alliance with those Southerners committed to a national Democratic party. Benjamin differed over an important political issue with the hot-tempered Jefferson Davis (q.v.), and exchanged insults led to a challenge. After both politicos thought better of their situation, they forged a political alliance. But once again the adopted Louisianan found himself embarrassed—this time by his wife who ran off to Paris with a young man. Humiliated, Benjamin planned to leave Washington and his regal home on Lafayette Square.

Soon even more important matters occupied his mind. The presidential contest of 1860 had broken the national Democratic party political alliance, and the senator from Louisiana found himself allied with the newly organized Southern nationalists. Ironically, that citizen of the world, that adopted Southerner, had to join the minority of Louisiana secessionists to survive in his own state. Benjamin became a reluctant secessionist. He took advantage of his new position to deliver a rousing secessionist speech in the U.S. Senate, one praised by a member of the audience, Varina Howell Davis (q.v.), who would become his devoted friend and even patron. When Louisiana seceded from the Union, the senator who had worked to keep his state neutral had to join the infant Confederacy.

Intelligence, keen knowledge of all forms of the law, and the bonds he had previously forged with Jefferson Davis soon elevated this reluctant man into the highest ranks of the newly formed Confederate government. His quick study of the many issues presented to him, even if at times he appeared to exercise poor judgment, sustained him in high office over the next four years. In Richmond, Benjamin cut a splendid figure in an expensive frock coat, a silk waistcoat, a beaver hat, and felt gloves. Always impeccably dressed, even in a society that soon revealed its shabby side, he had grown stout with success, although he looked young because of his ruddy complexion, black beard, and bright, alert eyes. Sorrowfully, no Natalie occupied his attention. But there always was a coterie of nephews or wards to keep him company. Mainly, he fell in with the great politicians' wives in Richmond, as Mrs. Davis took him under her care, perhaps for the gossip they provided one another. This further solidified his connections with the president, which was handy because the secretary of many hues became one of the most controversial cabinet members in the Confederacy.

Initially summoned to Montgomery, Alabama, to advise the president-elect, Davis named him attorney general of the Provisional Confederacy in February 1861. While in Montgomery he assisted the president to form his cabinet and select a team of bureaucrats to take to the permanent Confederate States government in Richmond, early dealt with legal issues surrounding governance, and gained a reputation for organization, administration, and long working hours. His attention to detail became legendary. But he also lorded his legal skills and his connections over lesser leaders and thus earned their enmity. To the president, however, he always appeared loyal and the one who would volunteer for even the most arduous of tasks. He couldn't wait to leave Alabama for the supposedly more sophisticated and open atmosphere of Richmond. But in the new capital city, he discovered the difficulty of communicating with the powerful, particularist governors of the states with whom he had to do legal business.

Having found the position of attorney general confining, Benjamin longed to have overseas duty or to return to the more pleasant confines of New Orleans. But he always kept faith with his boss, and on September 17, 1861, he accepted the post of Secretary of War. It was a position for which he was not equipped, neither in temperament nor in skill. Immediately he clashed with the heroes of First Manassas, P. G. T. Beauregard (q.v.) and Joseph E. Johnston (q.v.). Both generals had many friends in high political circles, and both believed themselves to be great leaders. Johnston felt underused and accused the secretary of poor procurement policies that hampered his organization of the army. Nursing his own vanity, the Creole Beauregard believed that Benjamin was a traitor to the interests of Louisiana. Then, with the excellent owner of the Tredegar Ironworks, Joseph Anderson (q.v.), he fought over military contracts. Soon, his supposedly loyal "war clerk," the traitorous John B. Jones, began to describe in his *Diary* a sleazy, cheap, slave driver who had lost the confidence of the generals and the support of the staff in his own agency. Finally, the blame Benjamin took for the loss of Roanoke Island destroyed his effectiveness in the War office. Political and military leaders alike accused him of refusing to provide reinforcements at a crucial time, and that key North Carolina coastal defense was lost along with some sons of important political figures, and they wanted revenge. To make matters even worse, events surrounding the debacles at Island No. Ten on the Mississippi River, and Forts Henry and Donelson in Tennessee, in early 1862, turned the upper South's political leaders against him. Henry Foote of Tennessee then introduced a no-confidence bill against him in the Confederate Congress, which meant he had to go. To protect his friend and ally, the president relieved him from office. But he did not want to lose his talents and advice, so he appointed Benjamin Secretary of State, a post in which he would make use of his years of practicing international law. Perhaps he had at last found his proper place in the Confederate government.

To some extent, however, whatever success he had in diplomacy would always be undermined by the cloud of failure in the War Department. Edward A. Pollard (q.v.), the Richmond newspaperman, had already published his first volume of the war's history, and he attacked the activities of Benjamin in part to get at President Davis, his real villain. Thus, whatever Benjamin did in any office was always linked with the reputation of the president. Of course, the secretary also had his own problems at State, in part because he had accepted the arguments of the cotton diplomats who believed they could use the threat of refusing to export that staple to coerce European governments to support the Confederate cause. In that policy he failed miserably. He also was haunted by the hostile activities of Virginia politicial leader Robert M. T. Hunter (q.v.), who had wanted the secretaryship for himself. Always there was a frustrated Congress looking over his shoulder.

It is probably true that prejudice against him and the president disrupted any real opportunity to make his job work out well. However, there were a few successes. The secretary did assist in raising funds abroad for the financially strapped Confederacy. In late 1863, he secured the Erlanger Loan from France, even if the Confederacy never received the full value of that loan. But there also were other failures, at least in the view of the press. Perhaps out of frustration with the confines of the office, Benjamin turned to international intrigue, activities that some thought fit his personality. Smuggling, profit making for favored friends, personal gain—all were charges leveled at him. The abortive attempt to invade the Northeast through southern Canada in late 1864 also gained him enemies. Events surrounding secret negotiations with France over Mexico led others to insist that Benjamin all along had desired a separate Gulf Coast Confederacy.

The worst was soon to come. Pollard and his radical friends claimed that Benjamin had become a Reconstructionist because he had persuaded the president to support the Hampton Roads Peace Conference late in 1864. Indeed, to read Benjamin's speeches and watch his activities during the last months of the Civil War is to wonder just what he was up to. He seemed to waffle between support for peace and urging the president to stay the course. He advocated arming the slaves to aid the war effort, even though he knew that action would lead to the end of slavery. Because of Benjamin's persistent call for the use of slaves in the army, Congressman Hunter again went after his reputation. When he joined the entourage around the president that fled Richmond just ahead of the Union Army's capture of that capital city in early April 1865, some Confederates accused him of stealing what was left of the treasury for his own use. Yet Benjamin was the only cabinet member to urge President Davis to carry the war into the Southwest. Then, after Appomattox and on the eve of Bentonville in May 1865, he advised General Joseph E. Johnson to sign an armistice. At the last, he deserted President Davis—or was he given permission? He lit out for Florida and a boat that would take him from the battered and failed Confederate South. Benjamin once again had found the means to gain another chance. Many of those leaders who remained in the prostrate South believed his flight was proof that he had never been loyal to the Confederacy.

To look again at Benjamin's escape to safety in England is to see a survivor, a man who quite frankly believed that he was hated by anti-Jewish Southern leaders and that the Northern government planned to try him for murder. In England he would be reunited with his wife and, more particularly, with his beloved daughter. Whatever his reasons or secret motivation, Benjamin's rise to legal prominence in London was as extraordinary as his earlier success in New Orleans. He had arrived in England with only a few cotton investments and no other visible means of support, save his intelligence. He parlayed his talents into a career as one of the greatest trial lawyers at Lincoln Inn after he joined the bar in January 1866. Once again, he used his abilities to write on the law to gain fame, as his *Treatise on the Law of Sale of Personal Property* (1868) revealed his knowledge of English law and brought clients to his door. He came to specialize in international law, in part because of his cases dealing with the American Gulf Coast business trade, and climbed to the top of his field. Soon he practiced in the highest courts, although perhaps for reasons of prejudice, he never took silk (became a Queen's Council).

Benjamin refused to discuss his former life in the Confederate government or in Louisiana, and he even advised former President Davis to avoid contending with his detractors over past events. He claimed that the past no longer interested him. Instead, he devoted his life to his daughter, to his London friends, and to his legal practice. But those years of perfecting his talents in different places finally wore the lawyer down. He had a heart attack and had to reduce his practice. He died on a visit to Paris, no doubt to his estranged wife and his daughter, on May 6, 1884. There was much praise for his career in England and almost no mention of his passing in the South.

Perhaps being forgotten in the South was what he had wanted. His unwillingness to defend himself certainly left him vulnerable to his enemies and to those historians who later would use his contemporaries' negative writings to evaluate his career. Pollard's immediate accusations of failure and deceit, the rebel war clerk's venomous memories, and countless memoirs of the great and near great who never liked his closeness to Davis would haunt his reputation. For example, the conflicted Henry S. Foote, in *Casket of Reminiscences* (1874), so loathed Benjamin that he even resurfaced the Yale case and accused him of dishonest legal practice in Louisiana and of gambling in Richmond during the war while the Confederacy burned. Both Beauregard and Johnston labeled him a fiend. When his so-called friend Jefferson Davis brought out his own apologia, he did not even bother to defend Benjamin.

Only Pierce Butler, in the first biography of Benjamin, published in 1906, insisted that the secretary for all seasons had made major contributions to Confederate governance. But Butler the Southerner claimed that Benjamin was hardly a Confederate patriot. "Though he felt for the South," said Butler, "he felt that there was no obligation upon him to share her adversities" (8). A later biographer, Robert D. Meade, insisted that the immigrant had spent his life overcoming adversity. Meade resurrected a life that was exotic, even mysterious, perhaps because that was how Benjamin actually had wanted to be seen. Benjamin and his wife Natalie have even been the subject of a romantic novel, *Beloved* (1956), by Vina Delmar. It is a love story filled with falsehoods, as Benjamin the Jew was supposed to have become a Roman Catholic on his deathbed to please his wife. The best scholarly study of his life, that of Simon I. Neiman, depicted him as colorful, a man with a protective mask. Neiman at least has been the only person to attempt a full analysis of Benjamin's career as Confederate Secretary of State. His pursuit of cotton diplomacy he finds plausible. But always the personality gets in the way of the substance. Even the latest and most sympathetic study of his life, that of Eli Evans in 1988, cannot overcome the legend of the brilliant businessman-lawyer who failed in public life because he had no loyalty to any country. Perhaps that is the final tragedy of that tormented man. But it does not assist us in understanding his true place in the annals of Confederate governance.

BIBLIOGRAPHY

Judah P. Benjamin, *Digest of the Reported Decisions of the Superior Court of New Orleans and the Supreme Court of Louisiana* (New Orleans: n. p., 1834).

John B. Jones, *The Rebel War Clerk's Diary*, 2 vols. (Philadelphia: J. B. Lippincott, 1866).

Henry S. Foote, *Casket of Reminiscences* (Washington, D.C.: Chronicle Publishing Co., 1874).

Judah P. Benjamin, *Treatise on the Law of Sale of Personal Property* (1868; 3rd. ed., Jersey City, N.J.: F. D. Linn, 1889).

Pierce Butler, *Judah P. Benjamin* (Philadelphia: George W. Jacobs, 1906).

Robert Douthat Meade, *Judah P. Benjamin: Confederate Statesman* (New York: Oxford University Press, 1943).

Vina Delmar, *Beloved* (New York: Harcourt, Brace & Co., 1956).

Simon I. Neiman, *Judah Benjamin* (Indianapolis: Bobbs-Merrill Co., 1963).

Eli M. Evans, *Judah P. Benjamin* (New York: Free Press, 1988).

THOMAS STANLEY BOCOCK
(May 18, 1815–August 5, 1891)

Jon L. Wakelyn

Former antebellum U.S. congressman from Virginia, Thomas Stanley Bocock served as Speaker of the Confederate States Congress throughout the Civil War. A proud and committed Virginian, Bocock stands out as a major facilitator of wartime legislation and thus one of the Confederacy's most important congressional leaders. Wilfred B. Yearns, the most thorough historian of the Confederate Congress, says that Bocock eventually turned against President Jefferson Davis (q.v.) and led the Confederate Congress in opposition to executive policies. How he rose to such political prominence and why he turned against his leader require examination in order to assess that congressman's contributions to the Confederacy. Since Bocock has had no major biographer and no substantive study has been made of his wartime activities, his life's work will have to be reconstructed from local historical accounts, those around him who commented on his duties, and what little he left about his own thoughts and deeds.

Bocock was born in Buckingham County, Virginia, on May 18, 1815. His father, John W. Bocock, variously farmed, kept a school, and practiced law. The elder Bocock married Mary Brooke from Buckingham, a relative of the powerful Smith and Brooke families of that part of the Virginia southside. Given an early education in his cousin John T. Bocock's school on Burt Creek near Appomattox Court House, young Bocock was brought up in an upwardly mobile family that had extended connections throughout the region. His brother, Henry F. Bocock, became a successful lawyer, a Presbyterian lay leader, and a trustee of the small Hampden-Sidney College. No doubt under the influence of Henry and the locally powerful William Cabell family, young Thomas Bocock matriculated at Hampden-Sidney in 1837. His closest friend in school, Robert L. Dabney, later became an eminent Presbyterian divine and educator and a staff officer with Thomas J. Jackson (q.v.). Bocock and Dabney vied for first honors in the class of 1838. Another brother, John H. Bocock, who also attended Hampden-Sidney, later also became an important Presbyterian minister. Their older brother, Willis, the most successful lawyer in Buckingham County, served in state politics as attorney general and married a South Carolina heiress. The wealthiest man in the Appomattox area, Willis brought young Thomas into his law practice and encouraged his early political ambitions.

As his law caseload grew, Bocock also entered and eventually rose to leadership in Buckingham County politics and gained election to the Virginia House of Burgesses in 1842. He married Sarah Patrick Flood, daughter of a local political leader and prominent social lion. Henry D. Flood and Harry Flood Byrd, two of Virginia's most important twentieth-century leaders, also descended from that remarkable family. When the legislature formed Appomattox County out of part of Buckingham County in 1845, the voters elected Bocock as the county's first prosecuting and commonwealth attorney, and that office gave him the kind of public exposure certain to further his political career. His cousin, John T. Bocock, became first county clerk, and the family began to use his political prestige to promote Thomas's rise in public life. Family members also rallied around Thomas's successful campaign for the U.S. House of Representatives in 1846. Continuously reelected until the outbreak of the Civil War, Bocock rose in national Democratic politics, became an excellent parliamentarian, and at one time nearly gained election as Speaker of the House. In 1855, the adroit politico beat back a Know-Nothing and ex-Whig challenge to his post. Walter Watson, in his *Notes on Southside Virginia*, described the Bocock of that time as an attractive and persuasive lawyer, "a man of great simplicity and cordiality of manner" (209). At church meetings that he attended to learn much about local political opinion, Bocock always talked with the common sort, leaving his Flood wife to entertain the local quality.

John Goode, fellow Virginia congressman, and other political leaders remembered him as a committed Southern nationalist who often spoke out in Congress in defense of slaveholding interests. Bocock even praised Preston Brooks's outrageous attack on Charles Sumner (q.v.) in a memorable radical speech in Congress. But that canny political leader also tried to achieve compromise on the slave expansion issue, and he spoke out for recommitting the Kansas statehood bill to that territorial legislature. As the secession movement in Virginia exploded after Abraham Lincoln's (q.v.) 1860 election, Bocock positioned himself as a moderate Southern nationalist in Washington, while he encouraged the forces of separate state action back in Appomattox. He supported his ally the radical Lewis D. Isbell in his bid for election to the Virginia secession convention. His famous reply to the Force Bill, which he delivered in the U.S. House of Representatives on February 20 and 21, 1861, catapulted Bocock into a leadership position in the newly organized Southern Confederacy. He began that speech by saying that perhaps speaking was unwise when the times called for action. But he objected so much to that bill that gave the president authorization to raise troops in the event of insurrection that he just had to speak out. He characterized the bill as an act of war because the chief executive now for the first time held near dictatorial powers over the individual states. Obviously directing his remarks to his fellow Virginians, especially those who had for the time being taken a moderate position, Bocock had a pamphlet of his speech printed and widely circulated it among political leaders. The pamphlet became a topic of discussion at the Virginia secession convention, as a number of delegates there commented on its major issue, the rise to national power of the Republican party as a radical party, and its implications for Southern slavery. Bocock had even hinted that the Republican party had begun to show strength in those parts of Virginia where slavery was on the decline. Those who discussed his pamphlet then insisted that all Virginians would have to defend themselves against antislave insurrectionists. Shortly thereafter, Bocock resigned from the federal Congress and returned home to prepare for what he believed would be war.

Bocock had wanted to assist in drawing up the new provisional Confederate constitution. A number of state leaders believed he would have insisted the constitution contain rigorous statements about the rights of states in the new Confederacy. A boomlet of sorts even began among Virginia's radicals to nominate him for president of the Confederacy. Unfortunately for his ambitions and the state's rights forces, Virginia had not yet seceded from the Union. After Virginia seceded in April, Bocock accepted membership in the Confederate States Provisional Congress. Noting his years of congressional leadership experience, his fellow congressmen elected him Speaker. Because of his expertise in procedure and the methods of governance he displayed in those early days of the new Republic, his colleagues again made him Speaker in the first permanent Congress at Richmond. His only opposition for legislative leadership was the mercurial Henry S. Foote of Tennessee. Once Foote realized the amount of support for Bocock, he moved successfully that the Virginian be elected Speaker unanimously. At that time Bocock gave the appearance of a distinguished, knowledgeable leader who looked the part with his graying hair, trimmed beard, sharp and alert features, and a stern, determined look around the mouth. How well he would serve in that demanding office remains to be created from the fragmentary record of that national Confederate Congress.

The Speaker's acceptance address delivered on February 18, 1862, announced his priorities and perhaps signaled how he wanted to handle the task that had been thrust upon him. With the claim that he was humbled by the amount of confidence placed in him, Bocock promised to "maintain the dignity and preserve the decorum" of the House. He also vowed to support the welfare of the entire Confederacy and to govern for all of the people. Bocock then attempted to define what he believed already had caused internal resentments and jealousies in the infant new nation and to get rid of feelings of personal anger. He offered that "submission to contributed authority is the primary necessity of all communities" within the borders of the Confederacy. The new Speaker pledged to accept and to support differing economic interests, and asked especially that all his colleagues acknowledge the value of industrial development in the Upper South. Above all, Bocock stated with conviction, he worried about tyranny of the majority, as he feared for the special interests of his native state of Virginia. Then he pledged himself to defend constitutional limitations and to support the war effort to his fullest ability. But, Bocock concluded, he would support the taxing of the people only for such military expenses necessary to ensure victory.

In short, that speech invoked the dilemma that many able and just political leaders such as Bocock had to face during the war. Enormously disturbed that his beloved Virginia was under siege, worried over growing division among Confederate States' interests, and determined to use his authority to preserve civilized behavior, his pledge to force the unity of war effort in the Confederate House no doubt went against his own state's interests. But he persevered and in those early years behaved with much decorum. One incident in late 1862 showed his skills under fire. When a woman entered the House and threatened to cowhide Congressman George C. Vest, Bocock calmly showed her the door and stifled laughter by calling the House to order. Often against his own beliefs, which favored sound monetary policy, he shepherded Secretary of Treasury Christopher G. Memminger's (q.v.) questionable money schemes through the House. Though no great friend of the centralizationist Jefferson Davis, Bocock early defended the president's governmental policies and administration demands. He did, however, manage some degree of state particularism as he focused especially on promoting Virginians who served in the military and became an exponent of the advancement of the career of Robert E. Lee (q.v.).

But as the war wore on and on, as he watched more and more of Virginia come under Northern control, as friend after friend lost sons and land to the war, Bocock's resolve began to crack. An ally of fellow Virginians William C. Rives and Robert M. T. Hunter (q.v.), by 1864, like them, he had begun to ask whether the Upper South had already been defeated. Still, when the president wanted to use slaves to work in the trenches and behind the Confederate lines, Bocock supported that measure as a last-ditch means to gain needed labor for the defense of the Upper South. But when President Davis suggested arming the slaves, he joined Hunter in arguing vigorously that such an action would be the end of slavery, the protection of which was the only reason to resist the North. In late 1864, Bocock at last joined the opposition to President Davis and Secretary of War James A. Seddon (q.v.), a personal friend and former political ally. Bocock called for Seddon's resignation and promoted the candidacy of General John C. Breckinridge, in hopes of restoring unity to the Confederacy. He led the forces that wanted Lee to be declared military dictator, though that act of frustration actually seemed to repudiate his once-proud resistance to the 1861 Union Force Bill. Bocock's nationalism had given way to Virginia particularism, and he appeared willing to sacrifice the Confederacy in order to protect his own state.

Although the internal functions of the Confederate Congress await detailed analysis, especially the issues of how that body facilitated the war effort, it is clear that the Speaker of the House held a most important leadership role. For one thing, the Speaker named all committee assignments and thus could direct the best personnel to key positions. Of course, if he chose unwisely, then the processing of committee information as well as the facilitation of legislation could falter. The Speaker also could select what bills to bring before the House. Thus, the Speaker was in a position to stifle key administration measures or to give them priority. Lastly, the Speaker set up the operations that reconciled House and Senate bills. Bocock's ability to work with Hunter and other senators no doubt was at times extremely important to the war effort. So when Bocock went into opposition to President Davis, he was able to wreak havoc upon the administration's war policies, especially during the waning days of the Confederacy.

After the Confederate government had evacuated Richmond, in early 1865 Bocock returned to his own home, "Wildway," in Appomattox County. But he found no peace there, as soon he had to flee from invading Union troops. Tired, much of his property ruined, after the war ended, he returned home again to practice law. He found little work there and had to move to Lynchburg, where he would spend most of the remainder of his life, though he kept his country home in Appomattox. Eventually Bocock returned to Democratic party politics and later helped to form the Virginia Conservative party and even supported Andrew Johnson (q.v.) for president in 1868. Elected to the Virginia House of Delegates in 1870, he worked to restore his state's ruined financial base. Bocock supported Horace Greeley in 1872 and Samuel J. Tilden in 1876, always in the hope that the national Democratic party would resume its close ties to the South. In 1878, this moderate "funder" who wanted Virginia's debt credit restored sponsored a bill to stabilize Virginia bonds. But Bocock could neither slow down the Readjuster movement nor resist the rise of new, young political leaders in the state. According to Alexander F. Robertson, in his biography of Alexander H. H. Stuart, Bocock and his friend Hunter had come to realize that their prewar generation of state leaders must give way to new men. So he retired to his law practice and probably to his own bitter thoughts about why the Confederacy had failed. In the summer of 1891, he became ill in Lynchburg and returned to Appomattox to die at Wildway on August 5, 1891.

Thus passed a man who in his own contradictions—Southern nationalist and Virginia particularist—may have embodied the dilemmas within the Confederate government itself. But history does not yet know enough about this important leader to make such a judgment. Analysts of the Confederate Congress, from Yearns to Alexander and Beringer, say little about either his motivation or the quality of his performance. *The Official Record of the War of the Rebellion* revealed him to have been outspoken and to have been disliked by some of the members of the Richmond newspaper corps. Tidbits and snippets that elucidate his life are found in local histories and genealogies. The best of these are Eugene A. Maloney, *A History of Buckingham County* (1976), and Vera Smith Stanley, *Appomattox County, Past, Present, and Future* (1965). His student life is profiled in the *General Catalogue of the Officers and Students of Hampden-Sidney College* (1901). Jack Maddex, in *The Virginia Conservatives* (1970), described enough of his postwar activities to show that Bocock had played a most important part in Virginia's reconstruction.

BIBLIOGRAPHY

The Official Record of the War of the Rebellion (Washington: Government Printing Office, 1880–1901).

General Catalogue of the Officers and Students of Hampden-Sidney College (Richmond, Va.: Whittet & Shepperson, Printers, 1901).

Richard McIlwaine, *Hampden-Sidney as an Educational Force from the War of the Revolution to the War between the States* (Petersburg, Va.: Buckman Mfg. Co., 1903).

Alexander Farish Robertson, *Alexander Hugh Holmes Stuart* (Richmond, Va.: The William Byrd Press, 1925).

Wilfred Buck Yearns, *The Confederate Congress* (Athens: University of Georgia Press, 1960).

Vera Smith Stanley, *Appomattox County, Past, Present, and Future* (Appomattox, Va.: Times-Virginian, 1965).

Jack P. Maddex, *The Virginia Conservatives* (Chapel Hill: University of North Carolina Press, 1970).

Thomas B. Alexander and Richard E. Beringer, *The Anatomy of the Confederate Congress* (Nashville: *Vanderbilt University Press*, 1972).

Eugene A. Maloney, *A History of Buckingham County* (Waynesboro, Va.: Charles F. McClung, 1976).

Walter Allen Watson, *Notes on Southside Virginia* (Baltimore, Md.: Genealogical Publishing Co., 1977).

Jon L. Wakelyn, ed., *Southern Pamphlets on Secession, November 1860–April 1861* (Chapel Hill: University of North Carolina Press, 1996).

BRAXTON BRAGG
(March 21, 1817–September 27, 1876)

Steven E. Woodworth

Braxton Bragg has fared ill in history. Few other Civil War generals have suffered a press as unflinchingly and universally negative, both during the war and since. Perhaps only John C. Pemberton, among Southern leaders, and Ambrose Burnside, among the generals of the North, have suffered from historians a dismissal as curt, sweeping, and final as that accorded Braxton Bragg. Indeed, to read almost any modern campaign or battle study involving Bragg's army is to wonder not why he was still in command of an army but why he was still outside of a mental institution, few though such places might have been in those days.

Some modern students of the war would explain this phenomenon very simply: Bragg was indeed an atrocious general and a loathsome human being. Yet the more thought one gives to the situation, the less satisfying such an explanation becomes. Bragg possessed an excellent reputation in the pre–Civil War U.S. Army, was one of the most celebrated of the South's military leaders in early 1862, and won the grudging respect and admiration of Jefferson Davis (q.v.), a tough, experienced army officer and politician who had been on bad terms with Bragg while serving as Secretary of War during the mid-1850s. Nor was Davis his only admirer—others within the Confederacy, including officers and soldiers within his own army, retained a high regard for him throughout his tenure in command. Finally, his troops won at least tactical victories in three out of the four pitched battles they fought under his command, though facing numerous and well-equipped enemies led by some of the North's premier commanders. How could all of this be if Bragg were indeed the blundering miscreant often depicted? Clearly, something here needs explaining.

Born third of the twelve children of Thomas Bragg and Margaret Crosland Bragg, on March 21, 1817, in Warrenton, North Carolina, Bragg was the son of a successful tradesman. His two older brothers, John and Thomas, became an Alabama judge and a North Carolina governor, respectively. Braxton himself received as good an education as the state offered in those days before heading for the U.S. Military Academy.

Finishing fifth in West Point's graduating class of 1837, Bragg found himself posted to the 3rd Artillery. An early assignment carried him into a theater of combat—of sorts—in Florida's Seminole War. If anyone at all enjoyed the Seminole War (besides, perhaps, the Seminoles) or found it even as professionally rewarding as junior officers are wont to count such affrays, he seems to have left no record of it. Bragg certainly did not. In the fetid south Florida climate he fell ill, and his health deteriorated to the point that he requested and got a series of furloughs followed by assignments to less strenuous duty. During the rest of his life, Bragg frequently suffered from poor health—often described as dyspepsia, a sort of nondescript stomach complaint. Many have suggested that Bragg's assorted ailments gave him a chronically cranky personality. In his pain and physical misery, according to this theory, he lashed out at those around him, poisoning relationships and destroying his ability to work with his subordinate generals. Perhaps, but other generals with health problems included Robert E. Lee (q.v.) and Stonewall Jackson (q.v.). The latter was never accused of possessing winning personal charm, while Lee's aide recalled that "The Tycoon," as he called him, could be decidedly snappish when unwell, which he frequently was. Poor health was no help to the general, but neither was it a guarantee of military failure or of impossible working relationships with subordinates.

Another feature of Bragg's early years was a tendency to squabble with superior officers. The army frowned on insubordination but still tolerated a surprising amount of it among officers. Other pre–Civil War officers, Jefferson Davis for example, also engaged in behavior that would be unthinkable in most modern armies. Bragg merely carried contentiousness a little farther than most other officers, though not as far as some. At least one humorous story, reported years later by Ulysses S. Grant (q.v.), made the rounds about Bragg's alleged bickering, but it seems not to have been regarded as a serious reflection on Bragg's worth as an officer until after the events of the Civil War. After all, had an officer's Old Army reputation been decisive, few today would bother reading Grant's memoirs (Grant, 2:86–87).

In the Mexican War, Captain Bragg commanded a battery of the new horse-drawn light artillery in Zachary Taylor's army down on the Rio Grande and won notice for its efficiency and high level of training. His finest hour came at the battle of Buena Vista. Using a mobility hitherto unknown to artillery, Bragg raced around the battlefield to threatened points. "Captain Bragg . . . saved the day," Taylor reported (McWhiney *Braxton Bragg*, 34). Brevet Lieutenant Colonel Bragg returned from the war and married a beautiful young Louisiana heiress. Several years later he resigned and took up the life of the Southern gentry on his wife's Louisiana sugar plantation.

Thoroughly pro Southern and pro slavery, Bragg seems to have experienced not a moment's hesitation about bearing arms against his old flag in the name of his adopted state's claim of secession. Louisiana was glad to have him and made him commander of its (temporarily independent) forces. Once the state army was absorbed into Confederate service, Bragg's rank was brigadier general, and he commanded one of the two most important posts in the South.

By the time of Abraham Lincoln's (q.v.) inauguration on March 4, 1861, Southerners had seized every federal fort, arsenal, or other installation in the seceding states with two exceptions. One of those exceptions was Fort Sumter in the harbor of Charleston, South Carolina, the other, Fort Pickens, just outside the harbor of Pensacola, Florida. Lincoln meant to hold both; the Southerners were determined to take them. Louisianan Pierre G. T. Beauregard (q.v.) commanded the forces arrayed against Sumter; Bragg, those facing Pickens. Bragg's nearly twenty-year military career and especially his impressive performance in the Mexican War made him one of the most highly regarded soldiers to cast his lot with the Confederacy before the outbreak of hostilities, and his selection for such an important post surprised no one.

That Beauregard became the hero of Sumter while Bragg languished in drowsy Pensacola was a factor of politics and geography rather than the generals themselves. As the metropolis and most extreme city of the most extreme Southern fire-eating state, Charleston created its own impetus for an early resort to violence. Geographically, the location of Fort Pickens on Santa Rosa Island, outside Pensacola harbor, put it beyond the reach of practical attack by Confederate forces on the mainland in a way that was not true of Fort Sumter, inside the harbor at Charleston. Events, then, made Beauregard the conquering hero and Bragg primarily a drill master. Though Beauregard's flare for public relations led him to capitalize on his fortuitous success in ways Bragg could hardly have dreamed of, success is its own press agent, and even the most curmudgeonly of generals can become the darling of public opinion if only the people perceive him a winner. In that case, the general's contrariness becomes one more endearing eccentricity to the adoring public—as witness the case of Stonewall Jackson, the least suave of men but probably the most popular in the Confederacy by the time of his death. In short, circumstances beyond Bragg's control denied him an early and easy opportunity to establish his fame as a victorious general and place all his subsequent actions and the results in a far more favorable light.

After the collapse of the Confederacy's western defenses upon the fall of Forts Henry and Donelson, Bragg and his Pensacola garrison traveled northwest to Corinth, Mississippi, as part of the Confederacy's drastic concentration of forces in the face of impending disaster to the Southern heartland. During his months in Pensacola, Bragg's reputation had risen slowly but steadily as a result of his effective training and skillful administration of the forces under his command. By the time he moved to Corinth, Bragg stood high in Jefferson Davis's estimation, as well as that of others, as one of the best generals in the Confederacy. As part of Albert Sidney Johnston's army Bragg led his troops into the confused and furious battle of Shiloh and, under the circumstances, did about as well as anyone did, emerging with enhanced reputation, though the Confederate attack failed (Woodworth, *Jefferson Davis*, 93–94).

Johnston died in the battle, and that made Bragg second-ranking officer in the defeated Confederate Army that retreated to Corinth and then, six weeks later under pressure of a massive Federal army, further south to Tupelo. Beauregard, its commander, was in ill health because of his nerves and in bad odor with Jefferson Davis because of his actions—primarily retreats—during and since Shiloh. When Beauregard that summer granted himself a sick leave and headed for a health spa in south Alabama, Davis lost no time in turning over command of the Confederacy's chief western army to Bragg (Connelly, *Army*, 181–182).

Bragg's unenviable place in history is the product of his nearly year-and-a-half command of what would soon be known as the Army of Tennessee. The keynote of that tenure was his first campaign, and his course was largely set within his first four months at the helm. Though Bragg performed reasonably well in the fall 1862 Kentucky campaign, the strategic situation allowed little margin for error, and Bragg's superior and some of his subordinates both made a number of errors that canceled out some of Bragg's finest achievements.

Bragg took over an army in difficult straits, blocked by a mighty Union host in northern Mississippi while another powerful Federal army bore down relentlessly on the key rail junction at Chattanooga. Davis, and the Confederate public generally, expected Bragg to make a "desperate effort to regain what Beauregard has abandoned"—meaning all that the South had so far lost west of the Appalachians. The situation was ready-made for ruining a general's reputation.

In east Tennessee, Confederate department commander Major General Edmund Kirby Smith could do nothing to stop Don Carlos Buell and so appealed to Bragg. In response, Bragg transported his army by rail south to Mobile, then north through Atlanta, and finally to Chattanooga only a few days after leaving Tupelo. It was an enterprising use of the South's patchy and rickety rail system, and it not only secured Chattanooga from the threat posed by Buell's advance but also opened the way for Bragg to turn Buell and either destroy his army or drive it back, possibly fulfilling the South's expectations of him. His plan was to march north and then west into middle Tennessee and squarely into the rear of Buell's army. Somewhere near Nashville, where Bragg could draw supplies from the agriculturally rich and pro-Confederate Nashville Basin, Buell, desperate to restore his broken supply line, would be forced to fight a great battle at a terrible disadvantage.

That the plan never became reality was as much Davis's fault as anyone's. The Confederate president gave his blessing to the movement but crippled Bragg in two important ways at its very outset. The first was in neglecting to place Kirby Smith and his East Tennessee force under Bragg's direct command. Unrealistically, Davis believed voluntary cooperation between the generals would secure the necessary smooth cooperation of their armies. Second, Davis refused a request from Bragg to allow him to purge his army of incompetent senior generals and promote capable junior men in their place. Among those senior generals who would have gone into a well-deserved obscurity, however, was the president's close friend and former West Point crony Leonidas Polk. Polk's blundering had already cost the Confederacy dearly, but in Davis's eyes he could do no wrong. Bragg, the president declared, would keep the officers he had. These two failures on Davis's part hamstrung Bragg in the coming operation and shaped the course of his entire career in command of the Army of Tennessee.

Bragg's campaign plan went out the window at once when the headstrong Kirby Smith marched his force directly into Kentucky, where Confederate sentiment allegedly ran high, leaving Bragg to fight Buell by himself. Bragg's army was too small for that, and the best he could do was to march into Kentucky himself, skillfully keeping his army between Smith's force and Buell's larger Union Army. Smith, ignoring Buell and using troops borrowed from Bragg, won a victory over green Federal recruits at the small battle of Richmond, Kentucky, and ensconced himself in Lexington, in the heart of the rich Bluegrass region. Meanwhile, in a brilliant movement, Bragg saved Smith from the probable results of his irresponsibility and once again turned crisis into opportunity by establishing himself on Buell's supply line in Kentucky.

That should have given Bragg a decisive victory, but Buell had enough supplies on hand to sit cut off in southern Kentucky for some time. Bragg, who probably could have supplied himself in the Nashville Basin, could not do so in west-central Kentucky. Running low on food, he found that he and not Buell had to act quickly. While he had men enough to receive an attack from Buell, he did not have enough—without Kirby Smith—to deliver one. Smith would not join him, and so Bragg had no choice but to give up his commanding position, vacate Buell's supply line, and join Smith in Lexington, where he could at least feed his troops.

With the Confederate forces at last united, Bragg commanded by reason of his senior rank—regardless of Davis's failure to straighten out the command system. Yet by now the only real hope of holding Kentucky was based on its people rallying to the Confederate standard en masse, and this they did not do. Bragg tried to salvage a seemingly impossible situation by setting in motion the political process that would allow him to draft Kentuckians into Confederate ranks. Before he could get a Confederate state government up and running, however, Buell finally offered battle.

Forced to fight on whatever odds he could get, Bragg moved to strike one of Buell's several separated columns with his combined force but was balked when Leonidas Polk blandly refused the order to attack. At a severe political cost in the sensitive Bluegrass region, Bragg had to pull back to the southeast. Buell followed, and Bragg tried one more time. Again Polk refused Bragg's orders, and only when the commanding general arrived in person at his headquarters did the recalcitrant Polk comply. The resulting battle of Perryville was characterized by much confusion on both sides about the numbers and location of the enemy. Buell failed to get most of his troops into action, and Bragg's forces had the better of the scrap. Still, Confederate success fell short of something that would unravel Buell's whole army. Out of solutions at last, the badly out-numbered Bragg had to abandon Kentucky.

The Kentucky campaign crippled Bragg as an army commander. Roundly flailed in press and public for having led a failed campaign, he received even more damaging criticism from within his own officer corps, where generals who had blundered, or knew Bragg considered them incompetent, or were from Kentucky and preferred some other explanation for the campaign's failure than the apathy of their state, all strove to shift blame to Bragg. Perhaps a Robert E. Lee would have weathered such a storm, but Bragg was no Robert E. Lee, and his relations with a number of his generals grew steadily worse.

His reputation took a further blow when in December 1862 Davis divested him of 10,000 men, one-fourth of his infantry, to reinforce Mississippi. The move prompted an advance by Bragg's new opponent, William S. Rosecrans. In the resulting battle of Murfreesboro, Bragg gained a striking tactical victory in the first day's fighting but simply did not have enough men to finish the job. When Rosecrans failed to lose his nerve (as Joe Hooker did against Lee under similar circumstances the following May), Bragg, at the urging of his generals, was compelled to retreat again.

The volume of denunciation against Bragg now redoubled, with the anti-Davis faction now playing up the general's unpopularity in order to batter the president politically. Again, Bragg's own generals seem at least to have supplied am-munition to the politicians and editors, not all of it honest. Stung to indiscretion, Bragg ill-advisedly sought what amounted to a vote of confidence from his generals and got anything but. Davis would at that point have relieved Bragg of command, save that Bragg's immediate superior, Confederate theater com-mander Joseph E. Johnston (q.v.), through whom the president was trying to work, thwarted his commander in chief's intentions.

By the summer of 1863 the Army of Tennessee's command system had bro-ken down, with Bragg and a number of his generals hardly on speaking terms. When Rosecrans launched an extremely skillful and well-executed advance, Bragg's generals seemed ignorant of their commander's battle plans, which, though promising, were never carried out by an army that was now increasingly out of his control. The retreat that followed carried them all the way back to Chattanooga. After a six-week pause, Rosecrans advanced again, skillfully using the complicated terrain. Bragg had to abandon Chattanooga and fall back into Georgia.

Then, however, heavily reinforced by the now desperate authorities in Rich-mond, Bragg turned at bay. On at least two separate occasions, he got his army into prime position for defeating Rosecrans's widespread columns in detail, yet each time the refusal of his generals to cooperate allowed the Federals to escape. Finally bringing Rosecrans's now-united army to ground near Chickamauga Creek, Bragg tried to cut it off from its base and destroy it. Once again he was hindered by Polk's blundering and disregard for orders—as well as the heroic fighting of the Union troops. Though Chickamauga was a Confederate victory, it offered no opportunity for successful exploitation, and Bragg knew it—if many of his critics then and since did not. The best he could do was establish a virtual siege of Rosecrans in Chattanooga. That looked promising until one month after the battle the Federals, now commanded by Major General Ulysses S. Grant (q.v.), broke Bragg's grip on their supply line. The Army of Tennessee could fight and die, but with its command system having all but ceased to function, it simply could not win. This was dramatized even more clearly a month later when Grant's troops routed Bragg's army from the imposing high ground around Chattanooga.

That defeat marked the end of Bragg's tenure in army command. Bragg requested to be relieved of command, and Davis accommodated him. Although Bragg served in Richmond during the closing year of the war as nominal commanding general of all Confederate armies, his place in history was established by his unhappy seventeen months at the head of the Army of Tennessee. After the war, Bragg worked as a civil engineer in Galveston, Texas, where he died suddenly, of natural causes, in 1876, leaving no written memoirs.

Having fared poorly in the war, Bragg fared no better in the postwar "battle of the books." Many of the same who had savaged his record during the war—often in order to cover their own deficiencies—continued to criticize him roundly in writing their memoirs. Though some of his worst enemies, such as Leonidas Polk, left no memoirs, others, like James Longstreet (q.v.), did and included in them harsh and blatantly unjust criticism of Bragg. According to Longstreet, Bragg had been lethargic in his victory at Chickamauga, unaccountably ignorant of the enemy's movements afterward, and unpardonably slow to pursue—all untrue or at least badly distorted. "I was prepared for halting work," Longstreet wrote, "but this," speaking of Bragg's alleged failures, "was a little surprising." On went the narrative of Longstreet's service in the West, blaming Bragg for every debacle that had befallen the Confederacy there. It was wartime polemics carried on with a zeal undimmed by some thirty years of peace (Longstreet, 452–508).

Other former Southern commanders, with the benefit of not having been personally involved in the internecine bickering that rent the Army of Tennessee's high command—nor in a position to covet for themselves Bragg's position— wrote more objectively of his career as a Confederate general. Predictably, their accounts sometimes repeated the hue and cry of Bragg's many and vocal critics, but often, particularly when they had personal knowledge of the circumstances involved, they showed a clearer understanding of Bragg than many a latter-day historian.

One of these more reasoned pictures of Bragg came from the pen of the highly successful Louisiana general Richard Taylor. His 1879 history of the war and its aftermath, *Destruction and Reconstruction*, has been called by historian Grady McWhiney a well-written memoir. William T. Sherman (q.v.) rightly observed of Taylor's writing that he wrote with honesty and fairness, but that he could be unfair in his criticisms regarding events he did not observe. Taylor's modern biographer has observed that "he exercised a stridently opinionated and judgmental style." These elements colored Taylor's otherwise reasonable picture of Bragg (McWhiney, "Leadership," 350).

Taylor met with Bragg in Chattanooga in 1862 as Bragg was preparing to advance toward Kentucky. The two discussed Bragg's plan of campaign, and Taylor considered it "excellent, giving promise of large results," an accurate assessment based on Taylor's personal observation. Taylor then proceeded on to his assignment in the trans-Mississippi department and learned of Bragg's subsequent career mostly through secondhand sources. The failure of the Kentucky campaign he thus "ascribed to the infirmities of the commander," echoing the conventional wisdom then and since. Bragg he depicted as conscientious and hardworking but too exacting of his subordinates, the best disciplinarian among the high-ranking Confederate generals but harsh in his manner of administering discipline and "sour and petulant" of temper. One other point of direct observation enters into Taylor's account of Bragg. While Taylor was in Chattanooga on the eve of the Kentucky campaign, he found himself at a dinner with Bragg and a number of other officers. Taylor asked about one of Bragg's division commanders and, to his horror, heard Bragg reply, "General ———— is an old woman, utterly worthless." Later, in private, Taylor asked Bragg whom he intended to assign to take the place of the general thus spoken of. "No one," Bragg replied. "I have but one or two fitted for high command, and have in vain asked the War Department for capable people." Taylor suggested "that he could hardly expect hearty cooperation from officers of whom he permitted himself to speak contemptuously." But Bragg replied, "I speak the truth. The Government is to blame for placing such men in high position." In truth, Bragg had some reason to feel that way, but it was not a very constructive attitude, nevertheless. "From that hour," Taylor wrote, "I had misgivings as to General Bragg's success." Here Taylor had taken hold of a very important piece of truth: Bragg's failure to adjust successfully to the poor hand his commander in chief had dealt him. Yet proceeding from that insightful analysis, Taylor again returned to parroting the common line in stating that thereafter Bragg's lieutenants "supported him wonderfully, in despite of his temper," when in fact nothing of the sort was true. (Taylor, 99–101).

Another former highly successful Confederate general who afterward wrote intelligently of the war and Braxton Bragg was John B. Gordon, who spent his entire Confederate career in the Eastern theater and never had Bragg for a field commander. In his *Reminiscences of the Civil War*, written after the turn of the century, Gordon stressed the nobility of the American soldier, and so his accounts of generals are happily characterized by an attempt to understand their actions rather than to pass judgment and apportion blame.

Familiar with the Alabama-Georgia-Tennessee area where the late 1863 campaign for Chattanooga was played out, Gordon had a healthy respect for its complicated terrain and absolved Bragg for failure to accomplish the impossible in preventing Rosecrans's crossing of the Tennessee. He went on to aver that Bragg was "not only one of the boldest fighters in the Confederate army . . . but [also] an able commander." Regarding Bragg's much criticized decision not to mount a quick, aggressive pursuit of Rosecrans after Chickamauga, Gordon wrote that "a calm review of the situation, and the facts as they existed at the time," would show Bragg's action to have been "not only pardonable, but prudent and wise" (Gordon, 192–193, 196–197, 214–219). Unfortunately for Bragg's reputation, calm reviews of the situation he actually faced were not to be especially common, and the writings of Longstreet and others with personal vendettas against Bragg, came to set the tone for future historians.

In 1923 Don Carlos Seitz published the first biography of Bragg. To be sure, it was not long on analysis. Seitz tended to reproduce remarkably long and numerous dispatches, so that some portions of the work read like little more than an annotated wartime-papers collection, and to the frustration of future researchers, he omitted both index and footnotes. He perpetuated the image of Bragg as a bloodthirsty martinet, relating an unsubstantiated and probably false account of Bragg having a Confederate soldier shot for robbing a Kentucky apple orchard. On the other hand, however, he gave Bragg high marks for the Kentucky campaign generally, praising "his great achievement in the conduct of the venturesome campaign." Still, his final verdict was a negative one. He repeated the by-then already stock criticisms of Bragg's "supineness" after Chickamauga and his detachment of Longstreet to east Tennessee as "a gambler's chance" without weighing the odds that faced Bragg in any alternative course of action (Seitz, 174–175).

Eighteen years after Seitz wrote his biography of Bragg, the Army of Tennessee received its first major historical treatment. Stanley F. Horn's 1941 *The Army of Tennessee: A Military History* was a gigantic forward stride in Civil War history, reminding readers, as Horn pointed out in his foreword, that all of the war "was not fought in Virginia. There was another Confederate army, strangely neglected by most historians of the war." Indeed, there was two-thirds, at least, of the war fought across hundreds of miles of the continent and involving what was, as Thomas L. Connelly would one day make clear, the very heartland of the Confederacy. While Douglas Southall Freeman polished the historical monument to R. E. Lee and wrote with remarkable skill and careful research of the exploits of the Army of Northern Virginia, the Army of Tennessee had been apparently invisible to historians until Horn's work. Well researched and written and thoroughly endnoted, *The Army of Tennessee* immediately put future students of the Civil War deeply in Horn's debt.

However, perhaps as a result of relying too heavily on the wartime and postwar writings of Bragg's enemies, Horn marred his account with unreasoned criticism of Bragg. In Horn's reckoning, Bragg had given up his position between Buell and Louisville not because of lack of supplies but because "Bragg was unequal spiritually to the responsibility of precipitating a battle.'' If Kirby Smith would not join Bragg, that was somehow Bragg's fault; if his troops would soon be going hungry, that was merely ''cloak for [Bragg's] timidity.'' Horn could see no purpose in Bragg's installation of a pro-Confederate state government in Kentucky except that Bragg must have been ''carried away with the political implications of his presence in Kentucky.'' Yet Horn seems oblivious to how the move might have furthered Bragg's campaign by opening the possibility of conscription in the state as well as to what other course might have been open to Bragg by the time Buell had restored his connection with his base and the people of Kentucky had silently voted for the Union by the refusal to enlist in Bragg's ranks. In short, for every strange or unfortunate circumstance that beset the Confederates, Horn generally found it necessary to look no farther for an explanation than Bragg's supposed deformities of intellect and character. The same interpretive framework Horn carried through to the Tullahoma, Chickamauga, and Chattanooga campaigns, as well as Bragg's difficulties with insubordinate generals. Aside from being not quite an accurate depiction of Bragg's generalship, it also is less than satisfactory as a means of explaining what really did happen and why (Horn, 170–304).

The Army of Tennessee's most notable historian, Thomas Lawrence Connelly, entered the field in 1967 with his *Army of the Heartland: The Army of Tennessee, 1861–1862*, the first of a two-volume set chronicling and intensively analyzing that army's entire career. Connelly's work represented as great an improvement over Horn as the latter did over what had gone before, offering deeper and broader research and far more incisive analysis. Indeed, if the work has a major fault it is probably that it is too critical of practically everyone. Under his unblinking examination, virtually the whole of Confederate military and civilian leadership seems to be weighed in the balances and found wanting.

Naturally, in such a work, Bragg comes in for much criticism, as does Davis for sustaining him as long as he did. Still, in *Army of the Heartland* and its follow-on volume, *Autumn of Glory*, Connelly found Bragg to be an able strategic planner and a skillful organizer and administrator who nevertheless could not execute his plans, partially because he could not get along with his subordinates. Connelly also opened the way for a new and more measured assessment of Bragg by pointing out the degree to which the western Confederacy was slighted by Richmond in the allocation of men, weapons, and supplies, thus making success there far more difficult than it was in Virginia. Finally, his unflinching view of Bragg's subordinates exposed the incompetence of a number of them. Thus for Braxton Bragg, as for almost any other aspect of the military history of the Confederacy west of the Appalachians, Connelly has set the terms of historical research and opened the conversation that we continue to this day.

Appearing just two years after the first volume of Connelly's set was Grady McWhiney's *Braxton Bragg and Confederate Defeat, Volume I*. McWhiney has had an even greater impact on Bragg studies than has Connelly. The first truly scholarly biography of Bragg, it remains unchallenged as the definitive account of the general's life and early career up to the battle of Murfreesboro. As the title suggests, McWhiney is in some ways highly critical of Bragg. Yet what set McWhiney's work apart from previous forays against Bragg was that he carefully sifted the primary sources and made the "calm review of the situation, and the facts as they existed at the time," that Gordon had seen as necessary to assess a general's performance. Thus, McWhiney exposed even more about Bragg's enemies within the Army of Tennessee's officer corps and demonstrated with primary source evidence that in fact Bragg had possessed a considerable degree of affection and respect among at least some of the officers and soldiers of the army. He pointed out in greater detail than had previously been done the practical workability and high promise of several of Bragg's operational plans—in the Kentucky, Tullahoma, and Chickamauga campaigns—if his subordinates would but have obeyed orders.

For whatever reason—historian Richard McMurry suggested it was because he "found his subject so nauseous"—McWhiney never wrote the projected second volume of his Bragg biography, eventually turning the project over to one of his many able graduate students. McMurry's own 1989 book *Two Great Rebel Armies* was thus the next major work to deal extensively with Bragg. In this extended essay, McMurry took a new look at the disparity of Confederate success between the Eastern and Western theaters of the war and suggested that perhaps at least part of the explanation for this phenomenon—and one that historians have long overlooked—was that the Army of Tennessee was, in a number of important ways, inferior to its eastern counterpart, the Army of Northern Virginia. While McMurry repeats much of the wholesale criticisms that have previously been leveled at "the disgusting Bragg," his dissecting of the other problems of the Confederacy's western army does much to show that the situation there was more complex than merely a miserable commander sustained by a stubborn president (3–132).

The year after McMurry's thought provoking work appeared Steven E. Woodworth's *Jefferson Davis and His Generals: The Failure of Confederate Command in the West*. In as favorable a treatment as Bragg has probably ever gotten in print, this work argues that while Bragg had his faults, he was nevertheless a serviceable commander—and likely the best Davis had available—and that Davis could have supported Bragg in such a way as to prevent the destruction of his usefulness (125–255).

In 1992, Judith Lee Hallock, the McWhiney graduate student who took over the Bragg project, published her half of the set, *Braxton Bragg and Confederate Defeat, Volume II*. Relative to McWhiney, Hallock focuses more on personalities and relationships and less on campaigns and battles, though neither element is missing from either book. While according Bragg more criticism than does Woodworth, Hallock nevertheless points out that in many ways, during the closing months of his tenure in command of the Army of Tennessee, he was more sinned against than sinning (7–124).

While some of the more recent major works dealing with Bragg point in the direction of endeavoring at least to understand the man and perhaps even to show that he was a far better general than has been represented in most of the literature about him up to this time, such reinterpretations have yet to be reflected in the body of Civil War literature being produced today, and authors continue to repeat—and even to extend and exaggerate—the extreme criticisms of Bragg's wartime enemies within the Confederacy. Several recent battle and campaign studies have what can almost be described as a can-you-top-this style of making Bragg out to be a bigger fool and a more loathsome miscreant than heretofore suggested. One is led to believe, for example, that Bragg preferred having his army unsupplied than otherwise. Like Horn, such authors seem to find in the folly or knavishness of Bragg sufficient explanations for most of what went wrong for the Army of Tennessee, it only being necessary to amplify that folly and knavishness to an adequate degree.

In view of this, a recent essay by Edward Carter Franks is particularly refreshing. A Ph.D. economist, Franks carefully examines the numbers and other evidence pertaining to Bragg's detachment of Longstreet during the Chattanooga campaign and finds that it was not, after all, the unmitigated blunder hitherto depicted. As it turns out, when one endeavors to *understand* what Bragg is about, rather than simply exceeding previous condemnations of him, what he was doing can sometimes make a good deal of sense. Franks's findings are in turn reflected in Steven E. Woodworth's 1998 *Six Armies in Tennessee*, a study of the campaign in Tennessee from Tullahoma through Chickamauga and Chattanooga to Knoxville.

Signs exist, therefore, that historians may be willing to take another look at Bragg and reassess the validity of the stream of criticism that began with his wartime detractors and has been echoed down to the present day. What may well emerge from all of this is a picture of a human being, rather than a monster, an intelligent (though flawed) officer, rather than a blithering incompetent, and a good soldier who could perhaps have been made useful to the Confederacy.

BIBLIOGRAPHY

Richard Taylor, *Destruction and Reconstruction* (1879; New York: DaCapo Press, 1995).

Ulysses S. Grant, *Personal Memoirs*, 2 vols. (New York: Charles S. Webster, 1886).

Don C. Seitz, *Braxton Bragg: General of the Confederacy* (Columbia, S.C.: The State Co., 1923).

Stanley F. Horn, *The Army of Tennessee: A Military History* (Indianapolis: Bobbs-Merrill, 1941).

James Longstreet, *From Manassas to Appomattox* (Bloomington: Indiana University Press, 1960).

Thomas Lawrence Connelly, *Army of the Heartland: The Army of Tennessee, 1861–1862* (Baton Rouge: Louisiana University Press, 1967).

Grady McWhiney, *Braxton Bragg and Confederate Defeat, Volume I* (New York: Columbia University Press, 1969).

Thomas Lawrence Connelly, *Autumn of Glory: The Army of Tennessee, 1862–1865* (Baton Rouge: Louisiana State University Press, 1971).

Thomas Lawrence Connelly and Archer Jones, *The Politics of Command* (Baton Rouge: Louisiana State University Press, 1973).

James Lee McDonough, *Stones River—Bloody Winter in Tennessee* (Knoxville: University of Tennessee Press, 1980).

Gary Donaldson, " 'Into Africa': Kirby Smith and Braxton Bragg's Invasion of Kentucky," *Filson Club Historical Quarterly* 61 (October 1987): 439–448.

Richard M. McMurry, *Two Great Rebel Armies: An Essay in Confederate Military History* (Chapel Hill: University of North Carolina Press, 1989).

Steven E. Woodworth, *Jefferson Davis and His Generals: The Failure of Confederate Command in the West* (Lawrence: University Press of Kansas, 1990).

Judith Lee Hallock, *Braxton Bragg and Confederate Defeat, Volume II* (Tuscaloosa: University of Alabama Press, 1992).

John B. Gordon, *Reminiscences of the Civil War*, introduction by Ralph Lowell Eckert (Baton Rouge: Louisiana State University Press, 1993).

Edward Carter Franks, "The Detachment of Longstreet Considered: Braxton Bragg, James Longstreet, and the Chattanooga Campaign," in *Leadership and Command in the American Civil War*, ed. Steven E. Woodworth (Campbell, Calif.: Savas Woodbury, 1995), 29–65.

Grady McWhiney, "Leadership—Confederate Army Officers," in *The American Civil War: A Handbook of Literature and Research*, ed. Steven E. Woodworth (Westport, Conn.: Greenwood Press, 1996).

Steven E. Woodworth, *Six Armies in Tennessee: The Chickamauga and Chattanooga Campaigns* (Lincoln: University of Nebraska Press, 1998).

JOSEPH EMERSON BROWN
(April 15, 1821–November 30, 1894)

Jon L. Wakelyn

As governor of Georgia throughout the Civil War, Joseph E. Brown became, in the eyes of Confederate President Jefferson Davis (q.v.) and his allies, the supreme state's rights villain who sabotaged the government's war effort. That accusation has nearly sealed Brown's reputation and has made most difficult any realistic reappraisal of his amazing public political career. But Brown himself claimed that his defense of the parochial interests of Georgia actually assisted the Confederacy. In truth, his life story encompassed a number of contradictions, and he should be judged on his ability to have survived and even to have thrived in those most confused political times of the period of national separation. Destined by his family to become a preacher, he learned to wallow in the stink of antebellum politics; a man of the people, he nevertheless grew wealthy through railroad speculation; committed to the Democratic party, for a time he flirted with the postwar Republican party; and most challenging, he began as a vehement secessionist but spent the war obstructing the new Confederacy. Perhaps these seeming contradictions are clues to the true motivations of Joe Brown. Certainly, his life activities reveal much about the contradictions within the slave states themselves.

Joseph Emerson Brown came into the world in the dirt-poor hill country of Long Creek in Pickens District, South Carolina, on April 15, 1821. His Scots-Irish ancestors, originally from Derry in northern Ireland, moved often in search of better farmland in the Appalachian region before they finally settled in Union County, Georgia, not long after his birth. Young Joe took great pride in his grandfather's heroics during the American Revolution and that of his father, the dour and stern Mackay, who had fought alongside Andrew Jackson at the Battle of New Orleans. Mackay married Sally Rice, also from a poor farm family but imbued with ambitions for her eldest son. Young Joe took on the tasks of a farmer and soon learned to make profit from the sale of excess produce in the local villages. He also was a bright young man, and his family managed to send him to Pleasant Jordan's Academy in nearby Anderson District, South Carolina. Joe soon paid his own way at the academy by teaching at local schools. In 1840, he left his family home for good to take up the life of a peripatetic teacher.

By 1844 he conducted his own school in Canton, Georgia, where he fortunately became the tutor of Dr. John Lewis's young children. The ambitious teacher also read law at night and, in 1845, passed the Georgia bar. Obviously, he impressed Dr. Lewis with his seriousness of purpose, and the doctor loaned him the funds to attend Yale Law School during the 1845–1846 school year. In that way, Brown followed in the footsteps of his hero John C. Calhoun. Just how he performed or what friends he made at Yale remain unknown, as he returned to Georgia at the term's end and rarely spoke about that experience. Besides, he was busy riding the law circuit and soon developed a practice before the Georgia Supreme Court. Having made some success in his profession, in 1847 Brown married Elizabeth Grisham, the daughter of a prominent Canton Baptist minister. For a short time Brown thought of fulfilling his mother's hopes and entering the ministry, but instead he settled for a lifetime devotion to that church.

The young man from hardscrabble farmland had, through hard work, risen to become a success in business. With his marriage he settled into a place in the social life of his community. As his legal practice grew, like many others who wanted social standing and secure financial success, Brown began to acquire land. Tall, thin, his clothes always seeming too large for his body, he had assumed the guise of a middle-class provincial with the nasal voice to go along. But the poorer citizens who heard him speak did not forget that determined mouth of the awkward but self-assured man who seemed with his words to so capture their own sentiments. Their support, plus his own ambitions, no doubt led Brown to attempt to enter political life. Despite his own financial success, he would rise as a spokesman for those very people. As Emory Speer, one of his early biographers, said, "he had no particular reverence for great families or great names, and he said so"(19).

That talent for leading his audience to identify with his tales of his own rise in life, along with the sense of power that went along with it, soon earned him the prestige of public office. In 1849, those poor farmers from Cherokee and Cobb Counties elected him to the state senate. He soon became the ally of the wealthy planter and politically astute Howell Cobb. While in the senate, Brown also served as the judge of the Blue Ridge Circuit, where he gained a reputation as stern but fair, especially in his dealings with ordinary people. In the legislature, he opposed extremism in politics as he took a stand against both temperance reform and the rise of the Know-Nothing party in Georgia.

Brown's actions in politics showed that he had ambitions even for higher office. He ran for governor in 1857 as the "Mountain Boy," the embodiment of old Jacksonian politics, and he won. Part of his campaign had been directed against the so-called established leadership. They responded with charges of upstart and outsider. Indeed, that group of nabobs had good reason to fear the upstart. In rejection of powerful urban banking interests, he vetoed a measure to establish new banks with the charge that such a bill would deprive struggling farmers of much needed loans. He displayed hostility to federal government agents living in Georgia, charging them with interfering in the business of the ordinary citizens. Governor Brown also spoke in favor of reducing the size of the state legislature, perhaps reflecting an early aminus to any government's abuse of popular freedoms. If small government was good for the farmer, he said, then why need personal liberty laws?

Soon this state particularist became involved in the roiling national politics of sectionalism. As a loyal national Democrat he endorsed the temporizing activities of President James Buchanan and wrote him that he supported him for reelection. But his moderate stance proved only temporary, as by late 1859 Brown began to enlarge the state militia and to denounce antislavery politics in Kansas. Perhaps he sensed the desires of his followers. In his race for reelection in 1860, Brown called for Southern secession and endorsed the Southern Democrat John C. Breckinridge for president. The governor also began to gather various Georgia political factions under his wing, or at least those who favored secession. After Abraham Lincoln's (q.v.) election, he counseled with other Southern governors, and he covertly advised South Carolina's governor that Georgia would follow that state into secession. Michael Johnson, an astute student of antebellum Georgia politics, suggests that the state's radicals had persuaded Governor Brown to lead the nonslaveholders out of the Union. But Brown did not follow the state's elite leaders; he led them. A more plausible explanation of his actions is that he had decided that the interests of all Georgians at that time required secession from an oppressive Union. Unfortunately for the future of a Southern Confederacy, that did not mean that Brown desired unity with the other slaveholding states.

Immediately upon his own state's secession, Governor Brown began to prepare for war with the Union. But first he had to show his true colors by once again vetoing a state bank act, further evidence of his resistance to any form of central authority. He then seized Fort Pulaski and the federal arsenal at Augusta in order to arm his state's militia. The governor next persuaded the state legislature to purchase a large cache of weapons and advised the state's military officers to keep Georgia troops home to defend the people rather than send them to Richmond to support Virginia. Brown's primary concern, so he said, was the large and vulnerable coastline of Georgia, which he considered ripe ground for a Union invasion.

Those early declarations and defensive preparations revealed that Governor Brown may have lacked true commitment to the newly formed Confederacy. But he did seem consistent in his actions, as he rarely deviated from what he believed were the best interests of the citizens of Georgia. He also early displayed some fear of the potent powers of the Confederate national government. These assertions are best understood by evaluating just how he performed his wartime gubernatorial duties.

From the war's beginning, Governor Joseph E. Brown set as his highest priority the interests of the people of Georgia. During the crucial early days of the war, Confederate national officials also wanted to show their support for civilian actions and attitudes. But their priority was to defend the new country from federal invasion. Governor Brown, in contrast, set as his policy to avoid taxing Georgians or taking their goods to pay for the war being fought on the Confederate borders. He also wanted the state to assume the responsibility for the families of the soldiers. Brown believed that little help of that sort would come from Richmond. Accordingly, he set up volunteer stations to raise funds to purchase food and clothing for those families. Later in the war Brown organized his own state welfare system to take care of the needs of the citizenry on the home front. Obviously, his own plans for the defense of Georgia required that he attend to local civilian morale.

Brown's early policies faced much criticism, especially in his 1861 bid for a third term as governor. At first he resisted the idea of running for reelection. Then, with the support of Confederate Vice President Alexander H. Stephens (q.v.) and his allies, who had already turned against what they called national oppression, Brown relented. He chose as his campaign tactic once again to divide Georgians themselves as he fulminated against wartime speculators who exploited their fellow Georgians and who refused to participate in the defense of their homeland. The citizens reelected him after a bitter and divisive race. In early 1862 the state legislature offered to send the governor to the Confederate Congress in Richmond, but he refused to accept, stating that his first priority was the people of Georgia.

After his election victory, now secure in the governor's chair for the duration of the war, Brown continued his hostile behavior toward the Confederate government. He aligned with the opposition to the national Confederate government that Alexander Stephens and his brother Linton led. As did they, he focused on President Davis as the chief villain. Not only did Brown claim that Davis was a poor leader who could not inspire the people to resist the Union invasion, but he also had come to regard the president as a dictator bent on dominating the state governments. The headstrong Davis, of course, replied in kind. That battle of words resulted in mutual distrust that did not bode well for the future of cooperation in the Confederacy.

But if Brown had personal animus for the actions and the personality of the president, his actions toward the national government also reflected his analysis of events in Georgia itself. He had begun to fear internal dissent in Georgia and even suggested that insurrection leading to another civil war could happen at any time. Aggrieved nonslaveholders who bore the burden of the fighting especially worried him. Business interests in Atlanta and Augusta, in his estimation, gave little support to Georgia's defense and thus served as a divisive force. The governor determined at any cost to keep his state united.

Therefore, by mid-1862 he had fixed an agenda to oppose the transfer of any national burdens on the already hurting citizens of Georgia, and he renewed his hostilities to any federal taxing schemes. He became an enemy of Treasury Secretary Christopher G. Memminger (q.v.) when he rejected forced loans and a tax on state agricultural products. When the government in Richmond wanted to confiscate or at least direct state railroad shipments, the governor refused to countenance what he called an incursion on the rights of private business. Thus, to the war's end, Brown resisted any federal attempts to assume control of Georgia business or to drain funds from the state, even if that meant the Confederate armies had to go without.

The governor's most persistent activities in opposition to the Confederacy concerned policies for fighting the war itself. His biographer Joseph Parks insists that Brown always managed to underestimate the number of Georgia troops needed for national defense. What seems more precise is that the governor just did not want to deplete Georgia's home defenses. Especially after General William T. Sherman (q.v.) began the Atlanta campaign at the beginning of 1864, Brown proclaimed all of Georgia's resources would be devoted to self-defense through self-government. Some leaders even believed that Brown was prepared to sue for a separate peace for Georgians and thus would give no troops to the army of General Joseph Johnston (q.v.). But the evidence for this assertion remains unclear. He did, however, resist Howell Cobb, his former ally, in his entreaties to loan state troops to the federal army because he planned his own military defense of Atlanta. Still, Brown did assign some troops to John Hood's (q.v.) army during the final Union assault on Atlanta. Only after the fall of Atlanta did he again dig in and refuse to send Georgians to confront Sherman in the March to the Sea. His infamous exchange with Secretary of War James E. Seddon (q.v.), in which the proud Virginian accused him of populist demagoguery, did no good to either leader's reputation. Some believe that battle over who would use Georgia troops led to Seddon's resignation from the government. At the end of 1864, Brown's frustrations with Richmond's war policies led him to call for another Confederate States convention to allow each state to decide its own future, and he suggested a few states might wish to return to the Union.

Those financial and personnel issues over which the governor had resisted the national government, when combined with that final act of desperation, for some reflected supreme defense of Georgia and for others suggested the governor had been a traitor to the cause. His early postwar actions merely compounded the felony. Those activities unleashed a torrent of abuse from ex-Confederate politicians and resonate through the history of the New South. For, as the war came to its exhaustive conclusion, the governor sought a parole from President Andrew Johnson (q.v.) and joined his wing of the Union party. He next called on all Georgians to face up to reality, to accept defeat, and to get on with reconstructing their own lives. Brown then urged Georgians to join him in signing an oath of allegiance to the Union. Ever the realist, he thought he had acted in the best interests of his constituents.

The now ex-governor decided to remain in public life. He attended the state's Radical Republican convention called to revise the Georgia constitution. At that time he also advocated that ex-slaves be given the right to vote. In return for his most visible support, the Republicans named him chief justice of the Georgia State Supreme Court. In 1872, the man who seemed to have no clear political loyalties endorsed former abolitionist Horace Greeley for president on both the Liberal Republican and Democratic tickets. He had hoped to use this endorsement as a safe way back into the Democratic party, now on the rise again in the ex-Confederate states. In 1876, Brown the Democrat turned against granting further civil rights to the freed people. But his actions hardly assuaged hostilities toward him, as he became involved in a messy controversy with ex-Confederate general John B. Gordon. For the time being, at least, the great chameleon of politics had seemed to have worn out his welcome in Georgia politics.

In the meantime, in response to fluid business opportunities in the reviving economy of Georgia, Brown determined to refill his own depleted financial coffers. He grew wealthy by making shrewd investments in farmland and mines. He also became a railroad builder, which later led to accusations that he had received special favors from the legislature. But Brown's rise to wealth also helped his public image, as he used his gain to fund various charities run by the Baptist Church. His health for the first time began to fail him at that time. In the late 1870s, pneumonia laid him low. Still, he persevered in the struggle to rebuild his tattered reputation.

Then his political fortunes took a dramatic change for the better. In 1880 Gordon resigned unexpectedly from the U.S. Senate, and in a surprising move, the state legislature appointed Brown to replace him. Of course his political enemies claimed foul as they charged that he had purchased members' votes with gifts of railroad shares. In reality, Brown had gained the support of Henry W. Grady and the New South Georgia business community because they believed he would become the champion of a diversified economy, which was needed to wean Georgians from their disastrous dependence on staple agricultural crops. Brown also had taken to the lecture circuit to defend his career, and he backed a number of publishing projects that rewrote his past activities and corrected the wartime record his enemies had made for him. Brown had thus indulged in the game of historical revisionism, as he re-created his wartime career from resistance to the Confederacy to a vigorous defense of the property and personal rights of the people of Georgia. At least the legislature and the powerful Henry W. Grady had bought this version of his war governorship.

When Brown's first term in the Senate had ended, the legislature reappointed him. Back in Washington he became an advocate once again of the ordinary people. He opposed President Grover Cleveland's hard money policies as contrary to the interests of the farmers. But he also represented the position of New South businessman when he supported a protective tariff for new industrial production. Those were his last stands, as he had grown old and weary and the grind of national politics soon laid him low. In 1890 he retired from the Senate and left the political stage for good. He died at his home on November 30, 1894.

The ordinary people of Georgia mourned the passing of their champion. The Georgia press, or at least most of it, lauded his life's accomplishments in the public sector. He was seen as one who had adjusted to political changes, and he had always had the interests of Georgians at heart. His detractors, however, regarded him as a self-promoting demagogue, and they gleefully claimed that posthumous honors did not continue to accumulate. Even the famous statue erected on the state capital grounds, they asserted, had been built and paid for by his family.

How, then, has history treated this man who always seemed to rebound in his public life, even against the most heinous charges of disloyalty? In his memoirs, Alexander H. Stephens judged him to have been a loyal Southerner who supported the interests of Georgians. Even Brown's desertion of the Confederacy, said Stephens, was because the government leaders were unable to protect the Southern people. But newspaperman/historian Edward A. Pollard (q.v.) and ex-President Jefferson Davis obviously believed differently. Pollard called Brown an obstructionist. Davis simply regarded him as a traitor to the cause of a separate Confederacy. Brown's postwar friends and allies jumped to his defense. Herbert W. Fielder, in a thinly veiled campaign biography published in 1883, made the first historical revisionist claim that Brown had indeed done much to try to save the Confederacy. Fielder also stated that Brown's postwar career had well served Georgia. Emory Speer, an ally with impeccable wartime credentials, in a famous address in 1905, insisted that Brown had really supported the Confederate war effort and that he deserved praise for his sacrifices in defense of Atlanta. Even Brown's once bitter enemy Benjamin H. Hill at the end of the century called for Georgians to put the past behind them, to look forward, and to use Brown as a guide to future behavior.

But if some of his own state's early historical writers allowed him back into grace, the first important professional historians did not. Using Jefferson Davis's works, in 1910 George Cary Eggleston saw Brown's defense of state's rights as destructive for the Confederacy. Then came the famous Frank L. Owsley in his seminal *State Rights in the Confederacy* of 1924 to destroy utterly any credibility left in the activities of the war governor. For Owsley, Brown sabotaged the Confederate financial efforts to support the army. In 1939, Owsley's student, Louise B. Hill, systematically took Brown's wartime career apart. She called him a man without moral courage who had behaved shabbily during the war. Hill also took some pleasure in pointing out that Georgians never really loved him. In 1973, Derrell C. Roberts simply called Brown's Reconstruction policies crooked. Even the once sacred Jacksonian poor man's reputation fell with Michael Johnson's charge that Brown really supported the large planters during the Civil War. While purporting to be an objective observer, Brown's major biographer Joseph H. Parks concluded that the wartime charges against him were true, even if the governor sincerely believed that he had operated in the best interests of Georgians.

Most recently, Archer Jones and Herman Hattaway have tried to reassess

Brown's military activities. They insist that the governor "actually had aided the overall war effort, not only by taking appropriate steps for state defense and the continued functioning of the economy but also by making compulsory military services more efficient"(320). If his military role deserves revision, and it does, is there any way to restore Brown's tattered political reputation? Perhaps the place to begin is not with state's rights but with Brown's understanding of the creation of a new nation. Did Brown believe the Confederate government could protect Southern property, especially slavery? That the Confederacy as well as the United States might have presented a problem for the future of slavery he might well have understood. Until we have a full study of the meaning of Confederate governance, Brown's actions cannot receive the revision they deserve.

BIBLIOGRAPHY

Alexander H. Stephens, *A Constitutional View of the War between the States*, 2 vols. (Philadelphia: National Publishing Co., 1868–1870).

Jefferson Davis, *The Rise and Fall of the Confederate Government*, 2 vols. (New York: D. Appleton, 1881).

Herbert Fielder, *A Sketch of the Life and Times and Speeches of Joseph E. Brown* (Springfield, Mass.: Press of Springfield Printing Co., 1883).

Emory Speer, "*Joseph E. Brown of Georgia*" (baccalaureate address at Mercer University, Macon, Ga., June 7, 1905).

Frank Lawrence Owsley, *State Rights in the Confederacy* (Chicago: University of Chicago Press, 1924).

Louise Biles Hill, *Joseph E. Brown and the Confederacy* (Chapel Hill: University of North Carolina Press, 1939).

Derrell C. Roberts, *Joseph E. Brown and the Politics of Reconstruction* (Tuscaloosa: University of Alabama Press, 1973).

Michael P. Johnson, *Toward a Patriarchal Republic* (Baton Rouge: Louisiana State University Press, 1977).

Joseph Howard Parks, *Joseph E. Brown of Georgia* (Baton Rouge: Louisiana State University Press, 1977).

Archer Jones and Herman Hattaway, *Why the North Won* (Urbana: University of Illinois Press, 1984).

JOSHUA LAWRENCE CHAMBERLAIN
(September 8, 1828–February 24, 1914)

Kenneth Nivison

By issuing a "soldierly salute to those vanquished heroes" of the Confederate Army on April 12, 1865, Union general Joshua Lawrence Chamberlain solidified himself in the annals of the Civil War as a near transcendental figure. In a similar fashion, the extension of such a symbolic olive branch has transcended history as an event of supreme importance for the American nation, beginning the process of reuniting North and South. Chamberlain's actions that day also reflect how the leadership qualities of a college professor from Maine developed and crystallized in the bloody maelstrom that was the American Civil War. Moreover, they represent the culmination of his belief of what the Civil War was all about: creating an America of states *united*, a nation that was free for all of its inhabitants.

Historians have been quick to highlight three characteristics that gave force and meaning to the events of Chamberlain's life. The first of these qualities was Chamberlain's deep faith in God and his resignation of future events to Divine Providence. Second, Chamberlain is portrayed as having had a tremendous work ethic that manifested itself in his time as a student and professor at Bowdoin College as well as on the battlefields with the Army of the Potomac. Lastly, historians have emphasized Chamberlain's great vision, his ability to think and operate in bigger, philosophical terms. In illustrating these principal characteristics, historians have shown a great deal of consensus in their interpretation of the man. They all convey the admiration that the American public has had for Chamberlain.

Yet for all of the importance of these three characteristics, a fourth quality exists that served as a central element of his life and bound all of the particulars together in his actions as a leader in the Civil War. At every step, Chamberlain's sense of duty to his country—his deep sense of nationalism—drove his actions in the war and after the war. His first commitment was to his nation, and he fought not only to preserve its integrity but also to ensure that it became free

for all of its inhabitants. His was a democratic, cosmopolitan nationalism. Devoted not to extracting revenge from Southerners but to retaining what he considered a God-ordained nation, his actions made him a symbol of the kind of
citizenship expected of participants of the war. Nowhere was this realized more
forcefully than on that April day when Chamberlain stood opposite John Gordon
and issued a salute to his fellow Americans.

Born into a strict Congregationalist family in central Maine on September 8,
1828, Joshua Lawrence Chamberlain learned quickly the meaning of hard work
and discipline. Anecdotal stories of his childhood and young adult years serve
to illustrate how important those early lessons were in shaping the qualities of
character that would manifest themselves in the Civil War. Perhaps the most
telling of these stories is that of the effort put forth by him and his brothers in
moving a stone from a field on the family farm. Chamberlain had "told his
father that he and his brothers could not clear away a large stone from a field,
[to which] the older Chamberlain merely looked at him and barked, 'Move it!'
And the stone was moved" (Wallace, 20). Reflecting later on his upbringing,
Chamberlain said, " 'Do it, that's how!' . . . was a maxim whose value far exceeded the occasion." It became "an order for life" (Trulock, 33).

If his early years served to form his character, Chamberlain's time at Bowdoin
College in Brunswick would test those values. The first challenge was gaining
admission to the college. At the time, Bowdoin required a reading knowledge
of both Greek and Latin as part of its entrance examination. Knowing little of
the latter and none of the former, Chamberlain put to good use the discipline
instilled in him by his father, as he virtually locked himself away in the family
attic throughout the cold of winter in order to hone his skills and pass the exam.
Once admitted in February 1848, he then had to deal with the adjustment to
college life.

By the middle of the nineteenth century, Bowdoin College was a well-
established institution of higher learning. It was committed to providing an educational experience that formed the whole of the student character, not just his
intellect. In an environment where the curricular and the extracurricular complemented each other in a way that made it difficult to distinguish the two, the
college regulated the moral development and behavior of its students through
its rules and laws while introducing them to the wide array of intellectual and
professional areas of interest through its curriculum. This blending of rules and
instruction provided students with the skills they would need in order to become
the nation's future leaders.

The importance of his time at Bowdoin was not limited to his formal training,
however. Chamberlain also had the good fortune of being a student at Bowdoin
while Calvin Stowe was Bowdoin's professor of natural and revealed religion.
His high academic standing at the college helped make Chamberlain an occasional guest at the Stowe home for the many parlor-style discussions that took
place there. These talks were becoming of great interest in 1850–1851, for it
was in this time that Calvin Stowe's wife, Harriet Beecher Stowe, was sharing

with her discussants the most recent installments in her serial *Uncle Tom's Cabin*. Hence, Chamberlain was introduced to a world much larger than Brunswick, Maine, when invited to discuss pertinent issues of the day with the Stowes and their guests; he was given a glimpse into the cosmopolitan world of the Beechers and the Stowes. His budding romance with his future wife Fanny Adams, the adopted daughter of George Adams, pastor of the First Parish Church in Brunswick, gave the Bowdoin student yet another contact to a larger world than what a farmhand from Brewer would otherwise have had (Trulock, 42–43).

Following his graduation from Bowdoin and his subsequent training at Bangor Theological Seminary, Chamberlain returned to Bowdoin as a professor of rhetoric and oratory. In these years, he came under intense criticism from his fellow faculty members for the revolutionary oratory and rhetorical innovations that he taught his students. Despite their criticisms, Chamberlain's fellow faculty members could not help but be taken in by this likable young man. By 1862, they had finally persuaded him to accept the position of chair of the department of modern and romance languages. The position was prestigious indeed, and though he regretted having to vacate his position as professor of rhetoric, he took the new office, which carried with it the promise of a two-year, expenses paid leave for study in Europe. In large part, this offer was made to Chamberlain to prevent him from joining the war effort, which he had been discussing openly. While the faculty thought they had secured him from the war with this lucrative offer, President Abraham Lincoln's (q.v.) call for more troops in 1862 was one that he could no longer ignore. He would use the leave of absence in Europe to join the Union Army.

Thus, this kindly, humane intellectual from the middle of Maine, instilled with strict moral principles, possessing great strength of character and the courage of his convictions, and developing a strongly democratic view of American nationalism, was made a lieutenant colonel of volunteers in the U.S. Army. The many lessons of hard work and discipline accumulated up to this point would be called upon in great measure in the ensuing years. Moreover, Chamberlain would see the Divine plan as playing an ever increasing role both in the war as a whole and in Chamberlain's own place in the conflict.

The wartime exploits of Joshua Chamberlain are by now quite well known among historians of the Civil War. He was involved at the front at Fredericksburg; later saved the day at Gettysburg; was severely wounded at Petersburg; returned in the final campaign to play a decisive role at Petersburg yet again, as well as at Quaker Road, White Oak Swamp, and finally, at Appomattox. While his participation in these grand events of the Army of the Potomac can be (and often are) glorified for their own sake, they serve a greater purpose: to show how Joshua Lawrence Chamberlain responded as a leader in the horrific events of the war between August 1962 and April 1865.

Chamberlain's first few months with the 20th Maine proved to be the most important, for it was in this time that he used his skills as a student and quickly learned all he could about military affairs. In addition to reading every military work he could find, he gained much knowledge from the regiment's commanding officer, the stern West Point graduate and Maine native Adelbert Ames. This "schooling" was supplemented by something to which Chamberlain was no stranger: discipline and drill. The lieutenant colonel discovered very quickly that he agreed with this regimented side of army life. Chamberlain's youngest brother Tom, himself a member of the regiment, wrote in a letter to their parents that Lawrence was increasingly finding himself in his element (Pullen, 37). All of this initial training would be tested in the crucible of the coming years.

Fredericksburg is a first and important case study. Poor tactical command in the 5th Corps, and in the Army of the Potomac as a whole, caused an attack to be launched too late—and tentatively at that; the strength of the Confederate position was too great to be overcome. The 20th Maine regiment knew this firsthand; its men were among those sacrificed in great number on Marye's Heights. The folly of the attack was not lost on Chamberlain: "Our dead . . . had died in vain," he would write (Wallace, 61). In addition to opening his eyes further to the sacrifices of the war and to the need for solid-thinking leaders, the cost of the failed attempts at Fredericksburg also facilitated an important incident after the battle between Chamberlain and the commander of the Center Grand Division of the Army of the Potomac, General Joseph Hooker, in which Chamberlain sharply questioned the wisdom in the method of attack chosen at Fredericksburg. Although Hooker had not ordered the offensive himself, Chamberlain nonetheless called his superior to task for the assault, claiming that there was "not much intelligent design there" (Trulock, 104). The battle had taught Joshua Chamberlain an important lesson about leadership when it involved the lives of so many men, and in his pointed exchange with Hooker he displayed his customary straightforwardness. Fredericksburg was important for another reason, though; he quickly learned what the nature of this particular war would be, what the price was for preservation of the Union, and "what manner of men" were needed to win the war and construct a more fully democratic nation (Trulock, 62). Moreover, it would place him in a certain state of mind as he and his regiment marched north on the Baltimore Pike in late June 1863.

The events of Little Round Top on July 1863, are as famed as any in the entire Civil War. Moreover, Chamberlain's own actions at Gettysburg did not go unnoticed, as he was later awarded the Congressional Medal of Honor. The decisions he made that day represent nothing short of the first real culmination of his leadership qualities. Dispatching company B to guard his left flank; refusing the left flank of his line; rallying his men to hold their ground and, as always, fighting right alongside them; finally out of ammunition, ordering a bayonet charge with a "swinging door" maneuver down the hill in order to defeat the Confederate forces—every step of the way, Chamberlain acted increasingly more like a leader of men than a professor of rhetoric. "To his men it afterward seemed that the Colonel had the ability to see through forests and hills and to know what was coming" (Pullen, 111).

Chamberlain's actions at Little Round Top solidified him in the annals of American history as a most remarkable soldier. The role of Divine Providence, in Chamberlain's eyes, was as much responsible for the success of his regiment as anything or anyone else. In an attempt to understand how this could come to pass, Chamberlain wrote after being awarded the Congressional Medal of Honor that "[t]he inspiration of a noble cause involving human interests wide and far, enables men to do things they did not dream themselves capable of before, and which they were not capable of alone. The consciousness of belonging, vitally, to something beyond individuality; of being part of a personality that reaches we know not where, in space and in time, greatens the heart to the limits of the soul's ideal" (Trulock, 154–55). His "consciousness of belonging" was no doubt heightened when, during General Ulysses S. Grant's (q.v.) Overland Campaign in May 1964, Chamberlain was placed in command of the 1st Brigade, 1st Division, 5th Corps. While this assignment meant that he had to leave his beloved regiment, he quickly won the support and respect of the members of the First Brigade, composed entirely of Pennsylvania men. The ease with which he was accepted by the First Brigade is evidence of the fact that he put his country and its interests first, not allowing differences in state origin to stand in the way of national unity. As he would later write, "Our thoughts that day were not of States as States, but of the States United—of that Union and oneness in which the people of the United States lived and moved and had their being" (Chamberlain, "Dedication," 3).

Chamberlain's next major engagement came at Petersburg in June 1864. Here, as at Gettysburg, Chamberlain displayed his leadership qualities. In the ill-fated attack of June 18, Joshua Chamberlain received the most grievous of the six wounds his body would absorb over the course of his two and a half years of service in the army. As the ball tore through his torso and knocked him off of his horse, Chamberlain, more fearful that his men would fail in their assignment than he was of his own death, propped himself up with his sword and waved his men on, as blood swelled out of his body. His commitment and performance that day earned him a field promotion to the rank of brigadier general from General Grant, supposedly the only such promotion Grant ever conferred (Grant, 1:297–298). The degree to which Chamberlain was committed to leading his men by example is "exceeded in its notability only by the fact that he did not die that day, or any day in the near future, thanks in large part to the superhuman efforts of a team of doctors who labored over him in surgery through the night and kept careful watch over him in the ensuing days" (Trulock, 219).

Although the wound kept Chamberlain out of action for quite some time, he chose to return to duty as early as November 18, 1864, earlier than his doctors had anticipated or recommended. Explaining why he chose to return so soon, Chamberlain said: "I believe in a destiny—one, I mean, divinely appointed, and to which we are carried forward by a perfect trust in God. I do this, and I believe in it. I have laid plans, in my day, & good ones I thought. But they never succeeded. Something else, better, did, and I could see it as plain as day, that God had done it, & for my good'' (Trulock, 219). Yet again, Chamberlain yielded to Divine Providence as being the ultimate mover of events both in the war and in his life. For Chamberlain, the divine destiny was one that moved him to fight through immense pain and discomfort to create a new American nation that was inclusive of all its people.

In the spring of 1865, the final campaign of the war, Chamberlain assumed the role he had played ever since his first battle over two years ago—leading his men into battle. At the Battles of Quaker Road and White Oak Swamp, he caught the eye of both Generals Grant and Philip Sheridan (q.v.): "By God, that's what I want to see! General officers at the front!'' exclaimed Sheridan upon witnessing Chamberlain's attack at Five Forks (Wallace, 168). Though a bit slower due to his Petersburg wound of the previous June, Chamberlain commanded his brigade with the same zeal and conviction that had so marked his reputation to that point, earning him a promotion to the rank of brevet major general. His actions also prompted General Grant to accord him the honor of accepting the formal surrender of the Army of Northern Virginia a few days later, a job in which he demonstrated the kind of man, the kind of leader, he had become since leaving Portland in August 1862.

Chamberlain's postwar reputation, while certainly not of the same magnitude as those of some of the more high-profile, professional general officers, was nonetheless extremely favorable, and it was destined to remain so. Northerners came to see him as the hero of Little Round Top; Southerners quickly viewed him in the same vein as General John Gordon, as he became one of the most beloved Union officers among members of the former Confederate States. Indeed, he was a truly national hero, admired by Americans both North and South. Moreover, unlike many of his contemporary Civil War leaders whose postwar activities and comments often served to diminish their ''hero'' status, Chamberlain's reputation as a result of his activities after the war only grew.

Elected governor of Maine in September 1866, Chamberlain embarked on what would be the first of many high-profile civic positions following the war. In his first inaugural address in 1867, he displayed his vision and clarity of thought as he proposed to deal with many of the challenges that postwar Maine faced—a decline in the shipbuilding industry, the need to expand education, especially in the field of agriculture, and the desire to create an economic and social system that could halt the growing number of young Maine citizens who sought to make their livings elsewhere for want of opportunities in their native state (Wallace, 207–209). In addition to these internal issues, Chamberlain also addressed himself to the ongoing debate over the nature of Reconstruction. While by no stretch of the imagination a Radical Republican, Chamberlain nonetheless was clear in his belief that Southern states could not simply assume their prewar status as members of the Union without some set of guarantees and concessions. He issued a stern rejoinder to those members of the former Confederate States ''who with scorn and contumely spurned the Constitution, and defiled the Government, and sought with violence, without any apology for the past, without a guarantee for the future, the unconditional restoration of their rights under the Constitution, their places in the Union and their prestige in the Government. This is so little in the spirit of surrender as to seem like a mockery of triumph'' (Wallace, 207–208).

Another issue of national force that drew Chamberlain's attention was the impeachment proceedings of President Andrew Johnson (q.v.). In this heated controversy, Chamberlain sided with Maine senator William Pitt Fessenden, who was one of seven Republican senators who voted against Johnson's conviction. "In this," Willard Wallace writes, "he placed principle ahead of party, and the criticism that now poured upon his head was so vitriolic that friends feared not simply for his career but for his life as well" (215). Here again, Chamberlain showed the kind of fairness of mind that had so characterized his life up to that point. While this was the first substantial break Chamberlain would make from the position of his party, it certainly would not be his last; standing the middle ground and working from his own idea of American nationalism rather than accepting the party line became more the rule than the exception over the duration of his four terms as governor, from 1867 to 1871. The reforms in the economy as well as those in government and education that he would continually espouse in those years portrayed his ever increasing progressive vision for his state and nation; his difficulty in accomplishing many of them to the degree he sought led him, in 1871, to return to Bowdoin College and accept the then-vacant position of president.

Just as his time as governor was marked by his zeal for reform, so too was his tenure at the college. Chamberlain had three principal areas of reform in mind when he assumed the presidency: "a loosening of discipline with a view to treating the students henceforth as adults, a revision of the curriculum with a greater emphasis on science and modern languages as well as the inception of a graduate program leading to the Master of Arts degree, and the introduction of military drill" (Wallace, 229). In Chamberlain's eyes, these changes were necessary if Bowdoin was to prepare its students for the challenges that the late nineteenth century presented. The forces of modernization and industrialization were indeed strong, and Chamberlain was determined not to let Bowdoin drift in the backwash of these monumental changes. While some of the changes he proposed were adopted, others met harsh resistance. Despite the struggle over these changes, Chamberlain pursued them rigorously. In many ways, he had been ahead of his time in his thinking, for Bowdoin, along with many other liberal arts institutions, would later adopt many of the reforms proposed by his administration.

Following his retirement as president of Bowdoin, Chamberlain, never able to settle down completely, became involved in a number of civic organizations. While many heroes of the war simply lent their names to many of these "causes," Chamberlain felt bound to contribute his gifts to them. In addition to giving his time and talent to these activities, he became involved in business (though not entirely successfully) and continued to write and deliver memorial addresses on the war. In his final days, he was appointed surveyor of the Port of Portland, a job that required little actual attention but one into which Chamberlain customarily invested much time and energy.

Eventually, though, the wound he received at Petersburg, which never completely healed and in fact caused him to be in constant pain, finally forced him to scale back his activities. Though he remained active giving speeches, writing, and attending reunions, his health slowly continued to decline. On February 24, 1914, at the age of eighty-three, the wound that was supposed to have killed him on June 18, 1864, finally took his life. A state funeral was held in Portland, and he was buried in the family plot at Pine Grove Cemetery in Brunswick next to his beloved wife Fanny, just on the border of the Bowdoin College property. Despite his many accomplishments and contributions, Chamberlain's headstone bears only his name and the dates of his birth and his death:

Joshua L. Chamberlain
1828–1914

The last few years have witnessed an increased interest in the life and times of Joshua Chamberlain. John Pullen's history of the 20th Maine Regiment was reprinted in 1991 to meet demand, as was Willard Wallace's biography of Chamberlain. The number of visitors at the Chamberlain house and museum has swelled dramatically; the museum cannot keep enough photographs of the general in stock, as visitors from across the country flock to the home of the hero of Little Round Top.

There can be little doubting the reason for this increasing interest in Chamberlain. First, Michael Shaara's novel *The Killer Angels*, published in 1974, reintroduced Chamberlain to the American public. In 1990, Ken Burns's landmark PBS series *The Civil War* brought his extraordinary military career into the homes of millions. The 1993 motion picture *Gettysburg*, the film rendition of Shaara's novel, is the most recent piece on the Civil War to focus in depth on the character of Chamberlain, and it undoubtedly augmented the spread of Chamberlain's reputation.

While these events are the primary catalysts for the revival of interest in Chamberlain, they are not responsible for that interest being sustained. In truth, Chamberlain's reputation as a leader and as a man continues to soar not simply because of the exposure but more so because of the quality of the subject. As America looks to the Civil War in an attempt to define its nationalism, it finds in Joshua Lawrence Chamberlain a man possessed with many admirable qualities—an ordinary citizen of extraordinary talent and dedication who sought to make his country free for all its inhabitants and who sacrificed all that he held dear to defend a democratic, egalitarian version of American nationalism. Reflecting on his salute of Gordon's troops at Appomattox years after the event, Chamberlain took the opportunity to drive home a central theme that motivated him to participate in the war. Speaking of his Confederate foes, he said: "Although, as we believed, fatally wrong in striking at the old flag, misreading its deeper meaning and the innermost law of the people's life, blind to the signs of the times in the march of man, they fought as they were taught . . . Whoever had misled these men, we had not. We had led them back, home'' (Chamberlain, ''Appomattox,'' 20).

While Chamberlain's deep religious convictions and his great intellect explain much about the man, they do not tell all about his actions in the Civil War and the postwar years. These elements alone cannot explain why he has become such an icon—why people across the country admired him in his own day and continue to admire him today. The real force behind the phenomenon is the fact that Chamberlain emerges as a likable, national leader, fair, conciliatory, and upright. For many Americans, he was, and is, a model American citizen, a model leader, of the Civil War era.

BIBLIOGRAPHY

Ulysses S. Grant, *Memoirs*, 2 vols. (New York: Charles C. Webster and Co., 1886).

Joshua Lawrence Chamberlain, ''Dedication of the Maine Monuments at Gettysburg'' (address delivered October 3, 1889, General Collection, Library of Congress, Washington, D.C.).

Joseph Lawrence Chamberlain, ''Appomattox,'' (paper read before the New York Commandery Loyal Legion of the United States, October 7, 1903, General Collection, Library of Congress, Washington, D.C.).

John B. Gordon, *Reminiscences of the Civil War* (New York: Charles Scribner, 1903).

John J. Pullen, *The Twentieth Maine: A Volunteer Regiment in the Civil War* (Dayton, Ohio: Morningside House, Inc., 1957).

Willard Wallace, *Soul of a Lion: A Biography of General Joshua L. Chamberlain* (New York: Thomas Nelson and Sons, 1960).

Alice Raines Trulock, *In the Hands of Providence: Joshua L. Chamberlain and the American Civil War* (Chapel Hill: University of North Carolina Press, 1992).

SALMON PORTLAND CHASE
(January 13, 1808–May 7, 1873)

Frederick J. Blue

Nothing in the early life of Salmon Portland Chase suggested a career of anti-slavery leadership and later prominence among Republicans championing the cause of racial equality. Nor was there anything to suggest an insatiable desire to be president or play a central role in the Civil War cabinet of Abraham Lincoln (q.v.), to be climaxed by continued importance during Reconstruction as chief justice of the Supreme Court. Born in rural New Hampshire on January 13, 1808, Chase experienced little in his first twenty-five years to indicate he would live a life other than one in the schoolroom or before the bar. His father farmed the rock-strewn New England soil and dabbled in local Federalist politics. With the elder Chase's premature death in 1817, young Salmon was raised for a time by his authoritarian uncle, the aristocratic Episcopal bishop of Ohio, Philander Chase. On his return to New Hampshire, Chase enrolled at Dartmouth College while teaching school in a small nearby town. At eighteen and with a college degree in hand, he moved first to Washington, D.C. There he opened his Select Classical School for young boys, determined to earn enough money to pursue his chosen career as an attorney.

A protégé of Attorney General William Wirt, Chase found his already conservative views reinforced by his mentor, who became his model as both lawyer and politician. As Chase prepared to leave Washington to seek his fortune in Cincinnati in 1830, his elitism and pompous nature along with a degree of smugness, characteristics that later associates would find so disconcerting, were already revealing themselves. Nor did his early years in Cincinnati give any hint of the political conversion to come. As a young attorney, he held true to his Whig politics and espoused traditional causes even as he struggled to secure clients. He became active in the temperance crusade and in religious affairs, both within and outside his Episcopal Church. Numerous factors pointed toward a career as a traditional Whig attorney, including marriage in 1834 to the daughter of a prominent Cincinnati family, a developing legal practice that included being named solicitor of the Cincinnati branch of the Bank of the United States, and friendship with some of the wealthiest and most influential businessmen in the city.

Yet events in Cincinnati and elsewhere in the 1830s and 1840s moved him to an antislavery commitment and a central role in the Liberty and Free Soil parties. Alarmed by an antiabolitionist mob's attack on James G. Birney and his press in 1836, he was moved to defend first Birney and then the growing number of fugitive slaves seeking refuge from bondage on the northern side of the Ohio River. He quickly gained a reputation as a defender of fugitive slaves, the champion of civil rights for blacks, and advocate of the separation of the federal government from slavery, although in all of these areas, he spoke for only a minority of Northerners. Even as he moderated his position to better fit the Northern tone, many still saw him as an extremist. Surely his advocacy of eventual abolition and black suffrage won him few friends before or after the Civil War.

Chase's growing antislavery commitment was tempered significantly by his willingness to resort to political expediency to win office. This was most obvious when, after his key role in the Free Soil campaign of 1848, he gladly sacrificed the third party's independence to secure his own election to the U.S. Senate with the help of Democrats in the Ohio legislature. The bargaining antagonized many of his own supporters, but in gaining the Senate seat, he also forced Ohio Democrats to support the partial repeal of the state's racist black laws, including one that required African Americans to post a $500 bond before entering the state. Once in Congress he became the outspoken critic of Southern domination and the proslave policies of Millard Fillmore and Franklin Pierce. His term in the Senate climaxed with his dramatic effort to prevent passage of Stephen A. Douglas's Kansas-Nebraska bill in 1854. He joined with five other antislavery members of Congress in writing ''The Appeal of the Independent Democrats,'' which combined his free soil position with an effort to create a party dedicated to containing slavery within its existing boundaries. The following year he returned home to lead the newly formed Republican party to victory—a party that he had helped to create. That victory was the election of Salmon P. Chase as the state's first Republican governor.

In the fifteen years between 1840 and 1855 Chase had belonged to four parties, Whig, Liberty, Free Soil, and Republican, and had frequently allied with a fifth, the Democratic, in order to pursue his personal and antislavery goals. By the mid-1850s he finally appeared in position to achieve what had by then become his primary goal, the presidency. The governorship was to him a mere stepping stone to that goal, not an end in itself. Yet 1856 brought the first of four successive frustrations. Republican leaders regarded him as too radical on slavery and race and preferred the popular explorer-turned-politician John C. Frémont as their presidential candidate. In that struggle, Chase did not even have the united support of the Ohio delegation due to memories of his political expediency and fear of his advanced views.

Four years later he was back again and, in 1860, had probably his best chance at his elusive goal. The same problems hampered this effort, however, compounded by his own ineptness as a political organizer. Throughout the campaign for the 1860 Republican nomination, Chase proved unable to inspire others beyond mere rhetorical interest. Even many of his own supporters were concerned more with blocking his rivals than in forwarding his own candidacy. He had delegated no one to initiate the necessary collective bargaining with other state delegations at the Chicago nominating convention in May. His candidacy was flawed in other respects as well. His courageous stands on sectional issues alienated moderate and conservative Republicans. Although incorrectly labeled an abolitionist by his opponents, he was more willing to advocate the antislavery cause than most Republicans. He explained to John Sherman in 1858: "My best years have been devoted in no wild or fanatical spirit I hope to the advancement of the antislavery cause" (Chase, May 6, 1858). Unfortunately for him, too many Republicans viewed him as one who did have a "wild or fanatical spirit."

Despite the yeoman work Chase had performed in helping to build the Republican party of Ohio, he had not won the loyalty of the majority. His cold and aloof personality kept people at arm's length as did his morally righteous attitude. His role in politics before becoming a Republican had left too many enemies. Most Republicans reacted negatively to his single-minded desire to be president and his rather transparent efforts to mask his political ambitions. As Carl Schurz later reminisced about Chase: "I had never before come in contact with a public man who was . . . possessed by the desire to be President, even to the extent of honestly believing that he owed it to the country and that the country owed it to him" (2:172).

Chase did not let his bitterness over the loss of the nomination stop him from an active campaign for Abraham Lincoln. Although well aware of the possibility of a key cabinet position in a Republican administration, his enthusiasm for the candidate was sincere. Despite Chase's many disappointments, Lincoln's victory in November made possible what he had been seeking for so long. In congratulating the president-elect, he exclaimed: "The object of my wishes and labors for nineteen years is accomplished in the overthrow of the Slave Power." The way was now clear "for the establishment of the policy of Freedom" (Warden, 364). Lincoln's victory gave Chase the opportunity to forward his beliefs. Having earlier established a friendly and supportive relationship with the new president, he now hoped and expected to play an active role in his administration.

After lengthy deliberation and consideration of political factors, Lincoln rewarded Chase for his loyalty by naming him Secretary of the Treasury, a post for which he had only limited background or training. Chase would have preferred to head the State Department but gladly accepted the Treasury instead, never expecting to confine his influence to financial matters. Inheriting a difficult set of financial conditions, Chase dealt with the problems in a controversial yet satisfactory way. Initially, like most Union leaders, Chase had assumed that the war would be brief, necessitating only traditional means of raising revenue through increased taxes, tariffs, and borrowing. This hit-and-miss method designed for a simpler age would soon have to be augmented through more extensive loans and a modernized banking system when the prospect of a quick surrender of the Confederacy faded.

By 1862, Chase reluctantly accepted greenbacks as legal tender to help finance the war and, with the help of Senator John Sherman of Ohio, planned the national banking system embodied in the act of February 1863 (later revised in June 1864). The act created a system of federally supervised national banking associations empowered to issue banknotes guaranteed by the federal government and based upon U.S. bonds. This highly controversial system did create a more secure currency and helped to bring some order to the previously unstable Civil War economy. Another key ingredient to Chase's financial program included heavy government borrowing through bond sales. Most controversial was his arrangement with Philadelphia financier Jay Cooke (q.v.), who used his power and influence to facilitate his role as special agent for the sale of government bonds. By mid-1864 Cooke had announced bond sales of more than $500 million and had realized a handsome commission in the process. Chase made many mistakes as Secretary of the Treasury. Most seriously, he relied too heavily on private banker Cooke to sell bonds, but for the most part, the loans were wisely managed and Cooke produced the desired results. The Union debt, although huge, was not exorbitant when compared with debts incurred in later wars. Inflation was also kept as much under control as the chaotic conditions permitted. Paper money issued during the war totaled less than one-third that of the Confederacy. In all economic areas, the Union record compared favorably with that of the Southern government.

Chase's official duties as Secretary of the Treasury were not limited to financing the war. Also involved was the complex problem of regulating trade between Union-controlled areas and the seceded states. The issue was more complicated than simply preventing trade with the enemy; it also involved the desire of Union border states to keep old trade patterns open and the necessity of keeping such areas loyal. Trade in parts of the Confederacy under Union control, as in New Orleans and parts of Virginia, Tennessee, and the Sea Islands of South Carolina and Georgia, was also a Treasury responsibility. The Union need for Confederate products, especially cotton, meant that such exchange had to be carefully regulated to avoid excessive profits for speculators.

As Northern armies advanced into the Confederacy, Chase's responsibilities for all trade questions increased. Inevitably, trade restrictions and licensing became mired in a bureaucracy of regulations, and Treasury agents assigned to control the trade were subject to open invitations to corruption. Rooting out dishonest agents and developing a coherent policy that kept private citizens as well as army and naval officials happy and that produced an efficient system of control were beyond the limited resources and capabilities of the Treasury. Political favoritism, while never admitted, was evident to all. Despite Chase's concerted efforts and honesty of purpose, corruption among speculators and some Treasury agents was common. Nor was the secretary ever willing to accept criticism and admit errors. Yet despite the problems, Chase's adherence to principle and devotion to the Union cause produced a record of which he could be justifiably proud.

One of the areas outside of the scope of Treasury responsibilities where Chase became especially active and influential both within and outside of the cabinet was the momentous issue of slavery and race relations. Before the war, he had been consistently ahead of Lincoln in the efforts to limit the spread of slavery and to divorce the federal government from any responsibility for it. Yet with his appointment as Secretary of the Treasury, he had appeared for a time to be the model of moderation on slave-related issues. He even defended Lincoln against those who demanded immediate abolition. He appeared to appreciate the president's need to move with caution in order not to antagonize many Northern supporters or especially those in Union border slave states. Yet it was clear that Chase's goal of emancipation and Lincoln's prime concern of restoring the Union would soon clash.

Chase restrained himself when, in late 1861, Lincoln rescinded the order of General John C. Frémont freeing slaves of rebels within his Missouri command. In the spring of 1862 when General David Hunter did the same for slaves in his command in Georgia, Florida, and South Carolina, Chase urged Lincoln to recognize the order and complained bitterly when the president revoked it. By this time the secretary had concluded that federal action could be justified on the grounds of military necessity. Behind the scenes, he urged General Benjamin F. Butler, the commander in Union-occupied New Orleans, to free slaves in that area and enlist them in his army, because not to do so was to contribute to "the continued subjugation of nearly four million loyal people" (Schuckers, 375–76).

Yet even as Chase continued his efforts, Lincoln had concluded to move against slavery with a presidential proclamation. The president never explained what moved him to inform his cabinet on July 22, 1862, that he was prepared to use his authority as commander in chief to emancipate slaves in those parts of rebel states behind Confederate lines. Chase's efforts along with others both within and outside of government appear to have been among the more important influences in changing Lincoln's mind. Those others, most of whom were Radical Republicans, included members of the Congress like Charles Sumner (q.v.) and private citizens such as Frederick Douglass (q.v.).

The secretary did have some input in the final wording of the Proclamation agreed to in the cabinet in late December. Most significantly, the document urged the recruitment of freedmen into Union armies. Chase, who had argued for such a policy for several months, was satisfied that his voice had been heard by the president. On the issue of black troops Chase appeared to have had more influence than on emancipation itself. Now he rejoiced that blacks would "be called into the conflict, not as cattle . . . but as men." He also urged that they be used in all varieties of military effort, for in this way, "from a burden they will become a support" (*Lincoln Papers*, April 9, 1863). Chase and Lincoln had thus reached an accommodation satisfactory to both on racial issues. There had been many critical factors in Lincoln's decision, but among them was the constant pressure from the Secretary of the Treasury. Chase believed that he was at least in part responsible for Lincoln's advance. Long before this the differences between the two on political issues had intensified, but in this most crucial area, Chase's influence had prevailed to a remarkable degree.

It was the secretary's interference in military matters that helped bring his differences with Lincoln to a critical point. Although he had no military experience, he nevertheless believed that his advice on the movement of armies bore respect from both the War Department and the president. This became especially significant in regard to General George B. McClellan (q.v.), whose reluctance to engage the Confederacy in battle through late 1862 frustrated all Union leaders. It especially angered Chase because the general also had informed Lincoln of his opposition to "the forcible abolition of slavery" (*Lincoln Papers*, July 9, 1862), a position that Chase ironically regarded as unjustified interference in a political matter. Complicating the situation was the rivalry for Lincoln's attention between Chase and Secretary of State William H. Seward (q.v.), whom Chase desired to see removed from his cabinet position. Chase, in fact, became the leader in the movement to force Lincoln's hand. The Seward matter climaxed in December when Chase and a Senate delegation met with the president. With an eye toward using the meeting to forward his own nomination for president in 1864, Chase instead found his challenge resulting in Lincoln skillfully outmaneuvering him and leaving him with few congressional supporters.

Although frustrated and humiliated, Chase pressed on through 1863, believing himself a superior candidate to Lincoln. On occasion, he used his Treasury position to forward his candidacy by appointing key backers to party positions in Union-controlled areas of Louisiana and Florida. The degree to which he used his patronage in pursuit of the presidency is not easily assessed. Surely there were few active opponents of a Chase nomination among his key appointees, and many of his strongest political proponents held Treasury positions in both North and South. Clerks in his Washington department numbered 2,000 by the time he left office, whereas the number of special agents, internal revenue collectors, and custom house officials multiplied throughout the war. Chase vigorously denied using his power of appointment to promote his candidacy and in fact never admitted that he was even seeking a nomination. Yet few were convinced.

In early 1864, Chase had some reason to believe that he could successfully challenge Lincoln. The radical element of the Republican party had grown increasingly discontented under Lincoln's leadership, and many were eager to see him replaced by someone more closely aligned with their philosophy. Chase clearly fit that requirement, and because of his obvious administrative and executive ability as well as thinly disguised interest in a nomination, much of the anti-Lincoln sentiment naturally centered on him. His criticism of Lincoln's racial policy had sparked support among some, as had his dislike of the president's support of Seward. But because Chase and the congressional critics had been outmaneuvered by Lincoln in their December 1862 confrontation, most of them would hesitate before openly supporting a Chase candidacy.

There was a small group, however, led by Senator Samuel C. Pomeroy of Kansas, that persisted in Chase's behalf and in February published the Pomeroy Circular, which specifically proposed Chase for the nomination because his record was "clear and unimpeachable, showing him to be a statesman of rare ability and an administrator of the highest order" (Schuckers, 499–500). Chase himself had played no role in the committee's deliberations but must have known what it was proposing to do. The committee itself had badly miscalculated public opinion in its expectations of tapping a reservoir of anti-Lincoln and pro-Chase sentiment. Their attacks on the president instead revealed that most preferred Lincoln's moderate course on race issues to Chase's more advanced position. Thus, when the party moved quickly to consolidate support behind the incumbent, Secretary Chase again found himself embarrassed and outmaneuvered.

Chase's days in the Lincoln cabinet were now clearly numbered, and it remained only for the necessary incident to force his removal. In early June, the Union party renominated Abraham Lincoln at its Baltimore convention, and the president would no longer feel it necessary to keep his wayward Secretary of the Treasury in check within the cabinet. Thus, when a patronage dispute over the New York collectorship brought another Chase challenge to the chief executive's control, Lincoln gladly accepted his offer to resign in late June 1864.

Frustrated with his latest failure, Chase left the cabinet, beaten but still determined. He threw his support behind Lincoln's reelection drive, knowing that an appointment as chief justice lay in the balance. With the death of the eighty-seven-year-old Roger Taney and the president safely reelected, Lincoln appointed Chase in December 1864. The president had been warned by Chase's many opponents that as chief justice he would continue to intrigue for the presidency, and that he did. Lincoln had told these critics at the time of the appointment that Chase was a man of great ambition and that "if he does not give up that idea [the presidency] it will be very bad for him and very bad for me." Yet he concluded revealingly: "Chase is about one and a half times bigger than any other man that I ever knew" (Boutwell, 2:29).

Many factors contributed to the president's decision to appoint Chase chief justice, among them being "Mr C's ability" and his "soundness on the general issues of the war." As Lincoln explained to a friend, "We have stood together in the time of trial"(Lincoln Papers, Dec. 1864). Equally important, the president could expect that the new chief justice would provide judicial approval of the many changes that the Civil War had brought. Chief among those changes was emancipation. It had surely occurred to Lincoln that a court challenge of the constitutionality of his Emancipation Proclamation might jeopardize what had by then become a central part of his wartime strategy. What better way to assure its approval than to make the man who had urged him so strongly to free the slaves the head of the court that might have to rule on its legality?

Chase's reputation among his contemporaries was indeed a mixed one as the war drew to a close. At the time of his resignation from his Treasury post, Chase's friends quickly rallied to his support and expressed their dismay at his leaving the cabinet. Jay Cooke was "deeply pained," and Horace Greeley's *New York Tribune* regretted the loss of "one of the few great men left" (*Tribune*, July 1, 1864). Critics could not contain their relief on hearing of the resignation. Secretary of the Navy Gideon Welles confided in his diary that "Chase's retirement has offended nobody and has gratified almost everybody." Of the cabinet members, only Edwin Stanton (q.v.) expressed regret to Chase personally and showed the courtesy of calling on him before he left Washington. A similar reaction followed announcement of his appointment to be chief justice. His friends were quick to extend congratulations. Joseph Medill, editor of the *Chicago Tribune*, expressed confidence that Chase would defend the Constitution "in accordance with the principles of Freedom and Human Rights." Abolitionist supporters Lydia Maria Child and Lewis Tappan rejoiced that the proslavery days of the Court under Taney had given way "to the cause of Freedom." In contrast, his long-time nemesis Frank Blair told his brother Montgomery, the postmaster general, that "Chase's appointment *shakes my confidence in the President's integrity*" because "he must know that Chase is dishonest as well as an enemy to him and the Government." Chase's longtime Ohio antagonist Senator Benjamin Wade commented sarcastically on hearing of his selection: "Chase is a good man, but his theology is unsound. He thinks there is a fourth person in the Trinity" (Dennett, 53). Chase would thus remain as much a source of controversy in 1865 as he had been ever since assuming a prominent role in antislavery politics.

The new chief justice's remaining years did not always see him at his best. Occasionally at odds with Republican leaders over Reconstruction policies, Chase clashed with them over their efforts to deny him a major role in the Andrew Johnson (q.v.) impeachment trial of 1868. In many other aspects of Reconstruction, he agreed with radical leaders, and where he did not, he led the Court in avoiding an open confrontation with Congress. Nonetheless, he continued to push his twin goals of black rights and a Chase presidency, not necessarily in that order. With the Republicans determined on a Ulysses S. Grant (q.v.) candidacy in 1868 to capitalize on the general's military record, Chase would have to look elsewhere for a nomination. Not through switching parties, he now listened eagerly to flattering Democrats eager to find someone who might oust the Republicans from the White House. The problem was that Chase advocated black suffrage and most Democrats did not. Even though he moderated his position somewhat, the party could not accept a man so far in advance of their own racial views and one so long identified as a Republican. Chase nonetheless did help persuade reluctant Ohioans in the legislature to ratify the pending Fifteenth Amendment granting black suffrage.

Chase was destined to serve his remaining days as the nation's chief jurist, although he never reconciled himself to not becoming its chief executive. Even in 1872, a year before his death and after having suffered a paralyzing stroke, he listened rather pathetically to those who would have had him lead the Liberal Republican effort to prevent Grant's reelection. Chase died in New York on May 7, 1873, having never attained his primary goal of the presidency. A self-righteous and opinionated man, he held fast to his puritanical morals and was almost totally lacking in a sense of humor. Ambition for personal political power was so obvious that his enemies were many and constant friends few. Yet he maintained a moral courage throughout that helped push the country toward eventual emancipation and greater equality.

Always a source of controversy while alive, Salmon P. Chase continued to provoke disagreement among those attempting to assess his life and his role in the Civil War. The earliest efforts reveal much about Chase himself and his controversial daughter Kate Sprague, who had wanted so much for her father to achieve the presidency. In 1873, a few months before her father died, Kate had chosen a trusted friend, Jacob Schuckers, to produce an idealized biography. What she sought was a hagiology, a biography in the mode of family history in which the subject is eulogized. Her father, on the other hand, was so sure of his own place in history that he wanted an objectivity that would nevertheless appreciate his role in the past four decades, not apology. He sought some character analysis and a willingness to deal fairly with his life. He made these intentions clear in early 1873 to his private secretary Robert Warden and promised that he would assist him in gathering material and would place no restrictions on his using all available sources.

Following Chase's death, Kate did all that she could to gain control of many of the personal letters that her father had given to Warden and even tried to prevent his biography from being published. Once Warden's work was released, she attacked it in the press and defended the rival volume of Schuckers. Warden won the race to the printers by approximately two months. Not surprisingly, the two biographies were very different in quality and usefulness. Schuckers produced a strictly limited public life of Chase, making little effort to deal with the private affairs that Kate wanted so desperately to guard. Only those aspects of his public career that placed Chase in a positive light were dealt with at length, while the less favorable were glossed over or rationalized into praiseworthy action. Schuckers concluded his 600-page tribute to Chase by summing up his many positive qualities, including modesty, dedication to humanity, hard work, great achievement, deep religious conviction, and total honesty. Warden, on the other hand, produced a more reliable volume because of the greater number of letters and diary entries included with very little significant editing.

Neither volume did much more than compile the vast amounts of Chase material at their authors' disposal, and each is thus valuable mostly as a primary source. Yet as imperfect as both volumes were, the long-winded, yet sincere and honest, Warden produced a biography of more lasting and historical value. More in keeping with what Chase himself had wanted, it was as objective an account as a friend and admirer might produce.

Several of Chase's other contemporaries dealt with him in their diaries or memoirs. Republicans Carl Schurz, John Sherman, and Henry Wilson were among those who commented on Chase's personal and political goals and provided insight and an understanding of Chase and the period. Others such as cabinet members Gideon Welles and Edward Bates used their diaries, not published until after their deaths, to emphasize Chase's political maneuvering designed to promote his own career and goal of achieving the presidency.

As Civil War memories began to fade, these amateur, partisan historians gave way to those who were more detached and who could thus be more objective. In 1899, Harvard professor of history Albert Bushnell Hart produced *Salmon Portland Chase*, a volume in the famed American Statesmen Series. It is a complete life and a well-written analysis of his complex subject based on thorough research into Chase's letters and diaries and showing both the strengths and weaknesses of the Secretary of the Treasury. Hart's biography represented the triumph of realism and the scientific approach to history rather than the romanticism of Warden and Schuckers. Concentrating on Chase's public life and saying little about private matters, Hart's *Chase* took a highly effective life and times approach.

Following Hart, there was an eighty-eight-year hiatus in Chase biographies. In part, the lack of new scholarship was due to Chase's diversity, for his career included that of antislavery lawyer, Free Soil senator, Republican governor, Secretary of the Treasury, and chief justice. It was also due to the tremendous quantity of Chase letters and diaries and his horrendous handwriting. In 1954, David Donald edited his Civil War diaries and provided additional insight to his wartime activities. Some who have written about him in recent decades have stressed the view of many of his contemporaries who believed him to be little more than a selfish, grasping politician. Typical of this interpretation are Thomas and Marva Belden who, in their study of Chase and his daughter Kate during the Civil War years, painted a picture that added an unjustified twist, that of Treasury Department corruption, to that of self-seeking politician. Based on insufficient and circumstantial evidence and speculation, their study concludes that Chase's Treasury administration was characterized by "improper bonding, bribery, and favoritism" (143).

More recently, Chase has been the source of renewed scholarly interest, and while critical, for the most part, these historians have been more appreciative of his commitment to racial justice and equality even as they recognize his political maneuvering. Frederick J. Blue and John Niven have each written full-length biographies. Blue stresses Chase's life in politics, pointing out his political ambition and especially the maneuvering he went through to achieve the presidency but also his genuine concern for others, especially African Americans. Niven has taken a more life and times approach and presents his subject as a moralist torn by political ambition who deserves more attention and credit than has often been accorded him. Niven is also the author of a multivolume edition of the Chase papers, the completion of which will make Chase a more accessible figure.

Salmon P. Chase thus could engender both loyalty and distrust. His vanity and absorption with his own advancement made close personal friendships difficult; his political ambition appeared insatiable. But he is remembered also for his achievements. An intelligent, diligent, and efficient administrator committed to hard work, he effectively guided the Union through the financial difficulties of the war years. He maintained a reputation for honesty and fought consistently for a program of reform in terms of race relations. As Robert Warden concluded at the time of Chase's death, "[T]he real glory of his life" lay in his "persevering agitation against slavery" and all forms of racial injustice (816).

BIBLIOGRAPHY

Abraham Lincoln Papers, Library of Congress.

John Sherman Papers, Library of Congress.

Henry W. Wilson, *History of the Rise and Fall of the Slave Power in America*, 2 vols. (Boston: J. R. Osgood, 1873–1877).

Jacob W. Schuckers, *The Life and Public Services of Salmon Portland Chase* (New York: D. Appleton and Co., 1874).

Robert B. Warden, *An Account of the Private Life and Public Services of Salmon Portland Chase* (Cincinnati, Ohio: Wilstach, Baldwin, and Co., 1874).

Albert Bushnell Hart, *Salmon Portland Chase* (New York: Houghton, Mifflin, and Co., 1899).

George S. Boutwell, *Reminiscences of Sixty Years in Public Life*, 2 vols. (New York: McClure, Phillips and Co., 1902).

Carl Schurz, *The Reminiscences of Carl Schurz*, 3 vols. (New York: The McClure Co., 1907–1909).

Howard K. Beale, ed., *The Diary of Edward Bates, 1859–1866*, in annual report of the American Historical Association, Washington, D.C., 1930.

Tyler Dennett, ed., *Lincoln and the Civil War Diaries and Letters of John Hay* (New York: Dodd, Mead and Co., 1939).

David H. Donald, ed., *Inside Lincoln's Cabinet: The Civil War Diaries of Salmon P. Chase* (New York: Longmans, Green and Co., 1954).

Thomas G. Belden and Marva Robins Belden, *So Fell the Angels* (Boston: Little, Brown, 1956).

David Hughes, "Salmon P. Chase, Chief Justice" (Ph.D. diss., Princeton University, 1963).

Frederick Blue, "Kate's Paper Chase: The Race to Publish the First Biography of Salmon P. Chase," *Old Northwest* 8 (1982–1983): 353–363.

Frederick Blue, *Salmon P. Chase: A Life in Politics* (Kent, Ohio: Kent State University Press, 1987).

John Niven, ed., *The Salmon P. Chase Papers*, 5 vols. (Kent, Ohio: Kent State University Press, 1993–1998).

John Niven, *Salmon P. Chase: A Biography* (New York: Oxford University Press, 1995).

JAY COOKE
(August 10, 1821–February 16, 1905)

Charles F. Ritter

Jay Cooke made his reputation serving the Union during the Civil War. With two biographers celebrating that service, he continues to be known as "The Robert Morris of the Civil War" and "the financial wizard of the Union war effort." Some say he did as much to win the war as did the Union Army. Yet this is the same Jay Cooke whose banking house collapsed, ushering in the devastating Panic of 1873. Indeed, Cooke was more than a banker; he was a promoter, an entrepreneur, and a developer. These images do not attach to his memory. The survival of Cooke's high-toned reputation lies not only in the fact that he did rescue Union finances in the darkest hours of the war but in historians' focus on that aspect of his life.

Born outside the Ohio frontier town of Sandusky on August 10, 1821, Cooke was the third of four children and the second of three sons born to Eleuthoros and Martha (Carswell) Cooke. He traced his roots to the Plymouth settlement where the first Cookes arrived in 1638. His forebears followed a typical migration pattern from Massachusetts to Connecticut, across New York state and into the Western Reserve, first to Indiana and then back to Ohio.

Cooke's father was a prominent figure in Ohio political and legal circles. A lawyer by trade, Eleuthoros Cooke served in the Ohio House of Representatives in 1822, 1823, and 1825. Elected as an anti-Jacksonian to the 22d Congress in 1830, he ran unsuccessfully for reelection in 1832. After returning to his law practice, he was elected again to the Ohio House in 1840. In addition to practicing law and politics, Eleuthoros Cooke was also an entrepreneur. While in the Ohio legislature he successfully sought a charter for the construction of a canal from Sandusky to Cincinnati, and in 1826 the Ohio legislature granted him what is reputed to be the first railroad charter in the United States.

Jay Cooke was educated through home reading and at the village school until he was fourteen. He began his business career at the age of nine when he sold tin toys and picture books in a corner of his uncle's Sandusky dry goods store.

As his brothers departed the homestead for more schooling, Jay chose to enter business, and at fourteen he became a clerk at Hubberd and Leiter's store in Sandusky.

In 1836, at the age of fifteen, Cooke accepted an offer to go to St. Louis to work for the merchants Seymour and Bool. While this move changed his life, his sojourn in St. Louis lasted only a year, when the Panic of 1837 forced his employer to close. He returned to Sandusky with $200 in his pocket, furs and Indian blankets in his kit, and "the manner of a Southern gentleman and the feeling of the capitalist" (Larson, 17). In the spring of 1838 Cooke left Sandusky for Philadelphia, joining his brother-in-law William Moorhead, president of the Washington Packet & Transportation Company. This move connected a family interest in transportation with a family talent for promotion, both characteristics that Cooke would find useful in later life. In his new career, Cooke kept the books, solicited trade, and directed the company's publicity. He also worked briefly as a bookkeeper at the Congress Hall Hotel where he lived.

The packet company failed, another casualty of the Panic of 1837, and Cooke returned to Sandusky to farm with his brother. But in 1839 Enoch Clark and Edward Dodge, two bankers who admired Cooke's talents at the Congress Hall Hotel, invited him to join their firm. Cooke returned to Philadelphia in April 1839 to begin work at E. W. Clark and Company.

By 1839 Clark & Co. was one of Philadelphia's top "stock and exchange" houses. Cooke became a protégé of Enoch Clark and was the firm's principal "counterfeit clerk"—he had a unique ability to spot counterfeit banknotes. He also returned to his bookkeeping job at the Congress Hall Hotel, and he wrote a money matters column for the Philadelphia *Daily Chronicle*.

Cooke joined Clark & Company just as private banking flourished in the post-Jacksonian period, and he flourished along with it—in January 1843 he became a one-eighth partner in the Philadelphia house. Principally in the "exchange" business, Clark & Co. bought and sold all manner of funds through their offices scattered throughout the United States. The company also worked in conjunction with Corcoran and Riggs in Washington to help finance the Mexican-American War by selling two U.S. Treasury bond issues. In addition to absorbing lessons in government finance, Cooke learned about handling securities from various entities, especially railroads.

Clark & Co. went under in the Panic of 1857, although Cooke came out of the financial debacle with what he described as "a fair fortune" (Popowski, 30). His father enticed him to return to Sandusky, and once there, Cooke focused his attention on transportation matters. He conducted the reorganization of Pennsylvania's canal system under a single state agency, and he reorganized the Vermont Central Railroad. With the profits from these and other transactions, Cooke and brother-in-law Moorhead opened a bank in Philadelphia in 1861.

The timing of this move could not have been accidental since the times were precarious for banking. The Civil War had just begun, and Cooke must have seen the potential for handling government securities, just as Clark & Co. had a dozen years before. Cooke made contact with Secretary of the Treasury Salmon P. Chase (q.v.), informing him that he and Anthony Drexel, another Philadelphia banker, planned to open a branch of Cooke & Co. in Washington. "We would wish to make our business mostly out of the Treasury operations," he told Chase, and he thought he could "greatly help you in the management of your vast negotiations" (Josephson, 55).

The overture to Chase was not coincidental. The Treasury Secretary was a close friend of Cooke's father, and while governor of Ohio, Chase had been a favorite of Jay's older brother Henry's newspaper *The Ohio State Journal*, the most important paper in the state. Henry Cooke moved to Washington in 1861 to become Jay's agent there and used the family influence on the Ohio members of the Republican party. Jay drew especially close to John Sherman, who borrowed $3,000 from Cooke to finance his successful campaign for the U.S. Senate seat that Chase vacated when he went to the Treasury.

In spite of these avenues that Cooke had into Chase's office, the secretary was reluctant to bestow any special favors on the banker. Yet in 1861 Chase's problems were enormous. The U.S. Treasury was completely unprepared to deal with the war emergency. It had little cash to run the war and little power to raise capital. Indeed, in the wake of the Bull Run campaign, Chase was able to sell only half of a 6 percent bond issue, and he was forced to issue short-term Treasury notes to make up the difference. Banks that normally would have bought the securities were weary of the Lincoln administration and uncertain about the Union's fate. At this crucial moment the thirty-one-year-old Cooke stepped forward.

Cooke's first effort to sell government securities came in April 1861, when he received $200,000 in Treasury notes convertible into 6 percent bonds. He participated in a small way in other issues, always purchasing the bonds at a large discount. He was dissatisfied with the discounts, however, feeling that in this emergency the government should not have to sacrifice up to a third of the value of its securities. He thought that an emotional appeal to citizens would help the government sell its bonds at par.

An opportunity for Cooke to demonstrate his ideas appeared in the summer of 1861. Pennsylvania wished to sell bonds to raise cash for the defense of the state. Bankers estimated that at best the bonds would sell at 75 percent of their value. Cooke suggested a scheme to sell the bonds at par, and state officials accepted his offer, placing the $3 million loan exclusively in Cooke's and Drexel's hands. Cooke immediately applied his radical ideas to selling this loan. He placed advertisements for the loan in newspapers across the state, appealing directly to people's patriotism and informing them that the bonds would pay an untaxed 6 percent interest. To skeptics' surprise, banks, railroads, insurance companies, and ordinary citizens oversubscribed the load.

Building on the success of the Pennsylvania loan, Cooke renewed his overture to Chase for exclusive handling of Treasury business. Chase still resisted Cooke's offer, causing Anthony Drexel to withdraw from his planned venture with Cooke. Jay pressed ahead on his own and opened a Washington branch of his bank in February 1862. His partners were his brother Henry; his brother-in-law William Moorhead; and Harris C. Fahnestock, a Pennsylvania banker who would manage the new office.

By the time Cooke opened his D.C. branch he had ingratiated himself with Secretary Chase. After the Union debacle at Bull Run, Cooke helped promote the sale of 7.3 percent Treasury notes, which had virtually stopped selling in New York. Chase was so impressed that he offered Cooke the position of assistant treasurer at Philadelphia. But the banker had bigger fish to fry and turned the post down. However, he accompanied the secretary to New York in August 1861 to face down the Associated Banks of New York, Boston, and Philadelphia and persuade them to underwrite a $150 million loan to the government.

Chase appointed Cooke the Philadelphia area agent for this loan, and Jay used the opportunity to put his selling technique into high gear. He advertised the loan in over twenty newspapers and placed favorable editorials in three of Philadelphia's largest newspapers. By early September 1862 he had daily sales of $100,000 a day. Chase was so impressed with this performance that in October, when the government failed to sell its 1862 issue of $500 million so-called 5–20 bonds (6 percent bonds that were redeemable in five years and matured in twenty), he appointed Cooke the sole agent for this critical issue.

Cooke now expanded his promotional efforts. Employing an army of some 2,500 bankers and private subagents to market the 5–20s, Cooke supervised them by using the most modern communications technology, the telegraph and the railroad. Using his brother Henry's newspaper connections, he planted favorable stories about the issue in strategic newspapers. Through these means, Cooke peddled the 5–20s to anyone who would invest.

In conjunction with the 5–20 campaign, Cooke also helped Secretary Chase institute a national banking system. Although Chase had important support for this plan in Congress, in January 1863 he enlisted Jay and Henry to promote the idea. Again they wrote articles favorable to the new system and planted them in friendly papers. The Cookes went further; in another innovation they placed clippings of newspaper stories from hometown papers on congressmen's desks. Thus, Cook used his 5–20 system to promote the national banking idea. After the legislation passed, Secretary Chase wrote Jay that "your services . . . are fully appreciated by me" (Larson, 139).

Cooke's 5–20 campaign was such a brilliant success that Chase retained him as sole agent for the 5–20s after July 1, 1863, when he could have terminated the relationship. The move was generally well received. Union victories at Gettysburg, Vicksburg, and Chattanooga helped sell the bonds; by November the Treasury was $33 million in arrears on orders. Finally, the 5–20 loan sold out at $500 million on January 21, 1864.

The 5–20 campaign netted Cooke a profit of $22,054.49, out of which he paid his advertising costs, travel expenses of his agents, freight, and postage.

His risk had been high since he put the credit of his banking house behind the government's issue, but his profit was substantial.

When the 5–20 loan closed, Cooke's special relationship with the Treasury ended. Mounting criticism of the Chase-Cooke connection and a hint of scandal in Henry Cooke's involvement in an insider scheme made Chase shy away from another special relationship with the banker. Chase could have used Cooke's machine to help market the slow-selling 1863 issue of $900 million in 10–40 bonds (redeemable after ten years and maturing in forty), but he chose not to. Although the war was going well for the Union in 1864, the Treasury was still strapped for cash. At the close of the fiscal year, the government had $18.8 million in cash, $71.8 million in unpaid requisitions, and a $161.8 million debt. The war cost $2 million a day. Secretary Chase chose this point to resign from the cabinet.

Cooke was shocked at Chase's resignation. He had worked diligently for the Union cause and for the inside track to the secretary's office. He hoped that another Ohio friend, John Sherman, would replace Chase, but President Abraham Lincoln (q.v.) selected the Mainer William Pitt Fessenden. The new secretary made it clear that he would not employ Cooke as exclusive bond agent. However, in June 1864 Congress authorized a three-year loan of $300 million at 7.3 percent (called "7–30s"). As usual, sales were slow, and the secretary suggested a partnership between Cooke and the New York banker Morris Ketchum to market the issue. At first amenable to the deal, Cooke soon learned that Ketchum was trying to depress the government securities market. He was livid and exposed the nasty business to Fessenden, who ended the joint project. Shortly before he left the Treasury to return to the Senate, Fessenden made Cooke sole agent for the 7–30 issue and for the languishing 10–40s as well.

Cooke ran the 7–30 campaign much as he had the 5–20. His agents fanned out across the country to sell the bonds. They entered Southern communities that had recently fallen under federal control, and they sold bonds to soldiers in the field. He also advertised them widely in newspapers around the country. As his biographer Ellis Paxson Oberholtzer points out, Cooke brought the government money that people had hidden away.

The campaign was Cooke's triumph. By the end of February 1865 he was selling $9.5 million a day. The issue sold so well that in March Congress authorized a $300 million second series of the loan, and in May a third series of $230 million. When the loan closed at the end of July, Cooke had sold $830 million of the 7–30s. His reputation as a financial genius was now secure; his brilliant organization, his ambition, his dedication to the Union cause became legendary.

The war was barely over when Cooke received an overture from William L. Banning, president of the Lake Shore and Mississippi Railroad, seeking the banker's services as the fiscal agent of the road. Cooke declined the honor then, and again in 1866 and 1867. But by 1868 Cooke's circumstances had changed. With government business dropping off, Cooke's partners urged him to look for other opportunities. Fahnestock championed opening a London office and going after the foreign commercial business that other bankers were exploiting. But Cooke had never been much interested in European investment. Ever the patriot and nationalist, he sought his fortune in the American West.

Cooke was no stranger to western land speculation. Before the end of the war, he had purchased several thousand acres of Iowa farmland. The overtures from Banning and other Minnesota men no doubt drew his curiosity, and he sent his agent Rice Harper there to look around. Harper's report no doubt fired Cooke's developmental instincts, and in June 1868 he traveled there to see the place for himself. What he saw was the future—vast agriculture on the high plains and extraction of natural resources, principally iron ore, all moving by rail to Duluth, which Cooke hoped would be another Chicago, where it would be processed and shipped on the Great Lakes to eastern ports. He accumulated land in Duluth and farmland outside the village and purchased a $10,000 interest in the Western Land Association, which owned 7,000 town sites and 4,000 acres in St. Louis County. Word of Cooke's involvement caused a speculative boom in the town. By 1873 the population had swelled from 100 souls to 5,000.

The key to making these investments pay off was development of the Northern Pacific Railroad connecting Duluth with the Mississippi and Missouri Rivers, the Great Plains, and the Pacific. In May 1869, only a week after the linking of the Union and Central Pacific Railroads to form the first transcontinental railroad, Cooke signed an agreement with the Northern Pacific to sell $100 million of its 7.3 percent bonds and to be the railroad's banker. Attracted by the opportunity for development of his property, Cooke was also enticed by the sweep and boldness of the project. Whereas the Union Pacific–Central Pacific feat had been accomplished by two railroads that had the benefit of government largess, the Northern Pacific would accomplish a similar feat by only one company operating with a generous government land grant but no government cash. It would be the longest continuous rail line in the country and would spur the economic development of the entire region. It would serve as a giant promotional scheme to attract thousands of settlers to the area.

Cooke took on this project with characteristic energy and optimism. But significant hurdles lay in his path. His idea was to sell stock in the railroad through his usual publicity machine to raise the capital needed to start construction. That early construction would encourage immigrants, already approaching flood tide, to settle on the rich lands of the Great Plains. Cooke needed to encourage well-known businessmen and investors to buy stock in the railroad so he could use their involvement for publicity purposes. He did not succeed in that effort. Cooke also needed to get congressional approval for the railroad to mortgage its federal land grant. The request naturally drew opposition from competing railroads and the congressmen who supported them. It also drew a vigorous attack on the entire enterprise from the Philadelphia *Ledger*, which condemned the "huge robberies of the public domain" by the road and the huge commissions made by the businessmen involved in the project (Larson, 290). Cooke was not without political and journalistic resources in this struggle, and in May 1870, Congress passed the Land Grant Mortgage Bill.

Although successful with Congress, Cooke found marketing the Northern Pacific in the United States and Europe an uphill battle. From 1870 to 1873 he worked doggedly to make the operation go. Construction of the railroad commenced with seed money from Cooke and progressed toward the investors' first target, the Red River. Yet completion of track put more pressure on the company to spend money it didn't have on purchasing rolling stock. The effort to sell bonds in Europe, made difficult by the dubious reputation of American railroad enterprises, collapsed with the onset of the Franco-Prussian War in 1870. This meant that Cooke had to market the entire stock issue to domestic investors. His associates advised caution. Harris Fahnestock specifically urged him to stop pouring Cooke & Co. money into the railroad. But Cooke was not one to back away from a potentially profitable deal.

Financial markets forced on Cooke what he could not do himself. The tightening currency market and the resulting increased cost of money led Cooke to urge Treasury Secretary Hugh McCulloch to purchase $3 million in government bonds from the financial houses, thus putting more money in circulation. Indeed, Cooke was so desperate for cash that he wanted McCulloch to recirculate the $40 million in greenbacks that the secretary had retired.

None of these moves was sufficient to buoy up the deeply troubled economy. Cooke simply ran out of cash and could not pay the drafts that came due from the Northern Pacific. Unsuccessful efforts to find investors either in the United States or abroad led the Philadelphia house of Cooke & Co. to close on September 18, 1873. The closing came in the midst of a severely astringent market, and the news of the closing sent the stock market into a tailspin. The root cause of this vast collapse is not far to seek; Cooke and other money men simply forgot they were bankers and saw themselves as promoters.

James J. Hill completed the Northern Pacific Railroad in 1888. By that time Cooke had admitted defeat, declared bankruptcy, and moved on to an involvement in western mining. He sold his organizational skills for stock in the Horn Silver Mining Company and in January 1880 sold that stock for $800,000. Other mining companies clamored for his high-priced talent, and soon he had recovered his lost fortune and property. With his son-in-law managing his affairs, Cooke devoted his remaining years to fishing. He died on February 16, 1905.

The Cookes erected a monument to Jay Cooke in 1921. Commissioned from New York sculptor Henry Merwin Shrady, the Cooke family donated it to the city of Duluth after Philadelphia officials turned them down. Duluth dedicated a small park for the statue, adjacent to Lake Superior, across from an exclusive businessmen's club, and at the intersection of Duluth's main commercial street and its wealthy district. The statue depicts Cooke seated, hat on his crossed knee, faithful dog at his side. The words ''Pioneer-Patriot-Financier'' appear on the base below his name.

In 1921 Duluth was on the brink of explosive growth, and identifying with

Cooke connected the city to the reputed man of vision and genius. No ruthless and predatory entrepreneur he, Cooke was the archetype of the responsible and patriotic financier. When time eroded the beauty of the statue site in Duluth, city fathers faced a choice. Rather than move the statue to some remote location in the city, they decided to rehabilitate the site and thus preserve the association of Cooke with the lake, the railroad, and the town.

The fate of the Duluth statue reflects the trajectory of Cooke's reputation, which continues in a positive, upward direction. Yet Cooke's legacy to Duluth and to the nation is ambiguous. In 1870 the "Cooke Bubble" was well under way in the little village on Lake Superior. Two out of three residents worked for a Cooke enterprise, and the population swelled. When the economy collapsed and Cooke shut down in 1873, 75 percent of Duluth's population fled the town. In 1875 Duluth lost its city charter and became a village again. The "Cooke Bubble" had burst. But Duluthians, like the rest of the nation, prefer to remember Cooke as the "Robert Morris of the Civil War" and as a "Pioneer-Patriot-Financier."

Historians have contributed to sustaining Cooke's reputation as a patriot and visionary. There are only two biographies of Cooke, Ellis Paxson Oberholtzer's two-volume 1907 work *Jay Cooke: Financier of the Civil War* and Henrietta M. Larson's *Jay Cooke: Private Banker* (1936). Both works celebrate Cooke the financier, the patriot, the man of vision. Oberholtzer's is a comprehensive but uncritical biography. Larson's work, also laudatory, focuses on Cooke the businessman. She celebrates his linking personal gain with patriotism and sees him as a pioneer of modern American banking. The institutions he pioneered live on despite his failure, she says. Those he trained helped introduce modern banking practices.

The only other book-length study of Cooke's career is John S. Harnsberger's *Jay Cooke and Minnesota: The Formative Years of the Northern Pacific Railroad, 1868–1873*. A 1956 University of Minnesota Ph.D. dissertation, Harnsberger's work recounts in minute detail how Cooke assembled the properties to build the railroad. He is critical of Cooke for losing sight of his goals and overextending himself, although he notes that Cooke was not alone in this. Harnsberger drew on his dissertation for the 1960 article "Land, Lobbies, Railroads and the Origins of Duluth" in *Minnesota History*. Here again, he notes Cooke's failures but, like Larson, judges him to be a man ahead of his time, an ambitious builder and visionary, a precursor of the captains of American industry. He saw what the region would become but could not himself bring it to fruition.

Timothy Garvey offers a critical commentary on Cooke in two articles, "The Jay Cooke Monument as Civic Revisionism: Promotional Imagination in Bronze and Stone" (1983) and "The Jay Cooke Monument: A Postscript" (1984). Garvey portrays Cooke as a garden-variety capitalist, concerned about profits and unconcerned about the damage caused by the quest. He provides a penetrating insight into the power of Cooke's reputation by focusing on Duluth's persistent embrace of a man whose failure brought misery to the town.

Cooke makes an appearance in Matthew Josephson's *The Robber Barons: The Great American Capitalists, 1861–1901* (1934, 1987). Here he is a scheming capitalist with no redeeming value, like all the rest of Josephson's parade of horribles. A much more balanced view of Cooke's contribution to the Union War effort is in John Niven's *Salmon P. Chase: A Biography* (1995). Niven portrays Cooke as a banker who was bent on getting government business but who was deeply committed to the Union cause. He provides a tantalizing look at the Cooke political machine, spearheaded by brother Henry, which provided access to the highest levels of government.

Cooke's reputation has withstood a few attempts at revisionism. His wartime activities have been well formulated, although Niven's glimpse of the politics of banking suggests terrain still to be plowed. Except for Garvey's articles, revisionism has not disturbed his postwar reputation. Development, exploitation of natural resources, and dislodgment of indigenous peoples are fertile areas for scholarship.

BIBLIOGRAPHY

Ellis Paxson Oberholtzer, *Jay Cooke: Financier of the Civil War*, 2 vols. (Philadelphia: George W. Jacobs and Co., 1907).

Matthew Josephson, *The Robber Barons: The Great American Capitalists, 1861–1901* (New York: Harcourt, Brace and Company, 1934).

Henrietta M. Larson, *Jay Cooke: Private Banker* (Cambridge: Harvard University Press, 1936).

John S. Harnsberger, *Jay Cooke and Minnesota: The Formative Years of the Northern Pacific Railroad, 1868–1873* (Ph.D. diss., University of Minnesota, 1956; New York: Arno Press, 1981).

John S. Harnsberger, "Land, Lobbies, Railroads and the Origins of Duluth," *Minnesota History* 37, no. 3 (September 1960): 89–100.

Howard Popowski, "Grandaddy of the Greenback," *Civil War Times Illustrated* 21, no. 8 (1982): 28–35.

Timothy Garvey, "The Jay Cooke Monument as Civic Revisionism: Promotional Imagination in Bronze and Stone," *Old Northwest* 9, no. 1 (1983): 37–57.

Timothy Garvey, "The Jay Cooke Monument: A Postscript," *Old Northwest* 10, no. 2 (1984): 209–211.

John Niven, *Salmon P. Chase: A Biography* (New York: Oxford University Press, 1995).

CHARLES ANDERSON DANA
(August 8, 1819–October 17, 1897)

Charles F. Ritter

The Civil War saved Charles Dana's career. With a wife and four children to support in 1862, the forty-two-year-old newspaperman was out of a job, dismissed by Horace Greeley after fifteen years as managing editor of the *New York Tribune*. Dana quickly landed a position in the U.S. War Department and soon became a confidant of Secretary of War Edwin Stanton (q.v.) and President Abraham Lincoln (q.v.). The political and social contacts he made in his three years in the War Department enabled Dana to purchase the *New York Sun* in 1868 and launch a brilliant twenty-nine-year career as one of the most influential journalists of the Gilded Age.

Dana was born in modest circumstances in Hinsdale, New Hampshire, on August 8, 1819, the eldest of four children. His father was Anderson Dana, who James H. Wilson characterized as a "self-centered ne'er-do-well." A failed country store keeper, Anderson Dana was a poor relation to the more prosperous Massachusetts Danas. His mother, Ann Dennison, died in 1829 when Charles was nine years old. Financially unable and emotionally unwilling to care for his children, Anderson Dana abandoned them to various relatives. Charles went first to his uncle David Dennison's Connecticut farm, and in 1831, he was shipped off to Buffalo, New York, where he lived with his uncle William Dana and worked in the dry goods store of Staats & Dana.

Charles Dana was an ambitious young man, evidently determined not to have his hardscrabble background hold him back. Before he was twenty, and with only limited country schooling, he taught himself Latin, Greek, and the dialect spoken by the local Seneca. One member of his widening circle of associates, Dr. Austin Flint, was a Harvard graduate. Through him Dana matriculated at Harvard in 1835, where he excelled. Janet Steele says going to Harvard was an "astonishing achievement" for one of Dana's impoverished background. Deteriorating eyesight and perhaps tight finances forced Dana to leave Harvard in

1841; twenty years later Harvard awarded him an honorary B.A. as a member of the class of 1843.

At Harvard, Dana fell under the spell of Transcendentalists Ralph Waldo Emerson and George Ripley. By 1841 Emerson and Ripley and such other lights as Theodore Parker and Orestes Brownson had become disenchanted with the Unitarian Church's drift toward the Boston establishment. Ripley left the ministry and established the Brook Farm community in the winter of 1840 in the Boston suburb of West Roxbury. Invited to join, Dana purchased three of the twenty-four community shares and became Brook Farm's teacher of Greek and German—another of the half-dozen languages he learned during his lifetime—a trustee, and the director of the farm's finances.

At Brook Farm, Dana was exposed to the ideas of Fourierism, a social philosophy imported from France and based on the idea of the perfectibility of humankind living in small agrarian cooperatives. Given his economically marginal background, Dana readily took to the idea of producer solidarity. In his early writings for Brook Farm's publication the *Harbinger*, the future editor decried the "increasing poverty of the producing classes" and saw individualism as "the poisonous fruit" of an industrializing society. What he and other Brook Farmers derived from Fourierist ideas was a cooperative socialism in which joint stock owners profitted according to their share.

Dana met his wife at Brook Farm. Traveling with her family from Maryland to join the cooperative experiment, Eunice MacDaniel married Dana in New York City on March 6, 1846 (later Eunice's brother Osborne married Dana's sister Maria). Returning to the farm, the Danas discovered that the new Fourierist living quarters, the phalanstery, had burned to the ground on their wedding day. Uninsured, the building was a total loss and the experiment at West Roxbury was at an end.

After reading copy briefly for the Boston *Daily Chronotype*, Dana contacted Horace Greeley, a Brook Farm acquaintance, and got a job at the *New York Tribune*, first as city editor, then as the managing editor. In 1848 Dana traveled to Europe to report on political turmoil there, much to the displeasure of Greeley, who felt that one European correspondent was enough. But Dana wanted to see conditions for himself. What he saw undermined his Fourierist convictions— although not his faith in working people. Reporting first on the popular uprising in Paris and then in Berlin, Dana was sympathetic to the workers whom he saw as being caught in a class struggle with wealth and privilege. Yet the failures of the 1848 revolutions undermined Dana's attachment to radicalism and led him to advocate gradual reform.

Returning to New York, Dana settled into managing the *Tribune* for Greeley. In his fifteen years at the paper, he made it one of the most influential journals in the country by assembling an outstanding staff of writers—George Ripley, George William Curtis, Margaret Fuller, Karl Marx—and followed a strong Whig Republican editorial line. Ardently free soil and antislavery, the *Tribune* played a key role in bringing the Republican party into existence.

The events of the secession winter brought to the surface a long-smoldering conflict between Greeley and Dana. Dana did not believe secession was constitutional; Greeley would have allowed the "erring sisters to depart in peace." Despite his boss's timid attitude toward secession, Dana put the *Tribune* on record as forcefully opposing it; the paper carried the banner "No Concessions to Traitors!" After the firing on Fort Sumter, Dana beat out the refrain "Forward to Richmond" until the debacle at Bull Run. While Greeley apologized publicly for the *Tribune*'s banner campaign, Dana pressed his belief that the Union had to stamp out the heresy of secession. By then Greeley had had enough of Dana's freewheeling style and put an ultimatum to the *Tribune*'s board of trustees that either he or Dana had to go.

Out of a job and with no journalistic prospects, Dana had at least three offers from key members of Lincoln's cabinet whom the *Tribune* had supported. Dana chose the offer from Secretary of War Edwin Stanton and soon found himself in Cairo, Illinois, investigating government contractors. While in Cairo, Dana deliberately sought out military officials. He met Ulysses S. Grant (q.v.) at Memphis, Tennessee, in July 1862 and found him "a man of simple manner, straightford, cordial, and unpretending (Dana, 15). He told Secretary Stanton that Grant was pragmatic, a man of action.

His War Department job done, Dana briefly joined Roscoe Conkling and George W. Chadwick in a lucrative venture purchasing Confederate cotton for Northern mills. Sensitive to Grant's condemnation of this practice, Dana advised Stanton to put an end to the trade. Impressed with Dana's advice, which ran counter to his pecuniary interests, the Secretary of War gave Dana another mission. Ostensibly sent to investigate the pay service of the western armies, Dana's real mission was to spy on Grant for the secretary and the president. They wanted to "settle their minds as to Grant," Dana said in his *Recollections of the Civil War* (21). They had "many doubts" about the general, Dana noted, particularly about his drinking.

Dana caught up with Grant at Vicksburg, Mississippi, in April 1863. Despite Dana's cover story, James H. Wilson says in his biography of Dana that everyone on Grant's staff knew why the New Yorker was there and that their futures depended upon what he saw. They decided to bring him into the inner circle and keep him fully informed. Already predisposed toward Grant, Dana fell in easily with the group and sent Stanton glowing reports of Grant's plans. Seeing that the general's ability to lead men and win battles outweighed his occasional bouts with the bottle, Dana lied implicitly to the Secretary of War and explicitly to Senator Elihu Washburn about Grant's binge drinking, which he witnessed aboard the U.S.S. *Diligent* in early June 1863. There can be no doubt that Dana's discretion helped save Grant's career and thus influenced the course of the war.

Given Dana's status as "the eyes of the government at the front" (as Lincoln called him), he wielded considerable influence. He helped end the military career of a Grant opponent and obstacle, John A. McClernand, and he opened the way for Grant's ascendency by maneuvering the removal of William Rosecrans after the Union defeat at Chickamauga. Grant replaced Rosecrans at Chattanooga, and his success in breaking Braxton Bragg's (q.v.) siege sent Grant's star into the ascendency and him to the rank of lieutenant general with command of all the Union armies.

Named Assistant Secretary of War in July 1863, Dana returned to Washington from Chattanooga to work on supply contracts. But he preferred being in the field—''[C]ampaigning I found very agreeable and very wholesome,'' he wrote to his former reporter friend and then minister to Holland James S. Pike. He finished the War commuting between Grant's field headquarters in Virginia and the War Department in Washington.

With the war over, Dana found himself out of a job for the second time in three years, but this time he was not without journalistic prospects. Although he says in his *Recollections* that he did not consider pursuing a journalistic career again, in fact he wrote to his friend James Pike that ''I have various offers. . . . Among the best are 2 or 3 relating to newspapers in the west'' (Steele, 61). Indeed, his reputation as a Republican mover and shaker prompted a group of Republican businessmen in Chicago to invite him to take over their newly pur- chased and reorganized *Chicago Republican* and make it a rival to Joseph Me- dill's powerful *Chicago Tribune*.

Dana's career at the *Republican* was brief; taking over the paper in July 1865, he was back in New York in May 1866, after running afoul of the board of trustees' political sentiments by using the paper to attack Andrew Johnson's (q.v.) Reconstruction program, which he found too accommodating to the South. The trustees dismissed him when President Johnson disclosed that Dana had secretly sought the coveted and lucrative collectorship of the Port of New York. Dana, who could be idealistic, was periodically undermined by what Janet Steele calls his ''great thirst for money and power.''

Between May 1867 and the fall of 1868 Dana drew on his considerable in- fluence with prominent New York Republicans to raise $110,000, which he used to buy Moses Beach's *New York Sun*. Considering his syndicate of backers— which included William Evarts, Roscoe Conkling, Alonzo Cornell, and Cyrus Field—Dana's purchase of the venerable *Sun*, so long identified as a sensation- alistic sheet directed at the city's Democratic, working-class population, was astonishing.

Over the next twenty-nine years, Dana turned the *Sun* into one of New York's highest circulation newspapers, which generated interest far beyond the city's environs. This popularity reflected the trim look Dana gave his paper and the stable of high-quality editors and writers he assembled—among them Henry B. Stanton (Elizabeth Cady Stanton's reformer husband), Francis P. Church (''Yes, Virginia, there is a Santa Claus''), his old friend from *New York Tribune* days James S. Pike, and the socialist and labor agitator John Swinton. Dana's political views were too erratic for the *Sun* to be politically influential, but the sheet was widely popular with the working class; New York's bastion of Republican re- spectability, the Century Club, did not subscribe.

Dana did not condescend to his working-class readers but carried his own class sensibilities into the coverage of politics and labor affairs. From his modest background and socialist experiences, Dana more than most saw the class implications of industrialization. He also was sensitive to the class origins and implications of reformers' programs that lent support to the exploitation of labor by the postbellum industrial machine. Dana's emphasis on respect for cultural diversity and religious toleration, his support for civil rights for the freed people, and his adherence to Fourierist worker cooperativism rendered him a unique voice in an era when the party journalism of the postbellum period was dying and the commercial, business-oriented journalism of the twentieth century was aborning.

Aside from these dependable themes, no one could predict what would appear in the *Sun*. Dana supported Grant's presidential bid in 1868, perhaps as a quid pro quo to his Republican backers, and then turned against his former friend, perhaps because he lost out on yet another bid for the collectorship of the Port of New York. Although identified thereafter as a solidly Democratic paper, Dana's *Sun* opposed the nomination and then the election of Grover Cleveland in 1884. Calling Cleveland "a coarse debauchee" because he fathered an illegitimate child, Dana suggested that if elected he would "bring his harlots to Washington" (Steele, 131). Refusing to support the Republican nominee James G. Blaine against Cleveland, Dana threw his weight behind the marginal candidacy of the Greenback-Labor candidate, Benjamin Butler.

Dana's rejection of both major party candidates in 1884 was symptomatic of his distaste for establishment figures and programs. Regarding both as self-serving and hypocritical, he never tired of spewing his venom at them. Indeed, he never missed an opportunity to take down a prominent reform figure. Henry Ward Beecher (q.v.) is another example. An enormous icon of respectable reform—antislavery, abolition, temperance, woman suffrage—in 1872 Beecher was exposed in the press as having an affair with Elizabeth Tilton, a prominent member of Beecher's politically posh Brooklyn Heights Plymouth Church and wife of Theodore Tilton, a former Beecher associate and editor of the important Congregational journal *Independent*. Although exonerated of all charges by a jury of Plymouth Church parishioners, and by a hung jury in Tilton's $100,000 damage suit, Dana crucified Beecher in the *Sun* during the trials, after the trials, and even after his death. He characterized the pastor as a "perjurer," a "liar," an "adulterer," a "debaucher," and an "old grey-headed seducer." He even attacked Beecher's son Herbert, calling him an opium smuggler. In 1891 Dana revived the scandal upon the dedication of a bronze statue of the former minister.

The vitriol he heaped on the likes of Beecher and Cleveland cost Dana dearly. The *Sun*'s circulation fell precipitously after the election of 1884, from 145,000 a day to 82,300, losing 43.4 percent of his readers in two years. Since Dana restricted advertising to 25 percent of the *Sun*'s space, such a drop in readership was disastrous. Another reason for the circulation decline was competition from Joseph Pulitzer's upstart *New York World*. Purchased from Jay Gould in 1883, the *World* had a readership of 25,000, but it also had an Associated Press franchise. In three years Pulitzer had almost 150,000 working-class readers of his own special brand of traditional sensationalism—vice, crime, and violence. Pulitzer also stayed firmly attached to mainstream Democratic ideology.

Dana's anti-Beecher and anti-Cleveland campaigns, and the challenge from Pulitzer, gave the *Sun*'s board of trustees ample reason to remove the eccentric editor, although there is no clear evidence to support the rumors of an impending coup. Nevertheless, Dana moved quickly to save his job. He borrowed almost $40,000 from Samuel J. Tilden—whose political career Dana championed long after it was over—and he may have mortgaged his house to purchase more shares in the paper. He also modernized the paper's machinery—installing new presses and the Linotype, which once he had resisted. His updated and expanded paper (from four pages to six, eight, twelve, sixteen pages as the occasion warranted) met Pulitzer's competition head-on. By 1893 the *Sun* had regained a circulation of 120,000, although it still lagged behind the *World*'s 170,000 readers.

When the Democratic party succumbed to Populism and nominated William Jennings Bryan in 1896, Dana took the paper back to its original Republican home. He regarded the Democratic platform, with its appeal to an income tax and currency inflation through free silver, as "the wild light of anarchy" (Steele, 154). Although suspicious of the intolerance of the Republican proprietary class and its exploitation of workers, he remained confident in the ultimate benefits of industrial society for all people.

After 1873 Dana's home was on Deicers, an island attached by a bridge to the mainland of Long Island near Glen Cove. There he enjoyed a domestic life of entertaining American and European luminaries, supervising his exotic flower gardens, and entertaining his children and grandchildren. He died there on October 17, 1897. The *Sun* carried his death notice (no obituary) the next day on page two. As was his wish, it read: "Charles Anderson Dana, Editor of the *Sun*, died yesterday afternoon." His understated death notice emphasizes his wish to separate his public from his private life. He did not save his correspondence because he wished to be known from his editorials in the paper.

Although there is no full modern biography of Dana, he has not lacked for biographical treatment. James H. Wilson published *The Life of Charles A. Dana* in 1907. Wilson met the editor in 1862 when Wilson was on Grant's staff at Vicksburg. His bond with Dana was immediate and strong and they remained friends and confidants. Although hagiographical, Wilson's *Life of Dana* provides insights into Dana's character and some previously unavailable documentary material.

Frank M. O'Brien, a *Sun* reporter, published a biography of the paper in 1918, *The Story of the Sun*, where Dana makes an appearance midway through the story. On the other hand, O'Brien makes it clear that Dana *was the Sun*. That is Charles J. Rosebault's point in his biography *When Dana Was the Sun: A Story of Personal Journalism* (1931). Rosebault, another *Sun* reporter, gives equal treatment to Dana's career before and after 1865, as does Alfred H. Fenton in his *Dana of the Sun* (1941). Both are celebratory and uncritical works, although Rosebault's book provides some insight into the working of the *Sun*'s editorial office.

The best early biography of Dana is Candace Stone's *Dana and the Sun* (1938). Stone focuses almost exclusively on Dana's life at the *Sun*, devoting only her first chapter to his life before he purchased the paper in 1867. She deals extensively with Dana's various editorial positions, and provides a multidimensional picture of the editor in all his literary glory, his political eccentricity, and at his vitriolic worst.

Vernon Louis Parrington in *The Beginnings of Critical Realism in America, 1860–1920* (1930, 1987) puts Dana in an interpretive frame that characterizes the editor as selling out to industrial materialism. Calling Dana a "disillusioned idealist," Parrington saw Dana's life as a "cynical commentary on the changing spirit of America" (43), a spirit that Parrington says plunged the nation into acquisitiveness. In Parrington's hands, Dana became "the apologist and defender of capitalism" (44). He says that Dana's support for a high tariff and sound money and his contemptuousness of the farmer's plight indicated that he had abandoned the idealism of Brook Farm and embraced the material world of Mark Hanna.

In her fine book *The Sun Shines for All: Journalism and Ideology in the Life of Charles A. Dana* (1993), Janet Steele says that Parrington's view of Dana is lopsided. She argues that Dana carried his Brook Farm vision into the postbellum period and notes that his poll star was always the welfare of working people. He supported private property, she says, because he believed the benefits of ownership should accrue to all. He favored a protective tariff, she says, in order to protect workers' wages, and he supported sound money to ensure the integrity of those wages. She argues that he attacked reformers because he saw them as bigoted hypocrites who tried to confine diversity and homogenize people into an Anglo-Protestant ethic designed to control the lower and unruly orders. He opposed union-led strikes, but not unions, she says, because they were counterproductive, and he supported the old Fourierist idea of worker cooperatives instead. She concludes that he carried his social vision to the end.

In the hiatus between Stone's and Steele's biographies, most scholarly attention focused on Dana's Civil War career. Serving in the War Department for only three years, Dana cut a wide swath in Washington and in the field. In 1898, D. Appleton & Co. posthumously published Dana's *Recollections of the Civil War*. This book was ghostwritten by Ida Tarbell and comprised a series of articles she wrote for *McClure's Magazine*. Based on Tarbell's research into published and unpublished sources, *Recollections* consists of a series of interviews she had with Dana during the winter of 1896–1897. He saw only one article before he died. Appleton reprinted *Recollections* in 1902, and there have been two subsequent editions.

Recollections provides a bird's-eye view of operations in Grant's camp and in the field and catches a sense of urgency and breathlessness at certain moments. Yet his account can be remarkably deceptive. There can be no doubt, for instance, that Dana witnessed Grant's binge drinking aboard the *Diligent* on June 6–7, 1863. Yet Dana recorded that Grant became ''ill and went to bed'' (83), and never reported the incident to Secretary Stanton. William F. McFeeley provides a comprehensive account of the incident, and Dana's part in it, in *Grant: A Biography* (1981).

Another event recorded in *Recollections* in which Dana played a critical role was the removal of William Rosecrans after the Union defeat at Chickamauga. While Dana accurately reflects his ill feelings for the general, he is less than candid about his wish to remove Rosecrans to make way for Grant. William M. Lamers makes the case for Rosecrans and against Dana in *The Edge of Glory* (1961) and brings considerable contemporary evidence to bear against Dana's soundness of judgment. Roy Morris, Jr., is more severe on Dana in ''A Bird of Evil Omen'' (1987). Calling the Assistant Secretary of War ''inscrutable'' (20) and arguing that he represented a greater threat to Rosecrans than the Confederate Army, Morris makes clear that Dana wanted Grant in.

Charles Dana's wartime service is still controversial, but there seems to be a consensus regarding his journalistic career. There is no question that Dana was a great journalist, if an eccentric one. And there can be no doubt that he had a profound influence during the war. Whether that influence exceeded his abilities, whether he was a ''loathsome pimp,'' (Morris, 28) as General Gordon Granger called him, or whether he was a prescient observer and wise adviser to Stanton and Lincoln—these are open questions. Certainly events proved Dana right— Grant succeeded where others failed—and perhaps that is all he needs to keep his reputation intact.

BIBLIOGRAPHY

Charles Dana, *Recollections of the Civil War* (New York: D. Appleton & Co., 1898).
James H. Wilson, *The Life of Charles A. Dana* (New York: Harper and Bros. Publishers, 1907).
Frank M. O'Brien, *The Story of the Sun* (New York: George H. Doran, 1918).
Vernon Louis Parrington, *The Beginnings of Critical Realism in America, 1860–1920*, Vol. 3 of Main Currents in American Thought (1930; Norman: University of Oklahoma Press, 1987).
Charles J. Rosebault, *When Dana Was the Sun: A Story of Personal Journalism* (New York: Robert M. McBride and Co., 1931).
Candace Stone, *Dana and the Sun* (New York: Dodd, Meade and Co., 1938).
Alfred H. Fenton, *Dana of the Sun* (New York: Farrar & Rinehart, Inc., 1941).
William M. Lamers, *The Edge of Glory* (New York: Harcourt, Brace, and World, 1961).
William F. McFeeley, *Grant: A Biography* (New York: W. W. Norton, 1981).
Roy Morris, Jr., ''A Bird of Evil Omen,'' *Civil War Times Illustrated* 25, no. 9 (January 1987): 20–29.
Janet Steele, *The Sun Shines for All: Journalism and Ideology in the Life of Charles A. Dana* (Syracuse: Syracuse University Press, 1993).

JEFFERSON FINIS DAVIS
(June 3, 1808–December 6, 1889)

Jon L. Wakelyn

In order to set the historical record straight on the life and accomplishments of her much maligned late husband—the Confederacy's President Jefferson Davis—the grieving but determined widow Varina Howell Davis (q.v.) plunged into her account with the claim that "he was universally regarded, both at home and abroad, as pre-eminently the representative of a great era, a great cause, and a great people" (1:1). She had indeed described something of the swirl of defensiveness that has come down through history of a man considered by many to have been overmatched and underzealous for a revolutionary task, while many others claim no other could have done a better job. In her life of Davis, based mostly on his unpublished memoirs and her memory usually of the good times, Mrs. Davis gives historians a portrait at once distant and personal but often confused about the many skills her husband needed to govern a region in insurrection against its own country. Varina also had described a man deeply loyal to the idea of his native land, yet the leader of those who would make a separate nation. The true record of his accomplishments must then relate to a man confused over what his proper activities were to have been.

Perhaps another look at that leader's life will allow us to grasp the contradictions between talent and motivation that so marked his long and often useful life. All accounts of his early life state that young Jefferson Davis was raised in a successful border and later Deep South family. Rough, outgoing, and filled with a certain devilishness, Jefferson Finis was the youngest son of Samuel Emory Davis, a Revolutionary War veteran and an ever-moving small farmer. His mother was Jane Cook, whom his father met and married in Georgia. Soon after the war they left Georgia with their growing family and headed for the fertile lands of southern Kentucky. Eventually they settled in Hopkinsville, Christian County (later Todd County), where Jefferson was born on June 3, 1808. Like many a small slaveowner, Samuel and his sons worked hard to produce a meager crop. But they did not find success in Kentucky, and they removed first to Louisiana, then to Mississippi near rich bottom land. The family had followed a successful older son, Joseph, who soon would replace his elderly father as Jefferson's role model. Joseph became wealthy and then socially ambitious as he rose into a position of prominence in the newly developed region of the lower Mississippi Valley. The older brother doted on young Jefferson and sent him at the age of seven back to Kentucky to attend the prestigious St. Thomas Academy, a Roman Catholic preparatory school in Washington County. After two years in Kentucky he came back to school in Mississippi. In 1821 he went to college at Transylvania University in Kentucky, then a training ground for some of the wealthiest families in the upper South. If he learned little in the way of schooling at university, Jefferson had acquired the habits of a member of the Southern plantation elite.

But his brother had other plans than a life of leisure for his headstrong younger brother. Joseph used his political influence to get Jefferson appointed to the U.S. Military Academy at West Point, New York, in 1824. At the Military Academy the then gregarious Jefferson made many friends who would later assist his career, earned the wrath of his instructors, and incurred many demerits for his hard drinking and general rowdiness. A poor student, he graduated near the bottom of the class of 1828. At that time he was a young man with little ambition and less direction who assumed the life of an officer and a gentleman.

Tall, thin, erect, and considered quite handsome, Jefferson Davis entered the U.S. Army as a second lieutenant of cavalry and held various dull frontier posts, which included a fleeting moment of warriordom in the Black Hawk War. On the Wisconsin frontier he grew close to fort commander Zachary Taylor and to the commander's young daughter. He fell in love with Sarah Knox Taylor, and against the wishes of her father, they married in 1835. Determined to return to the life of leisure on his brother's Mississippi plantation, Jefferson resigned from the army. But the beautiful Sarah died of malaria only three months after the wedding, and the ex-officer himself contracted that dreaded disease, which periodically would sap his strength for the remainder of his life. Despondent, near desperation, he retreated under his brother's wing and took up planting in a desultory fashion. He read voraciously, traveled extensively, and lived a gloomy, isolated life. But he soon became a successful planter, the master of ''Briarfield'' plantation, and thanks to his brother's encouragement, began slow forays into local politics.

He became a state's rights Democrat in that staunchly Whig stronghold of the Natchez region and somehow gained a seat in the U.S. House of Representatives in 1845. Not content to see his younger brother waste the opportunity for additional family social prestige, Joseph contrived a meeting for Jefferson with Varina Howell, daughter of an impecunious but upper-class Yankee settler in Natchez. Struck by each other's good looks, and with the ambitions for prominence of Varina, the courtship led to marriage. Jefferson was considerably older than Varina, but the two people well understood how both could gain from their union. On their honeymoon they discussed politics and Jefferson's future and

.

attended political gatherings, which Varina loved. But they also visited Sarah's grave, and his weeping must have been something of a shock to Varina. Still, they were well matched, and they became close companions, even if Jefferson never regained his humor and playfulness nor forgot Sarah.

In Washington for the congressional season, the newly married couple mingled with that group of young nationalists who surrounded President James K. Polk. The Mississippi Democrat became something of a leader of the Gulf Coast and southwest expansionists and advised them to unite in support of the president's proposed war with Mexico to protect the newly annexed Texas. Davis then resigned his congressional seat and returned to Mississippi to raise a rifle company to fight in Mexico. A train ride led to a chance meeting with General Taylor, and Davis volunteered to join his former father-in-law in his march to south Texas. Davis fought alongside Taylor at the battle of Monterrey and in many other engagements. He became a hero in the popular imagination and, alas for his future problems, believed himself to have been the victor at the battle of Buena Vista because he had helped to halt the charge of the Mexican general Santa Anna. He then resigned from the army along with the disgruntled General Taylor and returned to Mississippi to a hero's welcome and a gubernatorial appointment to the U.S. Senate. Davis the expansionist voted for the treaty to end the war. But he also was a state particularist, and he refused to support President Taylor's desire to bring California into the Union as a free state. Davis, the staunch supporter of slavery, then resigned from the Senate to campaign for governor of Mississippi as a Southern sectionalist. Defeated in the race for governor, no doubt because of his rash radicalism, Davis changed his political tone and joined the moderate Southern nationalists.

When his former military colleague and old friend President Franklin Pierce named him Secretary of War in 1853, Davis's political maturity shown forth as he used his office to conduct an expansionist campaign, to advocate railroad building westward, and to help negotiate the Gadsden Purchase. He solicited funds and the means for enlargement of the U.S. Military Academy, supported technological training at the newly built Smithsonian Institution, and generally made his office a catalyst for financing internal improvements in the Southwest. By all accounts Davis had been an excellent and visionary administrator. Back in the U.S. Senate in 1857, his years of government experience and his deep, resonant debater's voice soon made him the leader of the Southern nationalist faction of the Democratic party. His rising national career, marred only by occasional bouts of illness and melancholy, and weakening eyesight, made many think of him as presidential material. But Davis also had the vain politician's flaw of believing himself always right, and he seemed prone to violent reaction if he did not get his way. Davis even managed to challenge the circumspect Senator Judah P. Benjamin (q.v.) to a duel, and only their sense of mutual interest kept them from actually fighting. As Davis said of himself at a later interview: "[W]hen I am aroused in a matter, I lose control of my feelings and become personal" (Davis, 264). Alas, politics for him often became personal.

By 1860, other Southern public figures considered Davis a national figure who had friends in all parts of the Union because he had become a major voice for moderation in that increasingly disputatious national scene. He opposed both the antislave expansion Republicans and his radical secessionist peers. But his own national ambitions and his leadership of the Gulf Coast Democrats led him to resist the candidacy of Stephen A. Douglas and to support John C. Breck-inridge for president. Soon, however, events caught up to him when the secession movement worked its way through the lower South after Abraham Lincoln's (q.v.) election. Mississippi firebrands then forced Senator Davis to defend the right of secession in speeches in Washington in order for him to keep power back home. On January 2, 1861, he resigned from the Senate. When Davis followed his state into disunion he hoped to parlay his military experience into commander of Mississippi troops in the newly forming Confederacy. But that was not to be. The delegates to the Montgomery convention named him provisional president of the Confederate States of America. Davis was at that time ill, overwrought, and certainly unsure of his skills as a leader. Still, after William L. Yancey of Alabama declared that "the man and the hour had met," Davis managed to convince himself of that fact.

The new president formed a cabinet and made plans to defend the new country he had helped to create. But events quickly got out of hand when the president tried to impose governance on that disputatious and divisive slaveholding people. Radical supporters of the Confederacy even accused Davis of having plans to lead the South back into the Union upon getting agreement on constitutional protection of slavery in the West. Though he believed strongly in the federal union, he had made a commitment to his new nation, and he would act accordingly. Perhaps because he feared that charge against him, or he believed that the Confederacy was unraveling, or he knew war was inevitable, President Davis ordered the Confederate military leaders near Fort Sumter, the Union fort in Charleston Harbor, to demand its surrender. Certainly he thought that the only way to force slaveholding states that had not joined the Confederacy to support their peers was to bring about civil war. In any case, when President Lincoln refused, Davis felt he had little choice but to order the fort to be fired on. To this day his and Lincoln's actions remain clouded in a maze of recrimination and misunderstandings of their motivations. It is clear, however, that Davis well understood that he had helped to start what would be a long and costly war. He also had confidence that he was the most experienced person to lead his new nation.

When he arrived in Richmond there was little time to think about leadership policy or to make his own war plans because a Union Army was threatening the capital city of the Confederacy. With his new cabinet in tow, many of whom had gained their posts because they would obey their president, Davis began to prepare the defense of Richmond. Defense it was, and for much of the war, Union Army initiatives forced the president into a reactive rather than an active military mode. Besides, the politics of nation building seemed to require him to defend his new country and to appear to the world as the victim of an aggressor. Davis also had learned much about defensive warfare in his old military career. He had been trained to use a well-coordinated, mobile, and concentrated force to resist a much larger military force. The president too was aware that the border slave states had remained neutral and that he did not have the support of all of the states in the newly created Confederacy. Any precipitate action might give the appearance that the Confederacy, not the Union, was the aggressor. Of course, some radical leaders in the slave states immediately attacked him for refusing to take the war to the North.

The first major engagement of the Civil War took place that summer of 1861 near Washington at the railroad hub of Manassas, Virginia. It proved a debacle for the Union Army, which ran helter-skelter in retreat from the battlefield. Immediately, the generals in command of the Confederate defenses attacked Davis for refusing to allow the army to pursue the enemy and "end" the war. He ran afoul of Generals Joseph E. Johnston (q.v.) and Pierre G. T. Beauregard (q.v.), two men who would never forgive nor support him, and their powerful congressional supporters. The president personalized those arguments over taking the offensive and made matters worse for himself as he proclaimed he would never forgive military insubordination.

As he early in the war made enemies, Davis also gained friends. Those who supported him earned his undying gratitude, devotion, and loyalty even when they later failed the cause. Such a bond had been formed years ago with the soon-to-be-vilified Commissary General Lucius B. Northrop, his West Point friend, who, when under attack from General Joseph E. Johnston, received the president's complete support. That flawed bully Braxton Bragg (q.v.), another old and loyal friend, received a number of major appointments from the president that proved beyond his capacity. Robert E. Lee (q.v.) understood that part of his leader's character and made the effort to appear always loyal and deferential, to his obvious advantage. Most tragic for the Confederacy, the president came to trust Lee completely, even at the expense of the war in the West. At the last, Davis supported Lee's choice of the loyal and sycophantic John Bell Hood (q.v.) to command the Army of Tennessee from Atlanta to Nashville.

If the president had troubles with difficult general officers and seemed too loyal to his friends, his temperament and belief that he was always right also made for problems with the Confederacy's political leaders. His opponents among the high command urged their congressional allies to attempt to influence military decisions of policy and personnel. Davis resisted their advice, often retreating into a shell from which he made his own military decisions. Having had previous military experience, Davis insisted he could conduct the war effort himself and that war secretaries need only serve as clerks to carry out his policies. Unfortunately, these actions led to many changes in that office, changes that made him enemies among the politicos who championed the many secretaries. Thus, able students of war were lost to the administration, and the turnover in office led to discontinuity in policies.

To make matters worse on the political front, a faction-ridden Congress from the first divided over the kinds of sacrifices necessary to conduct the war effort. For example, when Davis called for a military draft, a number opposed him. When he supported a rigorous tax-in-kind and other harsh means to raise necessary food and supplies for the soldiers, many congressmen resisted. Then, when his much maligned Secretary of the Treasury Christopher G. Memminger (q.v.) in 1864 ran afoul of the Congress because of his recalcitrance over economic changes, instead of bowing to its wishes and removing him, Davis stubbornly kept him in office until the political leaders forced him out. Even worse for his chances with the political leadership, the president never found a means to use the talents of his vice president Alexander H. Stephens (q.v.). Davis's cockiness so offended him that Stephens joined a faction of lower South governors in opposing the president's policies. A most dangerous opponent was Georgia governor Joseph E. Brown (q.v.), who regarded Davis as a dictator bent on taking control of state governments. The president never seemed to get along with strong governors, as he managed to alienate the different regions within the Confederacy and turn them hostile to the interests of the new nation as a whole. In all, Davis's poor dealings with civilian political leaders both in Richmond and in the states led to extreme divisions within the Confederacy.

Failure to control the politicos also affected the president's relations with the civilian population of the Confederacy. To sustain morale and enthusiasm for the war effort, the president just had to work to unify private citizens. It was not that he did not try. Davis spoke often and at times eloquently about sacrifice. His words just could not stir the increasingly hostile and discouraged Southern people. Even when he called for days of fasting and sacrifice, he could not rally the clergy to support his efforts. Perhaps he failed because he had to defend a way of life that numbers of people found indefensible. As a spokesman for the slaveholding aristocracy, he offended the nonslaveholding majority. Perhaps the military failures also tired out those who really wanted to make sacrifices for their new country. Certainly, those citizens who were trapped behind Union lines felt the president had deserted them. And those who faced future invasion began to question the ability of the president to lead them. Davis exhausted himself in his efforts to restore morale and thus weakened his own ability to make plans to resist the enemy.

Indeed, Davis often felt ill and ill at ease in the social whirl of Richmond. He suffered from severe neuralgia in one side of his face, which kept him in constant pain. He had lost sight in one eye and no doubt, in pouring over plans and long hours of work, strained his other eye. His so-called friends in that treacherous capital city spread rumors and gossip that redounded on the president's veracity. The city was awash in petty cabals. Friendships formed by Varina solicited cutting remarks and envy and made more enemies. Mrs. Davis's special relationship with Secretary Judah P. Benjamin illicited the worst gossip and jealousies. One need only page through Mary Chesnut's *Diary* to see how those social relations created divisions among the leadership classes. Only his deep and abiding faith—the president had joined the Episcopal Church in 1862—kept him at peace with himself.

But the president's faith could not protect him from his enemies, his friends, and himself. In the matter of military actions, to which he singularly devoted himself, Davis made many mistakes. Where to commit troops and who to lead them he decided himself, which gave truth to the critics' accusations that he personally had failed to achieve victories. That there were few clear-cut successes in that first of modern wars because of the power of defensive weapons hardly sunk into a public that required decisive actions. Thus, Davis received criticism for refusing to pursue a retreating General George B. McClellan (q.v.) after the Peninsula Campaign in mid-1862 and for misunderstanding how vulnerable the Union Army was after Second Manassas that September. Even when he allowed Lee to influence his plans and direct a Maryland offense, the president was blamed for the debacle at Antietam. That he also came around to Lee's view in the summer of 1863 and supported the Army of Northern Virginia's raid into Pennsylvania meant that he shared in the blame when Gettysburg nearly destroyed that army. From then on, Davis allowed Lee to make his own plans to protect Virginia. The result was that history would blame Davis for the Army of Northern Virginia's final failure at Appomattox Courthouse.

There were still other shortcomings in Davis's military decisions. For a number of historians, the most important being Thomas L. Connelly, Davis seemed preoccupied with the Eastern theater and never really grasped the importance of the West to the Confederacy's attempts to achieve separation from the Union. The president played favorites even more in the West, as his appointment of his hero Albert S. Johnston to defend Tennessee showed. His hatred of Beauregard meant that the president was never able to coordinate the military efforts there, and the result was Shiloh. Davis approved Bragg's gigantic turning movement, and that action resulted in the Confederacy's never again contesting for Kentucky. His defense of Bragg against the overwhelming hostility of his staff only made matters worse in the Western command system. Some historians believe that Davis stuck too long with the incompetent General John C. Pemberton because he hated Joseph E. Johnston and that his refusal to force coordination of military efforts led to the loss of Vicksburg in July 1863. Certainly coordination of the entire military effort rested with the commander in chief, and in the West, the verdict is that his policies had failed.

As the war ground down, Confederate politics became increasingly partisan and regional, the public lost heart, and the president continued to make personnel and strategic blunders. Worst of all in those dark days was the removal of Joseph E. Johnston around Atlanta in the late summer of 1864. Everyone knows the resultant debacle of John Bell Hood's command in the West after he replaced Johnston. Of course, general officers must bear blame for their actions, and the required number of troops never seemed available, but Davis must stand at the bar of history as one who planned poorly and neglected the most crucial areas of the Confederacy.

To add to Davis's wartime problems and to give fodder to postwar critics, the Confederacy's newspaper press attacked and second-guessed his every activity. Led by the *Richmond Examiner*'s Edward A. Pollard (q.v.) in his editorials and early histories of the battles, all of Davis's actions came under increasing public scrutiny. According to Pollard and the Robert B. Rhett, Jr., family of Charleston, South Carolina, Davis had failed as a military leader, lacked control of politics, and had little sense of what made the people willing to make sacrifices. Soon after the war came to an end, Pollard wrote its history and his verdict was that Davis had failed as a leader. In his 1869 biography of the ex-president, Pollard confirmed his wartime views of Davis. In his bestselling volumes on the war's history, Pollard defended the heroic soldiers and attacked the politicians, and Davis mostly. Above all, in the opinion of those early historians the president had used too heavy a fist to force compliance, to the point that his denial of state and individual rights had destroyed the reasons why they had fought in the first place. Pollard and his allies had fixed the way future historians would see Davis.

Pollard and others have described Davis's heavy-handedness as that of a dictatorial personality. They also found character flaws such as weakness of personality and resolve. The famous retreat from Richmond during the spring of 1865 not only led some to insist that Davis had stolen the Confederate Treasury but others insisted that when the Northerners found him, he had tried to disguise himself in women's clothing, thus proving his weaknesses. In fact, the very same critics who called him dictatorial also suggested he could not control the various groups who ran the war. Only his imprisonment for two years under quite squalid circumstances seemed to solicit any sympathy—and that was for the man, not his wartime behavior.

To make matters worse for his reputation, Davis's postwar writings showed his untoward anger and excessive defensiveness. In them he appeared insensitive to the politics of reputation making. At first, however, he attempted to forget the war and to make a living in insurance, but he failed at both activities. Blame for losing the war seemed to obsess his every action. So he sulked back at his Mississippi plantation, and he established a self-serving and vindictive correspondence with his most loyal sympathizers. After he learned that his two worst enemies, Johnston and Beauregard, had attacked him in their memoirs, he set about an elaborate defense of his actions. At his new home, Beauvoir, on the Gulf Coast, he began to revise his views even of his purposes for going to war. He now claimed that the Confederacy had been formed to support the rights of individual states. Too, the war had not been fought to defend slavery but to defend Southern rights. He changed from the leader who had created an effective central government to one who never had challenged individual rights. Self-justification had led him to historical revisionism of the worst kind.

If Davis had revised his purpose for fighting, in his dull, legalistic, two-volume *The Rise and Fall of the Confederate Government*, he also tried to revise his war record. One after another of those military leaders who had let him down came in for criticism. Tediously, he recounted how his plans had been disobeyed, how generals had fought poorly, and how they had little faith in the Confederate government or nation. Davis even attacked them personally. But his arguments and accusations against them hardly cracked their protective armor and led only to further recriminations from them.

But some of his old allies rallied around his new-found state's rights argument and even praised Davis for his wartime sacrifices. A number of ex-soldiers came to regard him as a defender of the common man. When he died in Mississippi on December 6, 1889, those supporters raised funds to build a monument to him in Richmond. The monument, however, rather than depict him as the warrior he regarded himself as, captured the ex-president as the political orator surrounded by a loving Southern people. Of course, that edifice got him all wrong.

If those who sought to give him his due seemed confused over what Davis had accomplished during the war, the historians during the early twentieth century who began to study his life with so-called detachment were bothered by the contradictions between his motivation and the reasons for his failure. The first major professional historian to look at his career, William E. Dodd, regarded the ex-president as one who had wanted to heal sectional wounds after the war. But Dodd's *Jefferson Davis* of 1907 took no position on why he had failed and only praised him for his courageous defense of state rights. Others, such as Hamilton J. Eckenrode, Robert McElroy, and Hudson Strode, applauded Davis for his heroic sacrifices, and all of them found his character central to any judgment of his success or failure. Some found him cold and austere; others saw in him a certain warmth and compassion. Recently, Clement Eaton and William C. Davis have analyzed Davis's efforts to create a viable Confederate government. They focus on his medical problems affecting his personality and his ability to function. Eye and nervous system problems, they suggest, contributed to his rigid character. So it goes, personality replaces serious consideration of his actions.

The best recent work on Davis and his wartime activities has rejected the personality theory and instead has turned to his life to understand larger questions about why the Confederacy lost the war. In *After Secession: Jefferson Davis and the Failure of Confederate Nationalism* (1978), Paul Escott suggests that neither Davis nor any other leader could have articulated a "unifying ideology" to unite that disparate and class divided people of the slaveholding states. For Escott, Davis was never able to disabuse Southerners of their "fundamental confusion . . . over the nature of their government" (74). In *A Long Shadow: Jefferson Davis and the Final Days of the Confederacy* (1986), Michael Ballard maintains that the federal government's immediate postwar attempts to discredit Davis contributed to the lasting image of a man unable to lead his people. Ballard finds that image flawed and instead claims that the president's aloof and calm control at the war's end "reinforced his status as the last beleaguered defender of the cause" and should be the image of him today (x). Steven E.

Woodworth, in *Jefferson Davis and His Generals* (1990), insists that the traditional historian's verdicts of flawed self-righteousness and poor leadership judgment have dimmed the bald fact that Davis simply never had the personnel to defend his beloved South. "He was spread far too thin from the beginning," says Woodworth, and that explained his inability to take decisive action (10). If, in Woodworth's words, Davis "was not quite good enough" (316), Allan Nevins perhaps has best said it when he asked, just who could have better led that flawed Confederacy? The answer is nobody.

BIBLIOGRAPHY

Edward A. Pollard, *Life of Jefferson Davis, With a Secret History of the Southern Confederacy* (Philadelphia: National Publishing Co., 1869).

Jefferson Davis, *The Rise and Fall of the Confederate Government*, 2 vols. (New York: D. Appleton, 1881).

Varina Howell Davis, *Jefferson Davis: A Memoir*, 2 vols. (1890; Baltimore: Nautical and Aviation Publishing Co., 1990).

Hamilton J. Eckenrode, *Jefferson Davis, President of the South* (New York: Macmillan Co., 1929).

Allen Tate, *Jefferson Davis: His Rise and Fall* (New York: Milton, Balch, 1929).

Robert McNutt McElroy, *Jefferson Davis* (New York: Harper & Bros., 1937).

Hudson Strode, *Jefferson Davis*, 3 vols. (New York: Harcourt, Brace, 1955–1964).

William E. Dodd, *Jefferson Davis* (1907; New York: Russell and Russell, 1966).

Clement Eaton, *Jefferson Davis* (New York: Free Press, 1977).

Paul D. Escott, *After Secession: Jefferson Davis and the Failure of Confederate Nationalism* (Baton Rouge: Louisiana State University Press, 1978).

C. Vann Woodward (ed.), *The Private Mary Chesnut* (New York: Oxford University Press, 1984).

Michael B. Ballard, *A Long Shadow: Jefferson Davis and the Final Days of the Confederacy* (Jackson: University Press of Mississippi, 1986).

Steven E. Woodworth, *Jefferson Davis and His Generals* (Topeka: University Press of Kansas, 1990).

William C. Davis, *Jefferson Davis: The Man and his Hour* (New York: HarperCollins, 1991).

William C. Davis, *"A Government of Our Own": The Making of the Confederacy* (New York: Free Press, 1994).

VARINA HOWELL DAVIS
(May 7, 1826–October 16, 1906)

Jon L. Wakelyn

Unfortunately for her own place in this country's history, Varina Howell Davis's considerable accomplishments are inseparably linked to those of her husband, Confederate States President Jefferson Finis Davis (q.v.). Some of her contemporaries viewed her as a cold and interfering woman, perhaps frustrated by her lack of personal political power. Others believed she wasted her own time in later life in the vain attempt to resurrect her husband's career through her book *Jefferson Davis, A Memoir* (1890). More careful studies of the woman herself reveal a deeply flawed, yet heroic person. She made incisive judgments about the strengths and weaknesses of Confederate leaders, judgments her husband took to heart and acted upon. If her friend Mary Chesnut labeled her a meddler for that activity, Chesnut all too well understood her powers. Chesnut, too, grasped Varina's calming effect on the president, as well as her efforts to set a proper social scene in beleaguered Richmond. Mrs. Davis's duty was always to appear calm, collected, and optimistic, even in the face of adversity. Thus, her activities in behalf of the Confederate war effort, if appearing to some historians as problematic, require objective evaluation.

Varina was born into an ex-Yankee family of enormous pride and status, if of modest income, in the clannish, rich Mississippi delta near Natchez. What income there was came from the family of her Virginia-born mother, Margaret Kempe. Her father, William Burr Howell, had been born into a prestigious family of New Jersey politicos. His father had been governor. But William, despite his advantages, seems to have had little ambition. For a time he wandered aimlessly through the Midwest, then served ably in the navy during the War of 1812, and later visited old war acquaintances in Natchez. A gregarious man, he became friends with Joseph Davis, the elder brother of Jefferson, who set him up in a law practice there. Howell met, courted, and married the heiress Margaret Kempe. That marriage allowed William to give up the law, become a planter, and purchase a modest home, ''The Briers.'' The young couple became supporters of the local Episcopal Church, entered the social whirl of that wealthy community, and depended upon Joseph Davis for financial support. Into that upper-class planter world Varina was born on May 7, 1826.

Raised to believe she belonged to the upper classes, Varina learned to dance, to ride, to develop the charms of a wealthy young woman. But that young woman also acted a bit rough in her play, seemed determined to enlarge her knowledge of the outside world, and early gained a reputation for outspokenness. At twelve, as was the custom in her family's circle of friends, she was sent north for further schooling in culture and refinement. At Madame Greenland's fashionable ladies school in Philadelphia, she hobnobbed with others of her class. But Varina's real education came from Massachusetts Yankee school-teacher George Winchester, who had come to Natchez to practice law. Winchester also became a distinguished judge. Local tradition, if not also legend, has it that Varina studied with him for twelve years and that the judge became her closest friend and confidant. Under his tutelage, that bright and quick young woman gained almost the equivalent of a college education, as he taught her Latin, mathematics, history, and literature. From the judge she also learned the rules of debate and discourse. Certainly that was not the traditional education pattern for one of her class. Of course, intelligent young men were drawn to her, but most of the local planters' sons found Varina much too quick, facile, and sharp tongued for their taste. So at eighteen Varina possessed an excellent education, sophisticated talents, and no venue in which to express herself outside of the parlors of wealthy Natchez.

Described at that time as having an intense and sultry look, she had beautiful dark hair, large and bright eyes, and a becoming smile. Certainly she was a most eligible young woman. In her eighteenth year, 1842, her father and her benefactor, Joseph Davis, contrived for her to meet the morose thirty-seven-year-old widower Jefferson Davis. They talked, rode, argued about politics (Davis belonged to the Mississippi Democratic party and Varina favored the Whigs), and gradually fell in love. Their courtship correspondence reveals a ritual of pressure, evasion, and coyness over how to proceed. Surely Varina understood that Davis's wealth was being used to lure a daughter of the profligate Howell family. Finally, in January 1844, Jefferson proposed marriage, and she accepted. The wedding, kept small and tasteful, was held at "The Briers," despite the bride's illness and probable reservations. On the honeymoon they visited the gravesite of Davis's late wife, and that image of his former love stuck with Varina for the duration of her life. They also, to her great delight, traveled together on the campaign trail in a quest for Jefferson's election to the federal Congress. A pattern developed between the two of them of conferring together in private over political plans and of extreme loneliness at being left out when Jefferson had to meet with the rough and tumble men of party. But Varina truly shared in her husband's political ambitions.

When Davis entered Congress in 1845 Varina traveled with him to Washington. She began to meet and to get to know some of the powerful denizens of that federal city. At times, however, she lived apart from her husband, and the long absences, her family's precarious finances, and his many illnesses surely began to wear on that vivacious young woman. While Jefferson fought in Mexico and made his reputation, she moped in Natchez. But her reward for that absence was her husband's election to the U.S. Senate and travel again to Washington. There, the twenty-three-year-old woman entertained the political elite and, more important for her own needs, studied carefully the workings of the federal power structure. Her brilliant notes taken on the frailties, excuses, and failings of political genius, if published as a social-political commentary of those times, would surely have given her an important place in American letters. Though there always were rumors of her speaking out in ways in which women of those times did not, she generally behaved herself and assisted her husband's career.

When Jefferson became President Franklin's Pierce's Secretary of War, Varina took her place as a famous Washington hostess. In party after party she touted her husband's abilities. Some thought that she was preparing him for a run at the White House. An insider would have seen how she personally evaluated the abilities of the military establishment. She became an intimate of President Buchanan's just as that man needed moderate friends. Along with Senator John Slidell and a few other Southern Democrats, Jefferson emerged as a leader of the moderates in the Senate. Varina applauded her husband's statemanship, and she often attended the vigorous Senate debates that announced the end of moderation. Exhilarated by the verbal pyrotechnics, she nevertheless feared the onset of civil war.

When the Civil War began in the spring of 1861, Varina was only thirty-five. Some said that childbearing had turned her matronly looking. Others saw her as a self-confident, stately looking woman who understood that she was always on display. She would play the role of the wife of the Confederacy's president brilliantly. If the man and the times had met, surely the same was true for the woman. She indeed was anxious to leave Montgomery and to go to Richmond, that proud and fashionable capital city of the Confederacy. She would throw herself into the endless round of state parties and at them cultivate the men of power while soothing their sometimes bored and neglected wives.

If being the best hostess and the image of solid support were part of her job, she also became a major adviser to her often beleaguered husband. Her years of learning about how political loyalty worked, at sizing up talent, and at studying the workings of government now had become quite useful to the president. Varina early discussed with her husband the disloyalty of Vice President Alexander Stephens (q.v.), and she helped him to set that Georgian aside. She liked the dour, methodical, and loyal Secretary of the Treasury, Christopher Memminger (q.v.), and perhaps persuaded Jefferson to stay with him too long. Political allegiances and confidences also flowed her way. Her close relationship with Judah P. Benjamin (q.v.), dating back to U.S. Senate days, may have had all Richmond atwitter. But they used each other well, and Benjamin remained intensely loyal to the president.

Varina also had learned much about the pitfalls of social politics, and her actions revealed her own strengths. She grew to hate the snobs of Richmond and their constantly destructive rumor mill. For a time she appeared to be under siege, but she rallied to keep up a strong public presence and to resist the pessimism of those upper South nabobs. Her husband had a number of serious ailments, and at times the pressures of office left him quite depressed. Today we might say that he suffered from clinical depression. Varina protected him from the outside world, took his place at important gatherings, and nursed his illnesses. In doing so, certainly she helped to preserve his fragile energy. Despite her own heartbreak after the accidental death of their beloved young son, Joseph, she revived her despairing husband. Through her personal faith, she brought Jefferson to convert to the Episcopal faith, which indeed gave him much peace of mind even in the direst of moments. In short, her social activities in public and in private were of incalculable aid to the Confederacy, its government, and its president.

What is most difficult to discern is what the first lady contributed in her own right to the Confederacy. Of course she conducted a working household, and she cut corners and consumed less to show others how it could be done. Household production continued during the war, and she helped to set up sewing groups to produce clothing for the soldiers. But Varina did far more. Her visits to hospitals and her encouragement to the nurses and orderlies helped their morale. She even became a recommending agent for promotion of hospital staff. She took on some of her husband's correspondence, even to the point of becoming a kind of personal secretary to him when staff shortages occurred. Varina was even said to have had a role in sorting out appointments and promotions. For certain, her hard work and many hours of effort in behalf of the president and the government hardened and aged her.

As the war came to its end, she had to flee Richmond without Jefferson and to give up all that she loved and cherished. When the Union imprisoned her husband, she worked indefatigably to obtain his pardon. Certainly her many letters to the newspaper editor Horace Greeley and her personal meetings with President Andrew Johnson (q.v.) helped gain his freedom. Embittered by those efforts, she developed a downward droop to her mouth. But she traveled with Jefferson to Canada and then to England, all the while nursing him back to health. She also began her quest to protect his good name. Her letters in response to Edward A. Pollard's (q.v.) unkind judgment that Davis had lost the war are a model of propriety and skillful argument about the nature of wartime leadership. Of course, she herself was branded by some as a woman who had stepped outside of her sphere to enter the hurly-burly of journalistic arguments.

As Jefferson and Varina aged together, she alienated some of her children because of her preoccupation with her husband's reputation. Rumors abounded that she had become hard and super-expectant for them to succeed in life.

Friends called her cold and a perfectionist, always expecting others to perform in as selfless and analytical a way as herself. But she was forced to move from place to place, from business failure to business failure as Jefferson became increasingly morbid, preoccupied with his past, and unwilling to face the needs of the present. To help him, she encouraged him to fight back against his detractors. She had hoped that his *Memoirs* would help rebuild their depleted finances, but they did not. Of course, she resented her old friend Sarah Dorsey for providing aid and comfort to Jefferson when he was writing his history of the Confederacy. Despite that hurt, Varina researched, edited, and even shaped the argument in Davis's *Rise and Fall of the Confederate States*. She had entered as a full partner in that battle of the books that would so influence the way the future evaluated the Confederate leaders' war activities.

Mrs. Davis broke down in 1889 after the death of Jefferson. For the duration of her life, she would be forced to forsake the land and people she loved, as she continued the crusade to restore her husband's reputation. In her *Jefferson Davis, A Memoir*, (1890) she singled out the Confederate villains who had destroyed her country. But the book sold poorly, as most people even in the South did not want to read yet another apologia. Perhaps also many Southerners desired unity and reunion and resisted her sharpened case for hostility and division. Today, however, that book is a major source for understanding the character of leadership in the Confederacy, as it reveals just what a student of politics she had become. As a means to make a living, Varina went on the lecture circuit. It seems that some people, as it turned out, especially Northerners, wanted to hear of the heroes of the past. With her daughter she settled in New York City, where Southern expatriates lionized her as a great woman. She continued to write, and her close friend Joseph Pulitzer hired her for the editorial page of the New York *Sunday World*. She even assisted John W. Burgess to write his revisionist life of Joseph E. Johnston (q.v.), no friend of her late husband. She herself had become a major historical source for the Civil War. Ever loyal to her own family, now grown close with her children, she helped her daughter Winnie's budding literary career. At her death on October 16, 1906, Varina had once again started to write her own history of the Civil War.

Her personal reputation that she also had wanted to protect had taken a beating after the war in the hands of contemporaries like Edward A. Pollard and Mary Chesnut. In part, she was identified with her husband; in part, Varina suffered from being a woman in public life, which was deemed inappropriate for one of her station. Most professional historians, many of whom have relied in their efforts on the nineteenth-century memorialists who disliked her, have not quite known what to do with her life. For example, Allan Nevins's monumental history of the Civil War mentions her only twice, and the recent Pulitzer Prize–winning history of the war, James M. McPherson's *Battle Cry of Freedom* (1988), cites her only once. Of course, popularists have often tried to capture her plight. Among the best are Eron O. Rowland and Ishbel Ross. But their works are dated, written for a general audience, and in no way analyze her accomplishments in the context of that war. Even among them, Varina's own life often gets lost in the criticism of her husband. It is hoped that Joan Cashin's eagerly awaited life will make an adequate evaluation of this great Civil War leader's wartime activities.

BIBLIOGRAPHY

Jefferson Davis, *The Rise and Fall of the Confederate Government*, 2 vols. (New York: D. Appleton, 1881).

Varina Davis, *Jefferson Davis, a Memoir*, 2 vols. (Baltimore: Belford Co., 1890).

Eron Ophal Rowland, *Varina Howell Davis: Wife of Jefferson Davis*, 2 vols. (New York: Macmillan Co., 1927).

Ishbel Ross, *First Lady of the South: The Life of Mrs. Jefferson Davis* (New York: Harper and Bros., 1958).

C. Vann Woodward (ed.), *Mary Chesnut's Civil War* (New Haven: Yale University Press, 1981).

James M. McPherson, *Battle Cry of Freedom* (New York: Oxford University Press, 1988).

DOROTHEA LYNDE DIX
(April 4, 1802–July 17, 1887)

Charles F. Ritter

Dorothea Dix's life's work evolved in three distinct stages. For nearly twenty years between 1818 and 1836, she supported herself as a teacher and writer. In 1841, she embarked on the second phase of her life's work, a nearly single-handed campaign to improve the care of the insane poor. The third endeavor of her life began in 1861, when Dix offered her skills as a hospital and nursing supervisor to the U.S. government during the Civil War. Dix later looked back with chagrin on that third stage of her life as superintendent of nurses: " 'This is not the work I would have my life judged by,' " she said (Tiffany, 339). Perhaps she felt her war work unworthy because it did not result in great physical structures such as the asylums she helped build during her two-decade labor as an advocate for the insane poor. But what she did accomplish in Washington during the war was extraordinary and exemplary. She recruited, trained, and placed hundreds of female nurses in Washington hospitals; coordinated the collection and distribution of vast amounts of clothing, foodstuffs, and hospital supplies to wounded soldiers; and urged hospital management reforms. This phase of her life was as noteworthy as the earlier phases. In acting boldly in America's greatest domestic crisis, Dix set standards for nurses' training and hospital management that would survive her and stand as a legacy that is perhaps more positive than the great asylums she willed into being.

Dorothea Lynde Dix was born in Hampden, Maine (then a district of Massachusetts), on April 4, 1802, the only daughter and first of three children born to Joseph and Mary (Bigelow) Dix. Joseph Dix was the ne'er-do-well son of Elijah and Dorothy (Lynde) Dix. Expected to pursue medical studies at Harvard and follow in his wealthy father's footsteps, Joseph Dix lacked drive and ambition and was dismissed from Harvard in 1797. His father tried to interest him in the apothecary trade, but that was a disaster. Joseph further alienated his father in 1801 by marrying Mary Bigelow, an impoverished woman in frail health. Joseph and Mary fled his family and moved to Vermont, where Joseph failed as a bookstore manager. Elijah Dix tried to rescue the young family by sending Joseph and Mary to the Maine District where Joseph served as sales agent for one of Elijah's big land development schemes. Joseph failed again, taking up drink and evangelical religion instead of real estate. As an itinerant preacher to the backwoods inhabitants, Joseph Dix rejected his parents' acquisitive lifestyle and subjected his young family to economic and emotional privation. Despite a second rescue attempt by Elijah in 1815, Joseph continued to drink and peddle his sermons, while Mary took to her bed. Worn down by the abuse of poverty and zealotry, Dorothea went to Boston to stay with her sixty-eight-year-old widowed grandmother Dorothy Dix (known to everyone as Madam Dix), where she found economic stability but not emotional succor.

In a year's time, Dix was back in Worcester living with her aunt, who also cared for Dorothea's younger brothers, Charles and Joseph, Jr. She found acceptance there and began what became the first of her three lifetime endeavors, teaching. At age sixteen and self-taught, Dix opened a school for young children where she conducted writing and reading sessions. In 1820, she closed the school, moved to Boston to manage her grandmother's household, and in 1821 opened a charity school in the barn at Dix Mansion. A few years later she opened a school for elite children. During her nearly twenty years of teaching, Dix was also a successful writer. In 1824 she published a children's reader, which went through sixty printings before 1860. A half dozen other inspirational readers followed by 1833.

Through her teaching and writing, Dix became a part of Boston's intelligentsia and formed associations with leading intellectuals, among them Ralph Waldo Emerson, Joseph Tuckerman, and William Ellery Channing. Having abandoned Methodism for Unitarianism, Dix fell under Channing's influence and in 1827 worked for him as a governess during the Channing family's summer retreats to Newport, Rhode Island, and on a trip to St. Croix in 1830.

Returning from the Caribbean with restored vigor, Dix reopened a school in Boston in May 1831 and for the next five years taught and pondered her future. Although school teaching was one of the few professions open to women in the antebellum period, Dix was dissatisfied with that role. By the end of 1835, she was depressed about the drift in her life. Never a robust person and probably suffering from chronic tuberculosis, Dix's health seemed to give way under the especially heavy stress caused by a failed romance with her cousin Edward Bangs. Accordingly, she closed her school and in April 1836 left Boston for a sojourn in England and Scotland. With nothing more than a letter of introduction from Channing, Dix met and developed a long-lasting relationship with Elizabeth and William Rathbone III. A wealthy and well-connected merchant, William Rathbone introduced Dix to some of the most important reformers in England. Dix was especially interested to meet the reformers who advocated state-sponsored poor relief, and she was impressed by the success of institutions like the York Retreat in curing the mentally ill through so-called moral treatment. An innovative approach to mental illness, moral treatment involved re-

moving the patients from society—thought to be the cause of mental illness—
and placing them in pastoral settings where they were treated with dignity and
humanity. Patients received a balanced diet, music, art, and physical therapy,
and the only restraint they encountered was a straitjacket, if necessary. This was
quite a remove from traditional methods of dealing with the insane, and it impressed Dix deeply.

Returning to Boston in August 1837, Dix was a woman alone—her grandmother died in April and her mother in May—but she was also now financially
independent, thanks to a legacy from Madam Dix. She traveled throughout the
East and, in 1838, moved to Georgetown, District of Columbia, where she began
visiting jails, asylums, and almshouses. In Baltimore she met Moses Sheppard
and advised him on his planned insane asylum patterned on the fabled York
Retreat.

Still at loose ends about how to employ her Unitarian-inspired commitment
to service to the downtrodden and poor, Dix returned to Boston in 1839, where,
in March 1841, she experienced what has come to be known as her epiphany,
her awakening to the plight of the insane poor and to the second phase of her
life's work. The stories of her ''sudden revelation'' are mostly ''legend,'' which
Dix herself began and encouraged (Gollaher, 125–126). It is true that James
T. G. Nichols, then a Harvard divinity student, asked her to recommend someone
to teach a Sunday School class for women in the East Cambridge jail. Dix took
the class herself and was appalled by what she saw. But what happened that
Sunday had its roots in her experiences over the previous decade.

Dix had been to the East Cambridge jail before 1841. She had seen the squalor
and was aware of the controversy over the treatment of prisoners and their
incarceration with indigent insane. She knew from her recent visit to England's
York Retreat and conversations with Whig reformers that there were better ways
to treat the mentally ill than locking them up in dungeons. Indeed, moral therapy
was already being practiced in Massachusetts, at the Worcester State Lunatic
Hospital, opened in 1833, and at the Boston Lunatic Asylum, which opened in
1839. Both asylums based their treatment on the York Retreat model.

What happened on that Sunday was that Dorothea Dix discovered a need that
she could fill. Urged on by fellow reformers like Horace Mann and Samuel
Gridley Howe, Dix first got heat for the poor souls in the East Cambridge jail
and then launched into her second two-decade career, as reformer of the treatment of the indigent insane. In a display of energy and determination unseen in
America before and seldom since, Dix traveled the length and breadth of the
country, from Massachusetts to Louisiana, from Rhode Island to Illinois, lob-
bying for the construction of new insane asylums or the expansion of existing
ones. She began by gathering data on the treatment of the insane poor in every
hospital and almshouse and jail in the state. Armed with eyewitness testimony
to the misery of the mad, she addressed a moral imperative to the legislature,
seeking a specific remedy. Supported by a skillfully conceived and managed
publicity campaign in the press and among the state's reform circles, and en-

listing the support of the most influential men both in and out of politics, Dix invariably prevailed. As success piled on success, legislators were either converted or intimidated, and her campaign gained momentum and irresistibility.

Cultivating a "lady in the inferno" persona (Gollaher, 133), Dix began her crusade in Massachusetts, where in 1842 she toured the state, gathering evidence on the treatment of the mad. In January 1843 she presented a memorial to the Massachusetts legislature (and simultaneously published 5,000 copies for general distribution) seeking funding to expand existing institutions so they could absorb the mad languishing in jails and almshouses. She wove a compelling narrative that incorporated the work of other reformers—especially the Boston Humane Society and the legislature's own 1827 committee on the insane—her experiences in England, and her observations in Massachusetts.

Gaining support in the press, and with the help of her well-connected Unitarian friends (Charles Sumner [q.v.] became a follower), the legislature appropriated $25,000 to expand the Worcester State Hospital. Although accused of fabricating her evidence, which she did embellish for dramatic effect, she used her image as a frail woman combating a large evil and her moral authority to disarm critics and bolster those who were sympathetic.

Success in Massachusetts spurred Dix on. In January 1844 she presented a memorial to the New York legislature. Since that state already had a large asylum at Utica headed by the able and articulate Amariah Brigham, her effort there produced no tangible result. Undaunted but wiser, Dix pressed her campaign into Rhode Island. Calling herself a latter-day Philippe Pinel, the Frenchman who broke the chains of the mad, she memorialized the legislature and succeeded in getting wealthy businessmen to help finance improvements to the Butler Hospital in Providence.

Her *idee fixé* throughout was that the care of the insane was a public responsibility, and as her reputation spread, her name became synonymous with lunacy reform. In 1845 she moved her campaign into New Jersey and Pennsylvania. Catching the flood tide of insane reform in the Garden State, Dix linked her campaign to one begun in 1837 by the state's medical association. In March 1845 the governor signed a bill providing for the construction of the New Jersey State Lunatic Asylum at Trenton, a facility Dix referred to as her "first-born child" (Tiffany, 122). There shortly followed a bill for the construction of a new state hospital at Harrisburg.

During the New Jersey and Pennsylvania campaigns, Dix added an economic argument to her humanistic one; she argued that treating the insane with moral therapy in asylums produced a far higher cure rate than housing them permanently in jails and thus was cheaper to the community. This proved a powerful incentive to economy-minded legislators in Dix's next targets—Tennessee, Kentucky, Ohio, and Maryland, which she visited in 1845–1846. Between 1846 and 1848 she took her campaign into the South and won legislative approval for institutions in North Carolina, South Carolina, Georgia, Alabama, Mississippi, Louisiana, and Arkansas. It was an impressive sight, this frail-looking woman, so politically savvy and knowledgeable yet without any medical or psychological expertise, prevailing upon reluctant legislators to provide state money for the treatment of the least of the population.

Keeping the states committed to supporting asylums was an ongoing struggle that required her to travel the country, answering calls from frantic legislators to stave off attacks on funding. In order to provide a source of permanent financial support for the state asylums, Dix developed her most audacious and far-reaching scheme. Drawing on the English example of a national system of government-supported asylums, Dix single-mindedly promoted the idea of a federal land bank of 10 million acres to be sold off as needed to support state mental institutions. The boldness and sweep of her proposal were breathtaking, yet her reputation and contacts both in and out of Congress were so powerful that the Senate established a select committee to study it and the Congress provided her with an office in the congressional library. She even developed a close and long-lasting relationship with President Millard Fillmore. She labored for six years to get the land bill passed. Finally, on March 8, 1854, the Senate passed it, 25–12, and the House followed on April 19, 81–53. President Franklin Pierce vetoed the bill, explaining that the business of public welfare belonged to the states.

Pierce's veto devastated Dix. Despite the fact that she had won congressional and presidential approval for a mental hospital in the District of Columbia in 1852, the land grant defeat was a crushing blow. In September 1854 she again left the United States for Europe. Over the next two years she renewed her acquaintance with the Rathbones in England, led an asylum reform campaign in Scotland, and traveled throughout Europe investigating the condition of the insane poor. Her fame was so great that even Pope Pius IX was moved to promise reforms in Vatican asylums. While in Europe, Dix was impressed with the success of Florence Nightingale, whose work in the Crimean War revolutionized hospital management and nursing.

Returning to the United States in September 1856, Dix quickly saw that her work for the insane poor was in trouble. Generally underfunded and chock-a-block with a rising patient load because of the rapidly increasing U.S. population, the asylums had become as bad or worse than the jails and almshouses Dix fought so hard to eliminate. With cure rates declining significantly, the mental hospitals that just ten years earlier were the cutting edge of enlightened treatment had become warehouses for the insane where treatment was impossible and neglect the norm.

Dix resumed her travels throughout the country, called hither and thither to support funding legislation. She mostly ignored the growing sectional crisis, as she had ignored most other social and political issues that distracted people's attention and threatened to undermine the national effort necessary to care for the mad.

When secession came, Dix was at the New Jersey Asylum in Trenton recuperating from her exhausting travels. News of the encounter between the 6th

Massachusetts Regiment and the citizens of Baltimore on April 19, 1861, spurred her to action. She entrained for Washington that day to minister to the soldiers from her home state. Arriving in the chaotic capital, Dix offered herself and some nurses " 'for Free service at the war department and to the Surgeon General wherein we may be needed' " (Marshall, 203). Like other women who responded to the war crisis, Dix saw herself as an American Florence Nightingale, an image supported by Louisa May Alcott, one of Dix's nurses. Dix copied Nightingale's dress, a simple black affair without ornamentation, and adopted the English nurse's attitude toward hospitals—that is, as places for shielding wounded soldiers from the corrupting influences of the world so their wounds would heal. Like Nightingale, Dix redefined the role of nurses as "nature's allies" in the healing process (Gollaher, 401), an idea that claimed the medical moral high ground from physicians who viewed curing in terms of aggressive treatment.

In this fashion the fifty-nine-year-old Dix launched the third phase of her life. At first rebuffed by Acting Surgeon General Clement A. Finley, Dix, who knew her way around Washington, saw members of Congress and the president, and on April 23, Secretary of War Simon Cameron accepted her offer. On June 10 he commissioned her superintendent of women nurses.

Although some criticized Dix for lacking organizational skills, Dix threw herself into organizing nurses and supplies for the military hospitals. Asked to raise 500 hospital gowns, Dix contacted her network of service organizations in Boston and raised 5,000. Believing that diet was an important part of recovery, a novel idea, she called for and received hundreds of pounds of canned food and preserves, which she distributed throughout the Washington area. Taking the nurses' role seriously, she set stringent (some say eccentric) standards for them: They had to be at least thirty years old, plain looking, and in simple dress. She would not accept women religious, who the military doctors especially admired, principally because she was anti-Catholic.

Interpreting her mandate from the War Department broadly, Dix assumed that she had "plenary power . . . of the hospitals," that she could remove and appoint nurses, at will, and that she "had general supervision of this department of the service" (Bigelow, 676). This assumption brought her into conflict with other service organizations. She found herself in a nasty dispute with the United States Sanitary Commission (USSC) over recognizing the Western Sanitary Commission established at St. Louis by Jesse and John Charles Fremont. Calling her a "philanthropic lunatic" (Nevins and Thomas, 3:165), George Templeton Strong, the treasurer of the USSC, complained that "Miss Dix has plagued us a little." She worked "on her own hook," he said, and noted that "no one can cooperate with her for she belongs to the class of comets" (Nevins and Thomas, 3:173–174).

Dix's interpretation of her commission also produced clashes with the medical establishment, which led to her undoing. The Army Medical Department was a small and insular organization in 1861 that expanded rapidly and without much supervision during the war. Dix regarded many of the army's surgeons as unenlightened hacks, and she tried to influence the way they ran their hospitals. She insisted that only her nurses serve on staff—no independents like Clara Barton (q.v.) or Mary Ann "Mother" Bickerdyke, or the Sisters of Mercy, whom the army doctors especially liked—and she began making surprise hospital inspections. She criticized the patients' diets, the sanitary conditions in the wards, and the duties assigned to her nurses, who comprised 20 percent of the total and who were paid $12.00 a month, as opposed to the $120.50 a month paid to male nurses. One observer noted that the doctors were " 'jealous of her power, impatient of her authority, [found] fault with her nurses, and [accused] her of being arbitrary, opinionated, severe and capricious.' " She thought the army surgeons were " 'wholly unfit for their office' " because they " 'fail to bring skill, morality, or humanity to their work' " (Brockett, 87). It was not long before the surgeons complained to the surgeon general, now William Alexander Hammond, and the new Secretary of War, Edwin M. Stanton (q.v.). Although both were Dix admirers, in the face of continued complaints from the doctors, they moved to rein her in.

In October 1863 Stanton, through Assistant Adjutant General E. D. Townsend, issued Order No. 351, which appeared merely to regulate the assignment of nurses but actually placed Dix's nurses under the control of senior medical officers. In effect, Dix's office became an employment agency. It took a person of "sheer grit" and "a large measure of denial" (Gollaher, 419) to keep going after being so rudely put in her place, but Dix persevered until the end of the war. She continued to organize nurses and distribute supplies, but her role as the government's head nurse was over. After the War Department closed down women's nursing on September 1, 1866, Dix remained in Washington helping nurses and soldiers find their way home.

Following the war, Dix organized a successful effort to build a monument at Fortress Monroe in Virginia to Union soldiers and then returned to her work on behalf of the insane poor. For the next sixteen years the then sixty-two-year-old reformer traveled around the country to raise money for existing asylums and spur the creation of new ones. During that time, another dozen institutions came into being, even as critics attacked the asylum movement for warehousing the mad rather than curing them. In the fall of 1881, Dix finally gave up the struggle. She moved into the New Jersey State Hospital at Trenton, her firstborn child, and died there on July 17, 1887. She kept no diary, and she fended off suggestions from friends that she write an autobiography. Her work, it seems, would speak for her life.

The great humanitarian work she engaged in made her an icon of progressive reform. At the same time, her reputation was intimately entangled with an asylum movement that received increasing criticism. Perhaps that explains the lack of serious attention given to her life, while those who chose to write about her emphasized her courage, individuality, perseverance, and humanism. Within four years of her death, the Unitarian minister Francis Tiffany published an authorized *Life of Dorothea Lynde Dix* (1891). Reprinted twice, in 1918 and 1919, Tiffany based his *Life* on her papers and on those of her correspondents. While Tiffany's biography touches all the aspects of her long career, it is an uncritical and celebratory portrait.

Subsequent accounts of Dix's life followed this iconographic path. Helen Marshall's 1937 *Dorothea Dix* is based on the then available Dix papers and other primary and secondary sources, but Marshall was in Dix's thrall and uncritically celebrated her as a great humanitarian and moral visionary. Other Dix biographies do not have the scholarly cache of the Tiffany and Marshall efforts. Dorothy Clarke Wilson's 1975 effort, *Stranger and Traveler*, is simply fiction based on fact. Indeed, Dix's life has been largely fictionalized in books directed at young readers, like Rachel Baker's *Angel of Mercy*. Joanna Scott's imaginative first-person narrative of Dix's life in *Epoch* is in a class by itself.

Some commentators have observed that Dix is not an icon of the women's movement since she did not share the first-wave feminists' passion for women's rights, was unsympathetic to abolitionism, believed blacks inferior, and was sympathetic to the South. Perhaps for these reasons, and because she is so closely associated with the controversial subject of institutionalization, she has not seemed a ripe subject for feminist scholarship. However, Sonya Michel's fine discussion of Dix's memorials in *Discourse* suggests the efficacy of gender analysis applied to her life and work.

The best comprehensive work on Dix is David Gollaher's 1995 biography, *Voice for the Mad*. Gollaher gives us a Dix for the ages—a woman of her time who took the imperatives of her society seriously and who focused single-mindedly on a pressing issue. This is a warts and all portrait, from which Dix emerges with the magnitude of her accomplishments intact, her dignity in place, and a greater admiration for her perseverance in the mind of the reader. Gollaher draws a flesh and blood woman, not an iconographic stick figure.

Little of the periodical literature focuses on Dix's civil war career. Jean O'Brien and Robert Hoffsommer's ''Personality Profile'' of Dix in *Civil War Times Illustrated* is one of the few pieces that deals with her experience as superintendent of nursing. Taking their lead from Dix, they regard her war work as ''only an interlude'' in her ''true life and work'' (44). On the other hand, Alfred Boe made a better point in a speech in 1888 when he called Dix ''The lady whose fame was equal to that of almost any officer in the Civil War. Similarly, Linus Brockett and Mary Vaughan's *Woman's Work in the Civil War* (1867) and Mary Holland's *Our Army Nurses* (1895) accord Dix first place among Civil War nurses. Eyewitness accounts like Louisa May Alcott's *Hospital Sketches* (1863) and Jane Woolsey's *Hospital Days* (1868) show us an enormously energetic Dix who was focused and disciplined and determined to serve.

Using reticence effectively and having an executor who guarded access to her papers, Dix managed to control subsequent accounts of her life. Focusing on her humanitarian legacy as manifested in the great mental hospitals, she drew attention away from her Civil War career. Yet if Dix's Civil War work failed, it failed because of chaotic conditions and a resistant medical establishment, not because of her unwillingness to serve.

BIBLIOGRAPHY

Louisa May Alcott, *Hospital Sketches* (Boston: J. Redpath, 1863).

L. J. Bigelow, "Miss Dix, and What She Has Done," *Galaxy* 3 (March 15, 1867): 668–676.

Linus P. Brockett and Mary C. Vaughan, *Woman's Work in the Civil War* (Philadelphia: Zeigler, McCurdy & Co., 1867).

Jane Stuart Woolsey, *Hospital Days* (New York: D. Van Nostrand, 1868).

Alfred S. Roe, *Dorothea Lynde Dix* (Worcester, Mass.: Private Press of Franklin P. Rice, 1889).

Francis Tiffany, *Life of Dorothea Lynde Dix* (Boston: Houghton, Mifflin, 1891).

Mary A. Gardner Holland, comp., *Our Army Nurses* (Boston: B. Wilkins & Co., 1895).

Helen E. Marshall, *Dorothea Dix: Forgotten Samaritan* (Chapel Hill: University of North Carolina Press, 1937).

Allan Nevins and Milton H. Thomas, *Diary of George Templeton Strong*, 4 vols. (New York: Macmillan, 1952).

Rachel Baker, *Angel of Mercy: The Story of Dorothea Lynde Dix* (New York: Julian Messner, Inc., 1955).

Gertrude Norman, *Dorothea Lynde Dix* (New York: G. P. Putnam's Sons, 1959).

Jean G. O'Brien and Robert D. Hoffsommer, "Dorothea Dix: A Personality Profile," *Civil War Times Illustrated* 4, no. 5 (August 1965): 39–44.

Dorothy Clarke Wilson, *Stranger and Traveller: The Story of Dorothea Dix, American Reformer* (Boston: Little, Brown, 1975).

Joanna Scott, "Dorothea Dix: Samaritan," *Epoch* 42, no. 1 (1993): 29–42.

Sonya Michel, "Dorothea Dix: or, The Voice of the Maniac," *Discourse* 17, no. 2 (Winter 1994–1995): 48–66.

David Gollaher, *Voice for the Mad: The Life of Dorothea Dix* (New York: Free Press, 1995).

FREDERICK DOUGLASS
(February 14, 1818–February 20, 1895)

Charles F. Ritter

By the time the Civil War began, Frederick Douglass was one of the best-known figures in America. As a former slave who became an abolitionist stalwart, Douglass was also known for his close involvement with other reform causes, principally woman suffrage and temperance. Traveling from slavery to freedom, from illiteracy to oratorical greatness, from poverty to material comfort and bourgeois values, from obscurity to worldwide recognition, Douglass was a real American success story. By 1860, while still in his early forties, Douglass's life had become a living symbol of the promise of America and the hope of his race. Yet despite his success as a reform speaker both in the United States and England, Douglass was still a black man in a racist society. He was vilified by opponents of abolition and discriminated against in free territory. The Civil War presented an opportunity to change that and found Douglass at the apogee of his activism and influence.

Frederick Douglass was born into slavery on Holme Hill Farm in Talbot County, about twelve miles east of Easton, on Maryland's Eastern Shore. Because slavery was an institution that regarded slaves as commodities, Douglass never knew his exact birthdate, calculating incorrectly that it was February 1817; in later years, his family celebrated his birthday on February 14, Valentine's Day. We now know that he was born in February 1818, but his paternity is still uncertain, although scholars assert with some confidence that his father was indeed his owner, Aaron Anthony. Anthony also owned his mother, Harriet Bailey, a member of the fourth generation of the Bailey clan to work as slaves in Talbot County. Harriet christened her son Frederick Augustus Washington Bailey.

Young Frederick Bailey was raised at Holme Hill by his grandmother Betsey Bailey, who was married to Isaac Bailey, a free black sawyer. He rarely saw his mother because she lived and worked a dozen miles away on another Anthony farm. Living with his grandmother and free grandfather, Frederick did not experience the Holme Hill slave quarters during his formative years.

As was the custom in slavery, when Frederick was six years old his grandmother took him to his master, Anthony, who lived on and managed the vast Eastern Shore properties of Edward Lloyd, three-time governor of Maryland and twice a member of the U.S. House of Representatives and the U.S. Senate. When young Bailey arrived at Anthony's house on Lloyd's Wye River plantation, he entered a new world, one comprising some 10,000 acres in thirteen farms toiled on by over 500 slaves. Here Bailey became aware of slaves' precarious existence and severe deprivation. Although he was in the care of his mother's cousin, he rarely received enough to eat, slept on the floor in a corner of the kitchen, and witnessed other slaves, including some of his relatives, being beaten. He also encountered blacks who were not far removed from their African roots, unlike himself and his siblings whose family was long assimilated into the Creole slave culture.

At Wye River, Frederick Bailey also had his first introduction to the white world. Befriended by twenty-year-old Lucritia Anthony Auld, he was chosen by her from eighty slave children to be servant and playmate to twelve-year-old Daniel Lloyd, Edward Lloyd's youngest son.

In late 1826 Frederick Bailey's world changed. His absent mother died and Aaron Anthony retired. All the Anthony slaves except Frederick were sent back to the Tuckahoe farms. Apparently through the intercession of Lucritia Auld and her husband Thomas, Anthony sent Frederick to Baltimore in March to Lucritia's sister Sophie Auld and her husband Hugh to serve as a companion to their son Tommy. When Anthony died in November 1826 and Lucritia Auld, Frederick's new owner, died in July 1827, Frederick was returned to Talbot County for a division of the slave property among the Anthony siblings and Lucritia Auld's husband, Thomas. Thanks to a ''kind of Providence'' (*Autobiographies* [*Narrative*], 47), Frederick went to Thomas, who promptly sent him back to Sophie and Hugh Auld in Baltimore.

Arriving in Fells Point in Baltimore in November 1827, Frederick reentered what he knew was a life unimaginable for a slave on the Eastern Shore. For the first time in his life he slept in a bed and ate at the Aulds' table. He played with Tommy Auld and his white friends without any consciousness of race. Most important, he learned to read, from Sophia Auld at first, and then, after Hugh Auld admonished her to stop because '' 'learning would spoil the best nigger in the world' '' (*Autobiographies* [*My Bondage*], 217), from his white companions.

Young Bailey took advantage of the many opportunities available in Baltimore. He experienced a conversion to Christianity and joined the black Bethel A.M.E. Church. He studied the Bible with Charles ''Uncle'' Lawson, a free black, and he acquired a copy of *The Columbian Orator*, from which he memorized long passages of great speeches from the past.

Frederick's stay in Fells Point was rudely interrupted in March 1833 when, after a falling out between Thomas and Hugh Auld, he was returned to the Eastern Shore. There, in the St. Michael's household of Thomas Auld, he experienced again the cruelties of slavery.

The fifteen-year-old rambunctious Frederick was constantly in trouble—not attending to his duties, questioning authority, and worst of all, starting a clandestined school to teach slaves to read. Discovering the school, Thomas Auld hired Frederick out to the notorious "slave breaker" Edward Covey. After repeated beatings by Covey in the early months of 1834, Frederick stood up to him and fought for his life. Unable to subdue the slave, Covey quit and, rather than have him arrested for resisting punishment, never hit Frederick again. It was another remarkable turn of fate for the young boy and a profoundly liberating experience. It "rekindled in my heart the smoldering embers of liberty; it brought up my Baltimore dreams, and revived a sense of my own manhood," Douglass later wrote. Before the fight "I was *nothing*"; after it "I WAS A MAN" (*Autobiographies* [*My Bondage*], 286).

Rather than leave him under Covey's brutality, Thomas Auld hired Frederick to William Freeland in 1835. Freeland was a master who never beat his slaves, yet Frederick was "still restless and discontented" (*Autobiographies* [*My Bondage*], 297)—he organized a school, and he planned an escape. Conspiring with five other Freeland slaves, Bailey planned to travel to the head of the Chesapeake Bay by canoe and then make for Pennsylvania and freedom. But someone informed on the conspirators, and they wound up in jail in Easton, Maryland, in April 1835. Rather than being "sold South"—a typical fate for attempted runaways—these slaves were returned to their masters. To Frederick's "surprise and utter astonishment" (*Autobiographies* [*Narrative*], 79), Thomas Auld sent the lad back to Baltimore, telling him that he would free Frederick at age twenty-five if he behaved himself and learned a trade. It was another remarkable piece of luck for the young slave.

Back in Baltimore after a three-year sojourn into plantation slavery, the eighteen-year-old Frederick arranged with Hugh Auld to hire himself out and to live on his own in return for a payment of $3.00 a week. He learned to be a ship's caulker and he joined free blacks in self-improvement associations. He even founded one—the East Baltimore Mental Improvement Society, a debating club. It was through this network that Frederick met Anna Murray, a free black domestic worker. They fell in love and wished to marry.

Perhaps because of the prejudice he encountered from newly arrived immigrants desperate for jobs, perhaps because he wished to marry Anna Murray as a free man, perhaps because Hugh Auld revoked his hiring and living privileges, Frederick Bailey decided in 1838, two years after returning to Baltimore, to seek his freedom. In early September, in a sailor uniform purchased with Anna's savings and papers borrowed from a retired merchant seaman, the twenty-year-old Bailey boarded a train in Baltimore and headed for New York City. He later referred to this day as his "birthday" (Barome, 219).

Avoiding the slave catchers and their informers who lurked in black areas of

New York, young Bailey made his way to David Ruggles, the secretary of the New York Vigilance Committee, who hid him. After Anna Murray arrived, she and Bailey married on September 15, 1838, and, at Ruggles's suggestion, headed for New Bedford, Massachusetts, a whaling port. Along the way, Bailey changed his name to Frederick Stanley, then to Frederick Johnson, and finally, at the suggestion of his New Bedford hosts, Mary and Nathan Johnson, to Frederick Douglass, after the Scottish character in Sir Walter Scott's poem "The Lady of the Lake." Along with the name changes, Douglass created a new identity, a new person based on a literary character who had "unflinching fortitude in adversities" (Walker, 256). He also abandoned the long name his mother had given him and its identification with five generations of slave ancestors.

For three years Douglass worked in New Bedford as a day laborer, because shipyard workers would not allow him to practice his caulking trade, and joined the black Zion Methodist Church when he found the white Methodist Church segregated. Shortly afterward, he began to read William Lloyd Garrison's *The Liberator*, and although he resonated to its sentiments, he did not dream "of the possibility of my becoming a public advocate of the cause so deeply imbedded in my heart. It was enough for me to listen" (*Autobiographies* [*My Bondage*], 363). And so he passed his first years in freedom, providing for his family, attending church and antislavery meetings, reading Garrison's newspaper, a free man. "I was now my own master. It was a happy moment, the rapture of which can be understood only by those who have been slaves" (*Autobiographies* [*Narrative*], 95).

Douglass emerged as a public man in 1841 after attending a Massachusetts Anti-Slavery Society Convention in Nantucket. He went there with followers of William Lloyd Garrison who knew of his activities in the Bristol County Anti-Slavery Society. At the convention, on August 16, Douglass addressed the crowd about the horrors of slavery and launched his fifty-four-year career as an orator.

For ten years Douglass represented the Massachusetts Society and its Garrisonian version of antislavery: abolition, anticolonization, nonpolitical action, and nonviolence. He traveled with the antislavery road show detailing the abuses of slavery and using himself as a prima facie example of the dignity, humanity, and abilities of blacks. He suffered heckling from hostile audiences, segregation from racist innkeepers, and the paternalistic nuances of his abolitionist handlers who tried unsuccessfully to limit his remarks to the Garrisonian script. Through it all, Douglass charted his own path with righteous dignity. He spoke so well, in fact, that critics charged he could not have been a slave. To counter these accusations, Douglass wrote the first of his three autobiographies, *Narrative of the Life of Frederick Douglass, an American Slave, Written by Himself* (1845). Written as a propaganda tract and published by the Anti-Slavery Society, *Narrative* was an instant hit, selling 4,500 copies by September and 30,000 copies in five years, with editions in England, Ireland, Holland, and France.

Publication of the *Narrative* rendered Douglass, still legally a slave, more vulnerable to capture than he already was. On August 16, 1845, therefore, he left the United States for England. This nineteen-month sojourn was a revelation for the orator. Despite the fact that he was constantly monitored by agents of the Anti-Slavery Society, lest he act up or speak out of turn, Douglass was celebrated in England. He spoke to huge crowds throughout the United Kingdom and found there a freedom from color consciousness absent in the United States. Garrison joined him in August 1846, and in December, his current owner, Hugh Auld, filed manumission papers for him in Baltimore after Douglass's English supporters paid $711.66 for the slave's freedom, an act that did not go uncriticized by Garrisonians who needed him to be an object for their cause rather than a free person.

Douglass returned to the United States in April 1847 a truly free man and an international celebrity. Against the wishes of the Garrisonians, and again with the largess of his English supporters, Douglass started his own abolitionist newspaper, *North Star*, in Rochester, New York, late in the year. The Garrisonians, chagrined at Douglass's independent course, and revealing more about themselves than they probably cared to, assailed him bitterly, eventually made the most highly charged accusation against him, that he had a sexual relationship with Julia Griffith, the Englishwoman who became his confidante and manager at *North Star*.

By 1851, his separation from the Garrisonians complete, Douglass emerged as a central figure in American racial reform. As James McCune Smith observed, he had "become a colored man!" He was, Smith said, "one newly born among us" (Walker, 246). Yet while his goal was always abolition and racial equality, he gave visible and wholehearted support to the women's suffrage movement and spoke favorably about temperance and prison reform. He also pursued strategies to achieve his ends. In June 1851, for instance, he merged *North Star* with Gerrit Smith's Liberty party newspaper to create a broadly based sheet called *Frederick Douglass' Paper*. He also shifted his program away from the Garrisonians. He urged direct political action, and he began to condone violence as a means of achieving his abolitionist and equalitarian goals. Denouncing the new fugitive slave law in 1852, he said that "the only way to make the . . . Law a dead letter is to make half a dozen or more dead kidnappers" (Foner, 2:207). Ever the pragmatist, however, he drew back from supporting John Brown's Harper's Ferry raid in 1859. Implicated in that action by circumstantial evidence, Douglass went underground and then to England for an already planned speaking tour.

By the time the Civil War began, Douglass spoke with the moral authority of an authentic African-American leader. He criticized Abraham Lincoln (q.v.) every time the president temporized on slavery and pressed his view that the war was primarily a war of black liberation. On this he was always clear: "The principles involved in the contest . . . demand the utter extirpation of slavery from every foot of American soil, and the enfranchisement of the entire colored population" (Foner, 3:402). He also argued the proposition that blacks should participate in their own liberation. Although Douglass was disappointed with

Lincoln's action, the Emancipation Proclamation was pregnant with implications, and the decision to organize black combat regiments gave blacks a visible presence in the struggle. Douglass was in the limelight; he recruited four black regiments, and two of his sons joined the fabled 54th Massachusetts and fought at Fort Wagner, South Carolina.

Emancipation prompted many abolitionists to feel that their work was completed, but such attitudes only confirmed Douglass's observation that abolition was the white man's agenda and did not take into consideration the best interests of blacks. For Douglass, emancipation was only the beginning—equality, integration, and assimilation were the goals. During Reconstruction, Douglass sought black enfranchisement. He urged ratification of the Fifteenth Amendment, despite the fact that it did not include women and led to a twenty-five-year breech in his relationship with the women's suffrage movement.

Achieving emancipation and Radical Reconstruction were the culmination of Douglass's public advocacy. Yet, in the years following Reconstruction, Douglass disappeared into the Republican party and lost credibility as a leader. Indeed, as he achieved respectability and middle-class status, he lost visibility as a leader as his life became less about black liberation and more emblematic of rags-to-riches material advancement. Before the war his life story was still vital; in 1855 he published his second autobiography, *My Bondage and My Freedom*. It sold 15,000 copies in two months. In 1881 he published his third autobiography, *The Life and Times of Frederick Douglass*. It sold so poorly that his publishers reintroduced it in 1882 but to no avail. Ten years later, yet a third edition appeared, again to a poor reception.

Circumstances conspired to remove Douglass from the center of the racial fray. For one thing, he was sixty years old in 1878, and while still vigorous, he longed for status and respectability, the rewards bought with years of struggle. President Rutherford B. Hayes appointed him U.S. marshall for the District of Columbia in 1877, and President James A. Garfield made him Recorder of Deeds for the District in 1881. These posts were more honorific than substantive.

Furthermore, there was little he could do or say to prevent the Republican party's retreat from supporting the so-called fruits of the war—African-American political and civil equality. He didn't give up the fiery rhetoric; it just didn't bear the weight it had before the war. He denounced the Republican party, saying in September 1883 that "if the Republican party cannot stand a demand for justice and fair play, it ought to go down" (Foner, 4:381). He condemned the Civil Rights Cases decision, which undermined the critical Civil Rights Act of 1875, saying in October 1883, "I look upon it as one more shocking development of that moral weakness in high places" (Foner, 4:397). But in the end, his efforts were useless.

Aside from two minor diplomatic assignments, one to Santo Domingo in 1871 and another to Haiti from 1889 to 1891, Douglass existed on the margins of politics. And despite his expressed indignation at the resubjugation of American blacks and his support of such new black leaders as Ida B. Wells, he became increasingly out of touch with the lives of his people largely owing to his second marriage to a white woman, Helen Pitts, in 1884 and his extensive, eleven-month European tour (1886–1887).

Douglass lived out the rest of his long life at Cedar Hill, in the Anacostia section of Washington, D.C. He purchased a twenty-room house on nine acres in 1873 and lived there in the bourgeois lifestyle that was regarded as appropriate for one who had succeeded in the capitalist system. Yet however removed Douglass became from the everyday life of other black Americans, he never lost sight of the goal of black equality and assimilation in America.

When he died at Cedar Hill on the evening of February 20, 1895, after attending a National Council of Women meeting and being escorted to the stage by his old friend Susan B. Anthony, Douglass was already a legend. Yet after an initial flurry, interest in his life fell into a deep trough until the 1940s. His own works remained virtually out of print until the 1960s. Since then, writing about Douglass has been a veritable cottage industry, more so than for perhaps any other black leader.

Frederick Douglass created his own story in three autobiographies. Although he lamented in later years that "I shall never get beyond Fredk Douglass the self-educated fugitive slave" (Barome, 217), his *Narrative of the Life of Frederick Douglass* (1845), *My Bondage and My Freedom* (1855), and *The Life and Times of Frederick Douglass* (1881, rev. ed. 1892) all projected the persona Douglass wanted the public to identify with. All these autobiographies remained out of print until 1941, when Pathway Press reprinted *Life and Times*. Finally, all three works reappeared in the context of the civil rights movement of the 1950s and 1960s—the *Narrative* in 1960 from Belknap Press, *Life and Times* from Collier Books in 1962, and in 1968 *My Bondage* from Arno Press. In 1994 the Library of America published all three in a critical edition called *Autobiographies* (used here).

For the most part, biographers have told the story as he told it—a morality tale of rags to riches, good triumphing over evil. Yet Douglass was such a protean character that he became a talisman for his biographer' respective agendas. Two early biographies, one in 1891 by Frederick Holland and the other in 1893 by James Gregory, uncritically celebrated Douglass the orator. Charles W. Chesnutt's 1899 *Frederick Douglass* celebrated his life and work as a refutation of then-current Social Darwinist theories. In 1906, Booker T. Washington weighed in with a portrait that had Douglass playing John the Baptist of industrial education to Washington's Jesus Christ. William Pickens's 1912 portrait *Frederick Douglass and the Spirit of Freedom* focuses on Douglass the abolitionist. After that, interest in the Sage of Cedar Hill faded.

The two historians responsible for bringing Douglass out of obscurity and fueling the explosion of work on him were Benjamin Quarles and Philip Foner. Based on original sources, Quarles's *Frederick Douglass* (1948) sought to put Douglass back into the story of antebellum and abolitionist politics, from which he had been excluded by the Dunning School historians. For Quarles, Douglass followed the Horatio Alger career path.

Despite Douglass's commitment to capitalism, Philip S. Foner portrayed him as a black Marxist who helped free the Negroes. Foner's great contribution to the Douglass story was to gather many of his speeches and letters into *The Life and Writings*, published in four volumes from 1950 to 1955 (with a supplementary volume in 1975).

Douglass's dramatic and ennobling story is ripe for treatment in juvenile literature and quasi-fictional biography. Among the better treatments in this genre are Shirley Graham's *There Was Once a Slave* (1947) and Arna Bontemps's *Free at Last* (1971).

Until the 1970s none of his biographers had challenged Douglass's portrait of himself or the way he emplotted his story. Peter Walker's *Moral Choices* (1978) brilliantly paved the way to a fuller portrait of Douglass by prying into his writings. Then, in 1980, Dickson Preston published *Young Frederick Douglass*, a work in which the author sought to uncover the details and context of Douglass's life in Maryland. Preston uncovered aspects of Douglass's lost past, and of the past that he obscured, that placed his life in an entirely new context. William McFeely's *Frederick Douglass* (1991) is the latest book-length biography. Richly detailed, and drawing on the torrent of Douglass primary and secondary materials, McFeely offers to the reader a multidimensional leader. Works like McFeely's are helped immeasurably by the publication of *The Papers of Frederick Douglass*. Under the editorship of John Blassingame, and now up to five volumes, the first series consists of his speeches and debates.

Surprisingly, until the publication of Waldo Martin's *The Mind of Frederick Douglass* (1984) and David Blight's *Frederick Douglass's Civil War* (1989), there had been no intellectual biography. These important works have been augmented by William Andrews, editor, *Critical Essays on Frederick Douglass* (1991), and Eric Sundquist, editor, *Frederick Douglass: New Literary and Historical Essays* (1990). These collections of essays assess Douglass's commitment to his race and help add dimension to the portrait he bequeathed to prosperity.

The periodical literature for Douglass is enormous. One can begin to access it in M. Thomas Inge and coeditors, *Black American Writers*. Much of the recent work on Douglass has been by literary critics who deconstruct his autobiographies. David Dudley's *My Father's Shadow* (1991) gives the reader a good sense of this development, as does Deborah McDowell's essay ''In the First Place: Making Frederick Douglass and the African American Narrative Tradition.''

Even as recent biographers and critics have begun to unravel the Frederick Douglass who has been obscured from history, they have not shaken his reputation. He remains today what he was when he died: a prodigious symbol for his race and an exemplar for all Americans.

BIBLIOGRAPHY

Frederick Douglass, *Narrative of the Life of Frederick Douglass, an American Slave, Written by Himself* (Boston: Antislavery Office, 1845).

Frederick Douglass, *My Bondage and My Freedom* (New York: Miller, Orton & Mulligan, 1855).

Frederick Douglass, *The Life and Times of Frederick Douglass, Written by Himself* (Hartford, Conn.: Park Publishing Co., 1881).

Frederick M. Holland, *Frederick Douglass: The Colored Orator* (New York: Funk and Wagnalls, 1891).

James M. Gregory, *Frederick Douglass: The Orator* (Springfield, Mass.: Wiley & Co., 1893).

Charles W. Chesnutt, *Frederick Douglass* (Boston: Small Maynard and Co., 1899).

Booker T. Washington, *Frederick Douglass* (Philadelphia: George W. Jacobs and Co., 1906).

William Pickens, *Frederick Douglass and the Spirit of Freedom* (Boston: The Arakelyan Press 1912).

Shirley Graham, *There Was Once a Slave* (New York: Julian Messner, Inc., 1947).

Benjamin Quarles, *Frederick Douglass* (Washington, D.C.: Associated Publishers, 1948).

Philip S. Foner, *The Life and Writings of Frederick Douglass*, 4 vols. (New York: International Publishers, 1950–1955).

Joseph A. Barome, ed., "Some Additional Light on Frederick Douglass," *Journal of Negro History* 38, no. 2 (April 1953): 216–224.

Arna Bontemps, *Free at Last: The Life of Frederick Douglass* (New York: Dodd, Mead, 1971).

M. Thomas Inge, et al., eds., *Black American Writers: Bibliographical Essays*, vol. I (New York: St. Martin's Press, 1978).

Peter F. Walker, *Moral Choices* (Baton Rouge: Louisiana State University Press, 1978).

John W. Blassingame and John R. McKivigan, eds., *The Papers of Frederick Douglass*, 5 vols. (New Haven, Conn.: Yale University Press, 1979–   ).

Nathan Irvin Huggins, *Slave and Citizen: The Life of Frederick Douglass* (Boston: Little, Brown, 1980).

Dickson J. Preston, *Young Frederick Douglass: The Maryland Years* (Baltimore: Johns Hopkins University Press, 1980).

Waldo E. Martin, Jr., *The Mind of Frederick Douglass* (Chapel Hill: University of North Carolina Press, 1984).

David W. Blight, *Frederick Douglass's Civil War: Keeping Faith in Jubilee* (Baton Rouge: Louisiana State University Press, 1989).

Deborah E. McDowell, "In the First Place," *The Invisible Majority* (New Orleans: The Graduate School of Tulane University, 1990).

Eric J. Sundquist, ed., *Frederick Douglass: New Literary and Historical Essays* (New York: Cambridge University Press, 1990).

William L. Andrews, ed., *Critical Essays on Frederick Douglass* (Boston: G. K. Hall, 1991).

David L. Dudley, *My Father's Shadow: International Conflict in African American Men's Autobiography* (Philadelphia: University of Pennsylvania Press, 1991).

William S. McFeely, *Frederick Douglass* (New York: W. W. Norton, 1991).

Frederick Douglass, *Autobiographies* (New York: Library of America, 1994).

JOSIAH GORGAS
(July 1, 1818–May 18, 1883)

Jon L. Wakelyn

During the Civil War a number of leaders deserted their homeland to enlist on the side of the enemy. The Pennsylvania-born and -raised chief of the Confederate Ordnance Bureau, Josiah Gorgas, was one such person. During that great war, ordinary men from ordinary backgrounds with supposedly ordinary skills rarely rose to become the great leaders of their respective sides. But the slow, deliberate, sad but stern-looking man of Dutch descent did just that. Undistinguished in his prewar profession, Gorgas was to have, in the words of his biographer Frank Vandiver, "a military career which was to contribute more than any other man, with the exception of Robert E. Lee, [q.v.] to the success of the Armies of the Confederacy" (Vandiver, 6). Gorgas nearly worked miracles in making an agricultural society into a well-armed military machine. Perhaps for that colorless man of few words, there is a connection between his traitorous behavior to his own people and his ability to turn his mediocre prewar career into wartime genius.

The Ordnance wizard who made Confederate logistics was born on July 1, 1818, in Daupin County, Pennsylvania, to a proud family descended from the Dutch patroons of New York State. His father Joseph made clocks, at times worked as a mechanic, farmed a bit, and even kept an inn. His mother, Sophia Atkinson, daughter of a sturdy middle-class Pennsylvania farmer, had few distinctive qualities, save a desire to see her son succeed. The family at times barely scraped by, and young Josiah remembered moving many times, growing up lonely and without friends. In his early life in middle Pennsylvania, the family finally ended up in Lebanon County, where young Josiah received a smattering of schooling. At seventeen he moved in with a sister at Lyons, New York, where he apprenticed in a printing office. In that town, the hard-working young man met and impressed U.S. Congressman Graham Chapin and began to read law in his office. Like many a poor but ambitious youth, Josiah jumped at the chance for technical training when Congressman Chapin recommended him for West Point.

Gorgas had no real reason for going to the U.S. Military Academy, which he entered in 1837, as his dreams were not filled with scenes of military valor. Perhaps instead he merely hoped for the kind of training that could make him a better mechanic than his father. At West Point, Gorgas fell into the routine of hard work, diligence, and obedience. A few of his classmates felt he seemed a bit too ambitious and too certain he was right. To none of his peers' surprise, the young man who graduated in 1841 number six out of fifty-two chose service in the Ordnance Corps. Stationed at first in upstate New York he worked on rebuilding a fallen fort, then transferred to Detroit to study river defenses. The ambitious young man soon wanted a chance to learn more about engineering by studying in Europe, so he pushed hard for overseas duty. Perhaps he pushed too hard. Gorgas's angry and untoward letter to Secretary of State James Buchanan in 1845 demanding such an appointment nearly scuttled his career. Labeled a hothead, the powers at Washington resisted giving Gorgas any special treatment.

Even when the opportunity arose to better himself during the War with Mexico, his constant squabbling kept him from receiving credit. He was with the Winfield Scott expedition to Vera Cruz where he did good work setting up batteries to fire on that coastal town. His reward was the duty of protecting the coastal ordnance supply for the advancing army. Of course, he adequately supplied Scott's army, but then he quarreled with a superior. The new first lieutenant finally got to move forward, only to discover that he had joined the army after the fighting had stopped. Gorgas received no brevet appointment for field duty, so the war proved a bust for his career.

After the war had ended, Gorgas wangled an appointment to Fort Monroe, at Hampton Roads, Virginia, where he got to know Joseph Anderson (q.v.), a Southern munitions factory owner who would become the Confederacy's largest supplier of arms. Gorgas did quality work on gun experiments and began to gain the reputation as an expert on ordnance. But once again letters to superiors asking for favorable positions branded him as a troublemaker, and he did not get the posts he wanted. In 1853, the future leader took on the unhealthy task of rebuilding a fort around Mount Vernon, near Mobile, Alabama, where soldiers from the North often succumbed to the swampy and humid climate.

To break the monotony and keep his health, Gorgas found living quarters on the higher ground around Mobile. There he met the beautiful and intelligent Amelia Gayle, daughter of Judge John Gayle, former Alabama governor and congressman. John Gayle owned slaves, had a successful plantation, and lived the life of a Southern gentleman. The young couple soon married. Amelia loved the lush coastal land that was her home. Gorgas, however, longed to satisfy his ambitions, so he sought duty elsewhere. When he was transferred to Maine in 1854 to work on arsenal repair, she refused to go north. In 1858 the frustrated, middle-aged captain finally received a plum position to work on Charleston

Harbor. But he gained little recognition from Washington until Southern-born Secretary of War John B. Floyd, friend of John Gayle, became his champion. Gorgas had become an expert on ordnance, and in October 1860, Floyd put him on the prestigious Ordnance Board in Washington City. His job was to survey and replenish federal military inventories.

While stationed in the federal city, Gorgas and his wife hobnobbed with Southern congressional leaders. He soon acquired the reputation of being too friendly with the Southerners in Washington. Gorgas also feverishly watched the fragile federal relations come apart. On March 21, 1861, he resigned from the U.S. Army. Some have said he was maneuvering for a good federal post. Others insist that his newly gained Southern family ties, plus pressure from his wife, led him to look for service in the recently organized Confederate States Army. Whatever his true reasons, he cut his connections with his former friends in the U.S. Army and went south.

Confederate General P. G. T. Beauregard (q.v.) recognized his talents and helped Gorgas to get an offer as chief of ordnance in the Confederate Army with the rank of major. In many ways the man and the moment had met. When war broke out, Gorgas discovered that many Confederate state governments had purchased weapons, ammunition, and other military supplies for their own defenses that they refused to share with the national army. In addition, there were modern weapons in the Federal arsenal that the Confederate state governments had confiscated. Without support from the states to gather the necessary ordnance, Gorgas had to build his weapons stockpile nearly from scratch. Not one to be disheartened, he turned to the task of purchasing war materiel and finding ways to pay for those goods and the means to deliver war products to troops in the front lines. Gorgas wanted to centralize the ordnance operation, so he took the post of acting chief of the Engineering Bureau in April 1861, only to be relieved of that duty in August 1861. To furnish the army's needs, the chief of ordnance planned to secure arms in Europe. He wisely chose as his foreign agent Major Caleb Huse, the quiet genius who was able to buy the military goods needed until the Confederacy could set up its own factories. In addition, Gorgas knew the importance of protecting the coast and running Union blockades. Thus, early in the war, even before he had been given federal authority, he combined successfully the guile of blockade running and the adroit purchasing of military goods from supposed neutral powers.

Gorgas next overhauled, enlarged, and purchased new Confederate arsenals. He also established powder mills in strategic locations. Angry and frustrated at the resistance of private companies to his plans, Gorgas nevertheless was aware that the central government had to get along with local authorities. He gained promotion to lieutenant colonel in September 1861. He shunned details as he plunged to the center of issues, and used his growing skills of persuasion to get local support for production. Gorgas became an excellent spokesman for the cause before the Confederate Congress, as he lobbied that body to persuade the states to overcome their resistance to the Richmond government's appropriation of state property. He also contracted with General Joseph Anderson of the Tredegar Iron Works to set up a Confederate Armory in the strategic location of Richmond in order to supply the needs of the Army of Northern Virginia. In early 1862, Gorgas again used his genius for selecting fine subordinates when he put George W. Rains in charge of Confederate States powder manufacturing at the works in Augusta, Georgia. At that time Gorgas, who understood the place of politics in his job, became the friend and advocate of President Jefferson Davis (q.v.). On May 6, 1862, the Reverend Charles Minnegerode baptized and confirmed him at St. Paul's Episcopal Church in Richmond. As Gorgas stated, ''I trust I shall benefit by thus linking myself to the visible church'' (Vandiver, ed., 11).

Always in search of weapons, in 1862 Gorgas expanded his overseas and blockade running operations. He used Huse to funnel cash to Europe, and he acquired much needed funds in trading cotton for money through setting up the Bureau of Foreign Supplies. Wilmington, North Carolina, became the port to ship cotton. Bermuda and the Bahamas became the ports to run the blockade with newly purchased military supplies, especially for the needy Trans-Mississippi Department, which had no means of making its own weaponry. When speculators tried to break into his market, Gorgas fumed over their disloyalty. But later he persuaded the state governments to compete with private companies for the purchase of cotton in order to supply the Bureau with currency. Thanks to the activities of Gorgas in running the blockade to raise money, fully two-thirds of Confederate small arms came from purchases abroad.

Not satisfied to rely on foreign supplies alone, Gorgas continued to expand home production. He organized the Bureau of Nitre and Mining to produce powder and metal for home production of war implements. Later he formed the Artillery Bureau, even though Congress initially opposed him. To protect those factories, he enlisted expert factory workers to train as a home guard. To test the quality of goods produced, Gorgas turned to field examinations of weaponry. He became an expert at finding substitute materials to use for making weapons. Alas, the shortage of lead in 1862 could not be replaced by ersatz goods. Often he clashed with the Conscript Bureau, which wanted his skilled workers for front line duty. He would never have enough workers to produce quality armaments. Still, Gorgas treated subordinates with care, gave them much freedom to experiment, and seemed to get the most out of his dwindling numbers. His workers respected his support and in turn came up with many new inventions, including the sophisticated detonating instrument the Bormann fuse. With all of that accomplishment, by early 1863 Gorgas knew that manpower and raw products shortages would destroy the Confederacy's abilities to produce enough arms for its troops.

Yet he fought on. Gorgas became more and more strident as prices went up. Personal hardship and sacrifices followed as his family fell victim to hyperinflation. His response was to work even harder to impress upon his superiors that he needed more raw materials despite the cost. He accused Southern businessmen, especially the rich ones along the Carolina coast, of price gouging their own country. Their actions at last led Gorgas to support government impressment of private goods. That driven Northerner seemed unable to grasp that a number of Southerners had less love for their new country than did he.

By 1863, circumstances had forced him to advocate localism, or the decentralization of his operation from Richmond's control. He encouraged home manufacturing. For a time Gorgas put the quartermaster general in charge of transporting goods from throughout the Confederacy to the front lines. But because of exceedingly poor transportation facilities, Gorgas decentralized that task, too. Adjusting logistics to supply at the local distribution point, miraculously he continued to supply troops in the front lines. But field commanders did not always coordinate their local efforts with him, and often supply depots were left unprotected.

Despite the dwindling resources for war, the Bureau chief continued his efforts. Increasingly operating without needed funds, he often could not pay the iron manufacturers. With federal troops occupying more and more Confederate land, Gorgas knew that mineral deposits such as the copper mines of east Tennessee had been lost to his producers. The labor shortage continued to grow. State governments such as North Carolina stopped producing military goods. Unpaid private armories closed. The dreaded yellow fever hit Bermuda in June 1864, and that port, formerly so useful for bringing in arms, shut down. For his extraordinary ability to readapt, reorganize, and redeploy war goods, in November 1864, Gorgas was rewarded with the rank of brigadier general.

At war's end, the general's operation was pared down only to the defenses around Richmond. He still tried to move armament works to Alabama. But General William T. Sherman's (q.v.) march across Georgia in the winter of 1864 meant Gorgas no longer could supply guns to troops in the lower South. When Columbia, South Carolina, was lost to the Federals, the lower South was completely broken from its supply line. Gorgas passed control of that sector to Rains, but even that able subordinate was forced to flee his works. Then, in March 1865, the lead supply ran out completely. Gorgas was forced to flee Richmond, leaving his beloved family to fend for itself, as he continued to attempt to organize resistance. At the last, Gorgas was alone with no one to give orders to. His health and his new country had collapsed.

Amelia, his beloved wife for whom he had sacrificed so much, was disheartened. The former bureaucrat promised to recoup the family losses. When it became apparent that the federal government would not arrest him, the ex-general began to look for work. He had little funds, and for a time, even he grew despondent. His old ally John W. Mallet joined him in a scheme to set up an iron works in Brierfield, Alabama, but Gorgas had little funds to invest. High freight rates and a poor product left him unable to compete in a local or national market.

Forced to sell out in 1869, he used old military ties to gain a teaching job at Sewanee, the newly reopened University of the South, in Tennessee. Named headmaster of the junior department, his skills for reorganization and the practical shone. He wanted to revise the curriculum, to build new buildings, to prepare Southern youth for competitive reentry into the newly restored nation. In 1872, he was named vice chancellor, but the school was poor. Gorgas had both to manage the school and to offer courses in engineering and physics. In 1878, having given so much to Sewanee, and in declining health, he was forced to resign. Friends got him named the president of the University of Alabama in 1878, but he was too ill to really assume the position. In 1879 he was made university librarian, but his wife actually ran that operation. On May 18, 1883, Gorgas died.

Before he died, the man of ordinary ability who had become so useful to his adopted South completed his journal in which he assessed "the abilities of his contemporaries" (Vandiver, xxiii) as well as their loyalties to his adopted homeland. He viewed most of the citizenry unfavorably. The journal also revealed his love for his family and his influence on them, even if he did not have the wealth to help them. Sarah Wiggins, in her article in Carol Bleser's (ed.) *In Joy & Sorrow* on Gorgas's relationship with his children, captured the connection between the leader's character, his acquired Southernness, and his family. Wiggins said that his favored son Willie provided Gorgas with the final hope that his many sacrifices for the South had not been in vain. Neither of them could ever resist the bonds of his adopted South. Willie went to West Point to try to replicate his father's fabled career. But Willie came home to become a famous physician. The son's life in many ways repeated his father's devotion to the South.

What, then, has history had to say about the proud father and loyal converted Confederate Josiah Gorgas? Immediately after the war he was lionized in both sections as a miracle worker. But as the New South slipped into the romantic and antitechnical behavior of the lost cause, it ignored the Yankee who had become the Confederacy's greatest technocrat. He was all but forgotten until Frank E. Vandiver recovered his wartime diaries in the 1940s. Vandiver, in search of the story of the romantic blockade runners, instead discovered what that great student of logistics had done for the Southern cause. His biography has led to a more sophisticated study of total war. Vandiver's verdict on Gorgas smacks of truth. Gorgas deserved to be a great leader because of his organizational ability, his management style, and his skills at judging the talents of subordinates. In Vandiver's words, Gorgas had the "capacity to command from his associates a high degree of devotion" (*Ploughshares*, 314). Building on Vandiver, Richard Goff, in the splendid study *Confederate Supply*, focused on Gorgas's ability to supply the Confederate Army.

Most recently, Sarah W. Wiggins, seeking to understand the man behind the ordnance genius, has edited Gorgas's *Journals*. She has done a brilliant job, especially in the ways she linked the ex-leader's loyalty to the South and his abilities. But other than family ties and perhaps the opportunity to rise faster in the Confederacy, just why Gorgas sold out his homeland remains a mystery.

What is not a mystery, however, is what Gorgas thought of others who sacrificed too little for his cause. Gorgas, himself, leaves the final irony of his genius in his rousing anger against the effete aristocrats with whom he so wanted to identify yet who became traitors to his adopted country.

BIBLIOGRAPHY

Frank E. Vandiver, ed., *The Civil War Diary of General Josiah Gorgas* (University, Alabama: University of Alabama Press, 1947).

Frank E. Vandiver, *Ploughshares into Swords: Josiah Gorgas and Confederate Ordnance* (Austin: University of Texas Press, 1952).

Richard D. Goff, *Confederate Supply* (Durham: Duke University Press, 1969).

Mary Tabb Johnston, *Amelia Gayle Gorgas* (University, Alabama: University of Alabama Press, 1978).

Carol Bleser, ed., *In Joy and Sorrow* (New York: Oxford University Press, 1991).

Sarah Woolfolk Wiggins, ed., *The Journals of Josiah Gorgas, 1857–1878* (Tuscaloosa: University of Alabama Press, 1995).

ULYSSES SIMPSON GRANT
(April 27, 1822–July 25, 1885)

John T. Hubbell

Ulysses S. Grant, general in chief of the Union Army, was born Hiram Ulysses Grant on April 27, 1822, in Mt. Pleasant, Ohio. His great-grandfather was killed in the French and Indian War, and his grandfather, Noah Grant, served six years in the Revolutionary War, reaching the rank of captain. His father, Jesse Grant (1794–1873), married Hannah Simpson on June 24, 1821. Jesse and Hannah were attentive parents to ''Lyss'' and encouraged an independence in him that bordered on the indifferent. Grant learned to ride early and well. He trained horses and by age twelve drove teams and wagons long distances, sometimes 200 to 250 miles. He also became an excellent marksman, although he never liked to kill animals.

When Grant entered the U.S. Military Academy in 1839, he stood five feet one and weighed 117 pounds. He was a casual student who tended toward slouchiness in dress and military bearing, but he excelled at horsemanship and long carried the reputation as one of the best riders in the army.

Grant graduated in 1843, twenty-first in a class of thirty-nine. He still weighed 117 pounds but had grown to five feet seven. His first assignment was to the 4th U.S. Infantry at Jefferson Barracks near St. Louis, where he met and became engaged to Julia Dent, the sister of Frederick Dent, his West Point roommate.

In June 1844, the 4th Infantry was deployed to Louisiana and then to Texas, whose annexation to the United States became a political issue and a cause for war with Mexico. In early 1846, Grant was a company officer in the army of Zachary Taylor, which pushed to the Rio Grande, opposite Matamoros. He believed that ''a better army, man for man, probably never faced an enemy'' (*Memoirs* 1:168). Some 90 percent of the 3,000 enlisted soldiers were regulars, and most of the junior officers were West Point graduates. In their first action, at Palo Alto, on May 8, 1846, Grant did not remember ''any peculiar sensation,'' although he appreciated the effectiveness of the American artillery and reflected on ''what a fearful responsibility General Taylor must feel, commanding such a host and so far away from his friends'' (1:94). After a second engagement at Resaca de la Palma, on May 9, Grant wrote Julia, "There is no great sport in having bullets fly about one in every direction, but I find I have less horror when among them than when in anticipation." He still sympathized with the Mexican people, but "now that the war has commenced with such a vengeance, I am in hope my dear Julia that we will soon be able to end it" (1:86).

In August 1846 Grant was named regimental quartermaster, a responsible and demanding assignment, although he would have preferred to remain a line officer. At Monterrey, September 21–22, Grant rode into battle with his regiment, although his orders were to remain with the supply wagons. He had taken it on himself to replace the regimental adjutant, who had been killed. At one point he volunteered to go for ammunition, riding his horse "Indian style" through the streets of Monterrey and the gunfire of the enemy.

Grant missed the fighting at Buena Vista, February 22–23, 1847, as the 4th Infantry had been ordered to service with Winfield Scott, who landed his army near Vera Cruz on March 9 and laid siege to the city rather than order an assault. The Mexican defenders surrendered on March 29, and on April 8, Scott began the march to Mexico City with an army of some 11,000 men. Victories at Cerro Gordo (April 18) and Puebla (May 15) preceded the final assault on the Mexican capital, beginning August 15. To this point Grant believed that Scott's tactics were flawless, but he also came to believe that the direct and bloody assaults against Mexico City were ill considered. He would have advised an encirclement of the city and an attack from the north, where the ground was solid and natural obstacles less formidable. However, in his *Memoirs* he wrote: "[M]y later experience has taught me two lessons: first that things are seen plainer after the events have occurred; second, that the most confident critics are generally those who know the least about the matter criticized." Further, "General Scott's successes are an answer to all criticism" (1:165–166).

Grant emerged from this war with a reputation for modesty, competence, and coolness under fire. He won brevets to first lieutenant (September 8, 1847) and captain (September 13, 1847) and was "mentioned in dispatches" by John Garland, the lieutenant colonel of the 4th Infantry. His Mexican War experience "was of great advantage" to him, as there were "many practical lessons" taught in the field, and the "war brought nearly all of the officers of the regular army together so as to make them personally acquainted" (*Memoirs* 1:191–192). In the Civil War, he knew that the Confederate generals, even Robert E. Lee (q.v.), were mortal and not to be feared.

On August 22, 1848, Grant married Julia Dent, his first and enduring love. They were stationed at Sackett's Harbor, New York, and Madison Barracks in Detroit until June 15, 1852, when Grant left for California. Julia and his sons, Frederick Dent (May 30, 1850) and Ulysses, Jr. (July 22, 1852), stayed behind. For the next two years Grant served at Fort Vancouver in Washington Territory and Fort Humboldt in California. He was promoted to captain on August 9,

1853, but could not withstand the loneliness, the boredom, and an overwhelming sense of personal and professional inertia. Business investments failed, and he began to drink excessively. Grant was a binge drinker and not especially tolerant of alcohol. He may have been encouraged to resign because of his "bad habits" and did so effective July 1, 1854.

Jesse Grant was disgusted with his war hero son and tried to persuade Secretary of War Jefferson Davis (q.v.) to delay the resignation. Nor did Julia seem especially overjoyed to see her husband. At age thirty-two Grant was to begin a new life. He tried farming and real estate and applied unsuccessfully for a government job. Old army friends pitied him and reported that he appeared to be depressed. In his own mind he had failed, especially as compared to his father and father-in-law. Still, he was steadfastly true, as always, to Julia, and he was not drinking, notwithstanding the incentives. In 1860 he moved to Galena, Illinois, to manage a tanning business with his brother Simpson, who was dying of tuberculosis. He now had two more children (Ellen, July 4, 1855, and Jesse Root Grant II, February 6, 1858).

After the election of 1860, friends reported that Grant spoke more often of his military experiences and expectations of war. When Galena raised a company after the firing on Fort Sumter, Grant refused the captaincy, because of his age and experience, but helped with recruitment and drill and continued to serve as a mustering officer while seeking a colonelcy and regimental command. He had been a combat soldier, to be sure, but he also knew how to "move paper," to process government forms. This last skill was of particular value in his first assignments, as a staff officer in Springfield and as commander of the 21st Illinois Volunteers.

Grant and his regiment learned together and grew in confidence together. On their first march, into Missouri to deal with that distracted and divided population, Grant said that his soldiers "behaved admirably." He knew that this war would be fought by volunteers—citizen soldiers—and he would have to be both teacher and commanding officer. He also learned from his first brush with the enemy that his counterpart "had as much reason to fear my forces as I had his. The lesson was valuable" (*Memoirs* 1:250). Indeed, he may have learned the lesson too well, as he was given to taking too little account of the opposition. Because of the need to expand the army, President Abraham Lincoln (q.v.) on July 31, 1861, submitted twenty-six names to Congress for promotion to brigadier general. Grant, who stood sixth on the list, thanked his congressman Elihu B. Washburne for his support, but in fact he had already attracted attention for his early effectiveness.

In early September 1861 Grant was posted to Cairo, Illinois, strategically situated at the confluence of the Ohio and Mississippi Rivers. There he was to resist Confederate probes northward and to plan Union movements via the western rivers into the Southern interior. He also demonstrated his early grasp of the political dimensions of the war, namely, the need to hold Kentucky for the Union.

On September 6, Grant took Paducah, at the mouth of the Tennessee. In November, he moved with a force of some 3,000 men to attack a small Confederate force at Belmont on the Missouri side of the Mississippi. It was a Union victory, but Grant neglected a proper reconnaissance, established no reserve force, and finished the day at the rear of a chaotic withdrawal in which he might have been captured. Grant chose to see the battle as a tactical success, as it encouraged his men and seemed to unbalance the Confederates.

Engagements at Forts Henry and Donelson in February 1862 gave Grant national attention and one of the classic military nicknames, "Unconditional Surrender." Fort Henry, on the Tennessee, and Fort Donelson, on the Cumberland, stood in the way of Union gunboats and a general advance up those rivers. Fort Henry was poorly situated and fell early. Fort Donelson was held by a considerable force and not as open to an attack by gunboats. A Confederate counterattack on February 15, while Grant was consulting with Andrew Hull Foote, commander of the gunboat squadron, almost broke the Union lines. When Grant returned, he reorganized the demoralized soldiers, saw to it that ammunition was distributed, and ordered an attack, which carried the day. As Grant put it, "The men only wanted someone to give them a command" (*Memoirs* 1:308). It was not the last time that he would take control of a bad situation and turn it to his favor. To Confederate commander and old army friend Simon Bolivar Buckner, he wrote: "No terms except an unconditional and immediate surrender can be accepted. I propose to move immediately upon your works." Buckner accepted the "ungenerous and unchivalrous terms" and surrendered the garrison (1:311–312).

Fort Donelson was Grant's first great victory. He had understood and acted on the need to control the Tennessee and Cumberland Rivers. He had forced the Confederates from western Kentucky and opened Tennessee to invasion. The South lost a vital recruiting area, and the political effect on the Northwest was immediate and pronounced.

Grant wanted to press his advantage and urged moves on Memphis and Nashville and in fact dispatched troops up the Cumberland to the Tennessee capital. His actions, while eminently sensible to him, brought on him the resentment of Don Carlos Buell and the outright enmity of his department commander, Henry Wager Halleck (q.v.). Halleck tried to parlay victory at Fort Donelson into overall command in the West for himself and promotions to major general for Buell, Grant, and John Pope. But within weeks, he also tried to have Grant removed from command of a projected movement up the Tennessee. He told General in Chief George B. McClellan (q.v.) that Grant's army was in disarray and that Grant himself refused to forward the proper reports and returns to department headquarters in St. Louis: "It is hard to censure a successful general immediately after a victory, but I think he richly deserves it," (*Papers* 4:320). McClellan added his bit to this extraordinary exchange by authorizing Grant's arrest and removal from command. In response, Halleck reported that Grant had "resumed his former bad habits," and while it was "not advisable to arrest him at present,'' he had placed Major General Charles F. Smith in charge of the Tennessee River expedition (*Papers* 4:320).

Smith had been commandant of cadets while Grant was at West Point, and a generation of cadets regarded the tall, imposing officer as the *beau ideal* of a soldier. In his *Memoirs*, Grant recalled that Halleck believed Smith to be ''a much fitter officer for the command of all the forces in the military district than I was. . . . I was rather inclined to this opinion myself at that time'' (1:328). He assured Smith that he would cheerfully cooperate in making the expedition a success, but he also defended himself to Halleck in terms both pointed and dignified. And he sent copies of his letters to his political patron, Congressman Elihu B. Washburne, who had the attention of the president. Grant was also supported by his staff officers and by his senior subordinates. In the face of this powerful support, Halleck restored him to command.

The Tennessee River expedition was to cut the major railroads that crossed at Corinth, Mississippi. In a strategic counterstroke, a Confederate Army under Albert Sidney Johnston began to assemble at Corinth with the intent to strike the Union forces before they could reach full strength. Grant in turn was to await the arrival of Buell's army before he initiated a general engagement. His forward division commander, William T. Sherman (q.v.), was to remain at Pittsburg Landing, ''making such fortifications as may be necessary for temporary defense'' and through ''frequent and extended'' reconnaissances to ''keep well informed of the strengths of the enemy'' (*Papers* 4:379). Grant did not expect Johnston to attack him and was clearly eager to begin offensive operations as early as possible. He wrote to Halleck on April 5, ''I have scarcely the faintest idea of an attack, (general one) being made upon us but will be prepared should such a thing take place'' (*Papers* 5:14). Early on the next day came the battle of Shiloh.

The Union Army suffered significant casualties on the first day, April 6, and during the counterattack on April 7. Grant took control of the field and proved once again to be an effective and courageous battle leader. But for the rest of his life he was obliged to defend the deployment of his army and against the charge that through his neglect his forward divisions were surprised and subjected to needless casualties. In his *Memoirs* he commented on the ''all day struggle'' and that for the most part he maintained a ''continuous and unbroken line.'' There were no entrenchments because he believed that his inexperienced soldiers, officers, and men needed drill and discipline ''more than they did experience with the pick, shovel and ax,'' (*Memoirs* 1:342, 357).

Grant did not think in terms of what the enemy might do; his instinct for the offensive was not balanced by appropriate caution or respect for the enemy army. The greater tactical error was in not preparing for a pursuit on the second day. Grant rather weakly explained that his army was exhausted, and he did not feel easy enough with Buell to order or even request that he organize a pursuit with his fresh troops. Nor is there any record of Buell urging such a move.

After Shiloh, Halleck took command of the now-massive Union Army, whose resources and initiative he frittered away over the next several weeks. Grant was effectively shelved at Memphis and given nominal command of West Tennessee, where he entertained and set aside the idea of resigning. His prospects were revived when Halleck was posted to Washington as general-in-chief.

Grant's preoccupation was Vicksburg, the fortress city that prevented Union control of the Mississippi. After setbacks at Holly Springs and Chickasaw Bluffs in December 1862 and a modest victory at Arkansas Post on January 11, 1863, Grant took overall command (over McClernand and Sherman) of the campaign to open the Mississippi. The plan that he eventually followed was the simplest: to get his army below Vicksburg and on the east bank of the river, where he would have room to maneuver. On April 30, he landed three corps near Bruinsburg. In Grant's words, "When this was effected I felt a degree of relief scarcely ever equaled since." He "was on dry ground on the same side of the river with the enemy. All the campaigns, labors, hardships and exposures from the month of December previous to this time that had been made and endured, were for the accomplishment of this one object" (*Memoirs* 1:480–481). In a series of engagements Grant forced the Confederate Army under John C. Pemberton into the formidable works around Vicksburg. Two bloody assaults failed on May 22 and then Grant settled in for a siege. On July 4, the Confederate garrison surrendered, and on July 9, Port Hudson, below Vicksburg, fell. As Lincoln later phrased it, the "Father of Waters again goes unvexed to the sea" (*Works* 6: 409).

Grant now thought in terms of a large movement on Mobile, in concert with the Army of the Cumberland's pressure on Braxton Bragg (q.v.) in central Tennessee. Unfortunately, the Lincoln administration was interested in Texas and cotton—hence, the ill-advised and ill-fated Red River Campaign. On September 19–20 came the Union reversal at Chickamauga and the subsequent bottling up of the Army of the Cumberland at Chattanooga. Its commander, William S. Rosecrans, was thoroughly demoralized by the defeat, and his army was in danger of starving. In consequence Grant was given command of all Union forces in the West (except for those of Nathanial Banks in Louisiana). He immediately moved his headquarters to Chattanooga and replaced Rosecrans with George H. Thomas (q.v.), a formidable personality and commander with whom Grant had an uneasy personal and professional relationship. Grant had never liked or trusted or respected Rosecrans. His differences with Thomas were more complex. They were strong-willed men of powerful intelligence, but Thomas was often slow to act, while Grant understood that decisiveness, a clear idea, was essential to command. But decisiveness could become impatience, even rashness, as at Shiloh and again at Chattanooga.

In November 1863 the Army of the Cumberland was not ready for a sustained offensive, a circumstance of bad weather, short rations, and the recent beating at Chickamauga. When Braxton Bragg detached James Longstreet's (q.v.) corps to attack Ambrose Burnside at Knoxville, Grant wanted Thomas to attack the northern end of Missionary Ridge. Thomas thought the better course was to wait for Sherman to arrive with reinforcements from the Army of the Tennessee. In any case, it would be best to attack Lookout Mountain, on the Union right, where Joe Hooker (q.v.) was in command. Grant agreed to wait for Sherman, whom he trusted, but he harbored misgivings about Thomas.

The battle of Chattanooga on November 23–26 was a significant victory for Grant but one that again left him vulnerable to criticism. The plan was for Sherman to seize the high ground on Bragg's right, especially Tunnel Hill. Unfortunately and inexplicably Sherman failed, mainly because he misread the terrain and allowed Patrick Cleburne's Confederate division to seize the tactical advantage. At this point Grant still could have made better use of Hooker, who more or less on his own took Lookout Mountain. Grant ordered Thomas to attack the Confederate center, which was effected amidst great command confusion. The Union forces took the rifle pits at the base of Missionary Ridge and after a slight pause moved to the crest and drove Bragg's demoralized soldiers before them. The credit for the Union success lay with the division and brigade commanders who kept the attack moving. Grant seemed surprised by the continued attack, and the confused and vague orders could have produced a disaster. Neither Thomas nor Grant were at the top of their form. Nor was Sherman, for that matter.

Grant wrote in his *Memoirs* that he had in fact given Thomas authority to carry Missionary Ridge and expected him to do it. He forgave (and promoted) Sherman and implied that his attack was meant to be a diversion. He never lost his confidence in Sherman or his lack of confidence in Thomas. It is not altogether clear why Grant did not pursue Bragg's army; he seems not to have had a plan beyond driving the enemy away from Chattanooga. He did send a force under Sherman to relieve Burnside at Knoxville, an unnecessary mission as it turned out. No Union general present thought in terms of a full-blooded pursuit of Bragg.

Grant's reward for Chattanooga was his elevation to general in chief, on March 3, 1864, and to the rank of lieutenant general. It was an appointment applauded by those who believed that he would bring both energy and vision to a central command too long occupied by reluctant warriors such as McClellan and Halleck. His approach to the larger war was evident in January 1864 when at the invitation of Halleck he proposed early movements from Chattanooga and Mobile and against Raleigh. These grand excursions into the interior would disrupt Confederate communications and lessen their ability to concentrate or take the offensive. Halleck did not accept Grant's ideas, preferring, as did Lincoln, that he focus his attention, at least in Virginia, on Lee's army.

Grant adapted to political realities, that the administration and the public preferred that the Eastern army close with Lee's, which by the spring of 1864 was the political and military center of gravity of the Confederacy. Thus Grant of necessity confronted the South's premier army and its foremost commander. The Virginia campaign of 1864–1865 is the campaign for which Grant is most remembered, overshadowing even his great successes in the West.

Grant established his headquarters not in Washington but with the Army of the Potomac, which was still commanded by George G. Meade (q.v.). Meade had graciously offered to step aside, should Grant wish to take direct command or name a commander of his choice. It was an awkward arrangement, but it is unlikely that Meade could have handled Lee on his own.

The opening battle, that of the Wilderness, May 5–6, 1864, was tactically in Lee's favor, but it forced him to remain on the defensive for the remainder of the war. Grant's decision to "move South" inspirited his army, but the bloody second round at Spotsylvania, May 10–13, was predictive of the carnage ahead. Grant proposed "to fight it out on this line if it takes all summer," but in the process he almost used up the old Army of the Potomac. Once again, the failures stemmed from faulty execution of plans, perhaps inevitable given the "dual command" of the Army of the Potomac. Faulty execution there was, but Grant chose to advance through the Wilderness, which negated his numerical advantage, his freedom to maneuver, and the effectiveness of his artillery. His habitual loose rein on his commanders, noticeable at Shiloh and Chattanooga, was more costly in Virginia. Illustrative is the debacle called the Battle of the Crater, which failed because Grant and Meade had little interest in it and Ambrose Burnside was, as usual, ineffectual. Equally illustrative is Grant's reaction to Jubal Early's actions in the Shenandoah Valley. Grant had written that Sheridan was to "put himself South of the enemy, and follow him to the death." Lincoln approved of the sentiment but said: "I repeat to you it will neither be done nor attempted unless you watch it every day, and hour, and force it" (*Papers* 7:343, 344). Grant never did "watch it every day and hour," except at Vicksburg. It was an inexplicable flaw in an innately clear-minded man.

Grant's reputation as a general brutally unmindful of casualties was sealed at Cold Harbor on June 1–2, 1864, where thousands of Union soldiers paid the price for an assault against the entrenched Confederates. He later expressed regret for his decision, but little excuse can be found for his lapse into impatience and fatalism, akin to that of Lee on July 3, 1863.

Grant did not sink into self-recrimination. Only days after Cold Harbor he skillfully withdrew his vast army from Lee's front, crossed the James River, and reached Petersburg before Lee fully recovered. His lead corps commanders, William F. Smith and Winfield Scott Hancock, did not press their advantage against the as-yet weakly defended city, while Lee steadily and rapidly reinforced P. G. T. Beauregard (q.v.). After belated and failed assaults, the Union Army settled in for a long and arduous siege. It was a disappointing end to what many observers, at the time and after, called a failed campaign. In six weeks, Grant's army had suffered 60,000 casualties, a large price for a long-delayed victory—a victory delayed until he wore down Lee's army through months of incessant pressure and bombardment.

Grant now moved to a new arena, and not reluctantly. President and cabinet officers asked his opinion on political matters, and he willingly responded, suggesting that he had given considerable thought to national issues. The assassination of Lincoln brought him even more center stage and into the politics of

Reconstruction. Outwardly, he stood aside from the conflict between President Andrew Johnson (q.v.) and the Congress, secure in his status as general-in-chief. A careful reading of events suggests that Grant was protecting not only the nonpolitical tradition of the army but his own position as a possible political leader. The political adroitness glimpsed during his western campaigns was now honed to a fine edge. He supported military Reconstruction, to a point, yet maintained a public deference to the president. Johnson tried to rid himself of Edwin P. Stanton (q.v.) by appointing Grant Secretary of War ad interim. Grant was rescued from an increasingly awkward situation when the Senate voted to reinstate Stanton. This move allowed Grant to retreat gracefully from a tactically untenable position. Johnson's impeachment trial occupied his last year of office and opened the way for Grant to become the Republican candidate for president in 1868 and reelection in 1872.

Grant is usually portrayed as a failure in the White House, his administration being marked by corruption and the abandonment of the freed people to the tender mercies of the white South. Only as slight mitigation is the fact of general corruption among public and private men in the mid-nineteenth century and that if Grant, or any other president, had tried to protect the African-American population, he would have had to mobilize the full force of the national government, including the army, to do it.

After his presidency, Grant traveled and enjoyed his fame. Business connections turned sour cost him his financial security, which he recovered by publishing his *Memoirs*. It was a success made heroic because he wrote it while dying of cancer. His passing, on July 25, 1885, was widely mourned by a grateful and forgiving public.

Grant's rank as at least one of the dominant generals of the Civil War (Lee and Sherman being his primary rivals) has survived his contemporaries and three generations of military historians.

In the monumental *Battles and Leaders* (1887), reviews were mixed. Lew Wallace, who had some reason to resent Grant, praised his restraint and balance at Fort Donelson. "He knew how to keep his temper. In battle, as in camp, he went about quietly, speaking in a conversational tone; yet he appeared to see everything that went on, and was always intent on business" (*Battles and Leaders* 1:404). Don Carlos Buell was much less generous in his account of Shiloh. He chided Grant for deploying his lead divisions in an exposed position at Pittsburg Landing and none too subtly suggests that he rescued Grant and his army. Nor was Buell impressed by Grant's leadership in the field. "The record is silent and tradition adverse to any marked influence that he exerted upon the fortune of the day. . . . We read of some indefinite or unimportant directions given without effect to straggling bodies of troops in the rear. That is all" (*Battles and Leaders* 1:536).

Confederate Major General E. M. Law's assessment of Grant "from the Wilderness to Cold Harbor" aptly summarized not only the opinion of his army but a characterization of Grant that remained for decades. Confederate officers believed that his success in the West was "due more to the weakness of the forces opposed to him and the bad generalship of their commanders than to any great ability on his part" (*Battles and Leaders* 4:142). They expected him to pursue a "policy of force" but were not prepared for the unparalleled stubbornness and tenacity with which he persisted in his attacks in the Wilderness and at Spotsylvania. The "universal verdict was that he was no strategist and that he relied almost entirely upon the brute force of numbers for success" (*Battles and Leaders* 4:142).

Adam Badeau noted that Grant "had fought and beaten every important rebel soldier in turn." He grew in experience, skill, and confidence, but the essence of his generalship was evident at the beginning. These were "steadfastness under difficulties," "invention in unexpected emergencies," daring, fortitude, a "quick intuition," and a genius for grasping the critical stage of a battle.

There were no comments in *Battles and Leaders*, negative or positive, about Grant at Chattanooga, but William Farrar Smith's critique of Grant's own article states that he was "unjust to the memory" (*Battles and Leaders* 3:715) of General Thomas. Specifically, Grant was given credit for (or took credit for) plans that had been developed by Thomas. Smith, and other admirers of Thomas, continued to believe that both Grant and Sherman were ungenerous in their appraisals of Thomas.

Sherman admired Grant, to whom he owed much, but was often patronizing even while praising him. In 1862 he remarked that Grant was "not himself a brilliant man" but was a "good and brave soldier . . . sober, very industrious and kind as a child" (Hart, 149). After Vicksburg, Grant was still "a good plain, sensible kind-hearted fellow" but perhaps susceptible to flattery (Hart, 200). In 1864, Sherman asked his senator brother to "give Grant all the support you can." He "is as good a leader as we can find. He has honesty, simplicity of character, singleness of purpose, and no hope or claim to usurp civil power. His character, more than his genius will reconcile armies and attach the people" (Hart, 229).

In his *Memoirs* (1875), Sherman published a letter of March 10, 1864, in which he replied to Grant's statement that to Sherman and James B. McPherson, "above all others," he was "indebted for whatever I have had of success." Sherman wrote that he gave them too much credit. Grant was like Washington,

brave, patriotic and just; as unselfish, kind-hearted, and honest, as a man should be; but the chief characteristic in your nature is the simple faith in success you have always manifested, which I can liken to nothing else than the faith a Christian has in his Savior. This faith gave you victory at Shiloh and Vicksburg. Also, when you have completed your best preparations, you go into battle without hesitation, as at Chattanooga—no doubts, no reserve; and I tell you that it was this that made us act with confidence. . . . My only points of doubt were as to your knowledge of grand strategy, and of books of science and history; but I confess your common-sense seems to have supplied all this. (*Memoirs* 399–400)

This remarkable encomium contains the essence of the praise that Grant's admirers have written since that time.

Sheridan (*Personal Memoirs* 1888) credited Grant with an "imperturbable tenacity" without which he could not have beaten Lee. During the campaigns in Virginia "he met with many disappointments—on several occasions the shortcomings of generals, when at the point of success, leading to wretched failures." These disappointments did not unsettle his "well-ordered military mind. He guided every subordinate . . . with a fund of common sense and superiority of intellect." In all his campaigns "he was the steadfast center about and on which everything else turned."

James Harrison Wilson served sixteen months with Grant as a staff officer and in his autobiography *Under the Old Flag* (1912) described him, as did Sherman and Philip Henry Sheridan (q.v.), as the central military figure in the Union Army. He was "modest and unpretentious," of "even temper and exceedingly sound judgment. . . . He dealt with large things in a large way, and left details of every sort as far as possible to those below him" (322). Sherman and McPherson especially had his confidence, and he left much to their initiative. Indeed, some, "especially . . . professors at West Point," credited those two generals "with supplying him with brains." This notion was, according to Wilson, "not only baseless but absurd" (323). The greatest influence on Grant was John A. Rawlins, who often had the "controlling" opinion on Grant's staff.

The common theme that pervades these memoirs is that Grant knew early successes, but his character, personality, and common sense set him apart from other generals. This theme has been reflected in the writings of military historians for over a century. An early and persuasive defender was J. F. C. Fuller, especially *The Generalship of Ulysses S. Grant* (1929, 1958, 1969) and *Grant and Lee: A Study in Personality and Generalship* (1932, 1957). Before Grant, wrote Fuller, Lincoln's generals were amateurs in that they did not "understand that a general is an instrument of government. They had no concept of grand strategy, that is, of the relationship between policy and war" (*Generalship*, 182–183). In 1861 such a general did not exist, "circumstances had to create him, to educate him, to point him out" (183). Grant possessed common sense, a kind of genius, an intuitive understanding that "war is nothing more than an equation between pressure and resistance . . . action adapted to circumstances" (184). He evinced a moral and physical courage, whether in Mexico or during the Civil War. His energy was "quite extraordinary." He always stood "ready to act." He was "never obsessed by difficulties" or given to "painting mental pictures of imaginary situations" (189). Yet he could change the means or the direction without losing the idea or the objective. As general in chief he understood the need to concentrate the force of the Union Army, to maintain a continual pressure, in Virginia and in Georgia. Grant's failures, though Fuller seldom called them that, stemmed from the "faulty tactics and indifferent leadership" (297) of subordinates, especially in Virginia. More telling was Fuller's observation that Grant never appreciated the effectiveness of modern firepower.

James Marshall-Cornwall, in *Grant as Military Commander* (1970), agreed that Grant's "success as a commander rested on . . . solid qualities: A fixity of purpose, balanced judgment, imperturbable courage, and, above all, sturdy common sense. As Wellington once said, 'when one is strongly intent on an object, common sense will usually direct one to the right means' '' (221). Grant grasped a "wide strategic vision," much more so than his contemporaries, whatever their qualities as field commanders.

T. Harry Williams, in *Lincoln and His Generals* (1952), stated simply that Grant was the "greatest general of the Civil War." He stood "head and shoulders" over them all as an "over-all strategist," and was a "brilliant theater strategist, as evidenced by the Vicksburg campaign, which was a classic field and siege operation." He was a "better than average tactician," although he shared the tendency of the "best generals of both sides to underestimate" the increased firepower of Civil War–era armaments (312).

Allan Nevins described Grant as a general who grew in the job, just as Lincoln had mastered the presidency. "At Belmont he had been an amateur relying heavily on luck. At Forts Henry and Donelson his luck held, though some of his movements compared dubiously with those of the older, more experienced Charles F. Smith. At Shiloh he was still amateurish, making dire blunders before the battle just as did Sherman. But he enjoyed three blessings: the opportunity to rise gradually from low rank; the capacity to learn rapidly from his errors; and the assistance of loyal and discerning men who divined his potentialities." But his "principal gift" was his "strength of character." Nevins ranked Grant "below the major strategists of the war"—Joe Johnston (q.v.), Sherman, and Thomas—and "far below" Jackson and Lee. Yet his "logical vision" and "clear, simple" thinking allowed him to see the essential elements of complex situations. His "soundness of judgment," akin to Lee's and Wellington's, was buttressed by a "decisive promptness," strong nerves, and tenacity that never let him believe that he was beaten. He had "elemental strength when the republic needed precisely that" (15–16).

Perhaps the most forceful, certainly the most eloquent, of Grant's modern advocates was Bruce Catton, especially in *Grant Moves South* (1960) and *Grant Takes Command* (1969). Even the titles suggest energy and purpose. Grant's inner balance or stability set him apart from his principal lieutenants and adversaries, and his public modesty did not reflect a lack of confidence in his own abilities or purposes. His "deepest instinct as a soldier was to keep a beaten foe off balance," but this notable virtue could carry him beyond prudence (*South*, 190). He "had the defects of his qualities," and experience, as at Shiloh, did not necessarily supply a corrective. Yet he always placed himself in the responsible position, whether in the West or in Virginia. And he won notable victories.

A later generation of Civil War historians were less taken by Grant, but most of them were writing about particular battles or situations in which Grant made serious errors of judgment. Some of the most pointed criticism was of his actions at Chattanooga by Peter Cozzens in *The Shipwreck of Their Hopes: The Battles for Chattanooga* (1994) and Wiley Sword, *Mountains Touched with Fire: Chat-*

tanooga Besieged, 1863 (1995). Cozzens believes that Grant began by ''blithely and egregiously'' overestimating the readiness of the Army of the Cumberland to take the offensive. Further, he attributed the lack of readiness not to the recent fighting at Chickamauga and Chattanooga, but rather to General George Thomas's apparent slowness or lack of energy and initiative. Cozzens could appreciate Grant's confidence in Sherman but was less appreciative of Grant's tendency to overlook Sherman's errors and failures. After the Union attack carried Missionary Ridge, Grant did not seem to know how to exploit his victory, but even more harsh is Cozzens's assertion that Grant lied in his account of Chattanooga, deliberate misstatements designed to denigrate Thomas and elevate Sherman. ''Time would not mellow'' Grant's belief that Thomas was ''slow and argumentative,'' while Sherman was purposeful and energetic.

Sword praises both Grant and Thomas as ''men of strong will, with nerves of steel.'' Unfortunately their ''divergent personalities and perspectives'' never could mesh. Grant understood that the Army of the Cumberland was in poor condition but deemed it a passive force when compared to Grant's own Army of the Tennessee. Grant was disappointed in Thomas' apparent ''inability to conduct operations rapidly with his army. In Grant's mind it seemed to imply an unreliability, or at least a want of opportunistic perspective. . . . Accordingly, the cautious, methodical Thomas was not to be relied upon beyond a secondary role.'' Grant never really changed his opinion of Old Slow Trot.

According to Sword, Grant's handling of the actual battle, and especially Missionary Ridge, ''was so faulty in planning, concept, and out of touch with reality as to presage a total disaster'' (264). Success derived from Grant's luck and the initiative of the brigade and division commanders who stormed the Confederate Center.

James L. McDonough criticized Grant's neglect of security in *Shiloh: Hell before Night* (1978) and was almost as harsh as Cozzens and Sword in his *Chattanooga: A Death Grip on the Confederacy* (1984). Grant's first order to attack the north end of Missionary Ridge (November 7) would have been a ''colossal blunder'' but was reversed on the sound advice of Thomas and William F. Smith. Grant agreed with his subordinates but always believed that Thomas was ''slow,'' an ''ungenerous'' opinion, according to McDonough. Indeed, ''if not for Thomas, Grant well might have made one of the worst mistakes of his career'' (108). After all, Sherman failed at this same point, with fresh troops and more time to prepare.

J. F. C. Fuller gives positive reviews to Grant's conduct of the campaigns in Virginia, as do historians writing more recently. Fuller believes that Grant ''showed remarkable courage in shouldering the whole onus of the war, and in fixing the responsibility of defeating Lee, or being defeated by him, on his own shoulders'' (381).

As general-in-chief, Grant's central idea was to effect a concentration of force and conduct an unceasing and unrelenting offensive against the Confederacy's armies, resources, and morale. As a necessary corollary, he also became the *de facto* commander of the Army of the Potomac. Meade on his own could not have dealt with Lee, but had Grant actually replaced Meade, he could not have directed the war. According to J. F. C. Fuller: "In the circumstances, not only do I consider that Grant was right to act as he did, but that he showed remarkable courage in shouldering the whole onus of the war, and in fixing the responsibility at defeating Lee, or being defeated by Lee, on his own shoulders" (*Generalship* 210).

Grant's first challenge was to overcome the "inferiority feelings" among the officer corps of the Army of the Potomac. In *Our Masters the Rebels* (1978) Michael C. C. Adams argues that Grant, unlike many officers in the East, was "immune to the awe of Lee and the Rebels in general." He saw "no special virtue in the aristocratic way," which gave him a "moral unshakability. . . . Having no gentlemanly pretensions he presumably felt no particular awe for the gentleman image of the Southerner" (157). He was guided by "rational probabilities," which also explains his relationship with Lincoln. Grant "was one of the few top generals who managed to avoid looking down on the common-man president" (158). Adam's apt observation illustrates Grant's understanding, evident from the beginning of the war, that military commanders were obligated to obey the policies of the government. And he summarizes a consensus that perhaps the "incessant fighting was necessary to make up for the failures" of earlier commanders (159).

Gordon C. Rhea, in *The Battle of the Wilderness* (1994), suggests that Grant may have regretted not taking the Army of the Potomac more firmly in hand, notwithstanding that the Wilderness Campaign was a "Confederate failure" in that Lee's "offensive capacity was spent. . . . The grand maneuvers that had served Lee so well in the past were no longer possible" (441).

Richard Sommers, in his insightful *Richmond Redeemed* (1981), notes that Grant won major victories in the West by "carrying the war to the enemy strategically and tactically" (423). In Virginia he gave up the direct approach in favor of attacking apparent weak points in Lee's lines. In this sense, attrition was not "mindless butchery," nor was it "brilliant genius." Rather, it was the most efficacious way to defeat a formidable enemy. It was Grant's preoccupation with strategic considerations that prevented him from taking advantage of tactical opportunities. In Sommers's words, Grant was "tactically rigid, strategically flexible, grand strategically unrelenting" (443).

Herman Hattaway and Archer Jones, in their magisterial *How the North Won* (1983), give Grant small credit for his early successes, at least through Shiloh, but praise Halleck for guiding his sometimes erratic subordinates. They give great credit to Grant for his Virginia campaigns, even if they "blemished" his reputation. Grant was a man whose very subtlety of mind made his original plans, especially a proposed raid into North Carolina, unacceptable to Halleck and Lincoln. He was further handicapped by Benjamin F. Butler's command of the Army of the James, a task clearly beyond the capabilities of that political worthy. As a balance, Sherman's success in Georgia was made possible because Grant had "fixed" Lee and made it impossible to detach reinforcements to the

West. Even when his "strategy of exhaustion" was not obvious to the public, Grant persevered: "I shall necessarily have to take the odium of comparative inactivity [in 1865], but if it results, as I expect it will, in the discomfiture of Lee's army, I shall be entirely satisfied" (663).

William S. McFeely's *Grant: A Biography* (1981), which won the Pulitzer Prize, is not particularly sympathetic to its subject but contains pertinent comments on Grant as general. With reference to Virginia in 1864:

They [his generals] played it Grant's way. He never mapped strategy, never put pins in charts or moved counters over simulated terrain. Everything was in his head. He heard all that was said around him, he took in every message, he said little. What he wanted people to know he wrote out in his own hand, so there could be no misunderstanding. His crisp clear orders were almost impossible not to comprehend. Those who did not carry them out either chose not to or lacked any ability to translate words into action (186).

He was a capable quartermaster because when he thought of a general in the field, "he could see all the blankets, and bacon, and bullets that had to be there, too" (188). He could despair of sluggish or unimaginative generals, but he was "remarkably unenvious" of the successful ones, especially Sheridan and Sherman. But at the end, "he could not let the war end. . . . The war was not a discrete event with finite walls of time, separate from something called peace; rather, it was the core of his life. Ulysses Grant was reluctant to let go of war" (221). He was not the first or the last soldier to hold these feelings.

Russell F. Weigley, in *The American Way of War* (1973), observed that the war planners of World War II knew that "to destroy the enemy army, the only proven way remained the application of mass and concentration in the manner of U. S. Grant" (313). Yet Grant was not an "unsubtle general who bulled his way to victory over the butchered bodies of his troops" (139). He was flexible, "viewing battles as means rather than as ends" (139). His skill at maneuver was most evident at Vicksburg, when circumstances allowed. In 1864 a new policy was demanded. The destruction of the two major Confederate armies would not follow from "mere maneuvers and stratagems" (142) but from a policy of concentration, mass, and overwhelming force. Grant did not ignore "Jominian territorial objectives. It was threats against the political and logistical centers of Richmond and Atlanta that compelled Lee's and Johnston's armies to fight" (144). Grant knew that the price would be high but saw no other way to win the war. Weigley approvingly quotes Adam Badeau that "this enemy did not yield because he was outwitted or outnumbered" (151). Armies and resources had to be destroyed, leaving "no alternative but destruction or submission" (151). The annihilation of armies and resources thus became, according to Weigley, "The Strategic Tradition of U. S. Grant" (312).

Grant's comment that "General Scott's successes are an answer to all criticism" encapsuled his own experience in the Civil War. Missteps and mistakes, real or attributed, would be forgotten in victory. Yet the great triumph over Lee was never a sure thing to Grant. Prior to Appomattox he suffered one of his periodic sick headaches, which did not disappear until Lee agreed to surrender his army. Grant's terms were a mix of steel and compassion and his telegram to the Secretary of War read: ''General Lee surrendered the Army of Northern Virginia this afternoon on terms proposed by myself. The accompanying additional correspondence will show the conditions fully.'' The elegance of that message to his civilian superior was characteristic of the man. He had won on his own terms, and that was enough.

BIBLIOGRAPHY

William Tecumseh Sherman, *Memoirs*, 2 vols. (New York: Charles L. Webster, 1875).

Ulysses S. Grant, *Personal Memoirs*, 2 vols. (New York: Charles L. Webster, 1885).

Clarence C. Buel and Robert U. Johnson, eds. *Battles and Leaders of the Civil War*, 4 vols. (New York: Century, 1887–1888).

James Harrison Wilson; *Under the Old Flag* (New York: Appleton and Co., 1912).

John Frederick Charles Fuller, *The Generalship of Ulysses S. Grant* (1929; New York: Kraus Reprint, 1969).

J. F. C. Fuller, *Grant and Lee: A Study in Personality and Generalship* (1932; Bloomington: Univ. of Indiana Press, 1957).

T. Harry Williams, *Lincoln and His Generals* (New York: Alfred A. Knopf, 1952).

Roy P. Basler (ed.), *The Collected Works of Abraham Lincoln*, 10 vols. (New Brunswick, N.J.: Rutgers University Press, 1953).

B. H. Liddell Hart, *Sherman: Soldier, Realist, American* (New York: Frederick A. Praeger, 1958).

Bruce Catton, *Grant Moves South* (Boston: Little, Brown, 1960).

John Y. Simon (ed.), *The Papers of Ulysses S. Grant* (Carbondale: Southern Illinois University Press, 1967).

Bruce Catton, *Grant Takes Command* (Boston: Little, Brown, 1969).

James Marshall-Cornwall, *Grant as Military Commander* (London: Batsford, 1970).

Russell F. Weigley, *The American Way of War* (New York: Macmillan, 1973).

Michael C. C. Adams, *Our Masters the Rebels* (Cambridge: Harvard University Press, 1978).

James L. McDonough, *Shiloh: Hell before Night* (Knoxville: Univ. of Tennessee Press, 1978).

William S. McFeely, *Grant: A Biography* (New York: W. W. Norton, 1981).

Richard Sommers, *Richmond Redeemed* (New York: Doubleday and Co., 1981).

Herman Hattaway and Archer Jones, *How the North Won the War* (Urbana: University of Illinois Press, 1983).

Wiley Sword, *Shiloh: Bloody April* (Dayton, Ohio: Morningside Bookshop Press, 1983).

Brooks D. Simpson, *Let Us Have Peace, Ulysses S. Grant and the Politics of War and Reconstruction, 1861–1868* (Chapel Hill: University of North Carolina Press, 1991).

Peter Cozzens, *The Shipwreck of Their Hopes: The Battles for Chattanooga* (Urbana: University of Illinois Press, 1994).

Gordon C. Rhea, *The Battle of the Wilderness* (Baton Rouge: LSU Press, 1994).

Wiley Sword, *Mountains Touched with Fire: Chattanooga Besieged, 1863* (New York: St. Martin's Press, 1995).

HENRY WAGER HALLECK
(January 16, 1815–January 9, 1872)

Jon L. Wakelyn

Those of his contemporaries who described the manner and mien of Henry Wager Halleck, general in chief of the Union Army for a time and the country's first chief of staff, have left an indelible and damaging portrait of that military genius. Too chubby and too slow in his actions to be a successful field commander, he also was described as pop-eyed, always scratching his elbows, and rude to all who came across his sights. To subordinates he was curt, asking them in a surly fashion what business they had with him. Perhaps because of his abrasiveness and his lack of field command, Halleck was discarded at the war's end by the higher-ups. Most modern historians have followed their lead. Until the laudatory 1962 biography by Stephen Ambrose, his real role in the war had been overshadowed by comments on his sour personality. Ambrose points out that, in tandem with President Abraham Lincoln (q.v.), General in Chief U. S. Grant (q.v.), and Secretary of War Edwin Stanton (q.v.), Halleck helped to forge an effective and victorious Union war machine. Even with those duties in mind, many of his peers suggested Halleck acted too scholarly for the great leaders to take him seriously. But his activities in behalf of the Union war effort indeed were quite important. To understand that critical role he played and still to grasp why so many of his contemporaries attacked his actions requires a reconstruction of his life, another appraisal of his wartime record, and a look at just how history has treated this testy and talented captain.

Halleck came from sturdy old American stock. The Hallecks and the Wagers lived in the rich farming country of the Mohican Valley of New York. Strict and strong willed Joseph Halleck married Catherine Wager of a middle-class Syracuse family, and their son Henry Wager, the first of thirteen children, was born in the Valley on January 16, 1815. For the first sixteen years of his life Henry worked on his father's farm and picked up what schooling was available from local teachers and his mother. He was expected, like so many of the agricultural middle class, someday to assume ownership of the family farm. But

Henry had other plans for his life. Fortunately, his Grandfather Wager took an interest in his education and sent him to Fairfield Academy, where the young man showed special gifts as a quick learner. From there he went to the fine Union College in Schnectady, New York, a place that also trained Henry James, Sr. Quick, perhaps too quick in debate and in the classroom, Halleck seemed to antagonize his classmates. He graduated Phi Beta Kappa and was tempted by an offer to study engineering at Harvard.

But Henry instead learned engineering and much more at the U.S. Military Academy at West Point, which he entered in 1835. He graduated number three in the class of 1839. That next year he taught French at the Military Academy and debated taking a job teaching at Harvard. In 1840 the second lieutenant of engineers took up his military duties in earnest to work on fortifications around New York City. While at the Academy, he had become a favorite of his professor Dennis Hart Mahan, as he had shown great skills in learning military strategy. Mahan arranged for him to go to France to study military tactics. There Halleck wrote *Elements of Military Art and Science*, a paraphrase of the work of the great student of warfare the Baron Jomini. Halleck's book, published in 1841, extolled the ideas of concentration of force and fighting on the interior line and, as an early primer on modern warfare, would influence a generation of young students of war.

Upon his return to the United States, engineering duties and teaching occupied his time and soon bored that ambitious young officer. When war with Mexico broke out in 1846, Halleck gladly traveled to the California coast to a position in military governance. With little to do, he began to speculate in land and to study Mexican and American law. So when the California constitutional convention met in 1849, he was employed to help write the laws of governance for that new state. A staunch Democrat, grown politically ambitious, in 1849, while still on active duty, he formed the San Francisco law firm of Halleck, Peasley, and Billings. Because of pressing legal business, Halleck formally retired from the army in 1854. He soon grew rich in land speculation and in the practice of law. He had begun to build a place of prominence for himself in California society. In 1855 he married Elizabeth Hamilton of San Francisco. She was the granddaughter of the famous New York lawyer and Secretary of Treasury in the Washington administration of Alexander Hamilton.

The growing sectional conflict back East seemed far removed from his active life. But Halleck retained a loyalty for the Union. When the Civil War broke out, he debated his future action with friends and associates and discussed his options with former army colleagues. In August 1861, Halleck decided to enlist in the army. His military experience, fame from his manual of military tactics, and California business expertise earned him the rank of major general. According to Stephen Ambrose, at this time both "army officers and Washington leaders considered him the foremost exponent of the art of war in America" (10). In November 1861, President Lincoln assigned him to the command of the Department of Missouri whose base of operations was in St. Louis. That vital place alongside the mighty Mississippi River was much in need of organization and training of the raw army recruits, having been neglected by the previous commander. That Halleck also belonged to the Democratic party and would not make the same mistake of freeing slaves, as had his Republican predecessor, no doubt also influenced the president's decision. Halleck understood that he had to protect St. Louis and the rest of the state south of the Missouri River from the marauding Confederate Army of former governor Sterling Price. By January 1862, he had taken control of the state for the Union. He then began to make plans to send troops into Arkansas to wrest that state from the Confederacy. In part because of his success at Pea Ridge in Arkansas on March 7, 1862, President Lincoln put Halleck in command of the newly organized Department of the Mississippi.

The new commander convinced the authorities in Washington to allow him to fight the Confederates in Tennessee. But Halleck grew frustrated once he understood that he had to share authority for his invasion with General Don Carlos Buell. When at last he advanced, Halleck did so on many separate fronts, in violation of Jomini's maxim of concentration of force. He sent a subordinate with a not-too-clean reputation, General U. S. Grant, to invest the Confederate forts Henry and Donelson on the Cumberland and Tennessee Rivers. For Halleck understood that if he controlled those vital river forts, he would force the Confederate armies to evacuate central Tennessee. Halleck also sent General John Pope to take Confederate Island #10 in the Mississippi River. That supreme strategist had chosen to command his far-flung armies from St. Louis, certain he could direct the invasions of Tennessee from there. Halleck had come to believe that those in command on the ground were best able to know what to do in battle and that the general in chief should leave them to their task without interference. His duty, once the object of attack had been determined, was to support those in the field and to be the supplier of military materiel.

Although Halleck theoretically now commanded General Buell and his army in east Tennessee, he could not get him to move and assist in concentrating the army for its next major advance into south-central Tennessee. Halleck had wanted to concentrate at Corinth, Mississippi, the major supply area for the entire western Confederate Army. But Confederate General Albert Sidney Johnston had other plans. In April 1862, Johnston attacked the small army of General Grant at Shiloh Court House. When Buell finally arrived on April 7, Grant was able to drive off the Confederates. But Grant had failed to entrench to protect his troops, so Halleck, under considerable pressure to remove him, took the field himself. Fortunately for the Union's future, Halleck absolved Grant from any wrongdoing and gave him a new command.

Then Halleck concentrated all of his troops under his own command, and he slowly and carefully marched them toward Corinth, the major Confederate supply depot in northern Mississippi. Super-cautious, he entrenched every few miles and soon was seen as a plodding commander who perhaps was better placed at his desk in St. Louis and not in the field. To be fair to Halleck, he in fact was beset by rainstorms that turned his advance into a sea of mud. At last he set a siege of the vital storage center at Corinth, only to fall afoul of the Union newspaper press corps, which he banished from his camp and which resulted in a frontal assault on his reputation. The Northern press would rarely again say anything nice about Halleck. When the Confederate General P. G. T. Beauregard (q.v.) brilliantly evacuated Corinth and deceived Halleck, the Union general was too slow to pursue the Creole. Then Halleck dispersed his army and began to fortify and to repair railroads. If Beauregard had escaped Halleck's clutches, the Union commander nevertheless had succeeded in breaking the Confederate hold on his army's center. The Union now controlled the vital supply artery of the West. That action was to be his last in the West and his last as a field commander.

Halleck's commander in chief, President Lincoln, grown out of sorts with eastern General George B. McClellan (q.v.), brought the successful Halleck to Washington, and on July 11, 1862, named him general in chief of all the Union armies. President Lincoln had picked the best staff mind to coordinate all the Union war efforts, and Halleck was to operate as a kind of chief of staff of the newly organized Union high command. Along with Secretary of War Stanton, the president, and later General Grant, Halleck helped to forge a new way of conducting warfare. If, as Ambrose says, "as a field commander he had shown utter lack of imagination and audacity" (63), Halleck had nevertheless brought order out of chaos in the West. Perhaps he could do the same for the eastern army. His efficiency, however, would be sorely tested in that political-military hothouse called Washington, D.C.

During his entire time in command of the East, Halleck would never cease to fear Confederate attacks on Washington. After all, he wanted to do the same for Richmond. Thus, when Union General George B. McClellan launched his infamous campaign up the Virginia peninsula, Halleck fretted that the Confederates would gladly trade Richmond for the nation's capital. At that time the general in chief also continued to maintain the importance of protecting place and not attacking the enemy's armies in the field.

In addition to his problems over Washington, Halleck also faced the issue of his eastern general's inability to act in consort, of achieving the vital unity of command. Thus, he always feared that his armies were not united enough to concentrate against the enemy's well-coordinated advances. Even when he wanted to use the western army to relieve pressure on the East, he was unable to bring important generals east because he actually feared to hurt the feelings of the proud, political generals under his command there. One major and disastrous example of failed eastern unity of command occurred after McClellan's army had bogged down east of Richmond. Halleck had to get McClellan's army off the Peninsula to use it to defend the real threat of a Confederate attack on Washington. The braggart General John Pope, whose task it was to protect Washington, desperately needed help from McClellan. Instead, McClellan did not unite with Pope, and Pope was nearly destroyed at Second Manassas in late

August of 1862. One good thing did come out of that debacle. Halleck learned to trust General Herman Haupt, who commanded the railroad transportation system, because Haupt had managed to evacuate from the battlefield what was left of Pope's army.

The general in chief then studied the location of Lee's army as it moved into Maryland in September 1862 and realized that a strong confrontation with united forces could either drive Lee back into Virginia or destroy his army. On September 17 and 18, he watched in frustration as McClellan drove Lee from the field but declined to advance. Also, during that campaign, McClellan, unforgivably, had refused all communication with his chief, thus leaving him without knowledge of his general's whereabouts. Halleck vowed to get rid of McClellan. Fortunately for him, Halleck had come to understand something of the politics of war. Himself a Democrat in a world of Republican leaders, in part he sympathized with fellow Democrats Buell and McClellan when they were under siege from politicians. But he supported the president when he removed both men and replaced them with loyal Republicans because that was what Halleck too had desired. Of course, Halleck would have no better luck with their successors, Generals William Rosecrans and Ambrose Burnside. Eventually, he would be the one to remove them. In fact, Halleck had become the dismissal instrument of Stanton and Lincoln, as he was forced to respond to the politics and necessities of finding successful wartime leaders. He finally even convinced other officers in his department to take equal responsibility for the removal of failed generals.

As he directed the fighting and responded to the politics, Halleck had come to grasp the full meaning of military governance in modern warfare. Although he never really liked Secretary Stanton, he joined him in politics, in reorganizing the high command to make it an efficient arm of field operations, and in understanding the true meaning of total war. Halleck the Democrat had ceased whatever sympathy he had for the South and for Southern prosperity in slaves. He also came around to the use of slaves to support the Union Army, and he arrested Southern civilians who assisted the Confederate military. His love for the Union and his frustrations over the way the Confederate armies foiled his advances led Halleck eventually to endorse and to begin to plan total war against Confederate armies and their civilian partners.

His newly acquired political skills, grasp of the significance of organization, and understanding of the role of noncombatants in warfare led Halleck to place Grant the professional soldier in charge of nonprofessional political generals in the siege of Vicksburg. He also knew the consequences of failure to capture that vital place on the Mississippi River. With Grant in total command, land and sea operations were coordinated easily. Halleck also understood that a captured Vicksburg would give the Union Army a base of operations on the Mississippi River right in the midst of heavily civilian centers of population. He now believed that Southern private citizens' property had to be confiscated or destroyed in that region in order to break the will of the Confederacy. Halleck then put his friend, the brilliant political theorist Francis Lieber, to work on developing a policy for the conduct of armies in the field. Lieber's code of war gave Union generals in the field the authority to control the actions of civilian noncombatants. The age of total war had begun.

In addition to his genius for strategy and his new political awareness, Halleck was an excellent administrator, perhaps even a genius. In the words of Stephen Ambrose: "[h]e was, in short, the manager of the Northern effort—the man who brought about the professionalization of the army, supplied it, gave it rules and regulations while serving as military liaison with the civilian government"(160). Working alongside President Lincoln, the two of them informally used Halleck's staff to weigh military decisions. For the president he became a sounding board of wartime ideas and translated some of the president's brilliant hunches into the language of warfare. The usually contentious Halleck rarely overstepped his position and almost always deferred to the president's judgments. Because of Halleck's skills in working with the president, Russell Weigley, one of the best students of modern strategy, claims that the Union strategic policies soon became brilliant. As manager and strategist Halleck also knew he had to work with the equally contentious Secretary of War Edwin Stanton in order to place in the hands of the army the military wherewithal to fight a successful engagement. Although Stanton was in overall charge of procurement and transporting goods to the front line, Halleck was the brains behind what was needed to fight the war. His and Stanton's use of Herman Haupt to coordinate communications was well planned. When Stanton wanted action out of Quartermaster General Montgomery Meigs, it was Halleck who translated those orders. What a team: a tall, gangly, understated president; a fat, irritable Secretary of War; and a pop-eyed, often seemingly subservient general in chief. Together, those leaders created the first modern war machine.

Alas, General Halleck also had to try to get his generals to fight. For a leader who believed that career officers, once given their charge, could go at it, that phase of Halleck's war was a constant sore. Even when Grant desperately needed General William Rosecrans, then stationed around Nashville, to keep Confederate General Braxton Bragg (q.v.) from putting pressure on the siege of Vicksburg, Halleck seemed unable to get his German friend to move. He hoped General Nathaniel Banks would move north from New Orleans to help Grant, but Halleck couldn't seem to get that civilian general to follow orders. When his near pathological desire to protect Washington led Halleck to replace General Joseph Hooker with General George Meade (q.v.), he at last felt he had an officer to fight the splendid General Robert E. Lee (q.v.) and defeat the Army of Northern Virginia. Then, when Meade for good reasons failed to follow a defeated Lee after Gettysburg in early July 1863, Halleck took the blame. Halleck knew he had a fine subordinate in Meade, and he endeavored to keep up his fellow Democrat's spirits in the wake of Republican criticism. But the constant personal attacks on Halleck's judgments about good generals finally forced him to lose confidence in himself and to contemplate resigning his staff position.

Fortunately, Halleck did not lose all perspective. He was able to supply Rose-crans at the vital strategic location of Chattanooga until Grant arrived to push the Confederate Army south. Fortunately, too, Grant's success at Chattanooga led President Lincoln to put him in command of the entire Union war effort as a true general in chief. When Grant, perhaps learning from Halleck's experience, decided to forsake the hot political climate of Washington for the front lines, the seemingly irrelevant Halleck was asked to remain in command there. He did not have to tell Grant to fight. Instead, Halleck became the first formal chief of staff with duties to coordinate the overall Union war effort. Working with President Lincoln and General Grant he was able to see the Union advance whole and to offer sage advice on where to strike the enemy. Understanding the genius of Generals William T. Sherman (q.v.) and George Thomas (q.v.), if at times he made mistakes in orders to them, Halleck was able to give them support. He knew the reasons for and gave permission for Sherman's March to the Sea because that action fulfilled his own idea of total war. Halleck defended and supplied General Thomas and kept Grant from relieving him as the defender of Nashville. If he did not much care for General Philip Sheridan (q.v.), Halleck managed to make General Meade tolerate the feisty Irishman. Above all, work-ing with the intense Secretary Stanton, during that last crucial Union offensive in late 1864, he helped keep fresh troops and experienced soldiers in the field and to clothe, arm, and feed them. And as Ambrose shows, "Halleck approved taking or annihilating anything that could possibly be of service to the enemy" (181).

But for all of his usefulness to Grant and the armies, Halleck turned into a bitter man. His final actions during the war got him into trouble with the public and with his superiors. The newspaper press willfully and gleefully continued to attack that unpleasant man. One policy explains his unpopularity. Paying the bills of the quartermaster corps to ensure a steady supply of war materiel before he paid the troops meant that the soldiers got paid last. That policy left a sour taste among the people. Of course, the Republican politicians blamed him for any errors in the field. Even the usually supportive General Grant resented his interfering to save General Thomas's command. At the war's end, as he worked to make final transfers of Grant's troops to concentrate with Sherman in North Carolina, Secretary Stanton ordered Halleck to go to Richmond, where he lan-guished. Halleck had tilted with Sherman over how to treat the defeated enemy, and Stanton no doubt thought he had overstepped his authority. Sherman, like the elephant, never forgot Halleck's interference. Then the general who had hoped to set up military commands in the South himself turned conservative. Instead of being punitive, Halleck wanted to rebuild destroyed Richmond. He saw Richmond's recovery as part of the Union's responsibility to rebuild the South and bring it back into the Union. This did not fit the Republican's ideas of retribution.

Accused of appeasement, the Democrat was transferred to the Division of the Pacific to fight Indians. Even when in 1869 Halleck became a commander of the Division of the South, he was kept isolated in Kentucky. Halleck had given his all to the cause of war and then peace. He grew tired and old, and he was only in his mid-fifties. He turned to the church for solace and was baptized an Episcopalian by his cousin Bishop Joseph Whipple. On January 9, 1872, Halleck died in Louisville. At his funeral in Brooklyn, New York, attended by only a few fellow soldiers, no one spoke favorably of Halleck's wartime career.

Halleck soon was completely forgotten, save for comments in an occasional memoir of former subordinates, most of whom found him too bright, too sloppy, and too unpleasant. Old soldiers seemed not to know where to place that non-fighter in their memoirs of that war. Sherman, of course, neither forgot nor forgave. He judged Halleck bright but ineffectual. Grant, whose memoirs be-came the arbiter of a Union general's success or failure, did not remember him fondly. Halleck's texts were still used at the War College, but students were advised to avoid studying his politics or his personality. Only Emory Upton, a gifted young staff officer, in his history of military organization, gave Halleck credit for being a brilliant administrator. When the professional scholar Stephen Ambrose, who built on Upton's work, took on Halleck's life despite many friends who advised him not to, interest in that staff officer began anew. But Ambrose was perhaps too laudatory when he compared Halleck to George C. Marshall. At the same time Ambrose was writing, political historians Benjamin Thomas and Harold Hyman wrote their seminal biography of Secretary of War Edwin Stanton and almost completely ignored Halleck's role in the war. They simply repeated the wartime rap: "Halleck was a desk man rather than a field soldier, and he waged war according to rules"(285). Thomas and Hyman judged those rules inadequate.

Not until historians turned from writing stories of blood and thunder to study war in its entirety did Halleck's luck (reputation) begin to change. If Halleck only "partially fulfilled the promise that might have been expected from the first systematic and comprehensive American analysis of strategy, he understood the logistics of war," said the eminent student of strategy Russell F. Weigley (429, 430). In their magisterial *How the North Won the War*, Herman Hattaway and Archer Jones allowed that "Halleck completed the effective Union organ-ization when he began exploiting the informal unity of the staff" (689). They also found him loyal to the president, a soldier who deflected criticism from his chief (690). In the view of Edward Hagerman, in *The American Civil War and the Origins of Modern Warfare* (1988), Halleck has received too little attention from Civil War historians. Hagerman praised him for persuading Grant to pin down Lee at Petersburg, protect his inner line at all cost, and use his army to exhaust the Confederacy (244). For Hagerman, Halleck was the first of the great modern military leaders, an engineer rather than a fighter (237). That was the best review Halleck would get. Joseph Glatthaar, in *Partners in Command* (1994), insists Halleck "could serve a useful purpose, explaining military mat-ters to the president, advising subordinates, and preventing the most egregious blunders in the field" (231). The emphasis was on useful, not able. David Donald, in his brilliant *Lincoln* (1995), put finish to the recent Halleck revival. Donald believes Halleck was a good staff officer, but he failed as a general and as a modern student of war. Reiterating the old accusations, Donald proclaimed that Halleck "had more experience with theories of warfare than with realities of military politics"(370).

So Halleck, for all his genius at warfare and organization, remains the one great officer with only a meager following. Ambrose's short biography did little more than show Upton had a point about the importance of staff. Halleck's personality, curiously imperious, continued to haunt him. His lack of fighting skill leads many today to ignore him or to fail to place him in the context of that war. Even the charge that Halleck the general could not perform well politically has been used against him. What is left is the importance of his staff leadership to the Civil War. Perhaps when Upton's work gets studied by modern historians of warfare, when Hattaway and Jones's excellent but short analysis of staff activities gets expanded into a full-scale volume, the light will shine on Halleck's work—despite his personality.

BIBLIOGRAPHY

Henry Wager Halleck, *Elements of Military Art and Science* (1841; Westport, Conn.: Greenwood Press, 1971).

Emory Upton, *Military Policy of the United States* (Washington, D.C.: Government Printing Office, 1917).

Fred A. Shannon, *Organization and Administration of the Union Army* (Cleveland: Arthur H. Clarke, Co., 1928).

Stephen E. Ambrose, *Halleck: Lincoln's Chief of Staff* (Baton Rouge: Louisiana State University Press, 1962).

Benjamin P. Thomas and Harold M. Hyman, *Stanton: The Life and Times of Lincoln's Secretary of War* (New York: Alfred Knopf, 1962).

Herman Hattaway and Archer Jones, *How the North Won the War* (Urbana: University of Illinois Press, 1984).

Russell F. Weigley, "American Strategy from Its Beginning through the First World War," in *Makers of Modern Strategy*, ed. Peter Paret (Princeton, N.J.: Princeton University Press, 1986).

Edward Hagerman, *The American Civil War and the Origins of Modern Warfare* (Bloomington: Indiana University Press, 1988).

Joseph T. Glatthaar, *Partners in Command* (New York: Free Press, 1994).

David Herbert Donald, *Lincoln* (New York: Simon & Schuster, 1995).

JOHN BELL HOOD
(June 29, 1831–August 30, 1879)

Jon L. Wakelyn

Throughout his post–Civil War life, Confederate General John Bell Hood often defended himself from others' accusations that he had exceeded his capacity and too often had fought foolishly on the offensive in battle. Those who have commented on his written defense have questioned whether he made a proper or articulate case for himself. Few have found that Hood had redeemed his failed military career. Some who have done research beyond Hood's memoirs maintain that during the war he at times had responded brilliantly in a subordinate position, meaning, he knew how to take orders. But when the burden of decision making was placed on him, they say, he mainly made excuses for his poor leadership. Others have found a paradox in a man who constantly defended himself but had the reputation for taking an offensive stance, often just to push forward without regard to the cost. How does one evaluate that general's actions when the Confederacy itself behaved audaciously in a defensive posture to protect its own land? Hood entitled his memoirs *Advance and Retreat*, and that truly summed up his own life story.

To grasp that seeming contradiction in his title and to assess his actual wartime practices, the world that spawned him must be understood. His most thorough and compassionate biographer, Richard McMurry, has said: "The milieu in which the Hood family lived was crucial in shaping the personality of the general" (1). But McMurry also warns that Hood's formative years have been studied poorly, that Hood himself in his memoir of the war had little to say about his youth, and that the memoirs, anyway, is a "self-serving apologia." Indeed, Hood seemed somewhat unclear about what had formed him and instead seemed singularly intent on showing that he took his life and the development of talents into his own hands. The reality of just how that milieu shaped him bears a closer look.

The fifth child, and youngest, son of the physician John W. Hood and Theodina French, he came into this life on June 29, 1831, near Owingsville, Butler

County, Kentucky. The Hood family first had settled in Frederick County, Virginia. An ancestor, Luke H. Hood, a Revolutionary War veteran, was deeded land in Pennsylvania, then in 1784 removed to Lincoln County, Kentucky, where he became an Indian fighter, a hero at Fallen Timbers in 1811, and a small landowner. John W., the father of John B., was Luke's ambitious son, who hoped to rise in that Kentucky Bluegrass plantation culture through income gained from the practice of medicine. On young Hood's mother's side, he was descended from the Kentucky emigrant land promoter and Indian fighter Richard Calloway, whose daughter married into the family of James French, a Revolutionary War hero. The family background was of great importance to young Hood. For not only did he find militarist role models for his choice of career, but in later life, he claimed descent from Bluegrass gentry. That lineage no doubt meant a great deal to that young man on the make.

John Bell Hood's pride in land and slaves, in being a Southerner, was exacerbated by the way he was raised. With his destined-to-be-physicians but later ne'er-do-well brothers, he led the life of a typical planter's son. He rode, hunted, did little work, and received a decent but hardly proficient education at the hands of local masters and in a private school. John Bell spent what money he could get his hands on, was reputed to be a ladies' man, and grew to be handsome and dignified-looking, fully six feet two, and long and lean. After his mother was left land by her father, in 1836 the family moved to the rich soil, planter world of Montgomery Co., Kentucky. His mother indeed became the major influence on his life because his eccentric and absent-minded father was often away supposedly studying medicine at Jefferson Medical College in Philadelphia. Perhaps that is why young John Bell was headstrong, purse proud, and himself absent-minded. But the family became successful in the world of planter slaveholders, and something had to be done with the young adventurer. Probably against the father's will, his uncle, Judge Richard French, then a congressman from Kentucky, managed an appointment for him to the U.S. Military Academy at West Point in 1845.

The young Hood had found his calling, but he would struggle mightily with self-discipline and mathematics at West Point. At the military academy Hood flunked courses, received numerous demerits for sloppiness, and graduated near the bottom of his class in 1849. But he made many friends and gained the reputation of being a good, loyal, and fearless comrade in arms. Many of the lessons taught to him at the academy, however, such as never to confront a superior force, obviously did not stick. Upon graduation, Hood entered the cavalry, because he rode well. His first posting, to California, improved his financial position, even if he was bored by inaction. Hood would soon get all the action he wanted. He was sent to Texas in 1857 to serve in the Second Cavalry under Robert E. Lee (q.v.). In July 1857, First Lieutenant Hood, while on reconnaissance, engaged a superior force of Indians. He attacked, showed little regard for his personal safety, fought bravely, and was badly wounded. In his memoirs, in virtually the only substantive statement he made about his pre–Civil War military career, Hood narrated a harrowing tale of fighting in hand-to-hand combat on horseback, with little room for maneuver. He was lucky to escape with his life. But his exploits did catch Lee's eye.

During those pre–Civil War years Hood's allegiances to the South and his heritage surfaced often. When his father, with whom he barely got along, was dying, Hood traveled home to care for the family property. His physician brothers by that time had either left home or were incapacitated by drink, and the staunch Methodist soldier had to take charge. His pride in land and slaves, in the heritage he thought belonged to him, grew when his father died. No doubt his father had also come to see the merits of his soldier son. Also, while home in Kentucky, Hood spent time with a number of Southern colleagues, and they exacerbated his growing dissatisfaction with the North and abolitionism. When offered a staff position at West Point as chief of cavalry in late 1860, Hood declined. Perhaps he knew he wasn't made for staff duty, or more probably he already had decided to go with the South in the event of secession.

The loyal Kentuckian responded to his state's passive behavior by volunteering for Confederate military service from Texas, and thus was born the false moniker of "the gallant Hood from Texas." After his resignation from the United States Army on April 16, 1861, he was sent to join his old colonel, Robert E. Lee, to train troops in Virginia for the future Army of Northern Virginia. The story of his career to that point would not have led one to hope that the barely thirty-year-old former captain would rise to command an entire army and become one of the eight full generals in the Army of the Confederate States of America.

Why he would rise to such high command has confounded many students of the Civil War. In his own memoirs, *Advance and Retreat*, Hood gives scant attention to his early Civil War career, content only to show with whom he had grown close and who he admired. He commented that he had performed well and that only after he had been sent west, in October 1863, that "a storm arose which lasted not only to the close of the war, but a long period thereafter" (68). Indeed, Hood was correct in his assertion that he had performed well during the early stages of the war. In late May of 1861, Lee assigned him to instruct the cavalry around Yorktown. Appointed a major, he soon commanded most of the cavalry at the foot of the Virginia Peninsula. Next he was put in charge of the 4th Texas around Richmond and promoted to colonel. Hood also entered the social whirl of town society and military politics. In March of 1862 he was named a brigadier general, having had little battle experience save for the defense of crucial artillery outposts.

In early April 1862, Hood received orders to move to the Virginia Peninsula in anticipation of a major Federal offensive against Richmond. In May, he took part in important engagements around Yorktown. In late May 1862, he fought in the battle of Seven Pines, near the Chickahominy River, where General Joseph E. Johnston (q.v.) was wounded. At Gaines Mill he charged the enemy and helped to save Lee's offensive maneuver, at the loss of many of the men called "Gallant Texans." On that day, June 27, Hood became a heroic general. Then sent on the offensive, in late August 1862, to Bull Run Creek, he was placed under General James Longstreet (q.v). Hood took the lead in Longstreet's offensive against the Northern General John Pope at Second Manassas. Again, his troops took heavy casualties. In early September, his division joined the army's march into Maryland, but Hood had been placed under arrest for refusing to turn over Federal ambulances to a commanding officer. Lee suspended the arrest so as to get Hood back in command. At Sharpsburg he held a defensive position and gave Confederate troops time to regroup on the left. Again, his troops suffered heavily. But Hood had learned much in 1862, especially what he felt was the success of making a frontal assault on the enemy. For his services to the Army of Northern Virginia, Hood was promoted to major general in October 1862.

Now commanding four brigades, in November 1862 he was sent to Fredericksburg to defend against General Ambrose Burnside's river offensive. After that victorious battle, Hood and his troops settled into winter quarters near Richmond. The gregarious young general then made the rounds of Richmond society, where supposedly he fell in love with young Sallie "Buck" Preston, a lower South heiress. When that romance failed, Hood was hurt deeply. In April 1863, he took part in Longstreet's Suffolk campaign, which kept him from the battle of Chancellorsville where Stonewall Jackson (q.v.) fell. Considered for commander of the third corps in Lee's newly reorganized Army of Northern Virginia, Hood lobbied mightily for the post. Instead, Lee gave the assignment to the Virginian Ambrose P. Hill, which pleased a number of young generals who had taken a disliking to the self-promoting Kentuckian. Hood had already gained the enmity of a number of officers because he had been overly praised in one of the early histories of the war. The generals were referring to Nicholas A. Davis's 1863 history of the Texas Brigade, *The Campaign from Texas to Maryland*, which fulsomely praised the performances of Hood. Already, then, had commenced the so-called battle of the books where the war's participants had begun to value the creation of a historical record in their favor.

If Hood had learned the politics of military history, indeed even commissioned them, he was soon to learn another lesson on the hills around Gettysburg, Pennsylvania. On the second day of Gettysburg, as part of Longstreet's corps, Hood was placed at the right of the Confederate Army. The general wanted to turn the Union-fortified Round Tops, but Longstreet said no. Hood was ordered to attack along the Emmitsburg Road. He received a serious wound to his left side and arm and was carried from the field, away from the devastation at Gettysburg. He would forgive Lee and later praise his audacity, but Hood never comprehended why Longstreet rejected his suggested flanking movement. Some say he drowned his sorrows in a proposal to Sally Buchanan; others say he sought further military glory as he volunteered to accompany Longstreet west to the rendezvous at Chickamauga Creek.

In north Georgia, Hood joined General Braxton Bragg's (q.v) Army of Tennessee. On September 18, 1863, he was on the battlefield at Chickamauga, where he eventually commanded the center of the Confederate line. On September 20, he led the attack and prevailed. But once again he was wounded, this time in the right leg. He lost the leg and perhaps "the wounds altered Hood's psychological makeup" (84), said McMurry. McMurry also suggests that the loss of his leg merely agitated Hood's headstrong personality. Again, a direct attack, even with his and his troops' losses, had shown him what he perceived as the value of his audacious actions. While recovering from his wound the young hero struck up a correspondence with President Jefferson Davis (q.v.), then traveled to Richmond to become a confidant of the president. Following his leader, Hood joined the Episcopal Church. He also basked in his glory, sulked over Sallie's fickleness, and learned too well the value of military intrigue. Davis appointed him to the rank of lieutenant general, which made Hood the youngest man in that grade. His rank meant that he had to be given an important command.

Hood was sent back to the Army of Tennessee, which had become a cesspool of intrigue against General Bragg and had eventuated in his being replaced by General Joseph E. Johnston. Hood had become a close friend of the despised Bragg, who in turn was a favorite of President Jefferson Davis. Some generals thought Hood was a spy sent to inform on Johnston; others that Hood intrigued for his chief's position. It will probably never be known whether Hood was the instrument of others' politics or the clever and ambitious general who played on the bad blood between Davis and Johnston. Two things are certain. The president believed Hood to be a talented general, and Johnston did not trust him. On February 28, 1864, Hood assumed command of a corps around Dalton, Georgia. He seemed to get along well with Johnston, but he also secretly corresponded with Secretary of War James Seddon (q.v.) about the retreat toward Atlanta. For certain, he began to train his troops to take the offensive, something he claimed they were not allowed to do under General Johnston. Hood took part in many skirmishes, advised Johnston to find a proper way to take the offensive, and continued his correspondence with Richmond. He fought a pitched battle at Resaca in May and was forced back to the outskirts of Atlanta later that month. Hood wanted to take the offensive, and in *Advance and Retreat* he wrote again and again of opportunities to prevail against General William T. Sherman (q.v.). He claimed that General Johnston believed there were not enough Confederate troops to stop General Sherman. By June, Johnston and Hood had begun to squabble, and Richmond's political leaders had begun to worry a great deal about the fate of Atlanta. President Davis insisted that General Johnston could not deliver a proper plan for the protection of Atlanta. In mid-July Bragg visited the western army and conferred with General Hood. On July 17, 1864, President Davis removed General Johnston from command and replaced him with General John Bell Hood. Hood's place in history would be fixed in the results of that action.

Now in command of the defense of Atlanta, Hood began to reorganize the

Army of Tennessee. Restricted in his own mobility because of his old wounds, and unable to control unruly subordinates, the new commander hoped that his reputation as an audacious fighter would somehow encourage the troops to take the offensive initiative and thus drive Sherman north. He received almost no help from General Johnston and thus was left to figure out the strategy of the entire army by himself, something the young corps commander had never done before. Hood immediately turned to the area north of Atlanta, where General George Thomas (q.v.) had prepared a massive offensive. On July 20, 1864, Hood's troops fought the enemy along Peachtree Creek, and he was badly defeated. He blamed General William J. Hardee for being tardy. Again and again, he would blame others for his ill-considered offensive against superior forces. In actuality, Hood must bear some blame for failure to supervise his corps commanders. On July 22 he attacked, this time over poor roads, and was driven back. He then moved back into Johnston's old Atlanta defenses. On July 28, he planned to flank General Sherman near Ezra Church but reconsidered. In all he had lost 17,000 troops and was too weakened to mount another major offensive.

Hood then dug in and in August awaited Sherman's siege, as the Union Army extended its ranks south and west of the city. Somewhere around that time, Hood gave up on defending Atlanta and began to make plans to maneuver Sherman out of north Georgia, so as to save the industrial center of the Confederacy. He hoped to place cavalry troops behind the Union lines in order to cut Sherman's supplies from the south. But in sending out his cavalry, he had lost the ability to follow Sherman's movement. On September 1, 1864, Sherman attacked Hood's troops near Jonesborough, captured his railroad communications, and forced the Confederate general to leave Atlanta. The battle for Atlanta was over, and Hood had wasted precious troops in a futile defense. Perhaps Richard McMurry, Hood's most sympathetic modern analysist, in summing up why Atlanta was lost, said it best: "Hood's defense of Atlanta has never been adequately evaluated" (149). Further, McMurry pointed out, the general would spend "the rest of his life" in trying "to prove that somebody other than himself had been responsible for the loss of the city" (152).

But the "Gallant Hood" soon would have much more than Atlanta to explain to posterity. But he should not bear the entire blame for his fiasco at Franklin-Nashville. Both President Davis and General Pierre G. T. Beauregard (q.v.) approved his plan to drive the Union out of Tennessee and mount an offensive up to the Ohio River. Before that decision to go west was made, Hood made plans to fight Sherman again. He reorganized his army, forced General Hardee's transfer out of his command, and probably put inferior leaders in crucial corps command. Most of all, he hoped for other armies and lower South volunteers to join him in his efforts to rescue the Southern heartland. He tried but failed to disrupt Sherman's supplies from the North. He soon came to believe that he could not stop Sherman from moving east.

His only course, Hood insisted, was to get Sherman to chase him west in order to protect the Union stronghold in middle Tennessee. Although General

Beauregard questioned the judgment of Hood's move west, he in no way attempted to alter the plan. Beauregard believed Hood could get neither enough troops nor enough supplies to challenge for middle Tennessee, and President Davis appears to have misunderstood the general's objectives. Hood himself suffered from various illnesses, not the least of them being able to move with enough speed to challenge what he hoped was a divided enemy. Poorly prepared, with little understanding of where the enemy was because of almost no reconnaissance, in November 1864, Hood began his ill-conceived mission.

Thomas L. Connelly claims that Hood moved on Union General Richard Schofield at Franklin without a plan of where he was going and why. Probably Hood wanted to capture Nashville and then move his troops to the Ohio River. Alas, a powerful and large Union Army was in his way. And his audacity at attacking the enemy with speed and concentrated forces deserted him. On November 29, attack he did. Hood ordered a full frontal advance against well-entrenched Federal troops. Again he attacked on November 30. Then, Union General Schofield retreated into General Thomas's entrenched lines around Nashville. The results of Franklin for the Army of Tennessee were disastrous. Hood had lost 6,000 troops, which included twelve general officers and fifty-three regimental commanders.

He then asked President Davis to send him fresh troops from General Edmund Kirby Smith's trans-Mississippi department, but that general never responded to President Davis's request. It seemed as though each western army was acting on its own. But even without those troops Hood planned yet another grand attack. Moral was poor, desertion was up, and the army had no stomach for an attack. Then, on December 15, 1864, Union General Thomas attacked the Army of Tennessee, and the army broke apart. Hood had left Georgia with over 30,000 troops. He would return east with less than 12,000. The campaign had failed. On January 23, 1865, John Bell Hood, once a hero, resigned his commission in disgrace.

General Hood was a broken man. Yet President Davis still had hope of using him. On March 8, 1865, Hood asked to be sent to the trans-Mississippi to organize troops for continued resistance. If President Davis had been able to read Mary B. Chesnut's diary account, he would have responded with silence. That ex-senator's wife spent some time with him in late February and March as the general again courted "Buck" Preston. Mrs. Chesnut suggested there were rumors that Hood had been drunk at Franklin. She reported that with hindsight General Wade Hampton allowed Hood had been promoted too fast. Worst, she described him as red-faced, a melancholic man sitting by a fire nursing his wounds, with the agony of defeat in his face (Vann Woodward and Muhlenfield, 708, 222). She said of him that he was simple, transparent, without guile. "Buck" Preston rejected him, and soon Hood rode off to the Southwest. At the war's end, he surrendered, was paroled, and traveled to New Orleans to make a living, lick his wounds, and plan a way to save his tattered reputation.

One modern historian, John P. Dyer, said that soon after the war had ended,

Hood contemplated setting down his memoirs "so that everyone might know the true story of his failure" (360). For a time he lived in Texas; then in October 1865 he went to New Orleans. He entered business as a cotton factor and commission merchant and did well. In 1870 he became president of the Life Association of America, a large life insurance company. On April 13, 1868, he had married Anna Marie Hennen, perhaps following the advice of General Lee, who had suggested the once-handsome officer marry for money. His wife was Roman Catholic, but Hood remained an Episcopalian. They had eleven children. If Hood had found some kind of happiness with his family, he remained embittered over his wartime career. Perhaps his old wounds and memories hurt him. What hurt most was when General Johnston published his own memoirs in 1874, in which he made Hood one of the scapegoats of the Confederacy's defeat. Hood immediately began his own memoirs. By 1879 the memoirs were ready for publication. But Hood would never see them, for he contracted yellow fever in New Orleans and died in that city on August 30, 1879.

The reputation of that line commander has never really recovered from his short year as general in chief of the Army of Tennessee. The earliest work on his life, that of the Richmond journalist and early historian of the war Edward A. Pollard (q.v.), did not spare him. Mrs. Chesnut's diary, when published toward the end of the century, added to the burden of military defeat by making him a fool for love. Her comments on Hood's relations with "Buck" Preston showed him a failure in affairs of the heart, a simple man who had exceeded his capacity. General Joseph E. Johnston, whom history also has treated badly, fixed Hood among nineteenth-century students of the Civil War as a man who cheated and schemed his way to command, only to fail completely. Hood himself, in his own defense, so tried to curry favor with the Lee fans that he forgot there could be only one Robert E. Lee. Hood's own charges that Joseph E. Johnston had ruined the army's will to take the offense pales beside the lame excuses he made for the debacle at Franklin. Hood's linking the Atlanta campaign with his excuses for Franklin only look foolish. To some extent, he was his own worst enemy. He had committed a major offense of a military commander: Simply, Hood had overreached himself.

Modern scholars who have studied his personal defense do not disagree with Hood's verdict about his role in the Civil War. Instead, they have tried to explain why and how this man, who succeeded in many earlier battles, ultimately failed. His first major biographer, John P. Dyer, in an attempt to revise Hood's reputation upward, praised his early career. However, Dyer could only explain the failure in Tennessee as the actions of a man whose emotions exceeded his intellect, as his impetuosity led him to defeat. That he also had fought for an abstraction led Dyer to label him a failed romantic. Taking up this charge, Hood's most thorough biographer, Richard McMurry, judged Hood's great attachment to the Southern way of life and the image he created for himself to have been the great flaw in his behavior. Hood had to attack—that was the Southern way. But McMurry also studied Hood's campaign objectively. If Hood blamed others for Atlanta, McMurry saw some truth in it. He shows that Hood might have succeeded there. Only at Franklin, insists McMurry, did Hood take on an army he could not defeat. Most recently, Stephen Woodworth has acknowledged that Hood had been foolhardy, but he has added a twist. Woodworth blames Beauregard and Davis for allowing him to fail. Winston Groom, himself tormented by Franklin, has added yet another psychological flaw to Hood and to his South. Groom says that honor took over as the only means to face certain defeat. Of Hood, Groom said: "It was more judicious that that man should face a decisive issue, rather than retreat—in other words, rather than renounce the honor of their cause, without having made a last and manful effort to lift up the sinking fortunes of the Confederacy" (287–288). Rather than Groom's, I prefer McMurry's straight-out judgment that despite his many flaws Hood simply could not prevail at the last against such superior numbers. But, then, should he have attacked at Franklin?

BIBLIOGRAPHY

Nicholas A. Davis, *Campaign from Texas to Maryland* (Richmond: Office of the Presbyterian Committee of Publication of the Confederate States, 1863).

John Bell Hood, *Advance and Retreat: Personal Experiences in the United States and Confederate States Armies* (New Orleans: Hood's Orphans Memorial Fund, 1880).

John P. Dyer, *The Gallant Hood* (Indianapolis: Bobbs-Merrill Co., 1950).

Thomas L. Connelly, *Autumn of Glory: The Army of Tennessee, 1862–1865* (Baton Rouge: Louisiana State University Press, 1971).

Richard M. McMurry, *John Bell Hood and the War for Southern Independence* (Lincoln: University of Nebraska Press, 1982).

C. Vann Woodward and Elizabeth Muhlenfield (eds.), *The Private Mary Chesnut: The Unpublished Civil War Diaries* (New York: Oxford University Press, 1984).

Stephen E. Woodworth, *Jefferson Davis and His Generals* (Topeka: University Press of Kansas, 1990).

Peter Cozzens, *This Terrible Sound: The Battle of Chickamauga* (Urbana: University of Illinois Press, 1992).

Winston Groom, *Shrouds of Glory: From Atlanta to Nashville* (New York: Atlantic Monthly Press, 1995).

ROBERT MERCER TALIAFERRO HUNTER
(April 21, 1809–July 18, 1887)

John Allen

On the eve of secession, Robert M. T. Hunter stood among the most prominent Southerners in the federal government. Numbered with Jefferson Davis (q.v.) and Robert Toombs in the Senate's "southern trio," Hunter had distinguished himself as Senate Finance chairman while concomitantly receiving acclaim in the South for being a consistent proslavery advocate. During the 1850s, he twice turned down cabinet appointments from Presidents Pierce and Buchanan and, in 1860, organized an unsuccessful run at the Democratic party's presidential nomination. Although he served the Confederacy briefly as Secretary of State (July 1861 to February 1862), Hunter spent most of the Civil War replicating his antebellum service as head of the Confederate Senate's Finance Committee. Historians have virtually ignored Hunter, especially when compared with the treatment received by his contemporaries Davis, Toombs, Alexander Stephens (q.v.), and Howell Cobb. Why has so distinguished a figure as Hunter received so little scholarly attention?

Robert Mercer Taliaferro Hunter grew up in Essex County, Virginia (date of birth, April 21, 1809) within a network of prominent Virginia families including the Mercers, Taliaferros, and Garnetts as well as the Hunters. His kinfolk included two maternal uncles who had served in Congress and two Garnett cousins who would become Confederate brigadiers in addition to his beloved nephew, Muscoe Russell Hunter Garnett, who would follow Hunter into the U.S. and Confederate legislatures. Robert received private tutoring before entering the University of Virginia's first class in 1825. Although a serious scholar, Hunter received the sobriquet "Run Mad Tom" (highlighting his initials) from his fellow students. After two years in Charlottesville, he joined the Winchester Law School of well-regarded jurist Judge Henry St. George Tucker, half brother of John Randolph of Roanoke. Tucker stood at the top of his profession and ran the most eminent law school in Virginia at this time. In 1830, Hunter returned to Essex to practice law and to construct a political career.

Hunter's family connections, landownership, and education (prestigious for that era) ably prepared him for either a legal or a political career. When he first entered the local bar, Hunter complained of the competition among attorneys and expressed qualms about the money-making potential of country lawyers. Whether he had always intended on politics or whether he envisioned this arena as more economically viable than a country legal practice is unclear; however, Hunter shortly became politically active, locally, as a strong supporter of John C. Calhoun. Hunter won election to Virginia's House of Delegates in 1833, the Virginia Senate in 1835, and established himself as the leader of Calhoun's supporters in the Old Dominion.

At this time, Hunter undertook two additional endeavors. In 1836, he married Mary Dandridge, the niece of his law tutor Judge Tucker; they subsequently had eight children. He also began a lifetime career as an occasional speaker. As the first prominent alumnus of the University of Virginia, Hunter delivered the address at the organizational meeting of the alumni association. He was later the featured speaker at the Washington Statue dedication in Richmond's Capitol Square and delivered the main eulogy at former President John Tyler's funeral. Henry Simms, Hunter's principal biographer, noted that he served as a frequent orator in Virginia on notable occasions and was known for his breadth of knowledge, eloquence of style, and beauty of diction. Mary Chesnut commented that when Mr. Hunter lectured, it was worth recording even if "his waistcoat wanted pulling down, and his hair wanted brushing." She spoke of "Mr. Hunter's wisdom as unanswerable" (Vann Woodward, 54).

In 1837, Hunter took a further step up in his political career by winning election to the U.S. House of Representatives where he continued to support Calhoun. In 1839, Hunter benefited from a deadlock over the selection of the House Speaker. According to historian Daniel Walker Howe, John Quincy Adams used his prestige and knowledge of parliamentary procedures to resolve this organizational paralysis by promoting Hunter for Speaker; even antislave Whigs such as Joshua Giddings supported this tactic. Hunter served in this position until 1841 and continued to lead the congressional supporters of Calhoun.

Working from outlines and notes supplied by Calhoun himself, Hunter, in 1843, wrote a political biography of the South Carolinian, which was to be used for the 1844 presidential campaign. Hunter's authorship was widely disputed; however, historians Anderson and Hemphill have argued convincingly that both Hunter and Calhoun acknowledged Hunter's effort. Hunter noted that "not quite half of it mine"; Calhoun said that Hunter had "rewritten most" of the manuscript "so much so as fairly to be entitled to the authorship." Hunter had produced the longest sketch of Calhoun's political career published in his lifetime—an effort that redounded to Hunter's benefit and enhanced his political reputation (Anderson and Hemphill, 472).

In 1847, the Virginia legislature selected Hunter for the U.S. Senate, and while in Washington, he shared room and board with three other proslavery congressmen: Andrew P. Butler of South Carolina, David R. Atchison of Missouri, and James M. Mason of Virginia. He voted for the annexation of Texas and supported Franklin Pierce for president in 1852. Even though he had acted as a Calhoun protégé by promoting conservative issues, Hunter, by the time of Calhoun's death, had already emerged as a political power in his own right: From 1850 to 1861, he chaired the Senate Finance Committee. John E. Fisher, whose dissertation covered Hunter's mature years (after 1847), held that Hunter maintained his ties to the reactionary political philosophy of Calhoun; however, Simms portrayed Hunter as a quiet, unobtrusive moderate who became the financial brain of the Senate. Hunter certainly remained a strong proslavery advocate.

Speaking on the Kansas-Nebraska legislation, Hunter argued that a territory should determine the question of slavery when its convention drew up the constitution for statehood; however, he eventually supported the Douglas position: a difference only in nuance. Hunter also spoke in favor of, and voted for, the Lecompton Constitution. As Senate Finance chairman he consistently voted for lower tariffs, supported the Tariff Act of 1857, opposed internal improvements, and voted to postpone the Homestead Bill in 1858 and 1859.

Even though he spoke before the Senate on all the aforementioned issues, Hunter's political skills were as much rhetorical as oratorical. He excelled in logically presenting his side of a position and worked to sway individual legislators, behind the scenes, with his brilliance. His reputation for effectiveness in the Senate resulted largely from these endeavors.

Hunter, although a consistent proslavery supporter, was not necessarily a firebrand secessionist; he hoped to be the Democratic candidate for president in 1860. The splintering of the Democratic party, however, dashed these hopes; nevertheless, John E. Fisher and John B. Jones contended that Hunter carried this ambition with him into the Confederacy. In addition, Fisher classified Hunter as a conditional Unionist; however, Jon L. Wakelyn characterized Hunter as a "subtle secessionist living in a border state." Hunter said that "I believe in the right of secession—[yet] each state must judge for itself" (Wakelyn, 261).

Although Hunter concurred in the right to secede, he struggled to prevent a complete rupture: He served on the Crittenden committee and supported its efforts in trying to preserve the Union. In January 1861, Hunter delivered two addresses to the U.S. Senate. In the first, he tried to warn his colleagues of the dangers of the Fort Sumter situation and also of the need to retrocede Federal posts to the respective Southern states in order to prevent war. This speech, in addition, included a novel proposal for a dual presidency based on slave and free state alignments. He believed that the "social system of a people is its moral being"—that Southerners could claim equal standing would not suffice; Northerners must also acknowledge it—the morality of being pro slavery (Wakelyn, 268–269).

In the second, Hunter argued in favor of the right of secession and predicted a rosy future for a Southern confederacy. He felt, however, that both sections complemented each other economically and together could forge a brilliant future:

When we come to see what we might be, and how we might become the master influence of the universe, if this Union were properly administered according to the principles of justice and the Constitution, the imagination halts at the mighty conception, and the mind, rapt in the contemplation of the giant shadows of our future progress, as they sweep across the perspective, sinks under the effort to realize that glorious pageant of human grandeur as it passes before view. (Hunter, 15)

Shortly thereafter, in March 1861, Hunter resigned from the U.S. Senate, supported Virginia's secession, and headed the delegation that invited the infant Confederacy to locate its capital in Richmond.

In July 1861, Jefferson Davis appointed Hunter to be Secretary of State to replace Robert Toombs, who had grown frustrated with the Davis government and sought military accolades in the field. Davis selected Hunter not only because of his desire to include a Virginian in his cabinet but also because of Hunter's résumé of accomplishments and history of political effectiveness. John B. Jones noted that being Secretary of State likewise removed Hunter as a potential competitor to Davis by relegating him to an ''obscure'' place (60).

As Secretary of State, Hunter proclaimed the principles that explained Confederate diplomatic policies: He put forth resolutions that acknowledged privateering; he defined a blockade—a blockade in order to be binding must be effective; he accepted the rules of the Paris Conference of 1856; and he proceeded under the theory that the Confederacy now belonged to the family of nations. In addition, Hunter dispatched envoys to Spain and wrote the instructions to James Mason and John Slidell (soon to be involved in the Trent Affair). How much this reflected the hand of Davis, resulted from joint collaboration, or evinced Hunter's own individual initiative is unclear. Douglas Ball, in his discussion of these events, always used the phrase ''Davis and Hunter'' (Ball, 64). Historian Rembert W. Patrick, however, contended that Davis and Hunter worked together in a fair degree of accord with there being no reason to believe that the Secretary of State was not treated with respect or that the president slighted his advice (Patrick, 100).

Hunter's tenure in the Confederate State Department ended in February 1862 when Virginia selected him for the permanent Confederate States of America Senate. Writers have differed over their interpretation of Hunter's departure from the Davis government. The gossipy Edward A. Pollard (q.v.) described a cabinet meeting during which Davis admonished Hunter for offering unsolicited advice. A man of Hunter's stature could hardly remain as ''Davis's clerk'' (Pollard, 151). John Fisher reiterated Hunter's longtime ambition that led the Virginian to believe that the Senate offered a better route toward his ultimate goal, the presidency. War Department clerk Jones, however, thought that Hunter was miffed because Judah Benjamin (q.v.) held Davis's ear and therefore had become the most important cabinet member even though Hunter held the higher-ranking State portfolio. Historian Patrick offered an entirely different scenario; he suggested that Davis may have supported Hunter's departure since the executive needed a strong voice in the Senate. Furthermore, Patrick contended that Hunter's initial course in the legislature, showing firm administration support, demonstrated a possible collaboration with Davis.

Moreover, the appointment of James A. Seddon (q.v.) as the new War Department Secretary provided Hunter with a conduit into cabinet deliberations. Seddon, a fellow Virginian and likewise a University of Virginia alumnus, had been Hunter's political ally for over twenty years. According to Jones, Hunter called on Seddon daily and spent most Sunday mornings closeted with him in the War Department offices.

Furthermore, Jones proffered a physical description of Hunter at this time. He described the Virginia senator as a short, rotund man always walking quickly or in a hurry. Fisher likewise described Hunter as corpulent but added that the senator's makeup included a certain lazy slowness or inertness. Patrick contended, however, that even though Hunter was short, portly, had sleepy eyes, and gave the impression of polite indolence, his performance belied his appearance; he found Hunter to be efficient, cultivated, knowledgeable, and someone who completed his tasks with a methodical thoroughness. Patrick described Hunter's papers as well written in a plain, direct, and effective language (100).

Hunter, as president pro tempore, often presided over the Senate in the place of the frequently absent Vice President Alexander H. Stephens—in one instance for a period covering a year and a half. In addition, Hunter continued to be involved in financial affairs as the head of the Confederate Senate's Finance Committee. This committee, under the signature of Hunter and Thomas Semmes, offered a bill in January 1864 for reforming the Confederate currency. The House bill had been submitted by Hunter's nephew Muscoe. The adopted version had some success, initially, in reducing the redundancy of paper money. Hunter also provided Robert E. Lee (q.v.) a legislative ear that the general used to plead his case for more supplies and logistical support.

Remaining optimistic for the Confederacy at least through spring 1864, Hunter saw the possibility of "peace, liberty, independence, unrivaled opportunities for moral, material, and social development, and a renown which the proudest nations on earth might admire and envy" (Coulter, 58). By the end of that year, however, he had become far less sanguine. Hunter split with Davis over the necessity of conscripting slaves, to which Hunter never acquiesced. He had reached the most disturbing conclusion: If slavery had caused the war, and if the Confederacy had abandoned the war goal of the preservation of slavery, then how could it justify the loss of so many lives to save it? How could one justify the expenditure of so much blood and treasure? "Who was to answer before the bar of heaven" (Beringer et al., 391)?

Nevertheless, Davis chose Hunter to participate in the Hampton Roads conference. By this time, Hunter had veered far enough away from the Confederate president that he seemed to have joined Alex Stephens in the category of Davis political opponents. The unsuccessful conference not only increased Hunter's pessimism, but it also provided the fuel for a festering quarrel with Davis over the instructions, agenda, and symbolism of this meeting—a controversy that continued into the 1880s.

Unlike many others, Hunter remained in Virginia after Appomattox. Due to his public acknowledgment of Confederate defeat, Union General Ulysses S. Grant (q.v.) initially left Hunter alone; however, upon receiving instructions from War Secretary Edwin S. Stanton (q.v.), the Union general arrested Hunter in May 1865 and imprisoned him at Fort Pulaski, Georgia, with other high-ranking Confederate politicians.

After his release in January 1866, Hunter returned to Essex but faced a greatly changed world. Not only had his personal finances, based largely on a plantation mill (burned by Ben Butler), deteriorated, but illness and accident had also removed two sons, a daughter, and beloved nephew Muscoe from the family gathering. His daughter Martha felt he never quite overcame these family losses and never fully regained his verve for future political struggles.

In the 1870s, nevertheless, Hunter reentered the public sphere when elected Virginia's treasurer by the state legislature. He attempted to organize a tax-free issue of state bonds to help the Old Dominion's finances but did not succeed. Hunter, unlike some other politicians, remained in the good graces of the group of former Confederate military figures (Jubal Early, William Allan, J. W. Jones, and Walter Taylor) who became the primary interpreters of the Civil War experience from the Virginia perspective. Not only did he serve as vice president of the Southern Historical Society (their primary organ), but he also wrote the introductory article in its first volume; however, his stature as a prominent figure diminished.

How should R. M. T. Hunter be evaluated? Many contemporaries viewed Hunter as an eloquent orator whose capacities better suited peace than war. Biographer Fisher argued that Hunter, after Appomattox, could not understand the new political relationships and was quickly dismissed as a political dinosaur (Fisher, 273). Except for his quarrel with Davis and some mention in the gossipy stories of Mary Chesnut and E. A. Pollard, Hunter largely disappeared from historical view after 1865. Historian Charles Ambler described Hunter as an altogether insignificant figure. The lack of success the Confederate government had in providing sufficient resources for Lee and other heroes of the "Lost Cause" probably colored the public perception of Hunter as well as the historical focus on military affairs and military leadership.

R. M. T. Hunter died on July 18, 1887; old friends and scions of Hunter's large family network sought to remember his life and contributions. These groups planned to remove his remains to Hollywood Cemetery in Richmond and erect a suitable memorial. Colonel L. Quinton Washington delivered an eloquent eulogy, Hunter-style, on behalf of this effort; however, the attempt proved futile. Popular sentiment did not materialize, and the state offered no financial support. As future generations of historians looked back upon the Civil War crucible, the figure of R. M. T. Hunter largely disappeared from collective historical memory. The myth of the Lost Cause that so dominated Southern thinking at this time had no room for politicians such as Hunter. As current historians remove these layers of myth, perhaps the role of Confederate legislators such as Hunter can be more fully evaluated.

BIBLIOGRAPHY

John B. Jones, *Rebel War Clerk's Diary* (Philadelphia: J. B. Lippincott, 1866).

Edward A. Pollard, *Life of Jefferson Davis* (Philadelphia: Books for Libraries Press, 1869).

John C. Swab, *The Confederate States of America: A Financial and Industrial History of the South during the Civil War* (New York: Charles Scribner's Sons, 1901).

Martha T. Hunter, *A Memoir of Robert M. T. Hunter* (Washington, D.C.: Neal Publishing Company, 1903).

Charles H. Ambler, "Correspondence of Robert M. T. Hunter," *American Historical Association Annual Report*, vol. 2 (1916).

Henry H. Simms, *Life of Robert M. T. Hunter* (Richmond, Va.: William Byrd Press, 1935).

Rembert W. Patrick, *Jefferson Davis and His Cabinet* (Baton Rouge: Louisiana State University Press, 1941).

E. Merton Coulter, *The Confederate States of America, 1861–1865* (Baton Rouge: Louisiana State University Press, 1950).

John Eugene Fisher, "Statesman of the Lost Cause: R. M. T. Hunter and the Sectional Controversy, 1847–1887" (Ph.D. diss., University of Virginia, 1968).

James L. Anderson and W. Edwin Hemphill, "The 1843 Biography of John C. Calhoun: Was R.M.T. Hunter Its Author?" *Journal of Southern History* 38, no. 3 (August 1972): 469–474.

C. Vann Woodward, ed., *Mary Chesnut's Civil War* (New Haven: Yale University Press, 1981).

Richard Beringer, Archer Jones, Herman Hattaway, and William N. Still, *Why the South Lost the Civil War* (Athens: University of Georgia Press, 1986).

Douglas Ball, *Financial Failure and Confederate Defeat* (Urbana: University of Illinois Press, 1991).

Jon L. Wakelyn, ed., *Southern Pamphlets on Secession, November 1860–April 1861* (Chapel Hill: University of North Carolina Press, 1996).

THOMAS JONATHAN JACKSON
(January 21, 1824–May 10, 1863)

Jon L. Wakelyn

The Confederacy's famous General "Stonewall" Jackson belongs to that special category of heroes who transcended the reality of their accomplishments. Despite being one of the Civil War's leading generals, the myths that have grown around his war record make it quite difficult to evaluate Jackson's actual military contributions. But that does not mean that history has ignored his life. Except for Robert E. Lee (q.v.), no Southern hero has had more words written about him or more analysis of the deeds of his short life. Jackson remains a hero for the South and is a large part of its legends and myths. Yet although Virginia born and a hero of the Army of Northern Virginia, Jackson's own life hardly fits the stereotype so necessary to a re-creation of that romantic past. How, then, was he made a hero, and why has he remained one?

As with so many famous figures, some of what may be understood about his own persona and of what others made of him surely comes from his upbringing. Yet even his early life is shrouded in myth, in part because those who have created the great Jackson image also have made legends of his youth to establish the adult hero. At times reality conflicts with myth, but reality does much to uncover the motivation behind the driven life of the ambitious Tom Jackson. Tom may have been of old Scotch-Irish and English Virginia stock, but he was born and grew up in the rocky hills of western Virginia, near Clarksburg, in a land of rocky soil hardly redolent of wealthy plantation slave society. He also was born into an ordinary Virginia family unencumbered with the burden of a colonial heritage. On January 21, 1824, Jonathan Jackson and Judith Beckwith (Neale) brought their second child into this life. The father was a bit of a ne'er-do-well, a country lawyer who owned some land, practiced a little law, and always seemed in debt and under the threat of lawsuit. Despite the fact that he was the father of a future great hero, the elder Jonathan probably was a bit crooked. Fortunately for those who make legends, he died in 1826, which meant that his son hardly knew him. Young Tom's mother soon remarried, but she died in 1831, leaving Tom and his brother and sister orphans.

There were many relatives available to care for the children. Tom was raised near Jackson's Mill, Virginia, in the household of his uncle Cummins Jackson. Tom hunted, fished, rode poorly, and got himself into a number of youthful scrapes. He also worked in a mill and later was named a sub sheriff of the town. This left little time for schooling for the young man. His uncle, accused of counterfeiting, hardly gave his nephew a positive family image. From time to time, young Tom's debts made trouble for him with the law. They were the typical debts incurred by the sturdy western Virginia middle classes forced to live by their wits and their skills to survive in that hilly land with such poor soil. No wonder the youth was ambitious to break that cycle and to make something of himself.

The sub sheriff, who perhaps was one step away from jail, managed to escape his surroundings and enter the U.S. Military Academy at West Point. He seems to have had little interest at the time in the military, but the Academy provided a free education and perhaps the finest science and engineering training in the country at that time. When Jackson went there in 1842 he had to struggle to survive. His early education hardly prepared him for the rigors of mathematics, and his country manners left him outside the ranks of elite young Virginian gentlemen who were his classmates. Legend has it that he clashed with his upper-class classmate Ambrose Powell Hill over a slight and that the dispute would end only with Jackson's death twenty-one years later. The young and ambitious mountain man at first ranked near the lowest in the class, but through perseverance and working hard to memorize facts, he rose to a respectable place. Jackson also developed severe health problems in the cold climate along the Hudson River, although some of them probably were psychosomatic. He gained the reputation of being subservient to superiors almost to a fault, and that obedient young man received only a few demerits in his four years at the academy. Most of all, Jackson learned discipline, at least self-discipline, for he seemed to abhor going along with the crowd. He graduated in the class of 1846 high enough to be able to choose the artillery over the cavalry, and he was assigned to the First Artillery and posted to the New York border. The future military hero's preparation had begun.

By all reports, military duty at that time was dull and lacked any glamour. That changed quickly in September 1846 when Jackson was sent to Mexico to serve under General Zachary Taylor. For a time he languished as company commissary officer, but soon he gained a transfer and joined General Winfield Scott in his southern Mexican invasion of Vera Cruz. At first he was given garrison duty, but later he was allowed to join Scott's expedition to Mexico City. Scott had chosen to live off the land with his small army, and there would soon be fighting enough for any ambitious young man seeking advance in rank. Jackson was in on the capture of Pueblo and served under John B. Magruder as an artillery officer in the battles of Molino del Ray and Chapultepec. He

received praise for expert firing on the enemy and the brevet as major. After
Mexico's surrender, Jackson stayed on there doing garrison duty. He was later
to say that that duty was nearly the happiest of his life. In June 1848 he was
transferred east to New York.

The boredom of garrison duty at Fort Hamilton, New York, left Jackson time
to nurture his hypochondria and to seek relief in religion. In 1849 he was baptized into the Episcopal Church, but that broad church soon would not suffice.
Jackson would find a Protestant church more suitable to his dour and earnest
personality when he joined the Presbyterians. In 1850 he was ordered to Fort
Meade in Florida to guard against marauding Seminoles. There his ambitions
and his arbitrariness surfaced as he was arrested and accused of intriguing
against a commanding officer. When offered a job at the Virginia Military Institute in 1851, he eagerly extricated himself from his legal difficulties, resigned
his commission, and went home to the valley near the hills of western Virginia.
At the time Lexington was a bustling town anchored by Presbyterian Washington College and the elite Military Institute. Jackson took on the duties of instructor in science and military tactics. He seemed to have found a home.

What a picture the handsome but awkward ex-soldier must have made for
those young men. Jackson could not teach worth a lick. His means of instruction
was to memorize and deliver his lectures in a monotonous tone, and he refused
to entertain any student questions. He treated them like subordinates, constantly
accused them of being slackers, and at one time nearly was killed when some
students took revenge against their enemy. But Jackson had found peace, and
in 1853, he married Elinor Jenkin, daughter of a local leading Presbyterian
divine. When she died in childbirth, the ambitious professor married again in
1857, this time to Anna Morrison, daughter of a wealthy planter. The parsi-
monious teacher soon began to make money and acquire land and slaves, but
he never took to that life of leisure and power. He later owned a tannery and
became a bank director. His ambitions also led him to a fruitless application for
an appointment at the University of Virginia.

In those years, Jackson vigorously defended his native Virginia, although
friends thought that, like his sister, he also favored the Union. But the winter
of 1859 changed Jackson, as he led his cadets to control the crowd at the hanging
of John Brown at Harpers Ferry. He came to favor secession and became an
adviser to the Virginia governor on the purchase of weapons. After Fort Sumter
he placed his name for military duty before the Virginia convention and was
named a major of engineers in the Virginia state army. It was not long before
this man of few words, this mountain recluse, would become the stuff of legend.

Charles Royster, among other scholars, revised much of the legend of a self-
effacing hero and saw Jackson for what he was, a clumsy but savvy promoter
of his own career. For Jackson soon learned that his earnest personality appeared
newsworthy and that his dedication in habit of command displayed leadership
potential. He gained promotion to colonel and was sent back to Harpers Ferry,
this time to defend the Confederate arsenal there. He trained raw civilian recruits

and placed them along the heights in Maryland, though that state had remained neutral in the war. Put under the command of Joseph E. Johnston (q.v.) in mid-May 1861, Jackson intrigued with friends in Richmond to get promoted to brigadier general in the Provisional Confederate States Army. On July 18, 1861, Jackson accompanied Johnston's move from Harper's Ferry to Bull Run to join General P. G. T. Beauregard (q.v.) in preparation for battle. Jackson knew the land and was able to march his troops rapidly, and he arrived on July 21 to shore up the Confederate state defense. There, behind a stone wall, the legend of Jackson and the First Virginia Brigade, later the "Stonewall" brigade, was made. The new general with his raw troops halted the Union advance and then countercharged. General Barnard Bee was supposed to have said, "[T]here stands Jackson like a stone wall." The legend also began with Jackson's brigade sustaining the largest losses of any in the army and Jackson's excellent use of artillery to stop Union General Irwin McDowell's last charge. As Jackson's recent hostile biographer Byron Farwell said, it was indeed strange that the legend of "Stonewall" Jackson began with a defensive maneuver and that Jackson himself would become famous as a man of movement, a great offensive warrior.

Of course, General Jackson also talked to the press and claimed that he could have gone on to Washington. Perhaps he could have, but he never got the opportunity, as he was ordered to encamp near Centerville to prepare his hurt brigade to fight again. In October, for his heroics, he was promoted to major general. Later in the autumn he was sent to the Virginia frontier as commander of the Valley District with the assignment to hold Winchester for the Confederacy. Jackson had an independent command and a clear mandate, and he began to clamor for additional troops. He also earned the reputation for harsh judgment toward his subordinates, as he refused to allow slow or incompetent officers around him. When he did not get what he wanted, the soon to be legendary man of loyalty and perseverence threatened to resign. He was appeased by higher-ups who believed he could fight and did not want to lose him. Jackson then prepared for his most famous adventure when, in March 1862, he faced Union General Nathaniel Banks and began his celebrated retreat up the Shenandoah Valley of Virginia that would result in the legendary Valley Campaign.

The Valley Campaign has become so famous that it is said the German General Irwin Rommel studied it to learn about how to move men and materiel and how to concentrate an inferior force to take advantage of a larger, spread-out enemy. It should also be seen as an audacious, if at times foolhardy, set of maneuvers of advance and retreat buttressed by great luck. It began on March 23, 1862, when Jackson fought the Union General James Shields at Kernstown. Jackson gave confused orders to his subordinate General Richard B. Garnett, which resulted in a forced retreat and for which Jackson wanted to court-martial Garnett. Shields thought he had won the field, so he turned defensive and began a buildup of troops, perhaps thinking Jackson wanted to move on Washington City. But Jackson had other plans. He enlisted Major Jedidiah Hotchkiss to make him maps to use in his maneuvers against weak Union positions. In May 1862 he confronted General Irwin McDowell and forced a Federal withdrawal. From the mountains to the west, he moved back into the valley at Front Royal, where he superbly adopted the use of interior line to concentrate against the enemy. He was after supplies for his small army, but he also was under orders to keep Union General Nathaniel P. Banks from joining forces with General George B. McClellan (q.v.) on the Peninsula of Virginia. This he would accomplish, always in peril and with a bit of luck.

On May 25 Jackson's cavalry raced into the town of Winchester to keep General Banks out of that supply center. Banks's troops scattered before the charge of Colonel Richard Taylor, son of the late President Zachary Taylor, and Jackson was able to control the high ground around the town. When local citizens fired upon retreating Federal troops, Jackson encouraged their carnage. But Jackson never took advantage of his position because he did not send the cavalry to follow the Federals. Banks got out of the valley but not without surrendering some 3,000 troops to Jackson. When the Federals next concentrated around Harpers Ferry, Jackson's small army was nearly trapped. But at the end of May, Jackson audaciously escaped just before the troops of Generals John C. Fremont and Irwin McDowell converged to cut him off. "Stonewall" then burned bridges behind him to hinder the Federal attack.

Even with all his success, by early June the Confederate general and his troops seemed confused and unable to grasp Federal intentions. Tired and anxious about his precarious position, Jackson hoped to cross to the east over the Blue Ridge. Instead, on June 8, 1862, at the village of Cross Keys, he again found high ground and adroitly placed his artillery under General "Baldy" Ewell to defend against Fremont's attack. Defend they did, as the artillery stopped Fremont completely. Jackson again retreated, then counterattacked at Port Republic, and the Federals retreated. The Federals again lost sight of Jackson, were befuddled, and the Confederate general succeeded in defeating any rendezvous of Banks with McClellan. Of course, the ambitious general had used the press to trumpet his exploits and had not hesitated to praise himself, if not his "incompetent" subordinates, in his reports to Richmond. True, his exploits of advance and retreat were the stuff of heroics; truer, his self-aggrandizement was palpable. He had also gained a reputation of being loyal to his troops and was, as Byron Farwell says, "abusive and clumsy in his personal relations with subordinates" (332).

The legend of his valley exploits, partially of Jackson's own making, traveled to the new Confederate commander on the peninsula, Robert E. Lee, who held him in great respect. At first Lee thought of sending Jackson to Maryland and Pennsylvania to relieve pressure on Richmond but, instead, in mid-June, brought him east. A tired and beleaguered Jackson at first resisted this order, perhaps because he too much enjoyed independent heroics. To some extent his reputation would have benefited if he had remained in the valley. For on June 26, 1862, at Mechanicsville, he lost contact with the rest of the army and was slow to advance, thus damaging the coordination of Confederate efforts. At Gaines Mill, on June 27, Jackson got lost. At White Oak Swamp on June 30, he fought poorly and indecisively. Again he lost contact with Lee's army and displayed poor coordination. On July 1, 1862, in the disastrous Confederate advance on Malvern Hill, Jackson foolhardily attacked well-positioned Union fortifications and again had to retreat. But the Union Army under McClellan had had enough. Beating Confederates obviously was hard work. McClellan retreated, so Lee and Jackson claimed victory. Jackson had failed in those Seven Days, probably because he was worn out but also because he just didn't seem to get the hang of coordinated military efforts.

Lee would not often in the future make the mistake of counting directly on Jackson's support. He would give him his head to assume a kind of independent command. And "Stonewall" would respond by becoming again the brave, gambling, rash, and successful general who seemed reluctant even to tell his staff how he planned to fight the men in blue. At Cedar Mountain on August 9, 1862, in an independent action Jackson confronted the advancing General Nathaniel Banks. The Confederate general once again placed his artillery in such a way as to command control of the enemy advance. But the man famed for his mobility may have liked his defensive placement too well. Banks nearly turned Jackson's left flank, which would have resulted in defeat. Instead, the intrepid Jackson turned on his own retreating troops and forced them to mount a counterattack. Although Jackson prevailed that day, Banks's claim to have hurt the Confederate held some truth. But again the publicity machine geared up as Jackson once again became the audacious Confederate hero who routed the enemy.

Near Manassas, Virginia, Lee united with Jackson to concentrate his troops before Union General John Pope. But Pope retreated, and Lee divided his troops. Independent Confederate armies moved toward Pope as he retreated to Manassas Junction. In a prelude to Second Manassas, Jackson, on August 27, 1862, attacked the Yankees at Groveton, forcing an unnecessary encounter. In the battles of August 28–30, Pope and Joseph Hooker united to attack Jackson, who used the intrepid Ambrose P. Hill to create a strong defensive position. Pope attacked again on August 30, and fortunately, James Longstreet (q.v.) had united with Jackson to drive him back. But at Chantilly, Virginia, on August 31, Jackson's attack could not overcome Pope's strong defense. When Jackson did not combine with Longstreet there, Pope was enabled to save his Union Army and retreat to the safe confines around Washington. Jackson again in official reports and newspaper accounts was the Confederate hero. But he had lost many troops, could not fight alongside other generals, and probably was responsible both for Confederate victory and for allowing Pope's successful escape.

Some of his fellow generals suggested that Jackson's inability to grasp orders to unite with others was because of his growing deafness; others said he sought personal glory too much to link his fortunes with other parts of the Army of Northern Virginia. In early September, the petty Jackson placed A. P. Hill under arrest, perhaps thus avenging the slight of so many years ago at West Point. At any rate, as Farwell says: "[T]he hostility of these two brave, capable, and prickly men festered like a cancer in the body of Lee's army"(422). Despite these personality flaws, Jackson as a solo operator would do anything to win a battle. Lee had sent his general to Harpers Ferry to search for supplies, which forced the Union Army to divide its strength. On September 14, 1862, Jackson allowed Hill a reprieve, and at Harpers Ferry together they captured 13,000 Federal troops. No doubt that was a splendid victory, but would it allow Jackson to unite quickly enough with Lee when the Union Army under the beleaguered George B. McClellan concentrated around Sharpsburg, Maryland?

At Sharpsburg, or Antietam as the Yankees called it, on September 17, 1862, Jackson arrived on Lee's left wing to receive the blows of Union General Joseph Hooker. Unable to create a defensive position, Jackson's army attacked, retreated, counterattacked, slaughtered the enemy troops, and lost many of its own. Like a whirling dervish, Jackson was everywhere at once, and as usual, he shouted orders, countermanded them, and gave orders that his staff could not understand. But he held the Confederate position, even if he was too weakened to fight the next day. Instead, on September 18, he assisted in the Confederate retreat and managed to save much of Lee's artillery. A thoroughly busted Confederate Army then managed to escape near annihilation, in part because McClellan did not know how to take the offensive. Jackson conferred with his commander, and he was remanded to the valley. In December, "Stonewall" was made lieutenant general, ostensibly for his heroics in Maryland. Rumor had it that he planned a raid on Washington. Other more sinister rumors spread about officers grumbling over his disorganized leadership planning. For certain, Jackson had few friends left in the military command when he left the valley at the end of the year.

Reunited with Lee in the defense of Fredericksburg against Union General Ambrose Burnside in late December, Jackson joined an excellent Confederate defensive position. But he was not dug in, and his secure position on Marye's Heights was subject to Federal penetration. Both Jackson and Longstreet, however, were able to devastate the Union attack when they used cannons to fire down on them. Jackson's line was indeed breached, but he counterattacked, amid much confusion among his staff and troops, and stopped the Federals. On December 15, the devastated Union Army withdrew, but the Confederates had too few troops to follow them. Jackson at last took time to rest, but he remained with his troops to discipline deserters. Again, he quarreled with subordinates at the very time that his own public position had grown in stature. He had become, for Southern citizens at least, one of the Confederacy's greatest heroes, the stuff of legends.

Jackson and his Corps in the Army of Northern Virginia would see no action until the spring of 1863. During the lull, he met with his wife, wrote letters, and fleshed out reports of his own accomplishments. At last, north of Richmond, around Chancellorsville, Virginia, Lee would once again face "Fightin Joe"

Hooker. Lee had not wanted to fight, but Hooker had outmaneuvered him, and it was time to stand. Again, Jackson seemed to take matters into his own hands. Confident, again independent, on May 1, 1863, he advanced and pushed back Hooker and the Yankees. On May 2 Jackson was ordered to cross in front of Hooker and to flank him on his right. His attack resulted in a rout of the enemy camp, but then Jackson's troops became a disorderly mob, robbing, pillaging, and filling their stomachs. Jackson, out on personal reconnaissance, mistakenly was fired on by troops from the 18th North Carolina regiment. He was wounded just at the time Hooker counterattacked, but his personal guard managed to take him to the rear. The general was left unattended for some time. Finally, his physician, Dr. Hunter H. McGuire, a Virginia aristocrat, arrived and made the instant decision that to save his life he must amputate Jackson's right arm. Jackson's wife came to his camp with his two children, Julia and Hetty, in time to see him succumb to pneumonia. On May 10, 1863, Lee's "right arm" died.

Never before in this country's history had the death of a general been covered so thoroughly by the press. Even his last words were recorded. In a war where the images of heroics constantly were paraded before the public for purposes of morale, Jackson's funeral was spectacular. In Richmond, 5,000 weeping citizens and solemn officers marched by the bier. Flags were flown at half mast, the dirges sounded from the bands, and all heads were uncovered. Charles Royster called the response "oppressive pageantry" in his detailed description of the last days and funeral of "Stonewall." Some Northerners also made Jackson's death a spectacle, and many articles were written that displayed their high regard for the Southern hero. Of course, other Northerners boasted that Jackson's death would make Union victory certain. For the South, says Byron Farwell, Jackson's death resulted in "increased bitterness against the North" (531).

Biographies of Jackson soon began to appear, as people could not get enough of their hero's life story. According to Farwell, "the wealth of Jackson legends and his near apotheosis began immediately" (529). If there were murmurings that he failed to obey orders or that he was a brutal commander, there was also praise from the Richmond newspaperman and historian Edward A. Pollard (q.v.) in search of a bonafide Virginia hero. In 1863, one Markinfield Addey, in *The Life and Military Career of Thomas Jonathan Jackson*, described Jackson as another Cromwell. He used that avenging angel to show how Northerners had strayed from the path of piety. If they would only learn from that man of God, said Addey, they could resist sectional hatred, end the war, and make peace in the land. A "Virginian" wrote *The Life of Stonewall Jackson* in 1863, also to make him into a religious hero. Others in the South, including Pollard, proclaimed that their fallen hero could do no wrong.

So it went even after the war had ended, although Jackson's name was linked increasingly with that of the great Lee, as the memory of his audacity was used by the Lost Cause writers to claim that if not for Chancellorsville the Confederacy would have prevailed. By the 1880s, Jackson seemed for a time to fade from memory, as his life did not quite fit the go-getters of the New South creed.

But that would not last. In 1899, British career officer Colonel G. F. R. Henderson published *Stonewall Jackson and the American Civil War*, and the legend was confirmed by a professional military historian. Henderson depicted Jackson as a general of great military skill but, above all, as a man of honor. His story, said General Henderson, belonged to all military history. His life of complete dedication was a message for all people.

In the twentieth century the legend continued, aided by his family, in the writing of nephew Thomas Jackson Arnold. Arnold wanted to cover up the early shady blemishes of family crookedness and to re-create his uncle as an authentic Virginia gentleman, albeit with a Western common touch. Arnold also suggested that Jackson's life was studied everywhere. Certainly Jackson inspired one of the Fugitive poets of the 1930s, Allen Tate, to write a biography, very much in novel-like form, that went through many editions and was read by every young Southern white boy. Tate criticized all those around Jackson, save for Lee, to make his hero even more of a legend. Tate even went so far as to revise history to claim: "At Gettysburg the tactical situation eminently required Jackson's peculiar genius for swift and overwhelming attack" (320). In short, Lee could have won at Gettysburg if only Jackson had been there.

The finest modern biography of "Stonewall," that of Frank Vandiver, raised the question of why the fame continues. He knew the memory of Jackson was good for the South and called him "the treasured possession of the Southern people" (1). Vandiver created an image of the Southern frontiersman, the loyal Virginian, and the icon for all Southerners. But criticism of that fame was not far away. In 1991, in a brilliant analysis of military history, Charles Royster linked Jackson and William T. Sherman (q.v.) as the great butchers of a destructive war. Royster revealed in detail Jackson's ambition, desire for fame, and self-aggrandizement. But Royster also understood why "Stonewall" had become such a legend, as he depicted a general who was one of the few who had fought hard for a separate Southern nation and was willing to destroy any and everything in his way to gain it. For Jackson, as Royster said it, "the South as an independent nation was the next step in Christian history" (68). Even more iconoclastic than Royster was 1992 biographer Byron Farwell, who created the image of Jackson as a Virginia slaveowner fighting to defend his homeland. But Jackson hardly appears in this biography as a Southern gentleman or a man of honor. Jackson becomes for him the shoddy character who made money in slaves, the true Southerner. Unlike almost any other biographer, Farwell also gave Jackson mixed marks as a fighting machine. The legend of audacity becomes, in Farwell's opinion, the action of a blundering soldier unable to fight alongside others. But if Royster and Farwell have done much to give history a more realistic view of the man, they have been unable to penetrate the legend with truth. To visit the average Southern home even today is to find the twin portraits of Lee and Jackson hanging in the parlor.

BIBLIOGRAPHY

Markinfield Addey, *The Life and Military Career of Thomas Jonathan Jackson* (New York: Charles T. Evans, 1863).

[By a Virginian], *The Life of Stonewall Jackson* (New York: Charles B. Richardson, 1863).

Colonel G. F. R. Henderson, *Stonewall Jackson and the American Civil War* (1899; London: Longmans, Green, and Co., 1943).

Thomas Jackson Arnold, *Early Life and Letters of Thomas J. Jackson* (Richmond, Va.: Fleming H. Revell Co., 1916).

Allen Tate, *Stonewall Jackson, the Good Soldier* (New York: Milton, Balch, and Co., 1928).

Frank E. Vandiver, *Mighty Stonewall* (New York: McGraw-Hill, 1956).

Charles Royster, *The Destructive War: William T. Sherman, Stonewall Jackson, and the American Civil War* (New York: Alfred Knopf, 1991).

Byron Farwell, *Stonewall: A Biography of General Thomas J. Jackson* (New York: W. W. Norton, 1992).

James I. Robertson, *Stonewall Jackson: The Man, the Soldier, the Legend* (New York: Macmillan and Co., 1997).

ANDREW JOHNSON
(December 29, 1808–August 1, 1875)

Jon L. Wakelyn

Few of this country's presidents' brief moments upon the political stage have been so picked over by historians than those of Andrew Johnson, the only chief executive the Congress has impeached. Schools of historians of those fatal years of Reconstruction have analyzed that man's life in order to make their judgments of that crucial period's success or failure. Many of them have decided that to understand the Civil War's meaning they must grasp its outcome. This means that the failed presidency of Andrew Johnson has dominated the study of his life. Yet during the Civil War he served as a U.S. senator from Tennessee, the early Reconstruction occupation governor of Tennessee, and the vice president of the United States. His actions in political life and in Abraham Lincoln's (q.v.) administration were most crucial to the Union war effort, but historians have usually given those years short shrift. If Johnson's contributions to the war itself are to be understood and evaluated, even if most historians merely want to relate the war experience to that of Reconstruction, what prepared him to take the actions he did requires some comment. His career is perplexing enough, and it is made more troublesome by ignoring so much of what he did in his life before he became president.

Although Johnson's name would be inextricably linked to the fate of Tennessee, like a number of other future political leaders', his story begins in North Carolina. Remember, Andrew Jackson, William Blount, and James K. Polk, among others, all came from the poor soil and status-conscious Old North state. Though none of them, including the Johnsons, descended from poor families, all thought that better opportunity for their ambitions lay elsewhere than the South Atlantic. Johnson's life, then, follows an interesting migratory pattern of other emigrants to the new Southwest. How he got to Tennessee requires some study of his early life in North Carolina.

On December 29, 1808, Johnson was born in the town of Raleigh, North Carolina, the state's capital and its center of commerce. His roots thus were in the city, not the hardscrabble farmland. Andrew's father, Jacob, came from a family that had already lost its land, and he had gone to the city to seek his fortune. That ambitious young man at first found employment in a mill and later became a bank porter. A likable and popular man, the citizens of Raleigh also made Jacob the town constable. He married Mary McDonough, a proud seamstress, who also had urban roots. Unfortunately for that rising middle-class family, Jacob died three years after Andrew was born, leaving Mary to care for her young family. Young Andrew, unlike his father, grew up illiterate. A wild youth who joined local gangs, nevertheless, Andrew learned the useful trade of a tailor. But he was unsure of himself, and he disliked being an apprentice to a senior tailor, especially one who exploited Andrew's abilities and hard work for his own gain. The young man ran away from his indenture, first to western North Carolina, then to Laurens, South Carolina, later to Tennessee, and finally on to Mooresville, Alabama. He worked in those towns as an apprentice tailor, perfected his craft, and grew ever more restless. He returned to North Carolina for a time, then in 1826 went back to east Tennessee, where he made his home permanently in Greeneville.

During his travels in search of the right place to settle, Johnson learned to read and write, married Eliza McCardle in 1827, and eventually opened his own tailor shop in that growing east Tennessee town. As his business developed— he became a most able tailor, especially to the town's quality—Johnson joined the other members of the rising commercial class and bought farmland. His object, however, was not to become a country squire but to speculate in good real estate. He bought a few slaves, mainly for use in the household, as gardners, and to work in his own tailor shop. Along the way, Johnson discovered that he had talent for public speaking; he had a deep, sonorous voice and could weave brilliant verbal images. He used that ability to enter public service in hopes of gaining local prestige and status, and that required a career in politics. Like other young men on the make, Johnson joined the local militia, and he used the friends and contacts found there to gain election as a town alderman in 1829. In 1834 he became mayor of Greeneville and in 1835 entered the state legislature. At first he flirted with joining the east Tennessee Whig leadership, but he opposed that party's investment in transportation growth and soft money. The dominant Whig party defeated him for reelection in 1837, and Johnson vowed to build a constituency among the ordinary Democrats, who in outward manner he resembled.

From his early political experience, the middle-class professional businessman had learned that to succeed in east Tennessee politics he must build his own Democratic political machine throughout the state. In that way, he hoped to become a political leader back in Whig east Tennessee. He reentered the state legislature in 1839, this time as a committed state's rights Democrat. Now a staunch follower of Jacksonian politics, Johnson spoke out against state banking schemes, blamed the Whigs for the deepening economic depression, and became a Democratic presidential elector in 1840. Johnson's political opponents labeled him a demagogue who stirred up class conflict. In fact, the young politico actually represented the interests of many citizens of the state. In 1841, he took over a large portion of the east Tennessee Democratic party and gained election to the state senate. Soon he had become the hero of the state's farmers and small businessmen, who had lost their land and businesses in the depression of the 1840s. His most thorough biographer, Hans Trefousse, labeled Johnson the political spokesman for and representative of old-fashioned small farmer interests (53). In fact, that political man whose ties were mainly to the urban trade class merely had become adroit at recognizing where the interests of the largest part of the state lay. What Johnson had accomplished was to invent a populist political persona, in part because he believed in it and in part from knowledge of what it took to appeal to Tennesseans.

In 1843, the east Tennessean gained election to the U.S. House of Representatives and launched his national political career. He soon earned the reputation of being extremely conscious of his constituents' interest. But Johnson also was quick to take offense at any slur on his motives, and he early became known as one who would attack the personal motives of those who opposed him. He was also an adroit leader at developing successful coalitions to get his policies passed. For example, he had long disliked James K. Polk as a party rival, but he nonetheless championed the president's positions on government. He opposed tariff measures, and like many an upper South Democrat, he wanted to annex Texas. That Tennessean became a strong supporter of the War with Mexico. Johnson desired more land in the Southwest for his constituent farmers to move to and, as such, also advocated the expansion of slavery. His great cause, which he linked to all other issues, was the homestead bill. But his repeated call for getting government out of the economy and his opposition to internal improvement and education spending bills soon alienated him from some of his east Tennessee constituents. Accordingly, after he had realized that his isolated region desperately needed adequate transportation in order to ship goods to the western market, he switched positions and favored government investment in railroads. But for the time being he had acted too late to save his political position. After the Whigs had gerrymandered his congressional seat, he lost his bid for reelection to the House in 1854.

Undaunted, the so-called populist leader used his statewide Democratic party machine to get elected governor at the end of 1854. Again, he vigorously advocated homestead measures, seemed safe on slavery expansion, equivocated on the tension between slave and white labor in Tennessee, and boasted of his rise out of poverty to represent the underclass of the state. Johnson appeared to love the limelight, as he basked in the opportunity to make rousing speeches. He was building his reputation as a leader of the entire upper South. But he also showed impatience at the powerlessness of a state governor. In fact, most governors at that time held largely ceremonial positions, as they could make only a few appointments but could not veto legislative bills. Governor Johnson chose to exploit his lack of power as he began to shift his once-held Jacksonian ideals.

Perhaps that small-town businessman who always appeared in public exquisitely attired in his own made clothes had come to understand the changes coming to the upper South. He shifted on support of expenditures as he spoke out in favor of taxes to support the public school system. Johnson hoped to use the power of public opinion to rouse the citizenry to force their representatives to endorse his proposals. No doubt the governor understood that an educated citizenry would be better prepared to make the shift from agrarianism to trade and merchandising. Indeed, Johnson wanted to expand labor opportunities in his state. So when Tennessee Whigs turned anti-immigrant and nativist, he resisted and called for toleration of immigrant labor. Of course he held to his useful populist persona and publicly condemned the Bank of Tennessee. Some citizens, however, believed that the governor had hopes for a local banking system that could facilitate economic growth.

Despite his effective appeal to the voters, Johnson continued to chafe at his political confinement. After a serious injury in a railroad accident, his famous temper grew even more vehement, especially in his dealings with opponents. But his ambitions knew no end, and during the late 1850s, he politicked among legislators for election to the U.S. Senate. Once again, a coalition of east Tennessee farmers and middle Tennessee small businessmen and planters ensured him enough legislative votes to win that office. In Washington, Johnson lived a lonely life without his wife, his partner and best friend, and he worried a good deal about his sons, who seemed to lack his drive and ability. He would spend the rest of his life finding jobs for and otherwise supporting his debt-ridden and alcoholic sons. Yet once again he found the energy necessary to espouse his old dream of a homestead bill to assist in the settling of an agrarian West, perhaps to become a trade partner of the growing commercial upper South. Now, however, the issue of the government's role in western development commingled with Southern worries of slaves going west, and the senator from Tennessee found himself nearly alone among his fellow Southerners in his desire for a homestead bill. He defended himself against attacks by lashing out at the agrarian slaveocracy that he insisted dominated the U.S. Senate. Those aristocrats fought back by attacking his personal integrity.

Soon the debate over western lands took on an ominous tone, and the rising tide of secessionism forced the Southerner from Tennessee to reassess his ties to the Union. He defended slavery and the federal Union and hoped that his middle position would elevate him to the vice presidency in 1860. When denied second place on the national Democratic party ticket by Stephen A. Douglas, he shifted his support to John C. Breckinridge, the state's rights candidate. Despite his choice of Breckinridge, Johnson remained a staunch nationalist and insisted that the interests of Tennessee, which included slavery, would best be served within the Union. Courageously, if foolishly, he fulminated against the secessionists, as he vigorously attacked both the arguments and the integrity of Southern senators Judah P. Benjamin (q.v.) and Jefferson Davis (q.v.). As I have pointed out in a study of Johnson's famous Senate speeches of December 18 and 19, 1860, he hinted that he was playing for larger stakes as he sought to capture a Northern audience and make himself the South's leading unionist (Wakelyn, 13). Of course, both Benjamin and Davis retaliated passionately and spoke derogatorily of the integrity and intelligence of the Tennessean. But Johnson persevered. He supported the Crittenden compromise, which called for federal protection of slavery in the territories, and he accused the lower South's leaders of foolhardy ambitions destined to lead to civil war. Trefousse claims that Johnson had become the spokesman for the small slaveowners against the planter class (*Andrew Johnson*, 134). Another view suggests that the senator well understood that Tennessee's long-term economic interests did not coincide with those of the lower South.

On February 15, 1861, speaking from Washington, Johnson forcefully urged the people of Tennessee to resist secession. The newly elected Republican administration rewarded him with all of the patronage for Tennessee. President Lincoln hoped that the Unionist Johnson would assist in keeping the upper South states neutral in the coming conflict. Johnson went home and traveled throughout the state, working himself into a frenzy against Tennessee secessionists. When his state seceded, the senator, as leader of the state's Unionists, traveled to Washington to confer with President Lincoln. As the highest-ranking Southerner left in the U.S. Congress, he continued to speak out in defense of the Union and yet defended the rights of states against unwanted federal legislation. Johnson published pamphlet after pamphlet and had them franked back home, in hopes of expanding the Unionist movement in Tennessee. He traveled to the border states of Kentucky and Ohio and lectured the citizens on the need for a military invasion into the central South in order to restore the Union. Back in Washington, Johnson became a member of the powerful Committee on the Conduct of the War in order to urge an investigation of the weak Union military effort. His Unionist activities resulted in the Confederate government's putting a price on his head and declaring him a traitor to that new nation.

President Lincoln had taken notice of his staunch activities in behalf of restoration of the Union and, on March 4, 1862, after the central part of the state had been reclaimed for the Union, sent Johnson to Nashville as military governor of Tennessee. Though he faced insurmountable problems of persistent disloyalty among Nashville's citizens, and often lost his temper and political poise, he was to be the longest-serving and most successful military governor sent south during the Civil War. He also would display great physical courage, as his life was under constant threat. Though safe for the Union, Nashville and vicinity were unsafe for its Unionists. Johnson chose to take advantage of the presence of Confederates in the redeemed state. The angry Tennessean wanted to divide his state along class lines to build his own base of political support. But he also went beyond personal political gain, as his governorship provided the base for Northern government control and military power in the upper South.

Never did Johnson have full control of the state. Still, he persuaded his Unionist friends to support Nashville as a major supply depot for the Federal armies' advance into Mississippi and east Tennessee, and even northern Georgia. Although without gift as an administrator, he nevertheless managed to coordinate the military defense of Nashville and middle Tennessee. Along the way, of course, he fought with everyone. First, in the autumn of 1862, fearing another Confederate movement into Tennessee, the governor quarreled so much with Union commander Don Carlos Buell that he forced that recalcitrant general to heed his warning and come to Nashville. Johnson probably was the instrument of Washington's dismissal of Buell. Next, he nearly met his match in a power struggle with General William S. Rosecrans, whom he could not get to move. Johnson had demanded additional troops for the defense of his military supply dump and foodstuffs for civilians, and Rosecrans had refused. Pressure from Washington finally forced Rosecrans to cooperate with the governor. Johnson also tilted with the provost marshall's office when it failed to keep order among the Union troops in Nashville.

In regard to the Lincoln administration's policies to end slavery in the Confederacy, Johnson faced a most delicate problem. At first he attempted to persuade the president of the dangers to neutrality if slavery were ended. But by the summer of 1863, he bowed to the inevitable and supported emancipation. His official position was that black troops could then be used in lieu of whites to fight for the Union in Tennessee. Closer to the truth was that Johnson simply realized that union and slavery did not mix and that slavery was no longer necessary in Tennessee given the growth of a white working-class population. Certainly he forged ahead of his fellow Tennesseans on the slavery issue, and for that he would incur much hostility from some of his allies. But his actions also had catapulted him into national political attention. The Northern press treated him as a patriot willing to sacrifice all to save the Union, and Northern political leaders regarded him as a leader to be reckoned with.

At the same time the national Republican party, renamed the Union party, had become aware of its need for votes from the border state Unionists. Johnson's name then began to surface as a potential choice for vice president in 1864. As Lincoln himself sought to make plans for a reconstructed South, he met with the Tennessean to discuss them. Realizing also that Johnson had strong ties to the western farming community because of his having championed the homestead bill, the president offered him the second spot on the ticket. Assured of border and western state support, the Republicans prevailed in 1864. But whatever hopes Lincoln had had to build his own party coalition to deliver his plan of Reconstruction died with the assassin's bullet.

Johnson was sworn in as president on April 15, 1865. He would make his own Reconstruction policies for his cherished South and deal with the ex-Confederate elite whom he abhorred. Johnson's biographer Hans Trefousse insists that the president's Reconstruction program "was very different from anything Lincoln might have designed in the postwar period" (*Andrew Johnson*, 196). Whether Trefousse is correct or not, the ambitious new president, an ally neither of the Union party nor the ex-Confederates, would have to form his

Reconstruction policies using his own political faction. Again, as in the old days in Tennessee, he had to create his following outside of any formal party structure. Better able to win statewide than sectional elections in Tennessee, he would need to create a national coalition to overcome his weakness in certain radical Northern states.

At first, Union leaders and abolitionists believed he wanted to deliver the Reconstruction they advocated. But the president knew they were not his political friends. Accordingly, he refused to support their program. Instead, like Lincoln, Johnson proceeded on the notion that the Southern states had never legally left the Union, and he acted on that notion. Still, he never acknowledged that Southern Unionists like himself needed protection. At first he was shocked over the Southern imposition of the black codes that sought to control the movements of the ex-slaves. But his natural bias against the black people led him to attempt to build support for those heinous laws. However, he had underestimated the Republican party's ability to rally voters against activities that would set back their political gains. When the Democrats recovered in the election of 1866, Republicans united against the president and worked to rally Northerners against supposed Southern repudiation of the Union war victory. The Republicans plotted to remove him from office.

Perhaps because of Watergate in the early 1970s, historians have studied Johnson's impeachment trials quite carefully, but at the expense of the political context of the 1860s. Most have not linked Johnson's wartime agenda and activities to his postwar actions. His entire life has had to bear the brunt of his digressions during 1866–1868. At that time, the partisan Republican press attempted character assassination as it labeled him a drunk and a failed leader who was forcing the country into ruin. In fact, he was neither. Johnson was a man of principle with well-worked-out political positions on the issues of the day, even if his policies on Reconstruction were proved wrong. The former state's righter actually believed the Fourteenth Amendment would give Congress too much power. The Republicans used his actions to repudiate Johnson as an opponent of their attempts to control the war's losers. When he employed his veto powers to resist the imposition of a military government in the Southern states, opponents claimed he exacerbated the plight of Southern Republicans and Unionists. Certainly, those partisan accusations of treason, bribery, and high crimes and misdemeanors were never proved. The impeachment trial, however, did manage to weaken the office of the chief executive. But Johnson remained president.

What had Johnson himself done to keep from being removed from the presidency? Because of the controversy over his Reconstruction policies, few scholars have looked at the president's own plans for saving himself. Trefousse, however, has offered a plausible analysis of Johnson's activities and describes how he wilfully had trapped the Republicans into the radical action of trying to remove him from office. Certainly Johnson knew that he would not be removed for violating the tenure-in-office act because he had fired Secretary of War Edwin Stanton (q.v.). He also was certain that conservative border state Republican senators could not vote to remove him and still have credibility in their home states. So he goaded the enemy into personal and unprovable attacks, and he survived. But Johnson had also hoped that his victory would force the Democrats to make him their candidate in 1868. He was wrong because he had underestimated how much ex-Confederates hated him. At the end, Johnson was left without any political friends, and he returned to Tennessee a broken and defeated leader.

His reception in his beloved Tennessee was mixed. Often in the past his political enemies had written him off as dead. But Johnson wanted vindication, and his only route was to restore his position in his own state. This time, however, he had no machine, little favorable press, and no one to write a biography singing his praises. He nevertheless knew that to keep himself prominent before the citizens of Tennessee he would have to speak out on issues that concerned them. If disdained in the central and western part of the state, he believed he had friends in Unionist east Tennessee. Johnson attacked the Republicans in that part of the state in his 1872 campaign for Congress, but he lost. Meanwhile, he restored his lost wealth, gave much to charities for the state's poor, and sought to ingratiate himself with old friends. For a time in 1873, after a serious bout with cholera, he thought he would never again hold public office, but he took one last chance and joined the fledgling Granger movement of middle-class farmers. He changed his views against paper or inflationary money in hopes of appealing to the state's Greenback party, which so needed an infusion of cash to restore small businesses and small farms. Johnson also praised old line Tennessee Whigs, attacked militant former secessionists, and labeled himself a Union Democrat. His political sleights of hand paid off, and the legislature appointed him to the U.S. Senate in 1875. The new senator sat with the Democrats, even though many of them spurned him. In Washington, he spoke eloquently and urgently about the plight of the middle classes. Once again, he began to make plans for bigger things. But he was weak, tired, and quite sick. On August 1, 1875, he succumbed to a stroke.

Immediately after his death the people of Tennessee lauded his contributions to ordinary folk, while the rest of the country either ignored his passing or took the opportunity once again to attack his Reconstruction activities. His first biographer, Frank Moore, however, set a pattern of how he would be regarded among many popular commentators for the rest of the century. Moore collected and published his speeches up to 1865, only covering the period when Johnson had been most highly regarded by the country. Those who wrote about him after his death used Moore's book to describe their hero. Moore had used Johnson's own interpretation of his life's accomplishments, for Johnson had created the image of a young man who had risen from poverty and illiteracy through honesty and hard work and of a dedicated public servant loyal to the plain folk. Before the century had ended, Northern papers reassessed his war record, and Southern papers praised his prewar service to the South. The federal government, during a Democratic administration, turned his small tailor shop into a national shrine. So the once vilified, impeached, and disgraced leader became the symbol of success, a model for an emerging and dynamic middle-class capitalist society. Samuel S. Cox, a Democrat who had served with him in the U.S. Senate, said in 1885: "[H]e knew the ex-President would be vindicated, because there was no justifiable cause for his impeachment" (330).

Cox was correct, even if he had focused only on Johnson's presidency and had ignored his war record. When the early twentieth-century nationalist historians began to write about him, they targeted his failed presidency. James Ford Rhodes called him a sloppy administrator, a poor political leader, and an opponent of the war's major accomplishments. As with so many who concentrated on the personality of that angry and impetuous man, John W. Burgess simply stated his character was deeply flawed.

However, during the reform and racist 1920s and 1930s, a time of recovery for the Democratic party and its populist heritage, Johnson was again resurrected, often to defend the Southern version of Reconstruction. In *The Age of Hate: Andrew Johnson and the Radicals* (1930), George Fort Milton regarded him as honest and generous. His war against dis-Unionists was linked with his opposition to radical Reconstruction. Claude Bowers simply regarded him as a Southern progressive, much needed in his own times and in Bowers's. Howard K. Beale also saw Johnson as a victim because he had opposed the Republican policies that had built the hated modern industrial state.

But the civil rights movement of the 1950s and 1960s, and the messy politics of Nixon's Watergate in the 1970s, led to another revision of Johnson's career. Again, the war years gave way to Reconstruction policies, as the most important intellectually rigorous study of his life written to date concentrated almost exclusively on the postwar years. Eric McKitrick rejected the efforts of the 1930s generation of historical revisionists, attacked Johnson as psychologically flawed, and regarded him as a failed political outsider. For McKitrick, Johnson's behavior disrupted "the political life of the entire nation" (14). Likewise, Michael Les Benedict's two fine studies *The Impeachment and Trial of Andrew Johnson* (1973) and *A Compromise of Principle* (1974) regarded Johnson as an archconservative on race who deserved to be removed from the presidency. Benedict's carefully documented legal dissection of those times left Johnson's career in shreds.

Most recently, now that the Nixon years are behind us, some attempt has been made to see Johnson's actions as at least reasoned. Trefousse's *Impeachment of a President* (1975) claims that Johnson was an able politico who bested the majority Republicans (xi). In his recent biography *Andrew Johnson* (1989), Trefousse has built a complex life that might fit into present-day politics. Ambitious, opportunistic, Johnson carefully planned his entire career in order to rise in public life. But Trefousse's reading of that life may be too cynical and too narrow. Certainly Trefousse made little attempt to connect the war career to the presidency, and he does not set Johnson's actions into the political realities of the mid-nineteenth century. Perhaps the recent project to make a detailed study of Johnson's career through the publication of his personal and public papers will set to rest the flawed personality and evil genius theses and give way to a reasoned assessment of that man's true accomplishments—that is, until the next generation of historians needs him for other purposes.

BIBLIOGRAPHY

Frank Moore, *Speeches of Andrew Johnson* (1865; New York: Burt Franklin, 1970).

Samuel S. Cox, *Three Decades of Federal Legislation* (1885; New York: Books for Libraries Press, 1970).

John W. Burgess, *Reconstruction and the Constitution* (1902; Westport, Conn.: Negro Universities Press, 1970).

James Ford Rhodes, *History of the Civil War* (New York: The Macmillan Co., 1917).

Claude G. Bowers, *The Tragic Era* (Cambridge: Houghton Mifflin Company, 1929).

Howard K. Beale, *The Critical Year* (New York: Harcourt, Brace and Company, 1930).

George Fort Milton, *The Age of Hate: Andrew Johnson and the Radicals* (New York: Coward-McCann, Inc., 1930).

Eric McKitrick, *Andrew Johnson and Reconstruction* (Chicago: University of Chicago Press, 1960).

Michael Les Benedict, *The Impeachment and Trial of Andrew Johnson* (New York: W. W. Norton, 1973).

Michael Les Benedict, *A Compromise of Principle: Congressional Republicans and Reconstruction, 1863–1869* (New York: W. W. Norton, 1974).

Hans Trefousse, *Impeachment of a President* (Knoxville: University of Tennessee Press, 1975).

Leroy P. Graf and Ralph W. Haskins, eds., *The Papers of Andrew Johnson*, Vol. 5 (Knoxville: University of Tennessee Press, 1979).

Hans Trefousse, *Andrew Johnson: A Biography* (New York: W. W. Norton, 1989).

Jon L. Wakelyn (ed.), *Southern Pamphlets on Secession, November 1860–April 1861* (Chapel Hill: University of North Carolina Press, 1996).

JOSEPH EGGLESTON JOHNSTON
(February 3, 1807–March 21, 1891)

Frank Everson Vandiver

Was Joseph E. Johnston a military genius or a marplot?* This question almost splintered the Confederate States of America and continues to intrigue historians to this day. His partisans regard him as a brilliant strategist and sound field commander whose talents were stifled by a rancorous chief executive. Foes point to constant retreating, absence of victories, and a petty punctilio to illustrate an almost pathological unwillingness to make decisions. He was, they argued then and now, temperamentally unsuited to be a general. Thus, this enigmatic Confederate general has both attracted and repelled biographers, most of whom have been perhaps overconcerned with his personal flaws rather than with making systematic analyses of his accomplishments. His own *Narrative of Military Operations*, which he published near the end of his life, has been regarded with lofty scholarly suspicion and pointed to as an example of the bad taste that characterized so many former Confederates' efforts to defend their own places in history. Another look at his life and activities as well as how he defended himself could assist in the attempt to reevaluate the wartime career of this important Confederate general.

Except for an occasional aside, in the *Narrative*, Johnston glossed over his youth and early training. He should not have, for much of the feisty and self-defensive older figure was formed in the years before the Civil War. What becomes apparent in looking at how he grew up is that Johnston's Virginia lineage marked him for life. His father, Peter Johnston, had served under "Light Horse" Harry Lee in the American Revolution and had been proud of his service in the making of the country. After the Revolution, Peter married Mary Valentine Wood, a niece of the legendary Patrick Henry, and they settled at the

*In this study of Johnston I have drawn on my 1959 introduction to Johnston's *Narrative* for the Indiana University Press. I thank that press for kind permission to reprint parts of that introduction. While I have not changed my mind about General Johnston, I have deepened in my appreciation for the world he inhabited.

Johnston plantation, "Longwood," in Prince George County. Joseph, the seventh of their children, was born there on February 3, 1807. Peter served in the state legislature, where he became an outspoken opponent of the Alien and Sedition Acts. He parlayed his political experience into election as a county judge. In 1811, believing there were better opportunities in the western part of the state, Peter took a judgeship in Abingdon, in the far southwestern mountains of Virginia. As part of the Abingdon gentry, Peter took his place in the political world of that Virginia frontier. Through his position as a county judge, he managed to get a son elevated to the federal Congress.

Young Joe grew up in a world part frontier and part Virginia gentry. Like other youths of his time, the outdoor life appealed to him. His prized possession as a young man was his father's Revolutionary sword, and he obviously reveled in the tales of military heroics that he heard at home. As was his place in life, young Joe attended the prestigious Abingdon Academy, where he interacted well with his peers. Of Peter's eight sons, Joseph was chosen to follow a military career. He went to West Point, studied hard, and was well behaved, and his superiors regarded him as an obedient young man. His best friend at the Academy was Robert E. Lee (q.v.), the son of his father's commander. They graduated together in the class of 1829, with Joe finishing thirteenth out of forty-six in the class.

This Virginia gentleman had chosen the career path open to one who wanted to serve his country and who resisted the idea of just being a planter. Serve he did, as early in his career he saw duty in the Indian wars. In 1832 he participated in the Black Hawk War. Johnston also held a few posts in the South. He was at Fortress Monroe during the Nat Turner rebellion in southside Virginia. During 1832, at the height of the nullification movement, he saw duty at Charleston Harbor. No doubt he would have obeyed orders to put down the nullifiers, though his family supported that South Carolina movement. But he found service in the Florida Seminole War of 1835 distasteful. Even though he was given a prestigious post as aide to General Winfield Scott, in 1837, believing promotions came too slow, he resigned from the army. Poor, disillusioned, he made plans to use his excellent military-technological education to become an engineer. He took a position in the Topographical Bureau in Florida. In 1838, weary of civilian life, Johnston reentered the army as a member of the corps of engineers.

Johnston's career took a turn upward when, in 1845, he married Lydia McLane, the daughter of powerful Delaware senator Louis McLane. Her family owned a large plantation on the eastern shore of Maryland, and she was also connected to the prestigious Preston family of Virginia and Kentucky. Although theirs was a childless family, Lydia and Joseph became a close-knit team as he increasingly relied on her advice. Detailed to duty in Mexico during the war, he hoped to fight a European-style engagement. Instead, the United States used heavy artillery to defeat a well-emplaced enemy. Johnston was wounded at Vera Cruz, but the headstrong and brave young warrior fought again at the final attack on Mexico City. He had envisioned a great American Pacific Empire but also worried about the political interference in the affairs of the military. Back in the dull routine of the peacetime military, he grew disenchanted with the Topographical engineers and wished for an offer of better and more exciting duty. In 1855 he transferred to the cavalry. Some said he dreamed of joining the filibusterers to invade Central America and spread slavery southward.

At that time the aristocratic-looking officer chafed over his military duties. His looks and manners confirmed his refinement but belied his spirit and ambition. His close friends in the cavalry, Gustavus W. Smith and Mansfield Lovell, noticed his increasing dissatisfaction with the military and his worry over the growing sectional tensions. In June 1860, Johnston at last realized his dream when his kinsman Secretary of War John B. Floyd promoted his fellow Virginian to brigadier general. But he was general in the quartermaster division, a position hardly satisfying to his ambitions. To make matters more difficult for his feeling about his post, Johnston may also have been advising the infant Confederate government on the purchase of war materiel. On March 17, 1861, Confederate Secretary of War Leroy Pope Walker offered Johnston an appointment as brigadier general in the Provisional Army. His chief of staff, the Virginian Winfield Scott, told Johnston he could resign from the Union Army but that he should not join the Confederate. His wife pithily remarked that her husband had no money and only knew the profession of soldiering, so what was he to do? Without much joy, Johnston traveled to Richmond to offer his services to his governor. If he were to fight for the Confederacy, he wanted to serve in Virginia.

In Virginia and elsewhere he would serve, and serve always with dignity. Perhaps it was his dignity and sense of position that first got him into trouble. Early in the war, Johnston ably assisted in the Confederate victory at First Manassas. For that he expected to receive the rank that he felt he deserved. As Craig Symonds, his latest biographer, says, "Johnston's quarrel with Jefferson Davis [q.v.] was the decisive event of his life" (125). In the late summer of 1861, President Davis, acting under a law passed in May, nominated five full generals for approval by Congress. Johnston had reason to consider himself the senior general in the Confederacy, for he had been brigadier general in the Union Army, and no other Confederate had achieved rank beyond brevet brigadier in the U.S. service. Johnston was surprised to see himself fourth on the president's list of full generals. Honor demanded a protest. Protest he did, in the form of an angry letter to the president. Davis thought the letter insubordinate. Moreover, it did no good, and the result was that Johnston's resentment would smolder throughout the war.

Sent to Centreville, Virginia, to guard Confederate provisions, the general seethed, and their mutual distrust became entrenched. When he left behind war goods after evacuating that post and the Federals captured them, the president blamed him. Disagreement on matters of strategy further alienated Davis and Johnston. When he proposed plans for halting Union General George B. Mc-

Clellan (q.v.) in April 1862, he clashed with Johnston again. Johnston wanted to avoid having to fight McClellan on the Peninsula. He insisted that a line close to Richmond would reduce the danger of flanking and offer opportunity for effective attack. As the Federals advanced from their base, their gunboats would be left behind, the Peninsula would grow wider, and finally their expanding front would be bisected by the treacherous Chickahominy River. Although overruled, Johnston would soon be proved correct, as the decisive Peninsula battles would be fought near Richmond. During the early days of June 1862, Johnston attacked McClellan near Seven Pines. At the height of the battle, while trying for more coordination of his confused units, Johnston was unhorsed by a severe wound. Incapacitated for some time, a new commander would take credit for driving McClellan off the Peninsula. Throughout the remainder of his life, Johnston believed that victory had been snatched from him at the crucial moment.

For almost six months he fretted through convalescence, and he became easy prey to a growing anti-administration cabal. Louis T. Wigfall (q.v.), a senator from Texas, helped organize a pro-Johnston faction in Congress that continually urged the general be given important posts. A seasoned veteran was badly needed for an experiment that the changing nature of war forced upon Davis. He decided to create a large geographical—or theater—command in the West. Johnston was to have overall charge of the Department of the West, and he was given absolute logistical authority to assist his operations. He accepted the assignment in November 1862 and journeyed to Chattanooga to establish Department Headquarters. But Johnston never fully appreciated the possibilities of geographical departments, and he was unable to make intelligent and systematic use of his authority. Unable to move his subordinates Braxton Bragg (q.v.) and John C. Pemberton to take action, he came to believe he had only nominal command. When the danger to Vicksburg reached a peak in April and May 1863, no amount of cajoling from an exasperated Secretary of War or critical president could induce the department commander to violate a basic military principle by taking personal charge of Pemberton's army. Instead, he remained at Jackson, Mississippi, urging Pemberton to evacuate Vicksburg and avoid a siege. The loss of Vicksburg, attributed by Davis to Johnston's failures, confirmed his every suspicion concerning the general. Vicksburg was gone, and with it, virtually all contact with the trans-Mississippi Confederacy. The Southern people wrathfully blamed the general. The months following the loss of Vicksburg were filled with black recrimination.

Johnston then accepted a small command in Mississippi. With few infantry and overridden cavalry, Johnston did his best to protect the area from the Georgia-Alabama line to the Mississippi River. He might well have served the duration of the war in Mississippi, had not friend Braxton Bragg muffed the aftermath of the Confederate victory at Chickamauga in eastern Tennessee. Even Davis had to admit that Bragg seemed to have lost the confidence of the Army of Tennessee. At this critical moment, Davis received an avalanche of requests to appoint his old foe to command. And Johnston wanted that command. If it could not be the Army of Northern Virginia, then the second-most important field force in the Confederacy would do. He found his army in camps around Dalton, Georgia, and assumed command on December 27, 1863. A veteran army it was, one cursed with a succession of bad leaders and abortive battles. It knew when it had a general, and for Johnston, it would try anything. In the upcoming battle for Atlanta, it would have to.

The Southern commander made ready as best he could to oppose Union General William T. Sherman's (q.v.) huge aggregation. Although anxious to attack, Johnston refused to take suicidal risks with inadequate numbers, and again, his caution impressed Davis as cowardice. Without substantial aid, he could do nothing more than retire before the Yankee advance, which began in early May 1864, but his retreat from Dalton to Atlanta stands as a model of operational strategy. In almost constant contact for over seventy days with an army at least twice the size of his own, Johnston contested every mile, deftly eluded Sherman's flankers, avoided general combat unless he had advantage of ground, struck as he saw a chance, and conserved men and equipment with parsimony. Sherman's superior numbers enabled him to continue inching toward Atlanta, but he understood clearly when he crossed the Chattahoochee and approached heavy Rebel works that as long as Johnston's army held those lines, the campaign had failed. Both the Confederate Army and its Atlanta base were still intact.

Comfortably entrenched, and readying an attack on Sherman as he ventured across Peachtree Creek, Johnston suddenly received peremptory orders to turn over command to one of his subordinates, General John B. Hood (q.v.). On July 18, 1864, Johnston left the army. His removal may well have been Davis's greatest blunder of the war. It is probable that Johnston had not firmly decided on a plan when the Army of Tennessee occupied the Atlanta lines. He had nothing but contempt for Davis's dedication to ground and doubtless would have evacuated the city if strategy so dictated. The general believed that everything had been done on the retreat to Atlanta that could have been done, and there need be no self-doubt. He was to spend six months in exile. Finally, in February 1865, Johnston left the comforts of civil life at the behest of General Robert E. Lee. Hood had failed utterly, and Johnston once again took command of the Army of Tennessee, reduced now to a hard core of iron men.

Sherman was still the foe. Against his large and rugged blue horde, Johnston's handful could offer little resistance as they retreated toward Durham Station, North Carolina. For a brief moment at Bentonville in March, the old spirit flashed again, but it was an afterglow. Lee's surrender doomed the Army of Tennessee, and on April 26, 1865, Johnston surrendered it to his old enemy. According to Craig Symonds, President Davis considered his surrender an act of treachery (357). Unlike most fellow Rebels, Johnston's war was not over. Although he looked to the future and refused to bemoan a lost cause, he still fought with Jefferson Davis. But before he could take up the defense of his career and his honor, the ex-general would have to make a living.

At first Lydia and Joseph went to a resort in order for her to recover from the war's devastation of her health. Then they traveled to visit friends in Maryland. By November 1865, they were in Richmond where he entered the insurance business to recoup lost finances. Finally they settled in Savannah, where he could continue his war through writing his *Narrative*. In 1878 he was elected to the U.S. House of Representatives from his beloved Virginia. He served ably on the Military Affairs Committee, but he refused a second term. He settled into retirement at home. His wife died in 1887, and Joseph was heartbroken. His last years were spent traveling to gatherings of old veterans, where he was uniformly cheered. If his enemies reviled him, the ordinary soldiers knew they had served under a leader who supported them at all cost. Finally, old and weary from the battles to defend himself, Johnston died in Baltimore on March 21, 1891. There he is buried, the only Confederate full general with no memorial to his name.

Johnston had meant his *Narrative of Military Operations* to be both his rock of remembrance and his vindication. Davis had attempted to destroy his reputation in history, and the ex-president's acolytes had followed close behind. Johnston's version of events, his story, say biographers Gilbert Govan and James Livingood, "is written as concisely as a military report" (385). In it, Johnston pulled no punches, as in detail he entailed the weaknesses of the Confederacy. At the last, he said, all was lost, not for disloyalty or not for trying but because the government failed in the sale of cotton to raise the finances necessary to conduct the war. Of course, on all fronts he defended his own war record. In doing so he wrote his own version of the weaknesses of others. More than is true of most memoirs, the *Narrative* bears the mark of its author. It puzzles, irritates, lulls, and charms; it misinforms in one passage and enlightens in the next, and from it comes a glimpse into an enigma and an insight into a war. But the book received a mixed reception and merely stirred up old memories many perhaps wished put to sleep. The result was that if it enlightens much about the man, it has had its problems with historians.

What about the life of Johnston, his frailties and his accomplishments? What have those who have written about the Civil War had to say about that general from Virginia? The enigma of Johnston has both attracted and repelled biographers. Davis contributed to the damage done to Johnston's reputation with the publication in 1881 of his *Rise and Fall of the Confederate Government*. His carefully constructed case against Johnston had force and the ring of truth. In 1891, Bradley T. Johnson, an old military associate, edited *A Memoir of the Life and Public Service of Joseph E. Johnston*. A polemical book, it accepted Johnston's prejudices and assumed his ability. Sixty-five years were to pass before the publication of another biography. The long silence was prompted more by the difficulty of the subject than by lack of interest.

In the 1920s the controversy between Davis and Johnston again erupted. Articles in scholarly journals sought to reevaluate Johnston's military career. Especially was the Atlanta campaign revisited, with telling arguments made on both sides. In 1956 Gilbert E. Govan and James W. Livingood published the first full, scholarly biography of Johnston under the perceptive title of *A Different Valor*. They described him, sympathized with him, went with him into battle, and yet failed to understand him. Perhaps, after all, Johnston best understood himself, and because he was a mass of so many contradictions, even he often understood imperfectly.

Recently, Craig L. Symonds has revisited that important general's life. In *Joseph E. Johnston: A Civil War Biography* (1992), Symonds in part sought to get at the man by rereading all of Johnston's contemporaries' accounts of his wartime activities. Symonds pointed out that Grant and Sherman both found him to have been an excellent general. Some contemporaries regarded him as the greatest Southern field commander. But Symonds also found wide disagreement over his record. Often those who wrote about him reverted to comments about his troublesome, proud, sensitive, and sullen personality. It was as if Johnston hurt himself by his personal behavior. Symonds's own verdict was that Johnston was neither a genius nor incompetent. He made a fatal alliance with Louis Wigfall, which showed him to have been a poor politician. Often Johnston was unspecific in his orders, requested that superiors constantly reaffirm their orders to him, and in short seemed vague to many around him. For Symonds, Johnston's life remains elusive. But Symonds in fixing on Johnston's vagueness suggested that perhaps, like many others, he did not fully grasp modern warfare. Perhaps only a study that evaluates him as a flawed modern leader will tell us if that bundle of contradictions was indeed a great commander.

BIBLIOGRAPHY

Bradley T. Johnston, ed., *A Memoir of the Life and Public Service of Joseph E. Johnston* (Baltimore, Md.: R. H. Woodward and Co., 1891).

Gustavus Woodson Smith, *Generals J. E. Johnston and P. G. T. Beauregard at the Battle of Manassas, July, 1861* (New York: C. G. Crawford, 1892).

Gilbert E. Govan and James W. Livingood, *A Different Valor: The Story of General Joseph E. Johnston, C.S.A.* (Indianapolis: Bobbs-Merrill Co., 1956).

Joseph E. Johnston, *Narrative of Military Operations* (Bloomington: Indiana University Press, 1959).

Craig L. Symonds, *Joseph E. Johnston: A Civil War Biography* (New York: W. W. Norton, 1992).

ROBERT EDWARD LEE
(January 19, 1807–October 12, 1870)

Leonne M. Hudson

Confederate General Robert E. Lee was born on January 19, 1807, at Stratford in Westmoreland County in Virginia. His father, Henry "Light Horse Harry" Lee, served with distinction in the Revolutionary War. He was selected as the governor of Virginia in 1791 and elected to Congress eight years later. In 1793, Henry Lee married Anne Hill, daughter of the wealthy Charles Carter, uniting two of the most prominent families of the planter aristocracy of Virginia. Henry Lee's propensity for wreckless investments in land destroyed the family's fortune. Following his release from debtor's prison, he relocated his family to Alexandria, Virginia, in 1810. Misfortune continued to plague Lee when he was seriously injured in Baltimore in 1813 by a mob. To escape the scene of his troubles, Light Horse Harry sailed to the Caribbean, determined to rebuild his fortune. Robert was six years old when his father left home.

In 1825, Robert enrolled at West Point. His academic background, perceptive mind, and strict discipline helped him to excel at the academy. Because of Lee's exemplary deportment, he did not receive a single demerit during his years at the military institution. Charles Mason of New York and Lee graduated first and second, respectively, in the class of 1829, which consisted of forty-six cadets. After graduation, Lee, the newly minted second lieutenant of the engineer corps, reported for work as a construction engineer on Fort Pulaski in the Savannah River. In June 1831, Lee married Mary Anne Randolph, daughter of George Washington Parke Custis, who was an heiress to the Arlington estate on the banks of the Potomac River. Somber and pious, Mary Anne Custis enjoyed the luxuries derived from wealth.

It was paradoxical that Lee, who relished the chance to establish his own family, would have to endure a painful marriage. The union, which lasted nearly forty years, was bedeviled by extensive periods of separation. Adding to Lee's frustration was his wife's poor health and the difficulty she experienced in transitioning from Arlington to the humble quarters of military life. In search of relief for his wife, Robert and Mary frequented several spas in Virginia, believing that the mountain waters possessed curative powers. Lee's sense of reason was obscured by his faith in nature as a healing agent.

When the Mexican War started in 1846, Lee, who had served in the army for seventeen undistinguished years, was anxious to join the fight. With the assistance of Colonel Joseph G. Totten, chief engineer, Lee was mustered into service and reported to General John E. Wool at San Antonio in August 1846. In January 1847, Winfield Scott, the commanding general of the American forces, selected Lee and other officers to serve in what he called his "little cabinet" to advise him on technical matters. Lee's daring reconnaissance work during the march of Scott's army from Vera Cruz to Mexico City was spectacular. By the time the U.S. Army reached Mexico City, Lee had won the admiration of Winfield Scott, who regarded him as a fine soldier. Lee received three brevets for his meritorious service in Mexico, emerging from that war as a brevet colonel. When Lee returned to the United States in the fall of 1848, he put his engineering skills to use in Baltimore, where he was in charge of the construction of Fort Carroll.

In May 1852, he received a letter from General Totten offering him the superintendency of the U.S. Military Academy. With reluctance, he accepted the position in September and quickly established a reputation as a strict disciplinarian, a conscientious academician, and a competent administrator. President Franklin Pierce signed a bill in 1855 creating four new regiments. When the time came for Secretary of War Jefferson Davis (q.v.) to appoint officers to command the new units, Lee was one of his first selections. Lee was commissioned a lieutenant colonel and placed second in command of Albert Sidney Johnston's Second Cavalry regiment. After serving twenty-six years in the Army Corps of Engineers, Lee was leaving that prestigious corps to become a line officer. This transfer signaled a significant change in the military life of the soldier. Lee's new rank combined with the opportunity to command troops pleased him very much. He resigned from his West Point post in March 1855 and was ordered to west Texas.

The pastoral quiet that Colonel Lee was enjoying at Arlington while on leave from his post in Texas was interrupted on the morning of October 17, 1859. Cavalry officer Lieutenant James Ewell Brown (J. E. B.) Stuart brought him a note ordering him to report at once to the War Department. The night before, the old delusional abolitionist John Brown had initiated a raid on the federal arsenal at Harpers Ferry. Lee hurried from Washington to the site of the disturbance with orders from Secretary of War John B. Floyd to suppress the uprising. Under Lee's direction, the Brown-inspired insurrection was ended. Lee clearly demonstrated his leadership qualities by decisively bringing the Harper's Ferry affair under control.

Shortly after the Harpers Ferry incident, Lee was ordered by the U.S. Army to report to San Antonio to take command of the Department of Texas headquarters there. Lee had the unenviable task of controlling Indians and Mexican bandits on the Texas frontier. By the summer of 1860, the presidential campaign was in full swing, with slavery and sectionalism occupying the center of the political stage. By then, Southerners had turned up the volume on their rhetoric that a Republican victory would lead to secession. The momentum with which secession swept the lower South after Abraham Lincoln's (q.v.) triumph disturbed Lee. The crisis in the country in the winter and spring of 1861 was symbolic of the crisis then raging in Lee's life.

While stationed at Fort Mason in Texas, General Winfield Scott ordered Lee to report to him in Washington. While en route to the nation's capital, Lee told a confidant in San Antonio, "I will follow my native State with my sword, and, if need be, with my life." During the April meeting between Lee and Scott, the dissolution of the Union and the impending war were no doubt items of discussion. In the meantime, the seceders had created the Confederate States of America in Montgomery, Alabama, with Jefferson Davis as president. As the country spiraled toward an abyss, the Confederates added a new dimension to the crisis by firing on Fort Sumter. This attack was the beginning of a revolution that would change both Lee and the United States forever.

April 17, 1861, was a momentous day in the life of Robert E. Lee because on that day Virginia adopted an ordinance of secession. Simultaneously, he was offered command of the U.S. Army but declined the overture. At Arlington on April 20, Lee penned a terse letter of resignation to Secretary of War Simon Cameron. Lee had turned his back on more than thirty years of military service to his country. Lee, the private citizen, left home and traveled to Richmond, marking the last time he would ever see Arlington. With Lee's reputation preceding him to Richmond, the handsome and muscularly built fifty-four-year-old Virginian accepted the invitation of Governor John Letcher on April 22 to command the military forces of his native state. According to Douglas Southall Freeman, Lee's decision to join the Confederacy was "the answer he was born to make."

Less than two months after assuming command of the Virginia forces, he tendered them to the Davis government to become a part of the national Confederate Army. Shortly after this transfer, Lee was commissioned a full general by the Confederate government. He was immediately sent to the Kanawha Valley to offer resistance to Union soldiers marching through the western part of the state. Lee returned to the Confederate capital in October 1861, following his disappointing sojourn in western Virginia. Davis then assigned him to assume command of the Department of South Carolina, Georgia, and Florida. In early 1862, Lee fortified several places along the Charleston and Savannah Railroad, one of which was Honey Hill. This fortification paid huge dividends when a Confederate force defeated a Union Army at the battle of Honey Hill on November 30, 1864. This made possible the evacuation of William J. Hardee's Savannah garrison in December of that year.

Lee returned to Richmond from South Carolina in March 1862 to serve as military adviser to the Southern president. Lee was one of a handful of generals of the Confederacy whom Davis truly respected. The juxtaposition of Lee between his chief and commanding generals tested his diplomatic skills as he soothed officers who often possessed more ego than talent. Events on the battlefield, however, would soon change Lee's status and with that the nature of the war itself. By this time, Abraham Lincoln had placed the hopes of the Union Army in the East in the hands of George B. McClellan (q.v.). McClellan and the Confederate Army of the Potomac commanded by Joseph E. Johnston (q.v.) would clash at the battle of Seven Pines on May 31, 1862. It was at that battle that Johnston, Lee's West Point classmate, was wounded. The army then devolved upon the next ranking officer, the Kentuckian Gustavus W. Smith, whose ineffectiveness displeased Davis. Convinced that Johnston's subordinate was not the right man, Davis removed Smith and replaced him with Robert E. Lee on June 1, 1862. Under Lee's command, the Army of Northern Virginia would be involved in some of the more historic battles on the North American continent. It was Lee's successful defense of Richmond that helped to prolong the war, thereby transforming it into a true revolution.

A few weeks after Seven Pines, Lee and McClellan fought each other in what came to be known as the Seven Days' battle. With McClellan's army poised for a strike against Richmond, Lee took the initiative. To better gauge the strength and position of the Union commander, Lee sent J. E. B. Stuart on a reconnaissance expedition in which he completely circled the Federal Army of the Potomac on horseback. Lee, in preparation for the coming battle, ordered Thomas ''Stonewall'' Jackson (q.v.) from the Shenandoah Valley. In a series of battles from June 25 through July 1, 1862, Lee bested McClellan, forcing him to retreat to the safety of Harrison's Landing on the James River.

In August 1862, Henry W. Halleck (q.v.), general in chief of the Union armies, ordered McClellan to relocate his forces from the Peninsula to form a junction with John Pope's Army of Virginia at Fredericksburg. Lee's army was in a perilous position nestled between the two Union commanders. Lee fully understood that if McClellan and Pope could join forces, the Army of Northern Virginia would be crushed by the overwhelming power of the two Union armies. Defying prevailing logic, Lee divided his army. He sent Stonewall Jackson with about 25,000 troops on a long march with instructions to keep an eye on Pope. James Longstreet (q.v.) would soon follow Jackson with the remainder of Lee's army. Twenty miles to the rear of Pope, Jackson found the Northern general's supply base at Manassas Junction and destroyed it. As Pope was searching for the elusive Jackson, Lee and Longstreet were moving into position a few miles from where Jackson had camped near Manassas.

On August 29, the first day of the battle of Second Manassas, the impatient Pope essayed an assault against Jackson, who was protected by an abandoned railroad embankment. Pope wasted his numerical advantage by committing his troops in piecemeal fashion. He resumed the battle on August 30; however, by then the remainder of Lee's army had reached the field. During the night, the defeated Pope withdrew and marched in the direction of Washington. Lee's audacity for offensive warfare had helped to propel the Confederates to victory over a powerful Federal army at the battle of Second Manassas.

As the end of summer approached, Lee made plans to invade Maryland. He commenced his invasion by crossing the Potomac River and establishing his base a short distance from Frederick, Maryland. Having settled into camp, Lee once again did the unthinkable, dividing his army by sending an advance force under Longstreet to Hagerstown. One division was placed under Daniel H. Hill and ordered to protect Turner's Gap in South Mountain. The remainder of Lee's army was entrusted to the command of Stonewall Jackson, who had been directed to capture the Federal garrison at Harpers Ferry. McClellan, who was eager to meet the enemy, marched from Washington to Frederick, reaching that place on September 12. The next day a copy of Lee's orders outlining the objectives for his army was found, wrapped around cigars, by two Federal troops at the site of an abandoned Confederate camp near Frederick and delivered to McClellan. Not only was Lee facing a much larger Federal army at Sharpsburg on the banks of Antietam Creek, but his back was also pressed against the Potomac River. Although it was risky to wage battle under these conditions, Lee was aware that the benefits of success would be of historical proportions. The Confederate commander knew that a victory on Northern soil would be a devastating military and psychological blow to the United States. That combined with the possibility of European recognition of the Confederacy outweighed any negatives that might have resulted from defeat.

It was not until the morning of September 17 that McClellan opened the battle of Antietam. During this day of horrific slaughter, Lee's army bent but did not break. Lee displayed brilliant generalship in handling his army by shifting his men along the line to meet exigencies during the battle. The following day found Lee in position with his exhausted warriors contemplating an attack on McClellan's right flank. He, however, accepted the counsel of his corps leaders Longstreet and Jackson and ordered a withdrawal. On the night of September 18, Lee's battle-tested soldiers crossed the Potomac River back into Virginia. Although Antietam, the single bloodiest day of the war, was tactically a draw, President Lincoln used it as the pretext to issue his preliminary Emancipation Proclamation.

After that day of carnage in Maryland, both armies enjoyed a respite from battle. In October 1862, Lee took advantage of the lull in fighting to meet with Davis in Richmond. In the meantime, Lincoln, who had become thoroughly frustrated with McClellan's cautious approach to warfare, was urging him to take the offensive. Finally, in late October he crossed the Potomac River with Richmond as his destination. Because of the Federal army's agonizingly slow advance, Lee had ample time to block its path. Losing all patience with McClellan, Lincoln removed him from his post as commander of the army in November and replaced him with Ambrose E. Burnside. The new commander got his chance to show what he could do at the battle of Fredericksburg on December 13, 1862.

Lee's battle plans allowed Burnside to cross to the south side of the Rappahannock River without opposition. Having forded the river, the bluecoats were
confronted by a heavily fortified Confederate Army. Lee observed the battle of
Fredericksburg from his vantage point atop Telegraph Hill. Believing he could
overwhelm Lee's army with his numerical superiority, Burnside ordered his men
to attack in waves. This tactic proved futile against the well-entrenched Southern
soldiers. With the memory of a campaign gone bad, Burnside led his vanquished
army back across the Rappahannock on the night of December 14. The coming
of the new year brought yet another change in the leadership of the Federal
army. Having ousted Burnside as commander of the army, President Lincoln
appointed Joseph "Fighting Joe" Hooker to take his place on January 25, 1863.
On April 29, Hooker ordered his army to cross the Rappahannock and march
toward Chancellorsville.

Lee's performance in "the Wilderness" at Chancellorsville added to his reputation as an outstanding strategical and tactical general. Under his direction,
one of the more famous military maneuvers of the war was executed. In a bold
move, Lee sent Stonewall Jackson, his best corps commander, through the Wilderness with instructions to attack the exposed right wing of Hooker's army.
Jackson reached Hooker's right flank on May 2 and found Oliver O. Howard's
brigades preparing for dinner. He immediately launched a furious attack that
routed the unsuspecting Federals. As the victorious Jackson was riding back into
camp that night, he was mistakenly wounded by his own men. J. E. B. Stuart
assumed command of the fallen hero's corps. The Confederates renewed their
attack on the morning of May 3. When the right wing of the Army of Northern
Virginia had affected a junction with Stuart's left, Lee ordered his men forward
in a powerful assault.

On May 6, Hooker led his beaten army back over to the north side of the
Rappahannock. Not only would Chancellorsville be remembered as Lee's
greatest victory but also as Stonewall Jackson's last battle. Jackson, whom Lee
characterized as an "illustrious man," succumbed to his wounds on May 10.
The day after the death of his corps commander, a grief-stricken Lee issued a
general order to his army in which he called Jackson a "great and good soldier"
who possessed an "invincible determination." Once the battle of Chancellorsville was over, Lee again turned his attention to invading the North. Lee reorganized his triumphant army and moved into the Shenandoah Valley. In June
1863, he began his trek northward with his eyes fixed on Pennsylvania. Lincoln
by then, however, had become displeased with Hooker's performance and allowed him to resign. On June 28, 1863, Lincoln appointed George G. Meade
(q.v.) to replace him.

Within a few days after becoming the supreme commander of the Federal
army, Meade was tested in battle at Gettysburg against the Confederacy's best
general. Longstreet and his chief arrived at the town of Gettysburg on the morning of July 1, the place where Lee would have his climactic battle. When Lee
finally reached the battlefield on that afternoon, a portion of his army had been

fighting a contingent of Union soldiers for several hours west of the town. The Confederates eventually forced their adversaries to abandon their position, at which time they occupied Cemetery Hill. Richard S. Ewell halted his advance so as not to risk a full-scale battle with only a portion of the Army of Northern Virginia on the scene. Detecting a tinge of hesitation during his meeting with Ewell, Lee informed him that Longstreet would initiate the main assault on Meade's army the next day.

Lee had planned for Longstreet's corps to begin the attack early on the morning of July 2. His delay was symptomatic of the chaotic attacks carried out by the Confederates during the second day of action. When Longstreet began his attack later that day, a terrific battle ensued at Little and Big Round Tops. Still hoping to crush Meade's army, Lee decided to continue the battle for a third day, with Longstreet and Ewell leading the charge. It was on July 3 at about 2:00 P.M. when George E. Pickett began his fateful charge across an open field. Pickett's division attacked the center of the Union Army at Cemetery Ridge with deadly results. The courage of the Confederates was no match for the accuracy of the Union artillerists and infantrymen on that day at Gettysburg. Lee observed Pickett's charge of carnage from his post on Seminary Ridge, knowing that he had mortgaged the Confederacy's future at Gettysburg and had lost. He accepted responsibility for the annihilation of Pickett's men and the defeat of his army. Lee's army hobbled back into Virginia after the famous battle and set up camp on the Rapidan River a short distance from Orange Court House.

Confederate politicians and newspapers criticized Lee for the debacle at Gettysburg. Believing he could no longer be effective and suffering ill health, Lee submitted his resignation to Davis on August 8. The Confederate president in rejecting Lee's offer to step down reminded him that he still had "the confidence of the army." Davis stood by his embattled general, stating that the military effort of the South would succeed or fail with Lee as the commanding officer. Davis's unqualified commitment to Lee was a resounding affirmation of his faith in the Virginia general to prolong the war.

In October 1863, Lee's army crossed the Rappahannock River in pursuit of Meade. When Lee halted to feed his men, the retreating Meade hurried his army along the Orange and Alexandria Railroad to Bristoe Station. As Lee's advance guard under Ambrose P. Hill approached the army in blue, they were attacked on October 14 by Gouverneur K. Warren's Second Corps, inflicting heavy casualties. The day after the battle of Bristoe Station, Lee and Hill surveyed the field where the latter's division had been defeated. After listening to Hill's explanation for the cause of his failure, a disappointed Lee retorted: "Well, well, General, bury these poor men and let us say no more about it."

Four days after the fight at Bristoe Station, Lee relocated his army to the Rappahannock, leaving two of Jubal Early's brigades to guard the bridgehead on the river. Meade chased Lee, and on the night of November 7, 1863, the Federals assailed the two detached Confederate brigades and captured the bridgehead. Lee then withdrew his army from the Rappahannock and established his base on the Rapidan River. With winter approaching, Meade crossed the Rapidan in pursuit of the Confederate Army. Lee then ordered his men to construct fortifications on the west bluff of Mine Run. On December 1, Meade called off the attack because of Lee's strong defensive works. Determined to take the offensive, Lee instructed two of his divisions to attack the left flank of the Army of the Potomac at dawn on December 2. To Lee's surprise, Meade's men had recrossed to the north side of the Rapidan the previous day. Mine Run, the last active operation in 1863, was a disparaging campaign for Lee.

Anticipating tough campaigns ahead, Lee used the winter months to conduct inspections of his army. When Lee resumed active combat, he faced a new foe in the person of Ulysess S. Grant (q.v.), general in chief of the United States Armies. In May 1864, Grant initiated the Overland campaign with the destruction of Lee's army and the capture of Richmond as his objectives. Cooperating with Grant and Meade were Benjamin E. Butler and his Army of the James, which consisted of several thousand U.S. Colored Troops.

On May 4, Meade's Army of the Potomac accompanied by Grant departed from its base on the north shore of the Rapidan. Lee decided not to contest the passage of the Union Army across the river, preferring to allow them to rush into the thick forest and underbrush known as "the Wilderness." Once the Federal army had crossed to the south bank of the Rapidan, Lee ordered his army to concentrate at Mine Run. With Grant in the same imbroglio as Joe Hooker was a year earlier, Lee was confident of duplicating the same success against his new antagonist. On the afternoon of May 5, the competing armies collided, and the furious engagement raged until halted by darkness. The battle of the Wilderness consisted of thousands of courageous troops who desperately grappled not only with their adversaries but also with the obstacles of nature. There in the Wilderness, Longstreet was wounded by his own troops. The incapacitation of the "Old War Horse" forced Lee to take command of his corps. The misfortune that had suddenly descended upon Longstreet was reminiscent of what had happened to Jackson a year earlier near the same spot. Lee, however, could still take comfort in knowing that he had successfully halted Grant's advance in the two days of fighting, much to the consternation of the new general in chief. Grant's introduction to the Wilderness was the commencement of a deadly and protracted struggle between Lee and himself that would last until the end of the war.

Among the qualities that made Lee a first-rate general was his ability to anticipate the movement of the enemy and to prescribe an effective counter-strategy. Lee's thorough understanding of warfare combined with excellent reconnaissance work were important factors in helping him to predict accurately that Grant's next move would be toward Spotsylvania. Realizing the need to block the Northern general's march, Lee ordered Richard H. Anderson, who then commanded Longstreet's corps, to take up a defensive position just north of Spotsylvania Court House. When the Federal vanguard reached the outskirts of the village on May 8, they found Anderson's corps in place and ready to resist them.

The fog and drizzle that greeted the soldiers of the Union Army at daybreak on May 12 did not slow their advance. They moved forward and launched a thunderous attack at a salient called Mule Shoe or Bloody Angle at the center of the Confederate line. The fighting there was among the most ferocious of the war. Lee responded to the breaching of his fortifications by constructing a new line of earthworks across the base of Bloody Angle. Late in the evening, the weary Southern warriors withdrew to the new entrenchments. On the same day as that brutal combat at Mule Shoe, Lee received word that J. E. B. Stuart, the intrepid cavalry leader of the Army of Northern Virginia, had died in Richmond. He had been fatally wounded in the fighting at Yellow Tavern the day before. Heavy with melancholy, Lee knew he had lost a valued comrade.

After the battle of Spotsylvania, Lee and Grant continued their sparring for several days. Lee relocated his army to the south of the North Anna River and prepared a defensive line. Lee's position on the North Anna was ideal from which to attack the approaching Army of the Potomac, which was divided by the river. Grant's army no doubt escaped a telling blow because Lee was suffering from an intestinal ailment at the time. By early June, Grant, whose army was less than ten miles from Richmond, made another attempt to destroy Lee's forces. Grant's effort to break through Lee's defensive line resulted in the battle of Cold Harbor. Beginning at dawn on June 3, the Federal soldiers stormed the Confederate line with tremendous energy, only to be repulsed. The bloody affair at Cold Harbor was a stunning defeat for Grant.

Lee's performance during the campaign from the Wilderness to Cold Harbor served as evidence that his reputation as a great captain of war was well deserved. Although Grant's casualties in the spring campaign of 1864 were substantially higher than those of his Southern adversary, he could more easily supplement his army from a huge reservoir of men. By contrast, a man lost to the Army of Northern Virginia could not be replaced. Grant's implementation of his war of attrition was one strategy that even the ingenious Lee could not counter.

The failure of Grant at Cold Harbor did not lessen his appetite for battle. By June 16, the Union general had moved his entire army to the south side of the James River with the capture of Petersburg as his objective. Lee's army scurried down from Malvern Hill to the city under attack and occupied prepared defensive works just in time to assist Pierre G. T. Beauregard (q.v.), who was facing imminent danger. Grant's inability to conquer Petersburg in his operations against that city from June 16 to June 18 did not demoralize his spirit. Grant, whose options were limited at Petersburg, decided on a siege. For the remainder of the summer of 1864, the dueling armies strengthened their fortifications at the city that stood as the gateway to Richmond.

The sight of exhausted soldiers watching each other across a battle-scarred field convinced the Federals of the need to attempt to break the impasse. Grant accepted the recommendation of his engineers that the fortifications of the enemy could be severely wrecked by tunneling under a portion of the Confederate line and exploding gunpowder. On July 30, shortly after 4:30 A.M., an enormous gunpowder explosion created a massive hole in the earth, commonly referred to as the Crater. By congregating in the Crater, the Union soldiers made themselves easy targets for the Rebel sharpshooters. When the battle of the Crater was over, Lee's troops had again defeated the supreme commander of the Union Armies.

The serious reduction of manpower in Lee's army did not dampen his enthusiasm for offensive warfare. In June 1864, he designated Jubal Early's corps to carry out a demonstration toward Washington. By the middle of July, Early's army had marched through the Shenandoah Valley and had reached the outskirts of the Northern capital. The strong fortifications around that city caused the Confederates to halt their advance. With Federal reinforcements pouring into the nation's capital, Early was compelled to retreat. The threat of Washington being invaded by the enemy was a disturbing psychological blow for Northerners. The stalemate around Petersburg combined with plummeting morale caused many of them to doubt the Union's ability to win the war.

During the long siege at Petersburg, Grant had steadily extended his line, forcing his Southern adversary to match him. It was obvious that he was making plans to topple Lee by way of a grand assault. Lee accurately predicted that the Army of the Potomac would attack his western flank. The arrival of Philip H. Sheridan (q.v.) from the Shenandoah Valley with his cavalry in March 1865 bolstered Grant's offensive scheme. Sheridan moved to Dinwiddie Court House to position himself for an attack on Lee's western flank with a force consisting of infantry and cavalry. On March 30, he attacked Lee's defenses but was repulsed.

With the end of the war at hand, it was only a question of when Lee and the Southern nation would capitulate. Sheridan attacked the enemy's line on March 31, causing the right flank of the army to collapse. On April 1, Sheridan's forces combined with Warren's corps defeated Pickett's Division at the battle of Five Forks. The success of the Union Army on that day was the prelude for Grant to order a full-scale attack along the entire Confederate line at Petersburg. Under the weight of that powerful assault, Lee's defenses caved in at several places along the line, and the guardians of Petersburg and Richmond were forced to evacuate. On April 3, Union soldiers triumphantly entered the abandoned cities.

What followed was a retreat of Lee's exhausted troops. On April 7, Grant presented Lee with a summons to surrender. Two days later, Lee handed over the remnants of his army to Grant at Appomattox Court House. The surrender, the final act of Lee's military career, was carried out with dignity. On April 10, Lee issued his Farewell Address to the soldiers of his famous army. Following Lee's surrender, the old general traveled to the former Confederate capital as a paroled prisoner.

Within a few months after Appomattox, he accepted the presidency of Washington College in Lexington, Virginia. When Lee arrived on campus to assume his post in August 1865, he was already in poor health. Lee, the universally respected general of the Civil War, lost his final battle on October 12, 1870, when death claimed victory. He died of heart disease that had manifested itself during the war.

Novelists, journalists, and historians formed the core of writers who analyzed Lee's military record immediately after the conflict. Lee's generalship in several engagements, most notably Gettysburg, came under attack from writers such as William Swinton, John Esten Cooke, Edward Pollard (q.v.), and James McCabe. While their analysis of Lee's wartime record was not flattering, they still regarded him as the Confederacy's most outstanding general. Their criticism of Lee caused his defenders to take the offensive.

Jubal A. Early, who commanded the Second Corps of the Army of Northern Virginia, surfaced from among the legion of Lee admirers to lead the campaign to rehabilitate his chief's name. He was an influential writer of the postwar era who had a knack for making enemies because of his "haughty and disdainful" temperament. Early's book *War Memoirs: Autobiographical Sketch and the Narrative of the War between the States* was left untouched until his niece brought the manuscript to publication in 1912, eighteen years after her uncle's death. Frank E. Vandiver edited Early's *War Memoirs* in 1960. Early used a great deal of ink attacking James Longstreet, who was especially critical of Lee's generalship at Gettysburg. Early states that errors were made at that battle, but they "were not attributable to General Lee" (278). Early maintains that Lee was a Confederate nationalist who was motivated by an "ardent desire for the success of the cause of his country" (467). Although this volume is propitious toward Early and occasionally exaggerative, it is nonetheless an important book on the Civil War.

Among the more influential memorial organizations created after the war was the Lee Monument Association of which Jubal Early was president. This association gave him an excellent forum from which to extoll the virtues of Lee, including a portrayal of him as a flawless general. With Early leading the charge, Lee's reputation as a cult phenomenon became evident. The historical writing after the Civil War laid the foundation upon which the heroic image of Robert E. Lee was built. Lee's christening as the most important symbol of the Lost Cause coincided with his emergence as a God-like figure. The adulation that Southerners showered on him during the postwar years approached mythical proportions. Embodied in his persona was the belief that the South was still a land of virtuous people.

Forty years after the death of Early, Douglas Southall Freeman published the preeminent study of Lee. His Pulitzer Prize–winning four-volume work *R. E. Lee: A Biography* was published in 1934–1935. This prolific biographer sees Lee as the shining example of all that was noble and righteous in American life. To Freeman, Lee was the paragon of simplicity, spirituality, and magnanimity. According to the author, the ambitious and virtuous Lee was a man whose "conspicuous qualities" were apparent for all to see. Freeman concludes that there was nothing mysterious about Lee, but rather he "was one of the small company of great men in whom there is no inconsistency to be explained, no enigma to be solved" (4:494). Prodigiously researched, Freeman used a plethora of sources that had been ignored up to that time.

In the years after the publication of Freeman's monumental work, several historians attempted to knock Lee off his saintly pedestal. The most thorough revision of Lee came from the pen of Thomas L. Connelly. In 1977, he published *The Marble Man: Robert E. Lee and His Image in American Society*. This is a superb analysis of the historical and sociological forces that operated in the former Confederate States after Lee's death to create his heroic and legendary status. Connelly, in shattering Lee's spotless image, maintains that his life was filled with disappointments, turmoil, and self-doubt. Connelly penetrates the halo surrounding the Christ-like Lee, revealing that he was a man beset by trouble who was "convinced that he had failed as a prewar career officer, parent, and moral individual" (xiv). Connelly concludes that Lee's image as "the invincible general" was among his achievements that "were deliberately magnified at the expense of the reputations of others" (78). This book remains the most powerful intellectual challenge to Freeman.

Continuing along the line of revision is the controversial *Lee Considered: General Robert E. Lee and Civil War History* by Alan T. Nolan, who admits his debt to Connelly. Despite the body of literature on Lee, Nolan believes that he has never been really considered. The author presents a careful consideration of the Southern icon in his 1991 monograph. Nolan provides evidence to challenge what he calls "the major aspects of the Lee tradition." While this work is not biographical, Nolan uses Lee's life as the backdrop to illustrate that he was a study in paradox. Lee hated slavery and secession but waged a gargantuan struggle to preserve the Southern way of life of which the peculiar institution was a cornerstone.

In dismantling the prevailing view of Lee, the author contends that his postwar thoughts were in keeping with those of his Southern contemporaries. According to Nolan, Lee's embracement of states' right and white supremacy substantiates the fact that the general "was human, not the unlikely paragon that the tradition has created" (152). Nolan devotes a chapter to refuting the aspect of the Lee tradition that holds that he exhibited "great magnanimity toward his adversaries." On this point, he argues that the evidence clearly shows that such a claim "is manufactured and unhistorical." Nolan argues that Lee's offensive campaigns were detrimental to the Confederate cause because of the exorbitant number of casualties they produced in the Army of Northern Virginia.

Emory M. Thomas uses the methodological genre that Freeman used six decades earlier in the writing of his book *Robert E. Lee: A Biography*. Thomas describes his 1995 biography as "post-revisionist." This judicious evaluation of Lee falls somewhere between Freeman's idolatry work and *The Marble Man*. While there is little new information in this volume, its treatment of Lee as both man and general is balanced. As a man, the author reveals that Lee, "the patron saint of the American South,'' was an extraordinary person, though he was a tortured individual who experienced many failures and was consumed by self-doubt. While Thomas agrees with Freeman that Lee was an exceptional human being, he also concurs with Connelly and Nolan that his life was characterized by a ''series of paradoxes.'' The author concludes that Lee ''spent his life working with men . . . yet he lived for women—his real friends were female'' (413). Thomas maintains that he enjoyed the company of young women. The notion of Lee as a flirt is documented by Charles Bracelen Flood in his 1981 volume *Lee: The Last Years*. By limiting his study to the last five years of Lee's life, Flood depicts him as a national leader of reconciliation during the turbulent period of Reconstruction.

Thomas emphasizes that Lee enjoyed numerous triumphs during his life of sixty-three years. He was arguably the finest soldier of the Confederacy, and his leadership of the Army of Northern Virginia was brilliant. In the words of Thomas, ''Lee defined audacity and won victories in apparently impossible circumstances'' (19). This is an excellent biography, objectively written and meticulously researched.

Shortly after the publication of Thomas's book, Gary W. Gallagher's edited work *Lee: The Soldier* appeared. The purpose of this volume, according to its author, is to provide ''convenient access to assessments of Lee's generalship that reflect the interpretive sweep of the literature'' (xvii). The focal point of this book is the twenty-one essays, sixteen of which have previously appeared in print. The reader of this collection of analytical writings on Lee's wartime record will gain an appreciation for the voluminous literature both for and against him as a great Civil War general. Moreover, these essays provide a broad conceptualization demonstrating the way in which historians and others have critically evaluated Lee's generalship over the past 130 years. The last part of this volume contains an impressive annotation of 200 titles on the military career of Robert E. Lee. Students of the Civil War will doubtless find this bibliography helpful. The historiography on Lee as a soldier has been made richer by the publication of this book.

An analysis of Lee's wartime record reveals that he was a brilliant chieftain who won many victories, a yardstick by which to measure military greatness. Despite facing tremendous odds, Lee's confidence in his ability to win inspired his men to fight with dogged determination. The soldiers of the Army of Northern Virginia earned their reputation for courage and tenacity. Lee's daring spirit, bold maneuvers, and strategical sense made him the envy of his contemporaries. Lee was a great general who knew how to fight but not when to surrender. In reality, he had no chance of winning the war after the battle of Antietam. As Lee continued to lead the military effort of the seceded states, he knew that the Union Army posed a formidable obstacle to Southern independence. Lee, the gifted general of the Confederate States, used his military genius to prolong the war. The Confederacy's failed revolution, of which Lee was a prominent participant, taught the nation a valuable lesson. Never again would a state or section of the country use secession as a means of exercising political autonomy.

During those tumultuous four years of the Civil War, Lee left an indelible imprint on the pages of the nation's history. As a historical figure, he will continue to attract scholarly attention from both defenders and detractors. The historiographical debate over his place in the Civil War will rage well into the next millennium. The historical profession will no doubt witness a renewed interest in Robert E. Lee—the man and the soldier—as the bicentennial of his birth approaches.

BIBLIOGRAPHY

Robert E. Lee, Jr., *Recollections and Letters of General Robert E. Lee* (New York: Doubleday, Page, and Co., 1904).

Douglas Southall Freeman, *R. E. Lee: A Biography*, 4 vols. (New York: Charles Scribner's Sons, 1934–1935).

Stanley F. Horn, ed., *The Robert E. Lee Reader* (New York: Bobbs-Merrill Company, 1949).

Jubal A. Early, *War Memoirs: Autobiographical Sketch and the Narrative of the War between the States*. Edited by Frank E. Vandiver (Indianapolis: Indiana University Press, 1960).

Clifford Dowdey and Louis H. Manarin, ed., *The Wartime Papers of R. E. Lee* (Boston: Little, Brown and Company, 1961).

Thomas L. Connelly, *The Marble Man: Robert E. Lee and His Image in American Society* (Baton Rouge: Louisiana State University Press, 1977).

Charles Bracelen Flood, *Lee: The Last Years* (Boston: Houghton Mifflin, 1981).

Alan T. Nolan, *Lee Considered: General Robert E. Lee and Civil War History* (Chapel Hill: University of North Carolina Press, 1991).

Emory M. Thomas, *Robert E. Lee: A Biography* (New York: W. W. Norton, 1995).

Steven E. Woodworth, *Davis and Lee at War* (Lawrence: University Press of Kansas, 1995).

Gary W. Gallagher, ed., *Lee: The Soldier* (Lincoln: University of Nebraska Press, 1996).

ABRAHAM LINCOLN
(February 12, 1809–April 15, 1865)

James A. Rawley

Abraham Lincoln, Civil War president of the United States, was born in a log cabin in Hardin County, Kentucky. He had an American lineage that reached back to 1637. Abraham's father, Thomas Lincoln (1776– or 1778–1851), born in Rockingham County, Virginia, moved to Kentucky, where his father was killed by Indians. Thomas in 1803 bought a 238-acre farm in Hardin County. He married Nancy Hanks (1784–1819), a Virginian about whose ancestry little is known; she was perhaps illegitimate. The couple had three children: Sarah, the firstborn who died in childbirth in her late teens; Abraham; and Thomas, who died in infancy.

Thomas Lincoln was not the shiftless father sometimes portrayed. A farm owner and carpenter possessing scant education, he conscientiously served his church and community. Three farms he bought each failed to give him a clear title, because of Kentucky's defective land laws. Early in 1816 the family moved to better surveyed land in southern Indiana, near Gentryville. Abraham later said the move was "partly on account of slavery."

A strapping boy, Abraham worked hard, cutting wood and planting and harvesting crops. Until he was twenty-one, the youth, growing in height and muscular strength, performed farm labor. Pioneer life, pretty pinching at times, he later observed, offered little by way of education. He went to school "by littles" in his quaint phrase, in all less than a year.

What was remarkable about the pioneer farmboy was not only his enthusiasm for learning but also his mastery of several fields by self-education. The family apparently owned a Bible, an influence that increasingly shaped his outlook in mature years. Libraries were nonexistent, and books in the neighborhood were few. But Abraham borrowed *Aesop's Fables, Pilgrim's Progress*, Parson Weems's *Life and Memorable Actions of George Washington*, and *Robinson Crusoe*. As a youth he read inspirational and patriotic literature. In his maturing years, he avidly read newspapers, and as president he read Shakespeare often.

Fond of the political plays, he favored *Macbeth*. The Bible and Shakespeare wrought profound influence upon his thought and prose style.

At the age of nine Abraham lost his mother to the "milk sickness," with what effect upon the boy it is hard to say. His father soon married a Kentucky widow, a fortunate choice for the youth, who called her his "angel mother" and who encouraged him to pursue an education. Lincoln enjoyed a closeness with his stepmother that he never had with his father.

Thomas Lincoln restlessly again moved his family, this time to Illinois, Abraham driving a team of oxen. By 1831 the Lincolns had settled in Coles County, and Abraham, now six feet four inches tall and powerful in build, once more performed the taxing labor of clearing, fencing, and plowing land. Unwilling to be a farmer, after two journeys as a flatboatman down the Mississippi River, Lincoln in 1831 left the farm and moved to New Salem on the Sangamon River. The hamlet offered Lincoln the opportunity to be a storekeeper, at which he failed, and postmaster, enabling him to read incoming newspapers.

The New Salem years were formative. Lincoln taught himself surveying and became deputy surveyor of Sangamon County. When the Black Hawk War broke out in 1832, Lincoln enlisted and was elected captain of his company, a shaping circumstance in his life.

His company never saw action, and Lincoln, home in New Salem, continued his upward course by entering politics and studying law. In 1834 he won election to the state legislature; his victory at the age of twenty-five, a relative newcomer, meagerly educated, was a notable event in a life that became famous for political skill. Reelected as a Whig in 1836, he officially became a lawyer in 1837. That year he moved to the new state capital in Springfield, with its larger opportunities for a political and legal career.

Lincoln formed a law partnership with a fellow Whig and legislator, John Todd Stuart, who soon entered Congress. Lincoln himself continued to serve in the state legislature until 1840. In 1844 he formed a partnership with William H. Herndon, a relationship that endured until Lincoln departed for the presidency in 1861. Lincoln spent much time riding circuit, leaving records of thousands of cases, mainly small, spreading statewide a reputation as a sagacious lawyer and becoming acquainted with a wide circle of men who were to be associated with him during his presidency.

A close relationship with Ann Rutledge tragically ended with her death at nineteen. His hesitant courtship with Mary Todd led to marriage in 1842. A Kentucky aristocrat, sister to the socially prominent Edwards family in Springfield, she enhanced Lincoln's social standing in the community and encouraged her husband's political ambition. Her membership in the Presbyterian Church, whose services Lincoln attended, doubtless exerted an influence on his religious development. The couple had four sons, only one of whom lived to maturity—a series of blows to the devoted parents.

Politics fascinated Lincoln. An ardent Whig, admirer of Henry Clay, he served one term in the House of Representatives (1847–1849). His congressional career had two highlights; one was his challenge to President James Polk's claim that the fighting in the Mexican War started with Mexican aggression on U.S. soil. The other was his unsuccessful proposal for gradual and compensated emancipation in the District of Columbia, with approval by slaveowners. Failing to gain a federal appointment after his term, he returned to his law practice, growing in prominence in his profession.

The dramatic crisis of the Union, provoked by Stephen A. Douglas's bill to organize the Nebraska Territory, while repealing the thirty-four-year-old prohibition on slavery in the region, aroused Lincoln's animosity. During the next six years, opposition to extending slavery and concern about preserving national unity occupied his life. In late 1854 he delivered an impassioned speech attacking Douglas, repeal, and slavery. In 1856 he adhered to the new Republican party, espousing its stand against slavery expansion in more than fifty speeches. Becoming the most prominent Republican in Illinois, he garnered 110 votes for the vice presidency at the party's first national convention in 1856.

Two years later Illinois Republicans nominated Lincoln for U.S. senator, to run against Douglas. In accepting, Lincoln made his celebrated speech, "A house divided against itself cannot stand." The campaign became drama when Lincoln challenged the redoubtable Douglas to a series of debates. The confrontation offered Lincoln the opportunity to expose the inconsistency between the Dred Scott Decision that protected slavery in the territories and Douglas's insistence that the people in the territories could exclude it. Lincoln boldly applied the Declaration of Independence to blacks, while disavowing abolitionism and sympathizing with the Southern people. Though he lost the election, he won national recognition.

Early in 1860 New York Republicans invited him to give an address in New York City. At the Cooper Institute, he delivered a carefully thought-out speech that increased his national stature. He argued that most of the Framers of the Constitution were antislavery, attacked Douglas and the Dred Scott Decision, repudiated John Brown, stressed the Republican principle of excluding slavery from the territories, and passionately charged that slavery was wrong.

The Republican national convention, held in his home state, awarded Lincoln the presidential nomination on the third ballot. During a four-cornered contest that underscored the Republican party's stand against expansion of slavery in the territories, Lincoln refrained from speech making but quietly sought party unity. Voters in November accorded him the presidency by a minority and sectional vote. Three of every five ballots were cast for Lincoln's opponents; in ten Southern states no ballots were cast for him.

The house was dividing. Within weeks South Carolina announced its withdrawal from the Union, and by February 1, 1861—a little more than a month before Lincoln took office—seven states in the Deep South had seceded and formed the Confederate States of America. Congressional efforts to effect a compromise encountered Lincoln's inflexible opposition to slavery expansion, which he feared would further divide the Union. His strong nationalism stood behind his message to General Winfield Scott to hold the forts.

In his inaugural address he sought to assure Southerners he did not intend to interfere with slavery in the states. Having sworn an oath to execute the laws, he would enforce them, including the Fugitive Slave Law, and appealed for use of political institutions—the Supreme Court and the ballot—to resolve political differences. He made a strong case for the Union, arguing it was older than the Constitution and perpetual. Secession, he said, "is the essence of anarchy" (as well as physically impracticable) (Basler, 4:263). In an emotional closing he averred that if there is to be a civil war, the government would not be the aggressor. He made a final appeal to "the better angels of our nature" (Basler, 4:271).

The day after the inaugural address the first test of Lincoln's leadership presented itself. A memorandum lay on his desk starkly saying Fort Sumter in South Carolina could be held only by supplying more Federal troops; otherwise, the garrison must be given up. To do the first risked war; to do the other meant abandonment of Unionism and Republican party unity and hazarded charges of cowardice. The president's major advisers, Secretary of State William H. Seward (q.v.) and General in Chief Winfield Scott, urged abandonment, and at first so did most of the cabinet. In the end Lincoln rejected the advice of Seward and Scott, secured the sanction of most of the cabinet, held firmly to his stated purpose to hold "places belonging to the government" (Basler, 4:268) and planned to sustain the fort. The Confederacy replied with a successful assault on the beleaguered garrison.

The loss of the Federal fort—symbol of the clash between state's rights and national power—further challenged Lincoln's leadership. Congress was not in session; and the president acted swiftly. He summoned the militia to put down the rebellion, blockaded the Confederate coast, suspended the privilege of the writ of habeas corpus, enlarged the standing army and navy, and entrusted unappropriated funds to private citizens. All these bold acts stepped on congressional toes, and some were plainly congressional prerogatives.

Lincoln conducted the war himself, inciting cries of dictatorship, until Congress met at his call on July 4, 1861. The Congress, strongly Republican, sustained the president but failed to endorse suspension of habeas corpus. Though a federal circuit court, presided over by Chief Justice Roger Taney, had ruled against him and Congress would not support him, Lincoln steadfastly continued to suspend.

Militia by federal law could serve only ninety days. When the enlistment period was about to end, Confederate troops stood astride a railroad junction not far from the nation's capital. A popular clamor demanded a fight, thinking it might terminate both the rebellion and the possibility of foreign intervention on the Confederacy's behalf. Again overruling General Scott, Lincoln as commander in chief ordered a Union advance against the Confederates at Bull Run. The outcome was a disheartening repulse to Union forces and hopes.

Lincoln took increasing control of military affairs. He appointed George B. McClellan (q.v.) as general in chief after Scott retired; began to formulate a grand strategy of the war, rejecting Scott's plan of a slow, relatively bloodless constriction of the enemy; and replaced incompetent Secretary of War Simon Cameron with Edwin M. Stanton (q.v.), a dedicated, efficient war Democrat. As commander in chief he entered into a direct correspondence with his generals in the field, counseling them, prodding them, praising them, raising questions about strategy and tactics, and frequently changing them. Within twenty months, desperately seeking a winning general, he made six changes in the great Union Army in Virginia. Exasperated by McClellan's slowness, he would remove him as general in chief, replacing him with General Henry W. Halleck (q.v.), relieved and restored him to high command, and relieved him again. For a period in 1862 Lincoln in effect acted as general in chief. After Halleck's appointment, the trio of Lincoln, Stanton, and Halleck functioned as a war council, though at times the president acted on his own.

Following Bull Run Lincoln formed a conception of strategy that embraced recognizing Union superiority in manpower, probing the enemy forces for points of weakness, aggressively attacking such points simultaneously, and defeating the enemy army rather than conquering the enemy capital or defending Union soil.

Placed in charge of the Army of the Potomac after the Bull Run rout, McClellan served splendidly in organizing the army and raising morale. He was, however, slow to engage the enemy, secretive about his plans, and deliberately snubbed his commander in chief. Lincoln finally intervened, ordering a ''general movement'' against the enemy for February 22, 1862. McClellan ignored the order, disagreed with Lincoln over strategy, and prevailed in his plan to move his forces circuitously by way of the peninsula formed by the York and James Rivers. Fearing that McClellan's move left Washington exposed, Lincoln ordered retention of some forces to protect the capital.

Thereafter, Lincoln and McClellan engaged in a lively correspondence, interspersed with visits by Lincoln to McClellan's headquarters. The general maintained a drumbeat of unreasonable requests for more men and complaints against ''the hounds'' in Washington, all the while excelling in moving his forces but failing to defeat the enemy. With measured patience Lincoln forthrightly told McClellan, he must act soon.

The two men, military and political leaders, sharply differed in their conceptions of the conduct of war. McClellan believed, once given command, a general should have a relatively free hand in fighting. War, he advised Lincoln, should be directed against armed forces and political organizations, not against slavery. Lincoln, on the other hand, discerned a need to counsel his generals, who seemed not to understand they must destroy the enemy's military power; and he had begun to contemplate an Emancipation Proclamation and had signed confiscation legislation.

After General John Pope's defeat at Bull Run, on August 31, 1862, Lincoln

again gave McClellan charge of the Army of the Potomac. General Robert E.
Lee (q.v.) seized the opportunity opened by the Confederate victory to invade
Northern soil. Aided by discovery of Lee's orders, McClellan halted Lee at
Antietam in Maryland. In spite of presidential prodding, McClellan allowed
Lee's defeated army to escape and return to Virginia. Weeks later, claiming he
needed fresh horses to move, McClellan met with an unwonted sarcastic pres-
idential retort, "Will you pardon me for asking what the horses of your army
have done since the battle of Antietam that fatigues anything?" (Basler, 5:474).

McClellan's repulse of Lee ironically had provided the occasion for Lincoln
to issue his Emancipation Proclamation. The famous fiat set aside the assurances
of the Republican party's platform and Lincoln's inaugural address. It disre-
garded doubts, held in 1861, that he had authority to proclaim freedom for
Rebels' slaves. Such an act, he had said, was beyond "the range of *military*
law, or government necessity" (Basler, 4:532). When General John C. Frémont
had proclaimed freedom for Rebels' slaves in Missouri, Lincoln had forced
Frémont to revoke the order. When General David Hunter had essayed the same
policy in the lower South, Lincoln overruled him. All this, however, was attended by his personal wish—which he carefully separated from public policy—
that all men everywhere should be free.

Early in the year Lincoln had proposed a plan of voluntary state emancipation,
to be accomplished gradually, with federal compensation to slaveowners and
colonization of freedmen. He hoped the loyal slave states would grasp the offer
and show the way of an inevitable future of black freedom. Appeals to border
state congressmen, urging that the policy would shorten the war, failed to
achieve acceptance. Lincoln determined to proclaim freedom but prudently disguised his purpose. When the influential editor of the *New York Tribune*, Horace
Greeley, chided him for not having an antislavery policy, Lincoln publicly answered, "My paramount object in this struggle *is* to save the Union, and is *not*
either to save or destroy slavery" (Basler, 5:388). Five days before he issued
his preliminary proclamation he told an audience of Chicago Christians that such
a document "must necessarily be inoperative, like the Pope's bull against the
comet" (Basler, 5:420).

The proclamation deferred action for 100 days. It allowed Rebel states, meanwhile, to return to the Union with slavery untouched, provided they had placed
properly elected representatives in Congress. In his annual message to Congress
in December, recognizing "great diversity of sentiment" among Unionists about
slavery and the African race, he proposed three constitutional amendments. They
would, if ratified, provide for emancipation, a thirty-seven-year span of time for
accomplishing it, and compensation, which he artfully pointed out, would be
paid by a later and larger population.

No state availed itself of the offer to return to the Union on his terms, nor
had the Congress approved his proposed amendments when the 100 days expired. After conferring with his cabinet and accepting suggestions, Lincoln, on

January 1, 1863, issued his formal Emancipation Proclamation. He overcame his earlier doubts about constitutionality, justifying his decree by his power as commander in chief in time of war. Appropriately in this view, he exempted those parts of the Union not in rebellion against the United States, leaving several hundred thousand slaves in thralldom. He urged the freed people to abstain from violence, work for wages when allowed and importantly, added that blacks would be received into the armed service of the United States.

Legal barriers to black service had been cleared away by Congress in 1862. Even so, Lincoln had been reluctant to give guns to blacks. A few weeks after passage of the Militia and Confiscation Acts authorizing enlistment of black soldiers, Lincoln told a delegation, ''To arm the negroes would turn 50,000 bayonets from the loyal Border States against us that were for us'' (Basler, 8: 303). Not long later he said, ''[I]f we were to arm [the blacks], I fear that in a few weeks the arms would be in the hands of the rebels'' (Basler 8:304).

The Emancipation Proclamation evidenced a new outlook, and in the ensuing months, with growing zeal, Lincoln urged enlistment of blacks. To his military governor in Tennessee, Andrew Johnson (q.v.), who was contemplating raising a black military force, he declared, ''In my opinion the country needs no specific thing so much as a man of your ability and position to go to this work'' (Basler, 6:149). To General David Hunter, whose edict on emancipation he had overruled a year earlier, he now said, ''I am glad to see the accounts of your colored force'' (Basler, 6:158).

He sent none other than the adjutant general of the United States to enlist blacks in the Mississippi Valley. An overoptimistic president wrote Ulysses S. Grant (q.v.), ''I believe it [raising black troops] will soon close the contest'' (Basler, 6:374). In an eloquent letter to Illinois Republicans he asserted that some generals ''believe the emancipation policy and the use of colored troops constitute the heaviest blow yet dealt to the rebellion'' (Basler, 6:409).

Lincoln maintained his espousal of black service to the end of the war. He praised black bravery, and when the Confederate Congress threatened to enslave and kill black Union soldiers, he issued a general order threatening retaliation in kind: hard labor and death for Rebel soldiers. At the war's end, when nearly 190,000 blacks had seen service in Union forces, Lincoln told a group of anti-slavery men, ''I have done what no man could have helped doing, standing in my place'' (Carpenter, 77). Lincoln's vigorous championing of black service gave an impetus to winning both the war and black equality.

While Northern conservatives were alarmed over the president's policies for black freedom and military service, they were no less alarmed over his abridgment of the liberties of whites. Disregarding Taney's adverse opinion and Congress's unwillingness to approve his suspension of habeas corpus as well as charges of dictatorship, Lincoln proceeded to make arbitrary arrests. Two days after issuing the preliminary Emancipation he suspended habeas corpus nationwide, mainly to curb resistance to military service. The Thirty-seventh Congress, on the day before it expired, at last authorized presidential suspension.

The cause célèbre of suspension occurred in the spring of 1863 when an eloquent ex-congressman, long a critic of the president, was arrested by the military, tried before a military commission, and denied habeas corpus. Clement L. Vallandigham was convicted of publicly declaring sympathy for persons in rebellion against the United States and expressing disloyal opinions.

Lincoln was pained by the military proceedings, which had been carried out on an order from the overzealous general Ambrose Burnside. In a wry gesture Lincoln commuted the sentence and banished Vallandigham to exile in the Confederacy. A storm of criticism rained on the administration. Democrats exploited the infringement of civil liberty. Albany Democrats cried that military arrests should not occur beyond "the lines of military occupation."

In a notable reply on June 12, 1863, Lincoln argued that such arrests were constitutional "wherever the public safety does require them" (Basler, 6:311). Vallandigham, he charged, was endangering the military power of the Union, discouraging enlistment, and advocating desertion. With a skillful appeal to public support he asked, "Must I shoot a simple-minded soldier boy who deserts while I must not touch a hair of a wily agitator who induces him to desert?" (McPherson, 166). A fortnight later, replying to protesting Ohio Democrats, he justified suspension on his power and responsibility as commander in chief in time of rebellion. He persisted in suspending habeas corpus throughout the war and in using military courts. The Supreme Court ruled against him, but not until 1866.

Freedom of the press also was imperiled during the war. Many newspapers were extremely partisan, pushing the limits of freedom in wartime. It was again General Burnside who provoked a crisis when on June 1, 1863, while the Vallandigham affair was still raging, he suppressed the Chicago *Times* for expressing "disloyal and incendiary sentiments." Caught between upholding the military and freedom of the press, Lincoln acknowledged he was embarrassed. A mass meeting in Chicago urged him to revoke Burnside's order, which he did on June 4.

A good many newspapers suffered suppression during the stress of a civil war, but in the main, an opposition press continued to function. Lincoln showed his respect for civil liberties in an order to General John M. Schofield: "You will only arrest individuals, and suppress assemblies, when they may be working palpable injury to the Military in your charge" (Basler, 6:492). Throughout the war Lincoln tolerated a torrent of criticism, some of it outrageous. The Vallandigham and the Chicago *Times* infractions, it should be noted, were not his work but that of an injudicious general.

During most of 1863 Congress was not in session, enabling Lincoln to devote himself to military affairs and molding public opinion. The year 1862 had ended not only with disappointment in McClellan's failure to pursue Lee but also with Burnside's disastrous loss to Lee at the battle of Fredericksburg.

After removing Burnside as commander of the Army of the Potomac, Lincoln, without consulting others, appointed Joseph Hooker to the command. It was a curious choice, because Lincoln acknowledged to his appointee, "I have heard, in such a way as to believe it, of your recently saying that both the Army and the Government need a Dictator" (Basler, 6:77–78). The president pointed out other disabilities, including excess ambition and injudicious criticism of Burnside. He then continued, "What I now ask of you is military success, and I will risk the dictatorship" (Basler, 6:78). To a private secretary Lincoln confided he had appointed Hooker because of his popularity with the country.

The president kept watch on Hooker as his army moved against Lee across the Rappahannock River. With sharp insight and homely phrases Lincoln proffered advice to Hooker. Lee outgeneraled the Union commander, administering a smashing defeat at Chancellorsville. Emboldened by success, Lee once more invaded Northern soil. Just days before Lee and Union forces clashed in Pennsylvania, Hooker resigned, and General George G. Meade (q.v.) took command. For three days, July 1, 2, and 3, a great battle raged at Gettysburg while Lincoln anxiously sought news. Recognizing "the magnificent success" of Meade's victory over the invaders, Lincoln soon was "distressed immeasurably" by Meade's failure to pursue Lee.

In the West simultaneously General U. S. Grant accepted the surrender of besieged Vicksburg, the fort that dominated the lower Mississippi River. In a gracious and generous letter Lincoln confessed he had thought Grant had made a series of mistakes in his campaign. "I now wish to make the personal acknowledgment that you were right, and I was wrong," he wrote (Basler, 6:326). The episode—the president's self-restraint in allowing Grant to proceed and admission of error in military judgment—was a mark of Lincoln's qualities as commander in chief.

The July victories not only failed to foster Northern unity but also were accompanied by widespread complaint about fighting without uniting the North and South, emancipation, and black military service. In a masterly public letter, sent to a mass meeting of Springfield Republicans, Lincoln addressed all three issues. His Emancipation Proclamation, he claimed, was constitutional, justified by his role as commander in chief in time of war. Black soldiers were contributing to Union victories, weakening the enemy, and leaving "less for white soldiers to do. . . . The signs look better," he said, pointing to Gettysburg, Vicksburg, and other successes (Basler, 6:409).

With Union armies progressing on Southern soil, Lincoln tried a further approach to reuniting the nation. He had appointed military governors in three states—Tennessee, Louisiana, and North Carolina—and two border states were contemplating emancipation. He proposed to employ his pardoning power to extend amnesty to Southerners who would take an oath of loyalty to the Union and to the laws and proclamations concerning slavery. When 10 percent of the 1860 voters had sworn their allegiance, and had formed a loyal state government, republican in form, he would recognize the government. Mindful of a constitutional provision, he acknowledged Congress had the authority to seat members. So far as the freedmen were concerned, he would sanction any temporary arrangement consistent with their homeless condition, but providing for freedom and education.

Lincoln's amnesty plan, intended to undermine rebel resistance, was at first hailed by Congress. Second thoughts raised a doubt as to whether 10 percent was a sufficient base for a loyal government. More important, Congress took a stance that Reconstruction was a legislative, not an executive, prerogative. Rejecting Lincoln's leadership and leniency, Congress passed the Wade-Davis Bill, which insisted on a majority base for loyalty and the lawmakers' right to reconstruct the Union and to abolish slavery.

The measure won nearly unanimous Republican support, pitting the Republican Congress against the Republican president. Five opponents absented themselves. Lincoln vetoed the bill and by proclamation stated his reasons. He was not prepared to see set aside the free-state governments in Arkansas and Louisiana or to recognize the authority of Congress to abolish slavery.

The episode provoked the most serious crisis of the entire war between Lincoln and Congress. James G. Blaine, a Maine congressman, said that if Congress had been in session, "a very rancorous hostility would have been developed against the President" (Blaine, 2:43). Wade and Davis, the bill's sponsors, in an ugly manifesto cried, "A more studied outrage on the legislative authority of the people has never been perpetrated" (McPherson, 332).

In the subsequent session some members of Congress unsuccessfully sought to effect a compromise. Lincoln continued with his plan, and Louisiana became the focus of controversy. In his last public address, he argued in a characteristic figure of speech, "Concede that the new government of Louisiana is . . . as the egg is to the fowl, we shall sooner have the fowl by hatching the egg than by smashing it" (Basler, 8:404). Had he lived and persisted, a crisis of incalculable size might have erupted. At the same time, however, he gave a sign that he was moving in the Radicals' direction by favoring black suffrage.

A second challenge to Lincoln's leadership in 1864 arose when opposition to his reelection sprang up within his party. The first challenger was his Secretary of the Treasury, Salmon P. Chase (q.v.), whose name was put forward by a Kansas senator in a move that proved short-lived. Next came John Frémont, the party's nominee in 1856, whose candidacy enjoyed the backing of some Radical Republicans. Though Lincoln's control of party machinery effected a facile renomination, widespread internal opposition and a strong peace movement endangered his reelection. The Democrats' folly in adopting a peace plank almost simultaneously with General William T. Sherman's (q.v.) conquest of Atlanta dissipated the internal opposition, enabling Lincoln to retain office with a popular majority of 400,000.

Important tasks remained. There was congressional approval to readmit Louisiana, which Lincoln failed to secure. There was the war to conclude, for which he called upon an additional 300,000 men. There was the Thirteenth Amendment stalled in the House, which he pushed through to passage.

His second inaugural was a magnificent musing on the cause of the war: "One eighth of the whole population were colored slaves . . . localized in the Southern part of the [Union who] . . . constituted a peculiar and powerful interest" that divided the insurgents and the government. An increasingly pious president wondered whether "this mighty scourge of war" was God's punishment for the offense of slavery. He closed with memorable words intended to effect sectional reconciliation: "With malice toward none; with charity for all; with firmness in the right, as God gives us to see the right, let us strive on to finish the work we are in" (Basler, 8:332).

The work of war soon was finished; but assassination foreclosed the prospect of seeing sectional harmony and made Lincoln a martyr. The Civil War had lifted him to great leadership—first among all American presidents.

For three decades after Lincoln's death, men who had been close to Lincoln dominated biographical writing about him. William H. Herndon, who from 1844 was Lincoln's law partner, was an early shaper of the Lincoln portrait. Upon Lincoln's death, Herndon began assiduously collecting materials from people who had known Lincoln. He shared his trove with various Lincoln biographers.

Meanwhile, he gave a series of lectures on Lincoln in 1865–1866. In these he sought candor, producing consternation among Lincoln admirers. He portrayed a man who was greedy for public office, characterized by mind rather than heart, and not a formal Christian. He asserted that Lincoln's failure to appear for his wedding on January 1, 1841, was owing to temporary insanity. In a sensational lecture, he argued that the death of Ann Rutledge caused a melancholy that endured the rest of Lincoln's life. In 1889, Herndon collaborated with Jesse Weik to write *Herndon's Lincoln*, a book that challenged an apotheosis with its assertions that Lincoln's mother was illegitimate and reiterated the baleful effect of Ann Rutledge's death on Lincoln's life.

Ward Hill Lamon, associated with Lincoln in legal practice and marshal of the District of Columbia during the Civil War, was "my particular friend," the president said. Lamon bought transcripts of Herndon's notes and, in secret collaboration with a partisan Democrat, published *Life of Abraham Lincoln* in 1872. Like Herndon's book, it attempted a realistic portrayal. Lamon's Lincoln told earthy stories, had a shrewish wife, was of doubtful Christian piety, and was the child of a couple for whom there was no proof of marriage.

Isaac N. Arnold, who had known Lincoln as lawyer and president, was shocked by Lamon's book. He undertook to write a biography that would set matters right. Arnold conducted a wide search for materials, and in 1885 his *The Life of Abraham Lincoln* was published posthumously. The work, which among other topics asserted Lincoln was a religious man, for a time was the best biography of that leader.

John George Nicolay and John Hay, Lincoln's secretaries, who lived in the White House, wrote a comprehensive biography of the man they idolized. They owned the advantages of familiarity with their subject, a diary that Hay kept, notes that Nicolay made, and access to Lincoln's papers. They were the first and until 1947 the only biographers given access to the papers. Their *Abraham Lincoln: A History* appeared in ten stout volumes in 1890. Favoring Lincoln, partially censored by Lincoln's son Robert, it took its place as the most significant study of his life, presenting documents, opinions, and observations and devoting eight volumes to the presidency.

It remained to a twentieth-century generation to present a more balanced and accurate view. Leading the way was Ida M. Tarbell, a journalist, skilled writer, discoverer of new materials, open-minded yet critical. She interviewed Robert Todd Lincoln and Nicolay and stressed frontier influence on Lincoln. Her two-volume *The Life of Abraham Lincoln* appeared in 1900 and ran through eleven editions by 1928. Her book brought to light some 200 Lincoln items omitted by Nicolay and Hay in their two-volume edition of Lincoln's *Works*.

In 1917 a brilliant analysis of Lincoln appeared in a biography by Godfrey Charnwood, a Briton. Rather than finding new materials, he reflected deeply on what was in print. He asked penetrating questions; with a foreign perspective, he offered his judgments and saw Lincoln as a war strategist, a man who grew in religiosity as the war progressed; and in a world perspective, he limned his subject as a democrat, an emancipator, and a nationalist.

A thorough and fresh examination of Lincoln's life to 1858 appeared in two big volumes in 1928. The author's credentials included twelve years as an eminent U.S. senator and authorship of a four-volume life of John Marshall. Albert J. Beveridge possessed political insight and had a name that opened doors to correspondence with academic authorities and others. Beveridge searched for every fact he could discover, surprised to learn how little had been done about Lincoln's years in the Illinois legislature and in Congress. On Lincoln's early life he was skeptical about much of what had been written. A sturdy imperialist, Beveridge was dismayed by Lincoln's opposition to the Mexican War and saw little that was new in Lincoln's 1854 Peoria speech or in his debates with Douglas. Indeed, Douglas takes center stage. "How Douglas does loom up!" the Republican biographer exclaimed. Death closed Beveridge's account in 1858, before the years of greatness.

To his time, nonacademics had held the field of Lincoln biography. James G. Randall of the University of Illinois was the first major academic biographer. After publishing in 1926 a brilliant monograph, *Constitutional Problems under Lincoln*, he turned to writing a Lincoln biography, beginning where Beveridge had left off. Four volumes appeared between 1945 and 1955, the last completed by one of his students, Richard N. Current, himself a renowned Lincoln scholar. Randall cleared Lincoln of the charge that he maneuvered the Confederacy into starting the war, defended McClellan as general, discounted the possibility of foreign intervention, and provided a penetrating analysis of Lincoln's progress to emancipation.

The advent of Randall ushered in a series of professionally trained biographers. Benjamin P. Thomas, holder of a Ph.D. from Johns Hopkins University, in 1952 produced *Abraham Lincoln: A Biography*, which exploited the newly opened Robert Todd Lincoln Papers. Authoritative, reflecting Thomas's score of years as secretary of the Abraham Lincoln Association, balanced and well written, it took rank as the best one-volume life. A rival volume appeared in 1977 when Stephen B. Oates, recipient of a doctorate from the University of Texas, published *With Malice toward None: The Life of Abraham Lincoln*. Oates had the advantage of a quarter of a century research to draw on. He placed fresh emphasis on racism, Mary Todd Lincoln, and psychology. The author asserted he aimed to rescue Lincoln from the "mists of legend."

Mark E. Neely, Jr., for many years director of the Louis A. Warren Lincoln Library and Museum, possessing a doctorate from Yale University, in 1993 wrote *The Last Best Hope of Earth*. He focused on Lincoln's political life, particularly as president. A short book, written with erudition and insight, it had a sense for the times and admiration for the subject—but not without criticism—and furnished a brilliant chapter on Lincoln as commander in chief.

The following year another brilliant, informed study appeared, written by Phillip S. Paludan, who held a doctorate from the University of Illinois. *The Presidency of Abraham Lincoln* was from the hand of a specialist in constitutional history, who examined Lincoln through the prism of political-constitutional ideas. Paludan's Lincoln from the outset of his presidency had two goals—to save the nation and to free the slaves. The two goals were linked: Saving the Union would make possible freeing the slaves. With insight and a critical eye, Paludan freshly examined the Lincoln presidency.

In 1995 David Donald published *Lincoln*. Awarded a doctorate by the University of Illinois, where he had studied under James G. Randall, Donald launched his career with *Lincoln's Herndon* in 1948, at last providing a life of the controversial law partner and myth maker. A substantial volume of 600 pages, covering the whole life, and deeply researched, *Lincoln* portrayed a man who was a master politician, shaped by events, a moralist who was committed to reuniting the nation.

The next year a short biography appeared: James A. Rawley's *Abraham Lincoln and a Nation Worth Fighting For*. The work of a historian trained by Allan Nevins at Columbia University, it concentrated on the presidency, portraying Lincoln as president and commander in chief, dextrously using the latter role to justify his nonbelligerent acts such as suspension of the privilege of habeas corpus, emancipation of slaves, and reconstruction of the Union.

BIBLIOGRAPHY

Edward McPherson, *Political History of the Great Rebellion* (1865; New York: DaCapo Press, 1972).

Francis B. Carpenter, *Six Months at the White House with Abraham Lincoln* (New York: Hurd and Houghton, 1866).

Ward Hill Lamon, *Life of Abraham Lincoln* (Boston: J. R. Osgood, 1872).

Isaac N. Arnold, *The Life of Abraham Lincoln* (Chicago: James, McClurg, 1885).

James G. Blaine, *Twenty Years of Congress*, 2 vols. (Norwich, Conn.: Henry Bill Publ. Co., 1884–1886).

William H. Herndon and Jesse Weik, *Herndon's Lincoln*, 3 vols. (Chicago: Belford and Clark Co., 1889).

John George Nicolay and John Hay, *Abraham Lincoln: A History*, 10 vols. (New York: Century Co., 1890).

Ida M. Tarbell, *The Life of Abraham Lincoln*, 2 vols. (New York: Macmillan Co., 1900).

Godfrey Rathbone Benson Charnwood, *Abraham Lincoln* (New York: Garden City Publ. Co., 1921).

James G. Randall, *Constitutional Problems under Lincoln* (New York: D. Appleton, 1926).

Albert J. Beveridge, *Abraham Lincoln*, 2 vols. (Boston: Houghton Mifflin, 1928).

James G. Randall, *Lincoln, the President*, 4 vols. (New York: Dodd, Mead, 1945–1955).

Benjamin P. Thomas, *Abraham Lincoln: A Biography* (New York: Alfred Knopf, 1952).

Roy P. Basler (ed.), *Collected Works of Abraham Lincoln*, 8 vols. (New Brunswick: Rutgers University Press, 1953–1955).

Stephen B. Oates, *With Malice toward None: The Life of Abraham Lincoln* (New York: Harper and Row, 1977).

La Wanda Cox, *Lincoln and Black Freedom: A Study in Presidential Leadership* (Columbia: University of South Carolina Press, 1981).

Mark E. Neely, Jr., *The Last Best Hope of Earth* (Cambridge: Harvard University Press, 1993).

Phillip S. Paludan, *The Presidency of Abraham Lincoln* (Lawrence: University Press of Kansas, 1994).

David Herbert Donald, *Lincoln* (New York: Simon & Schuster, 1995).

James A. Rawley, *Abraham Lincoln and a Nation Worth Fighting For* (Chicago: Harlan Davidson, 1996).

JAMES LONGSTREET
(January 8, 1821–January 2, 1904)

Jon L. Wakelyn

"He served the rebel cause from Bull Run to the last day of Appomattox and ended his career as the respected senior corps leader of Lee's Army of Northern Virginia," stated Thomas L. Connelly and Barbara L. Bellows in 1982 in their reappraisal of famous general James Longstreet. But those authors' support for Longstreet's role in the war flies in the face of the near universal negative evaluations of his performance. Few Civil War military leaders who had served so well and so long have received the criticism from military historians that Longstreet has. Even despite the recent Longstreet revival, many scholars continue to insist that he failed the Southern cause when it counted. Some have attributed his shortcomings to an excessively defensive posture in a world of romantic and audacious Cavaliers. Others have claimed that Longstreet's post-war thoughtless attacks on General Robert E. Lee (q.v.) revealed his wartime insubordination. Still others have mingled what they believed was a lack of enthusiasm for the Confederate cause with his realistic yet naive acquiescence to the plans for Reconstruction of the Northern conquerors. In short, those who have analyzed his career have done so by judging Longstreet's flawed personal character and his loyalties and generally have dodged an assessment of his accomplishments. In order to give Longstreet's activities just reconsideration, the life of that great leader requires exploration.

In some ways the story begins before Longstreet was born, during the Revolutionary War era, when William Longstreet, the headstrong Dutchman and failed inventor, stubbornly took his family from New Jersey to unfamiliar South Carolina. William's son James, the father of the future Confederate general, was born in New Jersey. Young James, born in South Carolina's Edgefield district on January 8, 1821, was quite obviously destined to come under the influence of those stern Dutchmen. But his father died when he was young, and James's mother and his father's cotton-planter brother, the famous humorist and college president Judge Augustus B. Longstreet, together raised him. (Curiously, in his

Memoirs Longstreet does not mention the judge. Perhaps he wanted to separate himself from the extreme secessionist wing of his family.) His mother, Mary Ann Dent, from a Maryland planter family, with whom he was quite close, removed to Alabama with her children but left James to the care and schooling of his uncle Augustus. Raised in that still semi-frontier region of Piedmont Georgia, he hunted and played like most other rural Southern youths. But the family had other plans for him than the life of a farmer. His late father had recognized intelligence in young James and hoped someday to send him to the U.S. Military Academy. Although the family belonged to the class of small planters, no one in it had previously attended college. Living with his uncle, who understood the value of good preparation, young James was sent to private school and educated at home. Later he attended the Richmond County Academy, where he earned the reputation of being decisive and hardheaded. Uncle Augustus no doubt also taught him the ways of legal disputation, as he learned how to persuade others to his views. Well prepared and well treated, young James came to see himself as the center of family attention.

In 1838 he ventured north to the cold and unfriendly banks of the Hudson River to face an unfamiliarly regimented life. At times Longstreet rebelled against the rigid army educational system. He did not like school, and his conduct at times was poor. But in some areas Longstreet thrived. He became known as a man's man, quite popular among the hardheaded old Yorkers and resented by those from romantic Virginia. Surely friends came easily, but his own kind of snobbishness based on strength and endurance made him a problem for some. A close friend, U. S. Grant (q.v.), then called "Sam," would loom large in his later life. Quite obviously, friends and soldierly training—he rode well and led well—meant more than studies to that young man. Early in his days at the academy the curriculum nearly defeated him, and James almost had to leave school because of poor grades. But he always managed to take advantage of second chances, and with short bursts of intense work, he pulled through. Fifty-fourth in the 1842 class of fifty-six, he was relegated to the lowly infantry, but that was where he wanted to be.

Longstreet entered the military in dull peace times, and his first assignment to confront Indians at Jefferson Barrack in Missouri he found tedious and dull. He also did not like to take orders. Soon, however, his ambitions got the best of him, and he became known as an organized and well-prepared soldier who in turn could train his troops. Longstreet also took up again with his old classmate Grant. Grant was to join Longstreet's extended family when he married Julia Dent, a cousin of the Georgian's mother. Longstreet also met and fell in love with Maria Louisa Garland of Virginia, whose family had military connections. His peaceful career, though dull in routine and filled with friends, soon was to change after Longstreet was sent to the Louisiana border in 1844. Stationed in Florida in 1845 to guard against the threat of an Indian uprising, he gained promotion to second lieutenant.

Later in 1845 Longstreet was placed under General Zachary Taylor and went with him to Texas. Although in his memoirs he said little about his service in the Mexican War, save that he came to understand the value of studying hostile terrain, that war would reveal him to be a talented fighter. He fought at Palo Alto and at Resaca de la Palma early in the war, and he distinguished himself at Monterrey. Longstreet was rewarded for his accomplishments in 1847 with the rank of first lieutenant and made adjutant in charge of supplies. He then gained a transfer to serve under General Winfield Scott and became that famous general's supply officer. But Longstreet was not partial to such inaction, and he managed to persuade the general to allow him to take part in all of the overland battles from Vera Cruz to Mexico City. Wounded at Molina del Ray, he still served at Chapultepec in the decisive battle of the war. During the Mexican War, Longstreet displayed traits that would become his trademark as a soldier. Bravery under fire and intense physical stamina led others to believe he was fearless and never tired. But most of all he learned more than the textbooks had taught about how to maneuver troops to best advantage. He also had seen how well the concentration of force behind barriers worked.

After his duties in the Mexican War had ended, Longstreet married Maria and thus in 1848 joined, perhaps reluctantly, the Virginia planter society. But he was not to stay settled for long. Longstreet held numerous military duties, including service at Carlisle Barracks with Grant and as a commissary officer in Texas in 1849. His family soon grew, but Longstreet was a cold father, unlike others who talked of leaving the army and settling down with their families. The thought of becoming a Virginia squire never appealed to him, as even years of boredom in frontier duty fighting Indians never tempted him to resign. In 1858 he was promoted to major, then sent to Kansas to help calm divisions in that frontier territory.

In those duties along the border, Longstreet often was reminded that he came from the South and that his country was being torn apart. Usually silent about his beliefs, there remains much confusion over his plans as secession loomed. Jeffrey Wert, his most recent biographer, has called him devious and claims he had a secret military commission, or offer of one, from the Confederate government before he resigned from the U.S. Army. What is clear is that the threat of Civil War made much difficulty for him, because he was trained enough in the art of warfare to know that the South faced a long conflict ahead. Nevertheless, Longstreet chose to join his mother's adopted state of Alabama's army and became its senior professional soldier. In June 1861, President Jefferson Davis (q.v.) brought him to Richmond, appointed him a brigadier, and put him under Pierre G. T. Beauregard (q.v.) around Manassas. From then until the war's end he would usually serve under great leaders and in the thick of battle. No other corps commander would fight in as many engagements or perform so consistently at such a high level.

There were signs, however, quite early in the war that Longstreet would not be satisfied serving under others. He certainly believed, perhaps justifiably, that his military judgment was of the highest quality. Near Manassas the new brigadier took charge of ''green'' troops, marched, drilled, and cared for them, and turned them into loyal and able fighting men. Ordered to build field works near Bull Run, he was to become a hero in the defense of Blackbrine Ford. When under attack there, he rallied his troops, held the line, and mounted a brisk counterattack. Longstreet's appearance of self-confidence energized the able staff with which he surrounded himself, and they assisted him admirably when he turned to the offensive. In fact, Longstreet was one of the Confederate generals who believed that after the victory at Manassas he could lead his men to Washington. He was sadly disillusioned when those plans were dropped. Again he drilled troops. Then the Georgian was given line command of four Virginia regiments, and he traveled with them to Fairfax Court House to protect against a Yankee attack that did not materialize. Rough, blunt, and early confident in his own abilities, when recognition of his deeds was not forthcoming, he talked of resignation. But on October 7, 1861, he was promoted finally to major general.

Soon, however, horrible discord entered Longstreet's life. First and worst, three of his children died that fall, and his grief knew no end. Those who were close to him believed Longstreet then became the dour Dutchman of postwar folklore. Next, his loyalty to Beauregard and Joseph Johnston (q.v.) made President Davis wonder about his judgment. The president thought him too political and unreliable. But fighting once again intervened to take Longstreet's mind off his personal and political problems as Union Commander George B. McClellan (q.v.) advanced up the Peninsula of Virginia in late spring 1862. When McClellan divided his troops in May 1862, Longstreet advised his commander General Johnston to make a right turning movement. He was to be a major part of that maneuver. His means of fighting, learned early in the war, was to keep his own counsel, say few words, give direct orders, and then stay out of his men's way. But from May 31 to June 1, at Seven Pines, that policy backfired, and he failed for the first time. Slow, stubborn, refusing to reinforce his troops, even ignorant of the fighting in front of him, he was forced to give way, and the movement failed. When his friend and protector Johnston was wounded and forced to give up command, Longstreet wondered if President Davis had gone daft when he named Robert E. Lee as commander of the entire eastern army. Did the Virginia gentleman Lee, the beautiful and brilliant staff officer, understand fighting? said Longstreet rhetorically. Whatever his reservations, Longstreet would join Lee, and the two would make a great, though often strained, military marriage.

Lee certainly knew how to use ''Ole Pete,'' as he called Longstreet. The two would gain much fame in the month of June 1862. At Mechanicsville, Gaines Mill, and Frayser's Farm, Longstreet fought well. Even at the debacle of Malvern Hill he managed a gallant retreat to live to fight again. Lee's confidence in his general during the Seven Days battles produced a calm leader who knew how to use the best strengths of his own subordinates. But Longstreet's seeming need for attention from Lee provoked disagreement with the Virginian Ambrose Powell Hill, which earned the Georgian the enmity of many a Virginia general.

If he had had success in the later stages of the Peninsula campaign, during the summer and early fall of 1862, Longstreet would earn mixed reviews as a warrior. At Second Manassas, his careful, slow, at times uncooperative activities, some said, allowed Yankee General John Pope to escape back to Washington. The famous Lee biographer and apologist Douglas S. Freeman accused him of violating Lee's orders for an attack on August 29. In reality, Longstreet had taken the battle to the enemy, had sustained many casualties, and had again earned Lee's gratitude. He became his leader's most trusted adviser, and when Lee wanted to invade Maryland in September 1862, Longstreet reluctantly went along. Perhaps he supported that Maryland invasion in order to find food for his hungry troops. However, when Lee divided the army and sent Stonewall Jackson (q.v.) on a wild goose chase to Harpers Ferry, Longstreet at last demurred. Still, on September 17, he helped to save Lee's army by standing bravely at the infamous "Bloody Lane." After the debacle at Sharpsburg, Longstreet vigorously made judgments about his subordinates. He praised the activities of that much underrated warrior Daniel H. Hill and arrested John Bell Hood (q.v.) for his sloppy behavior. Perhaps that cautious general who liked to fight on terrain of his own choosing was so vicious to his own lieutenants because he had sustained 40 percent in casualties, a figure that appalled such a man beloved of his troops.

After Sharpsburg, Lee crept back into Virginia. On October 9, 1862, he named Longstreet lieutenant general and put him in charge of one of the two corps of the newly reorganized Army of Northern Virginia. Together the two vowed never to lose such numbers of troops again. They developed the idea of a tactical defense and a strategic offense. At Fredericksburg in December 1862, in the defense against General Ambrose Burnside's attempted offensive, Longstreet revealed the genius of the tactical defense. He dug in and deployed his famed artillery officer E. Porter Alexander on Marye's Heights, the hills behind the city and south of the Rappahannock River. Longstreet then built major field works and awaited the foolish Burnside's attack. Almost single-handedly his troops slaughtered the Union offensive and proved the strength of entrenched, defensive firepower. But Longstreet did not handle success well. He quarreled with Hood and minced no words about his desire for independent command. The hero of Fredericksburg wanted to go west, to join his old commander Joseph E. Johnston, and to mount a defense of Tennessee.

But Lee had other plans for his unruly subordinate. During the late winter of 1863 the First Corps was sent to Petersburg to use that southern Virginia city as a base to protect North Carolina as well as to gather food for the spring offensive. Longstreet took part in the Suffolk campaign of April 1863, in a successful raid to protect the North Carolina coast. In doing so he never did get to participate in the May 1863 battle at Chancellorsville, where Jackson died. In reality, what Longstreet was planning, since he saw the war whole, was a major strike to relieve beleaguered Vicksburg. Certainly an ally of what Thomas L. Connelly called the Western Bloc, Longstreet wanted to use the idea of an interior line of battle to concentrate against the Union Army under William Rosecrans in Tennessee. With Lee in Virginia, Longstreet in Tennessee, and Johnston in Mississippi, the Union would face a coordinated Confederate Army, well supplied from its rear. Instead of supporting the simultaneous actions of three major Confederate armies, Lee persuaded Longstreet to support yet another Maryland invasion, an act that would forever damage the Georgian's reputation because of that fateful place called Gettysburg.

As the Army of Northern Virginia crossed the Mason-Dixon line during that summer of 1863, Longstreet wondered if it would be possible to force the Union Army to attack where the Confederates wanted them to. The answer was no, because General George Meade (q.v.) commanded the enemy. So after the first day at Gettysburg, on the evening of July 1, 1863, Longstreet advised either a turning movement or a tactical retreat. Instead, Lee ordered his ''Old Warhorse'' to take the tactical offense on the second. Historians have said Longstreet was slow to attack the Union left flank, that he took too long to march, and that his failure allowed the Yankees to reinforce Little Round Top. Anyone who has seen that peach orchard can only wonder whether any Confederate general could have prevailed that day. Badly defeated, angry and sulky, Longstreet still hoped to maneuver Meade into attacking on the third of July. Instead, his commander ordered a frontal assault that Longstreet did not believe in. Indeed, Longstreet's deployment was probably flawed, although the gallant, stupid George Pickett would curse Lee, not Longstreet, for the destruction of his division. Again, Longstreet was proved correct. But he found no solace in the fact. The Army of Northern Virginia would never again fight an offensive battle. After the retreat back to Virginia, Longstreet nearly begged to transfer west. Lee accommodated him.

What Longstreet hoped to gain in that assignment to north Georgia and east Tennessee, his most recent biographer claims, was command of an independent western army. Certainly his ties to Texas Senator Louis Wigfall (q.v) and his certainty of the failure of Confederate commander General Braxton Bragg (q.v.) may have spurred Longstreet to grandiose dreams. But the truth is probably simpler. He wanted to get away from Lee and the memory of Gettysburg, and he desired to defend his homeland of Georgia. Once again, Longstreet would reveal his genius, slowness, stubbornness, ambition, and pettiness. Unfamiliar at first with the terrain around Chickamauga, he studied his position, employed the concentration of force, and became a hero at Chickamauga between September 20 and 23, 1863. Again, he did not lead personally but instead gave the orders to attack with superior numbers and prevailed. He had displayed his ability to learn and to grow as a commander. Then he ruined it all. Longstreet's role in the plot to get rid of Bragg, though Bragg needed getting rid of, failed, and Bragg would not trust him in combat again. In late October 1863, at Lookout Mountain, Longstreet seemed to willfully misunderstand Bragg's orders, and the two leaders never coordinated their efforts. To save what remained of the western command structure, President Davis transferred Longstreet to east Tennessee. There, poor supplies, inadequate transport, and too few troops doomed him to fail against Burnside, of all men, at Knoxville. Longstreet's assaults over poor land against superior forces nearly destroyed his troops, men he had so carefully cultivated to believe that he would protect them at all cost. The general lashed out, blamed subordinates, sought revenge in time of war, and failed miserably. He then countered his critics with plans for a major Kentucky offensive, but no one would go along. Finally, in April 1864, the Georgian was ordered back to the Army of Northern Virginia.

Once again in the arms of Lee, he would take part in the foolhardy defense of Richmond. Longstreet faced his best friend Grant at the Battle of the Wilderness on May 6, 1864. Again, he was slow to let the battle develop, but he used the advantage of favorable terrain to counterattack and assist the Confederacy in an amazing delaying action. But his own troops shot him mistakenly, paralyzing his right arm and forcing months of recovery time at home with his family. Longstreet journeyed to Georgia to heal his wounds and salve his conscience. Back in Virginia with Lee in October, he played again the role of the great defender in the trenches around Petersburg. At the end, long knowing that the Confederacy could not prevail, he nevertheless advised Lee to hold out. Was Longstreet just being perverse? Wisely, Lee surrendered.

Longstreet's own wartime record was mixed, to be sure. But certainly those around him at the war's end regarded him as the best corps commander of the Army of Northern Virginia. Wert, his latest and most careful biographer, insists: "History had a part of Longstreet now. In its hands he would not be accorded the status he had earned on some of the conflict's greatest battlefields" (404). But Wert's timing was surely a bit off, for the initial response to Longstreet's actions were favorable. Perhaps the historian was referring to how soon Longstreet would exercise his own inimitable talent for hurting himself.

The general's activities during the postwar period certainly figure into history's treatment of him, and in those actions he caused great troubles for himself. First, he accepted the $100 the Yankee army gave him at the war's end. Then Longstreet met with his family in northern Virginia to decide on their future. Practical, shrewd, and deeply committed to success, the ex-general settled in New Orleans, the city poised to return to its prewar opulence through trade along the Mississippi. Longstreet bought in to a New Orleans cotton trade business and began to thrive financially. He then went to Washington to try to obtain a pardon from President Andrew Johnson (q.v.), perhaps because he knew that he must make peace with the victors and get along with his civilian career. Johnson turned him down, but in 1868, his close friend U. S. Grant helped him obtain that pardon. Longstreet had begun to look to the future, to a new South that could use its rich land to produce the goods that would restore its wealth and allow it to become an industrial power. In an act that would soon come back to haunt him, on March 18, 1867, he published an article in which he identified himself as a Republican, instructed the South to acquiesce in equality for ex-slaves, and supported other Northern demands. Longstreet next became active in New Orleans Republican politics. Then President Grant named him to the lucrative post of Surveyor of Customs in 1869. Longstreet also assumed the thankless task as head of the local militia. When called to quell a race riot, he used federal troops to fire on ex-Confederate soldiers, was temporarily put under arrest by the Southerners, and his life was threatened. More than that, he became for many Southerners, especially Democrats, not a visionary but a hated ''scalawag.''

Perhaps because of these suicidal political actions, even if financially profitable and displaying a certain practicality, ''Old Pete'' became the victim of a publishing industry that sought profit in exploiting the doctrine of the Lost Cause. Put simply, many ex-Confederates would neither accept defeat nor the loss of what they believed was an idyllic plantation South. So, the idea that the war should have been won by superior Southern leaders if the South had not been undermined by a few failed military and political leaders began to appear in selected publications. Led by Virginians such as Jubal Early, a propaganda industry grew up to deify General Lee and, of course, seek scapegoats on whom to blame defeat. Although Lee himself had borne the responsibility for the failure at Gettysburg and thus the irreversible slide to defeat, Longstreet, the turncoat Republican, soon became the target of the Lost Cause propagandists. His slowness on that famous second day, July 2, became in their view the single cause of defeat. Where Longstreet had urged caution and retreat in the face of superior force, that caution was turned into slowness and disloyalty, and the once famous corps commander became in the eyes of Virginians the man who lost the war. Longstreet, practical, litigious, and enormously proud, responded in kind. In article after article, he matched the Virginians' venom with a supposed reasoned defense of his actions. Ostracized by some former friends, in constant pain from his wartime wounds, he sought to set the record straight by attacking the very General Lee who had become the symbol of all that was good about the Old South. He could not win that battle for history, and he became the enemy of all loyal Southerners.

But the ex-general soldiered on. In 1870 he became a railroad president in New Orleans. As Republican party power began to ebb in the rapidly reconstructing lower South, Longstreet attempted to extricate himself from that political and emotional burden. In 1875 he moved to Georgia, bought a farm and opened a tourist hotel, and brooded over his dwindling wartime reputation. As he grew older his behavior became increasingly aberrant. Longstreet often attended Confederate reunions where he was mostly welcomed by aging ordinary soldiers and derided by ex-officers bent on helping their political careers. He would put on the old uniform and perhaps dream and reconstruct his own wartime career. In 1889 his wife died. He also began his memoirs in hopes of telling his side of the story in depth, and he remarried. Longstreet's second wife, Helen Dortch, much younger than himself, turned into the keeper of his reputation. She urged him to complete his memoirs, helped to edit them, and established a correspondence with his ex-subordinates such as E. P. Alexander to rebuild the phalanx of support for his place in history. Also during the 1890s, the "Old Warhorse" became U.S. commissioner of railroads, largely a token if also lucrative position, and one that reconfirmed to his enemies that he had sold out.

In 1896 at last appeared the long-awaited *From Manassas to Appomattox: Memoirs of the Civil War in America*. The publisher had large sales, printed a second edition in 1903, and a third in 1960. The *Memoirs* were Longstreet's detailed answers to all who had criticized him. The efforts of that ex-general, now grown old, forgetful, and pained in body and soul, make for fascinating reading on many levels. For one, they showed how faulty memory could use selected records to rewrite the past. Second, they capture just how much personal historical place meant to that great leader. And third, they reveal once again the precise legal mind, the detailed tactician, the brilliant defender of and user of men, the leader who grasped the importance of war along interior lines, and a man who seemed to falter when given the task of conducting an entire campaign. Longstreet's wartime treatment of Braxton Bragg is revealed here even as more self-serving and devious. In recounting action after action, Longstreet defended himself, gave excuses, blamed others. But there is more to this work than the feeble old warrior trying to regain a place in history. There is his shrewd argument that he had become the victim of the Lost Cause in part because he opposed a romantic defense of the image of Old Virginia. In those *Memoirs* Longstreet also questioned the cause: As a general, he stated the South could never win; as a practical man, he stated the South should never have won. On January 2, 1904, he died, full of pain and regret. In 1905 his widow continued the task of restructuring his reputation, as she sought to show that he had always been a loyal Confederate.

How has history treated the man Lee called the "Old Bull of the Woods" and the finest Corps commander in the Confederate Army? The judgments of Edward A. Pollard (q.v.) in *Lee and His Lieutenants* (1867) that Longstreet was slow and of Mary B. Chesnut that he was dull and devious were used by the Virginia revisionists to bury him. Only the memoirs of Edward P. Alexander (1907) tried to show him in a good light as a fine warrior on the defense. Longstreet's own arguments for his reputation made matters worse, and the first generation of professional historians tended to agree. General Gamaliel Bradford, in *Confederate Portraits* (1914), judged him as neither brainy nor speedy. With psychological daring, Bradford suggested that maybe Longstreet's self-confidence hurt him. Certainly, insisted Bradford, his jealousy made for bitter recrimination against lesser subordinates.

The first major attempt at a dispassionate view of Longstreet's accomplishments, Donald B. Sanger and Thomas R. Hay's *James Longstreet* (1952), praised him for his leadership and tactical abilities but questioned whether he had strategic brilliance. Their verdict was that "on his own, Longstreet was never an effective force, either in peace or in war" (444). But Sanger and Hay at least give him credit for elevating able subordinates and for attempting to be a team player. In the 1960s, Michael Shaara's brilliant historical novel *The Killer Angels* appeared to rekindle interest in Longstreet's actions at Gettysburg. The talented Floridian Shaara, in his praise for that general's caution, perhaps identified more with Longstreet's Georgia than with Lee's Virginia. At any rate, Longstreet's reputation was on the road to recovery. Added to this revision of the record was the brilliant work of Thomas L. Connelly and Barbara L. Bellows, *God and General Longstreet* (1982), a further upgrading of Longstreet through an attack on Lee, the Lost Cause, and the Virginia revisionists. Connelly later unleashed his student William Garrett Piston, who wrote *Lee's Tarnished Lieutenant* (1987). Piston showed in much detail how Longstreet's reputation had been destroyed in the battles of the memoirists and the postwar historians. But Piston made no case for Longstreet's real accomplishments. That was left most recently to Jeffrey D. Wert in *General James Longstreet* (1993). Wert regards Longstreet as the ''Confederacy's most controversial soldier'' (subtitle), and in minute detail he reconstructs where Longstreet succeeded and failed. The judgment on success is mixed, but Wert nevertheless has done excellent service to Longstreet's memory. Best of all, says Wert, his men knew ''he had the soul of a soldier and they never forgot it'' (13).

Indeed, ''Old Pete'' never wanted to endanger his troops unnecessarily, believed in the use of superior force, and knew that all too frequently his Confederacy could not muster that force. Perhaps that is the best verdict on the man's abilities that history will allow. Longstreet understood that the Confederacy could never win the war and that too much had been invested in the defense of Virginia. Did his actions betray those convictions?

BIBLIOGRAPHY

Edward A. Pollard, *Lee and His Lieutenants* (New York: E. B. Treat & Co., 1867).

James Longstreet, *From Manassas to Appomattox: Memoirs of the Civil War in America* (1896; Bloomington: Indiana University Press, 1960).

Helen Dortch Longstreet, *Lee and Longstreet at High Tide: Gettysburg in the Light of the Official Record* (Gainesville, Ga.: Helen Dortch Longstreet, 1905).

Edward Porter Alexander, *Military Memoirs of a Confederate* (New York: Charles Scribner's Sons, 1907).

Gamaliel Bradford, *Confederate Portraits* (Boston: Houghton Mifflin, 1914).

Thomas L. Connelly and Barbara L. Bellows, *God and General Longstreet: The Lost Cause and the Southern Mind* (Baton Rouge: Louisiana State University Press, 1952).

Donald B. Sanger and Thomas R. Hay, *James Longstreet* (Baton Rouge: Louisiana State University Press, 1952).

C. Vann Woodward, ed., *Mary Chesnut's Civil War* (New Haven: Yale University Press, 1981).

William Garrett Piston, *Lee's Tarnished Lieutenant: James Longstreet and His Place in Southern History* (Athens: University of Georgia Press, 1987).

Jeffrey D. Wert, *General James Longstreet* (New York: Simon & Schuster, 1993).

GEORGE BRINTON MCCLELLAN
(December 3, 1826–October 29, 1885)

Thomas J. Rowland

Union commander of the Army of the Potomac until October 1862, General George B. McClellan was born on December 3, 1826, in the comfortable surroundings of his family home in Philadelphia. His father, Dr. George McClellan, a renowned physician, had founded the Jefferson Medical College and enjoyed a successful ophthalmological practice. His mother, Elizabeth Steinmetz Brinton, came from a leading Philadelphia family and was viewed as a woman of considerable grace and refinement. Despite Dr. McClellan's evident stature, the practice of medicine was not so financially rewarding in those days, a circumstance that only compounded the outstanding debts he had inherited from his own father. Moreover, the financial constraints placed upon the family by sending the eldest son John to medical school played a role in guiding his second son, George, to a free education at West Point.

George McClellan was the middle sibling among five. In addition to John, there was an older sister, Frederica, and a younger brother and sister, Arthur and Mary, respectively. Personal fortunes notwithstanding, the McClellans saw to it that no expense was spared in young George's education. As a child he benefited from instruction in private school and was tutored by a trained scholar of the classics. Prior to his admission to West Point, he enrolled in a preparatory academy at the University of Pennsylvania. Two years later, at the tender age of thirteen, he entered the university itself. Excelling in school, McClellan had nearly completed the curriculum in the spring of 1842 when his father engineered his nomination and eventual acceptance to West Point. When academy officials waived the minimum age requirement for entrance in McClellan's favor, he arrived there as the youngest cadet in his class, six months shy of his sixteenth birthday.

After a brief bout of homesickness, McClellan flourished at the Point. By all accounts, he was well liked and respected, and most of his classmates believed he was the most promising of all in the class of 1846. One of his instructors,

Erasmus Keyes, who later would serve briefly as one of his divisional commanders, recalled that McClellan was a cooperative and intelligent student. McClellan excelled in all of his studies, save drawing, which he found difficult and which earmarked him for a class filing only behind Charles Seaforth Stewart. An ambitious young man, McClellan was disappointed with his second-place ranking, and although he never allowed it to poison his relationship with fellow cadets, he did complain about it in a letter to his sister Frederica. Most of his classmates predicted that he—George McClellan—would be the shining star in the military firmament in the years ahead. As was true in most graduating classes, however, class rank generally was no prescient indicator of future stardom. In the class of 1846, Thomas "Stonewall" (q.v.) Jackson struggled to achieve seventeenth place, and few saw any promise in him. Moreover, Stewart would serve in relative obscurity during the war, attaining but a colonel's commission in the last year, while Cadmus Wilcox, who ranked near the bottom at fifty-fourth, became one of Lee's best division commanders.

Socially, McClellan mixed best with those cadets who hailed from the South. Jimmy Stuart, Dabney Maury, Cadmus Wilcox, and Ambrose Powell Hill were among his closest friends. This affinity for aristocratic Southerners gave McClellan what he believed to be a solid understanding of the Southern mind. This insight into Southern culture would at times aid, while at other times handicap, his appreciation of the political and military implications to the sectional debates leading to the outbreak of civil war.

Cadets of McClellan's generation imbibed deeply from the teachings of engineering, fortifications, and military tactics instructor Dennis Hart Mahan and from the theoretical strategic principles of Baron Henri von Jomini, a Swiss military historian who had served under Napoleon Bonaparte. McClellan excelled in Mahan's class and received the expressed approbation of this instructor. Years later, while serving a tour of duty at the Point, he would join Mahan's exclusive Napoleon Club, where he delivered a number of speeches based upon his widespread readings in military history. While most of his generation had also intently studied Jomini, few like McClellan had as broad and deep an understanding of this theorist.

No sooner had McClellan graduated from West Point and received his commission as brevet second lieutenant in the highly regarded corps of engineers than the Mexican War broke out. He arrived in Mexico in October 1846 and was assigned to General Winfield Scott's staff. There he participated in the amphibious invasion and subsequent siege of Vera Cruz, where his engineering talents were first tested. At Cerro Gordo, McClellan learned the beauty of a well-executed flanking maneuver that completely surprised Santa Anna's army. It was a lesson he took to heart, and to his own thinking, he emulated this feat in his campaign in western Virginia in 1861. He also played conspicuous roles in the battles for the approaches to the Mexican capital, particularly at Contreras, Churubusco, and Chapultepec. Following these battles, he earned two brevet promotions, and he ended the war as a breveted captain. After serving several months in the occupying army, he was assigned to duty at West Point. In addition to the valuable battlefield experience he gained in Mexico, McClellan also came away with an undisguised contempt for volunteer soldiers, particularly when commanded by political figures who cared nothing for discipline and training. In this regard, McClellan was not alone in his sentiments, as virtually all regular officers in the old line army felt exactly the same.

With the restoration of peace, junior officers like McClellan resumed their former grades and could expect long years of boring posting as they awaited turnover in the top-heavy seniority system. McClellan, however, received a progression of interesting and challenging assignments. Following his tour at West Point, he worked briefly on the ongoing construction of Fort Delaware before arriving at Fort Smith, Arkansas, to begin exploration along the Red River of Texas and Oklahoma. In his assignment as the party's engineer, he met his commanding officer and future father-in-law Captain Randolph P. Marcy, one of the few senior officers he liked during this stage of his career. After a brief stint along the Gulf Coast of Texas, McClellan was invited by a former engineering officer, territorial governor Isaac Stevens, to survey the land upon which a proposed transcontinental railroad, running from St. Paul, Minnesota, to the Puget Sound, would be built. He argued with Stevens over the best routes through the passes of the Cascades, even refusing in the end to supply the governor with his survey journal for the drafting of a report. Finally, in 1855, McClellan, who had only recently been promoted to first lieutenant, received his commission as captain of the newly created First Cavalry. This recognition also garnered the attention of then Secretary of War Jefferson Davis (q.v.), who selected McClellan as a military observer to the Crimean War.

McClellan was hugely flattered by his selection and was determined to absorb as much information and insight into European military tactics as he could. He became bored and impatient with the inordinate delays that greeted the commission before he could get to the scene of the fighting at Sevastopol, where he would become fascinated with the progress of the siege there. At one point he would write his brother John that he had become exasperated with his fellow commissioners, Majors Richard Delafield and Alfred Mordecai, declaring them out of touch with military affairs. This remark has been seen by many McClellan observers as consistent with his penchant for expressing discontent and impatience with superior officers. Yet it does not seem to be particularly unusual for the time. Many junior officers complained of the social and professional stagnation while serving under older men. During his first assignment, Ulysses Grant (q.v.) wrote to his wife Julia that of his two superior officers one was "a preacher and the other a member of the Church" and that he doubted he would ever be able to raise a "game of Euchre with them" (*Personal Memoirs* 1:29). As for McClellan, upon his return from Europe, he spent several months drafting his share of the report, which was published in 1857. His analysis of the siege and the organization of European armies was so well received that many perceived its author as one of the leading national military authorities. It was reissued in 1861 when the Civil War broke out. Upon completion of this report, McClellan resigned his commission and left the army on January 15, 1857.

In the handful of years before the onset of hostilities, McClellan served in numerous executive capacities for a couple of important regional railroads. He proved to be a very capable and energetic administrator. During this time, his services were sought by those who desired his military expertise in the many filibustering schemes throughout South America, but he prudently declined. Nevertheless, McClellan continued to keep abreast of military affairs, and he relished studying engineering and military history. After several years of contested courtship, he married Ellen Marcy on May 22, 1860. Following a brief sojourn in Chicago, the couple settled in Cincinnati, where the outbreak of civil war would find them. It proved to be a loving and nurturing relationship, marked by detailed correspondence during times of separation. The content and nature of these exchanges, however, would have decidedly deleterious implications for the McClellan legacy.

Days after the firing upon Fort Sumter, George McClellan accepted the position of major general of volunteers and commander of all troops from the state of Ohio. He quickly launched himself into the great task of readying the hastily mustered volunteers into a respectable fighting force, a trait that became the one generally undisputed hallmark of his career. The western Virginian campaign began on June 2, 1861, when McClellan's forces commanded by Thomas A. Morris routed a Confederate force at Philippi. McClellan joined his troops near Grafton on June 23. Opposing him on Rich Mountain was a Confederate force under the command of Robert S. Garnett. By a series of flanking maneuvers, McClellan and his leading brigadier, William Rosecrans, helped to turn Garnett out of his position, forcing him to retreat toward Beverly. There in a brief skirmish on July 13, Garnett was killed, and the remainder of his force hurried eastward, narrowly avoiding complete capture. Despite his impressive and comprehensive triumph, McClellan had not seen any of the hard fighting that Rosecrans had at Rich Mountain, as he was confused by the late start of the engagement and the precise meaning of the ferocious cannonading that accompanied it. Nonetheless, it had been his strategy that had defeated the rebels in western Virginia and destroyed any hope the Confederacy had for retaining this region in its fold. His victory here was welcome news in the North, especially in light of the Federal defeat at Manassas the following week. It had the effect of confirming earlier opinions of McClellan's promise and most certainly was instrumental in his being wired by Scott on July 22 to come to Washington to take command of the army there.

Throughout the remainder of the summer and well into the fall of 1861, McClellan was absorbed with the mission of creating, training, and disciplining what would become known as the Army of the Potomac—the largest assembled fighting force in American history—capable of waging successful offensive warfare. By nearly all accounts, he succeeded beyond all expectations, and this feat generally is viewed as his one inviolable contribution to the Northern war effort.

It began with his establishing martial law in the capital in the wake of the defeat and return of General Irvin McDowell's army. From there, he instituted organized instruction in drilling and training for the large number of recruits who streamed into Washington following Lincoln's call for volunteers. He addressed significant deficiencies in the officer corps by establishing qualifications for leadership that saw a large number of incompetent front line officers weeded out of the army. By the fall of 1861 he had transformed an immature, ill-trained collection of volunteers into a respectable fighting force.

The same public clamor to march on Richmond that had forced Abraham Lincoln (q.v.) to order McDowell out to Manassas in July had by October 1861 swelled to a chorus, placing overwhelming demands upon the president and cabinet to demand McClellan use this magnificent army of his. Despite indicating that the Army of the Potomac would be ready to march by December 1, it appears as though McClellan never intended to assume the offensive until the following spring. Lincoln did his best to ward off the radical wing of his party that was demanding either a movement by McClellan or his dismissal, but McClellan came to see the president as one with that clique. The distrust that began to build up between the commander in chief and his principal subordinate would ultimately affect the course of McClellan's spring campaign.

As the new year unfolded, Lincoln decided to force McClellan to share his strategic plans for all the Federal armies in the field, but particularly the one he commanded himself. Lincoln's executive order at the end of January, demanding that Federal armies begin campaigning by February 22, prompted McClellan to divulge his plans. In a lengthy memorandum, February 3, 1862, McClellan revealed that all Union armies would act in concert to begin the process of crushing the rebellion. The Army of the Potomac would play the principal role, and McClellan proposed a sweeping waterborne maneuver to bring his army between Joseph E. Johnston's (q.v.) at Manassas and Richmond. This was the genesis of the Urbana Plan. When Johnston suddenly pulled up stakes and moved his army below the Rappahannock River, the plan was altered to move the army to the base of the peninsula formed by the York and James Rivers. Lincoln doubted the benefits of this plan, preferring instead that the army march directly south to encounter the enemy. In the end, however, he gave his blessing with the proviso that McClellan attend to the defenses of the capital while the bulk of the army was away. The argument over whether McClellan fulfilled this condition would play a significant role in the progress of what became known as the Peninsula Campaign. Moreover, shortly after embarking for the peninsula, McClellan learned through the New York newspapers that he had been removed from overall command of the movement of Federal armies and relegated to sole command of the Army of the Potomac.

On April 1, McClellan set sail for the peninsula, trailing his huge flotilla of Union warships and transports already en route for Fortress Monroe. From the outset, things did not go according to plan. The day before his departure Lincoln had informed him that a division of McDowell's corps was being retained to deal with the first of several diversionary forays into the Shenandoah Valley by Stonewall Jackson. Moreover, all thoughts of establishing a base of operations up the James River were thwarted by the presence of the still formidable C.S.S. *Virginia* in anchorage at the Confederate naval base at Norfolk. Then, after marching the army up to Yorktown, McClellan could not obtain the navy's assistance in turning the defenses there by an amphibious invasion further up the York River. This left no choice but to overpower the Confederate force at Yorktown. As he was mulling over how to deal with this option, he learned that the remainder of McDowell's 40,000-man corps was being retained by Lincoln to help deal with confirmed reports of Jackson's activity in the valley.

McClellan's decision to reduce the fortifications at Yorktown by a textbook siege proved to be the wrong one. He spent nearly an entire month in this effort against a smaller defending force under John Bankhead Magruder that dazzled Union scouts with theatrical movements aimed at making McClellan believe he was facing a superior opponent. Clearly, McClellan was altogether too readily disposed to believe the inflated estimates of enemy strength that his amateur spy master Allen Pinkerton was supplying him. The delay at Yorktown eliminated any hopes for overwhelming the Confederate capital of Richmond before Johnston's army could filter down from the North.

Once Yorktown was abandoned by the Confederates during the darkness of night on May 3, McClellan's army trudged up the peninsula toward Richmond. Rapid movement was hampered by a combination of unlikely and unfortunate circumstances. Federal regiments frequently lost their way in the morass of swamps dotting the terrain because of the absence of any reliable maps or surveys of the land and by an unprecedented amount of rainfall that spring. Winfield Scott Hancock's defeat of the retreating Confederates at Williamsburg led the way to the establishment of the main Federal supply depot being based at White House Landing on the Pamunkey River, a tributary of the York. On Wednesday, May 20, Federal forces began to cross the southern side of the Chickahominy River, and by week's end, McClellan's left wing had come within eight miles of Richmond where front line troops could hear the church bells of that capital city. From higher ground, the Union Army could see the spires housing those bells. Meanwhile, McClellan's right wing continued to extend northward in order to link up with McDowell's corps whenever it should advance from Fredericksburg.

McClellan's methodical approach toward Richmond finally catapulted Johnston into action. In an uncoordinated attack on May 31, his army slammed into the Federal left in what would come to be known as the Battle of Seven Pines (Fair Oaks). Little by way of advantage was gained by either side in this fierce action, and the fighting was called off on June 1. On the first day of battle, however, Johnston was severely wounded, and command eventually devolved upon Robert E. Lee (q.v.).

Despite the inconclusiveness of this battle, it reinforced McClellan's conviction that a siege was his only realistic option. Many of his earlier hopes to overwhelm the Confederates with superior numbers had begun to unravel. Having lost the element of surprise, the Confederates were able to muster an army approximately equal to McClellan's, especially since the Lincoln administration continued to vacillate in its promise to send McDowell's corps to participate in the attack on McClellan's right flank. Again, on June 8, it appeared that McClellan would finally receive McDowell's force. Indeed, McDowell wired McClellan that it was the third time he had been ordered to link up with him. This assurance convinced McClellan to retain Fitz-John Porter's Fifth Corps on the north side of the Chickahominy. Under normal conditions, the Chickahominy was a lazy turgid stream, but given the record amount of rainfall that spring, it had become a raging torrent of a river. Nevertheless, the danger of Porter's force being isolated and overwhelmed by the Confederate left was minimized by the imminent arrival of McDowell. Meanwhile, McClellan engaged his left wing in the task of laying out siege lines in anticipation of moving the big guns up from White House Landing.

No one knew better of McClellan's real chances of succeeding in this mission than Robert E. Lee, who had just taken over command in the field. In blunt language he informed his superior that he would have to attack McClellan's well-entrenched defenses. Having observed the reflexive reaction of the Union government of retrieving McDowell every time Jackson wreaked havoc in the valley, Lee ordered that general northward again with the understanding that he would quickly return to Richmond once he had delivered the desired effect. Lee correctly interpreted Washington's reaction to Jackson's renewed activity in the valley. All but one division of McDowell's corps were ordered to halt, and Jackson quickly retraced his steps and rejoined Lee's army on June 24.

The following day, McClellan ordered Samuel Heintzelman's corps to carry the Confederate positions on the Williamsburg Road as a preparation to beginning his siege. Fearing that the Federals had fathomed his own plans for attacking, Lee ordered a general assault for June 26 that would mark the beginning of seven days of unrelenting fighting. At Gaines' Mill on June 27, Porter's corps was pushed from the field and survived only as a result of poor coordination on the part of attacking Confederate forces. This action convinced McClellan to withdraw Porter's corps to the southern side of Chickahominy, thus relinquishing his base at White House Landing. The Federal army was now in headlong retreat toward a new base being established on the James River with Lee in pursuit.

Despite his sincere conviction that the Federal army should have been annihilated during this retreat, Lee was plagued by the many problems inherent in delivering a crushing blow, particularly in this early stage of the war. In each of the three remaining battles of Savage's Station, Glendale, and Malvern Hill, he proved unable to ensure the proper coordination of all of his units, and in each case, McClellan's army was able to extricate itself from being overwhelmed. At Malvern Hill, in particular, the Federal force made Lee pay dearly for his ambition, as it mauled his army in its futile attempt to overtake Mc-

Clellan's entrenched positions. The conclusion of this battle marked the end of the Seven Days Battle, and McClellan retreated unmolested into his base at Harrison's Landing.

In retrospect, McClellan's campaign on the peninsula clearly had fallen way short of its strategic design. Lee had saved Richmond from capture, and he had seized the initiative away from McClellan. Moreover, McClellan had demonstrated a number of serious deficiencies as a field commander. Despite real operational challenges, he had failed to move his large army with deliberate speed in the early days of the campaign, particularly at Yorktown. His willingness to believe exaggerated estimates of enemy strength made him tactically timid. And he played a significant role in undermining the relationship with his superiors in Washington that was necessary for a successful campaign. On the other hand, there were promising signs. Lincoln, deploring the psychological impact of this ''half-defeat'' acknowledged the substantial punishment leveled at Lee's army, realizing that the rebel government could not long sustain such losses. Moreover, McClellan's army remained intact and in good spirits and was still only twenty miles distant from Richmond at Harrison's Landing.

Another month would pass before the official end of the Peninsula Campaign. During this time, Lincoln visited McClellan at Harrison's Landing, where McClellan handed him his now-famous letter, urging that the war continue to be fought along conservative and conciliatory lines. McClellan continued to plead that the Army of the Potomac renew fighting in its current position and that reinforcements be sent to support this effort. On July 25, General Henry W. Halleck, (q.v.) who had been called to Washington on July 11 to become the general in chief, met with McClellan to review operational plans for the Army of the Potomac, particularly in light of Confederate movements against General John Pope's newly created Army of Virginia. McClellan offered several options for renewing the offensive from the James, but each was predicated upon receiving substantial reinforcement. After returning to Washington, Halleck was greeted by McClellan's request for assistance over and above what had been discussed as practical. Consequently, Halleck was directed by Lincoln to recall the Army of the Potomac from the peninsula with orders for it to join up with Pope's command. On August 4, after protesting Halleck's directive one more time, McClellan was forced to accept the removal of his army from the James.

Over the next four weeks, McClellan was essentially a commander without a command. He remained on the James for the better part of this time, supervising the removal of the army. He arrived in Alexandria, Virginia, on August 27 to assist in unraveling the confusion surrounding efforts to forward units of his former command to Pope's army, which was settling in on the old battleground at Manassas. It was in this capacity that many of his critics in Washington, particularly Secretary of War Edwin Stanton (q.v.) and Secretary of the Treasury Salmon P. Chase, (q.v.) believed McClellan to have obstructed the timely flow of reinforcements to Pope. In response to Lincoln's inquiry of August 29 concerning the status of the military situation, McClellan responded that the army should concentrate near the capital and that Pope should be left to his own devices. Both the bluntness and the poor word selection obscured whatever possible wisdom resided in this advice and made Lincoln suspicious that McClellan wished Pope's defeat, a commander whose views of the political nature of the war conflicted squarely with his own. At any rate, Pope was soundly thrashed at Manassas by Lee and Jackson, and concerns for the safety of the capital resurrected in the wake of this defeat. Against the strenuous protests of his own cabinet, Lincoln reluctantly pressed command of the forces assembling around the capital upon McClellan. He reasoned that no other general commanded the respect of the army as much as McClellan and that McClellan's proven ability to organize an army into fighting mettle was indispensable to the crisis at hand. Consequently, on September 2, George McClellan once again commanded the Army of the Potomac, which now included Pope's former Army of Virginia.

The reorganization and restoration of morale were accomplished in a few short days, and McClellan's skill as a military administrator was a source of great relief to a worried Washington. Lincoln noted to his personal secretary that the general might not be an aggressive fighter himself but that he excelled preparing his troops for combat. During this time, dispatches arrived reporting that Lee had veered into Maryland rather than testing the defenses of Washington. On September 5, the first units of the Federal army departed Washington to find Lee in the open field and do battle.

Given the confusion as to Lee's location, and where he was heading, along with Halleck's repeated warnings that Lee was retracing his steps in order to attack Washington, McClellan still made steady progress toward Frederick. At any rate, he moved a great deal faster than Lee had predicted. On the evening of September 13, McClellan's suspicions as to Lee's whereabouts were confirmed by the discovery of a copy of that general's Special Order No. 191. An added bonus for McClellan was the insight gained into Lee's intentions and troop dispositions contained in those orders. He ordered his corps commanders to push through the passes of South Mountain and move to defeat Lee's divided army before it could reunite. Despite the failure of his left wing commander William B. Franklin to move with all possible dispatch, the Federals were successful in dislodging Confederate defensive positions from the mountains and were in position to move on Lee's army by the evening of the fourteenth. Meeting increased resistance from Confederate units freed up from the collapse of the Federal garrison at Harpers Ferry, McClellan slowed his advance and arrived on the east banks of the Antietam late in the afternoon of the fifteenth. McClellan wasted an opportunity to assault Lee's defensive positions before they were reinforced by spending most of the day, September 16, making sure that all of his units were in perfect assault position. McClellan moved against Lee's entrenched positions at dawn the following day. In what would prove to be the most sanguinary day in American military history, McClellan repeatedly hammered, but could not break, Lee's position. Critics have charged that he fought the battle in "driblets," failing to coordinate his three-prong attack strategy so as to maximize the pressure directed at Lee's defenses. The day's greatest failure occurred on the left flank under the command of Ambrose Burnside. Inordinate delays in commencing action there limited the chances for greater success. The next day saw both armies facing each other but neither offering a renewal of fighting. Lee vacated the field and crossed the Potomac back into Virginia during the night. McClellan offered but little harassment to that retreat.

Over the course of the next month, the Lincoln administration continually tried to prod McClellan into renewing offensive action, but even another personal visit by the president himself could not persuade the general that his army was capable of doing so. Finally, on October 26, McClellan's army began crossing the Potomac in pursuit of Lee and had advanced as far as Warrenton, Virginia, by early November. It was there on November 7 that an emissary from the War Department delivered the message that the president had relieved McClellan of command. He was ordered to report to Trenton, New Jersey, to await further orders. They never came. In 1864, McClellan resigned his commission in order to run as the Democratic candidate for the presidency. He was defeated in this bid in the November elections.

McClellan's stormy tenure as commander of the Army of the Potomac was only overshadowed by the controversy that ensued in establishing his place in history. Initially, as demonstrated in William Swinton's *Campaigns of the Army of the Potomac* (1866), McClellan's career received some balanced criticism. Swinton exposed McClellan's shortcomings but understood the trying conditions in the early part of the war, and in this light, he could see some of McClellan's virtues. During the Reconstruction era, when the Lost Cause myth began to forge the historical reputations of Southern leaders, the politically charged atmosphere in the North dictated much of the way McClellan's career was examined. As an elder statesman of the Democratic party, McClellan was a legitimate target for criticism. However, these critics, as well as the many apologists who rose to McClellan's defense, cared more for invective than impartiality. McClellan admitted as much in his 1881 introduction to his memoirs, by noting that "party feeling has run so high that the pathway to truth has been well nigh closed" (15).

If McClellan was overshadowed by Grant's and William T. Sherman's (q.v.) wartime accomplishments, he was again dwarfed by this pair in the war of the memoirs. His memoirs, published posthumously by his literary executor William C. Prime, contained many of his wartime letters to his wife Ellen that he most certainly did not intend for public viewing. Consequently, his memoirs, especially when compared to the highly regarded reminiscences of both Sherman and Grant, appear overly defensive. Historians have fallen in love with Grant's memoirs, in particular, while McClellan's have generally left them cold.

Despite the ascendancy of professional historical standards at the turn of the century, most Civil War literature dealing with McClellan continued to be tarred with either the panegyric or the vitriolic. Many of these works are favorable to

McClellan, as they were serving as official and moving testimonials to his career. Only James G. Randall's second volume of his study of the Lincoln presidency, published around the midway mark of the twentieth century, approaches objectivity. It renders a generally sympathetic portrait of McClellan's career, particularly in analyzing the context of the early period of the war in which he commanded.

McClellan's place in history today can be traced to the post–World War II period when what Joseph Harsh has coined as the "Unionist" interpretation was forged. Standing head and shoulders above all others in influencing the analysis of Northern Civil War commanders were the works of Kenneth P. Williams, T. Harry Williams, and Bruce Catton. Perhaps the greatest testimonial to their influence was rendered by one of today's leading Civil War historians—James M. McPherson. It was he who suggested that a "generation ago, fine studies by two historians named Williams—T. Harry and Kenneth P.—told us everything we might want to know about Lincoln's search for the right military strategy and for the right generals to carry it out" (McPherson, 35). Catton's influence, on the other hand, might well have exceeded the two Williams's, as his studies reached a much broader and less critical popular audience. In a nutshell, the Unionist interpretation holds that until Grant took command in the East, leaving the Western theater to Sherman, all that happened was an endless recitation of failure and disappointment. Ranking highest in the scales of failure and disappointment was George McClellan.

To wit, the Unionist interpretation upholds the veneration of Abraham Lincoln as both a masterful chief executive and an able military strategist. His flaws are but trivial, and they are obscured in the general apotheosis of his career as the martyred war president. Lincoln suffered greatly in his mission to reunite the nation until he found a military figure who would execute the war according to his vision. Kenneth P. Williams's very title to his study of Lincoln's quest only underscores the patient, suffering search the president endured until Grant arrived from the West. Of all Lincoln's flawed commanders, it was the arrogant McClellan who tried Lincoln's endurance the most. Williams could find nothing redeemable in McClellan's tenure of command, and his pithy conclusion as the general exited his study has been savored by students of the Civil War ever since. It reads: "McClellan was merely an attractive but vain and unstable man, with considerable military knowledge, who sat a horse well and wanted to be President" (K. Williams, 2:479).

T. Harry Williams was not as scathing in his indictment of McClellan and, at times, could sympathize with the general's difficulties with a Radical Republican Congress. All the same, he viewed McClellan as a professional pretender whose views of waging war were suspect when compared to Lincoln's intuitive grasp of military strategy. Consequently, McClellan, in his eyes, was "not a good general, was even a bad one" (T. Williams, 11). Catton merely added to the general denunciation of McClellan when he concluded that the general possessed "all of the virtues necessary in war except one—he did not like to fight" (Catton, 82).

Over time, the essentials of the Unionist interpretation became firmly entrenched in the literature and have been nuanced and expanded upon by the latest generation of Civil War scholars. Led by Stephen Sears, who has published the premier biography of McClellan, attempts have been made to link McClellan's dismal performance with psychological and personality disorders that precluded him from military greatness. Consequently, Sears unequivocally declares in *George B. McClellan: The Young Napoleon* (1988) that of all the commanders of the Army of the Potomac, McClellan "was inarguably the worst" (xii). Joseph Glatthaar follows suit by claiming that personality disorders and unbridled paranoia formed the basis for McClellan's failure. These sentiments are echoed by many other historians today and constitute the basis for assessing McClellan's career. They have also found their way into the many popular video documentaries and dramatic re-creations of the Civil War that have flourished in the last two decades.

McClellan has had few supporters in the literature over the last half century. Warren Hassler's more sympathetic biography in 1957 never gained as much influence as did the works of T. Harry Williams and his generation. Others, like Joseph Harsh, Edward Hagerman, and Rowena Reed, have explored specific aspects of the McClellan legacy to some effect but have not altered the prevailing view that McClellan was anything but a poor commander. The author's previous articles and forthcoming study on McClellan address the dangers of previous psychological profiling, as well as the inherent shortcomings in analyzing McClellan's performance in limited contexts. The chances, then, that McClellan's Civil War career will ever be reexamined will likely hinge on whether we are able to overcome the shortsightedness of earlier scholars.

BIBLIOGRAPHY

William Swinton, *Campaigns of the Army of the Potomac* (New York: C. B. Richardson, 1866).

U. S. Grant, *Personal Memoirs of U. S. Grant,* 2 vols. (New York: Charles L. Webster, 1885).

George B. McClellan, *McClellan's Own Story*, ed. William C. Prime (New York: Charles L. Webster, 1887).

James G. Randall, *Lincoln, The President* (New York: Dodd, Mead, 1945).

T. Harry Williams, *Lincoln and His Generals* (New York: Knopf, 1952).

Warren W. Hassler, Jr., *General George B. McClellan: Shield of the Union* (Baton Rouge: Louisiana State University Press, 1957).

Kenneth P. Williams, *Lincoln Finds a General*, 5 vols. (New York: Macmillian, 1949–1959).

Bruce Catton, *The Army of the Potomac*, 3 vols. (Garden City, N.Y.: Doubleday, 1962).

T. Harry Williams, *McClellan, Sherman, and Grant* (New Brunswick, N.J.: Rutgers University Press, 1962).

Joseph L. Harsh, ''On the McClellan-Go-Round,'' *Civil War History* 19, no. 2 (June 1973): 101–118.

Rowena Reed, *Combined Naval Operations in the Civil War* (Annapolis: Naval Institute Press, 1978).

Edward C. Hagerman, *The American Civil War and the Origins of Modern Warfare* (Bloomington: Indiana University Press, 1988).

Stephen W. Sears, *George B. McClellan: The Young Napoleon* (New York: Ticknor and Fields, 1988).

George B. McClellan, *The Civil War Papers of George B. McClellan*, ed. Stephen W. Sears (New York: Ticknor and Fields, 1989).

James M. McPherson, ''Lincoln and the Strategy of Unconditional Surrender,'' in *Lincoln the War President*, ed. Gabor S. Boritt (New York: Oxford University Press, 1992), 31–62.

Joseph T. Glatthaar, *Partners in Command* (New York: Free Press, 1994).

Thomas J. Rowland, *In the Shadows of Grant and Sherman: George B. McClellan and Civil War History* (Kent, Ohio: Kent State University Press, 1998).

STEPHEN RUSSELL MALLORY
(1811 ?–November 9, 1873)

Jon L. Wakelyn

A look through the literature written on the Confederate States Navy and its only cabinet secretary, Stephen R. Mallory, reveals an inverse proportion of scholarship to its and his importance in the South's efforts to sustain a separate nation. The secretary had the task to construct and finance a navy almost from scratch; to govern an agency with few trained staff members; and to win the naval war on the high seas, protect the ocean coastal towns and shipping, and control the inland waterways and rivers. In order to assist the government to raise necessary funds to conduct the war, Mallory had to break the Union blockade of the Atlantic and Gulf Coast south. Also, the secretary wanted to use the Confederate States Navy to damage Northern morale and hinder the federal government from purchasing war materiel through the destruction of merchant shipping on the high seas. How and whether Mallory accomplished all of these tasks require at least some attempt to look again at this all-but-forgotten man's extraordinary life.

Like a number of other important Confederate leaders, Mallory's origins did not begin in the South. The record of his birth is unclear, although he probably was born on the island of Trinidad between 1811 (?) and 1813. His father Charles had been born in Reading, Connecticut, and had trained to be a civil engineer. His profession took him to many foreign postings. Ellen Russell, Stephen's mother, came from County Waterford, in southern Ireland. Adopted at a young age by relatives who had immigrated to Trinidad, she met Charles Mallory, and they later married. They had two sons, the elder of whom died in infancy. Charles and Ellen moved often, and for a time they lived in Havanna, Cuba. Sometime around 1820, while doing a building job in Key West, Florida, the elder Mallory died, leaving Ellen to raise young Stephen. She brought him up Roman Catholic, although he would later convert to the Episcopal Church, and made certain he received a proper parochial education. She first sent him to the Jesuit school in Mobile, Alabama, and later to the Moravian School for

Boys in Nazareth, Pennsylvania. Perhaps he had all together a total of four years of schooling.

The bright and ambitious young Mallory soon determined to strike out on his own in hopes of rising in the world. At the tender age of nineteen, he obtained appointment in the office of the Inspector of Customs at Key West. It was a position that gave him many contacts and also taught him the value of the law. He also found time to study law, soon passed the bar, and became the Collector of Customs for lower Florida at the age of twenty-one. He also practiced law, beginning in 1839, and used his government office to build a lucrative maritime clientele. As with many an ambitious young man of the lower South, Mallory seized the opportunity to show his national patriotism by volunteering for service in the Seminole Wars. He also wanted the land and status that accrued to those who participated in those wars. Meanwhile, in 1838, he had married Angela Moreno, daughter of a powerful Pensacola businessman. His law practice continued to grow, and he soon owned fine homes both in Key West and Pensacola.

Like other successful lawyers, his career path soon led him into public life. His skills at business gained Mallory election to various Southern commercial conventions where he well represented the fledgling state of Florida and himself. In 1851, the Florida legislature elevated him to the U.S. Senate. By taking that office he earned the enmity of David L. Yulee and his powerful Florida Democratic party machine. In Washington, Mallory made many friends as he became a spokesman for Southern commercial and merchant interests. Perhaps because he came from a coastal state, he naturally became an expert on naval affairs. In his early days in the Senate, Mallory supported the movement to restore corporal punishment in the navy. Eventually he became chairman of the Senate Committee on Naval Affairs, where he began a campaign to modernize the navy, especially in the areas of ship design and ordnance. Mallory also took advantage of his position to speculate in Florida railroad building and in the fated movement to build a cross-Florida canal. Along the way, having become sensitive over his lack of education and training in navy affairs, he quarreled with other senators such as Robert Toombs of Georgia and with scientist Matthew F. Maury over navy policies. The tilt with Maury over naval experiments—Maury had pointed out that the committee chairman hardly knew anything about the navy— would come back to haunt Mallory. Nevertheless, despite his reputation for pugnaciousness and his quick temper, the Florida legislature returned him to the Senate in 1857, after his term had expired. No doubt he had served well his adopted state's maritime interests.

The senator suffered horribly from gout, which no doubt exacerbated his quarrelsome nature. In turn, Mallory's relations with his wife began to deteriorate as his political problems forced him to spend more and more time away from his family. Also contributing to his foul mood were Florida's radical sectionalists who began to clamor for secession. As his state's leadership became ever more hostile to the national party and resistant to compromise, Mallory attempted to hold on to his place in the moderate wing of the Democratic party.

Writing of his actions during the late 1850s, Mallory's biographer Joseph T. Durkin said: "Whatever might be the arguments in favor of secession as a remedy consistent with the theory of the Constitution, he regarded it as but another name for revolution justified only as a last resort from intolerable oppression" (113). The senator had become an ally of President James Buchanan, and that grateful leader offered him the ambassadorship to Spain, which he considered but declined. Nevertheless, all his Unionist hopes came to an end in January 1861 when pressures from home forced him to support secession and to resign from the Senate. But Mallory opposed civil war, and he advised his Florida allies that Fort Pickens in Pensacola harbor was not worth starting war over. His family life in tatters, his business interests in danger, his friends deserting him, Mallory sought to leave public life.

But retirement was not to be, because in February 1861 President-elect Jefferson Davis (q.v.) summoned him to Montgomery to join the provisional Confederate States government. Over the objection of the Yulee forces, Davis named him Confederate Secretary of the Navy. Davis no doubt chose him because he needed someone from Florida in the cabinet but also because the stubborn president believed Mallory had talent. Still, the question of his loyalty to the cause of a new nation lingered over his reputation, especially after his outspoken wife had declared for the Union. Throughout the war she would cause him no end of personal trouble. All that bickering aside, the secretary ably organized his office, brought in good talent to oversee the day-to-day running of naval operations, and slowly began to face the insurmountable task of creating a navy where none had existed. Fortunately, early in the war the Norfolk Naval Yard fell into the hands of the Confederates, and with careful dredging of the harbor, the secretary managed to have raised several vessels, including the frigate *Merrimac*, as well as a few cannons.

That was Mallory's major piece of luck in the way of acquiring materiel for war. He never found the funds to build a shipyard, and the many raw materials such as timber, pitch, and iron ore, which could be used to construct a navy, went unexploited. In addition, few trained naval officers lived in the South for Mallory to recruit, and little support existed in the government at first for the formation of a naval academy, which was so necessary to train a leadership corps. In 1863, nearly too late for any hope of navy wartime successes, he finally opened a navy training college. Even then, the army recruited a number of Mallory's newly commissioned officers for its own purposes. When he complained to President Davis, the chief executive told him that the priority for officers was with the land-based military defense. So he had to learn to make do with the talent left over. Mallory also adapted somewhat to lack of funds and shipping. He scrounged money to buy a few foreign vessels to use in the war against Union shipping.

The secretary soon focused almost exclusively on his "piracy" scheme. However, he clashed with Treasury Secretary Christopher G. Memminger (q.v.) over funding, because his needs were low among the Confederacy's priorities. He also fought with his old nemesis Matthew F. Maury over what kind of vessels to use to break the Union blockade or to fight on the high seas. Maury, the expert, resisted the expense of building ironclads, but Mallory insisted that only ironclads could run through the blockade. Even when he lost Norfolk and his source for ships, the secretary had the vision to refit a few conventional ships into ironclads. For a while they served his purpose. By February 1861, Mallory had convinced the Confederate Congress to support his scheme to purchase ships from abroad. He employed a trusted ally, James Bullock, to go to England, and later to France, as his personal emissary to buy ships, promote diplomatic pressure to lift the Union blockade, and buy other materiel of warfare. After the purchase of the fast-moving frigate *Alabama*, however, Union outrage forced the British to shut down his source of warships. Covertly, the secretary continued to buy merchant vessels that he turned into frigates of war.

At the most necessary task of finding experienced sailors or at least training a few landlubbers to do adequate service, Mallory displayed excellent understanding of talent. For the most important sea-time position of all, an audacious sailor who could attack the Union shipping lanes and thus disrupt merchant trades, he recruited Raphael Semmes (q.v.). Mallory encouraged Semmes's audacity, supported his unorthodox actions, and generally managed to protect his commander's career until the Union frigate *Kersarge* sank the *Alabama* and grounded that privateer. But Mallory did not fare well in his other selection to run Union blockades and disrupt its shipping. The spoiled John N. Maffitt would not only prove a failure at sea but would later attempt to destroy the secretary's reputation. Despite Maffitt's criticism, Mallory's hindering of Union commerce through the use of psychological warfare and the destruction of Yankee materiel of war contributed mightily to the Confederate overall war effort.

On the issue of providing adequate coastal defenses, however, Mallory had a decidedly mixed record. When he employed brilliant officers who understood how to build defense fortifications, like P. G. T. Beauregard (q.v.) in Charleston Harbor, he had much success. In part that was because Mallory insisted upon the use of torpedoes to sink the Union coastal war fleet despite the objection of Maury, his old enemy. The secretary even managed to protect Mobile from Union assault for a number of years, but the criticism against him that he was not prepared for the final Union invasion of that Gulf Coast port town was just. He also was unable to pacify the North Carolina Unionists who gave up Wilmington to the North. Most damaging for his reputation, Mallory completely misjudged the Union naval attack on New Orleans. He insisted that any assault on the "crescent city" would come from up the Mississippi River and failed to plan for or stop Admiral David Farragut's attack from the Gulf. The loss of the most important Confederate trading center of New Orleans led Congressman Henry S. Foote, who loathed Mallory, to call for an investigation into his conduct. The committee investigation that Louisiana Senator Thomas Semmes conducted fully exonerated the secretary, but history has not. Mallory would expend much needed energy to try to contrive schemes for retaking New Orleans.

If his record on coastal defenses proved spotty, Mallory's efforts to keep open the riverways generally succeeded. Using fast little gunboats, merchant ships refitted with cannons, and mines and torpedoes he gave Yankee vessels the fits. Only Ulysses S. Grant's (q.v.) running past the gun emplacements at Vicksburg marred Mallory's success. Still, the Confederacy kept open the Mississippi River throughout the war. Mallory also rendered the Tennessee River impassable for the Union flotillas, which delayed the attack on Chattanooga for some time. Most important to the Confederate government in Richmond, Mallory kept Union troops from advancing on the James River, first during George B. McClellan's (q.v.) Peninsula Campaign of 1862 and later during Grant's siege of Petersburg in 1864. Indeed, Mallory's understaffed office and underequipped river defense still managed to delay Union military movements at crucial periods and thus allowed the Confederate armies time to unify their defenses.

Mallory's success at delaying the Union victory was not without irony. He himself had early known that the Confederacy could not prevail against such an overwhelming Union materiel advantage. It was Mallory, during the Confederate government's evacuation of Richmond and its leaders' escape south, who told President Davis in April 1865 that the idea of extending the war through guerrilla activity was impossible. Yet the man who knew that to continue the war was hopeless had himself assisted in prolonging the war through his extraordinary ability to destroy Union war goods. A peace advocate at heart, he would pay for his successes. For his work of sabotage, the Union government imprisoned Mallory at the war's end and threatened him with execution. Treated abominably in a Union prison in New Jersey, Mallory wrote to President Andrew Johnson (q.v.) in June of 1865 and claimed that he had never been disloyal to the nation. He had always believed, he maintained, that Southern grievances against the North could have been assuaged within the Union. Mallory insisted to the president that he could be helpful in Reconstruction if he were allowed to return to Florida. For those words, and because he often was forthright and stubborn, a number of his Florida enemies would call him a traitor and resist his return to public life.

Finally, in March 1866 he gained his parole and left for Florida ill in health and in spirit as he contemplated the difficulty of restoring his lost wealth and providing for his family. During the war his fine homes in Pensacola and Key West had been burned. But Mallory was stubborn and courageous, and he somehow managed to put his law practice back together. His children soon gathered around him and gave him enormous pride. Mallory's namesake soon restored the family's political position, as he set out on a political journey that would take him to a long and able career in the U.S. House of Representatives. But his wife never returned to Pensacola. On November 9, 1873, he died in Pensacola and was buried in the Episcopal graveyard there. There, below the spanish moss, he lies today, nearly forgotten by his adopted state and by history.

Does Mallory deserve the reputation of a failed cabinet member that the more famous navy leaders Maffitt and Maury early gave to him? Certainly his equivocation over Southern chances in the war hurt him with loyal Confederates. But his devotion to resistance with such little in the way of usable resources showed an amazing ability to get the most out of what he had. The self-proud Raphael Semmes, who found little in others to praise, in his memoirs had much good to say about Mallory. President Jefferson Davis, who attacked all of his enemies and former allies alike in his later years, insisted Mallory had been a most loyal cabinet member. The first major historian of the Confederate Navy, John T. Scharf, writing in 1887, insisted that "the administration of Mr. Mallory is not to be judged and condemned by its failure, but it will excite surprise and win admiration for what was accomplished with the means and the resources at his command" (1:31).

Modern professional historians have commented on Mallory's wartime activities with mixed views. A most careful scholar of the wartime Confederate cabinet, Rembert J. Patrick, agreed with Scharf. Patrick rejected the Southern press's attacks on Mallory for being slow to build cruisers and found that his sober judgment of the art of the possible proved quite useful in the financially strapped Confederate war effort. Mallory's only modern biographer, Joseph Durkin, criticized his flawed personality and disrupted family life but believed there had been much merit in his actions. Although Durkin's favorable work is fact-filled, it lacks interpretative analysis and contains information that could be used to vilify the poorly educated and ill-prepared secretary. Other modern writers, such as Hamilton Cochran, have listened too much to Maffitt's political criticism. But Frank J. Merli, in his study of the relationship between Great Britain and the Confederate Navy, praised Mallory for his "balanced wisdom and audacity" (17). Most recently, the historian Robert M. Browning has shown that Mallory at least knew what a navy could do in time of war. Browning believes that the rest of the Confederate leaders misjudged the navy's usefulness and shortchanged it throughout the war and that other modern historians similarly have understudied naval warfare. Thus, Mallory remains a double victim; neither he nor the navy has received enough study to make an adequate judgment of his accomplishments.

BIBLIOGRAPHY

John Thomas Scharf, *History of the Confederate States Navy*, 2 vols. (New York: Rogers and Sherwood, 1887).

Burton J. Hendrick, *Statesmen of the Lost Cause* (New York: Literary Guild, 1939).

Rembert J. Patrick, *Jefferson Davis and His Cabinet* (Baton Rouge: Louisiana State University Press, 1944).

Joseph Thomas Durkin, *Stephen R. Mallory: Confederate Navy Chief* (Chapel Hill: University of North Carolina Press, 1954).

Hamilton Cochran, *Blockade Runners of the Confederacy* (New York: Bobbs-Merrill Co., 1958).

Frank J. Merli, *Great Britain and the Confederate Navy* (Bloomington: Indiana University Press, 1970).

Robert M. Browning, *From Cape Charles to Cape Fear: The North Atlantic Blockading Squadron during the Civil War* (Tuscaloosa: University of Alabama Press, 1993).

GEORGE GORDON MEADE
(December 31, 1815–November 6, 1872)

Jon L. Wakelyn

That taciturn Philadelphia gentleman commanded at the brigade level or above in every battle the Army of the Potomac fought, save its very earliest. Meade also held the post as the commanding general of the Army of the Potomac for the longest period of any Union general officer. From George B. McClellan's (q.v.) Peninsula Campaign through Appomattox Court House, he led and fought bravely and usually expertly, often in the front lines alongside his troops. If he does not rank with the greatest of Union officers, such as Ulysses Grant (q.v.) and William T. Sherman (q.v.), surely his wartime career equaled or surpassed any other. Yet Meade has never had a major biographer—the last rather superficial one appeared in 1960—and for many scholars today, he is remembered only for Gettysburg. Even with all his splendid effort at Gettysburg, he gained the reputation of excessive caution there and after. Accused of having failed to destroy Robert E. Lee (q.v.) and the Army of Northern Virginia at Gettysburg and later in the autumn of 1863 in Virginia, he has come down in history as General Grant's factotum during the crucial last year of the war.

Why has one of the Union's most significant commanders been relegated to the back bench of the officer corps? Why has he been so neglected by those who study that great war? Some have said that Meade's horrible and uncontrollable temper, often directed at politicians and the Northern press corps, left his reputation in shreds. But that is again the problem for those who have allowed personality to get in the way of the art of the military possible and the true accomplishments of the important commanders. Perhaps another look at Meade's life in full with concentration in particular on his wartime career will explain the reasons for his neglect and contribute to the revision of his place in that war and in this country's military history.

It is possible that Meade's own family's past figures large in why historians have treated him so poorly. He descended from some of those who held important place and position in the country's history, and thus from his privileged life students of the past have expected much. His father, Richard Worsam Meade, who had been born into a wealthy lawyer-merchant family of Philadelphia, employed his family's riches and his own skills to make a fortune by the time he had turned twenty-two. His mother, Margaret Coates Butler, the daughter of a wealthy Perth Amboy, New Jersey, merchant and shipper, descended from a well-placed old colonial family. George Gordon Meade, one of eight children of Richard and Margaret, was born in Cadiz, Spain, on December 31, 1815. He was baptized a Roman Catholic, although his mother later converted along with her children to the Episcopal Church. The family had lived in Spain for some time because of his father's merchant business and activities in diplomatic service for his country. Robert's secretive diplomatic negotiating eventually got him into trouble with the Spanish government and cost him much of his fortune. The family then returned to Philadelphia in June 1816, in reduced circumstances but still a part of the middle Atlantic merchant elite.

Educated for three years in Philadelphia's best private schools, young George suffered personally and socially after his father died in 1828. The family then removed to Washington, D.C., so that his mother could be close to family friends and pursue her indefatigable quest for restoration of the lost family fortune. George grew up in that young federal city among the politically, socially, and financially powerful. He was sent to the school run by Salmon P. Chase (q.v.), as his family moved comfortably in the ranks of the Episcopal Church elite. George later attended the famous military academy at Germantown, Maryland, where he no doubt recognized that he could get the mechanical and scientific training that would allow him to succeed in the increasingly technical world of American and overseas commerce. While at the prestigious Mount Hope Institute in Baltimore, he became a quick and smart student and a whiz at mathematics, despite having grown terribly nearsighted.

As was customary in such a mercantile family at that time, an older brother had joined the U.S. Navy and had begun to rise in rank (he would later become an admiral). The family decided that young George might also benefit from a military career. He was sent for engineering training to the U.S. Military Academy at West Point, New York, there then being no naval academy. Through family connections he entered the academy in 1831. George was a sloppy and disinterested young cadet who received many demerits. Although he found the curriculum to his liking and quite easy, his poor deportment cost him rank in his class. He managed only to finish in the middle of the class of 1835. That meant the prestigious corps of engineers was not open to him, so Meade joined the army's third artillery battalion. He had made few friends or contacts among his classmates or his superiors and in fact had alienated many of them because of his class-based pretensions. But that hardly mattered to him at the time. For, like others of the officer classes in the army, he found the duties distasteful, and he resigned his commission after only one year in service.

The ambitious but undirected young man then gained employment as a maritime engineer, as he hoped to parlay that career back into the front ranks of

Philadelphia's mainline merchant class. In 1836 Meade took a position in Florida as assistant surveyor on a railroad building project. But the depression of 1837 cost him his job and scuttled his plans. Family political contacts led to employment in the United States Topographical Bureau, and the bureau chief sent him to Texas to assist in the survey of the Louisiana-Texas border. Meade liked the adventure, and he thrived on the details of surveying. (Of course, years later that expertise gained in topographical analysis would serve him well in the modern army that would have to fight over so many miles of uncharted terrain.) When that job ended, he again was idled and broke. During 1840, he joined a team that surveyed the United States–Canadian border around the Great Lakes. All that time he worked with career military officers, and he soon developed those contacts that he had neglected while a student. In 1840, Meade also managed to find a bride. He married Margaret, daughter of Congressman John Sergeant, and entered the prestigious ranks of Whig political circles, which would one day be of assistance to him even though he came from a family of Democrats. Marriage forced the nomadic young man to become serious about a career, as he knew he needed steady work to provide for his family. Of course, the job must fit the prestige of his station in life. In 1842, he reentered the U.S. Army as a second lieutenant of topographical engineers. His position soon enabled him to live with his family in Philadelphia and to work on designs for lighthouses, which gave him much engineering training. No doubt that young man still had visions of joining the merchant classes.

But the Mexican War would change Meade's plans about a military career. In 1845 he joined General Zachary Taylor on the Mexican-Texas border, supposedly to help map that disputed territory. Often ill from stomach problems, Meade nevertheless managed to serve the general well, and he developed a personal respect for the gruff old man who expected efficiency, ability, and loyalty from his staff. Perhaps he also learned from the military-political ways of General Taylor. During March of 1846, Meade planned a line of march close to the Mexican army's military defenses and nearly was captured in an ambush. In that perilous event the young aristocrat discovered he enjoyed the thrill of combat. As his main topographical officer, he grew personally close to "Old Zach" and fought alongside him in the May 1846 battles of Palo Alto and Resaca de la Palma. Meade had become an indispensable officer, as his abilities to study and chart the local terrain assisted in the U.S. victory at Monterrey. For all of his success Meade gained no brevet promotion, perhaps because of his conservative Whig ties during a Democratic administration. He also watched as the partisan press vilified General Taylor, accused him of inaction, and then attacked the general for resigning his position. Those events were not lost on the young officer. Meade may have learned too much about the politics of war, for at that time he began to develop a distaste for the newspaper press and thus gained the reputation of one who had a short and abrupt temper, especially with inferiors and those who misunderstood the nature of warfare. For a time he, too, cooled his heels, then finally joined the army of General Winfield Scott. Meade participated in the storming of Vera Cruz in March 1847 but saw little action after that. In fact, he was one of a number of topographical officers available to his commander, and because he had been so close to General Taylor, he was relieved of duty and sent back to Washington.

At that time the tall, lean, hatchet-faced aristocrat with an aquiline nose filled his notebooks meticulously with plans and, alas, anger at being dealt out of the glory of victory. Just when he had found a real taste for fighting and had expected to rise in rank, enforced inaction hurt his chances for promotion. Finally assigned to duty in Philadelphia at the war's end, he again took up the post of designing lighthouses. Meade also held positions in Florida and Michigan. Finally, in 1851 he gained promotion to first lieutenant. Later named to the position of superintendent of the Seventh Lighthouse District in Delaware and New Jersey, Meade at last made captain. Military life for Meade had become tedious, but the attentive officer learned much about the military hierarchy and its function. The upper-class Meade also maintained an active social life among the young professionals of the Northeast coast, and his position led to connections with the business elite who had contracts with the federal government. For a time Meade also served in the Detroit area, where he surveyed the sea lanes of the Great Lakes. That activity placed him among those who stood to profit from that growing merchant trade. Life seemed safe and so secure.

But Meade had not learned about politics for nothing, and he well understood the dangers in the deep division in the country that had grown even worse during the 1850s. Although he belonged to the Philadelphia bluebloods, two of Meade's sisters had married into wealthy Southern slaveowning families, and he seemed sympathetic toward the South. Like many of his class who had shipping ties to Southern trade, he probably identified at that time more with conservative Democrats than he did with the rising Republican party. Still, Meade was a professional soldier, and he would obey orders and do his duty. But in those supersensitive days building up to Southern secession and declaration of war, a Michigan radical Republican congressman took objection to Meade's seeming pro-Southern sentiments and sought to relegate him to backwater duties in Detroit. The congressman had hoped to keep Meade from any military assignments. The headstrong Meade returned to Philadelphia on his own, then traveled to Washington to ask Secretary of War Simon Cameron to give him front line duties. Cameron only offered him the rank of colonel of a Michigan regiment, which would have kept him to the rear of the action. Then his wife, ambitious for her husband and her family, used her connections as a former congressman's daughter to get Meade promoted.

At last, in August 1861, he gained a commission as volunteer brigadier general in the Pennsylvania Reserves, and his commander gave Meade the task of making soldiers out of amateur troops. Placed under the supercautious General George B. McClellan, Meade's desire for combat was thwarted. Even when McClellan at last moved up the Virginia Peninsula in the spring of 1862, he left Meade behind in the defenses around Washington. Finally, on June 9, 1862, the Pennsylvania Reserves and their commander were put under General Fitz-John Porter's 5th Corps of the Army of the Potomac and allowed to join the army on the peninsula. For the duration of the war, Meade would serve ably in the front lines of the eastern sector.

Sent at first to Beaver Dam Creek, Meade witnessed in disgust a Federal fallback in the face of a smaller enemy force. But at Gaines's Mill on June 27, 1862, he assisted in building a strong defensive position. That activity was wasted, however, as the Union Army sustained major losses. At Frayser's Farm, the inexperienced general ably resisted the advance of Confederate General James Longstreet (q.v.). Praised for his bravery, Meade received a painful arm wound and was sent back home to Philadelphia to recuperate. Fortunately for his later career, he was not present at the ignominious Federal retreat from its strong position on the Virginia Peninsula.

Soon healed from his wound, Meade returned to his troops in midsummer. At Second Manassas, he displayed a canny use of artillery to delay a Confederate advance. Most important, the Pennsylvania Reserves were placed under General John Reynolds and saw major action in the battle to hold the Warrenton Pike, which allowed the defeated Union Army to escape a deadly Confederate trap. Meade's fame at being willing to fight had grown, but his distaste over Union defeat also had grown. In September 1862, Meade gained promotion to division commander and was placed in "Fightin' Joe" Hooker's famous First Corps of the Army of the Potomac. At the battle of Antietam on September 17, again he used artillery to defend his Union position at the bloody Turner's Gap. Also, when Hooker went down with a wound, Meade temporarily led the entire First Corps. After that so-called Union victory in which McClellan lost his command, the Pennsylvanian surprisingly said little despite his disgust over Union inaction. Perhaps because he had Democratic party ties, Meade had to remain silent. But in private he told others that his commander just didn't like to fight. Meade continued to soldier on, and in December he served under General Ambrose Burnside in the Federal debacle at Fredericksburg, Virginia. He led the Federal assault on Marye's Heights and sustained numerous casualties. But later historians, in reviewing that battle, acknowledge that Meade had become one of the finest generals in the Army of the Potomac. As A. Wilson Greene stated, "[L]argely on the strength of his accomplishments on the plains before Fredericksburg, George Gordon Meade became the last commander of the Army of the Potomac" (313–314). At the time, however, Meade only remembered the Confederate artillery barrage, which cost him 1,400 out of 5,000 Pennsylvania boys. But his penetration of Stonewall Jackson's (q.v.) lines had gained him the reputation of an audacious and fearless leader.

Considered a soldier who continued to learn about how to fight using a large and unwieldy number of troops over difficult terrain, as well as a careful student of the enemy's position, after Fredericksburg Meade became commander of the entire 5th Corps. In January 1863, he temporarily commanded the 3rd Corps, only to have it taken away when the intriguing and ambitious Joseph Hooker became commander of the Army of the Potomac. Yet for a man who had never held line command until the spring of 1862, Meade's rise was astounding. But on May 1–3, at the battle of Chancellorsville, Meade also showed his worst side in his public display of anger against Hooker's failures. Hooker, he claimed, not only gave up excellent military position to Confederate commander Robert E. Lee, but he had refused to allow Meade the necessary troops to hold the Union right. Meade had wanted to counterattack against the Confederate left, but instead the seemingly deranged Hooker had insisted on a Union retreat. After Chancellorsville, other Union generals began to regard Meade as a leader, someone to turn to for advice, and the eastern newspaper press for the first and, alas, last time touted him as a major commander.

The rising star was to reach his high point of command when he took charge of the entire Army of the Potomac around Gettysburg. Pennsylvania Governor Andrew G. Curtin, who had begun to panic as Confederate General Lee invaded the state, called on President Abraham Lincoln (q.v.) to replace Hooker with Meade, the Pennsylvanian, as commander of the Army of the Potomac. Meade himself favored his fellow keystone state General John Reynolds. But Lincoln gave Meade command, in part because Chief of Staff Henry W. Halleck (q.v.) believed him the more able leader of a large army. Given the impossible charge to protect both Washington and Baltimore, Meade hastened to place the Army of the Potomac between the routes to those cities and the advancing General Lee. Clearly, Meade knew what was at stake.

Some scholars believe that when Meade was given such an important command he grew cautious; others insist that he knew he could force Lee to attack and thus could stand on the defense. To prepare his position, Meade sent Reynolds to watch and maneuver on Lee's left flank. When the two armies clashed on July 1, 1863, Reynolds was killed. The reliable General Winfield Scott Hancock took over Reynolds's duties and held the high ground east of Gettysburg, thus making Lee choose between attacking a strong entrenched position or retreating back to Virginia and giving up his advance. Meade understood that Lee would have to fight, so he placed the able General Henry W. Sedgewick in the vital center defense position and General John Slocum on Culp's Hill to the north of Gettysburg. His army strung out like an inverted ''V,'' Meade coolly waited for Lee. Keeping his headquarters close to the front lines, Meade was well placed to know when Lee would move. The defense perimeter with cannon emplacements and troops dug in was prepared to protect the Baltimore Road at all costs. On July 2, Longstreet's corps struck at the exposed Little Round Top, but Meade moved up troops, and the famous Twentieth Maine held the line, forcing the Confederates to lose the initiative.

To prepare for the possible third day Confederate assault, Meade met with his staff to discuss whether he should attack or counterattack against the retreating enemy. Meade believed Lee would mount a frontal assault on Cemetery Ridge, but he also was certain that Lee held a strong position on the opposite Seminary Ridge. Meade focused on the enemy batteries firing on the Ridge and sent reinforcements to protect the flank. Then he moved forward guns loaded with cannister to deliver a withering fire upon the advancing General George E. Pickett. The Union center repulsed Pickett's charge, but the Union troops were then too exhausted to mount a counteroffensive. Besides, Meade knew that the well-placed Confederate artillery could stop his advance.

Meade's only important biographer, Freeman Cleaves, wrote: "No major counterstroke was believed possible under the circumstances" (168). But few other historians have accepted Meade's excuses, and his reputation has never recovered from those military, political, and press charges that he had allowed a defeated Lee to escape back to Virginia. To an urging President Lincoln, Meade explained that he had to rebuild his weakened army and at all costs to protect the roads to Baltimore and Washington. The reality of the situation was that the Potomac River had flooded, Lee had his back to it, and Meade only began to follow the retreating Confederates on July 6, 1863. Meade actually had appeared decisive as he maneuvered to attack the weakened Lee. But he never found the right moment to fight, and Lee managed to slip across the Potomac to the comparative safety of Virginia on July 14.

The newspaper tales of Meade's failure to engage Lee grew even more strident in September and October. Chief of Staff Halleck, also later accused of excessive caution, ordered Meade to maneuver in Virginia for the best ground on which to fight Lee. Meade, upset, feeling slighted, and certain of his position, threatened to resign from his command. He finally moved forward, but in an indecisive way. At Bristoe Station and again at Chantilly he checked Lee and countered Confederate advances. With his lines drawn close to the Rapidan River, Meade attempted to fight, but Lee would not engage him. In November, around Brandy Station, Lee wisely again refused combat. Meade then tried to turn Lee's right flank but failed. At Mile Run, Meade fought on the defensive, then retreated to a better position. Lee all the time had tried to get Meade to attack his protected front. Meade understood all to well what Lee was doing, and as winter advanced, he retreated carefully to avoid a trap. Historians should realize that Meade knew what he was doing. Even though he had failed to win a decisive and crushing battle, it was Meade who made certain the Army of Northern Virginia would never again fight an offensive battle or invade Union soil.

But the politicians and the press continued to attack his actions and hinted that the Democrat Meade actually wanted to allow the Confederacy a separate peace. Then, in January 1864, Meade came down with pneumonia. On March 3, General U. S. Grant was placed in charge of the entire Union Army, and he decided to command from the field instead of staying in political Washington. Meade hoped for a place in Grant's army but wondered whether his reputation had been so sullied because of the revisionist efforts to evaluate his recent activities that Grant would be forced to relieve him. Instead, Grant understood the man and his army, and he left Meade in charge of the Army of the Potomac. On May 3, Grant began a massive advance and placed Meade in command of the vital left flank, the wing that might have to defend against a counterattack on Washington. On May 5, during the Battle of the Wilderness, Meade made the mistake of quarreling with popular general Philip Sheridan (q.v.) over troop movements, and the feisty Irishman would never forgive him. At Spotsylvania Court House, Meade's lieutenant John Sedgewick was killed, and the Union Army then appeared poorly organized. When Grant chose to reorganize the army around two commanders, Meade resisted but deferred to his leader. By May 18 Grant had learned Meade's lesson to avoid a frontal attack on Lee. However, the press reminded Meade often that he was too defensive a commander and that the western Union armies were more willing to engage the enemy. He exploded over the unfavorable press coverage after the debacle at Cold Harbor. Meade had made the mistake of his career, and as his biographer Cleaver said, "[B]y a single act he made himself hated" (251). Meade's quick temper, his political ineptness at dealing with Illinois congressman Elihu Washburn's personal attacks on him, and his counterattack on the press had ruined his reputation.

Despite the press and the politicians, Meade resolved to support Grant any way he could. Grant chose his faithful commander to execute the grand turning movement in June 1864 that put the army in Petersburg south of Lee's lines. But Grant had given him no explicit instructions, so Meade was unable to coordinate his advance with that of General Benjamin Butler's movement up the peninsula. Neither general was able to penetrate Confederate General Pierre G. T. Beauregard's (q.v.) brilliant defense of Petersburg. The only choice for Grant was to mount a siege, an action widely unpopular with the army and the public. Grant nevertheless placed Meade in charge of the one around Petersburg. Republican politicians then asked that Meade be removed from command, but Grant refused. Even after Meade suffered blame over the fiasco at the Battle of the Crater, Grant stuck by him. In February 1865, Grant finally promoted Meade to major general. Grant and Meade then began to tighten their vise around Petersburg and stretched their lines to move on the vital Weldon Railroad, Lee's only escape route to North Carolina. At the decisive skirmish at Five Forks, Meade stopped the Confederate attempt to turn his flank, though again the press gave him no credit. Meade at last captured Petersburg on April 1, 1865. He seemed now to be in a hurry, lest General Sherman and the western army arrive to take the offensive. Though ill with a fever, after the victory at Saylor's Creek, Meade was present at Lee's surrender.

The war now over, Meade's reputation was in tatters. But he was a career officer, and he had duties to perform. Even when his sisters who had married Southern planters cut him off, he took on the politically difficult task of going south to command the Division of the Atlantic. Those with political ambitions knew that duty in the defeated South would keep their careers before the public. But Meade had no such ambitions, and instead he decided to be fair to the devastated Southerners. In the spring of 1866, however, General Grant sent him north into isolation to protect the Canadian border from the Irish revolutionary

Fenian army. In December 1867, President Andrew Johnson (q.v.) recalled Meade and ordered him to Georgia to soothe tensions with the old Confederate enemy. Of course he made mistakes, especially when he criticized radical Reconstruction. Still, Meade's symbolic act of assisting in the restoration of the great old Episcopal Church in Atlanta received favorable review in the South. After Grant became president, Meade's former trusted commander named Sheridan lieutenant general of the army, a direct slap at Meade.

Meade, the hero of Gettysburg, the last commander of the Army of the Potomac, continued to sink in reputation. He soon took sick, again with pneumonia. Allowed to return to Philadelphia to convalesce, the tired general took up personal and domestic interests. He worked for the Orphan's Home, and he helped to create parks for the city. But he again became sick, and on November 6, 1872, he died. For many in the North, he had already been forgotten. However, the people of Philadelphia mourned him. Lithographs, paintings, and statues all depicted his splendid wartime activities. His good friend Andrew Atkins Humphrey attempted to revive his reputation as a soldier. But others, like Sheridan in his *Memoirs* (1:355), were determined to render him a failure and themselves heroes. Meade never himself wrote in his own defense. Even his old friend Winfield Scott Hancock delivered an unkind cut in 1887 by taking credit for victory at Gettysburg. Only one lonely old voice, Meade's former staff officer Theodore Lyman, in 1922 praised him as a true hero. But even Lyman pointed out that Meade's anger at the press led it to destroy his reputation.

How have modern scholars dealt with his tarnished reputation? With his rapierlike skewering of those who had flinched in battle, T. Harry Williams, in his influential *Lincoln and His Generals* (1952), continued the attack on Meade. For Williams, Meade's "vicious temper" destroyed his usefulness. Grant himself gave Meade no real tasks in the final year because of his unpredictability, said Williams. Even if he was a fine handler of troops, and he was, Meade lacked glamor, or at least originality. At the last, said Williams, "he was willing to fight a completely defensive war" (289, 259–262). But most recently the record has begun to improve. Herman Hattaway and Archer Jones, in their magisterial *Why the North Won the Civil War* (1983) claimed that Meade's caution over Lee's retreat from Gettysburg was correct (471). If Meade suffered from self-pity, and he did, Hattaway and Jones nevertheless believe him to have been a master at logistics and of tactical skills and a genius at understanding topography. Above all, they claim, Meade understood the value of defense in that war, and "he made a dull but very capable army commander" (405). Favorable reviews of Meade's wartime activities continued when Edward Hagerman, in *The American Civil War and the Origins of Modern Warfare* (1988), insisted that Meade was correct in trying to stop Grant from continuous frontal assault in the Battle of the Wilderness (265).

When all is said and done, however, Meade remains a controversial figure. Because of his class and training, much was expected of that Philadelphia aristocrat. Perhaps more was required than he could have delivered. Because he knew about modern war and was a genius at military placement in difficult terrain, he never suffered fools who tried to tell him what to do. And they paid him back. Because he may have disdained the democracy of publicity, Meade hurt his chances to be seen as a popular hero. Because he sympathized with the Democratic party, Republican contemporaries took him to task. Others, whose military careers rose on Meade's decline, and whose reputations were based on Meade being seen as mediocre, such as Phil Sheridan, had much to lose if the Philadelphian was at all regarded as a success. Perhaps the final verdict of Grant, the general who used and discarded him, is one place to begin a serious professional reconsideration of Meade's career. Grant believed that Meade's temper was a drawback. Like so many other memoirists, Grant focused on personal failings and did not study military accomplishment. But Grant also suggested that Meade was a fine subordinate, most useful in ending the war. To Grant, "he was a most valuable officer and deserves a high place in the annals of his country" (771). Indeed, Meade does, if we are to give truth to the military past of this country's great Civil War.

BIBLIOGRAPHY

Ulysses S. Grant, *Personal Memoirs of Ulysses S. Grant*, 2 vols. (New York: Charles L. Webster and Co., 1885–1886).

Phillip H. Sheridan, *Personal Memoirs of P. H. Sheridan*, 2 vols. (New York: Charles L. Webster and Co., 1888).

T. Harry Williams, *Lincoln and His Generals* (New York: Alfred E. Knopf, 1952).

Freeman Cleaves, *Meade of Gettysburg* (Norman: University of Oklahoma Press, 1960).

Herman Hattaway and Archer P. Jones, *Why the North Won the Civil War* (Urbana: University of Illinois Press, 1983).

A. Wilson Greene, "Opportunity to the South: Meade versus Jackson at Fredericksburg," *Civil War History* 33, no. 4 (December 1987): 295–314.

Edward Hagerman, *The American Civil War and the Origins of Modern Warfare* (Bloomington: Indiana University Press, 1988).

Brien Holden Reid, "Another Look at Grant's Crossing of the James, 1864," *Civil War History* 39, no. 4 (December 1993): 291–316.

Joseph T. Glatthaar, *Partners in Command: The Relationship between Leaders in the Civil War* (New York: Free Press, 1994).

CHRISTOPHER GUSTAVUS MEMMINGER
(January 9, 1803–March 7, 1888)

Jon L. Wakelyn

The prevailing historical view of Christopher G. Memminger's performance as Confederate Secretary of the Treasury is that he was confused over policy and incompetent in running his office. His harshest modern critic, Douglas B. Ball, says that the fault with Confederate finances "lay particularly in the flawed policies and inept administration of the Confederate treasury" (9). Contemporaries of Memminger, too, judged him a failure, a weak, humorless man who had little understanding of politics. Yet President Jefferson Davis (q.v) kept him in office until the Congress forced the president into a wholesale reorganization of his cabinet late in 1864. The president had regarded his secretary as an able and loyal aide who had assumed an impossible task and, alas, had failed at it. But during most of Memminger's career, especially in his public service before and after the war, he had demonstrated an extraordinary ability and had had enormous success. Obviously, the pressures of wartime actions and peacetime accomplishments were dissimilar in scope, but that does not account for such differences between the two. Perhaps in the life history of that German immigrant who became the financial leader of the Confederacy there are answers to the contradictions in performance in his many different public spheres.

Born in Nayhingen, in the province of Würtemburg, Germany, on January 9, 1803, Memminger early learned about adversity and severe disruption in life. His father, the quartermaster of a military battalion, lost his life in battle. Christopher Godfrey Memminger had been university educated and had achieved much success before he died. After his death, the child's mother, Eberhardina Elizabeth Kohler, brought her young son to her parent's home in Charleston, South Carolina. She died there in 1807, leaving young Christopher an orphan. His grandfather John Kohler, unable to make a decent living in Charleston, soon thereafter left for Philadelphia. Fortunately for the young Christopher, John had had the foresight to place him in the Charleston Orphan Home, then run by members of the city's quality. Christopher showed early to be bright and diligent, and he soon came to the attention of members of the family of Thomas Bennett, a leader in Charleston society and political life. Bennett, who later served as governor of the state, no doubt believed that the dour but brilliant German boy would make a good example for his children, so he brought the youth into his household to be raised as one of the family.

Recognizing that young Memminger's brilliance as well as his diligence could lead to an important and useful career in Charleston, Bennett sent him at the age of thirteen to the South Carolina College in Columbia. At that time the young college had already achieved a reputation as being one of the finest and most demanding institutions of higher learning in the country and certainly held a place of utmost importance for wealthy and ambitious Carolina families. There, beginning in 1815, Memminger thrived as he made friends with many young men who would later rise in public life. He became an outstanding debater and an excellent student, graduating number two in his class. Yet those who knew him remarked that Christopher seemed just not quite able to fit into that Southern aristocratic world of gaiety and pretension.

After graduation, he followed a longtime practice of upwardly bound youth when he entered the Charleston law office of the governor's brother, Joseph Bennett. Barely seventeen at the time, his talents for careful and detailed legal analysis soon shone. Memminger also took advantage of the rich cultural world of antebellum Charleston, joined the local literary society, and there made a number of friends among the city's future leaders. In those society gatherings, bright young men and the town's elder statesmen gave papers on important topics and discussed the pressing issues of the day. But mainly the meetings served as stepping-stones to political preferment and social advancement. Memminger also made an early success in the law, as he soon established his own firm and pled some important cases involving the future direction of financial and business growth in that harbor city. Fame and friendships forged in the bonds of ability and propriety soon gave him entry into local and state politics in which public service would become his trademark in life.

As a young and ambitious politico, Memminger joined a number of others to oppose what he believed was the lunacy of the South Carolina Nullification movement. An ally of the moderate governor Thomas Bennett, he penned a satiric work, *The Book of Nullification*, which illustrated the ill-considered efforts of those who had defied the federal government on the tariff issue. Certainly at that time Memminger foresaw wider trade interests for Charleston and believed that the South itself should not become dependent on overseas cotton trade. Although he and his fellow Unionists were denounced by the radical nullifiers, Memminger gained election as a city alderman in 1832. In that office he supported the business community's desire to widen Charleston's major commercial thoroughfare, King Street. He also would lead in raising funds to restore those commercial parts of the city that had been burned in the fire of 1838. In 1834, Memminger took up his life's task of reforming the city's public school system, eventually turning the Charleston high school into one of the finest schools of its kind. Many of the youths who succeeded looked back with pride to their days in that school. Those activities reveal just how much civic responsibility Memminger had and how he was determined to employ his considerable talents in behalf of his adopted city.

During the 1830s, Memminger married Mary Williams, a member of a prominent Charleston family. With that marriage he gained access to various social clubs, prized law cases, and statewide public office. But one is hard-pressed to grasp much about the marriage itself, because in his letters and writings Memminger said so little about his wife. What is available—none of Mary's letters have been discovered—reveals a companionate marriage with Mary assuming the task of raising their children while Christopher enjoyed the public life. No doubt she shared in the perquisites of his fame. Certainly, she also shared in his adversity, as it is known that during the Civil War she grieved over the hostility shown to her husband. After she died, it seems that Memminger lost focus in his own life.

The two of them led an active social life in antebellum Charleston, and many rewards came to Memminger for his service to the city. When Memminger went off to Columbia to the state legislature sessions, which he did continuously for years, Mary remained in Charleston to attend to their affairs there. First elected to the state legislature in 1836, he came to specialize in education reform and in the state's finances and banking. Perhaps on account of his own past, Memminger opposed the formation of pauper schools because of the stigma attached to them and instead advocated free public schools for all children, an act far in advance of the country's public opinion. He also supported education for the deaf, dumb, and blind and led the legislature in the successful debate of a bill to fund housing and care for those people. Memminger became a trustee of his alma mater in 1837 and served the college ably continuously until 1877. He wanted to improve the quality of college education, so as to better prepare young men for future service in public life. He raised funds for a state Normal School, helped to define its function as a teaching school, and rejoiced when it opened in 1859. According to Mattie C. Kneece, he wanted a "corps of well-educated and intelligent young ladies, who will train in their turn, the minds and hearts of" the children of South Carolina (37). From 1854 until 1887, he served on the Board of Free School Commissioners for Charleston.

Memminger's other passion was state banking and funding reform. For twenty years he chaired the South Carolina House Committee on Ways and Means. A convinced localist, he opposed national banking schemes and wanted to limit the power of banks. An astute student of parliamentary rules, he used those skills to block the powerful Charleston politician and banker Franklin H. Elmore's plan to recharter the Bank of Charleston. He feared that Elmore would use his control of that bank to dictate state government's investment programs. Memminger also favored a conservative gold-based currency policy, as he wanted to avoid speculative fluctuations, which he believed hurt local businesses. If some of his fellow legislators regarded him as cold, calculating, and austere, he nevertheless gained fame for his fiscal conservatism as well as his accomplishments in promoting business growth in South Carolina. His reputation grew throughout the South when he achieved state funding for the Blue Ridge Railroad Company in order to open trade possibilities between Charleston and the Southwest. But in truth this larger economic vision hardly reflected Memminger's primary interest, which was to enhance local economic development. As such, when given the opportunity, he eschewed national office and fame to remain active in state and local public life.

This localist interest also led Memminger to support South Carolina's ties with other slaveholding states. Where in his youth he had opposed state particularist action, by 1852 he had become a sectionalist cooperationist, and some even regarded him as a secessionist. He supported the convention of Southern states that met in Nashville in 1852 and lobbied that convention to adopt a unified front against Northern attacks on slavery. Perhaps his loyalty to his adopted homeland and his subsequent belief in a benevolent slave society led this man of reform to radical action. For even though he believed that the Northern states would never allow peaceful separation, he supported secession of all of the Southern states as the only way to protect the way of life he had come to cherish. Therefore, in the aftermath of the bloody John Brown encounter, Memminger traveled as an emissary from South Carolina to Virginia to persuade that critical upper South state to join ranks with the lower South. Regarded at that time as a brilliant conservative and political realist, he spoke before the Virginia state legislature in January 1860 in an earnest fashion about the threat to that which all Southerners held dear. But his worries at least temporarily fell on deaf ears.

Upon his return to South Carolina, he informed Governor William H. Gist that he had contributed to that call for unity that should force adversaries to yield to Southern demands. But when South Carolina's legislature demanded a convention after the results of the presidential election of 1860, Memminger resigned himself to single state secession. As a member of that convention he voted for the secession of South Carolina. Because of his statewide reputation and because of his brilliance as a writer and analyst of public events, the convention chose him to draft the South Carolina secession message. He wrote most of the Ordinance of Secession, a document that revealed just how much slaveholding society feared from the Republican party's takeover of the entire North. Although the document also announced that South Carolina was prepared to act alone if necessary, it was sent throughout the slaveholding states with hopes no doubt to influence other conventions' actions.

In February 1861, when the seceded states met in Montgomery, Alabama, with the purpose of establishing a separate Confederate nation, Memminger attended as a delegate from South Carolina. He served on the committee that drafted the Confederate States Constitution and assisted in writing into that document a vigorous defense of the rights of individual states. Elected to the Provisional Confederate States Senate, his colleagues chose the talented financial leader as chairman of the Committee on Commerce. Although unpopular among his own state's leaders, being considered too conservative for a revolutionary movement, they nevertheless wanted his talents in the Confederate States cabinet. Others from the seceded states had major experience in business matters and even in national public life, but President-elect Jefferson Davis offered Memminger the post of Secretary of the Treasury. Davis no doubt selected Memminger to such an important position because of the place of South Carolina in the Confederacy and because of his abilities, but he also seemed to identify with the serious and dour immigrant. In his efforts and loyalty, the South Carolinian never disappointed his chief. At Montgomery, Memminger worked around the clock to secure funds for the infant army. He organized a most efficient office, set a standard of work habits among his talented staff, and managed to raise much money in those early days, despite precious little support from the other slave states.

In 1861, Memminger appeared to the public as stern looking, a man with sharp features, a small goatee as was the fashion, now gray haired, and fit looking despite a corpulent figure. One colleague said he looked smart and able. Certainly the work pattern set in Montgomery would be expanded in Richmond as the Confederacy's desperate need for funds continued to grow. Early on this hard-eyed leader seemed to have established rapport with the Confederate Congress, though few of those leaders liked his way of lecturing them on their duties. Always well prepared when he appeared before its members, he seemed so sure about finances, and so clear in his presentation, that they gave him nearly everything he wanted. But his schemes soon proved too conservative, the Confederacy grew increasingly financially strapped, and the Congress, sensing his patronizing and pompous tone, turned against him.

What had happened? Why had Memminger, the talented former political leader, lost the support of Congress? Some say the answer lay in his personality, but that argument from character hides the need to look carefully at his policies and possibilities for success. It is true that Memminger over time became morose, solemn, and mean. Perhaps that was because he knew that he had no answer to the desperate problem of raising funds for the war effort.

To be perfectly blunt, Memminger had only one major task as Secretary of the Treasury, that being to raise money for the cause. He could do so either by taxation or by the adroit development of a loan system. Taxes raised through a tariff bill in May 1861 at first helped, but he believed that taxing a people who already were taxed on the goods they produced was unthinkable. So Memminger had to rely on loans in the form of the public sale of bonds. An early letting of bonds to the public at 8 percent failed to get enough purchasers. Local and state governments themselves had issued notes, and the public seemed more inclined to invest in the needs of small governments. As inflation rose, federal bonds as a means to control the flow of money became increasingly necessary. The failure of the Richmond government to control inflation merely made the amount of funds required to fight the war and to conduct government affairs much more costly. Memminger next tried a scheme to accept produce (largely agricultural goods) as payment for the bonds he wanted to issue. But the produce loan never generated enough income. Out of desperation Memminger even asked Southern railroad and manufacturing concerns to take government bonds in payment for their goods and services to the government.

The secretary never really supported the one scheme that could perhaps have raised income, that of the issuance of Treasury notes. Because of his own conservative position on hard currency and coin, he distrusted paper notes and believed they would not receive popular backing, and he knew banks would refuse them as payment. As credit policy after policy failed, Memminger at last tried direct taxation. He convinced Congress to pass an agricultural, wages, property, and business tax. When the public grew upset over this intrusion into its financial affairs, the Congress deserted the secretary. After Memminger finally convinced the government to print certificates of indebtedness, there were no takers for that paper currency. His attempts to get foreign investors to give the Confederacy credit based on cotton production failed. By the time it was tried the Confederate Navy and Merchant Marine could no longer get cotton through the Union blockade. Even Memminger's congressional Funding Act of 1864 only served as a stopgap measure that did not halt inflation and only made the cost of raising the funds necessary to continue the war effort that much more difficult.

At last fed up with the secretary's failures, Henry S. Foote, spokesperson for the congressional majority, moved that he be removed from office. By May 1864, the president knew that his trusted secretary now had little or no support from Congress and that he had become a political liability. Memminger's resignation soon followed. The verdict of Congress was that his stubborn personality, his fiscal conservative opposition to speculation in Treasury notes, and a contemptuous public unwilling to invest in the Confederacy's future had made him expendable. Ever loyal to the cause, the outgoing secretary assisted his successor in organizing his office. Then, along with his wife, in July, Memminger retired for the duration of the war to a country home in Flat Rock, North Carolina.

After the war ended, always the practical man of public affairs, Memminger accepted the reality of emancipation. He returned to Charleston and set up his law practice with William Jervey, and they became experts in family bankruptcy proceedings. He vowed to help his beloved Charleston again to become prosperous. Accordingly, he reentered the fray in support of education reform with the belief that good public schools would make for an able workforce. He also assisted in the reorganization and refinancing of the College of South Carolina, recently renamed the University of South Carolina. Memminger wanted to assist in creating the next generation of educated business leaders and public servants.

Then, after he had provided for others, Memminger set about to attempt to retrieve his own damaged wartime reputation. On March 28, 1874, in an article in the *Charleston News and Courier*, he haltingly responded to former Confederate General Joseph E. Johnston's (q.v.) attack on his tenure as Secretary of the Treasury. Johnston had claimed that Memminger's failure to raise adequate finances had destroyed the Confederacy. Feisty, but still impervious to his own failings, Memminger replied that only people who believed that cotton had been the panacea for success could say he had failed. He poked fun at phantom ships filled with phantom cotton. Then he admitted tellingly that his prewar training had not allowed him to think about the needs of a large, central government. After that outburst of pique and candor, Memminger retreated into local public service and continued to nurse in private his grudges against those who had destroyed his reputation.

After a long illness, on March 7, 1888, he died in Charleston. The local obituaries all referred to his faith and his duty and ignored his wartime service. Mattie Crouch Kneece has pointed out that the bust of Memminger dedicated at the Charleston City Hall in 1888 gave tribute to his work for public schools, his devotion to the Episcopal Church, and even to his support for black youth, but said nothing about the Civil War. Unfortunately, the verdict of history has not passed over that war record.

Immediately after the war, the infamous Rebel war clerk John B. Jones published his *Diary*, in which he had noted on January 20, 1863, "Mr. Memminger should never have been appointed. He is headstrong, haughty, and tyrannical . . . and he deems himself superior." Jones then called him stupid and claimed that his resignation "caused much rejoicing" (1:242). The ever critical former congressman Henry S. Foote stated that Memminger was a poor economist. Only those closest to him, former clerks such as Henry W. Capers, defended his record. To Capers, Memminger had been a victim of others' poor management and had succeeded despite the failures of those around him. Capers personally had published large portions of Memminger's key financial reports because he believed they would vindicate his actions. Certainly the reports revealed a man who had become keenly aware of the need for his office to rouse public support for financing the war effort. But the reports also show a stubborn, conservative leader, unwilling to take risks, and the frustrations of a leader unable to cope with the national politics of Confederate governance and those unwilling to sacrifice for Confederate victory.

Sometime after that first generation of former Confederates' attempts to besmirch or resurrect Memminger's reputation, the professional historians tried their hands. The first serious reevaluation of his career came from Burton J. Hendrick, in *Statesmen of the Lost Cause* (1939), who depicted him as a useful citizen who was never bitter over attacks on him. Hendricks skirted making serious judgment of the former secretary's financial activities and instead showed him to have been a victim of an angry Congress. In 1944, Rembert W. Patrick, in *Jefferson Davis and His Cabinet*, also sympathized with Memminger's plight. Patrick castigated both Jones and Foote for their personal attacks on a man who had done his best. Even the author of the most thorough and sensitive portrayal of the travails of the Confederate Congress, Wilfred B.

Yearns, showed some feeling for the secretary who had to deal with such a divided Congress. Yearns suggested that Congress's forcing out of Memminger might not have been in the best interest of the Confederacy.

But those are the apologies of institutional-political historians. In the view of the new economic historians, Memminger's place in the war's history again sank. Robert C. Todd, in *Confederate Finance* (1954), gives him credit for having faced enormous economic obstacles. But he concludes that Memminger's unwillingness to print paper money until too late doomed the Confederacy to financial insecurity and finally squeezed it dry. Most recently, Douglas B. Ball, in *Financial Failure and Confederate Defeat* (1991), uses keen biographical insight and thorough understanding of financial matters to level Memminger's reputation in such a way that it is difficult to imagine that it will ever recover. The fault, says Ball, was the absence of a unified goal for the Confederacy. That absence was fed by Memminger's total failure to maintain a system of public finance. Not only did the secretary clash with other able financial leaders, but he refused to believe that the government should have assisted Confederate businesses. Finally, Ball states, Memminger "never seemed to get his priorities right." He "conducted economic affairs . . . in a manner reminiscent of the ir- responsible, transient rulers of a bankrupt banana republic" (268). In short, Memminger had only a localist politician's and small businessman's experience to apply to the science of finances for a new nation-state.

BIBLIOGRAPHY

John B. Jones, *A Rebel War Clerk's Diary at the Confederate States Capitol*, 2 vols. (Philadelphia: J. B. Lippincott and Co., 1866).

Henry D. Capers, *The Life and Times of Christopher G. Memminger* (Richmond, Va.: Everett Waddey Co., 1893).

Mattie Crouch Kneece, *The Contribution of C. G. Memminger to the Cause of Education* (Columbia: University of South Carolina Press, 1926).

Burton J. Hendrick, *Statesmen of the Lost Cause* (Boston: Little, Brown & Co., 1939).

Rembert W. Patrick, *Jefferson Davis and His Cabinet* (Baton Rouge: Louisiana State University Press, 1944).

Robert Cecil Todd, *Confederate Finance* (Athens: University of Georgia Press, 1954).

Wilfred Buck Yearns, *The Confederate Congress* (Athens: University of Georgia Press, 1960).

Douglas B. Ball, *Financial Failure and Confederate Defeat* (Champagne: University of Illinois Press, 1991).

OLIVER PERRY MORTON
(August 4, 1823–November 1, 1877)

Jon L. Wakelyn

As governor of Indiana throughout the Civil War, Oliver Perry Morton served the Union cause loyally and ably, despite having to deal with a recalcitrant state legislature bent on thwarting his policies. It is true that because of his devotion to the nation Morton at times used unusual and often illegal powers, which made him a despised figure among Democrats. Yet for most Republican or Union party leaders, other than Indiana's radical abolitionist faction, he became a wartime hero. After all, they knew that no state could have posed more of a problem to the Union cause than Indiana, a strong Democratic party bastion filled with recent immigrants from the slaveowning states. Accordingly, his actions received critical praise from his allies until after his death. But today his life largely goes unstudied, except for those historians who have begun to understand the centrality of state actions to the war effort. Perhaps a reconsideration of the life of this most important state leader could contribute to further analysis of the states' roles in the Civil War.

Oliver Hazard Perry Throckmorton, for that was his full name, began life in a typical migrant midwestern household that had achieved enough middle-class status among its extended family to give him the opportunity to profit from those fluid and affluent times. His hometown, the now-abandoned Saulsbury in Wayne County, Indiana, on August 4, 1823, when Morton was born, had gone from modest success to near-empty population as the state's wealth had passed it by. How did the family get to that desolate place? Oliver's father, James Throckmorton, descended from a successful New England colonial family that had removed to New Jersey, had married Sarah Miller, also from a family of substance. But the elder Throckmorton was a proud man who had fallen out with his older brothers over his being shortchanged in their father's will. In a fit of pique he dropped the "Throck" from his name, and as James Morton he removed to the Ohio frontier. He fought in the War of 1812 and thus probably named his son for his own hero Oliver H. Perry, the victor at the Battle of Lake

Erie. James later opened a tavern in one of the Ohio boomtowns. He then invested in the burgeoning canal building schemes, at first had modest success, and eventually went broke. The business failure led James to Saulsbury, Indiana, where Oliver was born, and later to Centreville, where he owned a shoemaking establishment. Neither of the parents had come from farm backgrounds, which made them atypical of their times.

The tale of young Oliver's rise to a profession and later to public prominence is related to the importance of an extended midwestern family's support of its own. In 1826, when Oliver was three, his mother died, probably in childbirth. His father sent him to Springfield, Indiana, to be raised by stern Presbyterian aunts, his mother's sisters, who forever weaned him of any church loyalties. Like other young men of his class, he attended school for a while. A man named Hoshour at Wayne County Seminary taught him the rudiments of reading and writing. Also, like others of his ilk, he was not allowed to have idle hands. His aunts put Oliver to work as an apothecary's clerk. The hotheaded young man soon clashed with his boss and left his service. Apprenticed to his older brother in the hatmaking trade, he soon decided that that kind of work was not for him. Fortunately, Oliver's grandfather had left him a small sum of money, and in 1843, he talked his family into allowing him to go off to the fledgling Miami University in Oxford, Ohio. There he mainly studied debate and played an early form of football. Successful at debate, Oliver won a number of prizes. But he had little patience for university life. He left school and returned to Springfield, where on May 15, 1845, he married Lucinda M. Burbank. Oliver was twenty-two years old and had no profession. Ambitious and in a hurry, he went to his father's town of Centreville and joined the lawyer John S. Newman as his stu-dent and general clerk. At first he loathed the technicalities connected to stud-ying law, but soon he came to realize that he could make a good case in court through his guile and verbal skills. Over the next few years he took on a number of law partners as he began to make a success of himself.

Along with other young lawyers in the ever-civilizing small towns of the antebellum middle west, Morton knew that politics and public service paved the way to a place in the community and to business success. In 1848, he ran for Wayne County prosecuting attorney and lost. His state's rights beliefs had led him to join the Jacksonian Democratic party in a district that was heavily Whig. Still, in 1852 the voters of Wayne County elected him a circuit court judge, then defeated him in the next election. Then Morton made an extraordinary decision for a thirty-year-old lawyer with a family and a mortgage. Realizing that he had little real refinement in the law and that he lived in a world grown more sophisticated in business practice, he went to study at the famous Cincin-nati Law School to sharpen his skills and learn more about the new practice of corporate law. While in attendance he made friends with Murat Halstead and a number of other young midwestern politicos who would fashion the Republican party. Back in Centreville in 1854, where he would soon become a famous trial lawyer, Morton joined the Odd Fellows society, at that time the organization to which all successful businessmen belonged. Morton then took on several railroad cases that he won. He soon gained financial security, bought land, and renewed his interest in public service.

To reenter the political fray, just as the cozy world of midwestern politics was becoming roiled by the Kansas-Nebraska crisis, must have shaken this man who was known as a Democratic party moderate who rejected the politics of those who too vigorously protested slavery. But Morton realized that there was no political future in his section for one who supported the expansion of slavery, so he turned against the Democratic party. At first he flirted with the new Temperance party, then joined the mildly nativist People's party, as he coupled antagonism to the extension of slavery with resistance to aliens voting in Indiana. By 1856 he had become a staunch Republican, having been in on the founding and building of that party in Indiana. He lost the nomination for governor that year when he tilted with the more radical branch of the party run by the abolitionist George W. Julian. In 1860, Morton was the successful candidate for lieutenant governor. His biographer William D. Foulke stated that "his great hold upon the people of Indiana was due to his conservatism" (83). Certainly Morton was one of those who believed that the inland states, as the future trading center of the country, needed one united nation. His moderate views and idea of nationalism were soon in for the test of the young country's life.

Just why Morton had become such a strong nationalist has never been documented fully. His hometown location of Centreville in Wayne County, situated on the Ohio border near rich farmland, although north of the region of intense Southern immigration, does not seem to explain his actions or beliefs. He had become quite successful in the practice of the new corporate law and accustomed to the life around Indianapolis, so perhaps he hoped to see Indiana become part of the new industrial world developing then in the Northeast. Morton had also imbibed the nationalist language of the new Republican party. In his cynical and harsh way, William B. Hesseltine claimed to have understood Morton's actions. Hesseltine charged that "Morton was an opportunist who adapted his principles to the demand of politics" (42). It is an accusation worth testing in that crucible of war. Certainly his ambitions had led him to support Abraham Lincoln (q.v) for president and to employ the language of national unity in his campaign for lieutenant governor. So, when shortly after his successful election Governor Henry S. Lane accepted the legislature's vote to become a U.S. Senator, the lieutenant governor, though not elected to the office, automatically became the governor of his state. His friendship with Lincoln, and he said his near total lack of elected office experience, seemed the only political advantage he had.

The new governor at least knew there soon would be war and that Indiana needed to be protected. That he set out to do. At that time he was equipped with a large and healthy frame, broad shoulders, black hair, searching and penetrating eyes, and a deep and resonant voice. At his inauguration in January 1861, he stated flatly that no state had the right to secede. Further, "I am not to argue questions of state equality, but to denounce treason and uphold the cause of the Union'' (Foulke, 1:102). So when on January 31, 1861, he was asked to appoint commissioners to seek peace at the Virginia Convention, Morton named those who would oppose compromise over the extension of slavery. He also knew that the state had few funds, but he nevertheless began to purchase weapons and to prepare to defend the Indiana border. He traveled to Washington to promise the new president his support in raising troops. On April 15, 1861, after the firing on Fort Sumter, when President Lincoln asked Indiana for troops, the governor pledged 10,000 men. During his war message in April, Morton defined treason as resistance to the needs of Indiana and called for raising $1 million through the sale of bonds. He hired detectives to cut off Indiana military supplies smuggled into the Confederacy. He bought arms in New York and set up a military communications network with friends in the East. When the three-month enlistments of Indiana troops sent to western Virginia ran out, Morton persuaded a number of them to reenlist. He led the charge in his own state to pass the Six-Regiment Bill that would guarantee a continuous flow of young Indianans into the United States Army. By January 1862 there were forty-eight Indiana regiments in the service. Those 53,000 men represented the largest percentage of troops sent in to combat of any state in the North.

Not only did Governor Morton work to recruit men and materiel in Indiana; he also solicited troops for the Union cause in Ohio and Kentucky. Perhaps the proximity of Confederate troops on the Kentucky border had quickened his actions. Certainly he knew Kentucky Governor Beriah Magoffin to be pro-Confederate, and that led him to assist that border state's Unionist contingent. Morton also resisted and attempted to undermine the rise of a peace movement in the border states. He advocated that Kentucky allow Union troops to pass through on their way to fight in Tennessee and Missouri. Despite President Lincoln's fears of losing the support of Kentucky Unionists, Morton persuaded him to keep a sizable army in that state. Morton personally sent troops to Kentucky. He even traveled to Kentucky to raise a home guard to protect the border. That the vital trading center of Louisville remained in Union hands was in part due to Morton's willingness to protect that river city. At all costs for him, Indiana's border had to be protected, and Kentucky's Unionists were essential to that scheme.

The governor also knew quite early in the war the importance of public opinion in keeping Indianans loyal to the Union. His gestures to assist Indiana troops at the front and to provide food and shelter for their families behind the lines reflected his knowledge of public image making and were vital to the Union war effort. Morton went beyond word to deed as he made urgent appeals to private citizens and personally raised funds for food, blankets, and clothing for the troops and their families. He sent agents behind the military lines to collect soldiers' pay to take to their families back home in Indiana. In February 1862, the governor organized the Indiana Sanitary Commission in order to handle medical problems of the troops. He did not work well with the national Sanitary

Commission, but he established an excellent reputation among the Indiana women who handled most of the work of the State Commission. He sent extra surgeons south after the battle of Shiloh and made a concerted effort to appoint additional Indiana doctors to take care of the Indiana regiments fighting in the Western theater. Under the governor's instructions, officers rented homes in Tennessee for Indiana soldiers' families. A City Hospital was founded in Indianapolis to take care of wounded troops sent home. In a dramatic gesture Morton traveled to visit troops on the battlefield. Pay for the troops was always on his mind, and in late 1862, he petitioned the federal Congress for further compensation for them.

Along with his attention to the troops and their families, Morton also tried to devise strategies to counter rebel attacks on the border and to end the war as soon as possible. He asked the Union military high command to expedite the conquest of the West so as to divide the Confederate states along the Mississippi River. Not only did he believe that a conquered Southwest would hasten the war's end; he also wanted a neutral Missouri to counter the buildup of Confederate border ruffians. Of course, an open Mississippi River would also help the trade balance of Indiana, as its merchants and farmers could then send goods through the port of New Orleans. In addition to resisting border rebels, he assisted Ohioans with the defense of Cincinnati in late 1862. In September of that year, the governor declared martial law in the Indiana river counties, and he built a successful home guard. He loathed Don Carlos Buell, the Union commander in Kentucky, and became frightened of a Confederate military invasion after the near disaster at the Battle of Perryville. Morton went so far as to ask the president for an independent military command, which Lincoln wisely declined with the assertion that he was much too needed in Indiana.

In Indiana, the so-called harsh, intolerant, and repressive governor had to face the real possibility of the hated Democrats' reemergence to power in the state in the elections of 1862. Morton's greatest fear of the midwestern Democrats was that "they would array the Northwestern states against New England through the plea of mutual interest with the South" (Foulke, 1:205). When a secret association, probably the Knights of the Golden Circle, tried to disrupt tax collecting, he had a number of Democratic party opponents arrested. For this the peace movement opposition roundly denounced him as anti civil rights. Undaunted, he continued to shore up his base in Indiana and to work to unite the Northwestern states. Morton traveled to Pennsylvania to endorse the Emancipation Proclamation and to discuss plans to conquer the entire Mississippi Valley. A war to end slavery as well as economic gain, he believed, would unite Westerners. He also had come to see slavery as the major impediment to a restored Union. But Morton misunderstood that Midwesterners might want economic development and a united nation yet remain in favor of slavery. The result of his actions against slavery were that the Democrats carried the Indiana state legislature in 1862.

If Morton had been considered ruthless before in his fervent support of reunion, what would the governor do in 1863, now that the hated peace advocates controlled his state legislature? He resisted them on all fronts, and they attempted to stop all of his activities. The Democrats accused him of making arbitrary arrests and, worse, threatened the governor with court action over alleged financial misdealings. When the state legislature refused to allow him to collect taxes or to appropriate war-related funds for gubernatorial use, Morton virtually shut it down. When the Democrats voted to set up a state military board to take control of the war effort from him, the governor vetoed the measure and appealed to the troops in the field for support. In 1863, believing that the peace Democrats were united across state lines, an angry Morton went to Ohio to campaign against the election of Clement L. Vallandigham for governor. Adroitly, he raised funds outside of the normal channel of state taxes, received $250,000 from Secretary of War Edwin Stanton (q.v.) in order to build up state defenses, and organized an extralegal government Bureau of Finance to disperse funds for local defense. The state government then ran into financial trouble, and it was forced to default on loans. So Morton persuaded his friend Secretary of the Treasury Salmon P. Chase (q.v.) to back up and guarantee the state's indebtedness. In July 1863, without support from the state legislature, he organized a citizen's militia to ward off the threatened raid of John Hunt Morgan. He even offered the governor of Ohio 5,000 Indiana troops to protect that state's border. Of course, almost all of the governor's activities were considered illegal by the Democratic state legislature.

But the hatred of those peace Democrats for him was not supported by the state's Republicans, as they united behind Morton in his campaign for reelection in 1864. Morton stood against slavery and a separate peace with the Confederates. In what became a brutal campaign, both sides traded charges of treason and usurpation of the law. Morton also realized that he needed the votes of front line soldiers to win reelection, so he went to Washington to plea for allowing them to register their vote in absentia. Turned down in his request, he nevertheless managed to get enough soldiers furloughed to give him victory by over 20,000 votes. After his successful reelection, Morton traveled throughout the Midwest and spoke in support of the reelection of President Lincoln.

The Republicans also had retaken the state legislature in 1864, but Morton continued to conduct government affairs by himself. By then the state's reputation for vigorous pursuit of the war had become synonymous with the name of Morton. He continued to finance relief for soldiers and their families. The state's good credit rating was restored. Morton negotiated a bill to pay the claims of loyal Indianans who had been burned out in the rebel John Hunt Morgan's raid. In a dramatic move, he stopped a bipartisan effort in the legislature to colonize ex-slaves and charged that the country had a responsibility to care for them. As the war ground down, the full weight of years of frantic service began to tell on the governor's health. Stooped and graying, he began to look like an old man. When President Lincoln was assassinated, he took the news quite hard. Lincoln had meant union and had symbolized the cause for which Morton had fought. Even though he had worked well during the war with new President Andrew Johnson (q.v.) he hardly knew what to expect from that former Democrat.

Despite the change in national leadership, Governor Morton next turned to a vigorous pursuit of Reconstruction as the means to keep the country united. As wave after wave of Indiana troops returned home, he held parades and dinners in their honor, perhaps to remind them of what he had done for them and their families. He also, and more importantly, expected their support for Reconstruction. Morton formulated his own views of peace as he insisted the slave states had never left the Union, and therefore the federal government was not liable for their debts. At first he took a moderate view on what to do about the ex-slaves, as he refused to support black suffrage. Perhaps he thought that the black suffrage issue would lead to racial conflict. At least he appeared to believe that when he endorsed early enfranchisement for ex-Confederates. He then went to Washington to visit President Andrew Johnson and came away a supporter of the president's moderate plans for Reconstruction of the South.

Worn down from his efforts, during the autumn of 1865 Morton suffered a paralytic stroke, which at first left him speechless and unable to walk. Taken to Europe to convalesce—the president had given him a special mission to France—he gradually recovered his health, though he would never again walk without the use of a cane. When Morton returned to Indiana in June 1866, he discovered that in his judgment the president had betrayed the Union. He wanted to resume his political career in order to oppose the president's not-so-moderate Reconstruction plans, so he began to angle for election to the U.S. Senate. In order to carve out his differences with the president, Morton resorted to his old tactic of speaking often in public. To preserve the fruits of Union victory, Morton now claimed that ex-slaves had to be enfranchised in the South. The Republican party also had become for this former moderate the savior of the victory, and he wanted to expand its electoral strength in the ex-Confederate states. His most sympathetic biographer says that "Morton was an intense and bitter partisan, to whom the success of the Democracy meant the loss of all that had been won" (Foulke, 2:476). He broke with President Johnson and claimed that victory could only be preserved by awakening "old memories" of the war struggle (Foulke, 2:477).

Chosen by grateful Indianans in 1868 to represent them in the U.S. Senate, Morton immediately went to work to preserve that victory. For him, seating Southerners in Congress could only be tolerated if they endorsed ratification of the Fifteenth Amendment. Of course, along with most Republicans, he voted to remove President Johnson from office. In 1868, he campaigned throughout the Midwest in behalf of U. S. Grant's (q.v.) candidacy for president. His Reconstruction views continued to harden as he advocated the retention of military governors even in states that had been restored to the Union. But Morton also had hopes for the future economic growth of the Midwest, so he also turned his efforts to the issue of financial growth. Seeking a proper balance between farm and business interests in Indiana, he opposed financial contraction but also wanted to continue the specie payments, which would be of benefit to the business community. Taking an interest in foreign acquisitions, he supported President Grant on the Santo Domingo treaty but later refused the position of ambassador to England. Presidential powers to investigate the violence of the Ku Klux Klan he found necessary. Morton even favored some sort of civil service reform, though he feared the Senate would politicize any efforts at reorganization of the federal bureaucracy.

In 1872, the state legislature of Indiana again returned the popular ex-governor to the U.S. Senate. He took little time to plead his own case, as Morton soon mounted a speaking tour in Indiana and Illinois in support of Grant's second term. Morton became frightened over the deepening downturn of the economy in the wake of the depression of 1873. He now introduced bills to expand the currency in order to put more money into circulation. As an advocate of enlarging popular electoral power, he favored an end to the electoral college, and he supported the right of women to vote. As Republicans bore the brunt of blame for the depression, a politically hostile Midwest forced him to campaign feverishly to preserve its electoral majority in order to protect the war victory. Morton reminded his listeners again and again of their sacrifices in behalf of the Union against Confederate, or Democratic, traitors. In the presidential run-up to 1876 at first he had national ambitions but then loyally backed midwesterner Rutherford B. Hayes. Even though he believed the election vote was fradulent, Morton knew the party had to prevail. In his last political act, he voted for the compromise that sold out Southern Republicans to preserve the Northern Republican majority. He died in Indianapolis on November 1, 1877.

The immediate response to Morton's death was public remorse over the loss of a great patriot. He was eulogized in an 1878 Memorial Address in Congress as one who had given his life to the nation. Editor of the *Indianapolis Journal* Charles M. Walker, also in 1878, claimed that Morton had saved Indiana during the Civil War. In his two-volume tribute to his friend, William Dudley Foulke in 1899 regarded Morton as Indiana's most famous political leader. The state legislature had a statue of him placed in the Hall of the U.S. Capitol in 1900, and a monument was raised on the state capitol grounds in 1908. In his *Life, Speeches, State Papers and Public Service of Governor Oliver P. Morton*, published in 1900, William M. French sought to preserve for history the accomplishments of that famous war governor. For French, "it must be apparent to every reader of history that justice has not been done to Governor Morton" (iii). French obviously sensed that his hero's life was fading from public view.

For a time at least, professional historians did not forget his name. Instead, they worked him over as an anti civil libertarian and regarded him as virtually a dictator in wartime Indiana. William B. Hesseltine, in his seminal *Lincoln and the War Governors* (1948), regarded Morton as the most able of the wartime governors but perhaps too much of an opportunist to govern with principles. His verdict on Morton's wartime career was that the governor "had zeal and ingenuity and administrative skill, but his emotions were unstable, and he was frequently filled with unwarranted terror'' (391). In 1973, G. R. Treadway went even further as he built on the efforts of Kenneth Stampp, a former Hesseltine student, to judge Morton's actions as governor as "dictatorial." Treadway insisted that Democrats who had defended themselves against Morton were neither seditious nor disloyal (268). Viciously, Treadway claimed that Morton's so-called military arrests of Democrats in 1864 were only done to ensure his and Lincoln's reelection.

But there also have been some modest disclaimers over charges of Morton's heavy-handedness. Emma Lou Thornbrough, in a 1965 history of Indiana in the Civil War, defended Morton's actions as necessary to keep Indiana from internal civil war. Of course, in his "personality and methods" Morton "exacerbated the bitterness and fears of his Democratic opponents" (182). But Thornbrough insists that Morton was indeed remarkable in his efforts to fund the state's defenses, his stalwart support for the draft, and his courage in the face of Confederate raider invasions of Indiana.

Thornbrough also cited a Republican State Central Committee pamphlet of 1876 that "declared that Governor Morton was compelled to fight two rebellions—one in the South and one in Indiana" (180). That pamphlet perhaps points to why Morton has had so few present-day defenders. Morton's wartime efforts in behalf of preserving the Union were useful to Republicans as long as he reminded voters of their nationalism. In the twentieth century, when the bloody shirt no longer won elections for the Republicans, they deserted him. The man who had fought so hard to preserve the Union became an example of zealous and untrammeled bending of the laws to his personal cause. Presently, except for the occasional article that discusses his keen understanding of finances and administration, Morton is rarely studied. For those who so zealously support civil liberties he seems to have become an embarrassment. Perhaps it is time to revisit this life and to call into question Hesseltine's charges, as the country again faces the issue of what it means to support the idea of nation. Certainly, students of the Civil War period must know more about how the state governments performed, especially in view of the tensions that then existed between state and nation.

BIBLIOGRAPHY

Charles M. Walker, *Sketch of the Life, Character, and Public Services of Oliver P. Morton* (Indianapolis: Indianapolis Journal, 1878).

William Dudley Foulke, *Life of Oliver P. Morton*, 2 vols. (Indianapolis: Bowen-Merrill Co., 1899).

William M. French, *Life, Speeches, State Papers and Public Service of Governor Oliver P. Morton* (Indianapolis: S. L. Marrow and Co., 1900).

William Best Hesseltine, *Lincoln and the War Governors* (New York: Alfred A. Knopf, 1948).

Kenneth M. Stampp, *Indiana Politics During the Civil War* (Indianapolis: Indiana Historical Bureau, 1949).

Emma Lou Thornbrough, *Indiana in the Civil War, 1850–1880* (Indianapolis: Indiana Historical Bureau and Indiana Historical Society, 1965).

G. R. Treadway, *Democratic Opposition to the Lincoln Administration in Indiana* (Indianapolis: Indiana Historical Bureau, 1973).

Scott Roller, ''Business as Usual: Indiana's Response to the Confederate Invasion of the Summer of 1863,'' *Indiana Magazine of History* 88 (March 1992): 1–25.

BENJAMIN MORGAN PALMER
(January 25, 1818–May 28, 1902)

Jon L. Wakelyn

Both the Confederate government and the Southern people considered the Presbyterian minister Benjamin Morgan Palmer as its most famous preacher propagandist and regarded him as an important war leader. Ultraorthodox, prolific with pen and voice, he used his brilliant oratorical abilities throughout the war to stir his people to action. When he died, the press and the many attendees at his funeral eulogized him as the "preacher to the Confederacy." Shortly thereafter, however, the Presbyterian Synod diminished his importance, perhaps because in his later years he forsook Southern-wide fame to labor close to home. His name now has faded in history. Even those who today inhabit New Orleans, the city that he so marked with his words and deeds, ask, Who is Palmer Street named after? To restore his place in Southern history and especially his contributions to the Confederacy, it is important to review how he became such a famous clergyman and just why his reputation has declined.

Like so many other great leaders of the Confederacy, Palmer's American antecedents begin in the Calvinist Congregational world of New England. His grandfather, John, left Connecticut to become a contractor and builder in Charleston, South Carolina. He also served as clerk and sexton to the Congregational Circular Church there. Benjamin's father, Reverend Edward Palmer, had attended Phillips Academy in Andover, Massachusetts, and had studied for the ministry at the famous Andover Seminary. He later received an M.A. from Yale College. Edward returned home to hold pulpits in the Congregational churches of Dorchester and later Walterboro, South Carolina. Benjamin's mother, Sarah Bunce, who greatly influenced his life with her stubborn will, intelligence, and desire for him to succeed, had been born in Connecticut into a merchant family. Benjamin's namesake and uncle, Benjamin Palmer, also became a Congregational minister in Charleston and later edited an important religious journal. Into this family of powerful clergy, Benjamin was born in

Charleston on January 25, 1818. That strict and, some thought, unforgiving family obviously planned to raise young Benjamin to follow in its footsteps.

But young Benjamin was not predisposed to enter the church. In fact, he at first had hoped to use his great voice and speaking skills in the practice of law. Early educated at home by his parents, he showed a brilliant and quick mind and a gift for recall. In 1827 he was sent to the school of J. B. Van Dyck, a stern Calvinist minister, where he prepared for college. His father at first wanted to send him to the College of South Carolina but decided against that place because its president, Thomas Cooper, was a free thinker. Instead, Benjamin attended the ultraorthodox Calvinist Congregational Amherst College in western Massachusetts, founded only a few years before to train poor but bright boys to become teachers and preachers. Young Benjamin—he was only fourteen when he matriculated in 1832—soon earned the respect of his classmates with his speaking skills, and he rose to the head of his class. But Benjamin, even as a youth a fervent supporter of South Carolina's nullification movement and Southern sectionalism, no doubt felt a bit lonely and out of place at a college that had begun to acquire the reputation for antislavery activity. In 1834 an incident of personal honor led to his expulsion from Amherst. No doubt those troubles of a young Southerner in the North fed his growing animosity toward his college and that section. Although the facts surrounding his leaving Amherst remain largely unknown, it appears that school authorities had asked that he reveal the names of members of his literary society who had lampooned faculty members. When Palmer refused, the president expelled him. Whatever had actually happened, Benjamin's father did not take his son's disgrace lightly but blamed him and put him out to fend for himself.

Obliged to tutor at the homes of rich planters, Palmer was sorely tempted by the wild life he saw around him. For a time he rebelled against his religious family. Perhaps because of his poverty, or because Calvinism had seeped into his pores, he had a religious conversion that he later claimed had saved him from a wicked life. In 1837 Palmer carried his beliefs to Franklin College (later the University of Georgia), where he graduated number one in his class. While a student in Athens he worked as a tutor to earn his own way through that rich boy's college. Rather than join some of his classmates in the study of the law, Palmer decided to pursue the profession of his father and uncle.

To prepare for his life's work, in January 1839 Palmer entered the Presbyterian Theological Seminary in Columbia, South Carolina, to study a staunchly conservative curriculum, similar to the one his father had imbibed at Andover. There he grew close to a brilliant young minister and college professor, the Reverend James Henly Thornwell, who would influence his life immensely by confirming him in the Old School Presbyterian ways.

Upon graduation from the seminary in 1841 Palmer became the agent for the Charleston religious magazine the *Temperance Advocate*. He married Augusta McConnell of that city who would be his close associate as long as she lived. That same year the elders called him to the Presbyterian Church in Savannah,

Georgia, which had been the church of the Reverend Charles C. Jones until he resigned to minister to the slaves. During his years in Savannah, Palmer came under the influence of Jones and his reform attitudes about master-slave relations and preaching the gospel to the slaves. In 1843, Palmer received a call to the First Presbyterian Church in Columbia, South Carolina, a place where he would hone his orthodox skills and become one of the Old South's most famous preachers. Undeterred that the church had once employed the legendary preacher and his former tutor James H. Thornwell as its minister, Palmer's success in the pulpit led the church to outgrow its confines, and the church fathers elected to build a larger and more spacious building to house the growing congregation.

In 1847, Palmer joined Thornwell in founding the *Southern Presbyterian Review*, a journal that became a leading orthodox and extreme sectionalist publication. Palmer often wrote for it, as he used its pages to engage in religious and political battles. A man of vigorous opinions and a leader in the pulpit, it was not long before he clashed with what he believed were the loose ways of members of his Columbia congregation. Over the issue of his opposition to dancing in the church, many younger parishoners condemned him and demanded his resignation. He refused to resign his pulpit. Palmer also taught his Calvinist views to a generation of future clergy at the seminary. It is no wonder that he often was offered prestigious conservative pulpits elsewhere and that he was at one time tempted to go to Cincinnati, Ohio, and later to Philadelphia. But always the Synod found ways to keep him in Columbia, that is, until 1856 when he was called to New Orleans and finally accepted.

No doubt the defenders of the South and the powers of orthodoxy would have lost a great advocate if that keen student of church polity had moved to the North. But in New Orleans at First Presbyterian, in 1857 the Southwest's largest and most prestigious Presbyterian congregation, he continued his polemical preaching. The church grew and Palmer himself, as before in Columbia, became close to the city's leading business and political leaders. As his biographer said: "He was to become in the new and larger arenas not only a great religious leader, but in epochal moments the moral and political mouthpiece of the city, state, and section of his adoption" (Johnson, 169). Indeed, Palmer became a powerful force in the Southwest Synod, which allowed him to spread orthodoxy even further. But he also became a legendary figure in that region when he helped to battle the yellow fever epidemic of 1858. In addition, Palmer revealed other aspects of his own peculiar reformist sentiments when he developed a ministry to Louisiana's slaves. He worked indefatigably to dissaude slaveholders from treating their slaves harshly.

Some historians insist that Palmer's reform activities were related to his hostilities to what he believed were sanctimonious Northern abolitionist attacks on slavery. Palmer's resentment toward Northerners indeed had grown in the years building up to the Civil War. He wrote ever more impassioned defensive articles in the *Southern Presbyterian Review*. And he began a movement for a separate Southern Presbyterian Church. Northerners rightly accused him of advocating a

Southern Presbyterian Church as a means to resist the encroachment of the national church on Southern interests. During the secession crisis, because of his intense loyalty to his section, Palmer took the lead among the radical secessionist Southern clergy.

Most important for the political leaders of secession, Palmer used his oratorical skills and clarity of expression honed by years of experience and learning to persuade the public to support separation. In his famous November 1860 Thanksgiving Day Sermon preached in New Orleans, he claimed Southerners had many grievances against the North. Palmer also insisted that secession was a sovereign right, that it was sanctioned in scriptures, and that Northern government hostilities had forced the South to debate secession. A modern historian, Doralyn Hickey, believes that Palmer, in that sermon, had expressed fear that the North wanted to free the slaves (67). Some 50,000 copies of that sermon were printed in pamphlet form and circulated throughout the South. That pamphlet became a most powerful part of Southern secession propaganda. The fame he received from his pamphlet led the new Confederate government to expect much support from Palmer in the forthcoming Civil War. Its leaders were not to be disappointed.

Throughout the Civil War, Palmer would preach resistance to the Union in the pulpits of the South's largest towns and in the front lines among the soldiers. With his publications he also promoted the interests of the Confederate cause. In 1861 he was well prepared for his wartime leadership role. Short, slender, with penetrating eyes, a firm chin, he had the tone of voice and the rhetorical flourishes that could sway the multitudes. Palmer began his war activities that May when he preached to a group of soldiers who were soon to go into combat. To the famous New Orleans Crescent Rifles he invoked the scriptures to vindicate the propriety of fighting. He urged them to sacrifice and to labor in that war for the defense of their homeland. Speaking on another occasion from the steps of city hall to some 5,000 citizens and soldiers, he insisted that the Louisiana Washington Artillery resist the Northern invasion in order to protect the right of self-government. To them he advocated the pursuit of a holy war, a war of true Christian faith against fanaticism. Later in 1861, Palmer traveled to the front lines with those Louisiana troops as they moved up the Mississippi River to Tennessee. Before they went into combat, he preached to them that they were fighting for their homes and their families.

Not a few observers at that time questioned whether the New Orleans divine had crossed the boundary between church and state. But Palmer had taught church polity, and many years as a leader had drilled into him the importance of his religious duty to his people. So Palmer pushed on through that first year of the war. In the summer of 1861 he wrote a "Declaratory Act" to unite all the slaveholding states behind the Confederate war effort. He then assumed statewide leadership of the Presbyterian Church. At the October Synod that gathered all the church leaders of the Southwest, he was made moderator. On December 4, 1861, at the Synod's meeting in Augusta, Georgia, his fellow clergymen honored him with their request that he give the opening sermon. His close friend James H. Thornwell also attended, but that famous leader was unwell. When the delegation, with Palmer leading, voted to set up a separate Confederate States Presbyterian Church, its members made him their president. As the presiding minister of that new church, he stated that he would work tirelessly in behalf of the old school tradition as the true religious belief for the new Confederate nation. Palmer then joined the army of Albert Sidney Johnston just before the battle of Shiloh in April 1862. He preached to and exhorted the Tennessee troops to continue to fight. But for a few other forays into the Tennessee region in 1863 and 1864, that act before Shiloh would be his last effort in behalf of the Confederacy in the Southwest.

In the spring of 1862, his beloved adopted city New Orleans came under Union control, and the Federal commander, General Benjamin "Beast" Butler, declared Palmer an outlaw. Palmer's preaching thus had made him a marked man, and the Union troops would not allow him to return home. During the remainder of the war his name would be linked with Columbia, South Carolina, as he took his family there out of harm's way to continue his preaching, to use his rhetorical flare in behalf of the hoped-for new nation. Later in the war he would tour other lower southeastern towns to encourage resistance and to raise funds for the cause. During 1863 he served as Presbyterian Church commissioner to the Army of Tennessee when it fought in eastern Tennessee and north Georgia and preached to the troops and officers before many of the battles. To assist the seminary in Columbia, which had been depleted of its faculty, in 1864 he took an appointment there. His courses were well attended, as even some of the townspeople sought relief from the trials of war in them. In the churches around Columbia, Palmer again and again used his oratorical powers in support of resistance. Eulogies, harangues, and sermons spilled forth. Palmer also published many of his sermon masterpieces and thus spread far and wide his efforts in the propaganda war to bolster Confederate morale.

Two eulogies to fallen heroes stand out as examples of Palmer's vigorous support of the conflict. The first, delivered in Columbia on September 17, 1862, was for his mentor, spiritual guide, and close friend James H. Thornwell. Thornwell had died that September in the full flush of life, a martyr to his consistent defense of slavery and Southern life. Palmer believed that the great preacher had worked himself to death in support of his beloved South. The second, delivered also in the Presbyterian Church in Columbia, South Carolina, on December 20, 1862 (the second anniversary of South Carolina's secession, which he duly pointed out), was at the funeral of General Maxcy Gregg who had perished at the battle of Fredericksburg. Palmer employed the cadence and sound of weeping to create a consistent refrain of sorrow, which he hoped would stir his audience. He juxtaposed the people weeping over "the gallant chieftain who led the strife" in which other troops fell with the manliness, the courage, the honesty of Gregg the South Carolina native. Palmer depicted Gregg as the citizen-intellectual called to war to defend the rights of the South. It was Gregg's mission, claimed Palmer, "to stand sentinel over the master-principle of State supremacy, the cornerstone upon which rests the whole fabric of constitutional republican liberty" (7). But the war, and Gregg's role in it, was more than state resistance, said the preacher. It was also a religious war. Gregg's hardships in battles were juxtaposed with his Christian values. Thus was the redeemer's blood used to resist infidel fanaticism. Palmer stirringly concluded: "[N]o nation was ever called to conduct a great struggle so completely under the shadow of Jehovah's throne" (9).

The Presbyterian minister's fame as the preeminent Confederate orator grew. Even political leaders, aware of his attractiveness to the people, often called on him to preach before state legislatures. On March 27, 1863, he spoke before the Georgia legislature in praise of President Jefferson Davis' (q.v.) sacrifices for the Southern people, a speech that probably troubled its governor Joseph E. Brown (q.v.). Palmer went on to insist that the South was blameless in this bloody war because the North started it. It was the unjust actions of the federal legislature to drain Southern wealth to help their New England merchants that was the final straw. Again and again he lashed out at Yankee, mainly New England, avarice. This meant that God interposed in favor of the pastoral, victimized South. "Our cause," he ranted, "is preeminently the cause of God himself, and every blow struck by us is in defense of his supremacy" (Johnson, 268). Even Palmer's most sympathetic modern critic, T. Cary Johnson, had to interject that that sermon "makes pathetic reading now." But Palmer persisted. He spoke before a political audience in Columbia in April 1864 on the war's heroic soldiers. In that sermon, Palmer praised Wade Hampton as a mighty revolutionary who fought for freedom. For him, Hampton had become the Chevalier Bayard of the South. Since Bayard had used swords against guns, Palmer did not know how close he was to the truth during those last days of the Confederacy.

Palmer also kept up his support for the Old School Presbyterian Church of the Confederate States of America. Especially did he resist the actions of upper South Unionist Alexander H. H. Boyd of Winchester, Virginia, who wanted recognition of New School Presbyterianism in the Confederacy. In the last year of the war, Palmer often wrote to his former congregation in New Orleans to resist both the Yankees and church reform.

That Old School Presbyterian leader also continued his reform work in his beloved South. He called on the better-off to feed and clothe the poor whites who had sacrificed so much, even their sons, for the Confederacy. As always, he preached to the slaves. He sought to convert slaves and warned their masters to allow them to attend church. He helped to revise the Presbyterian hymn book so as to make it accessible to the unlearned. A student of church polity, he also was instrumental in revising the Book of Church Order for the Confederate States Presbyterian Church.

Once more, during the siege of Atlanta, Palmer, now tired from his efforts, tried to rally the citizenry of South Carolina and Georgia to mutual defense. He believed William T. Sherman (q.v.) planned to march on South Carolina, and he hoped Georgians would help that state in its defense. When it became clear that Columbia itself would be razed, he left with his family for a safe haven. Now without hope for his vision of a separate Christian South, after Sherman's army left, he nevertheless returned to help the people of Columbia. He raised funds for food and provided shelter to people who had been burned out by the Yankee invaders. War's end found Palmer hankering to get back to New Orleans, and he arrived there, his odyssey over, in July 1865.

The years after the war were busy ones, as the great preacher and unreconstructed rebel labored to uphold his Southern and Old School Presbyterian values. First, he rebuilt his old congregation. Then Palmer began the expansion of the church's membership, which made it the largest congregation in the Southwest. He stayed out of Reconstruction politics, but from the pulpit he preached resistance to continued Northern incursions. He became the leading spokesman for those who opposed reuniting Northern and Southern Presbyterian Assemblies. Palmer founded the *Southwestern Presbyterian* and, in his articles for it, made that magazine into a bastion of Southern Calvinism. Always concerned about education, Palmer founded and served as the first board chair of the Southwestern Presbyterian University, which he hoped would train future Old School clergy. For a time that school in Clarksville, Tennessee, thrived.

In New Orleans he became the friend of recent immigrants, working for toleration of the Jewish and Italian immigrants. Ever the moralist, Palmer opposed the Louisiana Lottery, which he called a get-rich scheme to bilk the less fortunate. In 1890, his claims about the lottery's crooked practices led to its demise. Ever the reformer, he served on the local Presbyterian orphanage board. For his work in behalf of a hospital, it was named after him. Ever civic minded, when asked to support the new Tulane University he became one of its chief fundraisers. But even this indefatigable worker began to fail in health during the 1890s. On May 5, 1902, on his way to a church gathering, the now poor-sighted preacher was struck by a streetcar. Palmer died of his injuries on May 28, 1902.

That great conservative preacher, social reformer, and Confederate patriot left another legacy through his many publications. He wrote with verve, as he had often given his stirring sermons with publication in mind. His own sense of family solidarity led to his writing two books, *The Family* (1876) and *The Broken Home* (1890). He also published *Formation of Character* (1899), *Theology of Prayer* (1894), and *The Threshold of Fellowship* (1902). Two of his works, *The Life of James H. Thornwell* (1875) and *Memorial Service in Honor of William Preston Johnston* (1899), gave proof that he remained unreconstructed. In his work on Thornwell, Palmer described the life of a great Christian proslavery advocate and a leader of the secession movement. William Preston Johnston, son of Palmer's hero General Albert Sidney Johnston, he eulogized as the ''consummate'' Confederate general, a man who never surrendered. Johnston became the great symbol of the early American Republic of 1789, as Palmer claimed that the Confederacy also was reflective of the values of true Americans. He linked Johnston with Robert E. Lee (q.v.) and used the life of that great Virginia warrior to beat again at flawed capitalist Northern values. In his view, Lee became the Christian soldier who in defeat taught Southern children "how to gather up the scattered fragments of their homes" and restore the South's lost splendor. To the end, Palmer used his oratory and printed versions of it to support the South he had created in his own mind.

So what does history say about the career of such a single-minded defender of his beloved South? The wartime Yankees well understood and feared the power of his words. Robert L. Stanton, in his 1864 *The Church and the Rebellion*, branded him a vicious rebel leader. Benjamin Butler, of course, had even put a price on his head. Southerners like President Jefferson Davis regarded him a major contributor to Confederate values. But biographer and friend Thomas Cary Johnson in 1906 wondered whether Palmer had sacrificed too much to the Confederacy.

The only systematic modern study of Palmer's life, the unpublished Ph.D. thesis of Doralyn Hickey, has attempted to revive interest in that most important of Southern preachers. Where she acknowledged his major contribution to the Confederate cause and the power of his words, Hickey also asked whether his Old School narrowness has not condemned him to parochial oblivion. James Silver both wanted him forgotten and forever cursed as a radical church voice. Penrose St. Amant insists that all that is left of his life is that lonely street named after him in New Orleans.

Most recently, excellent students of church history have attempted objectively to understand his flaws and to assess his accomplishments. Anne Loveland says that despite his Southern conservative radicalism, Palmer's support for slave religion and reform of their masters' treatment of them deserve reevaluation. Mitchell Snay, the best modern student of religion and disunion, has recommended that historians of the Civil War era study this man more fully. To Snay, "his linking the cause of orthodox religion to the destiny of the South reinforced the belief that slavery was a divinely ordained institution," which implies just how powerful his views were in persuading others to secede (180). To link Palmer's reasons for secession to his enormous wartime activities is the task for that much-needed future biographer of the Confederacy's most important churchman.

BIBLIOGRAPHY

Benjamin Morgan Palmer, *Address Delivered at the Funeral of General Maxcy Gregg* (Columbia, S.C.: Southern Guardian Steam-Power Press, 1863).

R. L. Stanton, *The Church and the Rebellion* (New York: Derby & Miller, 1864).

Thomas Cary Johnson, *The Life and Letters of Benjamin Morgan Palmer* (Richmond, Va.: Presbyterian Committee of Publication, 1906).

Lewis George Vander Velde, *The Presbyterian Churches and the Federal Union, 1861–1869* (Cambridge: Harvard University Press, 1932).

James W. Silver, *Confederate Morale and Church Propaganda* (Tuscaloosa: Confederate
    Publishing Co., Inc., 1957).
Penrose St. Amant, *A History of the Presbyterian Church in Louisiana* (Richmond, Va.:
    Whittet and Shepperson, 1961).
Doralyn Joanne Hickey, "Benjamin Morgan Palmer: Churchman of the Old South"
    (Ph.D. diss., Duke University, 1962).
Anne C. Loveland, *Southern Evangelicals and the Social Order, 1800–1860* (Baton
    Rouge: Louisiana State University Press, 1980).
Mitchell Snay, *Gospel of Disunion: Religion and Separatism in the Antebellum South*
    (Cambridge: Cambridge University Press, 1993).

EDWARD ALFRED POLLARD
(February 27, 1831–December 12, 1872)

Jon L. Wakelyn

As wartime editorial page editor of the Richmond *Examiner* and early historian of the Confederacy, Edward A. Pollard became one of the South's most important political and military propagandists. In his wartime editorials this peevish and peripatetic aristocrat vigorously criticized the new nation's leadership actions. For Confederate leaders he was little more than an opinionated and wrong-headed journalist. For others, especially Confederate legislators, Pollard's perpetual attacks on the high command's abilities, motivation, and decision-making skills became useful weapons in internal leadership struggles. President Jefferson Davis (q.v.) believed that Pollard's attacks on him undermined the war effort. Thus, at least for its participants, Pollard's sharp pen contributed to the story of Confederate success and failure.

In addition to his newspaper editorials, Pollard became the first historian of the Confederacy. Beginning in 1862, he began to write the history of the war. Each year thereafter, to the mortification of the Davis administration, he published another volume on the previous year's wartime activities. Thus Pollard was able to put his personal stamp on Southern motivation, actions, and leadership qualities. Alas, for the veracity of history, Pollard's efforts have set a standard for future historians' understanding of those events. Because he had been an eyewitness to events in Richmond, historians have ever since relied on that journalist for much of their judgment on the Confederacy's great leaders. What motivated this leader who had so welcomed the Civil War and so loved the South and slavery to wield his pen as a weapon of destruction against the Confederacy? To understand the seeming contradictions between his love for the South and his acquired hatred for Confederate leadership, Pollard's troublesome and often misunderstood life requires reconstruction.

To grasp the essence of Pollard's life requires perhaps more than in most leaders an understanding that place was central to his life. His roots in Virginia meant so much to him because in his later life he became a rootless wanderer.

He was born on February 27, 1831, at "Alta Vista" in Albemarle County, Virginia, to the well-connected aristocrats Richard and Paulina Cabell (Rives) Pollard. Married in 1814, Richard and Paulina's own lifestyles would come to mark this younger son of this large and eccentric Virginia family. The father, Major Richard Pollard, U.S.A., had been born in Virginia, studied law at William and Mary, and like many a younger son of Virginia's declining plantation wealth, joined the army and later served ably in the War of 1812. When he married into the prestigious Cabell and Rives family, some said to regain his family's place in Virginia society, Richard left the military to become a merchant and planter. But business never appealed to him, and he lost much of the poor land he tried to farm. Said to be an elegant and charming man, he managed to make friends wherever he went, including in high government circles. Those connections gained for him an appointment as U.S. Chargé in Chile. He used that position in part to recoup his financial losses. Richard moved around quite a bit, grew estranged from his wife, and died in Washington, D.C., in 1851, probably alienated from his sons. Paulina, the daughter of Robert Rives, a revolutionary war hero and descendant of wealthy planters, and of Margaret Jordan Cabell, of an equally prestigious Virginia planter family, grew up accustomed to wealth. Named after an ancestor who had supposedly married a rogue, she was the sister of the famous historian, lawyer, and politician William Cabell Rives, a staunch Unionist who nevertheless served in the Confederate Congress. Paulina's lineage was most prestigious, and she also had family connections to such Civil War leaders as James A. Seddon (q.v.) and John Cabell Breckinridge. But she died nearly alone and poor in New York City in 1854. Thus, young Edward was born name proud into the aristocracy but grew up without the wealth to live like one of his class.

As the seventh child of nine, Edward would have to make his own way. His siblings also became wanderers, adventurers, and proud people. A brother was killed in the Texas revolution, another died at Fredericksburg in 1862, and Edward's hero Henry Rives Pollard was assassinated in Richmond in 1868 by a political foe who had not liked what Henry had printed about him in his newspaper. Young Edward doted on these older brothers whose lives he wished to emulate. He also had the family brains and writing talent—and the lack of ability to fix on a given profession. Because there was little land for him to inherit, and what there was was poor, the supportive Rives and Cabbell clan sent him to the family college, Hampden-Sidney, then on to the University of Virginia from 1847 to 1849, and finally, following in the footsteps of his uncle, to the law school at William and Mary in 1850. From none of these schools did he acquire a degree or discipline, but rather he always managed to get into trouble over disobeying rules, gambling, and his penchant for hanging out with unsavory characters.

He later moved in with a brother in Baltimore to study more law, but the steady and dull work of a lawyer was not for Edward. Believing himself too good for his surroundings, he too became a wanderer. He first went to Europe, where he managed to scratch a living as a freelance writer. Pollard next moved to California, too late to make a fortune in the gold rush, to more journalistic work. In 1855 he traveled to Mexico, and later to Nicaragua, where he probably took up with slave expansionists in the abortive William Walker expedition. Along the way he may have acquired a wife and child, but neither showed up when he finally arrived in Washington to take a position, gained for him by relatives, as a clerk for the U.S. House Judiciary Committee. Perhaps sick of his wild life, he came under the influence of Virginia Episcopal Bishop William Meade and studied for holy orders. But Edward A. Pollard was too much the wanderer, too much the writer, and too much the failed aristocrat to settle into any profession.

That young romantic did, however, display one consistent pattern in his life, which was a love for Virginia. But he was hardly prepared in fact, if much in fancy, for his upcoming important role in behalf of Virginia during Civil War. Shortly before the outbreak of the conflict that led to war, he began to write his version of slave life in Virginia. In 1859, he published *Black Diamonds*. The book, a sort of romantic reminiscence of his own life in antebellum Virginia, became a bestseller and went through numerous editions. Pollard claimed that he wrote that book ''from what he found in his heart.'' His purpose was also political, as he hoped to counter Northern antislavery attacks on the peculiar institution by ''presenting some material portraits of Negro character.'' In his book, Pollard described happy slaves and kind planters in a rather idyllic life that hardly existed in fact. But he also favored reopening the slave trade, no doubt a means of preserving slavery in the upper South by negating the need to sell slave labor to the lower South. In these sketches, Pollard had created a fantasy world of old Virginia, a world he believed worth preserving.

The budding political propagandist next joined his brother Henry Rives Pollard to edit a pro-Southern newspaper in Baltimore. While there, during the spring of 1861 he published *Letters of a Southern Spy*, a vicious attack on the character of Northern leaders, especially President Abraham Lincoln (q.v.). These *Letters*, written in the form of a group of essays, indeed reflected Pollard's feelings and showed something of the uncritical and unstable side to his character. In those essays all Northerners were depicted as unscrupulous, radical antislavery advocates who would stop at nothing to foment class and racial unrest in the South. He predicted the North would wage unmerciful war against women and children and attempt to destroy the world that he loved. This bile obviously caught the eye of Richmond editors just as he was made to feel unwelcome in that border city of Baltimore. After he had written one last column in opposition to Northern troops being stationed there, he hurried, or fled, to Richmond to use his pen to continue to destroy Yankee character.

In Richmond, Pollard joined the staff of John M. Daniel's Richmond *Examiner*, as editor of its highly political editorial page. At first he worked tirelessly to support the war effort, praising Confederate civilian leaders for their efforts to promote patriotic loyalty. In his view the generals also could do no wrong, and the enemy was sure to fail. Pollard also began to keep careful notes in order to record the history of Confederate victories. But he soon changed his tune of hopefulness as he came to see flaws in the Confederate political leadership. He turned against the methods they employed to fight the war. Pollard's hostility seems related to the insider information he received about votes in the Confederate Congress from his uncle William Cabell Rives. Too, he spoke often with a bitter uncle, Alexander Rives, a Unionist member of the Virginia legislature. Together they must have given him just the kind of data he needed to use against the president and his cabinet. He persuaded the *Examiner*'s owner to turn that paper for a time into the leading opponent of the administration, and no doubt he did incalculable damage to unity in the Confederacy. Pollard set leader against leader, as his columns were full of ugly gossip about Judah Benjamin (q.v.) and Alexander Stephens (q.v.), certainly to the detriment of the success of their mutual activities.

As he continued to collect information about civilian failures for his editorials and his proposed history, Pollard still waxed eloquent over the achievements of the military leadership. But he also began to ask if the wrong officers had begun to receive preferment in promotion. Soon, he also attacked some of the Confederate generals as he played favorites with praise for certain actions and accused others of poor judgment. Only the Virginia generals received uniform praise from that journalist. Soon, his harsh and excessive accusations against civilians and generals lost Pollard the support of Daniel. Abruptly, Pollard resigned as editorial page editor of the *Examiner*.

The restless romantic, rootless wanderer then did what he had always done in the past when his affairs declined. In May 1861, Pollard booked passage on the frigate *Greyhound* bound for England. Supposedly, he planned to write pro-Southern newspaper columns there. But a Union frigate stopped his ship, and Pollard was arrested as a spy and sent to prison in Boston. When finally released, he stayed in the North, went to New York, and tried to get work on a pro-Southern newspaper. Arrested again and imprisoned in Washington, Pollard eventually won release and returned to Richmond around January 1865. True to his writer's craft he created again a legacy of hatred, as in 1865 he published *Observations in the North*, another account of Northern duplicity. Some say he finally got to England in the spring of 1865, but if he did it was too late to write for the cause of the South, which he had alternately praised and cursed throughout the war.

As if he had not done enough damage, that romantic adventurer also used his close proximity to certain leaders and his reporter's skills to begin during the war to write his own version of its history. Pollard's *Southern History of the War*, published in multivolumes during the war, and covering its events year by year, created a personal record of military activities and leadership decisions and probably has done more than any other of the early histories to fix the reputations of Confederate leaders for the future. He never dodged controversy as he wrote on political policies, economic practices, and firsthand events of battles and leaders. Mostly the histories depict failure, except for his Virginia heroes, who fared well. Robert E. Lee (q.v.), Stonewall Jackson (q.v.), Joseph E. Johnston (q.v.), and J.E.B. Stuart all received praise. Pollard no doubt sought to curry favor with the friends of his relatives. But Braxton Bragg (q.v.), D. H. Hill, James Longstreet (q.v.), J. B. Hood (q.v.), and others were rendered in pithy sketches as ineffectual officers, poor commanders, and sycophants of the political leadership. President Davis became the supreme enemy, as Pollard alternately described him as disloyal to the cause or as overzealous in delaying defeat. Worst of all for Confederate morale, Pollard claimed, Davis had done nothing to sell the cause to the people. Strategically, Davis made false military policy by undue dispersal of troops, which resulted in divided and weakened armies and in the loss of much Southern territory. In short, Davis was an incompetent meddler, too conceited and too provincial (read, he was not a Virginian) to lead the South to victory. There is no telling how these histories published during the war influenced events in the South.

According to his biographer Jack P. Maddex, after the war had ended, Pollard turned his efforts to making defeat a victory for Southern honor and virtue. He wrote a number of articles about the heroic behavior of the Southern people in the face of much adversity. Pollard also completed his history of the Confederacy. In early 1866 he settled for a time in Memphis as associate editor of the *Avalanche*, a decidedly anti-Reconstruction paper. It was then that he left his second wife and took a third, though much of his private life remains a mystery. Soon even Memphis gave him no solace, and Pollard returned to Richmond to help his brother Henry Rives Pollard edit the weekly *Southern Opinion*, also a newspaper opposed to Northern Reconstruction policies.

During that time Pollard revised his version of the history of the Confederate defeat. He published in 1866 *The Lost Cause*, a thematic one-volume condensation of his history of the Confederacy. In choosing that title, he had coined a term that not only reflected his own view of a lost great past but one that would soon enter into the romantic folklore of the pastoral New South. Pollard continued to write his version of why the war had been lost in his revision of the South's history. Again, he praised Virginia generals, attacked weak-willed politicians, and found the Southern people uninspired by the war efforts of the leadership. Former General D. H. Hill attempted to correct Pollard's interpretation of the War to protect his own reputation—but also out of fear that Pollard would fasten his own version of events on future historical interpretation. A nephew of Henry A. Wise, in November 1867, angered over Pollard's treatment of his family, took a shot at him on the streets of Baltimore. Tragically, perhaps because of his own venom against opponents, Pollard's brother, the editor of *Southern Opinion*, was shot down in Richmond in 1868.

Because of that murder and his own rethinking of the cause of the war in light of the needs of peacetime, say Jack Maddex, Pollard began subtly to revise his own revision of the history of those events. For a time Pollard held a job in the New York Custom House, but his savage writings against the hand that fed him soon forced him to return for one last time to Virginia. He went to Richmond and began to write again. His thesis this time was that the people's fears of race conflict was the main reason the South had gone to war. The North's attacks on slavery, said Pollard, had fueled the potential for race warfare throughout the region. He then settled in Lynchburg near his brother Richard and continued to write history. In *The Lost Cause Regained* (1868), a title taken from the English poet John Milton, he developed further his last great theme that the war had been fought to resist race war. The triumph of a white culture, even in defeat, had assured the South that its cause had been just and that its policies would prevail in the postwar world. For him, "the 'Lost Cause' needs no war to regain it." In *Lee and His Lieutenants* (1867), he wrote a biography as a model to guide Southern youth and especially those who would someday lead the restored and victorious South.

Pollard's studies of race fear and Southern heroes hardly meant that he had mellowed enough to forgive his old enemies and villains. His *Life of Jefferson Davis* (1869) twisted the president's action into betrayer of the Confederacy for pursuing too vigorous and destructive a war. Davis could never have achieved victory, as Pollard's verdict on his life was that he did not do enough for the Confederacy and that he had done too much to hurt the Union. In this new Unionist phase of his writing, Pollard even had cooled his hatred of the North. In 1868 he supported the Democrat Horatio Seymour for president because that Yankee understood the importance of racial control. By 1872, he had come to favor a revised version of Reconstruction in which a free labor system would encourage whites to unite behind racism. Perhaps he believed that in their mutual racism North and South could unite.

Mercifully, on December 12, 1872, after a long illness, the tormented Pollard died in his brother's house in Lynchburg. Ex-Confederate General D. H. Hill and other bitter enders immediately sought to diminish his reputation as they classified him as a loose radical cannon more obsessed with attacks on Confederate weakness than devotion to the cause. But the life, and importance, of that tormented journalist and historian is more complicated than that. James Wilson, writing early in this century in the *Library of Southern Literature*, maintained that most of Pollard's history was dated and would have no impact on future historians. In that assertion Wilson has been proved shortsighted. Vivid in style, Pollard's characterizations of the Confederacy's leadership continue to influence today's scholarship. In addition, those bitter twentieth-century neo-Confederates and literary critics who have found him useful to their cause themselves have not understood what motivated the man. Pollard's most thoughtful critic, Jack Maddex, in *The Reconstruction of Edward A. Pollard* (1974), claims that his racist beliefs led him even to repudiate plantation conservatism and embrace free market liberalism as a means of racial control. Maddex's own tortured rereading of Pollard reveals how close that journalist's later writings had come to reflect Southern as well as national values.

Perhaps there is even more to Pollard's life actions than Maddex's view, activities that suggest something of where that wartime journalist/historian's life and labors fit into the story of his class. For one should not forget the burden of being a Rives and a Cabell, a younger son of an aristocratic family who with them watched their beloved Virginia deprive them of their true heritage. Because of the paucity of land remaining for members of the great families, their off-spring were forced to fend for themselves. Never ceasing to defend Virginia and its elite, at the same time the wandering writer lashed out at what had destroyed his heritage. Pollard's life suggests that he was a victim who fought back con-stantly by revising his view of the South to fit his own needs. Future students of where this man belongs in the pantheon of Confederate leaders perhaps should look again at that world that was lost to E. A. Pollard.

BIBLIOGRAPHY

Edward A. Pollard, *Black Diamonds Gathered in the Darkey Homes of the South* (1859; New York: Negro Universities Press, 1968).

Edward A. Pollard, *Letter of a Southern Spy* (Richmond: E. W. Ayres, 1861).

Edward A. Pollard, *Observations in the North* (Richmond: E. W. Ayres, 1865).

Edward A. Pollard, *The Lost Cause* (1866; New York; Fairfax Press, 1988).

Edward A. Pollard, *Southern History of the War*, 2 vols. (New York: Fairfax Press, 1866).

Edward A. Pollard, *Lee and His Lieutenants* (New York: E. B. Treat & Co., 1867).

Edward A. Pollard, *The Lost Cause Regained* (1868; New York: AMS Press, 1974).

Edward A. Pollard, *Life of Jefferson Davis* (1869; Freeport, N.Y.: Books for Libraries Press, 1969).

Library of Southern Literature, 14 vols. (1909–1923; New York: Johnson Reprint Corp., 1970).

Michael Houston, "Edward Alfred Pollard and the 'Richmond Examiner': A Study of Journalistic Opposition in Wartime" (master's thesis, American University, 1963).

Jack P. Maddex, *The Reconstruction of Edward A. Pollard: A Rebel's Conversion to Postbellum Unionism* (Chapel Hill: University of North Carolina Press, 1974).

DAVID DIXON PORTER
(June 18, 1813–February 13, 1891)

Charles F. Ritter

Secretary of the Navy Gideon Welles knew his man. David Dixon Porter has "stirring and positive qualities," Welles confided to his diary on October 1, 1862. He "is fertile in resources, has great energy, excessive and sometimes unscrupulous ambition, is impressed with and boastful of his own powers, [and] given to exaggeration in everything relating to himself," a trait Welles thought was a Porter family "infirmity." Yet the Navy Secretary continued, he "is brave and daring like all his family" (Welles, 1:157). In short, Porter was the right man for the job.

The job was to relieve Charles Henry Davis as commander of the Mississippi Squadron above Vicksburg. Despite the eighty officers who preceded Porter in seniority, Welles chose the forty-nine-year-old commander who had a reputation for action and results. Sending Porter off to Cairo, Illinois, with the rank of acting rear admiral, Welles would see if that reputation were justified.

Porter's love for the navy and his aggressive attitude came naturally to one who was born into the culture. The third of ten children of Captain David and Evelina (Anderson) Porter, David Dixon was born on June 18, 1813, and traced his nautical roots to his great-grandfather Alexander Porter who captained a merchant ship out of Boston. His grandfather David Porter (1754–1808) fought in the Revolutionary War and became a naval officer. His father, also David Porter (1780–1843), and his uncle John Porter (b. 1833) were both navy commanders. David Dixon's father gained a reputation as a fighter for his efforts against the Barbary pirates in 1803, his exploits as a commerce raider in the War of 1812, and his foray against West Indian pirates in 1823. Court-martialed for a breech of diplomatic propriety and perhaps international law, David Porter resigned his commission and joined the Mexican navy in 1826.

Just as David Dixon's grandfather David had taken his son David to sea at age sixteen, so David Dixon's father took him to sea when he was but ten. And when Porter *père* joined the Mexican navy, he took the thirteen-year-old Porter *fils* with him and enrolled him as a midshipman in the Mexican navy. Young Porter received his first taste of battle in an encounter between the Mexican *Guerrero*, captained by his cousin David H. Porter (or D. Henry Porter), and the Spanish *Lealtad*. Hit during the action, his cousin David died in Dixon's arms.

Returning to the United States, Porter was commissioned a midshipman in the navy in 1829 and served in the Mediterranean Squadron on the *Constellation* and on the *United States*. On board the *United States*, the young midshipman met and courted George Ann Patterson, daughter of the ship's commander, Daniel Todd Patterson. He achieved the rank of passed midshipman in 1835 and then sought a position with the coast survey so he could be near George Ann, whose father was now commander of the District of Columbia Navy Yard. Porter married the vivacious George Ann Patterson on March 10, 1839.

Promoted to first lieutenant in 1841, a rank he would hold for more than twenty years, Porter engaged in routine duty until he was tapped in 1844 to conduct a secret mission to Santo Domingo to report on the stability of that country. When the Mexican-American War erupted, Porter sought sea duty but was sent to New Orleans to recruit sailors. In January 1847 he was ordered to duty at Vera Cruz, where he was assigned as first lieutenant on the navy's newly acquired light draft steamer *Spitfire* commanded by Captain Joseph Tattnall. It was here that Porter earned his reputation for boldness and independence and perhaps where some wag first observed that "a Porter plan takes a Porter to carry it out" (Soley, 59).

The port of Vera Cruz, a walled city, lay across a narrow channel from the rock fortress Castle of San Juan de Ulloa. After the U.S. Navy transports of the Mosquito Division had disembarked troops to envelop the city by land, the new commander of the division, Matthew Perry, ordered the bombardment of the city. But David Porter was not satisfied with this strategy; he wanted to attack the mighty castle fortress. During the night of March 22, 1847, Porter took a skiff and some sailors and chartered the dangerous channel in front of the fortress. The next day, rather than remain at the point from which they could bombard the city but avoid fire from the castle, *Spitfire* and her companion vessel *Vixen* sailed directly into the channel and began bombarding the fortress. *Spitfire* and *Vixen* ignored Commander Perry's semaphores to withdraw and continued to pound the fortress until Perry sent his personal skiff to order their retreat. Their comrades cheered as they returned to the main fleet.

Three months later, in July 1847, Porter executed another feat of derring-do. Seeking to capture the Mexican stronghold at Tobasco, the river fleet of three light draft steamers began a seventy-mile trip up the Tobasco River. Stopped by obstructions sixteen miles below the town, Perry chose to put his troops ashore and march the rest of the way. Not to be left out of the action, Porter had his men clear the obstructions and steamed ahead to Tobasco. There he took seventy sailors, overran the town's fortress, and waited for Perry to arrive after a hot march through the jungle.

Despite his standout performance during the war, Porter faced once again surviving in the peacetime navy. He was thirty-five years old in 1848 and still a junior lieutenant in a service top-heavy with officers. After two more years in the coast survey and watching the navy sell off much of the steam fleet, Porter took a leave of absence and sailed for several steamship companies, traveling to ports along the east and Gulf coasts, Cuba, and Panama. Back on active duty with the navy in 1855, he began a five-year period in which he made two trips to the Mediterranean to secure camels for the U.S. Army operating in the Southwest. He was then posted to the Portsmouth, New Hampshire, Navy Yard where, despite being surrounded by George Ann and their six children, he longed for sea duty.

By 1859 Porter also longed for a promotion. Now forty-five years old and a thirty-year veteran of the navy, he had held the rank of lieutenant for eighteen years. Although the prospects for conflict between North and South increased after Abraham Lincoln's (q.v.) election in 1860, Porter did not believe there would be a war to provide him with a career opportunity. Thus, when he returned to Washington in 1861, he arranged to transfer to the western coastal survey with the intention of leaving the navy for good and joining the Pacific Mail Steamship Company. At dinner with his family on April 1, 1861, the night before he was to leave for California, Porter was summoned to Secretary of State William. H. Seward's (q.v) office. Alerted by Quartermaster General Montgomery Meigs, Seward wished to hear Porter's plan to relieve Fort Pickens in Florida.

The meeting with Seward changed Porter's life. After briefing the secretary on his plan, Seward whisked him and Meigs to the White House for an interview with the president. Lincoln was so taken with Porter's plan that he agreed to a secret mission to relieve the fort with Porter in command of the steamer *Powhatan*. These plans were drawn up by Porter and signed by the president without the knowledge of Navy Secretary Welles.

The *Powhatan* affair was typical Porter. Arriving at the Brooklyn Navy Yard on April 2, 1861, Porter learned that Secretary Welles had ordered the *Powhatan* refitted for duty at Fort Sumter under Captain Samuel Mercer. By the time the ship sailed on April 6, 1861, Porter had hatched a plot with Mercer—the ship sailed under Mercer's command with Porter secreted in a locked cabin. Mercer left the ship at Statan Island as Porter emerged from his hiding place and took command.

Meanwhile, Navy Yard head Captain Andrew Hull Foote advised Welles of the goings-on. Infuriated that he was left out of the plan, Welles persuaded Lincoln to cancel Porter's orders. The president sent the cancellation through Seward, and it reached Porter as he cleared the New York harbor bar. "Give up the *Powhatan* to Captain Mercer" Seward telegraphed. With his usual aplomb and audacity, Porter replied to the secretary, "I received my orders from the president and shall proceed and execute them" (West, 86–87). And proceed he did, directly to Fort Pickens and on into Civil War legend.

Porter cut a wide swath through the naval portion of the war and was a key factor in several crucial operations. He arrived at Fort Pickens on April 17, 1861, but was restrained from taking dramatic action to liberate the fort. Having little to do at Pensacola, Porter was ordered to blockade first Mobile and then the South West Pass of the Mississippi River into the gulf of Mexico. Since there was more than one pass from the Mississippi into the Gulf, Porter's *Powhatan* and his companion ship, the *Brooklyn*, were unable to stem the flow of Confederate shipping in and out of New Orleans. He got nowhere with proposals to enter the Mississippi on raiding operations, but finally received permission in August 1861 to pursue the Confederate raider *Sumter* commanded by the wiley Raphael Semmes (q.v.).

After three months of shadowing Semmes from Cuba to Jamaica to Brazil and back, without ever sighting him, Porter took the broken down *Powhatan* back to Pensacola, where he learned that he had been advanced a grade in rank to commander. Arriving at the Brooklyn Navy Yard on November 9, 1861, Porter headed straight for Washington to see his family and Secretary Welles. "Father Neputne," as Welles was known, had never met Porter but had every reason to be wary of him based on the earlier "*Powhatan* affair." Without an appointment, Porter finagled his way into Welles's office in the wake of two members of the Senate Naval Affairs Committee. To this trio of civilian navy leaders Porter laid out his unorthodox plan for taking the Confederate stronghold of New Orleans.

In order to capture the hub of Confederate commercial activity, Union ships would have to pass between two forts located midway between the town and the Gulf. Fort Jackson, on the south (or west) bank of the river, had some sixty guns mounted in heavy casemates and a formidable water battery. Fort St. Philip, on the north (or east) bank, sported some fifty guns on a barbette protected by a low parapet and an equally formidable water battery. Confederate leaders regarded the forts as unpassable.

Porter's plan involved mounting thirteen-inch siege pieces, ordinarily used by the army, on to stripped schooners that would be towed into positions where they could bombard the forts before the big ships attempted to pass on their way to New Orleans. Intrigued by the idea, Welles took Porter to the White House, where the president heard and also liked the idea. They then proceeded to George McClellan's (q.v.) residence, where the flamboyant general, after some hesitation, gave his approval.

Displaying his usual energy, Porter spent the end of 1861 and early 1862 supervising the creating of the "mortar flotilla," which he would command. He ordered the schooners stripped and reconditioned in New York, the twenty mortars cast in Pittsburgh, and 30,000 shells. He also participated in recommending his foster brother, David Glasgow Farragut, to lead the entire operation.

The assault on New Orleans took four months to bring to fruition. Porter's armada of twenty mortar schooners and seven gunboats, plus fifteen large ships of war, all under Farragut's command, assembled at the Head of the Passes in the Mississippi River in April 1862. Porter had been ubiquitous in this part of the operation, pulling several of Farragut's heavy vessels over the bar as Pass l'Outre. He also supervised mapping the river up to the forts. On April 16, 1862, he conducted the towing and placing of the mortar flotilla along the banks of the river within 3,000 yards of the forts, and on Good Friday, April 18, 1862, he began the bombardment. Thinking he could reduce the forts in two days, Porter concentrated his effort on Fort Jackson and eventually shelled it for six, until April 24, when he was virtually out of ammunition. By then Farragut's patience was spent, and the assault began. Farragut ran the forts and captured New Orleans in two days, while the commanders of the forts surrendered to Porter.

At this moment, when Porter began to gain recognition as a naval strategist, he outspokenly criticized General McClellan. The incident, similar to the one that led to his father's court-martial in 1825, cost him a reprimand, loss of his mortar flotilla, and an assignment as an aide to Commodore Joseph B. Hull in Cincinnati, inspecting ship construction. Yet his exile did not last long. On September 22, 1862, he learned of his appointment to command the Mississippi Squadron.

Two features stand out from this phase of Porter's career: his ability to organize "a museum of naval freaks" (West, 173), as the Mississippi Squadron was called, into an effective fighting force and his ability to work with army commanders on joint operations. For all his ego and ambition, for all his bravado and manipulation of men, Porter's greatest gifts were his endless energy and his dedication to accomplishing the job at hand.

Arriving in Cairo, Illinois, on October 15, 1862, Porter took command of 1,500 miles of Mississippi River. He ordered the "naval freaks" refitted with armor and commanded the hasty construction of more ironclads. In due time Porter's "museum" fleet was known by the Confederates as the "terror of the Mississippi" (West, 179).

He also discovered an affinity with Generals U. S. Grant (q.v.) and William T. Sherman (q.v.). They were professional military men who sought to cooperate in order to win battles. Working with them, Porter led a successful operation against Port Arkansas, a Confederate stronghold, but had less success in March 1863 when he attempted to attack Vicksburg from the north via the Yazoo River. Indeed, the Yazoo expedition almost resulted in the capture of Porter's flotilla. Typically, Porter was full of self-confidence. Sherman observed wryly about the tough going in the narrow river bayous that form the Yazoo delta: "You won't have a smoke stack or a boat among you," to which Porter replied, "[S]o much the better; it will look like business. All I need is an engine, guns, and a hull to float them" (West, 209).

By April 1863 General Grant had decided on a plan to attack Vicksburg. Unassailable by water or by land from the north, he would march his troops down the west bank of the Mississippi, cross the river below the fortress, and attack from the east. Porter played his supporting role in this assault to perfection. He ran his boats past the Vicksburg batteries on April 16, 1863, a maneuver he had done a year earlier and accomplished with no loss of boats or lives. He then shelled the Confederate fortifications at Grand Gulf, Mississippi, and ferried Grant's troops across the river between April 30 and May 3. With Grant's army safely deposited, Porter began a forty-day bombardment of Vicksburg from the river, while Grant and Sherman enveloped it from the east. On July 4, 1864, when Vicksburg surrendered, President Lincoln advanced Porter three grades in rank, from commander to rear admiral.

The fall of Vicksburg left Porter with the enormous task of patrolling 3,000 miles of river with little to occupy his restless imagination. In the late winter of 1863–1864 his attention was attracted by a joint operation up the Red River to seize Confederate cotton, which, like capturing prizes, was rewarding both militarily and monetarily. The expedition would also expand Union authority deep into Louisiana. Porter was to steam up the Red River in support of General N. P. Banks's land operation.

After hauling his flotilla of eight warships and twenty-four transports carrying 1,600 soldiers over the Red River bar in March 1864, Porter proceeded up river as far as Alexandria, Louisiana, counting on the spring freshets to float his heavy boats. The spring rains were unusually slight—the river above Alexandria carried only six feet of water—but Porter did not miss the opportunity to capture salable booty, about 3,000 bales in all.

Fortuitous rains allowed Porter to push much of his fleet as far as Loggy Bayou, Louisiana, by April 10, his planned rendezvous with Banks. There Porter was stunned to learn of Banks's defeat at Sabine Crossroads on April 9 and of his intention to withdraw from Louisiana, leaving the rear admiral trapped deep in enemy territory.

Porter immediately turned his fleet around. Confederate raiding parties attacked the flotilla during its torturous retreat, and by the time he reached Alexandria in early May, his ships were badly mauled. But it was nature that provided Porter with his severest challenge—he had to get his fleet out of the river or lose it to the Confederates. The rapids and falls below Alexandria carried only three and one-half feet of water, too little for his heavy boats to pass over. With the help of some 3,000 men from Banks's army, a Wisconsin lumberman, Lieutenant Colonel Joseph Baily, conceived and supervised the construction of a dam at the upper and lower falls across the 758-foot-wide river, thus providing sufficient water depth to float Porter's boats over the 13-foot river drop and into deep water. It was a stunning engineering feat that saved the heart of the Mississippi Squadron and Porter's reputation. By May 15, 1864, Porter was back on the Mississippi, sick but safe. His mettle had again been tested, and he had survived an extremely dangerous situation.

Given a leave, Porter spent the summer with his family in Perth Amboy, New Jersey, returning to Washington in August to learn of his next assignment—an attack on the last Confederate port open to oceangoing commerce, Wilmington, North Carolina. As he did in 1862, Secretary Welles bet on Porter's determination and tenacity. Yet this was a challenging assignment. Writing in his diary on October 6, 1864, Welles noted that Porter reluctantly took the assignment. The secretary observed, "He will have a difficult task to perform and not the thanks he will deserve, I fear, if successful, but curses if he fails" (2:172).

The leaders of the North Atlantic Squadron had failed to close Wilmington because there were two channels into the Cape Fear River, about fifty sea miles apart, each protected by forts, Fort Fisher at the northern channel and Fort Caswell at the southern inlet. Taking Fort Fisher, the main point of concentration, would require a land and sea operation. Porter's energy and drive, his proven organizational and administrative abilities, and his success on the Mississippi with combined operations provided him with the experience to succeed in North Carolina.

Arriving at Hampton Roads, Porter energetically built the 87-vessel squadron into a floating fortress of 120 ships, the largest naval force assembled by the Union under one command. In addition to assembling a fleet, Porter had the delicate task of wooing the cooperation of General Benjamin Butler, commander of the Department of the James and North Carolina. Porter had clashed with Butler after the battle of New Orleans when Butler denigrated Porter's bombardment of Fort Jackson and attempted to take credit for the fort's surrender. Porter also had to coax troops out of General Grant, who did not give a high priority to closing the Wilmington port.

The operation began on December 23, 1864, with the detonation of an unsuccessful "powder boat" designed to weaken Fort Fisher and silence her guns long enough for the fleet to open a bombardment. It did neither, and although the powder boat was perhaps suggested by Porter and championed by Assistant Navy Secretary Gustavus Fox, blame for the unsuccessful effort was pinned on Butler, who had embraced the idea enthusiastically.

Despite this fiasco, Porter pressed on with the plan to bombard Fort Fisher and then land an amphibious occupation force. Still wedded to the idea that a naval shelling could reduce a well-made fort—Porter remained convinced that the bombardment of Fort Jackson in 1862 had rendered it ineffective in stopping Farragut—he intended to use the same strategy against this fort.

Shelling the fort for two days, December 24 and 25, 1864, Porter's guns fired an estimated 21,000 projectiles but caused little damage. Another pounding on December 26, intended to cover 500 soldiers landed on the beach, was also ineffective. In the waning winter daylight, Butler ordered his men to withdraw and Porter assisted. Although later critical of Butler and full of bravado that his bombardment had been effective, Porter in fact knew that his shelling had failed to injure the fort. Writing to Secretary Welles on December 31 he said, "We all know . . . that a fort on shore, unless attacked by troops at the same time ships are bombarding, will always hold out against the ships" (Reed, 438, n. 84).

Undaunted, Porter made a second run at the fort. Landing troops under Major General Alfred H. Terry, together with 2,000 sailors and marines, Porter opened up a seven-hour bombardment on January 15, 1865. The troops assailed the fort's works and took it by early evening. Wilmington fell on January 21, and General Grant opened a direct line of communication with Sherman's advancing army.

In a war where the navy played a minor role in the popular conscience, Porter stood with Farragut in popular esteem. Widely praised for his exploits and innovations, Congress voted Porter its official "thanks" four times. And when Congress created the rank of admiral of the navy for Farragut in 1866, it named Porter vice admiral.

Secretary Welles appointed Porter superintendent of the Naval Academy in September 1865. Long the bastion of antiquated naval studies, Porter overhauled the curriculum, emphasizing modern warfare and technology without sacrificing basic sailing and gunnery. He also introduced studies in history, politics, and etiquette, and required sports to cultivate self-reliance. In all, Porter made the Naval Academy a rival to West Point.

In March 1869 President Grant appointed Porter special assistant to Navy Secretary Adolph E. Borie, a Philadelphia businessman, making Porter effectively the acting secretary. But Borie resigned in April, and his replacement, George Robeson, wished for more control over naval affairs and eased Porter out.

When his foster brother David Glasgow Farragut died in August 1870, it seemed clear that Porter would be named admiral of the navy, but those who disliked him, and there were many, tried to block his promotion. When Grant proposed elevating Porter, the naval hero was accused of surrounding himself with favorites at Annapolis and using the post to launch his postwar career. Many resented bitterly the bureaucratic shakeups he instituted at the Navy Department. Former Secretary Welles denounced him in a series of articles in the November and December 1871 issues of *Galaxy* magazine, calling him an ambitious self-seeker. Former General Butler entered the fray, criticizing Porter for opportunism at New Orleans and Fort Fisher. Characteristically, Porter answered his critics by publishing documents that supported his behavior in the New Orleans and Fort Fisher engagements. Several members of the House of Representatives moved to abolish the rank of admiral. In the end the Senate confirmed Porter's appointment in January 1872.

Porter's promotion to admiral effectively removed him from the center of Navy Department affairs. He inspected navy yards, supervised the trials of new vessels, and prepared annual reports to the secretary that no one read. He also raised money for a statue to Farragut and another to seamen who died in the Civil War. He was comfortable on his $13,000 admiral's salary, supplemented by a seemingly endless flow of prize money.

Still, his restless energy was frustrated, and so he turned to writing. He first published a memoir of his father in 1875, giving a long account of Commodore Porter's humiliation by the navy that lifted the elder Porter out of obscurity. In addition, he wrote a self-promoting account of his own exploits, *Incidents and*

Anecdotes of the Civil War (1885) and a highly partisan *Naval History of the Civil War* (1886). He also wrote fiction and financed the production of one play.

Porter ended his career in the navy as he had lived it, in controversy. As part of the celebration of the centennial of George Washington's inauguration, Porter received temporary command of a flotilla in New York harbor in late April 1889. The press recounted his naval exploits, which brought a flurry of rebuttals from his enemies, including Butler who revived his charge that Porter ''ran away'' from Fort Jackson during the New Orleans campaign. This revival of wartime rivalries was bleak and unfortunate, for by 1889, few people were left alive who cared about those old battles. Porter died soon after, on February 13, 1891. Flags flew at half staff, and navy ships fired a fifteen-minute salute to the old man.

Despite the attacks on him by Welles and others, Porter's reputation has been well served by four biographers. Porter asked his friend James Russell Soley, a former Assistant Secretary of the Navy, to write a biography, which he did. His *Admiral Porter* appeared in 1903. Detailed with information about navy practices, this is a highly partisan view of Porter that judges all his moves as altruistic and all his efforts as successful. Richard S. West, Jr., produced a 1937 biography titled *The Second Admiral: A Life of David Dixon Porter, 1813–1891*. West's work has a scholarly cachet that Soley's lacks, but it is equally partisan regarding Porter's exploits and his conflicts with the likes of Butler and Banks. Noel Bartram Gerson's 1968 biography, *Yankee Admiral: A Biography of David Dixon Porter*, is a popular biography that adds little to Soley's or West's work. Perhaps the definitive work on Porter is Chester Hearn's 1996 biography, *Admiral David Dixon Porter*. Boasting an impressive array of original and secondary sources, Hearn's biography catches the essence of Porter as a great Civil War fighter who was rash, outspoken, daring, energetic, and ambitious. Hearn notes correctly that Porter eclipsed his foster brother David Farragut in the complexity of the operations he led and the importance of the campaigns he fought in. While noting Porter's ambition and his willingness to promote himself at others' expense, Hearn finds that on balance Porter ranks with U. S. Grant as one of the Union's best fighters. Rowena Reed is equally impressed with Porter's ambition and fighting ability in her *Combined Operations in the Civil War* (1978).

Porter's tenure as superintendent at the Naval Academy has drawn attention from historians. Harold and Margaret Sprout charged that he opposed modernizing the navy after the Civil War, especially the introduction of steam power. This charge may have originated with Francis Adams's similar accusation in 1876 and former Secretary Welles's remark that Porter was ''the most costly luxury the government had ever been compelled to indulge in'' (Adams, 77). Kenneth Hogan, writing in a 1968 issue of the *United States Naval Institute Proceedings*, and Lance Buhl, in a 1974 article, both noted that the second admiral may have been highly partisan and a self-promoter, but he was not a reactionary when it came to modernizing the navy. However, the Sprouts' assertion has been made anew in a 1990 reissue of their classic study.

Most of the periodical literature recounts and celebrates Porter's various campaigns. One observer, Maurice Melton, is less enchanted, noting Porter's failure to disrupt Confederate traffic on the Mississippi River in late 1862. Still, despite his arrogance and self-seeking, most historians agree that he was an innovative fighting commander in a war that had a dearth of them.

BIBLIOGRAPHY

David Dixon Porter, *Memoir of Commodore David Porter of the U.S. Navy* (Albany, N.Y.: J. Munsell, 1875).

Francis Colburn Adams, *High Old Salts* (Washington, D.C.: [n.p.], 1876).

David Dixon Porter, *Incidents and Anecdotes of the Civil War* (New York: D. Appleton and Company, 1885).

David Dixon Porter, *Naval History of the Civil War* (New York: Sherman Publishing Company, 1886).

James E. Homans, *Our Three Admirals, Farragut, Porter, Dewey* (New York: J. T. White and Company, 1899).

James Russell Soley, *Admiral Porter* (New York: D. Appleton and Company, 1903).

Richard S. West, Jr., *The Second Admiral: A Life of David Dixon Porter, 1813–1891* (New York: Coward, McCann, Inc., 1937).

Harold and Margaret Sprout, *The Rise of American Naval Power, 1776–1918* (Princeton: Princeton University Press, 1939; Annapolis, Md.: Naval Institute Press, 1990).

Gideon Welles, *Diary of Gideon Welles*, ed. Howard K. Beale, 3 vols. (New York: W. W. Norton, 1960).

Noel Bartram Gerson, *Yankee Admiral: A Biography of David Dixon Porter* (New York: David McKay Company, 1968).

Kenneth J. Hogan, "Admiral David Dixon Porter: Strategist for a Navy in Transition," *United States Naval Institute Proceedings* 94, no. 7 (July 1968): 139–143.

Maurice Melton, "From Vicksburg to Port Hudson: Porter's River Campaign," *Civil War Times Illustrated* 12, no. 10 (February 1974): 26–37.

Lance C. Buhl, "Mariners and Machines: Resistance to Technological Change in the American Navy, 1865–1896," *Journal of American History* 61, no. 3 (December 1974): 703–727.

Rowena Reed, *Combined Operations in the Civil War* (Lincoln: University of Nebraska Press, 1978).

Chester Hearn, *Admiral David Dixon Porter: The Civil War Years* (Annapolis, Md.: Naval Institute Press, 1996).

JAMES ALEXANDER SEDDON
(July 13, 1815–August 19, 1880)

Jon L. Wakelyn

Participants in great events, for their own personal reasons, write about their peers with such venom that they are able to sear into the consciousness a reputation that history really cannot shake. Such was the fate of Confederate Secretary of War James A. Seddon, who had the misfortune both of having been a personal friend of President Jefferson Davis (q.v.) and possessed of a secure place in the firmament of Virginia's antebellum "southside" aristocracy. For those sins, Henry S. Foote, in his *Casket of Reminiscences*, depicted Seddon as an arrogant tyrant in public who fawned before Davis in private. Foote described Seddon as a person possessed of an "atrabilarious visage," and "it may safely be asserted that he did not possess a single one of the qualities needed for a creditable and useful performance of the duties now devolved on him" (144–145). Incompetent aristocrat, sickly, ascetic to a fault, subservient to a president who wanted to conduct his own war policy, many historians have dismissed Seddon as a failure. Yet Seddon served in the war office for the longest period of any secretary, and he participated in many major decisions concerning the Confederate war effort. His life and accomplishments, then, require another look in order to uncouple him from Foote's lasting stain and to give his war record a fair assessment.

Seddon indeed was guilty of belonging to the Fredericksburg aristocracy, but it was not necessarily one that had evolved from the ancient FFV (First Families of Virginia) tradition. His father Thomas, a parvenu who began life as a Falmouth wholesale merchant, gained place among the old elite after he married Susan Pearson Alexander, descendant of a distinguished Fredericksburg planter family. Thomas became a planter after his marriage, but he also owned a bank in Fredericksburg, an occupation hardly thought genteel by the old, established families. James was born in Fredericksburg on July 13, 1815, and at an early age came under the influence of his aristocratic uncle Philip Alexander, an old-school state's rights local political leader. No doubt aspects of the Seddon family history also loomed large in James's life, since he certainly had heard the romantic tales about his father's brother John who had been killed in a duel, the result of a political quarrel. Young James surely admired his father's skills as a financier, even if he blanched over his middle-class labors as a bank cashier at the Farmers Bank of Virginia.

As befit his family's status, James attended the upscale Fredericksburg Grammar School, then went off to Yale College in 1831. Wealthy Southern boys had for some time attended that prestigious New England school. Shortly thereafter, both his father and older brother died, thrusting young James into the position as head of the family household. He invested shrewdly in a Louisiana plantation, the land in his part of Virginia no longer being much good for farming. He even contemplated removing to the Southwest but instead began the study of law with the idea of better handling the family investments. But young James also was stricken with political fever, perhaps under the influence of his uncle Philip, so at the age of twenty he entered the University of Virginia law school. He studied the works of states' righter John Taylor of Caroline, read the fiery antigovernment speeches of John Randolph, and became fast friends with his classmates Louis Wigfall (q.v.) and William J. Robertson, young men who would later help to further his career. Seddon graduated from the university as first orator in July 1836.

He again talked of going to the lower South, but the lure of state's rights Democratic politics in Virginia and the advice of his hero John C. Calhoun convinced him to settle in 1837 in Richmond to practice law and politics. He thrived in the law, became part of the bright young political circle around Robert M. T. Hunter (q.v.), and courted the beautiful, frail, and wealthy Anne Parke Carter. When she died just before their wedding, he was devastated. Unable ever to forget her, he later named a favorite child after her. Perhaps that later close relationship with Jefferson Davis in part stemmed from Davis's own tragedy over the loss of his first love. To overcome his sorrows, Seddon soon lost himself in the political whirl around Hunter. At that time he also experienced his first real signs of the many illnesses that would plague his life. Nevertheless, he spoke out fervently on issues of slavery and expansion. In 1845, he married the very rich Sarah "Sallie" Bruce at Richmond's elite St. Paul's Episcopal Church in the society wedding of the year. Also, like Davis, he took his young bride to Washington city to serve his first term in the federal Congress to which he had just been elected.

In Washington the young couple seemed to thrive. There he met Jefferson Davis, and the two low tariff and agrarian export advocates found much in common. Seddon also became a Southern spokesman against the Wilmot Proviso and thus joined the ranks of the young sectionalist faction of the party. But ill health led him to decline renomination to Congress. Once again, in 1849, he went to Congress. After his term was over, Seddon declined reelection to public office in order to buy a plantation, Sabot Hill, in Goochland County. But before he could become the gentleman planter and state's rights theoretician and adopt the image he had always wanted of his proper station in life, Seddon had to return to the law to make money. His investments in Louisiana sugar also grew, and soon he could nurse his various illnesses and grievances against the federal government as a gentleman farmer at Sabot Hill. "Sallie" entertained lavishly, as their parlor became a gathering place for southside society. His nephew, William Cabell Bruce, well remembered the stories of how the young radical state's righters gathered around Seddon for long hours of discussion and exchange of ideas.

Aside from living the high life and the bouts of illness, Seddon studied the political climate and became an increasingly radical defender of the Southern way of life. His February 18, 1861, speech to constituents, whom he hoped would elect him to the Virginian secession convention, centered on the sacred mission of a slave society to take care of its people and its slaves. Seddon had obviously entwined his material interests, his sense of place and class, and his views of the good of slavery for the master into a radical defense of secession. Earlier he had even broken with Hunter because of that leader's moderate stance during the secession crisis, and he had supported the radical Breckinridge faction in the 1860 presidential election. Seddon's radicalism no doubt led his constituents to reject him for the secession convention. But Governor John Letcher appointed him to the Washington Peace Convention, where he clashed with the Virginia Unionist William Cabell Rives, and did his best to scuttle the peace process. Seddon, some said, had begun to take on the manner of the late chaotic political personality John Randolph of Roanoke.

When the war came, he thought of doing his duty and joining the army, but poor health prevented that. His devotion to the cause soon changed a number of his old political ideas. As a member of the Confederate States Provisional Congress he became an advocate of nationalist activities and rejected his old state's rights pose. Seddon's call for sacrifices in behalf of the infant new Confederate nation gained the favorable notice of President Davis. When his term in the Provisional Congress ended, President Davis named him a prisoner exchange commissioner. But he again became ill and retired to Sabot Hill, where he proceeded to attack the Confederate Congress for an insufficiency of national spirit. He again urged the leaders to make any sacrifices necessary to win the war.

In November 1862, Seddon's new-found nationalism would face a real challenge. After the Confederate Congress had forced his friend Thomas M. Randolph, scion of an old and famous Virginia family and descendant of Thomas Jefferson, to resign as Secretary of War, President Davis turned to Seddon to replace him. Before the war had ended, President Davis would have six Secretaries of War, mostly because he wanted to conduct the war effort himself. Randolph had possessed a distinguished military record, but that did not keep him from running afoul of the fickle Southern press and the pressured Confederate president. Seddon had no military experience and had never held an administrative office. Just why did President Davis select him? Pundits such as newspaperman and petty bureaucrat Albert T. Bledsoe announced that Davis merely wanted someone he knew to carry out the chief executive's own plans for victory. Davis himself stated that Seddon had displayed a desire for victory at any cost and could work well with a Congress in which he had formerly served. Seddon also belonged to the Virginia upper class, and his appointment might appease those who had been angered over Randolph's dismissal. Perhaps more than any other reason, Davis felt he could communicate well with his old colleague and that they agreed on many aspects of the war policy. Yes, Seddon had been his ally; but would he be subservient to the Mississippian? What is certain is that many skeptical leaders would soon be surprised by the tenacity of that frail, scholarly-looking man of the Virginia gentry.

Certainly Seddon began in office as an ally of the president and as his forceful spokesman before Congress and the public. Seddon immediately reorganized the War Department. Under his predecessors it had become a den of gossip, political intrigue, and had become quite inefficient. The new secretary took an instant liking for his major subordinate, the former U.S. Supreme Court Justice John A. Campbell, but had serious problems with Chief of Staff General Samuel Cooper. Immediately they clashed over military promotions, which had been turned into the politics of regional preferment rather than choices of real merit. So Seddon relegated the talented Cooper to mere clerical duties, and the one senior prewar military officer with administrative experience in the War Department was all but lost to Confederate war strategy making. Early in his tenure, the gaunt and sallow secretary was able to reflect and to carry out the policies of his commander in chief. They got along famously, as Seddon spent many hours in his own former Richmond residence, now the executive mansion, conferring with the president.

The Virginian's first major task was to deal with the results of the debacle at Sharpsburg. He ably assisted Robert E. Lee (q.v.), during late 1862, to reorganize the Army of Northern Virginia. Seddon bucked up his fellow Virginia aristocrat and, more particularly, was able to get the necessary replacements for the army to protect against the next Yankee invasion of their homeland. Seddon seemed well in charge of his office and his officers. But by mid-1863, as pressures mounted, the secretary began to lose power. After first showing skepticism over Lee's planned invasion of the North in the summer of 1863, Seddon went along and suffered the loss of reputation that resulted from the failure at Gettysburg.

To be fair to Seddon, he had come to understand much about the Western theater of the war and its strategic importance to the Confederacy. He supported the relief of Vicksburg, even though he lost in the struggle to keep Lee at home and to send troops west. To the charge that Joseph E. Johnston (q.v.) was responsible for the fall of Vicksburg, he replied that the entire Confederacy was to blame. Later, he became obsessed with keeping Atlanta from being captured on his watch. It is clear that he came under the influence of Congressman Louis Wigfall of Texas, his old classmate, and those others who made up the western concentration bloc that Thomas L. Connelly and Archer Jones have so ably studied. Wigfall and Johnston were President Davis's bitterest enemies, and Seddon's connection with and support for them must have begun to undermine his position with the chief. Nevertheless, after the fall of Chattanooga, Seddon insisted Johnston replace Davis's favorite Braxton Bragg (q.v.) in the crucial retreat into north Georgia. He viewed Bragg a poor general and certainly befriended those generals who had intrigued against him. He even resisted Bragg being named chief of staff, fearing rightly that that disgraced general would surely undermine his authority as Secretary of War. That the secretary was forced to make major military decisions concerning the West during the summer of 1864 due to the president's illness allowed others to claim that he had taken on dictatorial powers. The fall of Atlanta destroyed his authority entirely, and it was only a matter of time before he would be forced from office.

But there were other problems with that secretary who understood where the Confederacy should fight more than he grasped the logistics and politics of warfare. He never got the hang of commissary and procurement issues. Coordination of military efforts, tactics, and supply for the army faltered under his leadership. That he roundly disliked Secretary of the Treasury Christopher G. Memminger (q.v.) hurt him in negotiations over funding priorities. That he could not communicate well with the Confederacy's major procurement officer General Josiah Gorgas (q.v.) meant that he could never get the supplies he needed for the front.

Because Seddon had once served in the Confederate Congress, at first his relations with those prickly state particularists went well. But when Seddon spoke in favor of a national strategy and of sacrifice of the parts for the whole, many of those pundits turned against him. He never got along with the state governors, and his celebrated feud with Georgia's Joseph E. Brown (q.v.) hurt his ability to function in office. When Brown refused to obey the secretary's demand for additional troops to defend Georgia, the secretary took his case public. Alas, he lost the newspaper publicity war to state's rights policies. When he linked Brown with parvenu planters who sold cotton to the Union, he had gone too far. To have turned loyalty into a form of class conflict showed that Seddon had been more of a political theoretician than a practical public leader.

Ironically, Seddon's own nationalist proclivities finally destroyed his credibility among, of all people, Lee and his fellow Virginia aristocrats. Virginians turned out to be as particularist as Georgians, and President Davis at last acknowledged that his gentry followers resented his secretary's harsh treatment of them. Seddon had become a liability. The enemies of Wigfall and Johnston, the nationalists, and the allies of Lee soon requested that Seddon be let go. Fellow Virginians Thomas Bocock (q.v.) and Robert M. T. Hunter, the powerful Speaker of the House and chair of the Senate Finance Committee, respectively, administered the final blow when they asked President Davis to remove him from office. The president, facing a wholesale revolt in Congress, like most trapped and discredited executives in that situation, reorganized his cabinet. Facing imminent dismissal, the proud secretary resigned from office in January 1864.

Tired and hurt by his hard handling, Seddon wished only to go home to Sabot Hill. But he couldn't even do that because the Yankees had taken possession of it and the whole region. Seddon was forced to remain in beleaguered Richmond. When the war finally ended, the Yankees for a short time incarcerated that frail and sick aging leader. When released, Seddon finally returned home to nurse his grievances against the Union and his former Confederate foes. His nephew William Cabell Bruce wrote that ''he was one of the individuals to whom the defeat of the Southern Confederacy was little less than the dissolution of the entire cosmos'' (19). Grieve he did, but he was not idle. For a time he practiced law in Richmond, and he served on various business commissions that had formed to find ways to restore the state's lost financial position. That old conservative even flirted with the Republican party and came to accept universal suffrage. He joined the new Virginia Conservative party in an effort to acquire credit for investment to rebuild war-torn Richmond. Soon he grew to disdain public activities, and he retired once again to Sabot Hill, surrounded by his memories of the Lost Cause. His children, finding little hope for success in Virginia, increased his sorrow by leaving home. A brilliant and ambitious son, Thomas, died far away in Birmingham, Alabama. His namesake James became a well-known judge in St. Louis, Missouri. At home, Bruces and Seddons intermarried, and he had many cousins to regale with stories about what might have been. That able man with a nationalist vision at last succumbed to his many illnesses, real and imagined, at his home on August 19, 1880.

The first flurry of memorials all praised him for his dedication to the Lost Cause. Friends rose to defend his record. But Seddon himself left no evidence of personal desire to correct the version of failure in which history had portrayed him. Unfortunately for the record, Edward A. Pollard (q.v.), in his early histories of the Confederacy, blamed Seddon for the losses at Vicksburg and Atlanta. In his *Diary* (1866), Seddon's own clerk, John B. Jones, created a vicious portrait of a boss completely under the control of President Davis. He accused Seddon of having been too political and too much the appeaser of civil unrest, as if the secretary could have done anything about that. With some glee, Jones even claimed that Seddon could not deal with failed Treasury Secretary Christopher G. Memminger. Then there is the previously mentioned Foote version of that man's performance that so stressed his frailty, aristocratic posing, and subservience to the president. Even Seddon's supposed wartime ally Joseph E. Johnston, in his own memoirs, designed to protect his record, claimed that the secretary had not done enough to defend Western policy.

Modern professional historians, such as Burton J. Hendrick, used Foote's and Jones's accounts to assess the secretary's career. Hendrick merely added to the existing portrait when he depicted Seddon as too much the Virginia aristocrat to understand the significance of popular, state politics. But the gifted historian Rembert Patrick eschewed the use of those old, personally biased sources and instead studied the war's official record to attempt to correct the general view of Seddon's Western policy. But Patrick, too, bought the old charge that Seddon had been subservient to President Davis. The only full-length study of Seddon's life, a 1963 doctoral dissertation, largely repeated what is already known about the war record but at least pronounced Seddon an able leader who had sacrificed his health in service to the Confederacy. In that dissertation, Gerald F. J. O'Brien, however, also provided some new thoughts on how that aristocrat had fought the substitution rules and actively favored conscription despite a hostile Congress. He concluded that Seddon had done the best he could with what he had, but perhaps he was too much under Davis's control.

The latest historian to comment at length on Seddon's wartime accomplishments is George Green Shackleford. In his biography of George Wythe Randolph, Shackleford, alas, compares Seddon unfavorably to his fellow Virginian. He claims that Seddon knew nothing about fighting a war, and his deficiencies ended any "bold schemes for the War Office." But that judgment is not good enough, because it in no way evaluates the way modern historians have come to study the policies and organization of warfare. Perhaps a future biographer of that significant leader will analyze in depth the administrative history of the Confederacy and place Seddon into context. Until that is done, we will not have a complete record of his value to the Confederacy or of the way the government led in the war effort.

BIBLIOGRAPHY

John Beauchamp Jones, *A Rebel War Clerk's Diary*, 2 vols. (Philadelphia: J. B. Lippincott, 1866).

Edward A. Pollard, *Southern History of the War*, 2 vols. (New York: Fairfax Press, 1866).

Henry S. Foote, *Casket of Reminiscences* (Washington, D.C.: Chronicle Publishing Company, 1874).

Joseph E. Johnston, *Narrative of Military Operations during the Late War* (New York: D. Appleton and Co., 1874).

William Cabell Bruce, *Recollections* (Baltimore: King Bros., 1936).

Burton Jesse Hendrick, *Statesmen of the Lost Cause: Jefferson Davis and His Cabinet* (New York: The Literary Guild of America, 1939).

Rembert Wallace Patrick, *Jefferson Davis and His Cabinet* (Baton Rouge: Louisiana State University Press, 1944).

Gerald Francis John O'Brien, "James A. Seddon, Statesman of the Old South" (Ph.D. diss., University of Maryland, 1963).

Thomas Lawrence Connelly and Archer Jones, *The Politics of Command* (Baton Rouge: Louisiana State University Press, 1973).

George Green Shackleford, *George Wythe Randolph and the Confederate Elite* (Athens: University of Georgia Press, 1988).

RAPHAEL SEMMES
(September 27, 1809–August 31, 1877)

Jon L. Wakelyn

Once fabled as a romantic navy captain whose derring-do against the hated Yankees made him a legendary figure to generations of Southern youth, now the life story of Raphael Semmes is barely known outside the confines of the Confederate Naval Museum in his hometown of Mobile, Alabama. Perhaps this neglect is related to the paucity of study of the Civil War navy and especially that of the Confederacy. Perhaps it is also because the South is a region that prides itself on law and order, and those who support the protection of private property do not know quite what to do with a leader whom history has accused of piracy and treason. Also, for anyone attempting to assess Semmes's life, the contradiction between the conservative, by-the-book career naval officer and the commander of the privateer *Alabama* who sank countless millions of dollars' worth of commercial shipping requires much explanation. Too, Semmes's own action-filled memoirs allowed him to create his own legacy, which most biographers generally have adhered to, at times at the expense of reality.

To place the man, his motivation, and his activities into perspective and to assess his accomplishments requires another look at the life itself. It begins with the history of an English Roman Catholic family that had come to Maryland during the seventeenth century. The men of that family had carved out great wealth as merchant seamen in that Chesapeake border region. Raphael's parents were Richard Thompson Semmes, of French origin, and Catherine Middleton, the daughter of a wealthy southern Maryland family. The future sea captain was born in Charles County, Maryland, on September 27, 1809. His parents died when he was quite young, but he had the good fortune of being raised in the family of his Uncle Raphael, a prominent Georgetown merchant and banker. Uncle Raphael brought up his nephew along with his son Thomas Jenkins Semmes, later a congressman from Louisiana and a Confederate States senator, who would be quite useful to the future admiral. Uncle Raphael enthralled his nephew with stories of his heroic naval service during the War of 1812. Young

Raphael later attended the prestigious Charlotte Hall Military Academy in St. Mary's City, a school famous for its training of naval officers.

The combination of his family seafaring history and perhaps not wanting to be a burden to his generous uncle led Semmes to go to sea. He became a midshipman in the United States Navy in 1826. Even as a youth, he served on sloops and frigates, then attended the Naval School at Norfolk, Virginia, in 1832. Like many of his class, he seemed to go in and out of sea and shore duty. While on shore leave, he managed to study and then to practice law in Cumberland, Maryland, and later in Cincinnati, Ohio. In 1837, he received a commission as lieutenant. That same year, he married Anne Elizabeth Spencer, daughter of a prominent Cincinnati businessman. They eventually would have six children, and she would become quite important to his career decisions. At that time Semmes was torn between a life at sea and a political or writing career. But the lure of the sea was strong, and the adventurous young man opted for the navy.

Even though he had a successful law practice in Cincinnati, he had managed to serve in 1835 aboard the frigate *Constellation* and had taken part in the Seminole War in Florida. In 1837, his officer's rank in hand, he did duty along the Florida coast and the Gulf of Mexico. Like so many young officers, Semmes clamored to get ship duty to gain promotion, but there were entirely too many officers and too few berths aboard ship. So he bought land along the coast in Baldwin County, Alabama, even practiced a bit of law, and permanently linked his name to the Mobile region, having given up his important Maryland ties. He seemed to thrive in the new Gulf Coast, as he became a pillar of the local Catholic Church and a trustee of the fledgling Jesuit Spring Hill College. For most of 1841–1842 he served near Pensacola, Florida, where he performed important coastal survey work, a task that taught him about safe harbors and hidden inlets. At last, in 1843, he went to sea in command of the U.S.S. *Poinsett*. His wife took the young children to Cincinnati to be with her family, a climate and political world she felt more hospitable than the Deep South.

During the Mexican War, Semmes served ably and came to the attention of higher-ups. He commanded the *Porpoise*, in which he performed well at the siege of Vera Cruz. In late 1846, aboard the blockader *Somers*, Semmes ran aground and sank his ship. But a naval enquiry fully exonerated him and allowed him to continue his rising career. He then joined General Winfield Scott around Vera Cruz and commanded a group of marines in the inland march to Mexico City. He supervised the use of howitzers, launching deadly fire upon Mexican fortifications. As staff officer to General Johnathan Worth, he made valuable friends and received a commendation for bravery. The brilliant, inquisitive, and self-promoting young officer then turned his considerable writing talent to his memoir of that war, *Service Afloat and Ashore during the Mexican War*, which he published to a wide reception in 1851. It remains today one of the best accounts of the role of the navy in that short war. The memoir reveals a staunch nationalist and expansionist, as well as shows Semmes to have been a keen student of military organization. Also, Semmes displayed a knowledge of the place of commercial power in warfare, as he described vividly how the United States overwhelmed the Mexican army with the ability to supply its forces in combat.

But the reality of peacetime navy boredom soon intruded on the romance of Semmes's narrative when his superiors placed him in charge of the coastal storeship *Electra* in 1848. He then held interminably long shore duty as inspector of the Pensacola Navy Yard. In 1849, he commanded the *Flint* but shortly thereafter was sent ashore where he again practiced law. While on inactive service, he took a legal case on behalf of the young naval officer John Kell, and they became firm friends and future shipmates. Again and again he asked for active duty, but his superiors refused him. While on shore duty, he worked on Winfield Scott's Whig presidential campaign in 1852. Semmes obviously hoped to meet powerful politicians who could get him a ship berth. Finally, in 1855 he gained promotion to commander and held ship duty for a short time in 1856. In late 1856 Semmes joined the Lighthouse Service and became inspector of stations. This duty sent him to Washington, where, until 1861, he held the post of Secretary of the Lighthouse Board. In Washington, his outgoing wife thrived, while the argumentative Semmes fell out with Matthew Fontaine Maury of the Oceanographic and Geodetic Service but made a favorable impression on Secretary of War Jefferson Davis (q.v.).

Semmes soon showed his sectionalist political colors as he increasingly grew sensitive over slights to his beloved South. He campaigned for a low tariff, argued against dominant Yankee control of the nation's industry and commerce, and talked openly of two separate economic interests in the country. In 1860 he made one last public attempt to remain loyal to the Union when he supported Stephen A. Douglas for president. He also secretly applauded the secession movement in Alabama, even though he held duty in the U.S. Navy. In mid-January 1861, raring to join the secessionists, he sought the advice of radical Alabama Senator Clement C. Clay. Semmes had seniority in the navy, General Scott asked him to stay in Washington, and his Yankee wife wished him to remain loyal to his country. But he could not. On February 14, 1861, ex-Senator Clay asked him to come to Montgomery, Alabama, and on February 15, he resigned from the U.S. Navy.

Many of his cousins and former Maryland friends had remained loyal to the Union. But Semmes felt the pull of the lower South and acted accordingly. Sadly for him, his wife went to Cincinnati to spend the war years with her family, estranged from her radical Southern husband. Semmes had stayed behind because he had a duty to perform. In a private meeting Confederate President-elect Jefferson Davis asked him to undertake a secret mission to purchase war supplies in New York City. Semmes accepted. In New York, Semmes took the measure of Union loyalty as merchants sold him goods that the Confederacy later would use to destroy their commerce. Federal agents soon discovered his secret work, so he scurried south in search of a commission aboard a Confederate naval vessel. At that time, Semmes advised the Confederate States Navy to organize privateer corps to be used to disrupt Northern commerce and to force the neutral Northern merchants to abstain from support of the Union war effort.

On April 18, 1861, he took command of the C.S.S. *Sumter* and began his fabled career as a raider. Seemingly too old for sea duty at fifty-one, in fact the swarthy, small, wiry, fit, tireless, and adventurous leader was prepared for arduous duty. With his dark, smoldering eyes, waxed mustache, and aristocratic bearing, he cut the perfect figure of a commander, or was it a pirate? As he commenced his venture as a raider, Semmes believed firmly that international law as he understood it ''made enemy property at sea subject to capture and confiscation.'' His old but fully armed steamship served him well against unarmed merchant vessels. Semmes learned the art of surprise, as he flew false colors, sneaked up on the enemy, and burned ships and their cargo. The U.S. Consuls in Latin America labeled him a pirate because he had wrecked the Yankee merchant Gulf trade. The sea lanes belonged to this man who was at times ill but always ill-tempered. In November 1861, having worn out his Latin American welcome, Semmes took the *Sumter* across the Atlantic. But his ship had grown old through constant use and soon developed a leak and had worn-out engines. In April 1862 he left it for good.

In June 1862, the man and the cruiser met. Through his overseas lieutenant and purchasing agent James Bullock, Confederate Secretary of Navy Stephen R. Mallory (q.v.) purchased a British-built, light, fast cruiser, which he renamed the *Alabama* and placed Semmes in charge of. With a trained and rough British crew in search of plunder, Semmes sailed to the Azores, and then in October on to Newfoundland, where he burned whalers and cargo ships. Supposedly loaded with war supplies, and sailing with U.S. papers, those vessels were headed for north Atlantic seaports. Northern papers claimed that Semmes often burned neutral ships that did not carry materiel of war. The Confederate commander would receive such bad press throughout the war. The European governments complained that the Union Navy could not protect their vessels. Still, President Abraham Lincoln (q.v.) continued to trade on the Atlantic. The Northern merchants constantly changed the sea lanes, but to no avail. By October 1862, Semmes had wrecked much of the overseas grain trade, forced a rise in Northern insurance rates, and roiled U.S. merchants. In November 1862, the wily Confederate shifted his position once again to the Caribbean, in hopes of avoiding an armed U.S. Navy squadron hot in pursuit. Near Galveston, Texas, in January 1863, Semmes clashed with and sank the U.S. warship *Hatteras* in his only open-sea naval battle of the war.

By March, 1863, Semmes had moved to the south Atlantic off the coast of Brazil. But he sailed alone, as John N. Maffitt, the commander of the Confederacy's only other privateer, and the headquarters in Richmond were never able to coordinate their activities with his. Semmes grew tired and lonely. His great accomplishments of sinking U.S. merchant vessels were nearly behind him, as the Union had begun to protect its shipping lanes with large war vessels that he could not engage in the open seas. He captured only twelve ships in 1863, as he and his ship lost steam. Ashore in South Africa his British crew deserted because Semmes failed to pay them prize money. He then had to take on untrained and mutinous crew members.

By September 1863, he was in the South China Sea, and in January 1864, he sailed his aging and leaking vessel into the Bay of Benzel. Supposed neutral ports had become unwelcome to the likes of Semmes; thus needed repairs went unmade. So in June 1864, at the French port of Cherbourg, he planned to scuttle the ship. He also had requested leave due to poor health. But he was to fight one last and heroic battle, or perhaps a foolhardy action by a sailor who knew his time was up. The U.S.S. *Kersarge* had finally found him, and its commander, John Winslow, had blocked the port. The feisty Semmes seemed compelled to fight for personal vindication—or perhaps because he was tired of being seen as a pirate. At last he could fight as a C.S.S. naval commander. On June 19, 1864, Semmes sailed out of Cherbourg to face a larger, more powerful vessel. The Confederate vessel carried wet powder and lacked the firepower to take on such a formidable adversary. As Semmes's ship sank, a British fishing boat snared him and he escaped to England. His last act before leaving his ship was to carry his journals with him. Of course, there was a controversy around that final battle, as Semmes maintained that the *Kersarge* had fought unfairly because its hidden iron chains around its bulkhead had turned it into an ironclad. Was this complaint that of a spoilsport or a true romantic?

In December 1864, after receiving many accolades in England and France, and commenting unfavorably about the number of young Southern men living abroad, the weary sailor went home to Mobile. January 1865 found him in Richmond, and in February he received promotion to rear admiral, and Mallory placed him in command of the James Squadron. His task was to use ironclads and marines to keep Union General U. S. Grant's (q.v.) army from using the James River as a base of operations against Richmond. For awhile he succeeded. But Semmes had become as ill as the Confederacy, and on April 2, upon word of Lee's evacuation of the defenses around Petersburg, Secretary Mallory ordered him to burn his ships. Semmes then served as a land commander, as he took the last train out of Richmond to join the guard around President Davis. The president named him a brigadier general in the Confederate Army and commanded him to go to Greensboro, North Carolina. Semmes had orders to continue to fight in the trans-Mississippi theater, but he never got there. He persuaded his Union captor to parole him as an army general with the full knowledge that he faced arrest if it were revealed that he had commanded a privateer.

Semmes returned to Mobile to practice law in that coast city. He hoped to restore his lost finances and to get on with his life. But that poverty-stricken coastal city had little need for a lawyer. In December 1865, a Union general arrested him and sent him to the Navy Yard in New York City. His wife now returned to his side and fought for his release. Fortunately for him, President

Andrew Johnson (q.v.) seemed uninterested in prosecuting him for piracy, despite the proddings of Navy Secretary Gideon Welles. When released, Semmes returned to Mobile to a life of constant surveillance as Union commanders sought to deprive him of any public office. For a while he taught at the Louisiana State Seminary and later edited the anti-reconstruction radical *Memphis Bulletin*, which again got him into trouble with the federal government. Then Semmes went on a lecture tour to preach opposition to Northern Reconstruction.

Mostly, the former naval hero worked on his memoirs. He wanted to put the record straight and to show how hateful the Yankees were. In 1869 he published *Memoirs of Service Afloat, During the War between the States*. To read those brilliantly written, self-indulgent musings is to be captured by the drama of a vain man who had no real private life. They also revealed levels of self-deception and pride in accomplishments and lacked any remorse for his terribly destructive actions. Filled with the drama of great escapes and worthy battles, rarely does the reader find in those memoirs the gory details of merchant vessels set aflame, or the civilian crews stranded in unfriendly ports. Nor does the man who knew the law tell the truth of the legality of the laws of the seas. If a few scholars have made use of the drama of that life as described in the memoirs, many others have wondered where truth begins and fiction leaves off.

Then the need to make a living called him back to the law. In 1870, Semmes became Mobile city attorney. In 1871, the grateful citizens deeded him a house in town. In 1872, he adroitly resisted the U.S. claims for reparations from the *Alabama*'s destruction of merchant cargo. Semmes actually bragged about what he had destroyed. By 1874, many of the restrictions against his activities had been lifted, but he was too tired and ill to seek public accolades. In August 1877, food poisoning sank him still further, and he died on August 31. His funeral in Mobile was a splendid affair, and lasting fame seemed assured. A former ally, James Bullock, in 1883 claimed that Semmes's deeds would long be praised.

How has history treated this great captain who had sought with his memoirs to protect his own fame? By some accounts, not so well. To begin, shortly after the war had ended, the acidic Mary Chesnut labeled him a pompous fool. Northerners of course held him in infamy, as former Union Admiral David D. Porter (q.v.), in his *Naval History of the Civil War* (1886), regarded him as only a pirate. The Lost Cause Southerners regarded him as a hero, always able to outsmart superior forces. In the years just before World War I, German naval historians called him a great warrior whose use of disguise was part of the art of modern war. John Kell, in *Recollections of Naval Life* (1900), praised his old commander. John T. Scharf, a Marylander who had written the first full story of the Confederate Navy, regarded Semmes as an audacious sailor and justified his acts of piracy. His shrine in Mobile pays him much tribute as a Southern hero. Listen to the propaganda from Caldwell Delaney of the Museum of the City of Mobile: "As the greatest commerce raider of all time, he is unique in the annals of the sea" (8). Following this pattern, his most famous biographer, the novelist and poet Walter Adolphe Roberts, depicted Semmes as a man forced to fight against his will. Thus, all except Chesnut, and the Northern critics have agreed that he first was a navy commander and only incidentally a pirate.

But for those few modern historians who have studied the naval history of that war, there remain lingering doubts about his activities. Semmes's most recent biographer, John M. Taylor, who wrote a comprehensive and thorough account of his exploits, raised a number of questions about him personally. Though Taylor praised Semmes's actions, he depicted him as selfish and a martinet. Personality, however, does not tell much about accomplishment. Taylor also has written a full account of just how much Yankee property his hero destroyed. It is appalling. But to listen to Taylor explain away the sinking of unarmed neutrals, the indiscriminate destruction of so much materiel, also is appalling. Perhaps the true verdict on Semmes's wartime activities may be found in his own memoirs. In them he revealed just how much damage he had done to unarmed merchant vessels. But he also gives the reader a sense of what history has seen as lawless. Semmes concluded his *Memoirs of Service Afloat* with the warning that the Yankee victory had changed our "form of government" in a revolutionary way but that the South would rise to "still other acts of the drama to be performed." One shudders over that warning's meaning for Semmes the true believer.

BIBLIOGRAPHY

Raphael Semmes, *Service Afloat and Ashore during the Mexican War* (Cincinnati, Ohio: W. H. Moore, 1851).

Raphael Semmes, *Memoirs of Service Afloat, During the War between the States* (Baltimore, Md.: Kelly, Piet, and Co., 1869).

David Dixon Porter, *The Naval History of the Civil War* (New York: Sherman Publishing Co., 1886).

John Thomas Scharf, *History of the Confederate States Navy*, 2 vols. (New York: Rogers and Sherwood, 1897).

John McIntosh Kell, *Recollections of a Naval Life* (Washington: The Neale Company, 1900).

Walter Adolphe Roberts, *Semmes of the* Alabama (Indianapolis: Bobbs-Merrill Co., 1938).

Charles G. Summersell, *The Cruise of the C.S.* Alabama (Tuscaloosa, Ala.: Confederate Publishing Co., 1965).

Caldwell Delaney, ed., *Raphael Semmes* (Mobile, Ala.: Museum of the City of Mobile, 1978).

John M. Taylor, *Confederate Raider: Raphael Semmes of the Alabama* (Washington, D.C.: Brassey's Inc., 1994).

WILLIAM HENRY SEWARD
(May 16, 1801–October 10, 1872)

Marianne Fischer and Charles F. Ritter

William Henry Seward's four-decade public career placed him in the center of one of America's most dramatic periods. Elected in 1830 to the New York State Senate, Seward became governor of the state in 1838 and again in 1840. In Albany he gained a reputation as a reformer and as an advocate of internal improvements. He carried his reformist faith to Washington, where, during his decade of service as senator from New York, he became a rabid opponent of slavery. A leading Republican in 1860, Seward was poised to win the party's nomination for president. Although he did not secure the coveted nomination, he took a prominent role in President Abraham Lincoln's (q.v.) cabinet and won accolades for his handling of diplomacy during the Civil War. He remained Secretary of State during President Andrew Johnson's (q.v.) administration. Although overshadowed by Lincoln in life and death, recent scholarship acknowledges Seward's many accomplishments.

Born on May 16, 1801, in the village of Florida, New York, sixty miles north of New York City, William was the fourth of six children of Samuel and Mary (Jennings) Seward. Of Welsh descent, his father was a doctor, a merchant, and a local land speculator; his mother probably descended from Irish stock. Young William—he preferred to be called "Harry"—was educated in Florida's one-room schoolhouse and at Farmer's Hall Academy in Goshen, New York. In 1816, at the age of fifteen, Seward's father shipped him off to Union College in Schenectady. He graduated with highest honors and a Phi Beta Kappa key in 1820.

Seward read law in Goshen and New York City and was admitted to the New York bar in 1822. Settling in Auburn, he joined Elijah Miller's law firm, married Frances Miller on October 20, 1824, and moved into the Miller household. Settling into a profitable law practice, Seward turned his attention to politics.

Although reared in a Jeffersonian household, Seward briefly supported Martin Van Buren's Albany Regency, then threw his support to the Democratic Republican John Quincy Adams in 1824. In 1828 the Anti-Masons nominated him for Congress from Cayuga County, but when the National Republicans hissed him out of their convention, he withdrew from the race.

In 1824 Seward met Thurlow Weed in Rochester. A young Anti-Mason, Weed ran the *Albany Evening Journal* and sat in the New York legislature. In 1830 Weed engineered Seward's nomination and election to the New York Senate. He served one term and rose to the position of minority leader. Refusing to stand for reelection in 1834, Seward was unanimously nominated for governor by the new Whig party but lost the election by 11,000 votes to the Regency candidate, William L. Marcy.

Although he returned to his Auburn law practice, Seward's heart was in the political world. Ambitious for office, he began active campaigning across the state in 1837 and, with Weed's indispensable help, secured the Whig nomination for governor in 1838. He won the election by 10,000 votes, defeating the incumbent and the fabled Regency. He was reelected in 1840.

Seward's reputation as a reformer began during his gubernatorial years. He advocated educational and penal reform, emphasized the need for internal improvements in the state, and promoted the protection of blacks' legal rights. In one of his most controversial proposals, he urged government aid to New York City Catholic schools, which educated large portions of the Irish immigrant population. The issue was exceptionally volatile. The New York City public schools were controlled by a private organization known as the Public School Society that ran the public schools in the interests of the Protestant majority. As the numbers of Catholic immigrants increased in New York, parents complained about the religious orientation of the public schools and refused to send their children to them. Seward argued that it was in the interest of universal education and civic order that all children be educated. He failed to move the legislators to fund Catholic schools in 1840, but in 1841, he persuaded them to extend the New York State school district system to New York City. This undermined the control of the Public School Society and opened the public schools to Catholic immigrant children.

Seward's school proposal had political implications; while it garnered him support among the increasingly large Irish population that affiliated with the Democratic party, it cost him Whig support in the early 1840s and was used against him as a symbol of his radicalism in the 1860 Republican presidential nominating convention.

Seward insured his reputation as a reformer by joining the prison reform movement. He also urged internal improvements like widening the Erie Canal and building three new railroads with government funds. While these proposals established his reputation as a supporter of social and economic improvements, his advocacy of blacks' rights went farthest toward raising his stature in the state and the nation.

Throughout the 1830s and early 1840s, antislavery sentiment grew rapidly in certain areas of New York, and Seward's antislavery actions attached his name to that rising political movement. In 1839 he refused to extradite to Virginia three New York black seamen who had attempted to smuggle a Virginia slave to New York. He became a hero to antislavery leaders, and the New York legislature passed his proposals that provided a jury trial for fugitive slaves, a bold proposal given existing law on the subject of fugitives. In 1841 Seward furthered his reputation among antislavery advocates by successfully proposing legislation that freed sojourning slaves the moment they arrived in New York State.

Despite his growing antislavery reputation, Seward decided not to run for a third term as governor. By 1841 his general optimism was in retreat. He had stress in his personal life; Frances Seward never cared for the political life and remained in Auburn, tending to her father, and his real estate deals in western New York had turned sour. He also believed that he was too progressive for his party. "My principles are too liberal, too philanthropic," he told Congressman Christopher Morgan (Taylor, 53). Yet Seward was not a failed governor. His internal improvements program had brightened New York's economic picture, his social reforms had made New York's public schools more inclusive and its penal system more humane, and he had thrust New York State into the forefront of the antislavery crusade.

Seward did not hold another public office for seven years. During the interval, however, his prominence in the antislavery campaign continued to grow owing to his involvement in two celebrated court cases. Seward defended William Freedman, a black man accused of killing four whites. He lost the case and was bitterly attacked for defending the man, but his stock rose among abolitionists. Seward also participated in the fugitive slave case of John Van Zandt, who was convicted of helping slaves escape into Ohio. Volunteering his services to Salmon P. Chase (q.v.) of Ohio, they appealed to the U.S. Supreme Court, where they lost. What could one expect "from a court of which half the judges are slave holders?" [,] Seward asked (Taylor, 70).

With Thurlow Weed's backing, Seward won election to the U.S. Senate in February 1849. It was a propitious moment for him as the slavery issue came to a boil in the aftermath of the Mexican-American War. Agitated by the question of the role of slavery in the territories newly won from Mexico, Congress prepared to debate a series of compromise proposals introduced by Henry Clay. The aging Kentuckian tried to mollify Northern congressmen by providing for California's admission as a free state, organizing the New Mexico and Utah territories without reference to slavery, and abolishing the slave trade in the District of Columbia. He offered Southern members a new fugitive slave law that placed federal commissioners squarely in the center of the process of returning runaways and that required citizens to participate. With the support of another aging Senate icon, Daniel Webster, Clay hoped to overawe the younger members of the Senate.

As a new member of the national body, Seward had an opportunity to promote his antislavery ideas and also put himself in the national spotlight. He did not shrink from the occasion. On March 11, 1850, in a powerful speech carefully crafted by himself, Weed and Frances Seward, the junior senator condemned the compromise and ridiculed the notion that the Union was in danger of breaking up over the slavery issue. He opposed any extension of slavery, which he considered a dying institution. He invoked "a higher law than the Constitution," which required that the territories be preserved as "the common heritage of mankind" (Van Deusen, 123).

Widely castigated in the South for his speech, Seward won renewed visibility in New York and a wider audience in the North. Horace Greeley printed the speech in the *New York Tribune*, and Seward sent out 50,000 copies of it to his constituents. He was, as John Taylor says, "in a single stroke . . . the leading anti-slavery spokesman in the Senate" (86). By 1854, the number of antislavery senators had grown, and Seward was their nominal leader. In that role he attacked Stephen A. Douglas's Kansas-Nebraska bill in a three hour Senate speech in February 1854. In it he characterized the slave power as insatiable for new territory and again denounced the Compromise of 1850 for encouraging slaveowners in their peculiar institution. He won much praise for the speech, including a congratulatory note from Abraham Lincoln, and emerged as the embodiment of the antislavery sentiment.

Seward won reelection to the Senate in February 1855 and joined the nascent Republican party in 1856. He fit well with the new group. He had long been an advocate of economic development and now supported construction of a transcontinental railroad and laying of a transatlantic cable. He was also strongly attached to Manifest Destiny and the Monroe Doctrine. But it was as an antislavery man that Seward developed into a leading Republican. He denounced the Dred Scott Decision of March 1857, characterizing it as a product of collusion between the slaveholding justices and President James Buchanan, who was beholden to the South for his election. He led the Republican charge against the administration's position on Kansas. Seward would admit the bloody territory under the free state Topeka Constitution, and his major speech on the subject in April 1856 was reprinted widely throughout the North. When Buchanan announced in 1857 that he would admit Kansas under the proslavery Lecompton Constitution, Seward was again on the barricades.

On October 25, 1858, he delivered an important speech on slavery in Rochester, New York. In almost ten years in the Senate, he said, he had seen too much antagonism over race to hold to the belief that the debate over slavery did not threaten the Union. Indeed, he thought that the conflict between freedom and slavery was an "irrepressible conflict between opposing and enduring forces." Echoing Lincoln's well-crafted remark of four months earlier, Seward said the country would "become either entirely a slave-holding nation or entirely a free-labor nation" (Taylor, 107). He raised the specter of the slave power expanding into the territories and repealing the 1808 ban on the international slave trade. Seward had solidified his position as point man for the Republican antislavery forces.

As the 1860 presidential campaign season loomed, Seward left his presidential ambitions in Weed's hands and took a trip through Europe from May to December 1859. Sectional tension was rife in the country and in Congress when he returned, and in February 1860, he delivered a major address in which he projected a much less radical image. Avoiding any mention of an inevitable conflict, he instead noticed the comparability of slave and free labor, and he argued that slaves were better cared for than free labor in the North. And while he continued to advance the admission of Kansas under a free state constitution, he denounced the recently hanged John Brown. It was a conciliatory speech, one designed to portray both himself and the Republican party as no threat to the South.

Despite his efforts to back away from his advanced antislavery position, Seward's reputation for inflexibility on the slavery issue was well set in the national perception. He had been the point man on the issue for too long. Furthermore, by the time of the national convention, his opponents in the Republican party had built a strong case for his radicalism. In this moment of great national tension, a candidate with less visibility, less of an outspoken record on the paramount issue of slavery, won the Republican nomination in Chicago and crushed Seward's longtime ambition to be president.

When Congress reconvened in December 1860 Seward became a leader of the effort to conciliate the slaveholding states. As a member of the Senate Committee of Thirteen he suggested that Congress fulfill a Republican platform pledge and assure the security of slavery in the South. In January 1861 he proposed a constitutional convention to protect slavery in the South and admit the remaining territories without reference to slavery.

President-elect Lincoln invited Seward into the administration as Secretary of State in early December 1860, and although the New Yorker had grave misgivings about being a part of the diverse group, the president persuaded him to accept.

During the six weeks between Lincoln's inauguration and the firing on Fort Sumter, Seward attempted to guide administration policy. He told his former Senate colleague Preston King that he "has acquired a very controlling influence with the President and is very much disposed to do, and be responsible for everything done, himself" (Bigelow, 1:366). Before Lincoln made a decision on Fort Sumter, Seward told the Southern "peace commissioners" on March 15 that the fort would be evacuated. Clear in his own mind that the government must give up federal property in the seceded states in order to avoid a clash and thereby hold the moderate upper South and border states, Seward became frustrated with Lincoln's decision on March 30 to resupply the fort. On April 1, 1861, he penned "Some Thoughts for the President's Consideration" in a vain attempt to recapture the initiative within the administration.

In the memo, Seward urged the president to develop a domestic and foreign policy rather than spend all his time on patronage matters. He noted that seven states had already left the Union and that European governments seemed to be ready to exploit that situation. He advised Lincoln to abandon federal property in the South, sacrificing the antislavery cause in exchange for preserving the Union. He urged that the president seek to know the intentions of England, France, Spain, and Russia in the Western Hemisphere and, if those intentions were not to the government's liking, to declare war on one or all of them. He noted in conclusion that the government needed someone who could consistently speak to this policy, whether it be the president or some member of the cabinet. As for himself, he said, "It is not in my especial province. But I neither seek to evade nor assume responsibility" (Nicolay and Hay, 3:445–446).

The coming of war shattered Seward's four-month attempt to find a compromise solution to sectional rift. For his effort to preserve the Union at the expense of the antislavery cause, John Greenleaf Whittier wrote a poem about him. "Statesman, I thank thee," the Quaker poet wrote, "for wise calm words that put to shame passion and party" (Crofts, 243). But Frances Seward took another view when she wrote to him in January 1861 after one of his conciliatory speeches: "Compromises based on the idea that the preservation of the Union is more important than the liberty of 4,000,000 human beings cannot be right," she said. "The alteration of the Constitution to perpetuate slavery . . . cannot be approved by God or supported by good men" (Crofts, 243).

Once war broke out, Seward threw himself wholeheartedly into using the State Department to bolster the administration's aim of reuniting the country. He sidetracked his imperialist impulses and concentrated on ensuring that no European power, especially England, recognized the Confederacy. His basic position was that the United States was dealing with an insurrection and hence would see any recognition of the Confederacy as a hostile act. Although the French were eager to exploit the American dilemma in order to establish a colony in Mexico, they keyed their behavior on England's.

Seward was able to maintain positive relations with the British through his evenhanded treatment of the *Trent* Affair in 1861, but he took a much tougher approach with the Palmerston government regarding the case of the Laird rams in 1863. The Confederacy had contracted with Liverpool shipyards to build blockade-running vessels and ships with ironclad prows to be used as rams. Seward sought to have the British government stop the construction of the ships, or at least detain them. After the government allowed one ship, the *Alabama*, to slip away, Seward assumed an aggressive stand regarding the dangerous rams. He authorized U.S. Ambassador to London Charles Francis Adams to say that the president would regard the Confederacy's use of the vessels as an act of war by England against the United States. Adams emphasized this threat, and the government seized the rams.

After Lincoln's assassination, Seward remained Secretary of State at Andrew Johnson's request. His reputation as secretary under Johnson, however, was tarnished by his support for presidential Reconstruction. Seward's overriding concern during Reconstruction was the restoration of peace and prosperity to the nation. Although he believed that the government had done the right thing to free the slaves, he felt that to give them full citizenship or suffrage would undermine the goal of restoring the Union. As a result of these views, he supported Johnson's program. He backed the president's veto of the Freedmen's Bureau and Civil Rights bills, even drafting the veto messages for Johnson. Unlike the president, however, Seward tried to find common ground with Congress. In the veto messages that he drafted for Johnson, the secretary praised the benefits of the Freedmen's Bureau and the attempt to provide blacks with citizenship and civil rights. Yet he supported the presidential vetoes by pointing to technical flaws in the legislation and by objecting to the wording of the bills. In his veto messages, the president deleted Seward's references to the bills' positive aspects.

Seward also supported Johnson's veto of the Fourteenth Amendment and gave speeches defending the president. He even joined Johnson on his disastrous "Swing around the Circle," which was designed to generate support for presidential Reconstruction. By 1866, however, many moderate Republicans had thrown their support to Johnson's opponents, the Radicals, and congressional backing for the president all but disappeared. Seward continued to support Johnson during the impeachment crisis, but by that time the secretary had few political friends and little influence among congressmen. In the end, all he could do was raise money for Johnson's defense. Seward's moderation in the face of Congress's increasing radicalism ensured that his reputation among members of his own party would plummet. As a result, when Johnson left office in 1869, Seward's long political career came to an abrupt end.

Before he completed his eight-year career as Secretary of State, Seward managed to secure Senate passage of a treaty acquiring Alaska for the United States. Throughout his life, Seward was an ardent proponent of Manifest Destiny and the peaceful commercial expansion of the United States. After the Civil War, he made a great effort to obtain new territories for the nation. He attempted to acquire two of the Dutch West Indies and the Dominican Republic, but congressional indifference and lack of interest from the countries involved thwarted his expansionist impulse. Seward finally met with success in 1867 when he secured congressional approval for the treaty providing for the purchase of Alaska from Russia for $7 million. Many in the Senate opposed the agreement because of its expense, and the press ridiculed him. But he did not allow this proposal to falter.

Seward left office on March 4, 1869, and returned to Auburn. He made an extensive trip into the western United States, visiting the new Alaskan territory. He then proceeded to travel around the world as if to emphasize his global ambitions for the United States. He returned to Auburn in 1871 and died there on October 10, 1872.

The struggle for Seward's reputation began immediately after his death and focused on his role in the Lincoln administration. Charles Francis Adams delivered a eulogy for Seward in the New York State legislature on April 18, 1873, and Thurlow Weed published it. Aside from favorably comparing the late secretary to Pericles, Gregory I, and Cardinal Richelieu, Adams made the mistake of portraying the New Yorker as superior to Lincoln in "native intellectual power . . . in breadth of philosophical experience and in the force of moral discipline." He concluded that Seward "could not have been long blind to the deficiencies of the chief in these respects" (Adams, 53). Such an assertion was not likely to go unchallenged.

Gideon Welles, Lincoln's Secretary of the Navy and a bitter enemy of Seward, responded to Adams's eulogy in three articles published in the October, November, and December 1873 issues of *Galaxy* magazine. Welles wished to set the record straight, he said, and argued that Seward was an aggressive and ambitious rival of Lincoln's who tried to wrest leadership of the administration from the president.

The source of Welles's animus is not far to seek. Seward clearly regarded himself as Lincoln's chief minister and the other cabinet members as his inferiors. Repeatedly treading on their turf, he deeply offended Welles early on when he interfered with, and perhaps deliberately undermined, naval plans for the relief of Fort Sumter. Thus, as Norman B. Ferris says, after the Adams eulogy, Welles colluded with former cabinet colleagues Montgomery Blair and Salmon P. Chase to destroy the secretary's reputation ("Lincoln and Seward," 32–33).

Seward was not without his supporters. His son Frederick published Seward's autobiography and Frederick's memoir of his father in 1877. In 1883 Harriet Weed published her late husband's *Autobiography*, which put a positive light on Seward's public career. In 1884, George E. Baker republished in five volumes his 1853 *The Works of William Henry Seward*, which brought the New Yorker's speeches and state papers back before the public. Also in 1884 Henry Cabot Lodge published a glowing appraisal of Seward's career in *Atlantic Monthly*. Donn Piatt included a flattering portrait of Seward in his *Memories of the Men Who Saved the Union* (1887). In 1891 Seward's son Frederick, prompted perhaps by the publication of John Nicolay and John Hay's massive biography of Lincoln in 1890, republished his 1877 edition of Seward's autobiography and his own memoir, bringing even more of Seward's papers to light. In 1892, at Cornell University, Andrew Estrem produced a Ph.D. dissertation on Seward. Covering the period up to the Sumter shelling, Estrem saw Seward as a high-minded progressive leader and an advocate of preserving the Union at all costs. Thornton Lothrop followed with an 1896 biography (revised in 1899; reprinted in 1908, 1909, 1972). Although the work lacks footnotes and a bibliography, Lothrop was a Boston attorney with a Harvard degree whose work was published in the prestigious American Statesmen series.

At the turn of the century, Frederic Bancroft published an important and still valuable two-volume biography (reprinted in 1967), and in 1910 Edward Everett Hale, Jr., published a popular biography. Bancroft had a Ph.D from Columbia; Hale's Ph.D. was from Harvard. Both were in academe and both based their studies on available primary sources. Bancroft's view of Seward is not uncritical but is well balanced; Hale's portrait is admiring. No other serious biography of

Seward appeared until Glyndon Van Deusen's scholarly account in 1967. Based on Seward's papers and an extensive array of other manuscript collections, Van Deusen produced a political biography that is thoughtful and judicious and not uncritical. Nicely summing up Seward's character, he says, "Politicians of the Seward stripe act from a mixture of motives." While they genuinely wish to serve, "they are aggressive by nature, and . . . seek to bolster [their] self-esteem. They covet power," he says, "and if convinced that a given political course rides the wave of the future they will be loyal to it" (25). John M. Taylor's 1991 biography (with a 1996 reissue) is a popular portrait based mostly on secondary sources.

While Seward's involvement in domestic affairs during the war and Reconstruction brought him only grief and ridicule, his greatest successes were in the field of diplomacy and foreign policy. While Norman B. Ferris in *Desperate Diplomacy* (1976) and Howard Jones in *Union in Peril* (1992) write approvingly of Seward's Civil War diplomacy, there is no comprehensive study of his diplomatic career. Henry W. Temple's essay on Seward in *The American Secretaries of State and Their Diplomacy* (1927–1929) is thorough but rather laudatory and uncritical regarding his imperialist urges. Gordon Warren takes a different tack in his essay on Seward in *Makers of American Diplomacy* (1974). After asserting the proposition that Seward was ill prepared to be the nation's top diplomat, Warren awards him kudos for preventing European intervention in the secession crisis and for being "the precursor of late nineteenth-century imperialists" (219).

Ernest Paolino takes the most expansive view of Seward's imperialism. He argues that not only were the so-called expansionists of the mid-nineteenth century the precursors of the late nineteenth-century imperialists; there was no distinction between them. By the time Seward became Secretary of State, Paolino argues, "he had already devoted a great deal of thought to the idea of an American empire" based not on vast territorial acquisitions but on commercial power (x). Such a commercial empire required a far-flung network of bases to support the American navy and merchant marine. Ironically, Seward the imperialist had to be Seward the diplomatist for four years while he struggled to keep the Europeans from meddling in the American crisis. When the war was finally over and Seward the imperialist proposed acquisitions in the Pacific and Caribbean, the construction of an isthmian canal, and transcontinental railroads, he encountered a Congress preoccupied with Reconstruction and in an antiexpansionist humor. That he was able to persuade Congress to approve the purchase of Russian America in 1867 was a major triumph.

One might agree with Gordon Warren that, taken as a whole, Seward's public life was a success. As governor of New York and as a member of the U.S. Senate, he took a strong position on the burning issue of the day, antislavery. When he failed to achieve his long-standing ambition of becoming president and then was thwarted in his attempt to be Lincoln's prime minister, he got down to the business of being Secretary of State. There he succeeded in keeping

European countries out of the American conflict and after the Civil War set the American imperial juggernaut in motion.

BIBLIOGRAPHY

Charles Francis Adams, *An Address on the Life, Character and Service of William Henry Seward* (Albany: Weed, Parsons and Company, 1873).

Harriet A. Weed, ed., *Life of Thurlow Weed Including His Autobiography and a Memoir*, 2 vols. (Boston: Houghton Mifflin and Company, 1883).

George E. Baker, ed., *The Works of William Henry Seward*, 5 vols. (Boston: Houghton Mifflin, 1884).

Henry Cabot Lodge, "William Henry Seward," *Atlantic Monthly* 53 (May 1884): 682.

Donn Piatt, *Memories of the Men Who Saved the Union* (New York: Belford, Clarke and Company, 1887).

John G. Nicolay and John Hay. *Abraham Lincoln: A History*, 10 vols. (New York: The Century Company, 1890).

Frederick W. Seward, *William H. Seward: An Autobiography from 1801 to 1834, with a Memoir of His Life and Selections from His Letters, 1831–1846*, 3 vols. (New York: Derby and Miller, 1891).

Andrew Estrem, "The Statesmanship of William H. Seward, as Seen in His Public Career Prior to 1861" (Ph.D. dissertation, Cornell University, 1892).

William H. Kirk, *William Henry Seward* (Philadelphia: J. B. Lippincott Company, 1892).

Frederic Bancroft, *The Life of William H. Seward*, 2 vols. (New York: Harper Bros., 1899–1900).

John Bigelow, *Retrospections of an Active Life*, 5 vols. (New York: The Baker & Taylor Company, 1909–1913).

Edward Everett Hale, Jr., *William H. Seward* (Philadelphia: George W. Jacobs and Company, 1910).

Henry W. Temple, "William H. Seward," in volume 7 of Samuel Flagg Bemis, ed., *American Secretaries of State and Their Diplomacy*, 10 vols. (New York: Alfred A. Knopf, 1927–1929).

Burton J. Hendrick, *Lincoln's War Cabinet* (Boston: Little, Brown and Company, 1946).

Allan Nevins, *The Emergence of Lincoln*, 2 vols. (New York: Charles Scribner's Sons, 1950).

Patrick Sowle, "A Reappraisal of Seward's Memorandum of April 1, 1861, to Lincoln," *Journal of Southern History* 33, no. 2 (1967): 234–239.

Glyndon F. Van Deusen, *William Henry Seward* (New York: Oxford University Press, 1967).

Major L. Wilson, "The Repressible Conflict: Seward's Concept of Progress and the Free-Soil Movement," *Journal of Southern History* 37, no. 4 (1971): 533–556.

Ernest N. Paolino, *The Foundations of the American Empire: William Henry Seward and United States Foreign Policy* (Ithaca, N.Y.: Cornell University Press, 1973).

Gordon H. Warren, "Imperial Dreamer: William Henry Seward and American Destiny," in Frank J. Merli and Theodore A. Wilson, eds., *Makers of American Diplomacy* (New York: Charles Scribner's Sons, 1974).

Norman B. Ferris, *Desperate Diplomacy: William H. Seward's Foreign Policy, 1861* (Knoxville: University of Tennessee Press, 1976).

Norman B. Ferris, "Lincoln and Seward in Civil War Diplomacy: Their Relationship at the Outset Re-examined,'' *Journal of the Abraham Lincoln Association* 12 (1981): 21–42.

Daniel W. Crofts. ''Secession Winter; William Henry Seward and the Decision for War,'' *New York History* 65, no. 3 (1984): 228–256.

John M. Taylor, *William Henry Seward: Lincoln's Right Hand* (New York: Harper-Collins, 1991).

Howard Jones, *Union in Peril: The Crisis over British Intervention and the Civil War* (Chapel Hill: University of North Carolina Press, 1992).

PHILIP HENRY SHERIDAN
(March 6, 1831–August 5, 1888)

Jon L. Wakelyn

"I came back to my native land with even a greater love for her, and with increased admiration for her institutions." Thus spoke the Irish-born General Philip H. Sheridan upon his return to the United States in 1871 from Europe. Considered by many who have studied the Civil War to have been one of the three most famous Union Army generals, his devotion to his adopted country may well explain the motivation for his heroic activities. Indeed, from the audacity of his troops at Missionary Ridge to his victory at Brandy Station in April 1865, in which he turned Robert E. Lee's (q.v.) troops, thus cutting off Lee's ability to move south and effectively ending the resistance of the Army of Northern Virginia, he was truly one of the great Union captains. At the time of his famous ride in late 1864 to relieve his embattled troops in the Valley of Virginia, he became the stuff of legends. His portrait was hung in many a Union home, and his exploits were the subjects of song and verse. Yet aside from the occasional contemporary pietistic outpouring of biographical sketches, and an excellent study of his command in the West after the war, his great Civil War career has not been the subject of modern biography or been reevaluated as to his true accomplishments. To discover the reasons for historians' neglect of this great leader requires another look at Sheridan's life.

The best work on his life, written by officers who had fought under Sheridan, attempted to construct an image of gallantry that would be useful to those changing times. Frank Burr and Richard Hinton, in devotion to his memory, in 1888 described a leader who struggled against the adversity of humble birth to become the head of the army. Indeed, Sheridan's life began most humbly. Supposedly, Sheridan was born on March 6, 1831, to poor Irish immigrants in Albany, New York. But Joseph Hergesheimer, the novelist, conjured up, in his *Sheridan, a Military Narrative* (1931), a birth on shipboard somewhere out on the Atlantic, having sailed from Dublin, the point of debarkation for many Irish immigrants. His father, John, had owned a farm in County Cavan, which he sold to raise the funds to seek his fortune in the new world. Along with two other children and his wife, Mary Minoregh, John Sheridan emigrated to Albany, New York, although others believe to Massachusetts, where he sought work on the railroads. Unable to make a living in the East, the father took his family to the fabled West in 1832, to Somerset, Perry County, Ohio. There he hoped for work building the turnpike, and there he gained employment dragging the locks on the Harding Valley Canal. By the early 1850s, rags had turned to success, and John had become a small subcontractor. In 1853 he lost everything. But in that Eden of Perry County, young Phil, the future audacious cavalryman, learned what it meant to transcend the poverty of the Irish immigrant.

Those who have written about young Phil described him as being a small, free-spirited youth. He also was full of pride, and he often got into fights with the local toughs who possibly belittled his family and his roots. Phil's father was away from home much of the time and unable to protect him, so his mother, Mary, became the defining role model of his youth. Mary was a purposeful woman who managed to hold the family together, and she had great ambitions for her sons, especially Phil, her favorite. She encouraged his attendance at Somerset's small schoolhouse, where he studied with the nomadic teacher Patrick McNaly and later a man called Thorn. Young Phil learned the rudiments of grammar, math, geography, and history. Especially did he find in history his love for war, and from events in the books he read, he devised war games with his friends. The many war heros who came through the town to speak also intrigued the young man. Sheridan's biographer, Paul A. Hutton, in setting the scene for the future, states "that Ohio was a miniature Prussia in the first half of the nineteenth century" (xiv). That Ulysses S. Grant (q.v.), William T. Sherman (q.v.), George A. Custer, and others were born in Ohio certainly suggests something military was going on in that state. It is said that the exploits of Ohioans in the Mexican War determined the warlike young man to want to attend the U.S. Military Academy.

But first Phil, having exhausted what local schooling was available, at fourteen had to find work because his family was in need. He found employment at a local general supply store, then at a tobacco warehouse. He served as a clerk and became quite good at figures and inventory keeping. In Somerset's dry goods store his math training and his skills at organizing made him the bookkeeper. Unfortunately for him, in the early stages of his military career, those skills would turn him into an inglorious supply officer. While earning his living Sheridan also developed fierce patriotic ties that led him to the Whig party and to extreme love of nation. Phil also had ambitions to rise in life, and early he planned on a military career. Because of that career interest, his older brother Patrick, a Whig politician, approached Ohio Congressman Thomas Ritchie for an appointment for Phil to West Point.

In 1848 Sheridan passed the entrance requirement and entered the academy. But Phil was little prepared either for academic rigor or for the discipline required of a plebe. He nearly flunked out, and only his natural ability and his determined hard work saved him. It is said that he learned enough math to stay in school by forcing a roommate to tutor him late into the nights. His pride, pugnaciousness, and indefatigable will caused him great trouble, almost ending his career before it had begun. In 1852, he had yet another scrape with a fellow student he thought had humiliated him. Only this time he took on a superior officer, and he was suspended from his own senior class. Phil went back to Ohio to work that year in a tobacco warehouse. But he did manage to graduate in 1853, thirty-fourth out of a class of fifty-three, which gave him few choices of a career. Sheridan joined the 1st U.S. Infantry.

His pre–Civil War military career led to few accomplishments as he held dull frontier duties with little excitement. First sent to Texas for fort duty, he immediately got into trouble with his commanding officer. In November 1854 he was transferred to the 4th Infantry and sent to the Pacific Northwest. At least there he received the useful duty of training war recruits, and he learned to organize them well. There, also, he fought in the little known Yakima Indian War, after which he received a commendation for bravery, if not foolhardiness. He was merciless in rounding up so-called Indian warriors, and he summarily executed a few of them. Sheridan gained no promotion for those exploits. Then life settled down to dull routine, which hardly advanced his military expertise. He did get the customary promotion to first lieutenant for time served.

In September 1861, after the war started, Sheridan finally got his promotion to captain and was sent to join the 13th Infantry in Missouri. The young officer commented little about why he joined the Union war effort except to proclaim his loyalty to nation, his desire to punish the enemy, and his duty to bring the Confederacy back into the Union. Sheridan's legendary devotion to his adopted country obviously would develop as his fame grew.

The young and inexperienced officer, however, would not get a chance to punish anyone during the Civil War's early days. In October 1861 he joined the staff of General Henry W. Halleck (q.v.) in St. Louis, and in December 1861, he was named chief quartermaster in the Army of Southwest Missouri. Left out of battles, and chafing at the bit, he demanded active duty, but Halleck refused and continued him as quartermaster. His accounting, bookkeeping, and thorough organizing skills had come back to haunt him. In March 1862, after refusing to purchase stolen horses from quasi-guerilla troops, he was demoted to staff duties. Finally, Sheridan talked Halleck into giving him a line position. No doubt Halleck was tired of listening to his complaints and probably needed officers in the field. He became colonel of the 2nd Michigan Cavalry and its regimental commander. At the battle of Booneville in Kentucky in July, he made a well-planned cavalry raid to burn Confederate supplies. Promoted to brigadier, his fame as a scout who remembered everything he saw led Halleck to make him reconnaissance officer in the march toward Corinth. Of course, Sheridan deplored what he thought was a demotion or at least a duty that again would deprive him of the glory of combat.

Finally, the young general got his break when Halleck made him a general of volunteers under General Don Carlos Buell, and Buell gave him command of the 11th Division in October 1862 to help in the Union defense of Louisville. Confederate General Braxton Bragg (q.v.) had launched a large turning movement northward that had caused alarm in Kentucky. Sheridan organized and drilled his green troops and prepared them to stand against Bragg. And stand they did, as Buell became confused and Sheridan himself had to mount a major defense perimeter at the battle of Perryville. He became a hero to the press, as great Union fighters then seemed in short supply. After Buell had lost his command to General William S. Rosecrans, Sheridan was sent south of Nashville to the area of Stone's River. At Murfreesboro in January 1863, Sheridan assisted in General George Thomas's (q.v.) fabled defense, then led a counterattack to rout the rebel army. His fame skyrocketed.

As part of the Army of the Cumberland, the thirty-one-year-old general received ever more important commands, and he soon was made a provisional army major general. Around Chickamauga, in the Tullahoma campaign, he was delegated to destroy the enemy's communications, and he did. His ability to train recruits with speed, make dangerous and decisive marches, use bold tactics, and understand bridge building, in the eyes of his first biographer and former subordinates Burr and Hinton, were the reasons for his early successes (109). In the celebrated breakout of Chattanooga where the Confederates had trapped the army, Sheridan showed his loyalty to Rosecrans. When the Union took the offensive at Missionary Ridge, Sheridan and his soldiers became legendary. His troops burst up the ridge and captured artillery, arms, and soldiers. The result of that famous charge meant that the Union had taken control of the central South. Western Union Army commander U. S. Grant personally praised Sheridan for his valor. Grant knew that he had found a soldier who could and would fight. But Sheridan again felt neglected as, during the winter of 1863–1864, he languished in Tennessee, now under the command of General George Thomas. Sheridan desperately wanted in on the proposed Atlanta campaign.

That was not to be. Sheridan would claim his place in this country's military history in another place. As soon as Grant was named general in chief he met with Halleck and Secretary of War Edwin Stanton (q.v.), and he persuaded them to place Sheridan in charge of the Army of the Potomac's cavalry. Although he resisted assignment to the East, and especially opposed being named what he thought was a mere scout, Sheridan soon received major assignments. He was at the Union debacle in the Wilderness on April 8, 1864. But soon he was operating as an independent cavalry officer, often using his troops as dismounted fighters, and usually running afoul of his superior General George G. Meade (q.v.). Without clear understandings about their respective command duties, the two headstrong and outspoken men were bound to clash. Finally Grant had to break up the fighting by making Sheridan an independent commander. Taking over what was a demoralized cavalry, at first he had orders only to protect Union supply trains and lines of communication. But he performed ably at the Battle of Spotsylvania. On May 6, 1864, he defended General Winfield Scott Hancock's left flank, then launched an attack on the Confederate cavalry. At Todd's Tavern he defeated General J.E.B. Stuart, the Confederacy's most famous cavalry commander. On May 8, 1864, Grant sent him on a celebrated ride around the Confederate capital of Richmond. He cut railroad lines and fought numerous skirmishes. But the young general realized he could accomplish little in Richmond and declined to enter that city. At Cold Harbor on May 31, 1864, he had to retreat against a withering Confederate fire. But he regrouped and held a position from which the Union Army would rally a defense.

Grant then made other plans for his most successful cavalry officer. After the mighty Army of the Potomac had turned the Confederate right and headed to Petersburg, Grant placed Sheridan in charge of attacking the area west of Richmond to keep Lee from escaping into the Valley of Virginia and to protect the defenses of Washington. On June 7, 1864, Sheridan destroyed the Virginia Central Railroad and the James River Canal. Confederate Generals Jubal Early and Richard S. Ewell were sent to the valley to deflect Sheridan's threat to Richmond. Only at Reams Station, south of Petersburg, on July 27, 1864, after he had destroyed a Confederate railroad, did Sheridan suffer a temporary defeat.

Again Grant had plans for his cavalry as dismounted troops in war. He directed Sheridan to destroy Confederate supplies in the Valley of Virginia. But first Sheridan had the unenviable task of making up for General David Hunter's having let General Early slip north toward Washington. On August 4, 1864, Sheridan defeated Early, and the last Confederate offensive raid was over. Then it was on to the valley.

The object of the Valley Campaign, as stated, was to damage the Army of Northern Virginia's food supply. But it was much more. Sheridan was to protect Washington and to devastate Confederate communications around Lynchburg. On August 10, 1864, he began to march up the valley to force Early to fight. In doing so, Sheridan would destroy the morale of the valley civilians, as they would then know that the Confederate Army could no longer protect them. Having no specific orders, Sheridan could act as an independent Union commander plundering and destroying whatever got in his way. In mid-September, at the Battle of Opequan, near Winchester, he routed the Confederates. On September 22 he was victorious at Fisher's Hill, and later at Port Republic. Sheridan had destroyed all Confederate supplies in the area from Winchester to Cedar Creek. Named a brigadier in the regular army, he then went to the federal capital to confer with superiors. But hearing of a Confederate rout of his troops at Cedar Creek, on October 19 Sheridan made his legendary ride to rally his troops once again to defeat Early.

Newspaper articles, stories, even poetry and songs were written and sung about his famous ride. Burr and Hinton wrote that "both poet and painter took up the theme of the ride and made it famous" (230). In November 1864, after a Washington tribute to his celebrated ride, Sheridan was made a major general, the youngest in the regular army. For a time he outranked his enemy General Meade. After Sheridan gave an interview to Assistant Secretary of War Charles

A. Dana (q.v.), that former newspaperman described for all the Northern people a leader who always fought in the front ranks of his men. Foolhardy or courageous, he had become in the view of the press and the Northern people the third most famous Union commander, only after Grant and Sherman.

But there remained a war to finish, which meant Sheridan had to help flush Lee out of the Petersburg defenses. He continued to break up Confederate communications, burn wagon trains and boxcars, destroy supplies, and threaten interior towns. On November 24, 1864, he was sent to stop Colonel John S. Mosby's legendary raids against civilians, and he all but destroyed what was left of Confederate guerrilla warfare. In early 1865 he burned part of Lynchburg. Then, on February 27, 1865, Sheridan focused on Charlottesville, so as to force General Early out of hiding. At Waynesboro he defeated the last of the Confederate cavalry presence. That victory allowed him to occupy Charlottesville on March 4, 1865. Sheridan then ravaged the countryside around Thomas Jefferson's home and the university. He captured military goods and burned grain and other forage supplies for horses. Then Sheridan tore up the Confederate railroad links between Lynchburg and Petersburg and burned bridges, depots, and factories in that area. Next he went after the James River Canal Company factory, the supplier of military goods to Richmond. He had destroyed all of the supplies to the rear of Lee's army. By March 26, 1865, when Sheridan gave up independent command to join Grant, he had quite literally destroyed the industrial capacity of the Army of Northern Virginia.

Sheridan next took on the task of turning Lee's army west of Petersburg, thus keeping Lee from escaping to the lower South. But there should have been little worry that there was all that much fight left in the demoralized Army of Northern Virginia. In the wake of Sheridan's destructive actions, Confederate soldiers slipped away to go home. Civilians were already devastated, and they conveyed their sentiments to the soldiers. On April 1, 1865, at the Battle of Five Forks, Sheridan turned General George Pickett's troops, thus cutting off the final Confederate escape route south. He had thwarted Lee's communications and now controlled the last of the Confederate railroad lines from Richmond south. That allowed Grant's forces to break the Confederate entrenchments and control Petersburg. Lee had to evacuate and retreat. Then Sheridan, with his powerful combination of cavalry speed and dismounted troops, went after Lee. At Saylor's Creek, Sheridan actually was in front of Lee's army and thus was able to fight a defensive engagement to slow up Lee. He captured Lee's last wagon train of food. Perhaps only the incumbrance of so many Confederate prisoners—he had taken almost 7,000—kept Sheridan from defeating Lee himself. At Appomattox on April 7, 1865, Sheridan had constructed what Burr and Hinton called ''a wall of infantry across Lee's path'' (269). The little Irishman not only contributed mightily to forcing Lee's surrender, but his actions over the past month had destroyed any chance of continued Confederate resistance in Virginia.

Victory for the Army of the Potomac hardly meant unity obtained among its ambitious and sensitive general officers. Sheridan continued his quarrel with

Meade over which general had been most successful around Petersburg. Perhaps to break up this too personal struggle, General Grant sent his trusted cavalryman south, not to mop up what was left of the Confederacy but to the Rio Grande, to keep Confederates from crossing into Mexico. He had been given, in addition, the delicate diplomatic mission of defending the Mexican government from France's threats. Sheridan was also to control Texas, to support Unionists there, and to protect the new loyal state government. After the French had left Mexico and Texas was at last in safe hands, Sheridan was sent to New Orleans and, in June 1865, made commander of the newly organized Department of the Gulf. In that difficult job, Sheridan, the nonpolitician and extreme nationalist, had to put down the New Orleans riot of 1866 and to declare martial law in that beleaguered city. In March 1867 he became commander of the 5th Reconstruction District to represent the interests of General Grant and the restive Republican party. Of course, the little general clashed with President Andrew Johnson (q.v.) when he removed J. Madison Wells as governor of Louisiana. In August 1867 the president relieved him from command. Sheridan desperately wanted out of the political limelight, as he hoped to keep free from the entanglements of Reconstruction's bloody quasi wars.

In September 1867, he was placed in command of the Department of Missouri, perhaps because he knew the West and the activities of the Indians. In fact, he was sent to remove those hostile Indians west of Fort Leavenworth in order to open up the land for railroad building westward. His campaign against the Indians was a success. When U. S. Grant became president he named Sheridan a lieutenant general and placed him in Chicago as commander of the Military Division of Missouri, which meant he was in charge of most of the western armies. Aside from his duties to protect settlers, Sheridan became a local hero, as he took part in much of the commercial development of the city. During the great Chicago fire of 1871 his troops helped to put out the blazes, and he kept order by declaring martial law. Chicago also provided the general with social diversion, and it was there in 1874 that he took a wife. He married the love-struck daughter of the famous General Daniel H. Rucker, who had powerful political ties in Washington. Irene M. Rucker was nineteen years younger than her husband but completely devoted to the little general. They had four children and quite a happy life.

But Sheridan never left his duties far behind him. During the Sioux War of 1875 he visited the West. While in the West he founded the famous officer's school at Fort Leavenworth to train future military leaders. Also in 1875 he was sent to New Orleans to put down the White League. Back in Chicago Sheridan ruthlessly broke up labor riots, as his nationalism left him little room to sympathize with those who resisted his government. He was heard to call the union strikers communists. Between 1883 and 1888 he served as commanding general of the U.S. Army and was stationed in Washington. In 1888 he was named a full general. At the height of his career, having grown sickly, Phil Sheridan died at his summer residence in Rhode Island on August 5, 1888.

Although ex-Union generals often squabbled in print, and it is known that Meade and a few others disliked Sheridan, his place in history after his death appeared secure. In his *Memoirs*, which have been used ever since to rate Union officers, Grant pronounced him an excellent general and the true winner in the cavalry war in the East. Sheridan, himself, got even with a few malcontents in his own *Personal Memoirs* (1888). But in those *Memoirs* what the boasting little general really wanted to do was to create his own personal interpretation of his greatness. Sheridan humbly acknowledged his task was to serve as "the source of information for future historians." His life, or personally created fable, was to be an example for others of how the self-made immigrant's son had risen to prominence because of talent, not politics. In them, he stressed that his militarist personality was the result of his love for the Union. The reader also is struck by the cold, nearly bloodless rendering of nerve and audacity that made him a fearless leader. As his subordinates Burr and Hinton acknowledged in their 1888 biography, that fearlessness led others to follow him. They also praised Sheridan's military skills. Especially did they acknowledge his use of spies and scouts and his expert ability to understand topography. But most of all they waxed eloquent over his modern skills at use of dismounted cavalry to destroy an enemy assault. For them, and most others at the end of the nineteenth century, he was the finest cavalry officer in the entire war.

Early twentieth-century interpreters of the war made no attempt to revise Sheridan's considerable reputation. The continuous outflow of poems and paintings of his famous ride fixed him in children's minds as a great hero. In 1931, the novelist Joseph Hergesheimer in his biography made some attempt at iconoclasm. But all Hergesheimer did was cast doubt on Sheridan's birthplace, and he deviated not at all from the traditional reputation. That biography was really the last until another effort in 1952 by T. Harry Williams, which also offered little new to understand what that general had accomplished. It is as if Grant's favorable verdict was so enormous that there is little reason to revise the reputation. Success almost killed history's interest in Sheridan.

Almost is the operative word, as recently a number of scholars have been trying to reevaluate the accomplishments of that great cavalry leader. A most important book, Paul Andrew Hutton's *Phil Sheridan and His Army* (1985), thoroughly revised his later career. Because Hutton was so incensed by Sheridan's brutal postwar Indian policy, he judged the general to have been a ruthless leader. But Hutton did give some insight into how the man fought, and he showed Sheridan's ability to get the most out of his troops. A critique against the great commander in the Valley came from Carol Reardon, who suggested that later military instructors have had their troubles with assessing Sheridan's abilities and activities. When they teach about him, she said, they fault him for disrupting Meade's line of march in May 1864. His raids now seem a bit uncoordinated, too independent, and even as showboating without purpose. Most recently, Joseph T. Glathaar in *Partners in Command* (1994), a careful study of military leaders' relationships, suggests Grant's great support for Sheridan dated from their success together in the West and that Grant favored his western officers. Even if Secretary of War Edwin Stanton doubted the choice of Sheridan for high command, states Glatthaar, Grant always protected his own. But Glatthaar also regards Sheridan as exactly what was needed in the valley. It was a "job for the feisty cavalry commander," the man best able to defeat the Confederate cavalry. So Sheridan's war reputation remains secure. But he certainly has been the least scrutinized of the great commanders. Fixed too much by the past legends of the self-made superpatriot, perhaps it is time now for a full-scale modern study to understand the man himself who became a great man on horseback, the stuff of poetry.

BIBLIOGRAPHY

Frank A. Burr and Richard J. Hinton, *The Life of General Philip H. Sheridan* (Providence, R.I.: J. A. and R. A. Reid, 1888).

Philip H. Sheridan, *Personal Memoirs of P. H. Sheridan*, 2 vols. (New York: Charles L. Webster and Company, 1888).

Joseph Hergesheimer, *Sheridan, a Military Narrative* (Boston: Houghton Mifflin Co., 1931).

T. Harry Williams, *Lincoln and His Generals* (New York: Alfred A. Knopf, 1952).

Paul Andrew Hutton, *Phil Sheridan and His Army* (Lincoln: University of Nebraska Press, 1985).

U. S. Grant, *Personal Memoirs of U. S. Grant* (1885; New York: Library of America, 1990).

Carol Reardon, *Scholars and Soldiers* (Lawrence: University Press of Kansas, 1990).

Joseph T. Glatthaar, *Partners in Command: The Relationship between Leaders in the Civil War* (New York: Free Press, 1994).

WILLIAM TECUMSEH SHERMAN
(February 8, 1820–February 14, 1891)

John F. Marszalek

One of the Union Army's most distinguished generals, William Tecumseh Sherman was associated with uncertainty from early in his childhood. Born on February 8, 1820, in Lancaster, Ohio, he was the sixth of eleven children in the family of Connecticut expatriates Charles and Mary Sherman. Charles was a lawyer and, beginning in 1813, a collector of internal revenue for the Third District of Ohio. In 1816, when the federal government began accepting for government obligations only specie or Bank of the United States notes, Sherman found himself with a pile of worthless paper and, despite heroic efforts, a huge debt. He could have declared bankruptcy but resolved, instead, to pay back all he owed. He went back to the practice of the law, in 1823 becoming a judge of the Ohio Supreme Court. In 1829, he collapsed suddenly of a fever, dying virtually penniless because of his internal revenue losses. His death left his widow no choice but to break up the family and parcel out the children to helpful friends and neighbors.

It was under these trying conditions that the nine-year-old Tecumseh Sherman, or Cump as he was known to friends and relatives, entered the home of successful Lancaster lawyer and politician Thomas Ewing. The Ewings lived just up the street from the Shermans, and the two couples had long been friendly, their children running in and out of each other's homes. Still, the move produced a lifetime of uncertainty for Sherman. He never ceased considering himself an orphan and chronically worried that, like his father, he would die in debt and leave his family in poverty.

The Ewings accepted Cump as one of their own, adding the name William at the time of his baptism into the family's Catholicism. He had a stable and enjoyable childhood, but he never overcame the trauma of his father's death. He developed an ambivalence toward the ever more publicly influential Ewing. He admired him and his success, but it bothered him to depend on his benevolence. The economic contrast between Thomas Ewing and Charles Sherman was obvious, and Cump felt conspicuously uncomfortable as he contemplated it.

In 1836, through Ewing's influence, the sixteen-year-old boy received an appointment to the U.S. Military Academy at West Point. Here his emotional uncertainty continued. He disliked the nitpicking discipline and the enervating dullness of the institution, but he also developed a closeness to the other cadets, acquiring a feeling of family he never experienced with the Ewings. In a telling letter to Ellen, one of his foster sisters, he expressed his obligation to her parents for all that they had done for him; at the same time, however, he indicated the confusion of his own feelings toward them. "Indeed I often feel that your father and mother have usurped the place which nature has alloted to parents alone," he wrote (*Papers*, Aug. 21, 1839). When he graduated in 1840, and the Ewings wanted him to resign his commission and enter a civilian profession, he irritatingly spurned their attempt to pull him away from his military family.

He remained in the army, moving to his first assignment, the swamps and hammocks of Florida to battle the Seminoles. Once again, as had been the case at West Point, he was bored; but he enjoyed the military camaraderie. He also learned an important lesson for his future in this conflict against the Seminoles: War was not simply fought between two professional armies but between two societies. This was a lesson he would put to good use during the Civil War.

Sherman remained in Florida until 1842, when he moved briefly to Fort Morgan, Alabama. There followed a four-year stint at Fort Moultrie in South Carolina (1842–1846) and, finally, four years in California during the Mexican War and the gold rush. Most of the time he felt bored and sometimes depressed. Yet he also developed his long-held support for slavery and his disdain for Mexicans and Indians, while gaining a knowledge of the geography of the South and an affection for its people that would later help determine his Civil War military strategy. He regularly corresponded with Ellen, several years his junior, and, through her, heard repeated calls from the Ewings to resign. When this correspondence resulted in his formal engagement to Ellen, her determined insistence that he resign his commission and come live in Lancaster and her even more determined demand that he become a practicing Catholic wore away at his self-esteem. "I am content and happy, and it would be foolish to spring into the world barehanded and unprepared to meet its coldness and trials," he said. As for Catholicism, he believed in "the main doctrines of the Christian religion," but refused to accept any one sect (*Papers*, April 7, 1842).

The long-distance courtship resulted in no agreement on these fundamental issues, but it did result in an 1850 marriage. What followed was a decade of repeated business failures, the birth of children, marital and family tensions, and more depression. Sherman remained in the military until 1853, when he resigned his commission to become manager of a San Francisco branch office of a St. Louis bank. He demonstrated a talent for finance, though he found the work stressful. Ellen's constant desire to be with her father and family in Lancaster rather than with him and their children in California only added to the tension.

He suffered from suffocating asthma, and monetary conditions outside his control forced the closing of his bank, leaving him feeling responsible for failed investments he had made for fellow army officers. His life seemed to be moving toward the poverty of his father. Would he, as an adult, have to depend on Thomas Ewing again as he had during his childhood?

Mired in depression, Sherman became manager of a New York City branch of the St. Louis bank; but it, too, collapsed, this time because of the Panic of 1857. He then moved to Kansas, where he failed as a lawyer and a real estate broker. Finally, he went to Louisiana as head of a military school, finding success despite the unceasing pressure from Ellen and the Ewings to return to Ohio. When secession came, he saw it as representing the bankrupting anarchy he had experienced in his life, and he battled it by refusing to stay in the South. He prepared to give in to his wife and in-laws and return to Ohio, but now they insisted that he rejoin the Union Army. Instead, he went to St. Louis as a street railroad official, convinced that the Union war effort was so unfocused that it would only drag him down if he joined it. He worried and he fretted, best expressing his feelings when, in Kansas, he said: "I am doomed to be a vagabond. I look upon myself as a dead cock in the pit, not worthy of further notice" (*Papers*, April 15, 1859). Sherman entered the Civil War years unhappy with his life and unsure about his future.

In Washington in early 1861, William T. Sherman had a most unsettling interview with Abraham Lincoln (q.v.), the president's seeming unconcern about the seriousness of secession stunning him. In St. Louis, he and his son found themselves in the line of fire during the blundering encounter between pro-Union and pro-Confederate militia. He decided to reenter the military anyway but refused any commission except that in the regular army. Soon, however, he found himself commanding volunteer troops in Irvin McDowell's invasion force in Virginia, worried about the competence of these citizen soldiers. At Bull Run in July, he was, according to that battle's historian, "the star . . . of the whole army that fought" there (*Sherman Memoirs* 1:185–186). Yet what he saw frightened him. He saw confirmation of his deepest fears. The Union military effort was anarchic, and the nation's future and his own were in dire peril.

Feeling this upset, he welcomed the chance to leave Washington. He agreed to go to Kentucky but extracted from Lincoln and Department of the Cumberland commander Major General Robert Anderson the promise that he would never be required to take command of the area. He refused to lead as long as the Union war effort was so chaotic, but he promised to remain steadfastly loyal no matter what happened. "Not till I see day light ahead do I want to lead, but when the danger threatens and others slink away I am and will be at my post" (*Papers*, Aug. 1861).

Sherman found in Kentucky an even bigger mess than he had witnessed in Washington; and, even worse, he was forced to take command of the department when an emotionally and physically exhausted Robert Anderson resigned. Sherman sank into such a deep depression worrying about conditions in Kentucky that officials there and in the nation's capital grew convinced that he was mentally ill. His almost hysterical warnings of impending doom to visiting Secretary of War Simon Cameron, plus his animosity toward all newspaper reporters, resulted in increasing public distrust of him. He demanded and received transfer from command in Kentucky to a subordinate role in Missouri under California friend Henry W. Halleck (q.v.). His continued eccentric warnings of military disaster there added to his reputation for unsteadiness. Army officials summoned Ellen, who took him away to the Ewing home in Lancaster to recuperate. Again, he became the recipient of Thomas Ewing's aid, a terrible added pressure on the already depressed man. Sherman was then further mortified on December 11, 1861, when the *Cincinnati Commercial* headlined an article: "General William T. Sherman Insane."

Other newspapers picked up the story, and it soon became the conventional wisdom. A modern biographer has disagreed with this assessment, characterizing Sherman's condition as "a neurotic depression" that is, he suffered from no psychotic breakdown—"he remained whole" (Marszalek, *Soldier's Passion* 169). A later writer disputed this interpretation. He argued: "Sherman's society recognized melancholy and mental breakdown much as we recognize clinical depression, not as psychosis . . . but as deeply painful and incapacitating mental stress, a condition surely characteristic of Sherman at this time" (Fellman, 99n). Clearly, Sherman suffered from terrible stress and depression during this time of personal crisis in Kentucky and Missouri. He was not insane, however; he never lost control of himself, as his contemporary opponents seemed to insist he had. The lack of order he witnessed in the Union war effort made him worry excessively about his own and the nation's future. He became severely depressed, but he never became insane.

Ellen and the Ewings led a frontal assault against these accusations of insanity. Ellen wrote and then visited Abraham Lincoln to demand unsuccessfully for corrective action. Meanwhile, Sherman received a lowly position, training recruits at Benton Barracks in Missouri. Henry W. Halleck watched him closely and, in February 1862, restored him to a more demanding leadership position, making him commander of the Department of Cairo, headquartered in the Mississippi River city of Paducah, Kentucky. Sherman's job was to send troops forward to the commander of the Department of West Tennessee, a rising star in the Union war effort, Ulysses S. Grant (q.v.). Sherman watched with awe as Grant won brilliant victories at Forts Henry and Donelson, demonstrating that the Union war effort could be organized, that is, nonanarchical and, consequently, successful. The two developed a friendship that would have enormous impact on both men and on the success of the Union war effort.

Sherman's good work in Paducah and, no doubt, continued Ewing family pressure resulted in further promotion. He gained command of a volunteer division in Grant's Army of the Tennessee. This force and Don Carlos Buell's Army of the Ohio were to mass at Pittsburg Landing, an obscure stopping point on the Tennessee River near a small church named Shiloh. From there, Henry

Halleck planned to lead this combined force in an assault on nearby Corinth, Mississippi, an important railroad center. Sherman felt that it was only in combat that he would be able to salvage his reputation from the insanity charges, and serving under Grant made him feel confident of impending success. All he and the army had to do was wait for Buell and then overwhelm Albert Sidney Johnston and the Confederate Army at Corinth.

Sherman clearly tried to be on his most restrained behavior, expressing none of the pessimistic panic of Kentucky and Missouri. He sent pickets out into the spring-warmed countryside but made no other special preparations, despite the misgivings of some of his subordinates. "I am satisfied they [Confederates] will await our coming at Corinth," he said, becoming even more content when Grant agreed with his assessment. Sherman was determined to raise no alarm, fearing "they'd call me crazy again." When Colonel Jesse Appler of his division's 53rd Ohio Volunteer Infantry Regiment insisted on issuing such warnings, Sherman told him to stop, or he "could take his damn regiment back to Ohio" (*Papers*, Apr. 4, 1862).

Unfortunately, Confederate general Albert Sidney Johnston proved Grant and Sherman wrong. Rather than wait in Corinth for the Union Army to attack him, he put his own force into motion and on April 6, 1862, gave the Union commanders the shock of their lives. Attacking near Shiloh Church, the Johnston-led Confederates drove the Union forces back toward the river landing. Sherman fought furiously and courageously against the Southern wave. By the end of the first day, Grant had managed to organize a final defense line, utilizing Buell's army, which had just arrived. Sherman prepared himself for withdrawal. To his amazement and excitement, Grant ordered an offensive the next day and drove the Confederates off the battlefield. Shiloh provided the rebirth that William T. Sherman had hoped such combat would bring, and importantly it sealed a bond with U. S. Grant. When the Union Army later captured Corinth, Sherman excitedly saw the "victory as brilliant and important as any recorded in history, and any officer [obviously including himself] or soldier who has lent his aid has just reason to be proud of his part" (*Papers*, May 31, 1862).

Although Union troops now clearly had the initiative in the West, Halleck did not press them forward. He broke up his huge army instead and ordered it to perform various organizational tasks. In July 1862, Sherman was named military governor of Memphis and soon started working hard to restore economic and social order and rebuild Unionism in the Mississippi River city. While he achieved observable success in this effort, the more important result of his time in the city was his realization that the conservative war of set rules that he had long believed in and supported no longer existed. Guerrillas fired into Union boats on the Mississippi River and harassed Unionists on land. Sherman realized, as he had in Florida against the Seminoles, that war was indeed fought between two societies, not simply between two military forces. The Confederate Army posed no danger in Memphis; it was the civilian irregulars who were causing the problems. Consequently, Sherman had to wage war against all Southern society, not just against the Southern army. Therefore, following shots on a riverboat from the area near the village of Randolph, he destroyed the town and even threatened the expulsion of ten Memphis families for every boat coming under future attack.

In addition to waging harsh war against all of Southern society, Sherman pushed his demands for a total effort on his own side. In Memphis, he made unapologetic attempts to censor the press to prevent reporters from providing any information to the enemy. He was not completely successful, and news leaked out of Memphis, but he went so far as to arrest a reporter from Chicago and detained and fined the editor of the army newspaper in the city. He now began to consider actions valid that previously his conservative philosophy of war had absolutely prohibited. For example, pillaging, if it helped the Union cause, was proper.

In December 1862, Sherman left Memphis by water to initiate an offensive against Vicksburg, Mississippi, the last major barrier to Union control of the Mississippi River. He led a flotilla against the heights outside the city, the plan calling for U. S. Grant to cooperate in the attack from the land side. The destruction of Grant's supplies at Holly Springs prevented him from arriving as planned, however, and Sherman's solo attack at Chickasaw Bayou proved to be a disaster. "Well we have been to Vicksburg and it was too much for us, and we have backed out," he disappointingly reported to his wife. And to make matters worse, John McClernand, the political general from Illinois who had done such yeoman work in recruiting troops for the Union war effort, arrived to take command of the flotilla. Sherman remained upset at his Chickasaw Bayou repulse, and he worried that McClernand would receive all the credit for the subsequent success at Arkansas Post. "As usual my troops had the fighting and did the work, but of course others will claim the merit and Glory," he groused (*Papers*, Jan. 4, 12, 1863).

Sherman vented his frustration on a favorite target, the press. Thomas W. Knox of the *New York Herald* had hidden aboard one of the ships in Sherman's flotilla and then written a scathing attack on Sherman's generalship. Sherman had him arrested and then court-martialed, the only such event in American history. The board of officers found Knox guilty of disobeying Sherman's orders to stay off the boats and expelled him from the area. Sherman was disappointed; he had hoped for the death penalty. He felt that strongly that the press was creating anti-Union anarchy on the battlefield by its publication of war news. His concept of totally organized warfare had progressed yet another harsh step.

As the Knox trial came to its conclusion in February 1863, Sherman continued as Grant's subordinate in the Union Army's attempts to dislodge the Confederates from Vicksburg. The various efforts, including a canal intended to direct the Mississippi River away from the town, failed; but then, in May, Grant began the spectacular movement that resulted in the surrender of that Gibraltar on July 4. Sherman participated wholeheartedly, cooperating as Grant separated himself from his base, pillaged the countryside to obtain supplies for his army, and destroyed civilian property that aided the Confederate effort. Pillaging and destruction to defeat the enemy were clearly now acceptable. Sherman would not, however, tolerate it for its own sake. When he spotted a soldier torching a cotton gin while the army was marching unmolested back to Vicksburg, at a time when the burning "in no way aided our military plans," he ordered the culprit court-martialed. He demanded hard war but a soft peace.

Sherman was proud of his role in the great Vicksburg victory, feeling a satisfaction new to him in this conflict. Then, disaster struck again. His son Willy, his favorite child, died from fever while visiting Vicksburg with Ellen and the family. Sherman suffered a wound that never healed. "His loss to me is more than words can express," he wrote Henry Halleck at the time. "Oh that poor Willy could have lived to take all that was good of me," he lamented to Ellen (*Papers*, Oct. 8, 1863).

Despite his heartsickness, Sherman participated in the successful lifting of the Confederate siege at Chattanooga in late 1863. When Grant organized the effort, he made sure that Sherman played the leading role, and Sherman expressed complete support for everything Grant proposed. Even when Sherman's attack failed, he erroneously convinced himself (and Grant agreed) that the unsuccessful thrust had caused the Confederates to shift troops from the middle to the threatened flank and thus provided the opportunity for George H. Thomas's (q.v.) amazing breakthrough. Then, when Halleck went to Washington to become commanding general, Grant assumed overall command in the West and Sherman took over the Army of the Tennessee. "With Grant, I will undertake anything in reason," he enthused (*Memoirs* 1:390).

During these months, Sherman also concluded that, from then on, he would try to avoid pitched battles, where not only his own soldiers were killed but so too were Southerners, so many of whom were friends from his prewar days. Rather than take the lives of friends, he decided instead to wage a war against property, hearts, and minds. Grant gave him permission to conduct a raid from Vicksburg through Jackson to Meridian, Mississippi. If this raid proved successful, Sherman believed it would provide conclusive proof that destructive war was better than conventional war in convincing Southerners to stop this conflict. And it would spare him having to kill his friends.

Sherman conducted his Meridian Campaign in February 1864, inflicting a wide swath of destruction on a belt of Mississippi but causing or suffering few casualties. He destroyed property, but he did not injure or kill civilians. He kept reporters away, so few people, friend or foe, knew what Sherman was up to; and he credited this secrecy as a partial reason for his success. Unfortunately, when slaves ran away from their enslavement and attached themselves to his army, he demonstrated his proslavery bias. Seeing these black people as a hindrance to his war effort, he either ignored them or tried to get them out of his way. Sherman did not see himself as an emancipator; he never recognized the fact that destructive war against the hearts and minds of Southern society included the destruction of slavery.

In the spring of 1864, Grant became commanding general of all Union troops and moved to Washington to undertake his new task. Sharing his glory with Sherman in a most thoughtful letter, Grant also made sure that his friend received something more tangible. Sherman became commander of the entire Western theater. The two men met in Louisville and Cincinnati to plan for victory, their friendship easing the way. Grant began an offensive against Robert E. Lee (q.v.) in Virginia, while Sherman attacked Joseph E. Johnston (q.v.) in Georgia, determined to keep the Confederate Army there under constant pressure to prevent unification with Lee in Virginia. Other Union commanders also went on the offensive at the same time, the strategy calling for unremitting pressure against the Confederate military wherever it might be.

Sherman's role in this plan, the Atlanta campaign, resulted in the replacement of Johnston with John Bell Hood (q.v.), the near destruction of the Confederate Army of Tennessee, and the September capture of Atlanta. Sherman repeatedly sent James B. McPherson's Army of the Tennessee on wide sweeps of Johnston's force, while keeping George H. Thomas's Army of the Cumberland as the anchor of the main Union line. Before his dismissal, Johnston parried these repeated threats to his flank by skillfully shifting his army to face them and then falling back to a new position. As the chief historian of this campaign points out, Sherman "overlooked, ignored, and even rejected opportunities to crush or fatally cripple the Confederate forces in Georgia. . . . He was, in short, a general who did not like to fight" (Castel, 565).

This evaluation is accurate. Sherman's heart had turned against the carnage of conflict, concluding that a war of destruction was preferable to a war of conventional tactics. Consequently, he held back rather than commit his troops to fatal battle against his Southern friends. The one time he attempted a direct attack, at Kennesaw Mountain, the piles of bodies convinced him never to do it again. When Sherman captured Atlanta in September of 1864, giving the Union side in general and Lincoln's reelection campaign in particular a significant boost in morale, he returned to the model of his successful Meridian Campaign and turned away completely from conventional war.

From November 1864 until the war's end, Sherman engaged in a warfare of destruction that gave him his fame and, in some minds, his infamy. He did not, however, burn Atlanta to the ground. He detached George H. Thomas's Army of the Cumberland to deal with John Bell Hood's Army of Tennessee and then marched 62,000 men through the heart of Georgia to the sea at Savannah. Once there, despite Grant's desire that he put these soldiers on board ships and move them to Virginia to help crush Lee, Sherman convinced his friend that a march through the Carolinas would more efficiently accomplish the defeat of the Confederates.

Sherman used the Meridian Campaign as a model for these marches. He split his force into two wings to allow his soldiers to cover a wide area for foraging and destruction. No effective military opposition existing before him, he encountered only isolated fighting as his army moved over the land. He instituted no scorched earth policy; rather, destruction was selective. Any property associated with slavery or prisoners of war was almost certainly destroyed, but occupied houses frequently were not. Many houses, barns, and other property in Georgia and the Carolinas survived the Union onslaught. Importantly too, Union and Confederate deserters, fugitive slaves, and Joe Wheeler's Confederate cavalry added to the terror with their own significant destructive activities. Sherman instituted anarchy to try to end the anarchy he believed was the Civil War.

After he held off the returned Joseph E. Johnston and his severely crippled Army of Tennessee at Bentonville, North Carolina, Sherman once more refused to take the opportunity to annihilate the opposing Confederates. "I would rather avoid a general battle, if possible," he told one of his officers, as he refused to exploit another subordinate's breakthrough (*Memoirs* 2:185). Sherman saw no need for the further loss of lives. He was prepared to stop hard war so that he might institute the soft peace that he had long promised to Southerners once they ceased fighting.

Sherman and Johnston met at Durham Station, North Carolina, on April 17, 1865, several weeks after Sherman had conferred with Lincoln, Grant, and David Dixon Porter (q.v.) at City Point, Virginia, and two days after Lincoln's assassination. The result of the Sherman-Johnston meeting was a surrender agreement so mild for the Confederates that some people, including Washington officials, wondered if Sherman had turned traitor. Secretary of War Edwin M. Stanton (q.v.) and General Halleck were especially suspicious, while numerous newspapers launched vicious attacks. Some newspapers questioned, as they had in December 1861, Sherman's sanity. Andrew Johnson (q.v.) and his cabinet ordered Grant to take Sherman's command, but the commanding general diplomatically left his friend in control. Sherman ignored Halleck in Richmond and snubbed Stanton during the Grand Review of Union armies in Washington, but there the controversy ended.

During the war years, Sherman's image had first been that of an insane general whose personal eccentricities and mental failings were a threat to the Union war effort. As the fighting progressed and he developed his military strategy of selective destruction, however, he became a hero to Unionists and a vicious brute to Confederates. His lenient surrender terms to Johnston at war's end softened his brutish image, as did his friendly attitude toward the South during Reconstruction. He supported white Southerners, his old friends, whom he considered the best hopes for restoring order in the postwar region. He opposed enfranchisement of blacks, agreeing with conservative whites that it was foolish and dangerous to do so. He took such strong pro-Southern positions that, in 1871 after a speech in New Orleans, there was a presidential boomlet for him in several Southern newspapers and among some Southern politicians.

The South held no one position toward Sherman during these immediate postwar years. Some Southerners despised him because of the humiliation they felt from his destructive activity and their inability to prevent it, while others saw his actions as simply part of the war effort. When Sherman toured the region in 1879, most Southerners greeted him warmly. Atlanta and other locales he visited on this triumphal tour displayed little animosity. In New Orleans, he was the honored guest of Rex during Mardi Gras, and General John Bell Hood also enthusiastically appeared with him in public. Since this tour occurred four years after the 1875 publication of his memoirs, it seems evident that these two volumes did not convince white Southerners to consider him a pariah. Conversely, his soldiers continued to idolize him in the postwar years and so did Northern civilians.

The first real indication of change in Sherman's reputation came with the publication of Jefferson Davis's (q.v.) *The Rise and Fall of the Confederate Government* in 1881. In this apologia for himself and the Confederacy, Davis lambasted Sherman's approach to war and likened him to the worst villains in European history. Later in the 1880s, Davis and Sherman became embroiled in a dispute over whether or not the ex-Confederate president had ever considered using Robert E. Lee's army against a state threatening secession from the Confederacy. This matter was even debated on the Senate floor. Davis later called Sherman a liar, but the general refused further comment, so the controversy ended there. In 1888, Sherman saw his status in the South drop even further when, disturbed at antiblack violence, he published an article calling for fair treatment of black people. Still, when the United States Post Office Department issued its Civil War stamp series in the 1890s and Sherman appeared on one of the new stamps, there was no Southern protest.

The late nineteenth century witnessed the growth of the Lost Cause, the conscious fostering of a Southern interpretation of the Civil War. A variety of Southern patriotic organizations, extolling the virtues of Confederate officers and soldiers, especially Robert E. Lee, sprang up. The Southern Historical Society, for example, began publishing its papers in 1876. As the North and South came together at the turn of the century, the unwritten agreement was to avoid the issue of slavery and emphasize instead the virtue of common soldiers on both sides of the conflict. Lee became the exemplar of all that was good in the war, and Sherman became the villain symbolizing its evil. Lee the saint and Sherman the brute became accepted fare of both popular and professional writing.

As early as 1865, books on Sherman had begun to appear, and there was a spurt of publication after his death in 1891. The first two modern studies of the general did not appear until 1929 and 1932, however. Basil Henry Liddell-Hart extolled Sherman's military greatness, insisting that the bloodbath of World War I might have been avoided had Sherman's Civil War lessons been followed. Lloyd Lewis wrote a sympathetic biography that long remained the standard study of his life.

A variety of publications appeared in later years on various aspects of Sherman's life and career. T. Harry Williams's *McClellan, Sherman, and Grant* (1962) was complimentary of Sherman as one of the first modern generals. John G. Barrett's *Sherman's March through the Carolinas* (1956) detailed the destruction that occurred in the second of Sherman's great marches. James M. Merrill's positive biography *William Tecumseh Sherman* (1971) was the first to utilize Sherman's family papers, as did John F. Marszalek's 1968 Notre Dame doctoral dissertation and his later published book *Sherman's Other War, the General and the Civil War Press* (1981). James Reston, Jr., in his *Sherman's March and Vietnam* (1984), attempted to equate the general's activity in the Civil War with that of the American military in Vietnam. Joseph T. Glatthaar's *The March to the Sea and Beyond: Sherman's Troops in the Savannah and Carolina Campaigns* (1985) explained Sherman's destructive warfare within the context of its acceptance by his soldiers who saw it as an essential way to defeat the Confederates. Marion B. Lucas, in *Sherman and the Burning of Columbia* (1976), meanwhile, argued convincingly that Sherman was not solely responsible for the burning of this South Carolina city. Conversely, John B. Walters, in *Merchant of Terror: General Sherman and Total War* (1973), compared Sherman to the Nazi generals of World War II.

The 1990s saw the publication of several important books. John F. Marszalek's *Sherman, a Soldier's Passion for Order* (1993) is a sympathetic study whose thesis is evident in its title. Cited by reviewers as the new standard biography, this book argues against the perception of Sherman as the vicious brute, insisting instead that his strategy of selective destruction was the result of his desire to end the war as quickly as possible with the loss of the fewest lives. Charles Royster's award-winning *The Destructive War, William Tecumseh Sherman, Stonewall Jackson, and the Americans* (1991) traces the development of the idea for war of destruction on both the Union and Confederate sides and among Americans generally. Mark Grimsley in his acclaimed *The Hard Hand of War, Union Military Policy toward Southern Civilians 1861–1865* (1995) argues that Sherman was hardly unique in his brand of warfare, demonstrating the point through earlier examples from the Civil War itself and from conflicts in other lands at other times.

The decade has not been without new criticism. Michael Fellman, in his *Citizen Sherman, A Life of William Tecumseh Sherman* (1995), insists that the key to understanding Sherman's personal and public life is suppressed rage. His portrayal depicts an unattractive individual who acted out his anger against the South in his marches and against his wife through a lifetime of marital discord. Albert Castel criticized Sherman's military tactics during the Atlanta campaign, and he was even more critical of his alleged lack of honesty. He entitled his analysis of Sherman's memoir account of the Atlanta campaign: "Prevaricating through Georgia." John F. Marszalek responded with an essay in the same issue of *Civil War History* (1994), insisting that "Sherman Called It the Way He Saw It."

It is fair to say, therefore, that, in the last decade of the twentieth century, as was the case in 1861, William T. Sherman remains a controversial figure. There now exists, however, a much more positive view of the man and his warfare. Sherman was a fallible human being whose quirks and weaknesses were traceable to the earliest days of his childhood. He rose above them all to become one of the major figures of the Civil War and of all American military history. He was an American pioneer in the use of destruction for the psychological purpose of convincing the other side to end the war. His psychological warfare was so effective, in fact, that it has affected the American mind from the 1860s to the present day. There seems no reason to think, moreover, that the controversy over Sherman's actions will disappear in the foreseeable future.

BIBLIOGRAPHY

S. M. Bowman and R. B. Irwin, *Sherman and His Campaigns: A Military Biography* (New York: Charles B. Richardson, 1865).

Joel T. Headley, *Grant and Sherman: Their Campaigns and Generals* (New York: E. B. Treat, 1865).

Jefferson Davis, *The Rise and Fall of the Confederate Government*, 2 vols. (New York: D. Appleton and Co., 1881).

Edward Chase, *The Memoiral Life of General William Tecumseh Sherman* (Chicago: R. S. Peale and Co., 1891).

Basil Liddell-Hart, *Sherman, Soldier, Realist, and American* (Boston: Dodd, Mead and Co., 1929).

Robert G. Athearn, *William Tecumseh Sherman and the Settlement of the West* (Norman: University of Oklahoma Press, 1956).

John G. Barrett, *Sherman's March through the Carolinas* (Chapel Hill: University of North Carolina Press, 1956).

T. Harry Williams, *McClellan, Sherman, and Grant* (New Brunswick, N.J.: Rutgers University Press, 1962).

James M. Merrill, *William Tecumseh Sherman* (Chicago: Rand McNally, 1971).

John F. Marszalek, "The Knox Court-Martial: W. T. Sherman Puts the Press on Trial (1863)," *Military Law Review* 56 (1973): 197–214.

John B. Walters, *Merchant of Terror: General Sherman and Total War* (Indianapolis: Bobbs-Merrill, 1973).

Marion B. Lucas, *Sherman and the Burning of Columbia* (College Station: Texas A&M University Press, 1976).

James L. McDonough, *Shiloh, In Hell before Night* (Knoxville: University of Tennessee Press, 1976).

John F. Marszalek, *Sherman's Other War, the General and the Civil War Press* (Memphis: Memphis State University Press, 1981).

James Reston, Jr., *Sherman's March and Vietnam* (New York: Macmillan, 1984).

Joseph T. Glatthaar, *The March to the Sea and Beyond: Sherman's Troops in the Savannah and Carolina Campaigns* (New York: New York University Press, 1985).

Joseph T. Glatthaar, "Sherman's Army and Total War: Attitudes toward Destruction in the Savannah and Carolinas Campaigns," *Atlanta Historical Journal* 29 (1986): 41–52.

William Tecumseh Sherman, *Memoirs of General William T. Sherman* (New York: Library of America, 1990).

Charles Royster, *The Destructive War: William Tecumseh Sherman, Stonewall Jackson, and the Americans* (New York: Alfred Knopf, 1991).

Albert Castel, *Decision in the West, the Atlanta Campaign of 1864* (Lawrence: University Press of Kansas, 1992).

John F. Marszalek, *Sherman, a Soldier's Passion for Order* (New York: Free Press, 1993).

Albert Castel, ''Prevaricating through Georgia: Sherman's Memoirs as a Source on the Atlanta Campaign,'' *Civil War History* 40 (March 1994): 48–71.

John F. Marszalek, ''Sherman Called It the Way He Saw It,'' *Civil War History* 40 (March 1994): 72–78.

Michael Fellman, *Citizen Sherman, a Life of William Tecumseh Sherman* (New York: Random House, 1995).

Mark Grimsley, *The Hard Hand of War: Union Military Policy toward Southern Civilians, 1861–1865* (New York: Cambridge University Press, 1995).

Mark Bradley and Nat Chears Hughes, Jr., *Bentonville: The Final Battle of Sherman and Johnston* (Chapel Hill: University of North Carolina Press, 1996).

EDWIN MCMASTER STANTON
(December 19, 1814–December 24, 1869)

Jon L. Wakelyn

Asthmatic, overweight, introspective, yet overbearing and abrasive, the Union Secretary of War seemed the very antithesis of the man needed to guide the fortunes of the machinery of fighting. He had never had any prewar experience with military affairs. In addition, he was a Democrat and former corporate lawyer who had never been elected to national office. Yet Edwin McMaster Stanton had to serve in the Union government alongside Republican politicos who had spent their lives in public service. Could he possibly have been a match for William H. Seward (q.v.) of New York or Samuel P. Chase (q.v.) of Ohio, those two stalwart leaders committed to victory and unwilling to allow amateurs to run their war? Stanton also labored under a folksy commander in chief, a master at politics, who seemed unwilling to give his war leader any governance guidance or battle plans other than platitudes. To make matters worse, his wartime accomplishments have become entangled in "the dark and bloody" legal shenanigans of postwar presidential removal maneuvers. Stories of the War Secretary bolted behind his office door unwilling to give way to President Andrew Johnson (q.v.) made Stanton look foolish. In short, his true merits in that office, whatever they were, have been obscured by the actions of political geniuses, military heroes, and the rise and fall of Johnson's reputation.

The secretary thus appears in history as subservient to those giants. In addition, his wartime activities have been studied mostly by military history analysts. Many of those writers have depicted him as the "soft" civilian competing with the likes of competent anticivilian General Henry W. Halleck (q.v.) and the genius of hard-line officers like U. S. Grant (q.v.) and William T. Sherman (q.v.) who delivered the military victories. Even political historians have found little good to say about Stanton's wartime public career. Why would history need to remember support staff when great warriors and brilliant politicos were the stuff of success or failure? How could a mere civilian function well among such paragons?

Perhaps it is time for another serious look at all of those great captains, even the civilians, who made the Union victory. Simply put, all of those who held major leadership positions in that first of modern wars were necessary to the Union victory. The dilemma before anyone concerned with the relationship between fighting and governance, especially with the accomplishments of Edwin M. Stanton, is to attempt to understand how a man who had had no experience at war, nevertheless, helped to run the largest war machine known in the West until World War I surpassed it. What, if anything, in Stanton's past prepared him for the task for which no one could have had enough preparation?

Edwin Stanton was born into a family of Quakers and Virginia slaveowners, a pedigree that seemingly did not bode well for a leader who would oppose a slave society. But Stanton's family had moved to Ohio to settle near the village of Steubenville in the southern part of the state in 1799 in part to escape the world of slavery. His father David Stanton became a successful Ohio physician. His mother, Lucy Norman, daughter of a planter, early in her life had had qualms about slave labor. Edwin was born on December 19, 1814, sickly and weakened by asthma, which would make him a lifelong partial invalid and give him an irritable disposition. He was raised in a family of ambitious people, participants in local civic activities, converts to Methodism, and fiercely opposed to slavery.

The Stantons were not affluent—few doctors were in those semifrontier days—but they were comfortable middle class and able to give their son a stake in life. Edwin attended local private schools and for a time went to the Latin School of George Buchanan, where he prepared for college and a career. A good student, he studied hard, did well, but often took sick. In hopes of strengthening their son, and because it was the custom, Edwin also worked on a farm, though the outdoor vigor nearly killed him. In that time, children and parents alike often took sick and died early. In 1827, when Edwin was thirteen, his father died, and the son would have to help support the family. Just when that society had come to believe that knowledge was related to success, instead of furthering his schooling, Edwin had to apprentice himself to a bookseller as a way to provide for the family. His desire for college did not abate, however, and in 1831 he borrowed from his book shop owner boss and the family lawyer to enter nearby Kenyon College, then conducted by Episcopal Bishop Philander Chase, uncle of Salmon P. Chase. In beautiful Gambier, young Stanton thrived. He was quick, ambitious, and an excellent debater. There he sharpened his skills at oratory, became an Episcopalian, allowed his antislavery views to flourish, and met the right sort to assist in his future career. But the soft life of a student would soon come to an end. At the end of his second year in 1832, Stanton left Kenyon to become the major supporter of his mother and siblings. He went to work in a Columbus bookstore. In that thriving new capital city he soon made friends. In 1833, Edwin returned to Steubenville determined to prepare to become a lawyer. In 1835, having served his apprenticeship under a member of the local legal establishment, he passed the bar.

The life of a young lawyer was hard work. But the skills of the debater, a sharp mind, and the ability to focus on the essentials of the case soon allowed Stanton to rise in his profession. In 1836, he formed a partnership with Chauncey Dewey in nearby Cadiz. Later he returned to Steubenville to practice law with the Democrat and dean of southern Ohio lawyers, the antislavery advocate Benjamin Tappan. Tappan's connections would open many doors to young Stanton. Success in the practice of the law gave him the income to marry an old girlfriend, Mary Lemon of Columbus, and they settled into a loving and mutually supportive relationship. The ambitious young lawyer also wrote for the local paper, joined the Anti-Slavery Society, and became involved in politics.

In 1837 he gained election as Harrison County's prosecuting attorney, which enhanced his already growing reputation, and procured him new clients. As a hard money and antibank advocate, he fit well into the Van Buren wing of the Democratic party, and his ties to Benjamin Tappan allowed him to join the leadership of the Ohio party. By 1842 he was a reporter for the Ohio Supreme Court, in which capacity he became an ally of Salmon P. Chase. In 1844 he campaigned for Martin Van Buren for president, only to see him lose the nomination to the Tennessean James K. Polk. Though Stanton favored the Mexican War, he ran afoul of those Ohio Democrats who supported the Black Laws, Ohio's laws segregating and depriving black people of legal rights. Stanton flirted with joining the Liberty party, and later praised the Free Soil party, but he remained a Democrat even as that party gained the reputation of being pro-Southern.

In 1844 Stanton's personal life became even more strained than his relations with his party. In that year his beloved wife died, leaving him with small children. His younger and much liked brother committed suicide. Friends say he drew closer to his family, withdrew from public life, and became a hard, secretive man. Biographers Benjamin Thomas and Harold Hyman suggest that Stanton turned inward to avoid being hurt by public friendships (59). Stanton also resolved to make enough money to support his family. He already had had some success in the southern Ohio real estate market. In 1847 he moved his law practice to the thriving city of Pittsburgh, Pennsylvania, and became a high-paid corporate lawyer. Stanton grew rich by taking on crucial cases in defense of local industry against immigrant strikers. Most important, through victory in a transportation case he saved Pittsburgh and even his own part of eastern Ohio from losing its place as a trade center for the West. He also became general council for the wealthy Erie Railroad. In 1856, Stanton married the prominent Pittsburgh socialite Ellen Hutchinson. Though this second marriage did not have the loving relationship of his first, he would forge a business and political partnership with his wife's family. Theirs became the typical upper-middle class Victorian companionate marriage.

That marriage gave him access to national clients, so they moved to Washington, D.C. With practices and partners in Ohio and Pennsylvania it seemed only natural to him that he represent their interests in the nation's capital. Though antislave and close to those who had joined the Republican party, Stanton remained an Ohio Democrat. He made a friend of the powerful Democrat Jeremiah Black, who had entered President James Buchanan's cabinet. Stanton served Black as an assistant attorney general. In 1860, no friend of Stephen A. Douglas, Stanton supported the Kentuckian John C. Breckinridge for president. On December 20, 1860, the day South Carolina seceded from the Union, President Buchanan named Stanton attorney general. In the cabinet he soon became a hard-nosed nationalist who opposed appeasing the slave states. He lobbied Congress to resist any support for a federal slave code for the territories. Stanton also wanted to reinforce the military defenses of Washington, because he said he feared a Confederate plot to invade the citadel of democracy. Even after he had left office, Stanton continued to advise and work with other cabinet members. He stiffened new Secretary of State William H. Seward's resolve to reinforce Fort Sumter. But Stanton did not care for President Abraham Lincoln (q.v.), and he worried over just how the new Republican government would find the means to defeat the Confederacy. His antislave sentiments and loyalty to the nation in that harrowing secession winter of 1860–1861 still did not lure Stanton from his Democratic party loyalties.

A talented and able ex-cabinet member, Stanton promised to support the government from the sidelines. He returned to his law practice, but he also intrigued against the incompetent Secretary of War, the Pennsylvanian Simon Cameron. Cameron had consulted Stanton on Pennsylvania patronage choices and had asked for assistance on the tricky business of government war contracts. But Cameron soon became embroiled in charges of corrupt purchasing policies that undermined his effectiveness. Meanwhile, Stanton joined ranks with a number of fellow Democratic military officers, including the then powerful General George B. McClellan (q.v.). The skillful lawyer had taken a position in support of restoring the Union, but he rejected warring against slavery. When Cameron resigned his office, the president turned to the Democrat with Pennsylvania ties, Edwin M. Stanton, a man with narry a bit of military experience and little sense of the politics necessary to conduct the government's large procurement policy. On January 20, 1862, this portly, unassuming lawyer accepted the post of Lincoln's Secretary of War.

In the political atmosphere of wartime Washington City, Stanton had first to confront the real issue of just who ran the war office, the president, General McClellan, or himself. He also had to determine how the war office was to be linked to army headquarters, to a vigilant and impatient Congress, and to the state governments that sent the troops to fight the war. Stanton began by talking, listening, observing, and reading military accounts. He learned to rely on the advice of the general staff. The officers talked over war policies with him. In addition, he often consulted the president on the politics of military decision making. In that way the secretary had created an informal central staff under him to deal with military and political constituents. He seemed to work all the time, or at least his wife claimed he did. Certainly to many subordinates and politicians he was curt and abrasive. But in those early days of the war, he also showed the good sense to feed the press stories, and he made an ally for life of the excellent journalist Charles A. Dana (q.v.), who would later become an Assistant Secretary of War.

When Stanton actually turned to the art of warfare, to conduct his part of the war effort, he faced the resistance of the career officer McClellan, whom neither himself nor the president could get to engage the enemy. He also hoped to coordinate Union war efforts east and west, but he failed in getting General Don Carlos Buell to cooperate with General Henry Halleck (q.v.) in the West. Only after Stanton placed Halleck over Buell did some kind of unity of command occur. In the East he would not achieve any unified military efforts as long as McClellan was in charge. McClellan's Peninsula Campaign that spring to capture Richmond not only left the federal capital exposed, but it seemed to bog down in the field. McClellan, in addition, often disobeyed the secretary's orders. Stanton was kept ignorant of the general's plans, subjected to insubordinate behavior, and constantly forced to supply military materiel to an army that did little fighting. Stanton really began to worry about his eastern generals when General John Pope was unable to defend Washington and lost the battle of Second Manassas. Stanton's relations with McClellan, his fellow Democrat, completely deteriorated. Then in the summer the press turned on the secretary and accused him of being unable to conduct the war.

By July 1862, Stanton was ready to unite his efforts with a career military officer, and he advised the president to create the position of general in chief for the irrascible Henry Halleck. Even though he never really cared for "Old Brains" Halleck, he came to appreciate the way they worked together. Slowly, the idea of a staff was forming, and the two of them would, they hoped, be able to deal with the popular George B. McClellan. Eventually Stanton was able to get Halleck to remove McClellan from command, and he could then plan to take the offensive. Although he did not want to appoint General William Rosecrans as commander in the West, believing him too strong-willed for his own good, Stanton knew that a unified offensive movement there required his removing General Buell. As the secretary, the president, and Halleck played musical chairs with generals, the lack of advances at the end of 1862, and the debacle of General Ambrose Burnside at Fredericksburg, Virginia, led many in Congress and the press to ask whether the secretary was up to the task of that most difficult office.

But Lincoln knew that Stanton had acquired a great deal of experience in his two years in office, and he had begun to forge an efficient, effective, and committed military machine, so he stuck with his hardheaded secretary. Stanton's biographers, Thomas and Hyman, say that by early 1863 he had received effective civilian control of armies in the field, had learned to coordinate his efforts with state government on recruitment, and had come to understand the politics of war (185). Certainly, by then he had understood the power of local and state authority, and he deferred to governors' prerogatives to recruit volunteers for the army. Setting quotas and competition among the states, Stanton kept the army supplied with recruits, even during the vicious killing time during Grant's battles in the Virginia Wilderness. His use of the provost marshals to put down draft riots in the Union states at times appeared harsh, but Stanton had concluded the war must be won at any cost. Even his willingness to silence newspapers and other forms of dissent against the war reflected that will. Stanton also worked well with Halleck to procure the railroad trains needed to transport troops. He also aided General Montgomery Meigs in the rapid transportation of troops to the West during the campaign to lift the Confederate siege of Chattanooga. On the purchase of goods for the military he displayed a genius for making the correct judgment on priorities. His staff of purchasing agents rejected poor-quality goods and made excellent contracts for well-produced articles of war. Most of all he developed the skills of buying the proper materiel of war, as he placed priority on acquisition of weapons before food and clothing. First, the troops had to kill, said Stanton, then they could find food in enemy territory.

Even though he held office as a war Democrat and his party questioned the aims to end slavery, Stanton united with those who supported using black troops in the army. He knew that action would make the continuation of slavery impossible, but victory was all that mattered to him now. He hired the lawyer and professor Francis Lieber to write a report on the use of escaped slaves in the Union Army. Stanton next helped to form the Bureau of Colored Troops, whose task was to recruit and to train black soldiers. Thomas and Hyman report that Stanton believed "rebel strength derived from slave labor and that the Union must turn black energy everywhere against the South in order to win" (243).

The secretary also realized that Republicans, even those who distrusted him, needed to win in politics to ensure Union victory. When midwesterners turned against the use of slaves as soldiers and opposed Republican reelections in 1862, Stanton used the provost marshals to make certain troops could vote. He deplored Republican losses in 1862. During the fall 1863 election, he helped Republican candidates by allowing troops to vote for them. And in the 1864 presidential election, despite his worries about some of the president's policies, Stanton's hatred of Democratic candidate George B. McClellan led him to support the policy of troops in the field to vote. He was reputed even to have offered gifts and bribes to governors to help get out the vote. Lincoln's reelection in 1864 assured Stanton that the Union would fight on to total victory.

The military and political activity of the secretary did not stop with getting out the soldier and civilian vote. No longer did he believe that Democratic generals were necessary to a balance against radical Republicans; no longer did he advocate that civilian generals be given equal rank with career officers. The civilian secretary had become the political champion of the regular army command structure. He sent the Democrat George Meade (q.v.) to stop Confederate General Robert E. Lee (q.v.) in Pennsylvania because he believed in Meade's abilities. To find other officers of quality he sent former newspaperman turned Assistant Secretary of War Charles Dana into the field. Perhaps Dana's praise of Grant led Stanton to support the general's actions around Chattanooga and to refuse Halleck's request that Grant go to Mobile. It was Stanton who, in February 1864, advocated putting Grant in charge of all Union military efforts. The secretary persuaded President Lincoln to set up a new command system in which Halleck, the first chief of staff, was assigned to work with him in the War Department. Together, they provided support for General in Chief Grant in the field. The new organization worked well, for Stanton was then enabled to concentrate solely on keeping Grant supplied in the field. He understood and supported Grant's unleashing Philip Sheridan (q.v.) in the Valley of Virginia, both to protect Washington and to devastate Southern civilian morale. He helped Grant to push the reluctant General George Thomas (q.v.) to defend Nashville, and Stanton gave Thomas the military wherewithal to defeat Confederate General John B. Hood (q.v.) and break the back of the western Confederate Army. As the war ran down, the secretary also kept the politicians at bay to protect Grant's costly maneuvers during the siege of Petersburg. The portly civilian had become, along with Halleck, the loyal administrator for professional soldiers. As such, his role in the war, standing always at his desk, often completely exhausted, was of utmost importance. Certainly at that time the military high command regarded him highly.

But with the end of war no real peace came for the tired and aging secretary. When his leader went down to an assassin's bullet, Stanton temporarily took over the government. At first he became an ally of his fellow Democrat, President Andrew Johnson. It was the secretary who expanded upon Lincoln's occupation policy to use the provost marshals as military leaders for reconstructing the Union. He planned to send Grant to control the South, in the belief that the military would create an orderly return to the Union. He stuck by the federal government's support for ex-slaves and admonished those commanders who aided Southerners and neglected the freedman. Stanton then drew up the first plans for Reconstruction and set the postwar policy toward the South.

During the spring of 1865 he also began to demobilize and redeploy the armed forces. The secretary reorganized the army to create a rapid strike force against marauding Indians on the western frontier. He sent troops to protect the construction of the western railroad system. And he cooperated with Secretary of State Seward to patrol the Mexican border in order to resist a feared French invasion of the Southwest. But mainly he moved troops south, he thought in compliance with President Johnson's desire to control public life and keep peace. As such he also helped enlist the military in protecting the Freedman's Bureau.

Stanton decided to support the Republican party in Congress, or at least the soft money Republicans. He opposed Johnson's policies of pardon and amnesty for ex-Confederates. He resisted the Southern states' new black codes. Secretly, the secretary allied himself with certain Radical Republicans who sought to protect ex-slaves. He supported the ratification of the Fourteenth Amendment to the Constitution. Publicly, he tried to be the compromising agent between the president and Congress. Stanton also attempted to protect the professional army's authority, and he often worked with General Grant on politically sensitive policy matters. Eventually, these political activities of the secretary, now grown sick and tired of intrigue, ran afoul of the president. In the fall 1866 elections, he openly turned against the Johnson administration.

Still, he hoped his opposition to Johnson's policies could convince the president to approve Reconstruction bills. But Stanton's support in July 1867 of the Third Reconstruction act that kept the military in independent command in the Southern states, further proof of his loyalty to the professional army, was the last straw for President Johnson. In early August Johnson asked for the secretary's resignation. The stubborn secretary refused and tried to hold on to his office until Congress returned in December. The president then suspended him, and the Senate put him back in office. In February 1868, the president ordered him to give up his office. After a smarmy and demeaning exchange of charges, he left office early in May. Both men appeared as laughing stocks, and humor began to tell on the secretary's reputation.

Sick and financially destitute, Stanton took his family back to Ohio. He had hoped to resume his law practice. Instead, ever loyal to the military, in the fall he campaigned for Grant's presidential election. Grant, who seemed to have regarded Stanton as washed up, offered him no reward for his support. Only late in 1869 did the president finally nominate Stanton to a prized seat on the U.S. Supreme Court. But it was too late. The loyal Secretary of War died in Washington on December 24, 1869, before he could take office.

History has been mixed on Stanton's accomplishments, as was Grant, perhaps because he was a civilian bureaucrat in the midst of military heroes, perhaps because his life became entangled in the inevitable revisions of Reconstruction historiography. But allies such as Dana, shortly after his death, wrote of his major wartime accomplishments. Other former allies turned enemies, such as Jeremiah Black, devastated Stanton's reputation. Neither Grant nor Sherman in their *Memoirs* gave him much credit for his support of their military efforts. His rival civilian government leader, Secretary of the Navy Gideon Welles, in his infamous *Diary*, vilified Stanton. All of his opponents accused Stanton of wanting excessive control, of an overbearing personality, and of political mistakes. Most of those who wrote about him during the postwar period regarded the secretary as an amateur who interfered with professionals.

At the century's end, his old friend George C. Gorham tried to set the record straight. The war long over, it was time, said Gorham, to be objective, to recognize the secretary's notable accomplishments. In *The Life and Public Service of Edwin M. Stanton* (1899), Gorham described Stanton as a great patriot. But Gorham's effort was too praiseworthy, too poor in analysis, and it could not overcome the verdict of the generals. The major biography of Thomas and Hyman, Stanton's only full scholarly treatment, attempted a dispassionate critique of his accomplishments. But their biography was too much a political, legal analysis, too much occupied with Reconstruction. The secretary's truly significant contributions to wartime military organization were never really fully developed in this important work.

Only most recently, as students of warfare have come to understand the place of civilian administration in the Civil War, has Stanton begun to receive his real due. Although Hattaway and Jones, in *Why the North Won* (1985), suggested that his personality hurt his effectiveness, they praise his "gifts as a manager" (99). Although he was, they say, hardly a great strategist, Stanton "provided the managerial and operational requisites for the big war in progress" (99). His creation of the War Board, insist Hattaway and Jones, increased "coordinations among the bureaus" and provided "a resource of informed advice on operational questions" (126). Also, Stanton made important contributions to logistics in the use of railroads and the telegraph, through standardizing tracks and creating a uniform signal system. He went to the American Telegraph Company and the National and Secret Service to recruit young men of talent and gather them around him to run the war. Most recently, Joseph T. Glatthaar, in *Partners in Command* (1994), also praises Stanton as an "excellent administrator" (203). A master of all details, he operated most efficiently, says Glatthaar. But his abrasiveness and his lack of understanding of military strategy, claims Glatthaar, "along with his passion for political intrigue" (231), left him a flawed leader. Again there crops up in analysis of the secretary's accomplishments charges of a civilian playing at combat and the personality flaws. Until historians are able to go beyond the character issue and the false idea that only military skills matter during war, Stanton's true importance as the one who conducted the administration of warfare will not receive its due. That means that until the roles of governance in war are studied as brilliantly as has been the military, Stanton's real accomplishments will remain in historical limbo.

BIBLIOGRAPHY

Ulysses S. Grant, *Memoirs and Selected Letters*, 2 vols. (1885; New York: Library of America, 1990).

George C. Gorham, *Life and Public Service of Edwin M. Stanton*, 2 vols. (New York: Houghton Mifflin, 1899).

Burton J. Hendrick, *Lincoln's War Cabinet* (New York: Doubleday and Co., 1946).

Benjamin P. Thomas and Harold M. Hyman, *Stanton: The Life and Times of Lincoln's Secretary of War* (New York: Alfred P. Knopf, 1962).

Herman Hattaway and Archer Jones, *Why the North Won the War* (Urbana: University of Illinois Press, 1984).

Joseph T. Glatthaar, *Partners in Command* (New York: Free Press, 1994).

ALEXANDER HAMILTON STEPHENS
(February 11, 1812–March 4, 1883)

Jon L. Wakelyn

Few of the Confederacy's great leaders disappointed fellow Southerners as much over his contributions to the defense of his homeland than did its vice president, Alexander H. Stephens. In his prewar career, Stephens had soared to the top of political life, as he displayed an enormous intelligence and a gift for political propriety the envy of his peers. Thus, when President Jefferson Davis (q.v.) selected him for vice president over a number of able leaders, many applauded that appointment. Certainly the Confederate leadership expected much from that talented public figure. Within months, however, Stephens became an impediment to the government as he pouted over supposed neglect by the president. Stephens soon began to fashion a phalanx of political opposition to the administration that he would use to do much damage. How does one explain the discrepancy between Stephens's great talents and reputation for moderate behavior with his seeming traitorous activities toward the government he had pledged to support?

On one level of analysis, students of the war have turned to the man's personal quirks and even his appearance to attempt a judgment of his supposed contradictory behavior. Most explicitly and brilliantly, Edmund Wilson described Stephens thusly: "It was as if he had shrunk to pure principle, abstract, incandescent, indestructible" (221). Those who knew him well, of course, contributed to the images used by later commentators. During the hectic and eventually frustrating negotiations at the Hampton Roads peace conference in February 1865, President Abraham Lincoln (q.v.) described his good friend as unhealthily thin and probably ill and that he took the longest time to shed layer after layer of clothing to get down to his essence. Much less charitably, Confederate President Jefferson Davis blamed Stephens's personality traits for his perverse resistance to the Confederate war effort. All of those critics had used the man's manners to sum up his actions. But doubt lingers that his appearance and mood alone led to his negative actions during the Civil War. Instead, he may well have acted on what he considered his values and in the best interests of his beloved South. Perhaps another review of his entire career could excise that concentration on personal image and get to the facts of just why he seemingly sold out the Confederacy.

Born into a struggling small farmer family on February 11, 1812, in Wilkes County, Georgia, his mother, Margaret Grier Stephens, died shortly after his birth. His father, like so many other men of his time who lost their wives, soon remarried. His stepmother, Mathilda Lindsey, soon had her own growing family and had little time for the pitifully small and sickly Alexander. His father, Andrew Baskin Stephens, worked hard to make a meager success on that poor soil of Piedmont Georgia. He even had to conduct a school to make ends meet. Clearly, he had little time to devote to his son, who had become moody and withdrawn. Then, at the age of fourteen, when most young men in those antebellum days tried to make choices about their lives and, in doing so, often feuded with parents, young Stephens lost both his stepmother and father to an epidemic. For a time Alec assumed the responsibility of keeping the family together, teaching and trying to farm, but soon all of his siblings had to be dispersed to relatives. Young Alec went to live with an uncle, who sent him to school in the wealthy village of Washington, Georgia. The diminutive, sickly, and sullen young orphan soon quarreled with his fellow students who remarked on his pride and no doubt were jealous of his quick mind and sharp tongue. Others in the village, especially the grown-ups, liked him and commented on his seriousness and his intelligence.

Perhaps because of his seriousness of purpose, Alec received a scholarship from the Georgia Presbyterian conference and aid from his uncle to attend Franklin College (later the University of Georgia). He had given them some hope that he would return home and enter the ministry. As a student he did not disappoint them. He graduated number one in his class. Excellent at debate, he thrived in that setting where clever phrasing and sharp repartee set the best apart from the others. Stephens also made friends with a number of his classmates from that rich planter's college who would rise in financial and political life.

However, Alec did disappoint those who expected him to become a great preacher. He had decided that clergy life would be stifling. But he had promised to repay his debt to them, so he took a job teaching at a rural school. Stephens hated trying to instruct the thick students, feeling the effort was beneath his dignity. At night, in order to avoid the nightmare of his lonely existence, the often exhausted young man read history, studied the civil code, and immersed himself in Blackstone. He soon moved to Crawfordsville, Georgia, where he studied for the bar, and passed it by the time he had turned twenty-one. Stephen's skills at debate, keen mind, and solemn demeanor made him successful in the practice of the law. Like a number of young Georgians from meager pasts who had begun to rise in business, the status and class partisanship of the Southern Whig party attracted him. Through his new political connections, he was given a case to argue on the opening of a railroad link from Georgia to the

West. He won and his success earned him both profits and fame. That led to his election in 1836 to a seat in the Georgia legislature. When his finances had grown, he adopted his own younger brothers and sisters and reunited the family he so loved. Stephens also gathered around himself a coterie of young male protégés, whose careers he assisted.

In his career path, now focused on public service, Stephens established the trust that comes from loyalty to friends and support for his local constituents. Soon he took over the leadership of Piedmont Georgia Whig party, even though that region was firmly Jacksonian Democrat. But Stephens knew that if he were to defend Whig business interests in Georgia, he would need to become a spokesman for local and later state's rights, just like the Democrats. His reward for loyalty was the Whig nomination of his district to the U.S. House. Friendships forged as he rode the legal circuit, such as that with the handsome, brilliant, and wealthy Robert Toombs, gave him their support in the race that he won.

The Washington he traveled to in 1843 was still primitive, lacking the social amenities even of decent housing. Stephens found rooms with a Southern Whig clique, and he settled in to master the procedural workings of Congress. He also imbibed the expansionist views of his Southern peers, opposed any national banking, but supported his hero Henry Clay on a protective tariff. He argued for annexation of Texas as benefiting the slave-state interest, yet loathed President James K. Polk for collapsing on the Oregon question. In an important speech on the Mexican War, Stephens revealed his true loyalties. "National honor," he said, "could be maintained only by demanding what was right, not by submitting to what was wrong" (Schott, 69). Despite his stubborn defense of what he called state's rights, Stephens rose in prominence in Congress. He had learned the intricacies of parliamentary procedure, and his devotion to party friends made him an indispensable and adroit floor leader for Whig policies.

His growing national fame led to even more lucrative legal cases and finally to enough wealth and security to buy a plantation, "Liberty Hall," and a number of slaves. Stephens called Liberty Hall his Piedmont retreat, a place where he could read and relax and talk politics with friends. But mainly he returned there to recover from illness after illness, which would have destroyed one with lesser drive. There, he also returned to promote the careers of his younger brothers, especially his favorite, the handsome and intelligent Linton.

The devoted national Whig would need that retreat more and more during the hectic days of political devisiveness of the 1850s. By 1850 he knew that supporting the national Whig party had become nearly impossible, as he often broke with his party over policies, especially those concerning racial expansion. For that moderate leader who had even been mentioned for the House speakership, no doubt those breaks were traumatic. But first and foremost he professed loyalty to Southern interests. Stephens supported his colleague Toombs's 1850 Southern rights manifesto, which demanded political equality in the Union. Stephens himself soon contributed to the frailty of national politics when he became an early supporter of a Southern Whig–based Constitutional Union party, which Southerners founded to defend slavery.

At that time, however, he disagreed with those who wanted to leave the Union. In 1852 he worked in behalf of Daniel Webster's national Conservative movement and later wept when his heroes Clay and Webster died during that year. He also toured the Midwest in behalf of moderate Northern Whigs. But he opposed all compromise over slavery expansion. His high-pitched voice became even more strident and excitable with each divisive issue. Yet, when some of his friends joined the newly formed Know-Nothing party just after the Whig party collapsed in the South, Stephens, who seemed to have little interest in religion, calmly spoke against such a party. He refused to attack Southern Catholics and pronounced them white voters who supported slavery. Georgia Democrats turned to Stephens for support, and in 1855 this loyal Whig became a national Democrat. He voted against the expulsion of Preston Brooks after the Sumner affair, maintaining that Southerners must stand together in Washington. He also supported Stephen A. Douglas for president and had no qualms over the election of James Buchanan. His sharp tongue nearly led to a duel with later friend Benjamin H. Hill, then even too much of a nationalist for Stephens.

But Stephens was trapped politically. As much as he wanted to remain in the nationalist camp, he had to support the interests of his state and section. He noticed the rise of Joseph E. Brown (q.v.) to power in Georgia politics with great interest. To protect his political flanks in Georgia, he made an alliance with that Democratic populist. Now continually in consultation with his half brother Linton, Stephens knew of the growing separationist movement in Georgia. Stephens still hoped to support the Union, even as he was drawn into the vortex of Southern political coalitions. Those Southern leaders in Washington supported him for speaker of the House in 1858, because they felt he could communicate with the Northern enemy. Nationalist leaders used him to help draft the English bill to recommit the dangerous Lecompton Constitution to the territorial legislature of Kansas. He also traveled north to speak in support of healing the country's divisions. But Stephens soon broke under the strain of being a nationalist in those sectionally divisive times, and in 1859 he retired from Congress to convalesce at Liberty Hall.

Sick in body and at heart, the emaciated politico nevertheless joined the political fray in the election of 1860 when he resisted the Georgia recession movement, as he attempted to hold Southern and national interests in a healthy tension. When Robert M. T. Hunter (q.v.) from Virginia, his candidate for president in 1860, faltered, Stephens stumped Georgia in behalf of Stephen A. Douglas. However, all of his years of skills honed on the lecture circuit and in Congress did him no good as the election of Abraham Lincoln as president catapulted Stephens into radical secession politics. When Georgians called for a convention and demanded the end to the Union, little Alec once again resisted their radicalism and spoke on November 15, 1860, against precipitant action. Elected a member of the convention, he called for moderation. But the former nationalist had to bow to the inevitable. In March 1861, he made a major speech in support of a separate Confederacy. In his famous "Cornerstone" address, Stephens stated that slave society defined the South and that he was willing to have civil war to protect that economic and social system. He had spoken to the core of his beliefs, as his effort catapulted him into the role of the symbolic leader of Georgia's secessionists. A member of the Montgomery Convention that met to form the new Confederate nation, he became the principal architect of a conservative constitution, an ardent advocate for the election of Robert M. Toombs as president, and perhaps intrigued in secret for the reconstruction of the federal Union. Chosen Confederate vice president against his will, Stephens vowed to support the policies of President Davis and to fight with all of his might to secure a separate Confederate nation. Alas for the Confederacy, it was an oath that proved impossible to keep.

In the formative early period of nation making, however, Stephens fervently supported the policies of, and advised skillfully, his new president. He also advocated a policy of allowing other states easy entry into the new Confederacy. Stephens had hoped to appeal both to upper South slave states and to midwestern free states, as he discussed the trade and transportation ties of the West and the Gulf South. He sought to construct an insurmountable financial and population advantage and to deter any Northern attempt to dismantle that powerful alliance. But, after Fort Sumter, when war had been declared, Stephens went to Richmond to take charge of the provisional Congress and to lead it in writing the legislation necessary to unite and defend the new nation. He also made friends with powerful Confederate generals in hopes perhaps of creating a separate power base for himself. While involved in the plans for the defense of the South, the often ill vice president appeared as a dynamo of action. But soon, perhaps because of his illnesses, or perhaps because of his own large and growing reputation as a leader, President Davis seemed to freeze him out of his inner council. Instead the president turned to Judah Benjamin (q.v.), no friend of the vice president's, as his stalwart supporter. Not one to let a slight go by—Stephens had a mean temper and a skill at flaying his enemies—he joined the opposition to presidential war policies. He would become the major leader of those who believed the cause was lost and thus desired a just peace in order to save slavery.

By February 1862, now completely in opposition to the Davis government, Stephens began to speak openly of his worries that warfare itself had taken on a life of its own that had become dangerous to the cause that he had once supported. He opposed conscription and the confiscation of goods for the war effort and joined the camp of the so-called state's rights Confederates. But he was not really an exponent at that time of individual state action. For him, the sovereignty of the Southern people, the rights of local governments, and personal liberties had become more important than Confederate independence. Back in Richmond, he became the leader of those who opposed the excessive power wielded by the War Department. He feared a chaotic military leadership that had taken liberties with individual rights. In short, the vice president opposed all government attempts to impose authority on the South.

Back in Georgia at the year's end, along with his half brother Linton's new allies, Stephens prompted Governor Joseph E. Brown to thwart Richmond's interference in Georgia's internal affairs and property rights. Though he denied any personal antipathy to the president, Stephen's attacks on the financial policies of Secretary Christopher G. Memminger (q.v.) struck at the heart of Davis's economic plans to link all Southerners to the war effort. Stephens knew that holders of Confederate bonds soon would come to believe how worthless their investments had been. Then, he hoped, the most important leaders back home would turn against Confederate policies. By 1863, the question for him had become, Was the struggle for a separate country worth it?

The vice president, now virtually a pariah to the administration, completely abdicated his responsibility of presiding over Congress's direction of the war efforts. He spent most of the rest of the war at his beloved Liberty Hall, sick over the government's radical measures to secure a victory he either no longer believed in or felt could not be achieved. As a result Stephens became an advocate of peace. In June 1863, he asked the president if he could visit Washington to see if a just peace were possible. He wanted to encourage Northern peace activities, to obtain prisoner exchanges, and to denounce what he believed was illegal warfare against noncombatants. It is possible that Stephens's activities influenced the growing peace movement in the Confederate States and helped to sap the morale of some military leaders.

During the winter of 1863–1864 Stephens became quite ill and his behavior became even more chaotic than usual. He insisted Georgia soon was to be invaded and that the Confederacy would be unable to protect his homeland. By that time President Davis considered him a Reconstructionist, and Stephens proved him correct when he met with Governor Brown to ask him to negotiate a separate peace with the invading Union Army. To the state legislature in March 1864 he spoke of local needs and of separate liberty and even suggested the formation of a formal opposition party to the Confederate government. To Northern General William T. Sherman (q.v.) he wrote that Georgians were ready to return to the Union.

Back in Richmond in late 1864, Stephens rejoined his peace allies. Relations with President Davis had so deteriorated that they communicated only through the mails. Stephens even joined with Speaker of the House Thomas Bocock (q.v.) in his efforts to discredit the Confederate cabinet. He urged senators to negotiate with Northern Democrats. Realizing what Stephens had become, and how he had influenced the views of the powerful congressman Robert M. T. Hunter, the president sent them to Hampton Roads on a peace mission that he knew would fail. Fail it did, and Stephens was publicly discredited as disloyal to the Confederate cause. But Stephens in reality had only acknowledged that the Confederate government no longer could defend slavery. He insisted to his allies that their only hope was that Northern conservatives could help to control the ex-slaves who surely would prove to be a disruptive labor force in the South. No doubt he welcomed the surrender at Appomattox.

As soon as the war ended, Union troops arrested the former vice president and put him in prison. Stephens even feared for his life. But he gained release because President Andrew Johnson (q.v.) knew he would be a voice for moderation in the reconstruction of Georgia. Stephens invested in a newspaper and used his paper to show his fealty to Georgia by approving the black codes that had been written to control freed black labor. His reward was election to the federal Congress. But the Northern Republicans refused to seat him.

The bitter Stephens then retreated into silence to write his defense of his wartime actions. He also authorized a biography in hopes of heading off misrepresentations of his political life. Published in 1868 and 1870, his two-volume *A Constitutional View of the Late War between the States* was his own tortured defense of his beliefs. As he said of his own role in the Confederate government, ''[N]o stronger or more ardent man ever lived than I was.'' But his first allegiance went to the slave South and not to an overbearing government. In that strange book, written in the form of a dialogue between two political thinkers, Stephens laid out his support for local institutions above the rights of federal interference. His works would become useful manuals for later state's rights activity, but it is doubtful that they achieved his purpose of explaining or justifying his wartime disloyalty.

Despite his illness and his obsession with past wrongs, Stephens was to have a role in postwar Southern politics. He wrote a now unreadable school history of the United States in 1872, which influenced a generation of Georgia youth. He returned to the practice of law in order to recoup his wartime financial loses. Stephens also worked closely with his former slaves to ensure they would someday own land, their stake in the future. No doubt he gained some solace as he watched his old enemies die off. When his restrictions on public officeholding were lifted, Georgians again elected their defender to a seat in the U.S. House, only this time as a member of the once-hated Democratic party. He refused to support Horace Greeley for president in 1872 but did come out for Samuel J. Tilden in 1876. In Congress Stephens spoke out in favor of economic diversification in Georgia, and he supported expenditures on road building and other internal improvements to rebuild Georgia's war-damaged communications system.

But years of controversy and steady activity to defend the world he loved had taken its toll on him. Sick in mind and body he resigned from the U.S. House in 1882. The old man rallied once more for what he believed was the defense of his homeland. He ran for governor, and his people elected their popular hero, but he managed only little more than 100 days in office. Even at the last, he busied himself replying to accusations of wartime misconduct from ex-President Davis, and he gave information to ex-General P. G .T. Beauregard (q.v.) to be used to discredit the wartime activities of Davis. Perhaps due to that harsh regimen of self-defense, Stephens again took sick and died on March 4, 1883.

To the end of his life, Stephens had tried to explain his own behavior, a task many others also have attempted. He had hoped that his friends would set the record straight and overcome the harsh early verdicts of Edward A. Pollard (q.v.) and John B. Jones, the Rebel war clerk. Of course, ex-President Jefferson Davis, too, had weighed in to attack the integrity and the activities of his former vice president.

But his enemies' views of him prevailed until Myrta L. Avary in 1910 published a magnificent volume drawing on the previous work of Stephens's old ally Henry Cleveland. Entitled *Recollections of Alexander H. Stephens*, Avary perhaps caught her hero's contradictions best in the verdict: "He was the one public man of his day who remained throughout the war neither Northern nor Southern but American" (96). Ulrich B. Phillips, the first professional historian to analyze Stephens's wartime activities in depth, in part echoed this view. But Phillips also insisted that little Alec had been a true state's righter. In his monumental history of the war, Allan Nevins used Phillips's views, and perhaps has permanently linked Stephens's actions to the fate of his native Georgia.

It was in 1949 that a professor of American literature, Rudolph Von Abele, concentrated on the tormented personal life of that sickly, never fully developed male to show that Stephens was deeply scarred psychologically. Von Abele linked Stephens's political behavior with his supposed psychological and physiological problems. Edmund Wilson in 1962, though taken with Stephens's literary merits, supported those who maintained that the Georgian's political philosophy was resistance to centralized authority. Another historian, Daniel Howe, attempted to create the image of Stephens as a national Whig but gave up in despair to say he "perverts Whig political philosophy into its opposite" (258). Most recently, in his definitive factual biography, Thomas E. Schott applies Von Abele's psychological analysis to the political thinker to come up with a thesis of an ambitious and often practical politician who actually did what he felt was best for his country.

It is certain that history will not forget this civilian leader and that each generation will probably find his important and tormented life necessary to interpret for itself. But future commentators should not pursue the path of the tortured psychological misfit. Nor should they insist too much on the nationalist theme. The centrality in Stephens's thinking of the importance of slavery in his region informed his actions. He believed in his nation, if it would protect slavery. Thus, only those who defended slave society earned his support. For Stephens, clearly the Confederate government sometimes had acted in ways that did not defend slavery.

BIBLIOGRAPHY

Henry Cleveland, *Alexander H. Stephens, in Public and Private* (Philadelphia, Pa.: National Publishing Company, 1868).

Alexander H. Stephens, *A Constitutional View of the Late War between the States: Its*

Causes, Character, Conduct and Results, 2 vols. (Philadelphia, Pa.: National Publishing Company, 1868, 1870).

Myrta Lockett Avary, *Recollections of Alexander H. Stephens* (New York: Doubleday and Co., 1910).

Ulrich B. Phillips, *The Course of the South to Secession* (New York: Hill and Wang, 1939).

Allan Nevins, *Ordeal of the Union*, 8 vols. (New York: Scribner, 1947–1971).

Edmund Wilson, *Patriotic Gore* (New York: Oxford University Press, 1962).

Rudolph Von Abele, *Alexander H. Stephens* (New York: Greenwood Press, 1964).

Daniel Walker Howe, *The Political Culture of American Whigs* (Chicago: University of Chicago Press, 1979).

Thomas E. Schott, *Alexander H. Stephens of Georgia, a Biography* (Baton Rouge: Louisiana State University Press, 1988).

George C. Rable, *The Confederate Republic: A Revolution against Politics* (Chapel Hill: University of North Carolina Press, 1996).

THADDEUS STEVENS
(April 4, 1792–August 11, 1868)

Charles F. Ritter

Thaddeus Stevens, one of the Civil War's most effective congressmen, was a local Pennsylvania political operator who lived and died by his wits in the maelstrom of Middle Period politics. Starting in 1833, Stevens was in and out of the state legislature and served two terms in the U.S. House of Representatives. But after 1853 he practiced law in Lancaster and, through skill and cunning, barely kept his political fortunes alive. In 1858 public sentiment finally caught up with this ambitious antislavery advocate and sent the sixty-six-year-old Stevens back to Washington after an eight-year hiatus to begin a rapid ten-year ascent during which the Great Commoner became known as the dictator of the House and launched his reputation as a bona fide American idealogue. While dictator may be a misplaced sobriquet, he was a moving force behind the radical program for Reconstruction and a prime mover in the attempt to impeach a president.

Born in Danville, Caledonia County, Vermont, on April 4, 1792, the second of four sons of Joshua and Sally (Morrill) Stevens, Thaddeus had a clubfoot, which some say accounted for his dour outlook and cynical attitude. In addition to this physical embarrassment, the young Stevens family, always lingering on the margins of poverty, suffered the loss of Joshua, a failed shoemaker and a drunk, who ran off and apparently died in the War of 1812. Sally Stevens moved her young brood to Peacham, Vermont, where Thaddeus attended the Caledonia County Academy and then went to Dartmouth, where he graduated in 1814. Eschewing the ministry, which his mother wished him to pursue, Stevens left New England and traveled to York, Pennsylvania, where he taught at the local academy and read law. Admitted to the bar, Stevens opened a small practice in Gettysburg in 1816, living and working there for the next twenty-six years. As his practice prospered, he purchased property in the town and surrounding Adams County and entered the iron business, building the Caledonia Iron Works near Chambersburg.

With prosperity came political prominence and service in the state legislature. There he established a reputation as a fearsome political opponent, one who was unsparing in his use of sarcasm and vitriol. He also gained a reputation for leading a lascivious bachelor's life; among other things, the rumor mill linked him to the murder of a pregnant black girl in 1831. Such rumors, which he mostly ignored but sometimes seemed to revel in, dogged him throughout his life. At this time, too, a fever caused his hair to fall out; for the rest of his life the ruggedly handsome but crippled Stevens wore a bad chestnut wig that made him the target of even more ridicule and gossip.

Elected to the Pennsylvania House in 1833 as an Anti-Mason, a popular political movement he helped found, Stevens rode this anti-Jackson party hard, keeping it alive in Adams County long after it had faded elsewhere. But he was no ideologue yet. Concentrating on legislative goals, many of which advanced his personal financial interests, his keen instinct for political strategy led him to make necessary alliances with the Whig opposition. In 1834, he worked tirelessly with Whigs to pass Pennsylvania's vanguard free public education act and a year later rallied his Anti-Mason/Whig coalition to defeat a repeal effort. Similarly, his apparent prejudice against privilege did not prevent him from working with the Whig Nicholas Biddle to recharter the Pennsylvania branch of the Bank of the United States as a state bank. In achieving the bank recharter he got Biddle to agree to make heavy contributions to public education and to internal improvements that led to the construction of the so-called tapeworm railroad, whose circuitous route ran past his iron foundries.

This skilled alliance builder was also a fierce partisan. His unsuccessful efforts to keep the Democrats from organizing the state legislature after the disputed election of 1838 led to the legendary "Buckshot War," during which the victorious Democrats expelled him from the House and his Adams County constituents quickly reelected him. He intended to run again in 1840, but William Henry Harrison sought his assistance in the presidential campaign, offering a vague inducement of a cabinet position. Stevens accepted his offer but did not get the cabinet post he sought from the president-elect, who wrote to Daniel Webster in December 1840: "We should have no peace with his intriguing, restless disposition. We will have nobody of that character" (Brodie, 83).

Harrison's rejection may have been the final disappointment that led Stevens to leave Gettysburg. His political fortunes were bleak with the Democrats in power, and although his legal practice flourished, he had mounting debts from his stumbling iron works and his compulsive gambling, especially the large losses he sustained from bets on the 1838 election. A lawsuit against him for bastardy and fornication kept rumors about his bachelor existence alive. In short, Stevens, who was fifty years old in 1842, was at the lowest point of his political life. He moved to Lancaster where, he told a friend, "appearances . . . seem very favorable" (Hoelscher, 160).

The appearances Stevens saw may have been Lancaster's phenomenal growth, which began in 1840. Population boomed in both the city and the county and new businesses arrived, particularly iron foundries and rolling mills, greatly diversifying this largely agricultural community. Steven's law practice expanded rapidly, and he worked his way out of debt. He kept his political fortunes alive as an active participant in the local Anti-Masons and Whigs. In 1848, Stevens ran for Congress as a "woolly headed," or antislavery, Whig and was elected overwhelmingly.

Entering the Thirty-first Congress in 1849, Stevens immediately confronted the slavery issue. Although in 1821 he had successfully defended a Maryland slaveowner's claim to recover his female slave from Pennsylvania, Stevens had long since gone on record as opposing slavery. He was no abolitionist, however, and took the politically safe position that Congress could not interfere with slavery in the Southern states. The Mexican-American War had added the vast southwestern territories to the United States and raised the issue of extending slavery there. Stevens announced his arrival in the House with a rousing anti-slavery speech in which he condemned provisions in the emerging Compromise of 1850 that would organize those territories according to the dictates of popular sovereignty and that proposed a new, pro-Southern Fugitive Slave Law. Despite his modest views on abolition, the Democratic newspaper in Lancaster, the *Intelligencer*, noted that Stevens was *"the sworn foe of the South"* (Current, 85).

Renominated for Congress in 1850, Stevens won reelection but ran 500 votes behind the statewide Whig ticket, perhaps because of his antislavery views. His hold on electoral support was further compromised by the Christiana Riot. Occurring in his district, this 1851 incident made abolition an issue of intense local concern. Stevens joined the team defending the thirty-nine persons accused of treason for shielding alleged fugitive slaves in violation of the new Fugitive Slave Law, which Stevens had opposed and condemned. Although the trial was held in distant Philadelphia, a jury acquitted the thirty-nine in fifteen minutes, and Steven's political fortunes suffered. He was dumped from the Whig ticket in 1852 by the conservative "silver grey" faction of the party, and returned to Lancaster in 1853 to focus on his legal practice and his still-ailing iron works.

He did not leave politics, however. When the Whig party collapsed, Stevens had a brief flirtation with Know-Nothingism. But when this nativist movement broke up on the slavery issue, Stevens joined the new Republican party in 1855, a decision that seems in retrospect both logical and inevitable. The new party's antislavery and entrepreneurial moorings meshed nicely with his emerging ideology—his long-standing interest in tariff issues (he was a protectionist), internal improvements issues (he was especially keen on railroad development), currency issues (he was an inflationist), and antislavery (but not necessarily abolitionism).

Aside from his more politically pragmatic positions like protectionism, Stevens's antislavery impulses seem to have been consistent with his commitment to egalitarianism. Perhaps originating in his economically modest and physically disabled background, and in his personal climb to professional success and political maturity, Stevens developed a hatred for economic and racial impediments to individual success in life. Nor did he seem reluctant to take unpopular positions to advance his ideas. His crusade for public education illustrates the point well, as do his anti-kidnapping resolution in the Pennsylvania legislature in 1836, his struggle for the black franchise in the 1837 Pennsylvania constitutional convention, and his attacks on the congressional Compromise of 1850 and the Kansas-Nebraska Act of 1854.

The sixty-six-year-old Stevens resurfaced in electoral politics in 1856. Perhaps motivated by a strong desire to defeat his fellow Lancastrian, Democrat James Buchanan, he organized Republicans throughout the state only to see the new party's ticket swamped. In 1858 he made a fight for the nomination to his old congressional seat, which he won on the second ballot. During the campaign, he reiterated familiar themes—attacking the low-rate Walker Tariff of 1857, and slavery extension. Stevens won the election and easily held the seat for the next decade, during which he experienced a meteoric rise in power and influence.

When Stevens arrived in Washington in December 1859, the sectional issue was at the boil. Kansas had been bleeding for five years, and John Brown's plot to unleash a slave rebellion had just failed. Stevens was uncompromising in his opposition to slavery now and hostile to all attempts by the new Abraham Lincoln (q.v.) administration to temporize with Southern leaders. Hating slaveholders not only for their human bondage but for their social and economic elitism, Stevens sought higher office from which to carry on the fight. For many years he had aspired to the U.S. Senate, and in 1861 he again hoped for a cabinet appointment. Continually blocked in these ambitions by his Republican rival in Lancaster County, Simon Cameron, Stevens carved out a key place for himself in the House of Representatives.

Stevens won the chairmanship of the House Ways and Means Committee in the special session of Congress that met on July 4, 1861. From this vantage point, he gained a guiding influence over financing the war and thus became one of the most important men in Congress. He worked closely with Treasury Secretary Salmon P. Chase (q.v.) in imposing new taxes—including an unprecedented income tax; fashioning the Internal Revenue Act of 1862; providing for the issuance of greenbacks—another profound innovation; and shepherding the creation of a national banking system. These were all measures that helped win the war and that addressed the Republican party's goals of entrepreneurial growth and political ascendency. Although much credit for this legislation belongs to subcommittee chairs, Stevens employed his considerable legislative skills to get it passed.

Stevens advocated a vigorous prosecution of the war. Since he regarded the Southern states as actually seceded, he saw the war as an opportunity to bring social reform to the South. Although he was no leveler, he did hate the aristocracy and sought to provide opportunities for the downtrodden to rise up, regardless of race. His bourgeois values fit perfectly with the midcentury Republican economic ideology of independent entrepreneurship. Thus, the war provided him an opportunity to crush the hated Democrats and advance the hegemony of the Republican party on the back of a vast social reform movement.

Known as a member of the Radical Republicans, all of Stevens's wartime and Reconstruction proposals addressed this dual agenda. Being in the forefront of such measures as the Thirteenth and Fourteenth Amendments and the Reconstruction Act of 1867, Stevens was a part of the general Republican consensus on extending civil rights to the freed people. The 1867 Reconstruction Act, also known as Military Reconstruction because it divided the South into five districts under rule by the military, anticipated the creation of civilian governments in the South based on black votes. The Fifteenth Amendment, of which Stevens was the spiritual father, was intended to guarantee those votes.

Steven's radical reputation derived from his proposals to confiscate Confederate property and redistribute it to the freedmen—the famous "forty acres and a mule" idea. Although passed with almost complete Republican support, Stevens and his radical friends were unable to prevent the party's moderates, led by the president, from watering down the Second Confiscation Act (1862) so that Confederate property would be subject to seizure only during the lifetime of the owner. Since this undermined Stevens's goal of a sweeping revolution in Southern land tenure, he and other Radicals got the law repealed before the end of the war. Radical attempts to provide land to freedmen in the Southern Homestead Act of 1862 and in the Freedmen's Bureau Act of 1866 also bore no fruit.

Stevens's failure to provide this economic protection to the freedmen came in large part from the party's unwillingness to follow him into politically dangerous waters. Most Republicans regarded private property as sacrosanct, even if it were held by Confederates; for them, government encouragement of economic development was one thing, confiscation was quite another. Finally, most Republicans were not committed to protecting blacks' freedom and creating a black property-owning class; they were committed to saving the Union and then reconstructing it as soon as possible, which meant, as Massachusetts governor John Andrew said, creating "an understanding [with] the natural leaders of opinion in the South" (Foner, 161).

Stevens's last great Radical campaign was to impeach President Andrew Johnson (q.v.). Lincoln's successor proved to be too anxious to reconstruct the South on its own terms and too shortsighted and inept to grasp the opportunity to work with the Republican moderate majority in Congress. Stevens was a driving force behind the attempt to impeach Johnson, and he served as a member of the impeachment committee. In extremely frail health, he helped draft the articles of impeachment but took little part in the trial. In a final disappointment, he saw the Congress fail to remove the president.

Shortly before he died on August 11, 1868, Stevens told a reporter that he regretted living "so long and so uselessly" (Current, 316). He was perhaps not in the best frame of mind to judge his life's successes. The father of Pennsylvania's free public education system was also largely responsible for important wartime measures. Yet he was hardly the dictator of the House that legend suggests. He failed to realize his vision of a society based on equality of opportunity for all people because it was too bold for a party caught in the thrall of survival following the shocking election reversals of 1867, when Republican candidates throughout the North went down to defeat. As usual, Stevens saw the problem clearly: "I live in a world of men, not of angels," he said (Foner, 152).

When he died, Lydia Hamilton Smith was at his bedside. A mulatto widow with two sons, Smith had been Stevens's housekeeper for twenty years. His treatment of her as an equal fueled more rumors about his lascivious bachelor lifestyle. Although one historian argues that they lived together as husband and wife, there is no direct evidence of that, and all other historians reject the notion. His body lay in state in the U.S. Capital, and there was an outpouring of sentiment for him that rivaled that expressed for Lincoln. He chose to be buried in Schreiner's Cemetery in Lancaster because it was the only cemetery in the city that was not restricted to whites. The inscription above his grave says he reposes there because he wished to show "in my death the principles which I advocated through a long life; equality of man before his Creator" (Palmer, 14).

The outline of Stevens's historical reputation took shape shortly after he died. In 1872, Alexander Hood, a Stevens protégé, characterized his mentor as high-minded in *A Biographical History of Lancaster County*. Alexander Harris, in *A Review of the Political Conflict in America* (1876), denounced Stevens as a dangerous revolutionary. Edward Collender's 1882 biography *Thaddeus Stevens: Commoner* and Samuel McCall's 1899 volume in Houghton Mifflin's important American Statesmen series both portray Stevens as highly principled. As McCall notes, "[a] truer democrat never breathed" (353). James Woodburn echoed these sentiments in his 1913 biography *The Life of Thaddeus Stevens*.

While biographers treated Stevens kindly, commentators on the Civil War and Reconstruction found his program malevolent. Beginning with John W. Burgess's *Reconstruction and the Constitution* (1902) and William A. Dunning's 1907 *Reconstruction, Political and Economic*, an entire generation of Reconstruction scholars subjected Stevens and the Radicals to a variety of charges—they were vindictive toward the South, unduly concerned about the fate of the blacks rather than the interests of whites, willing to throw the nation into political and economic chaos to satiate their pathological hatred of President Johnson, who had picked up Lincoln's mantle and tried to facilitate reunion. D. W. Griffith's epic motion picture *Birth of a Nation* (1915), forever engraved that view of Stevens into the popular consciousness.

Biographers continued to carry the torch for the Pennsylvania congressman. Thomas Woodley's *Great Leveler* (1937) and Alphonse Miller's 1939 *Thaddeus Stevens* both focus on his idealism. "No one," Miller notes, "devoted himself so consistently to patriotic purposes or the salvation of the underdog" (22). Similarly, in the midst of World War II, Elizabeth Lawson saw Stevens as "a thoroughly consistent democrat, who scorned to circumscribe or limit democracy'' (3).

The lone dissenter to this portrait of an idealistic Stevens was Richard N. Current. Writing his 1942 biography *Old Thad Stevens* in the wake of the Great Depression, Current promoted his *idée fixe* that Stevens was a complete politician—ambitious for power and ruthless in acquiring it. While he clearly admires the Pennsylvanian's political skills, Current nevertheless finds it ironic that "the great commoner" did much to ensure Republican party hegemony over the postwar economy, one consequence of which was the advent of "the Age of Big Business, with its concentration of wealth and its diffusion of poverty, its inequalities and its inequities" (320).

Ralph Korngold's 1955 biography *Thaddeus Stevens: A Being Darkly Wise and Rudely Great* continued the view of the congressman as an idealist and reflected historians' reassessment of Reconstruction then under way and the advent of post–World War II Republican prosperity. Fawn Brodie challenged this principled view in her 1959 work *Thaddeus Stevens: Scourge of the South*. Brodie portrays Stevens as a politician who used his power to work out his personal problems. Like Current, she sees Stevens driven by his personal relationships and circumstances. She is the only historian who argues that Stevens and Lydia Smith had a sexual relationship.

Hans Trefousse's remarkably concise yet full 1997 biography of the Commoner, *Thaddeus Stevens: Nineteenth Century Egalitarian*, results from his long study of the politics of Reconstruction. Trefousse offers a multidimensional Stevens—the practical politician, the *petit bourgeois* entrepreneur, the idealist fighter for equal rights for all persons. Trefousse concluded that Stevens was the "spark plug of the Republican party" and that his legacy is America's movement toward "an interracial democracy" (245).

There is a wealth of good periodical literature on Stevens, much of it in the *Journal of the Lancaster County Historical Society*. Most of this work deals with Stevens's Pennsylvania career and provides important insights into his early political and business activities. James A. Jolly's 1970 essay "The Historical Reputation of Thaddeus Stevens" touches on all the historiographical issues surrounding his life. Robert Hoelscher's 1974 piece "Thaddeus Stevens as a Lancaster Politician, 1842–1868" and Andrew Robertson's 1980 essay "Idealist as Opportunist: Thaddeus Stevens's Support in Lancaster, 1843–1866" help clarify how he preserved support in his conservative congressional district.

In 1992 a group of Pennsylvania public service organizations commemorated the two hundredth anniversary of Stevens's birth with a conference in Lancaster. Several of the papers from that conference were published in the April 1993 issue of *Pennsylvania History*. The selected papers, while not uncritical, all promote the view that Stevens was an idealistic egalitarian, thus undermining the Current-Brodie interpretation and providing support for Trefousse's account.

Whatever the source of Old Thad's motives, whether an idealism rooted in the Republican synthesis or political pragmatism and opportunism, it is clear that many of the issues he struggled with confront America still. And regardless of his motives, one can still contemplate, as he did, the meaning of freedom in America and the role of political leaders in achieving it.

BIBLIOGRAPHY

Alexander Harris, *A Biographical History of Lancaster County* (Lancaster, Pa.: E. Barr & Co., 1872).

Alexander Harris, *A Review of the Political Conflict in America . . . ; Comprising Also a Resume of the Career of Thaddeus Stevens* (New York: T. H. Pollock, 1876).

Edward B. Collender, *Thaddeus Stevens: Commoner* (Boston: A. Williams and Co., 1882).

Samuel W. McCall, *Thaddeus Stevens* (Boston: Houghton Mifflin and Company, 1899).

John W. Burgess, *Reconstruction and the Constitution, 1866–1876* (New York: Charles Scribner's Sons, 1902).

William E. Dunning, *Reconstruction, Political and Economic, 1865–1870* (New York: Harper and Brothers, 1907).

James Albert Woodburn, *The Life of Thaddeus Stevens* (Indianapolis, Ind.: Bobbs-Merrill Co., 1913).

Thomas F. Woodley, *Great Leveler: The Life of Thaddeus Stevens* (New York: Stackpole Sons, 1937).

Alphonse B. Miller, *Thaddeus Stevens* (New York: Harper and Bros., Publishers, 1939).

Richard Nelson Current, *Old Thad Stevens: A Story of Ambition* (Madison: University of Wisconsin Press, 1942).

Elizabeth Lawson, *Thaddeus Stevens* (New York: International Publishers, 1942).

Ralph Korngold, *Thaddeus Stevens: A Being Darkly Wise and Rudely Great* (New York: Harcourt, Brace and Co., 1955).

Fawn Brodie, *Thaddeus Stevens: Scourge of the South* (New York: W. W. Norton, 1959).

Hans Trefousse, *The Radical Republicans: Lincoln's Vanguard for Racial Justice* (New York: Alfred Knopf, 1969).

James A. Jolly, "The Historical Reputation of Thaddeus Stevens," *Journal of the Lancaster County Historical Society* 72, no. 2 (1970): 33–71.

Eric Foner, "Thaddeus Stevens, Confiscation and Reconstruction," in *The Hofstadter Aegis: A Memoriam*, ed. Stanley Elkins and Eric McKitrick (New York: Alfred A. Knopf, 1974), 154–183.

Robert Hoelscher, "Thaddeus Stevens as a Lancaster Politician, 1842–1868," *Journal of the Lancaster County Historical Society* 78, no. 4 (1974): 157–213.

Andrew Robertson, "Idealist as Opportunist: Thaddeus Stevens' Support in Lancaster, 1843–1866," *Journal of the Lancaster County Historical Society* 84, no. 2 (1980): 49–89.

Beverly W. Palmer, "Equality of Man before His Creator," *Pennsylvania Heritage* 18, no. 2 (1992): 10–15.

Hans L. Trefousse, *Thaddeus Stevens: Nineteenth-Century Egalitarian* (Chapel Hill: University of North Carolina Press, 1997).

CHARLES SUMNER
(January 6, 1811– March 11, 1874)

Michael Connolly

In early November 1856, the carriage carrying an ailing Charles Sumner weaved through the streets of Boston, hastened forward by the boisterous cheers of onlooking crowds. Recently beaten senseless on the floor of the Senate by the vengeful South Carolinian Preston Brooks, Sumner limped north to his hometown that turned out in concerned sympathy to welcome its wounded representative. Reportedly, however, when the procession came to Beacon Street—home of the city's mercantile and manufacturing elite—the shutters of the federal mansions were shut tight in disdain. Even in this moment of personal tragedy, Sumner's traditional opponents among conservative ex-Whigs would not consider him their own. The fiery antislavery advocate had repudiated the policies of the man he had replaced, Daniel Webster, and the scions of Boston Whiggery had never forgiven him.

This vignette is also illustrative of how historians have considered the life of Charles Sumner, one of the most important Civil War U.S. senators. His reputation ebbs and flows, depending on the social vision of each passing generation. In eras expressing the hope of racial harmony, valuing the rewards of egalitarian democracy, and celebrating the march of social justice, Sumner emerges as a hallowed icon and a rich symbol of what determined and principled activism can achieve. But in eras worrying over the agitations of those discontented with the social order, critical of those urging fundamental reorderings of the institutions of society, and uncomfortable with those whose passionate appeals to justice seem to spurn calm and reasoned thought, the reputation of Sumner suffers. As much as any actor of the Civil War era, Charles Sumner has transcended the context of his own time. Scholarly fascination with his long and varied career demonstrates that, in truth, every generation has its own Sumner.

Despite his later lofty achivements, Charles Sumner was not a child of privilege like so many of Boston's antebellum political and social elite. The son of a middling Boston attorney and county sheriff, Sumner was born on January 6,

1811. Although Sumner was never close to his father, a cold and rather distant patriarch, he did absorb some of his father's progressive opinions on religion, society, and race—"a humanitarianism tempered by stoic behavior" (Blue, 3). His attendance at Harvard from 1826 to 1829 was a liberation. Surrounded by new friends in an intellectually charged environment, Sumner thrived and devoured the great texts of literature and history. After some uncertainty on a career path, in 1830 he entered Harvard Law School. Enjoying the opportunity to study the more intellectual and literary aspects of the law, he soon became the protégé of Supreme Court Justice and Harvard lecturer Joseph Story. When Sumner passed the bar in 1834 and opened a Boston practice, he seemed on the threshold of a promising law career.

But Sumner found the law dull and disillusioning. Editing texts on admiralty law and occasionally lecturing at Harvard in place of the absent Story was unsatisfying. Taken with the reformist culture of antebellum Boston and liberal Unitarianism, much like his father, Sumner began to involve himself in a variety of causes, most particularly the local abolitionist movement of William Lloyd Garrison. In 1837, Sumner left for an extended tour of Europe, against the wishes of Story and his other benefactors in New England, to cure his boredom. Over two years, he visited the capitals of Europe, studied their social and political systems, and conversed with literary and political leaders like Tocqueville, Macauley, Wordsworth, and Carlyle. Upon his return, his boredom unsoothed, he pushed deeper into the reformist movement. By the mid-1840s, Charles Sumner was one of Boston's better-known humanitarian spokesmen.

His causes were varied—antislavery, prison reform, pacifism, public education—but on July 4, 1845, the reformer Sumner would officially introduce himself to Boston society as the holiday orator, delivering an address on international peace. "The True Grandeur of Nations" speech was the first of many shots by Sumner across the bow of conservative Boston, incorporating his customary vivid imagery and biting rhetoric. From this moment on they would never regard him with anything but suspicion. Facing an audience of politicians, military officials, and elite Bostonians, Sumner charged that Texas annexation was a veiled attempt to "fasten by new links the chains which promise soon to fall from the limbs of the unhappy slave," President James K. Polk's Oregon policy was an unwise maneuver to capture "a worthless territory," and war a waste of national time and treasure. The endless and spiraling preparation for future wars with unknown foes was akin to "the wild boar in the fable, who whetted his tusks on a tree in the forest, when no enemy was near, saying that in time of peace he must prepare for war." Armaments were not characteristic of civilization but barbarity. Truly glorious nationhood was "moral elevation, enlightened and decorated by the intellect of man" that assisted society's unfortunate and built institutions for human betterment. "The eagle of our country, without the terror of his beak, and dropping the forceful thunderbolt from his pounces, shall soar with the olive of Peace, into untried realms of ether, nearer to the sun" (Donald, 109–110).

Reaction was cold. Outside Sumner's own reform circles, most felt the young attorney had been reckless. Robert Winthrop's dinner toast later that day was revealing: " 'Our Country, whether bounded by Sabine or Del Norte—still our Country—to be cherished in all our hearts—to be defended by all our hands' " (Donald, 111). The lines were beginning to be drawn in a growing and bitter battle between Sumner and the Whig establishment surrounding Senator Daniel Webster. They too believed Democratic policy on Texas and Oregon to be dangerous and divisive, threatening to upset the sectional balance of 1820. But while the Websterians sought to assuage difficulties with compromises and appeals to national feeling, Sumner made a moral appeal. Compromise was unacceptable in the face of the moral degradation of annexation and was the abandonment of high principle for the nervous and shallow needs of the moment. Wielding "the glowing force of an overpowering conviction, admitting of neither abatement nor compromise," the emerging Sumner of 1845 had made a lasting and dark mark on the minds of established Boston society. A "Puritan idealist" was not their model statesman (Schurz, 25).

Rather than curbing his harsh words and intense involvement in humanitarian affairs, Summer dove deeper and began to dabble in "Conscience" Whig politics, making friends with the aging John Quincy Adams, his son Charles Francis Adams, John Gorham Palfrey, Henry Wilson, and others. This dynamic coterie of reformist Whigs was desperately trying to steer the Whig party toward a stronger stance against Texas annexation, the Mexican War, and slavery. In a dramatic 1846 outburst against Boston Congressman Winthrop, who had opposed American involvement in Texas yet voted for the war declaration, Sumner declared that the Winthrop vote approved "the darkest act in our history" and that "Blood! blood! is on the hands of the representative from Boston. Not all great Neptune's ocean can wash them clean" (Donald, 144–146). What doors among "the youth and beauty, the best society and pleasantest homes" of elite Boston were still open after his 1845 speech were now slammed shut (Shotwell, 204). A "deep and lasting bitterness" settled in, and Sumner was now "outside the pale of society" (Haynes, 108).

By 1848, unable to translate their antislavery platform into official Whig doctrine and incapable of denying the Louisiana slaveholder and Mexican War veteran General Zachary Taylor the party nomination—a process that Sumner decried as an "unhallowed union . . . between the lords of the lash and the lords of the loom"—the Conscience Whigs splintered from the Webster wing and formed the Free Soil party (Blue, 46–47). Sumner was an energetic and early proponent of separation, ran as a Free Soiler against Winthrop for the Boston congressional seat, and was trounced. The hard lessons of politics did not deter him from furthering his antislavery activism. In 1849–1850, Sumner was actively engaged in desegregating the Boston public schools, and the constitutional understanding he displayed in the courtroom would, according to recent Sumner biographer Frederick J. Blue, be built upon by the Supreme Court in deciding the *Brown v. Board of Education* case in 1954. This event would be buried, however, beneath the greater significance of 1850 in Charles Sumner's life.

Responding to Henry Clay's compromise proposals in the wake of Mexican peace, Daniel Webster came to the Senate floor on March 7, 1850, and in a grand, if infamous, address supported the bill, including the controversial Fugitive Slave provision so hated by the abolitionists. If the oration was seen as consistent with Webster's more cautious Unionist instincts by his traditional Whig supporters, it was treated with contempt by the reformist-abolitionist bloc of Sumner's circle. John Greenleaf Whittier's *Ichabod!* bespoke Free Soil bitterness:

> All else is gone; from those great eyes
> The soul has fled:
> When faith is lost, when honor dies,
> The man is dead!
>
> Then, pay the reverence of old days
> To his dead fame
> Walk backward, with averted gaze,
> And hide the shame! (*Norton Anthology*, 505)

The Webster address gave added energy to a Free Soil campaign already brimming with anticipation. Although Whig control of the Massachusetts legislature was nearly a given in every election cycle, there was hope that the controversy over Webster and the renewed agitation over slavery might offer an unprecedented opportunity—if the Whigs could be denied a majority, the Democrats and Free Soilers could form a coalition to choose a new governor and senator. After a heated and divisive autumn—Sumner ran unsuccessfully for Congress again and railed against his Websterite opponents with renewed vigor—that hope was realized. The new coalition cut a deal: The Democrats would have the governor's chair and the Free Soilers could name the next senator. Although he claimed not to want the office, when the legislature, after four months of deliberation, finally named Charles Sumner the new senator from Massachusetts, he quietly accepted.

In Washington, Sumner began his tenure as Webster's replacement without fanfare. He seldom spoke at first, much to the consternation of his abolitionist backers, and made fast friends among many of the national elite, including prominent Southerners. Friends in private were rivals in public, however, and when it became clear that Sumner planned to break silence on the fugitive slave issue in the summer of 1852, threatening the fragile sectional peace of the 1850 Clay bill, all the Senate mechanisms of delay were used against him. By August, Sumner found a window of opportunity and, at a moment when his opponents were lax, held the floor and gave his first antislavery oration to the Senate, "Freedom National, Slavery Sectional." More constitutional and historical than emotional, the address was greeted with scorn. Secretary Webster heard the speech from the back of the Senate, "moved from one side of the chamber to another, and after about an hour, he left, black and scowling.'' Senator Jeremiah Clemens of Alabama, representative of most Senate sentiment, waved off Sumner's challenge to the compromise lightly: ''[T]he barkings of a puppy never did any harm'' (Donald, 236).

But the silence was now broken, and the controversy over Kansas only exacerbated the sectional difficulties Sumner was trying hard to ignite. Not surprisingly, Sumner violently opposed President Franklin Pierce and Senator Douglas's efforts to bring Kansas and Nebraska into the Union as possible slave states. Over two years, he denounced the Kansas-Nebraska pact as contrary to the spirit and letter of the Missouri Compromise and the craft of dishonest slave hunters turned politicians. All the previous friendliness between Sumner and Southern senators had vanished as both recognized the sincerity of the other's purpose. Senate debate on constitutional matters became laced with invective and personal attack. Senator James Mason of Virginia became a demon to Sumner for his part in the Fugitive Slave bill: ''[F]rom his brain came forth the souless monster.'' Clement Clay called Sumner a ''spaniel'' and a ''serpent'' (Blue, 82). Andrew Butler of South Carolina thought his New England colleague a ''plunging agitator,'' preaching a false ''philanthropy that proposes much and does nothing with a long advertisement and a short performance''—Massachusetts was, after all, an ''anti-nigger state'' (Shotwell, 315).

The battle of words over Kansas came to a head in May 1856. Before a captivated Senate audience, Sumner gave his ''Crime against Kansas'' address, summing up over two days both the irreconcilable nature of the slavery issue and the new abrasiveness of public debate. He lashed out in personal terms at those he considered most culpable for the Kansas tragedy: Andrew Butler and Stephen Douglas. ''[Butler] has chosen a mistress to whom he has made his vows,'' fired Sumner, ''and who, though ugly to others, is always lovely to him; though polluted in the sight of the world, is chaste in his sight: I mean the harlot slavery. . . . The frenzy of Don Quixote in behalf of his wench Dulcinea del Toboso is all surpassed.'' To Butler and other Southerners threatening secession over slavery, he mocked their supposed chivalry: ''Heroic Knight! Exhalted Senator! A second Moses come for a second exodus!'' Senator Douglas, as Sancho Panza, was nothing more than a ''squire of slavery'' (Shotwell, 317).

The senators were stunned and replied with understandable wrath. Douglas cruelly imagined that Sumner's address had been practiced and memorized faithfully ''every night before the glass with a negro boy to hold the candle.'' James Mason of Virginia took the speech as an affront to his state and section: ''I am constrained to hear here depravity, vice, in its most odious form, uncoiled in this presence, exhibiting its loathsome deformities in accusation and vilification against a quarter of the country from which I come.'' Sumner seemed incredulous at their anger and perhaps in a moment of prophecy noted in reply that ''the bowie-knife and bludgeon are not proper emblems of senatorial debate.'' He then ripped Douglas as being unfit for public office and ''not the proper model for an American Senator.'' Finally turning to a visibly upset Mason,

Sumner declaimed that "hard words are not argument, frowns are not reasons, nor do scowls belong to the proper arsenal of parliamentary debate" (Shotwell, 326–328).

Two days later, as Sumner sat writing at his Senate desk, Preston Brooks, a South Carolina congressman and nephew of Senator Butler, attacked Sumner in retribution for the Kansas speech that had dishonored his uncle, beating him unconscious with a cane. Carried bleeding and senseless from the chamber in the arms of his friends, he would not return to his full-time senatorial duties for nearly four years. The beating of Charles Sumner, one of the most renowned events of American antebellum life, galvanized Northern opinion and transformed the nature of national debate. Whereas before May 1856, slavery, muzzled by compromise, shared the political stage with such potent ethnocultural issues like temperance, immigration, and religious freedom, "Bleeding Kansas" and "Bleeding Sumner" refocused political attention to slavery and its meaning to American liberty. No longer did the rambling orations of Sumner, John P. Hale, and Salmon P. Chase (q.v.) on Southern conspiracies against American freedom and ominous visions of the "Slave Power" trampling liberty in Kansas seem so radical and without foundation. Sumner's beating took on the appearance of a bold attack on "Northern rights" of free speech, free labor, private property, and peaceful participation in national government. "Both in Kansas and in the nation's capital, men seemed to be attacked for what they said and thought" (Gienapp, 359). What was only suspicious in Southern denunciations of John Quincy Adams over the gag rule seemed clarified in Brooks's attack (with wide-scale Southern approval) on Sumner. The usually staid and conservative Josiah Quincy spoke for many on the beating, employing Sumner's own terms: "It says to us that Northern men shall not be heard in the halls of Congress, except at the point of the bowie-knife, the bludgeon, and revolver." Jeremiah Chaplin, a Sumner biographer, asked, "Where was free speech, where was liberty of any kind, if such deeds of violence could be allowed?" (292–294). It is perhaps a cruel irony that Charles Sumner's words—which he prided himself in carefully crafting and framing with classical allusions and literary quotations—meant less to American impatience with the institution of slavery than his eventual savage beating in 1856. Sumner's absence was a constant paradoxical reminder of the new politics of the late 1850s.

To regain his health, Sumner spent most of the years 1856–1859 outside Washington and outside the country. Painful "treatments" by quack European doctors, recoveries, and sudden relapses punctuated his visits to spas and hospitals across Europe. By late 1859, however, he had returned to his Senate duties on a limited basis and, while keeping away from the treacherous waters of presidential politics that were consuming his associates William H. Seward (q.v.) and Salmon P. Chase, was planning another rhetorical broadside on Southern slavery. Called "The Barbarism of Slavery," the address has been ridiculed by many as notable only in its bad political timing, with the Republicans desperately trying to hold the party together and convince the nation of its moderation, and Sumner's continuing bad taste in personally attacking his political foes. Allan Nevins, for example, claimed the address was "a stilted, schematic piece of invective, not lacking in literary polish or pedantic learning, but abominable in taste . . . [and] simply impaired Sumner's influence, angered Southern leaders, and hurt the party" (300). However, its political fitness aside, the 1860 address was a rather clear explanation of the Sumner vision: why slavery was socially, constitutionally, and culturally unfit for American civilization.

For Sumner, slavery was barbaric, unconstitutional, and antisocial. It was barbaric because man could never justly be the property of another man (that was an irreligious "pretension"); it was antimarriage by its willful breaking up of man and wife for sale on the slave trader's block and was also therefore antifamily; and it was anti-intellectual—witness Sumner's own beating for daring to question its legitimacy: "St. Paul could call upon the people of Athens to give up the worship of unknown gods; he could live in his own hired house at Rome, and preach Christianity in this heathen metropolis; but no man can be heard against slavery in Charleston or Mobile." Slavery was unconstitutional in Sumner's mind for the simple reason of constitutional silence: The document was "without a single sentence, phrase, or word upholding human bondage." Finally, slavery was antisocial because of the crude public and private attitudes it encouraged in slaveholders toward their fellow man and the national institutions: "The swagger of a bully is called chivalry; a swiftness to quarrel is called courage; the bludgeon is adopted as a substitute for argument; and assassination is lifted to be one of the fine arts" (Nason, 261–262).

Southern senators were unimpressed by its clarity and expressed astonishment that Sumner had not learned any lessons since 1856. James Chesnut of South Carolina summed up Southern disgust: "It has been left for this day, for this country, for the abolitionists of Massachusetts, to deify the incarnation of malice, mendacity, and cowardice" (Nason, 256).

In 1860, by now a Senate leader as chairman of the Foreign Relations Committee, Sumner was a good Republican. Although he was thoroughly unimpressed by the rough manners of the nominee and eventual victor Abraham Lincoln (q.v.), Sumner promised to work with the new president and soon became a routine backroom adviser to Lincoln on international relations. A most unusual political union, "these two radically different men came to respect and ultimately to like each other. Lincoln knew the senator was incorruptible, if often irritating. Sumner found that the President wanted 'to do right and to save the country' " (Donald, *Lincoln*, 321–322). Using his overseas knowledge and connections, Sumner served as Secretary of State William Seward's foreign policy foil (to Seward's disdain), taking the edge off the New Yorker's often gruff and unwise actions. Sumner's most notable foreign policy contribution in the Lincoln years was his role in the *Trent* Affair of 1861–1862.

Tempering the joy of Lincoln, his cabinet, and most of the loyal North over the capture of James Mason and John Slidell aboard a British steamer, Sumner was quick to warn official Washington of British anger and resolve. The senator's close contacts in London informed him of the real possibility of war with England over the *Trent* Affair and, upon convincing Lincoln, shifted American policy toward conciliation. Mason and Slidell were soon released and the crisis passed. Cooled by Sumner's advice and ready access to English political circles, Lincoln reportedly quipped later, "[O]ne war at a time" (Rawley, 258).

While not overseeing American foreign policy from his perch in the Senate, Sumner was continuing his role as the nation's racial conscience. He took to heart his progenitor John Quincy Adams's opinion of the 1840s that, in time of war, the national government would be vested with the authority to emancipate the slaves unilaterally. "The excercise of the war powers was the means—otherwise constitutionally unavailable—by which freedom would come to all Americans. Adams was not quite sure whether Congress, the Executive, or the commanders in the field would be responsible for it" (Howe, 63–64). Sumner had no such doubts. Building on Adams and the sentiment of his own antebellum addresses, Sumner suggested that secession and war had rendered the Southern states into territories, thereby placing them under the ultimate jurisdiction of the Congress. Slavery could therefore be outlawed by congressional fiat, presidential authority be damned. Quoting Edmund Burke on postrevolutionary France, Sumner looked to the South and claimed, "It is but an empty space on the political map!" The power of racial reform was now congressional: "The jurisdiction, civil and military, centers in Congress, to be employed for the happiness, welfare, and renown of the American people, changing slavery into freedom, and present chaos into a cosmos of perpetual beauty and peace" (Nason, 280).

This policy was in stark contrast to that of congressional moderates and conservatives who supported milder terms of reunification and President Lincoln's own scheme of partial emancipation as announced in the Proclamation of 1863 and often led to fierce clashes between Sumner and the White House. The 1864 fight over the readmission of Louisiana was a prime example. Lincoln wanted to undermine the rebellion by admitting former Confederate states that professed loyalty to the Union, no matter if the new loyal governments had wholeheartedly embraced racial equality. When Lincoln pushed for recognition of a loyal Louisiana without such promises of equality, Sumner dissented in his familiar dramatic manner and helped defeat the president. The new Baton Rouge government was, according to Sumner, "a mere seven-month's abortion, begotten by the bayonet in criminal conjunction with the spirit of caste" (Donald, *Lincoln*, 564). His race speeches of the war years reconfirmed his leadership in a growing coterie of radical congressional leaders dedicated to "a utopian vision of a nation whose citizens enjoyed equality of civil and political rights, secured by a powerful and beneficent national state" (Foner, 230).

Sumner was genuinely grieved by Lincoln's death in April 1865 and was with the president when he died. He looked forward, now that wartime demands for national unity and Northern resolve were ebbing, to return to a serious and principled push for racial equality under the Reconstruction policies of Lincoln's successor, the loyal Tennessean Andrew Johnson (q.v.). After initial hope, Sumner was sorely embittered by Johnson's actions. President Johnson, in Sumner's and other radical eyes, defied the moral purposes of the recent war by denying federal authority to impose radical racial reorganization on the Southern states and by interposing himself, through the powers of the executive, between the South and the radical Congress. In both a spirit of retribution and desperation, Sumner was soon a leader of the unsuccessful Johnson impeachment movement and ruthlessly attacked the president in the proceedings with "lurid and furious invective" as an unconstitutional tyrant (Haynes, 324).

Sumner fared little better with Ulysses S. Grant (q.v.). The new president, used to relatively unquestioned military obedience from people he perceived as subordinates, could not understand or tolerate the authority Chairman Sumner had over foreign policy. "Ulysses Grant got along less well with that handsome, vain, lonely, and ambitious man than with any other person he encountered in his entire life," writes Grant biographer William S. McFeely. First, in the Alabama Claims controversy, Sumner demanded Britain pay huge "indirect" costs, perhaps even the cession of Canada to the United States, for shipping damages during the Civil War. "It was a kind of wild will to self-destruction. Sumner was asking for enough money to obstruct any peaceful settlement, and he was doing so in a way that would undermine everyone's confidence in his ability to provide the leadership for the attainment of that settlement, or any policy objective of the Grant Administration." Second, Sumner opposed Grant's proposed annexation of Santo Domingo (after supposedly agreeing to the plan in private), comparing it to accepting the pro-slavery 1857 Lecompton Constitution in Kansas. Furious with the aging senator's ability to complicate the president's policies, pro-administration forces in the Senate finally toppled Sumner from the chairmanship in 1871 (McFeely, 334, 352).

The last years of Charles Sumner's life were those of frustration and disappointment. No longer a Senate leader, yet still a political veteran of some clout, he steadfastly opposed Grant's neglect of Radical Republican policies. But he was increasingly a man alone. "[T]he more the Republican party changed, the more the senator remained committed to his old agenda. His foreign policy differences with party leaders were real, but his continuing insistence on racial equality became troublesome and tiring to many Republicans who were eager to deal with other domestic issues." Further alienating himself from mainstream Republicans, he openly supported Horace Greeley for president in 1872, vainly hoping the New York Liberal Republican could defeat what Sumner labeled "Grantism." In fragile health since his 1856 beating, Sumner began to weaken in the early 1870s and tire of the political life. In debt and sick, he wrote mournfully, "I am not of the stuff for these strifes" (Blue, 195, 207).

Sumner died on March 11, 1874, at his Washington, D.C. home. No sooner had he passed, the battle over his legacy began. Not surprisingly, the first treatments of Sumner were laudatory and hagiographic, viewing the Massachusetts senator as an prophet of social justice. Elias Nason's 1874 study was representative, defending the senator against the routine charges of being an American Jacobin. "Mr. Sumner was no revolutionist. He held in profound reverence the organic law of the land.'' Recent battles with the likes of Johnson, Grant, and various fellow senators must not color perceptions of a long career: "He was called a theorizer and a visionary; but his thoughts were in advance of his age; and his opinions rested on the solid basis of eternal truth and equity. He had reached a higher level than the mercenary politicians of his time; and hence they could not understand him" (Nason, 81, 116). For the remainder of the nineteenth century he would remain a hero to those of abolitionist sentiment who fondly remembered his battles on behalf of emancipation and racial equality.

But as new generations faced new problems and brought new experiences to the study of history, the historiographical treatment of Charles Sumner began to change. With American involvement in imperial ventures in the Carribbean and the Pacific after 1890, facing the determined problems of instituting democracy and order in foreign cultures—Cuba was an impoverished mess, the Philippines were in revolt, Mexico was a constant challenge to American policy makers—historians began to look askance at figures preaching the optimism of racial and democratic hope. Idealism was no longer a special quality of leadership. Charles Sumner appeared a foolish, if quaint, radical with no understanding of human potential and social realities and was no model leader for the present.

This critical turn began ironically with the work of Sumner's friend and colleague Carl Schurz. While Sumner was to be appreciated for the clear moral vision he brought to politics, such men brought as much danger as hope. Politicians like Sumner, "a moralist determined to make everything bend to his conception of right and justice," were rigid, dogmatic, and corrosive of republics dependent on the ultimate victory of compromise. Aloof and unaware of the social and political consequences of his actions, "[h]e was, unconsciously, seeking to revolutionize the Constitution in its own name. . . . He would rather consult on questions of right or wrong the heroes of Plutarch than men living around him under the influence of the interests of the day" (Schurz, 42, 43).

George H. Haynes's 1909 study was indicative of most critical Sumner historiography of the period and, like many, "reflected the segregated society and racist views of most white Americans" (Blue, 214). The world of 1909 was not that of 1856 or 1870. "Day by day," wrote Haynes, "our dealings with the peoples of our new insular possessions are bringing into question doctrines which Sumner held to be absolute and impregnable." A man of "aristocratic manners" and "portentous seriousness," he was above all a dangerous idealist. Echoing the old Webster Whig concerns, Haynes charged, "He combined the unyielding conscience of the Puritan with the burning zeal of a Hebrew prophet. . . . If all men were prophets, where were the making of laws or the administering of government?" The American black experience since Reconstruction and twenty years' experience with colonization showed, according to the racialist Haynes, that contrary to Sumner's wild beliefs, democratization was a slow and difficult process. Sumner was no hero for the age but merely "an unpractical idealist" (8, 393–448).

This critical approximation of Sumner lasted roughly till the rise of the civil rights movement, its last real spokesman being perhaps Allan Nevins and his multivolume *Ordeal of Union*. David Donald's two-volume investigation of 1960 and 1970, though certainly critical, restored Sumner to some of his former reknown as orator and devoted humanitarian and marked an upswing of Sumner historiography that continues today through the writings of most slavery and antebellum historians. Frederick J. Blue's 1994 *Charles Sumner and the Conscience of the North* is but the most recent example of this historiographical trend, considering Sumner, though flawed, a moral example and "a man well in advance of his times." "Sumner cannot be effectively evaluated without a greater acceptance of his moral commitment . . . [and] should be seen as calling attention to a racial situation that most white Americans preferred to ignore" (209, 216).

Undoubtedly the next generation of historians, considering the context and experiences of their own eras, will look upon Sumner in a new light. He may fall in estimation or retain his now-high esteem, but his role as a Civil War era leader is secure—even his staunchest critics, merely by considering his life, give him that title. In life and death, on every historian's page, Charles Sumner exemplifies John Quincy Adams's dictum to his young protégé, "No man is abused, whose influence is not felt."

BIBLIOGRAPHY

Jeremiah Chaplin, *The Life of Charles Sumner* (Boston: D. Lothrop & Co., 1874).

Elias Nason, *The Life and Times of Charles Sumner* (Boston: B. B. Russell, 1874).

George. H. Haynes, *Charles Sumner* (Philadelphia: G. W. Jacobs & Co., 1909).

Walter G. Shotwell, *Life of Charles Sumner* (New York: T. Y. Crowell & Co., 1910).

Allan Nevins, *The Ordeal of Union*, Vol. 2 (New York: Charles Scribner's Sons, 1947).

Carl Schurz, *Charles Sumner: An Essay by Carl Schurz*, ed. Arthur R. Hogue (Urbana: University of Illinois Press, 1951).

David Donald, *Charles Sumner and the Coming of the Civil War* (New York: Alfred A. Knopf, 1960).

David Donald, *Charles Sumner and the Rights of Man* (New York: Alfred A. Knopf, 1970).

Daniel Walker Howe, *The Political Culture of the American Whigs* (Chicago: University of Chicago Press, 1979).

William S. McFeely, *Grant: A Biography* (New York: W. W. Norton and Co., 1981).

The Norton Anthology of American Literature, Second Edition. (New York: W. W. Norton & Co., 1986).

William Gienapp, *The Origins of the Republican Party, 1852–1856* (New York: Oxford University Press, 1987).

Eric Foner, *Reconstruction: America's Unfinished Revolution, 1863–1877* (New York: Harper & Row, Publishers, 1988).

Frederick J. Blue, *Charles Sumner and the Conscience of the North* (Arlington Heights, Ill.: Harlan Davidson, Inc., 1994).

David Donald, *Lincoln* (New York: Simon & Schuster, 1995).

James A. Rawley. *Abraham Lincoln and a Nation Worth Fighting For* (Wheeling, Ill.: Harlan Davidson, Inc., 1996).

GEORGE HENRY THOMAS
(March 31, 1816–March 28, 1870)

Charles F. Ritter

Union General George H. Thomas ended the Civil War as he began it, with a decisive victory over Confederate forces. Indeed, during his thirty-year-long military career, he never lost a fight and is known to history as "The Rock of Chickamauga." Recognizing Thomas's important contribution to Union victory, Ezra Warner says that he was the "third of the triumvirate who won the war" (Warner, 500). In fact, George Thomas is the only Union general to do what President Abraham Lincoln (q.v.) wanted all his generals to do—destroy Confederate armies.

It is symptomatic of Thomas's historical reputation that he gained his well-known sobriquet from the Union defeat at Chickamauga but that he is little recognized for the Union's final victory in the Western Theater of the war, Nashville. No fewer than ten biographers have attempted to rectify this oversight in the last century and a half. Yet interest in Thomas is so low that one major university library has moved its four biographies of the general to off-campus storage. Perhaps this lack of interest stems in part from Thomas's own elusive nature. Another factor to explain his obscurity may lie in the price he paid for overshadowing Ulysses S. Grant (q.v.) and William T. Sherman (q.v.) at Chattanooga and for defying Grant at Nashville.

Born on a prosperous farm in Southampton County, Virginia, on March 31, 1816, Thomas was one of five children of John and Elizabeth (Rochelle) Thomas. He descended from English, Welsh, and French Huguenot ancestors long resident in the region. Educated at Southampton Academy, Thomas read law with his uncle James Rochelle, the clerk of the country court. But the law bored him. A family friend, Congressman John Y. Mason, suggested he go to West Point, where he graduated twelfth in his class of forty-two in 1840. Although the lively "Cump" Sherman was his roommate, his classmates called him "Old Tom" because of his serious demeanor. Commissioned a second lieutenant in the 3rd Artillery upon graduation, Thomas was sent to Florida, where he participated in the Second Seminole War in 1841. While there he received a brevet to first lieutenant for gallantry and good conduct; he received his promotion to first lieutenant in 1844.

Following a succession of postings in the South, Thomas and his artillery company were assigned to General Zachary Taylor's army in June 1845. He fought with distinction at Monterrey in 1846 and at Buena Vista in 1847, receiving a brevet as captain, and then as major, for gallantry. Honoring his service, the state of Virginia presented its native son with a silver sword. After the war Thomas was stationed in Texas, and in 1849 he returned to Florida to participate in another Seminole War.

Thomas received an appointment to teach artillery and cavalry at West Point in 1850. The four years he spent at the Military Academy were good for him, although he did engender John Schofield's undying enmity when Thomas voted unsuccessfully to sustain his dismissal from the academy. But his students admired him and affectionately called him "Slow Trot," apparently because he refused to work the old cavalry horses too hard.

Thomas also met his future wife while he was at West Point. A thirty-one-year-old widow and mother of two daughters from Troy, New York, Abigail Paine Kellogg was the daughter of a prosperous hardware and grocery store owner. They married in Troy on November 17, 1852.

Promoted to captain in 1853, Thomas was posted to Fort Yuma in California in 1854 and in 1855 won an assignment as a major in the 2nd Cavalry where he served under Colonel Albert Sidney Johnston and Lieutenant Colonel Robert E. Lee (q.v.). William Hardee was the Cavalry's senior major and Thomas the junior major. John Bell Hood (q.v.) and FitzHugh Lee were lieutenants. Created by Secretary of War Jefferson Davis (q.v.), the 1st and 2nd Cavalries were elite corps of the first purely mounted troops in the U.S. Army, and Thomas learned much that would be useful in later years from the experience. Stationed with the Cavalry at Fort Belknap, Texas, he occasionally led patrols against marauding Comanche Indians. On one such outing he was wounded in the cheek by a brave's arrow.

In August 1860 Thomas received a year's leave of absence. Heading east to join his wife, he may have pondered his fortunate army career. Recognized and rewarded for bravery in the Mexican-American War, Thomas had survived the doldrums of peacetime by exploring his ideas about soldiering at West Point and putting those ideas into practice with the 2nd Cavalry. Indeed, he was uniquely experienced in the three critical areas of warfare—artillery, cavalry, and command.

In Lynchburg, Virginia, Thomas fell on the train platform, injuring his back sufficiently to threaten his military career. He recuperated for eight weeks at his family's Southampton County home. While there, South Carolina seceded from the Union. By the time he reached New York City on January 18, 1861, Mississippi, Florida, and Alabama had seceded. Faced with the prospect of Virginia's secession, Thomas chose to join his fellow Virginians Winfield Scott and Philip St. George Cooke and remain in the Union Army. A convergence of factors no doubt contributed to his decision—his loyalty to the Union, his distaste for slavery, and his Northern wife. His Virginia family disowned him.

After a brief stint reorganizing the 2nd Cavalry at Carlisle, Pennsylvania, Thomas was assigned to Major Robert Anderson and the Department of the Cumberland whose task it was to keep Kentucky in the Union. Thomas was quickly promoted to colonel in the regular army and to brigadier general of volunteers in August 1861. In Kentucky he took charge of the chaotic Camp Dick Robinson, where he organized the First Division of the Army of the Ohio (the core of the Army of the Cumberland) and led 4,000 men into the Battle of Mill Springs (Logan's Cross Roads) in January 1862. This action was the first major clash since the Union debacle at Bull Run, and it was typical of what became Thomas's style of operation. He managed his forces well, brought up reserves at the propitious moment, and completely routed the enemy, killing their commander and driving his troops off in disarray. He suffered 40 killed compared to the Rebels' 529 dead. This battle and Grant's important victories at Forts Henry and Donelson in February and at Shiloh in April helped achieve President Abraham Lincoln's (q.v.) goal of keeping Kentucky in the Union and drove the Confederates into middle Tennessee. Although promoted to major general of volunteers in April 1862, Thomas was miffed that he did not receive a promotion in the regular army, and refused to wear the second star.

During the summer and fall of 1862 Thomas became embroiled in political intrigues not of his making. After the near disaster at Shiloh in April 1862, Grant was made second in command to Henry Halleck (q.v.); Thomas inherited four of Grant's divisions and the command of the Army of the Mississippi. He resisted this appointment, insisting that Grant's troops be restored to him. He was then ordered to succeed Don Carlos Buell as head of the Army of the Ohio. Again he refused, objecting to replacing a commander who had already issued battle orders to engage the Confederates at Perryville. Instead, he became Buell's second in command. While he no doubt had ambitions for his own command, he would not take it under questionable circumstances. Buell was relieved of his command after the Battle of Perryville, and the newly renamed Army of the Cumberland was given to Major General William S. Rosecrans, who began a pursuit of the Confederate Army, which had taken up a position just north of Murfreesboro, Tennessee. Thomas protested Rosecrans's promotion since he was Rosecrans's senior in rank, but since Thomas had twice declined command, the president settled the matter by predating Rosecrans's commission to give him seniority and remarking, "[L]et the Virginian wait." Thomas took command of the army's center corps for the coming campaign.

That campaign resulted in the Battle of Stones River (Murfreesboro), which brought a precious victory to the Union after a terrible defeat at Fredericksburg on December 13, 1862, and at the very moment that the administration launched the Emancipation Proclamation. But it was a close call. Confederate General Braxton Bragg (q.v.) had the battle won after the first day, December 31, 1862.

That night Rosecrans and his commanders discussed withdrawal. There are conflicting reports of who said what, but all note that Thomas advised against leaving, saying something like, "[T]his army can't retreat," or "General, I know of no better place to die than right here." On January 2, 1863, Rosecrans ordered a counterattack and drove the Confederates back. Throughout the action, Thomas held the center, shifting his troops back and forth to support the right and left wings of the Union line.

Rosecrans kept his army at Murfreesboro until late June 1863, when he began maneuvering south, pushing Bragg toward Chattanooga. By late August Bragg had reached the city and moved south of it where his 45,000-man Army of Tennessee took up positions along Chickamauga Creek. Rosecrans, believing Bragg to be in desperate retreat, followed in hot pursuit, allowing his corps to become spread out. Then Bragg hit him. In a fierce three-day battle, Bragg drove Rosecrans from the field by midday of September 20, 1863, sending him in full retreat toward Chattanooga. Only Thomas's 14th Corps remained concentrated on the fabled Snodgrass Ridge and Kelly Field. There he stood like a rock and fought off successive waves of Confederate assaults, holding his position until nightfall. His stern resistance and calm demeanor bolstered his troops' determination and allowed Rosecrans to get safely into Chattanooga. After nightfall he withdrew into the city.

Although the Army of the Cumberland was safely inside Chattanooga, it was also surrounded on three sides by Bragg's army, which cut off rail and road access to the city. Behind the army flowed a rain-swollen Tennessee River. And although Grant was coming with 15,000 men fresh from his triumph at Vicksburg and Ambrose E. Burnside was coming with 30,000 men (he never got there), Rosecrans's army appeared to be in a desperate situation—food and ammunition were in short supply.

Lincoln removed Rosecrans, and Thomas's friends in Washington—Edwin Stanton (q.v.) and Halleck in particular—pressed for him to replace "Rosie." But Lincoln decided to combine the Armies of the Ohio, the Tennessee, and the Cumberland under Grant as the Division of the Mississippi, and he gave Grant the option of retaining Rosecrans or replacing him with Thomas. Grant chose Thomas, who, on October 19, 1863, assumed command of 154,000 men and 274 artillery pieces. He also won promotion to brigadier general in the regular army on October 27, 1863.

Thomas's first task was to open a direct supply route to the beleaguered city, a task accomplished by the end of the month. Grant arrived on October 23, and in an incident that reflected the personal coolness between the two men, Thomas allowed him to sit in rain-soaked clothes before a member of Thomas's staff extended the usual military hospitality.

While Thomas saw to the supply of the Union Army in Chattanooga, Grant devised a plan to break the Rebel siege. Thomas's Cumberland army would hold Bragg at the center along a thirteen-mile front, while General William T.

Sherman's Army of the Tennessee and Joseph Hooker's troops would sweep Bragg's flanks.

On November 23 Grant ordered Thomas's men to make a reconnaissance of the center to verify the rumor that Bragg was in retreat. He was not. Four of Thomas's divisions, with a corps in reserve, drove across the mile and a half through Bragg's pickets, where they entrenched. It was a greater success than Grant might have hoped and intensified the tension between the two men and the rivalry among Union soldiers. Grant ordered Hooker to advance on Bragg's left on November 24; the resulting Battle above the Clouds allowed the Union to capture Lookout Mountain. Grant then ordered Sherman to advance on November 25. Attacking Bragg's right, Sherman got bogged down and was placed on the defensive by fierce Rebel resistance. Grant threw three of Thomas's nine divisions into a rescue operation for Sherman and detached two more to Hooker, who was having trouble against Bragg's left. Grant then asked Thomas to have his four remaining divisions demonstrate in the center to draw Bragg's attention and take the pressure off Sherman and Hooker. Thomas ordered his men to advance. As they did his four divisions of fired-up Cumberlanders swept through Bragg's rifle pits, and exposed to fire from above, they drove on up the 600-foot Missionary Ridge. Against all probability Thomas's troops carried the ridge and sent Bragg's troops fleeing. Grant was furious that Thomas's troops had carried the day and outperformed his friend Sherman. "Thomas, who ordered those men up the ridge?" he demanded. "I don't know," Thomas replied. The commander of Thomas's 4th Corps spoke up: "When those fellows get started all hell can't stop them" (McKinney, 296). Although Thomas had carried the day, Grant got credit for the victory and his career skyrocketed.

After Chattanooga, Grant was promoted to lieutenant general and given command of all the Union armies. Passing over Thomas, Grant named Sherman his successor as head of the Division of the Mississippi. Thomas remained at the head of the Army of the Cumberland and in the center of Sherman's force. While the Federals advanced against the Rebels, Thomas was also responsible for protecting Sherman's movable base.

The advance against Confederate General Joseph E. Johnston (q.v.) was slow. Beginning in early May 1864, the two sides were in almost constant contact as they moved toward Atlanta. After a month Sherman had not caught Johnston and in frustration criticized his three army commanders—especially Thomas, who he accused of being slow. Given the smooth operation of the Union advance, the charge had doubtful validity, though it stuck and was later amplified.

Sherman's frustrations only deepened as his effort to engage Johnston proved futile. On June 27 he fought the Confederates in the Battle of Kenesaw Mountain, an engagement Thomas advised against, with disastrous results for Union soldiers. Still Sherman continued to press the Confederate Army, now led by John Bell Hood. On July 20 Thomas engaged two corps of Hood's army at Peach Tree Creek. The action was a defeat for Hood at the hands of his former West Point professor, and he withdrew into Atlanta.

Under withering Union pressure, Hood took his army out of Atlanta at the end of August. Sherman occupied the city on September 2 and for the next month watched Hood, sent units to protect his communications with Chattanooga and Nashville, and sent numerous requests to Grant to authorize his scheme to march to Savannah. On October 1 Hood moved his battered army north across the Chattahoochee River, heading for Sherman's communications. Sherman, who had dispatched Thomas to Nashville to supervise the rearguard operation, gave chase. By October 31 Hood reached the Tennessee River and put a division across at Florence, Alabama, making clear his intention to move north toward the Ohio River. On November 2 Sherman received permission to march to the sea. Leaving Hood to Thomas, he sent Major General John M. Schofield's 23rd Corps, General Thomas J. Wood's 4th Corps, General James H. Wilson's Cavalry Corps, and Andrew J. Smith's third division to Nashville. Thomas requested his crack 14th Corps from the Cumberland army, but Sherman took it with him to Savannah. Thomas's task was to defend Tennessee and the Ohio River from Hood's army.

That defense became the Battle of Nashville, which some have called the decisive battle of the war.

After cobbling together an army, Thomas sent Scofield's corps and Wilson's cavalry to slow Hood down at Franklin, some fifteen miles south of Nashville. On November 30 Hood slammed into Schofield's defenses with disastrous results, sustaining 6,000 casualties. Meanwhile, Thomas's army began coming together.

While preparing to give battle to Hood, Thomas also had to struggle with his commanding officer, U. S. Grant. Thomas thought he would attack Hood on the tenth, by which time Wilson's cavalry would be fully mounted. By the ninth Grant was convinced that Thomas would not move and wanted to replace him with Schofield, who certainly intrigued for the place. Halleck prevailed on the lieutenant general to wait. By the eleventh Grant could wait no longer and ordered Thomas to attack. But an ice storm had made the ground treacherous, and Thomas refused to send his men forward on such dangerous footing. By the fifteenth Grant was so frustrated that he sent John A. Logan to Louisville with an order relieving Thomas of command. Meanwhile, he himself had left his headquarters at City Point, Virginia, and was in Washington en route to Nashville to take personal command of the situation. Again he issued an order relieving Thomas, but before that order was sent, news of Thomas's victory arrived in Washington. By the end of the following day Thomas had broken Hood's army, and on the seventeenth, it was on the run with Federals in hot pursuit.

Thomas received promotion to major general in the regular army on December 15, 1864, and he accepted accolades from his fellow officers, from the president, and in March 1865, from Congress. In the months following his decisive victory over Hood, his Army of the Cumberland was broken up and sent to other commanders. Grant and Sherman put it out that although Thomas had won at Nashville, he had been too slow and his pursuit of Hood inadequate. A deliberate commander who planned well and prepared fully before moving, Thomas lacked the bold impetuosity of a Sherman or a Grant. Yet, his action at Nashville was one of the few times that a commander coordinated the use of infantry, artillery, and cavalry to destroy the opposing army.

After the war Thomas remained in Nashville in command of the western departments. He was briefly caught up in Reconstruction politics when President Andrew Johnson (q.v.) offered to promote him to brevet lieutenant general and appoint him to Grant's place. Thomas refused the honor. In 1868 there was an effort to place his name in nomination for president. Again he refused. In 1869 he became commander of the Military Division of the Pacific with headquarters in San Francisco. He died there suddenly, apparently of a stroke, on March 28, 1870. Following Thomas's instructions, his aide burned his papers. His remains were brought to the East in a funeral train, and he was buried at his wife's home in Troy, New York. None of his Virginia family attended the funeral.

Although Thomas told his friend Thomas B. Van Horne that "time and history will do me justice," (Van Horne, v) he died preparing to defend his reputation from General Jacob D. Cox's *New York Tribune* article that asserted that General John M. Schofield was responsible for the Nashville victory. In 1875 William Tecumseh Sherman amplified the charges in his *Memoirs*, reproducing correspondence between himself and Grant in which they questioned Thomas's actions and marveled at his slowness.

Yet Thomas had his defenders. In an address to the Society of the Army of the Cumberland in November 1870, James Garfield, who stood with him at Chickamauga, compared Thomas to George Washington. Such high praise continued in annual addresses to the Cumberland veterans and at the unveiling of the Thomas statue in Washington. On that day in November 1879 Stanley Matthews likened him to a "sturdy oak," a "resolute" man "without pretension, boasting, self-assertion or noisy demonstration." (5) In addition to the many speeches and pamphlets produced in the years following his death, four full biographies of Thomas appeared before the end of the century. The first, Richard W. Johnson's *Memoir of Major-General George H. Thomas* came in 1881. Thomas B. Van Horne's *The Life of Major-General George H. Thomas* quickly followed in 1882. Johnson served with Thomas, and Van Horne was chaplain to the Army of the Cumberland and, by Thomas's order, the army's official historian. They both defended his reputation against the charge that he was slow at Nashville.

In 1885, however, Ulysses Grant threw his considerable reputation into the controversy. In his *Memoirs* Grant criticized Thomas for not reinforcing Schofield at Franklin and for taking a defensive posture at Nashville. Grant tried to soften his criticism of Thomas, saying "he could not be driven from a point he was given to hold," but he depreciated his value as a field commander. "I do not believe," he said, "that [Thomas] could ever have conducted Sherman's army from Chattanooga to Atlanta" (2:525).

In two 1893 biographies, Henry Coppee, and Donn Piatt and Henry Van Ness Boynton defended Thomas against these attacks and in 1896 Boynton challenged the accusation that Thomas was slow at Nashville. Charles Dana (q.v.) also praised Thomas's generalship and his integrity in his *Recollections of the Civil War* (1896).

The debate over Thomas revived in the twentieth century in books about Grant and Sherman. The response to this anti-Thomas onslaught began in 1937 with the "Note on Thomas at Nashville" in Walter Wood and James Edmond's *Military History of the Civil War* (1937). Wood and Edmonds found Sherman culpable for leaving Thomas shorthanded at Nashville and commended the Virginian for building a fighting force capable of dealing a knockout blow to Hood. Since then, five biographers have defended Thomas. There were two biographies in 1948: Richard O'Connor's *Thomas: Rock of Chickamauga* and Freeman Cleaves's *Rock of Chickamauga*. Cleaves's is a well-documented and -balanced account. Francis McKinney's *Education in Violence* (1961) is the most thorough and thoughtful treatment of Thomas. He shows the General to be a superior field commander who was ambitious for advancement but would not advance himself at others' expense. Wilbur Thomas's *General George H. Thomas: The Indomitable Warrior* (1964) tries too hard to put Thomas in a consistently good light. An excellent small work by Hans Juergensen, *Major General George Henry Thomas: A Summary in Perspective* (1980) puts the Thomas historiographic disputes in perspective. Finally, there are two fine pieces that go far toward assuring Thomas's reputation as one of the Union's top generals: Herman Hattaway and Michael L. Gillespie's "Soldier of Conscience" (1984) and Peter Andrews's "The Rock of Chickamauga" (1990).

All of these works reflect the emerging consensus that while Thomas may not have been the geopolitical and strategic visionary of a Grant or a Sherman, he was the epitome of a battlefield commander. He planned, he thoroughly prepared, he gave clear orders to his subordinate commanders, and he sought to defeat the enemy while always caring for the welfare of his men. As Juergensen says, Thomas "was [never] surprised with his tents up and his rifles down" (18).

BIBLIOGRAPHY

William Swinton, *The Twelve Decisive Battles of the Civil War* (New York: Dick and Fitzgerald, 1867).

Stanley Matthews, *Unveiling of Ward's Equestrian Statue of Major-General George H. Thomas* (Cincinnati, Ohio: Robert Clarke & Co., 1879).

Richard W. Johnson, *Memoir of Major-General George H. Thomas* (Philadelphia: J. B. Lippincott, 1881).

Thomas B. Van Horne, *The Life of Major-General George H. Thomas* (New York: Charles Scribner's Sons, 1882).

Ulysses S. Grant, *Memoirs*, 2 vols. (New York: Charles L. Webster and Co., 1885).

William T. Sherman, *Memoirs* (New York: D. Appleton and Company, 1886).

Henry Coppee, *General Thomas* (New York: D. Appleton, 1893).

Donn Piatt and Henry Van Ness Boynton, *General George H. Thomas: A Critical Biography* (Cincinnati, Ohio: Robert Clarke, 1893).

Henry Van Ness Boynton, *Was Thomas Slow at Nashville?* (New York: Francis P. Harper, 1896).

Charles Dana, *Recollections of the Civil War* (New York: D. Appleton and Co., 1898).

Walter Wood and James Edmond, *Military History of the Civil War* (New York: G. P. Putnam's Sons, 1937).

Freeman Cleaves, *Rock of Chickamauga* (Norman: University of Oklahoma Press, 1948).

Richard O'Connor, *Thomas: Rock of Chickamauga* (New York: Prentice-Hall, Inc., 1948).

Francis McKinney, *Education in Violence* (Detroit: Wayne State University Press, 1961).

Wilbur Thomas, *General George H. Thomas: The Indomitable Warrior* (New York: Exposition Press, 1964).

Ezra J. Warner, *Generals in Blue* (Baton Rouge: Louisiana State University Press, 1964).

Hans Juergensen, *Major General George Henry Thomas: A Summary in Perspective* (Tampa, Fla.: American Studies Press, 1980).

Herman Hattaway and Michael L. Gillespie, "Soldier of Conscience: George H. Thomas, A Virginian Fights for the Union," *Virginia Cavalcade* 34, no. 2 (1984): 64–69.

Peter Andrews, "The Rock of Chickamauga," *American Heritage* 41, no. 2 (March 1990): 81–91.

WALT(ER) WHITMAN
(May 31, 1819–March 26, 1891)

Jon L. Wakelyn

How does a mere poet become one of the Civil War's great captains? Walt Whitman held no wartime elective office, wrote no major treatise on that war, contributed too little journalism to influence events, fired no weapon, and influenced none of the war's events in any formal way. Yet that "Good Gray Poet" who spent much of the war attending sick soldiers and holding petty bureaucratic jobs indeed became a great captain. Whitman had hoped to write a definitive history of the war but never did. Even his most powerful weapon, his pen, which in letters, prose, and poetry so brilliantly captured the war's meaning, only partially explains why he ranks as one of that war's greatest leaders. His most important task, to nurture the sick, which commemorated what he called the "divine average," goes some way to make his wartime actions symbolically important. But there is more—there is the image of the man himself in history, self-created, to be sure. In that image, Whitman embodied the values of the country. In his personal dilemma over support of central government power versus the need to protect individual freedoms, he embodied the dilemma of the Union. Most important, in his view of one nation, both North and South, Whitman created an image of himself as symbolizing the Union itself. Thus, the man and writer, despite failing most tests of great leadership, truly became a great leader.

Where did Whitman develop this image of Union, and how would he become so obsessed with embodying that image in his own person? Perhaps through a look at the way he lived his life, combined with how he expressed and created himself, the answer will become apparent. Whitman of course attempted to control what history would say was most important in his own character formation. In *Specimen Days* he wrote of his Dutch and English heritage, the combination of pastoral Long Island and "teeming" Brooklyn and New York, and "my experiences afterward in the secession outbreak" (15). Certainly these themes have been studied by almost all of his many biographers, and perhaps far too many writers have picked over them without attempting to set those influences in the context of the world that spawned him. Fortunately, Whitman's most recent biographer, David S. Reynolds, has sought to "overcome the piecemeal approaches to literary history" (xi) in order to understand the events of his life that created Whitman the man of his times. Reynolds perhaps does not go so far as to claim Whitman was a great Civil War leader, but his seminal biography, a work of critical contextual and textual reconstruction, has set a standard as a guide to understand the life of the most representative man of that great war period.

The life of that future poet began on the family farm in West Hill, on far eastern Long Island, New York, on May 31, 1819. The son of Walter Whitman, farmer, house builder, carpenter, and oft-failed entrepreneur, and Louisa Van Velsor, Walt early experienced the instability of paternal business enterprise and the stability created around him by his Dutch-descended mother. Though Louisa grew increasingly eccentric with age, it was she to whom young Walt poured out his early hopes and fears and confided in throughout her long life. The early life of the poet was suffused with tales of the Revolutionary War. Himself descended from Revolutionary War heroes, the young man was made aware of the greatness of the Union's heritage. He also grew up in a rural agricultural world still containing slaves and indentured farmhands. Although the family would settle and resettle a number of times, due to his father's pitiful attempt to provide for their large numbers, the connection with that rich soil and the myriad of stories about life on the tip of Long Island would never leave him and would influence the images he would create of himself and of his society.

In 1823, the elder Walter uprooted his family and moved to the bustling city of Brooklyn across the East River from Manhattan in order to "make a killing" through building houses for that burgeoning population. While living in Brooklyn they moved constantly, usually keeping just ahead of bill and rent collectors. Walt attended Brooklyn public schools from 1825 to 1830, in which he acquired his only formal education, what little of it there was. He also went to local churches and learned much while attending services, not the least of which was the power of the cadences and refrains in the delivered word of the pastors. In 1830 he left school for good to go to work and earn wages to help feed his family. First he worked as an office boy for a local lawyer; then he became apprenticed to a newspaper. At the paper he learned all the procedures of producing a printed and bound sheet, a skill that would be useful in later life. Here also he began to write, to develop a feel for words. Walt also read a great deal of fiction and a few sermons and mechanics tracts. He often went over to Manhattan to the theater, which exacerbated his fantasy world as well as his feel for how words were spoken and the physical gestures of expression. The bustle of street life, the smell of urban filth, the quickness of the pace all excited the future poet and taught him much about the underside of life.

In 1833, Walt's father gave up on Brooklyn and took his large family back to West Hills, Long Island. Walt remained in Brooklyn, working for a newspaper. In 1835 he took a position as a compositor in Manhattan. He lived in rooming houses and rarely had enough income to send any home. When his father, in 1836, sold the farm that had been in the family for generations, Walt went back to Long Island to help out. Like many a self-educated, intelligent young man, he scratched a living teaching school, often moving among different communities. Somewhere near the village of Babylon, around 1837, Reynolds and others have pointed out, Walt was involved in some kind of imbroglio with the local town fathers. Although the actual details of the incident have never been established, it probably concerned young boys and ended in Walt's being tarred and feathered and run out of town. Reynolds believed the episode had a lasting influence on the sexual activities of Whitman and informed much of what he wrote during the period before the Civil War.

Certainly, for a time, Walt gave up the formal teaching of young boys. In 1838 he founded a newspaper in Huntington. In 1839, having lost his own paper, he became a writer for another newspaper. Then from 1839 to 1840, he again taught school. Whitman appeared to wander from job to job and to have little purpose in life. In reality he was sharpening his writing skills, learning to observe carefully, and becoming interested in events of the day. A committed Jacksonian Democrat, in 1841 he took a job in Manhattan on John L. O'Sullivan's partisan *Democratic Review*. In 1845, in order to be with his family and to assist in its support, he moved again to Brooklyn, where from 1846 to 1848 he edited the *Brooklyn Daily Eagle*. Though he moved often and had a number of friends, he remained close to his own brothers and sisters. While employed at the *Eagle*, ideas about his own relationship with the growing nation began to appear in his experiments in writing. Most of his efforts were journalistic pieces, at times lurid in nature, about the seamier side of urban life. He learned much about those lives from covering trials and reading police reports. He also wrote short stories, poems, and novels, which never were published. Much of this literary work appeared autobiographical in nature, although patriotic and sensational themes crept into those early efforts. His published novel, *Franklin Evans* (1842), ostensibly was targeted to appeal to the growing movement for temperance. Excessive drink had destroyed the central character of the story. Yet Reynolds and others who have studied the novel wonder whether Whitman actually had been trying to exploit the growing market in sensational literature. Certainly Whitman the newspaper man wrote in a realistic narrative style, as he was well aware of the current interest many readers had in the underworld of the urban Northeast. Thus, his early work of fiction is difficult to separate from the realism found in his newspaper pieces.

Whitman was sensitive to how people spoke and what they talked about. In his articles and fiction, Reynolds says, Whitman evoked "colorful personalities and rough language" (100). He also hung around the Union organizer and Irish tough Mike Walsh, and he picked up the slang of the Bowry B'hoys. But Whitman also worried about city crime and other problems brought on by urban poverty. He was intensely aware of the anti-Catholic sentiment that fueled political crises.

During those expansionist days, Whitman eagerly supported the Mexican War, perhaps because like many others he believed in the opportunities for ordinary people that derived from the continued expansion of an agricultural world. He also turned against slavery during that war, and in 1848 that got him fired from the *Daily Eagle*. Later that year, he took a younger brother to New Orleans, where he had landed a position on the *Daily Cresent*. Whitman loved that cosmopolitan, mixed racial and ethnic community, and there he developed feelings for a complex Southern society that he would never shed. Soon, though, he returned to Brooklyn to work for Free Soil politicians and to manage a bookstore and print shop.

Keenly aware of the rise of sectional politics, he wrote in opposition to the Compromise of 1850 and turned antiparty and antigovernment. He came to regard Democratic party leadership as incompetent and corrupt, and he became a bit of an agitator. But he also called himself a "supreme" Unionist who hoped for the gradual elimination of slavery. Whitman lived a nomadic life in a violent urban environment, roiled by ethnic, religious, and racial tensions. His response to chaos all around him was to announce his belief in the law and his devotion to all of his country.

This was the setting in which, in 1855, he had printed the first edition of his monumental—though hardly regarded so at the time—*Leaves of Grass*. Many who have studied that remarkable work have wondered how a journeyman journalist was able to create such sensitive poetry. Reynolds offers the theory that Whitman's great poem was driven by his belief in the nation's potential and the role he could have in it personally. Whitman the poet had become a participant in society, and the boundary between art and life had dissolved. That made him want to appear spontaneous, to capture in the cadence of his language the music of the people. Contained in *Leaves of Grass*, therefore, were the nationalist beliefs of the new Republican party, a plea in Victorian America for reform, the optimism of a growing business community, and the charged sexual atmosphere of "a seamy underside" to society (195). For Reynolds, Whitman was "haunted by the increasing conflict between the individual and the man, as in the harsh sectional conflicts of the fifties, he created a harmonic social space in his poems where individuality and togetherness flourished" (274). Thus rebelliousness was combined with a desire for unity. Idiomatic, filled with current slang, with a sure sense of American dialect, Whitman hoped to embody in *Leaves of Grass*, maintains Reynolds, the many "different cultural images of the nation" (322). With *Leaves of Grass*, then, Whitman wanted to make himself the spokesman for all of the conflicting feelings of the country.

Despite the fact that the first edition eventually sold out, and that it achieved critical acclaim, Whitman insisted that few readers had listened to his poem's healing message. As Reynolds and other biographers have said, thus began the poet's self-created image of himself as the outsider, never to gain real popular acceptance of his gifts. It is known that Ralph Waldo Emerson praised him and that the self-promoting Whitman would abuse that support when he reprinted Emerson's letter to him in his second edition. In that second edition Whitman also sought to promote himself as the poet of Union. But he grew disillusioned when his efforts were not seen as speaking for the country's values. To support himself he took on the editorship of the sensationalist *Brooklyn Daily Times*. True to form, he went too far in his editorial writing, as he proclaimed his sympathy for the South while attacking Democratic party political corruption. He was fired in 1859. But Whitman had other plans for himself, as he persuaded the Boston publishing house of Thayer and Eldridge in 1860 to print a third edition of *Leaves of Grass*. In this edition he specifically announced that his purpose was to heal the nation. His poem "Out of the Cradle Endlessly Rocking" was a political diatribe in which the poet searched for a leader to heal the nation's wounds. In that third edition, Whitman had cursed all dis-Unionists, as he announced when the Civil War broke out, "I will make the continent indissoluble" (Reynolds, 402).

After the war had begun, Whitman remained a civilian and watched when his younger brother George and others went off to fight. Too old for active duty, he seemed content to record his patriotism in "Beat, Beat the Drum." In that poem, the freelance journalist wrote of war as necessary and predicted it would have a stabilizing effect on the nation. Reynolds says the Civil War would give Whitman purpose, "would give him the sense of completion he lacked" (406). But he published little poetry during the war. Only his notebooks, which were in part printed in his postwar autobiographical writing *Specimen Days*, published in his 1883 volume entitled *Prose Works*, revealed the war's impact on him and how his own activities had embodied the war's purpose. Whitman seemed destined to spend the war in New York writing about its local impact.

But in December 1862, when he received word that his brother had been wounded at Fredericksburg, Virginia, he rushed south to be with him. George's wounds were only superficial. However, the stories George related to him about the horrors of combat, and seeing so many wounded young soldiers, led the poet to move to Washington to be close to the action. Whitman even tried to get to the front lines to participate somehow. Instead, the poet settled for a part-time position in 1863 in the army paymaster's office. While holding that job, he managed to write a few war stories for Northern papers. In 1865 he took a government clerkship. But mainly he spent the years in Washington visiting sick soldiers in the many hospitals around the capital. In his notebooks, Whitman recorded his impressions of those boys as well as of the leading figures of the war, most importantly President Abraham Lincoln (q.v.). Whitman lived simply in rooming houses, but his seeming unimportant activities would indeed become a part of the symbolic meaning of that frightful, bloodletting attempt to bind the nation's wounds.

Above all, Whitman made many visits, estimated at some 600, to countless thousands of wounded veterans of both the blue and gray persuasions who suffered in those often makeshift hospitals or places where soldiers waited to die. Descriptions of Whitman's behavior at that time revealed a man who nurtured the sick with gifts and with his own presence. Words of comfort, holding the hands of dying youth, and writing letters to their families occupied the poet. His various part-time jobs sustained him and allowed him precious hours with the soldiers. Some of those boys would become his friends; most remained anonymous. One biographer believes that Whitman's actions embodied both male and female sentiments, as he became a mother and father figure for the boys. Most important, he took unto himself the grief of the war of destruction. He grasped the horrors of the modern killing machine and sought to curb its expression. In those activities in the hospital Whitman also tried to understand the meaning of union and his role in sustaining it. He claimed to be on the side of the Union, to see the soldiers as fighting to restore the nation and himself through them as the great restorer.

Perhaps that is why Whitman so identified with President Lincoln. Before the war he had attacked weak leaders as unable to bind the nation, as corrupt and failed politicians. Lincoln's resistance to disunion and his sympathy for both sides at the same time resonated with the poet. He even imagined he saw the president on the streets of Washington, advised him, and soothed his weeping visage. Certainly Whitman's major poems about the fallen chieftain—"O Captain! My Captain!" and "When Lilacs Last in the Dooryard Bloom'd"—have come down in history as capturing the public sorrow over his death. More than that, says Walter Lowenfels, the editor of *Walt Whitman's Civil War* (1961), Whitman "identified" with the subject matter of the poems (xi). Reynolds believed that "in Lincoln's death, he saw a grand strategy that promised ultimate purgation and unification" (438). Certainly that is so, as both Lincoln's and Whitman's activities embodied the meaning of Union. Throughout the remainder of his life Whitman would wrap himself in the image of Lincoln. In his writings and his many speeches on Lincoln's character, he merged both personalities. Nurse and leader, in his mind, had emerged as one image.

Just after the war had ended, Whitman was fired from his government job because his kind was not considered proper for public service. His good friend, William D. O'Connor, published in early 1868 an article in defense of Whitman's war activities in which he called him "the Good Gray Poet" and thus created the image of America's poet spokesperson. For years Whitman had hoped for that designation; now he had linked his life and poetry with the meaning of his country's war. His immediate postwar writings, especially *Drum Taps*, published in October 1865, enlarged upon his patriotism. In them as well, he attempted to heal the sectional wounds. Whitman also defended new President Andrew Johnson (q.v.) when he pardoned many of the enemy. He believed Johnson was bent on reconciling state and federal interests, in supporting the individual as a part of the whole country. Never really supportive of racial equality, he hoped to ease the transition from slavery to freedom and to protect the South from too-rapid change. Whitman believed himself to represent the entire nation, and he called for the country once again to unite after the bloody war.

But all was not peaceful in the emerging industrial world of Reconstruction America, so the nation's poet felt he had to write about the dangers of rapid change. In his one attempt at political philosophy, *Democratic Vistas* (1871), once again he worried that social problems were unsolvable. Though he would never give up on President U. S. Grant (q.v.), the military hero who had helped to restore the Union, Whitman gravely worried about the political corruption that surrounded the warrior president. Depressed, he wondered, Had the Civil War failed? No, he said. The poet who embodied the values of that war could go only so far in his criticism. Instead, Whitman turned to the new great business leaders and found in them the values of Union and the hope for a growing country. Reynolds believes that Whitman had become the ''celebrant of main-stream institutions'' (494). The neglected outsider had for a time entered the mainstream. But his poetic talents faltered and he had trouble describing events, even as he tried to capture on paper those postwar dynamics. Still, praise for technology, the syncopation of the sound of machinery, and the noise of the industrial army, in his ''Song of Exposition,'' announced his role as an advocate for growth.

Soon the overworked and overwrought poet began to fade. The years of be-lieved neglect and the need to become the public spokesman for the age had worn him down. In January 1873 Whitman had a major stroke that left him paralyzed for months and probably sapped his writing talents. That year he moved to his final city, of all places Camden, New Jersey, across the Delaware River from Philadelphia. There, in that industrial town where his engineer brother George lived, Whitman at first was depressed. He seemed ambivalent over where the nation was headed. But he was determined to have a public image. Again the neglected outsider sought to make himself important. His first biographer, a friend named Richard M. Burke, actually allowed Whitman to edit his text in 1884. Once again the good poet turned optimistic, especially after a visit to America's West where he saw capitalism in action. Again, he linked the Civil War to progress, and Lincoln to the country's future. In his famous 1887 Lincoln lecture in Manhattan, in part paid for by industrialist Andrew Carnegie, he described the martyred president as fulfilling the image of sacred patriotism. If he at times worried about excessive materialism and centralization's threat to the individual, too much had been sacrificed to save the Union for the poet to turn into a pessimist.

Wrapping himself in the patriotism of proclaiming the Union, and his efforts during the war, perhaps more even than his poems, at last had made him famous. During the late 1880s he worked for the mainstream newspaper press and wrote often for the *Herald Tribune*. As he grew sicker and weaker, Whitman again dealt with themes of the Civil War and with the image of Lincoln. He wanted always to be identified with the fallen hero. At the funeral of General Philip Sheridan (q.v.) he praised military power and accomplishment. When Whitman himself died on March 26, 1891, his funeral became a national occasion. The once outsider, the man who had felt himself neglected, at least for intellectual and political America, had succeeded in making his own life the embodiment of his country's values of unity and hard work.

Of course Whitman had been his own best publicity agent and had done much to promote his own accomplishments. Certainly he had encouraged O'Connor's view of the representative "Good Gray Poet." He had edited his first biographer. He had created his public image around Lincoln and the Civil War. Burke, in his 1884 biography, had made the Civil War the turning point in the poet's life, proclaiming the war had changed him from a young man to an old man. If Whitman repelled some, and left the intellectuals cold, Burke had insisted that the people loved him. But the opposite was true. Since his death, the literary community has published hundreds of studies on all facets of his work, his personal life, and what he has meant to the country. Whitman himself would probably chuckle over how he had become the intellectuals' famous and representative poet.

Most of the best of the writings on Whitman's life and work have generally agreed with the image Whitman created for himself. One of the most thoughtful biographies, published during the worrisome days World War II, that of Henry Seidel Canby, *Walt Whitman an American*, believed that the poet's life would help Americans "feel the strength and continuity of their own traditions" (iii). For Canby, Whitman's own experiences in the Civil War constituted his most important legacy to his countrymen. But Canby was also part of the ahistorical new critics, and he worried that writing about where Whitman fit into his times would lose sight of his poetic genius. Richard Chase, in *Walt Whitman Reconsidered* (1955), fulfilled Canby's fears when he claimed that Whitman's work and life were "committed to the radical literary and cultural values of his time" (186). The war experience, for Chase, made Whitman a radical critic of industrial America. Probably nothing could have been further from the truth.

At the same time the ahistorical critics were writing, historical biographers were trying to place Whitman in his times and as representative of his times. Gay Wilson Allen's *The Solitary Singer* (1955), based on years of research, had trouble with placing Whitman's homoerotic poetry into the mainstream of his times. Allen, however, succumbed to Whitman's own self-representation and made his public activities crucial to understanding the poet's place in the country's history. With insight, he stated that in *Drum Taps* Whitman's life and the book became the same. Too, the French writer Roger Asselineau, in *The Evolution of Walt Whitman* (1960), who began his study during the German occupation of France, saw in Whitman's life the belief in optimism. Poignantly, he stated: "[H]e dreamed of himself as a prophet of a new evangel and it was in that aspect that he portrayed himself" (15). The image Asselineau used was of the mystical healer. Postmodern critic Betsy Erkkila, in *Whitman the Political Poet* (1989), has tried to make him a political leftist for use today. Her work goes into much detail on Whitman's political and personal views, linking his homosexuality and his left-wing politics. But even she sees the Civil War as central to his experience, and she called him the man who bound up the nation's wounds. Most important, Erkkila focused on Whitman's *Specimen Days*, which included his "Memoranda during the War," not published until 1882, as a valuable work that revealed the poet's beliefs and sense of himself. She admits that in those musings Whitman identified completely with the idea of nation, and all that he did he did to bring the country together.

Walter Lowenfels, who has done much to put Whitman together with the war, in *Walt Whitman's Civil War* (1961), insisted that Whitman lived the war. If he saw the young soldiers at the heart of the war, he also identified himself and his poetry with the war. Whitman himself, pointed out Lowenfels, said the Civil War was "the distinguishing event of my time" (3). Further: "I consider the War of attempted secession—not as a struggle of two distinct and separate people, but a conflict between the passions and paradoxes of one and the same identity" (286). David Reynolds, Whitman's best modern biographer, concludes his book on the context of Whitman's writings, actions, and beliefs with, "[N]o writer is regarded as more indisputably American than Whitman." And "by fully absorbing his time, he became a writer for all times" (590). Whitman thus belongs in the pantheon of great Civil War leaders because the very life he lived in the war made him the image of the healer who would do anything to reunite his nation. That belief in nation was the Union's most powerful weapon, and Whitman became the embodiment of that weapon.

BIBLIOGRAPHY

Walt Whitman, *Franklin Evans* (1842; New York: Random House, 1929).

Walt Whitman, *Leaves of Grass* (1855; New York: Mitchell Kennerley, 1914).

Walt Whitman, *Drum Taps* (1865; Gainesville, Fla.: Scholars' Facsimiles & Reprints, 1959).

Walt Whitman, *Specimen Days and Prose Works* (Philadelphia: Rees, Welsh & Co., 1882–83).

Richard Maurice Burke, *Walt Whitman* (Glasgow: Wilson and McCormick, 1884).

Walt Whitman, *Complete Prose Works* (Boston: Small, Maynard and Co., 1898).

Henry Seidel Canby, *Walt Whitman an American* (Boston: Houghton Mifflin Co., 1943).

Gay Wilson Allen, *The Solitary Singer: A Critical Biography of Walt Whitman* (New York: Macmillan Co., 1955).

Richard Chase, *Walt Whitman Reconsidered* (New York: William Sloane Associates, Inc., 1955).

Roger Asselineau, *The Evolution of Walt Whitman: The Creation of a Personality* (Cambridge: Harvard University Press, 1960).

Walter Lowenfels, ed., *Walt Whitman's Civil War* (New York: Alfred A. Knopf, 1961).

Betsy Erkkila, *Whitman the Political Poet* (New York: Oxford University Press, 1989).

David S. Reynolds, *Walt Whitman's America: A Cultural Biography* (New York: Alfred A. Knopf, 1996).

LOUIS TREZEVANT WIGFALL
(April 21, 1816–February 18, 1874)

Clayton E. Jewett

As a Confederate States senator from Texas, Louis T. Wigfall served in the Richmond government throughout the Civil War. In his capacity as chairman of important committees, he helped to make important political decisions in behalf of the Confederate war effort. As a close friend of leading generals Pierre G. T. Beauregard (q.v.) and Joseph E. Johnston (q.v.), Wigfall supported their careers throughout the war. He had been one of the slave states' most radical secessionists before the war. But during the war, he turned against the administration of President Jefferson Davis (q.v.) and, some thought, hindered the war effort. Why such a powerful public figure's onetime loyal convictions turned to opposition requires careful assessment of his political life and his Civil War career.

Louis Wigfall was born on April 21, 1816, in Edgefield, South Carolina, a place that many historians have called a breeding ground for extreme Southern conservatism. Wigfall came from an elite family. The Trezevants, his mother's side, descended from the French Huguenots and established themselves as part of the Tidewater aristocracy. Wigfall bolstered his ties with the Trezevant line in 1841 by marrying his second cousin, Charlotte Maria Cross. Likewise, the Wigfalls resided as one of the region's elite families. Louis's father, Levi Durand Wigfall, did well as a merchant in Charleston and bought a plantation in Edgefield, where Louis was born.

As a young man, Louis Wigfall did not have the guiding influence of his parents. His father died when Louis was just two years of age, and his mother passed away when he was thirteen years old. This proved a major factor in shaping Wigfall's course of life and his character. Without his parents' guiding hand, Wigfall became a product of his surroundings, mostly influenced by the words of John C. Calhoun, James Hamilton, and other nullifiers and state's righters, a result of growing up in Edgefield, South Carolina.

At age eighteen, Wigfall attended Rice Creek Springs School, a private military academy for elite children. From there he spent one year of school at the University of Virginia (1834–1835) and then graduated from South Carolina College in 1837. During his college years, Wigfall nurtured a proclivity for drink and dueling and became enthralled more by the military than the academic or religious aspects of education. Wigfall geared his actions and interests toward carving his own path in life without the aid of others, a struggle not uncommon for young men in those days. The patriarchal society in which Wigfall lived, posits historian Bertram Wyatt-Brown, "left young men desperate for purpose in life" (359). For Wigfall, the lack of parental figures intensified this search. His indulgences were a means for self-identification and self-vindication and a mark of "uncontrollable ambition" (359). This combination of violence and ambition became a defining characteristic in Wigfall's political career.

Wigfall first entered politics in 1844, elected as a delegate to the South Carolina state Democratic convention. His political career in that state did not last long, primarily due to his unpopularity for the dueling death of Thomas Bird and his subsequent battle with Preston Brooks. Historian C. W. Lord, in "Young Louis Wigfall: South Carolina Politician and Duelist," details his early political and personal struggles ending in violence but offers no analysis of these events nor of Wigfall's life after leaving South Carolina. Wigfall's principal biographer, Alvy King, argues, though, that Wigfall's predisposition for violence and pistols earned him the community's disrespect. Edgefield residents did not view him as an honorable man. As a direct result of his dueling and bad reputation, Wigfall left South Carolina for Texas. With no money and a worse reputation for violence, he sought to recapture the standing and honor that his family name symbolized in South Carolina.

His political career in Texas took off almost from the start. A successful lawyer, Wigfall carried into politics the reputation of being an avid state's righter and a strict constitutionalist. In 1849 he won election to the Texas House of Representatives. Historian J. L. Bagwell's study, focusing on the antebellum career of Wigfall with an emphasis on state and local affairs, reveals that early on Texans moved to support strong state's righters such as Wigfall. In 1850 the *Marshall Texas Republican* reported, "[T]he crisis that has arrived in the state of affairs requires that we should elect no one to fill the position unless he is sound upon Southern and Texas Rights. To this, all others must yield" (August 31, 1850). The *Austin Texas State Gazette* reported on Wigfall's Southern extremism and election in a positive note, saying, "[H]is course as a legislator will be firm and truly democratic, according to the Jeffersonian standard erected when democracy meant PRINCIPLE and not PARTY" (Wigfall Family Papers, BC Library).

Wigfall was not only a man of principle but a man devoted to party. During the 1850s Wigfall earned the reputation of being Sam Houston's principal antagonist. Wigfall railed against Houston's opposition to the Kansas-Nebraska Act and his affiliation with the Know-Nothing party, causing Houston to lose popular support. Wigfall's obsession with defeating Sam Houston at every turn helped organize the Democratic party in Texas. A member of the Texas Democratic Committee on Platforms, Wigfall endorsed the acceptance of the 1856 national Cincinnati Platform, holding that Congress had no right to interfere with slavery in the states or territories. By the mid-1850s, Wigfall stood as the strongest voice in the state Democratic party and earned the reputation of being a radical state's righter.

As a Southern Rights Democrat, Wigfall won a seat in the Texas State Senate in 1857. An ambitious man, he deeply coveted a place in the U.S. Congress. In 1859, he vacated his state senate seat to run for the U.S. Senate. The most recent work on Wigfall's U.S. Senate election, Billy D. Ledbetter's 1973 article "The Election of Louis T. Wigfall to the United States Senate, 1859: A Reevaluation" posits that his triumphant election resulted from "the Texas Democrats' desire to redeem the party from the defeat that it had so recently suffered; to a lesser extent it was a reward for his service and devotion to the party" (242). Viewing his election strictly as a product of party politics, however, obscures the fact that Wigfall found favor in the eyes of many Texans due to his strong pro-Southern, pro-slavery stance. Texas politics in the 1850s was still highly per-sonalized with people voting on principle and personality, not just by party affiliation. It is ironic that Wigfall, while attached to the most conservative strains of Southern politics and ideology, was not a man of property nor a great slaveholder. His election, however, signified the embodiment of Calhoun ide-ology in Texas.

By 1860, Wigfall's reputation had grown across Texas and the South. He avidly pressed to reopen the slave trade, sought expansion into Latin America for more slave territory, and pronounced the right and duty of secession for all Southerners. Wigfall defended the right of slavery and secession on constitu-tional grounds in order to make sense of Southern rights and the *peculiar in-stitution* beyond the confines of race. Shortly before the election of Abraham Lincoln (q.v.), whose prospective victory raised the fears of most Texans, Wig-fall delivered a speech in Tyler, Texas. He argued that states existed as separate political communities. As a result, Texas had the right to call a state convention for the purpose of deciding its relationship with the federal government. Wigfall argued that the federal government trampled on the rights of individual citizens and threatened their commercial interests, as evidenced in the free soil plank of the Republican party. With state sovereignty and economic freedom endangered, Wigfall insisted upon the undeniable right of secession.

Wigfall, though, did not view secession as a radical move but rather as a conservative step to upholding the original ideals of the Constitution. Indeed, Wigfall was more of a nationalist than an extreme radical. In December 1860, Wigfall stood before the U.S. Senate and urged Republican leaders to stand in solidarity and propose amendments to the Constitution that would secure the protection of property and save the Union. Senate Republicans, though, only laughed at him. As a result, Wigfall turned to the border state representatives and appealed to their economic interest in slavery and reminded them of the North's devotion to abolition, which would leave their section in ruin. Wigfall's attention to border state politicians reveals his understanding that the nation was hanging in the balance. For a separate nation to exist, the South needed all the support it could muster. Wigfall truly understood the importance of the border states and the necessity of their fidelity to the Deep South for the salvation of individual rights and property. More than that, he stood as one of the few leading men who truly envisioned a separate centralized nation as a means to upholding America's founding ideals, a vision that he retained until his death.

During the war, Wigfall maintained a strong line of conservatism, while his reputation grew and changed. He became known for his military strategy, his politics, and his criticism of the Jefferson Davis administration, while exhibiting a combination of ignorance and bravery. This is evident in the initial crisis over Fort Sumter. Wigfall did not believe that Northern forces would evacuate Fort Sumter, nor would they fight; they did not have the nerve to make a move against the South. "They are just in the condition of Buchanan," he stated, and "they will neither make war nor conclude peace, but will stand still till the country drifts into war." (OR, 1, vol. 53, supp., 133–134). Confused about the aims of the North, he did not realize the willingness of Union soldiers to put up a fight for Fort Sumter. Nevertheless, during this initial crisis, Wigfall marked himself as a man of bravery. In the Fort Sumter crisis, Wigfall went to the fort to inquire about Union surrender. Onlookers recalled that he acted with "great gallantry and his accustomed indifference to danger" (OR, 1, vol. 1, 23, 38, 57, 61, 65). His boat carried a white flag too small to be seen by other Confederate batteries, and shelling of the fort did not cease when he started out—his approach was "one of immanent danger." Because of the heavy firing, commanding Brigadier General James Simons wished to recall Wigfall. Simon's hesitation in doing so, though, allowed Wigfall to forge on. Upon his return to the company, with news of a complete surrender, fellow soldiers hoisted him upon their shoulders in jubilation. Documented in several official accounts and in newspapers across the South, virtually everyone knew of Wigfall's role in procuring the surrender of Fort Sumter.

Not only did the South hold Wigfall in high regard, but his actions won the devotion of his family. When his daughter Lulie read of the account in the newspapers, she remarked to her brother Halsey that she "fully realized how happy and proud we ought to be in having such a Father, and it seems to me as if every day he is adding another page to his reputation" (Lulie Wigfall to Halsey Wigfall, April 16, 1861, Wigfall Family Papers, TSA). His family credited Louis with saving bloodshed and admired him for risking his life for the sake of others. To his family and the nation, he "showed such a spirit of bravery and unselfishness, as was well worthy of Hon. Louis T. Wigfall" (Louise Wigfall to Louis Wigfall, April 20, 1861, Wigfall Family Papers, TSA).

After Fort Sumter, Wigfall was commissioned brigadier general in charge of the Confederate Army's "Texas Brigade." During his leadership, he did not show the previous signs of bravery but displayed a type of dysfunctional honor driven by his own desire for victory. Such is the case when he hoarded ammunition against authorization, creating a shortage for other companies. Wigfall also spent time attempting to procure favors for kinsmen, such as Lewis Cruger and brother-in-law Dr. George Warren Cross. As a commander Wigfall acted for his own benefit during the war. He often caused a great stir among other military leaders, who were quick to criticize Wigfall's judgment and ability to lead.

Wigfall's tenure as a military leader did not last long. He resigned his command in 1862 to take a seat in the Confederate legislature. From 1862 to 1865, he served in the Senate as a representative from Texas. During his political career in the Senate, Wigfall ironically became known for his military strategy and support of Confederate war policy. He ardently pursued an offensive scheme, against the wishes of many Confederate leaders including President Davis. Other leaders, though, were more congenial. He often spoke of such plans with General Beauregard and R. M. T. Hunter (q.v.), especially after the first battle of Manassas. Wigfall questioned Davis's neglect of a frontal assault. He often obtained specific information on the location and availability of troops for offensive measures and confronted Davis with the information, especially after Beauregard called for a frontal attack across the Potomac in 1861. Davis, though, denied that any of his officers made such a suggestion. Wigfall's pursuit of an offensive strategy and his willingness to confront Davis on the critical issue of military strategy gained him the respect of many military leaders, who revered him as a man who, according to Mrs. D. Giraud Wright, "has a head to comprehend grand war" (105, 106).

Part of this comprehension involved understanding the need for destruction as an integral part of war, victory, and nationhood. Destruction, according to historian Charles Royster, was a critical element in nation building. Those men who understood the need to destroy the enemy, he argues, truly comprehended the possibility of creating a separate nation. Wigfall not only desired a separate nation, but he also understood the integral role of war and destruction in creating one. When it came to defending the Mississippi Valley, he wrote, "[O]n whichever side of the river the enemy appears he should be met with our whole force, and crushed. . . . Whenever the enemy divides, concentrate and crush; and then follow up the hand, as at ten pins when you make a ten strike" (Wright, 102–103). Wigfall understood that the Mississippi River was critical for Confederate survival and a potential problem for Confederate defense. He knew that the only means for successfully defending that section of the country involved taking the war to the enemy and annihilating them in battle.

Wigfall's press for the offensive and his stay in the Senate marked him as a well-known critic of President Davis. As such, disgruntled military leaders often wrote to Wigfall expressing their dissatisfaction over appointments and conditions in the West. Both John B. Magruder and Joseph E. Johnston confided in Wigfall over their placement and rate of promotion. Wigfall especially had a close relationship with Joseph E. Johnston—bound together in their criticism of Davis and the administration. In times of trouble, Johnston refused to communicate problems to Davis for fear that Davis would take over all responsibilities in the West or that he would be forced to follow Davis's ill advice. Instead, Johnston turned to Wigfall, a proven friend, strategist, and politician. Other military leaders reacted in similar fashion. During the Union threat of the Mississippi, Beauregard devised a plan that in his view would rid the entire Southwest of every Yankee. Though he did not mention the specifics of the plan in his letter, he relied on Wigfall to make the pitch before the War Department for an offensive move. Beauregard, however, did not want his name mentioned for "fear that information would consign them to the tomb of the Capulets" (*OR*, 1, vol. 23, pt. 2).

It is Wigfall's criticism of Davis that most historians highlight as the defining characteristic of his wartime reputation. In his biography *Louis T. Wigfall: Southern Fire-Eater* (1970), Alvy King argues that Wigfall almost singlehandedly undermined public confidence in Davis and his military commanders, dooming the Confederacy to defeat. Though Wigfall desired a separate South more than any other person, King places him at the top of those who betrayed the Southern nation. In addition, King attributes Wigfall with a dual personality, exhibiting pathological symptoms of paranoia. By relegating such dissenters to the periphery of political leadership, though, King's analysis does not broaden our understanding of the larger crisis in Southern nationalism.

Historian Eric Walther, though, accurately portrays Wigfall as one of those radical fire-eaters who were committed to the idea of an independent slaveholding republic and places Wigfall in the mainstream of political leadership. This placement is necessary for Walther, who uses Wigfall to refute the status anxiety thesis by turning it on its head. It was not a fear of losing what one might have that motivated people but an inner belief that as an elite member of society such men as Wigfall had a special place and calling in Southern society. Walther portrays Wigfall as a selfish, reckless, and violent man who betrayed the code of gentlemanly conduct but whose social status enhanced his "sense of destiny," overshadowing any personal weakness (161–163). Although taking much of his information from King, Walther does expand this earlier view by arguing that criticism leading to a decay in morale was secondary to the fact that such mainstream leaders were unprepared to adequately govern a new nation.

Historian George Rable, though, reveals that such leaders as Wigfall had an adequate understanding of governing. Rable credits Wigfall with being politically astute enough to avoid a complete break with the administration, which in turn caused him to fail in shaking widespread confidence in the president.

Given his understanding of an offensive strategy, destruction, and a separate Southern nation, Wigfall appeared better geared to govern than did most leaders. Wigfall's primary weakness was that he did not understand the depth to which most Southerners refused to relinquish political and military control to the national government. He was a man cut off from his constituency, who had his own vision of what a nation should be and how it should function. He forged ahead on his own and abandoned the code of honor and the ideals of those who sent him to the Senate. He was not bound by the dictates of community but rather by his own individualism. In the very least, Wigfall did not understand the politics of Texas, as his activity in the Senate reflects. While Wigfall may have been the confidant of military leaders, he did not understand the people behind the lines. On April 16, 1862, the Confederate government passed its first conscription act. Wigfall supported the act over fellow senator Williamson S. Oldham and the wishes of most Texans. While Rable views this solely as a move toward creating a consolidated national state, Wigfall also had the protection of Southern commercial interests in mind and viewed a strong army as a means to secure those interests.

Wigfall especially found disfavor late in the war when he proposed resolutions directing laws to authorize the impressment of property for use by the army. Furthermore, Wigfall advocated abandoning the territory west of the Mississippi and transferring the trans-Mississippi troops to the East where the dominant battles took place. Though Wigfall pressed Congress for appropriations to protect the Texas frontier against Indian atrocities, he did not understand that Texans wanted to stay home and fight to defend their property more than they wanted financial assistance. In May 1864 Wigfall spoke before the Confederate States Senate and supported the right to suspend the writ of habeus corpus based on the notion that the purpose was ''to protect each of the States from domestic violence and invasion'' and to uphold a republican form of government (Wigfall Family Papers, BC). Due to the fact that the individual states had delegated power to the federal government to deal with foreign powers in the interest of individual states, the Confederate government, claimed Wigfall, held the right and authority to enact such measures as would best protect the lives and liberties of its citizens. In addition, Wigfall argued against the move by governors and state legislators to entrust the state militia with protecting state interests. Wigfall claimed that such powers were delegated to the Congress and not the state legislature. Wigfall's wartime failure in supporting Texas interests is best characterized by selfish ambition and ignorance, rather than criticism of the Davis administration or an unpreparedness to govern. It was not Wigfall's weakness as a politician and person that led to Southern demise. Southern defeat stemmed from state leaders and those behind the lines who were unable to envision and unwilling to support a separate nation. Wigfall's support of the administration's conscription and impressment policies and his insistence on military necessity over political considerations reveal his deep understanding of nation building, a vision that state politicians were unwilling to embrace. Rable's view of this conflict as part of a larger antiparty culture rather than an understanding of the basic necessities to winning war, however, obscures the reality of Wigfall's early devotion to the Democratic party on a national basis.

Immediately after the war, Wigfall set out for Texas, leaving his family behind. There he hid out until leaving for England in 1866. Wigfall's family soon joined him, and he labored to find a means of existence. Although Wigfall had many schemes, each fell through, and he was forced to rely on financial aid from his son and his mother-in-law. By 1869, heavy debt plagued the Wigfall family. In 1872, Wigfall moved back to the United States, temporarily settling in Baltimore, Maryland. Two years later, he and his wife moved to Texas.

There has been no real analysis of Wigfall's life after the war. Most likely this stems from the little surviving correspondence of Wigfall. Alvy King's biography is the only detailed account of his postwar life, and it follows the same general analysis of his wartime activity. The most that can be said of Wigfall's postwar life is that he died when the Confederacy died; he was unable to come to grips with the defeat of the South. Even when all was going wrong, Wigfall held to an unrealistic expectation that the Confederacy would be reborn. Only Joseph Johnston still looked to Wigfall after the war. In September 1868, he turned to Wigfall in an attempt to rescue his own honor and reputation, asking him to write a statement for publication that would have cleared his name and placed him in honorable light against false statements made by General John Bell Hood (q.v.). Wigfall was unable to save Johnston's reputation; he could do little to save his own.

For Wigfall, however, this was of no consequence. One thing is sure: He did not place a high value on reputation. Just prior to the surrender of Robert E. Lee (q.v.), when the defeat of the South became evident to most, Wigfall wrote:

The people of the Confederate States cannot bear the thought that the very pick and choice of the men of this land, the flower, the crown and pride of our race and blood, should be regarded as the mere material for building up the fame of some promising officer whom the President has resolved to make a great general, at our expense. To rescue and hold our country—to save our souls alive—this is the grand point at present; and, strange as it may seem, we do not care a button how all these military reputations will be rated in history—not even that of Mr. Davis. (Wigfall Family Papers, LC)

BIBLIOGRAPHY

Louis T. Wigfall Family Papers (Texas State Archives, Austin, Tex.; Madison Division, Library of Congress, Washington, D.C.).

War of the Rebellion: A Compilation of the Official Records of the Union and Confederate Armies (Washington: Government Printing Office, 1880–1901).

Richard Francis Lubbock, *Six Decades in Texas, or Memoirs of Francis Richard Lubbock, Governor of Texas in War Time, 1861–1863*, ed. C. W. Raines (Austin: Tex.: Ne C. Jones and Co., 1900).

Mrs. D. Giraud Wright, *A Southern Girl in '61* (New York: Doubleday, Page, 1905).

J. L. Bagwell, "The Life and Services of Col. L. T. Wigfall of Marshall, Texas" (master's thesis, University of Texas, 1923).

Charles W. Lord, "Young Louis Wigfall: South Carolina Politician and Duelist," *South Carolina Historical Magazine* 30 (March 1958): 30–54.

Alvy L. King, *Louis T. Wigfall: Southern Fire-Eater* (Baton Rouge: Louisiana State University Press, 1970).

Billy D. Ledbetter, ''The Election of Louis T. Wigfall to the United States Senate, 1859:
    A Reevaluation,'' *Southwestern Historical Quarterly* 77 (Oct. 1973): 241–253.
Thomas L. Connelly and Barbara L. Bellows, *God and General Longstreet: The Lost
    Cause and the Southern Mind* (Baton Rouge: Louisiana State University Press,
    1982).
Bertram Wyatt-Brown, *Southern Honor: Ethics and Behavior in the Old South* (New
    York: Oxford University Press, 1982).
Gaines M. Foster, *Ghosts of the Confederacy: Defeat, the Lost Cause, and the Emergence
    of the New South, 1865–1913* (New York: Oxford University Press, 1987).
Charles E. Royster, *The Destructive War* (New York: Alfred Knopf, 1991).
Eric Walther, *The Fire-Eaters* (Baton Rouge: Louisiana State University Press, 1992).
George C. Rable, *The Confederate Republic: A Revolution against Politics* (Chapel Hill:
    University of North Carolina Press, 1994).

INDEX

ABOUT THE CONTRIBUTORS

JOHN ALLEN is completing his Ph.D. dissertation at the Catholic University of America on the Virginia southside during the Civil War era. He teaches at Shepherd College in West Virginia.

FREDERICK J. BLUE is professor of history at Youngstown State University. He is the author of *The Free Soilers: Third Party Politics, 1845–1854* (1973), *Salmon P. Chase: A Life in Politics* (1987), and *Charles Summer and the Conscience of the North* (1994).

MICHAEL CONNOLLY is writing a Ph.D. dissertation at the Catholic University of America on railroads and antebellum northern New England politics. He is editor of the *Paulist Studies* and director of the Paulist Archives in Washington, D.C.

MARIANNE FISCHER graduated from the College of Notre Dame in Maryland in 1997. She is pursuing graduate studies at the Washington Theological Union.

HERMAN M. HATTAWAY is professor of history at the University of Missouri at Kansas City. Among his books are *Stephen D. Lee* (1976), *How the North Won: A Military History of the Civil War* (1984), and *The Blue and the Gray* (1997).

JOHN T. HUBBELL is professor of history at Kent State University and editor of *Civil War History*. He is the director of the Kent State University Press. Among his books are *Battles Won and Lost* (1975) and *A Biographical Dictionary of Union Leaders* (1995).

LEONNE M. HUDSON is a professor at Kent State University. He has published several articles on the Civil War and is the author of *The Odyssey of a*

Southerner: The Life and Times of Gustavus Woodson Smith (1998). Currently he is editing a book on the United States Army during the Mexican War.

CLAYTON E. JEWETT has finished a Ph.D. dissertation at the Catholic University of America on Texas during the Civil War. He has published a number of articles on the history and geography of Civil War Texas.

JOHN F. MARSZALEK is professor of history at Mississippi State University. He is the author of a number of books and articles. Among his books are *Sherman's Other War* (1981), *Sherman: A Soldier's Passion for Order (1993),* and *Encyclopedia of African-American Civil Rights* (1992).

KENNETH NIVISON is writing a Ph.D. dissertation at the Catholic University of America on upper New England higher education during the Civil War era. He teaches at St. Anselm College in New Hampshire.

JAMES A. RAWLEY is Carl Adolph Happold distinguished professor emeritus of history at the University of Nebraska. He is the author of a number of books and articles. Among his books are *Race and Politics: "Bleeding Kansas" and the Coming of the Civil War* (1969), *The Politics of Union: Northern Politics during the Civil War* (1974), *The Transatlantic Slave Trade* (1981), and *Abraham Lincoln and a Nation Worth Fighting For* (1996).

CHARLES F. RITTER is professor and chairperson of history at the College of Notre Dame in Maryland. He is coauthor of *American Legislative Leaders, 1850–1910* (1989).

THOMAS J. ROWLAND is an instructor at the College of Lake County in Illinois. He is author of the *George B. McClellan and Civil War History: In the Shadow of Grant and Sherman* (1998).

MICHAEL J. C. TAYLOR is pursuing graduate studies in history at the University of Missouri at Kansas City.

FRANK EVERSON VANDIVER is professor emeritus of history at Texas A&M University and director of the Mosher Defense Studies Center. He is the author of many books and articles. His books include *Rebel Brass: The Confederate Command System* (1956), *Mighty Stonewall* (1957), *Their Tattered Flags: The Epic of the Confederacy* (1970), and *Black Jack: The Life of John J. Pershing* (1977). Most recently he has published *Shadows of Vietnam* (1997).

JON L. WAKELYN is professor of history at Kent State University. He is the author and editor of a number of books and articles. His books include *Politics of a Literary Man: William Gilmore Simms* (1973), *Biographical Dictionary of the Confederacy* (1977), *The Web of Southern Social Relations* (1985), and *Southern Pamphlets on Secession, November 1860–April 1861* (1996).

STEVEN E. WOODWORTH is a professor of history at Texas Christian University. He is the author of *Jefferson Davis and His Generals* (1990); *Davis and Lee at War* (1995); and *Six Armies in Tennessee: The Chickamauga and Chattanooga Campaigns* (1998). His forthcoming book is *Victory and Defeat: Problems of the Confederate High Command.*

ISBN 0-313-29560-3

90000>

EAN

9 780313 295607

HARDCOVER BAR CODE